NORTH CAROLINA WESLEYAN COLLEGE

WISDOM AND COURAGE THROUGH CHRISTIAN EDUCATION

1956

ROCKY MOUNT, N.C.

Industrialisation and social change in South Africa

Industrialisation and social change in South Africa

African class formation, culture, and consciousness, 1870–1930

EDITED BY
Shula Marks and Richard Rathbone

Longman

LONGMAN GROUP LIMITED, LONDON AND NEW YORK

Longman Group Limited,
Longman House,
Burnt Mill, Harlow, Essex,
UK

Longman Inc.,
19 West 44th Street,
New York,
NY 10036, USA

First published 1982

British Library Cataloguing in Publication Data

Industrialisation and social change in South Africa.
  1. South Africa–Economic conditions
  I. Marks, Shula II. Rathbone, Richard
  330.968   HC517.S7

ISBN 0 582 64338 4 (cased)
ISBN 0 582 64337 6 (paper)

Library of Congress Cataloging in Publication Data

Industrialisation and social change in South Africa.

  Includes index.
    1. South Africa – Social conditions – Addresses, essays, lectures.   2. South Africa – Economic conditions – Addresses, essays, lectures. 3. Blacks – South Africa – Social conditions – Addresses, essays, lectures. 4. Blacks – Employment – South Africa – History – Addresses, essays, lectures.
    5. Social classes – South Africa – History – Addresses, essays, lectures. I. Marks, Shula. II. Rathbone, Richard.
  HN801.A815 1982   306.3'0968   82-7168
  ISBN 0 582 64338 4   AACR2
  ISBN 0 582 64337 6 (pbk.)

Printed in Great Britain by Butler & Tanner Ltd, Frome and London

Contents

Acknowledgements

The cover depicts diamond mining in Kimberley in the 1870s and (inset) the anti-pass demonstration in Johannesburg in 1919. The publishers are grateful to the BBC Hulton Picture Library and the Africana Museum, Johannesburg, respectively, for permission to reproduce these two photographs.

List of maps and figures

Abbreviations

ABM	American Board Mission
ANC	African National Congress
BMSC	Bantu Men's Social Centre
ERPM	East Rand Proprietary Mines
GNLB	Government Native Labour Bureau
IDB	Illicit Diamond Buying
ISL	International Socialist League
IWA	Industrial Workers of Africa
LMS	London Missionary Society
NAD	Native Affairs Department
NGR	Natal Government Railways
NRC	Native Recruiting Corporation
OFS	Orange Free State
PEMS	Paris Evangelical Mission Society
SAMR	South African Mounted Rifles
SANNC	South African Native National Congress (later, African National Congress)
SNA	Secretary for Native Affairs
TNC	Transvaal Native Congress
WHS	Women's Help Society
WNLA	Witwatersrand Native Labour Association

Fig. 1 Southern Africa, c. 1900

x

Introduction*

Shula Marks and Richard Rathbone

Since the late nineteenth century, South Africa has witnessed an industrial revolution which has profoundly transformed the lives of all its inhabitants, both black and white. Conquered and colonised, black peasants and workers have experienced changes at least as harsh and disruptive as those in early industrial Britain. Before 1870, the majority of Africans in southern Africa lived in independent chiefdoms, though few were untouched by the coming of merchant, missionary and settler. Even the growing number of Africans becoming incorporated into the settler-dominated world of the Afrikaner republics or the British colonies for the most part retained their access to land and control over their labour power. Less than fifty years later – in the period covered by this book – African chiefdom, British colony and Afrikaner republic had been swept aside; south of the Limpopo, all had been meshed into a single capitalist state dominated by whites.

The broad economic and political developments which accompanied this are well known: the discovery of diamonds in 1867 and the British annexation of the diamond fields shortly thereafter; Lord Carnarvon's schemes to confederate southern Africa in the 1870s; the conquest of the remaining independent African societies in southern Africa; the discovery of gold on the Witwatersrand in the 1880s, followed by the renewed assertion of British supremacy in the interior of South Africa, culminating in the Jameson Raid and the Anglo-Boer war; the unification of the South African territories in 1910 and the party political struggles of whites. Yet we know remarkably little of what these dramatic events meant for black South Africans, whether in terms of the changes wrought in their material conditions, or how these changes were shaped by, and in turn reshaped, their culture and consciousness. We are beginning to understand the political economy of industrial South Africa, yet we have little knowledge of how, in this hostile environment, Africans survived as

*We are grateful to Deborah Gaitskell, Kevin Shillington, Stanley Trapido, Rob Turrell, Jean Jacques Van-Helten and Brian Willan for their comments on this introduction.

autonomous human beings with a culture of their own within the white masters' world; and how, in the final analysis, these processes entailed the making of an African working class.[1]

The South African working class has historically been divided. It is not the intention of this volume to perpetuate or sanction the divisions by its emphasis on the African working class. Indeed it cannot be understood without taking account of the relationship of black and white workers to one another as well as to other class forces. Nevertheless we know far more about the small white working class and its confrontations with capital in the first couple of decades of this century than of the black.[2] The literature is almost in inverse proportion to their ultimate historical significance.

While, therefore, we have largely excluded a detailed consideration of the white working class from these pages, it has proved less justifiable to exclude either African peasants or the petty bourgeoisie. The very nature of conquest and colonisation, of racial as well as class subjection, has made it impossible to consider African working-class culture and consciousness as in any sense watertight or closed off from the rest of the black population. Not only were the connections between workers and peasants intimate and continuous; they were also frequently the same people at different but often closely juxtaposed periods of their lives. Moreover, as the essays in this collection, especially those by Bonner and Coplan, reveal, to understand the making of an African working class in these years, it is necessary to think also about the making of an African petty bourgeoisie. Ironically, in a colonial context, where their opportunities were limited and finally stifled by the very forces which gave them birth, the petty bourgeoisie achieved, as we shall see, a degree of class coherence and self-consciousness only rarely achieved by the working class.

This collection makes no claim to being comprehensive. It still reflects immense gaps in research and in our understanding both of the overall contours of the political economy and more especially of the black experience.[3] Indian and Coloured workers have been excluded from these pages, partly because of the dearth of research available to us, partly because of the focus on Kimberley and the Rand. The roots of the African working class and petty bourgeoisie go back before the mineral discoveries to the mission stations and towns of the Cape and Natal. As the paper by Coplan shows, the continuities are important. Nevertheless the concentration on Kimberley and the Witwatersrand is deliberate: the central theme of this volume is not simply urbanisation, but South Africa's industrial revolution, a revolution based upon and fuelled by the mineral discoveries. The transformations of production and of social and economic relations in the north were far swifter, and more far-reaching and complete than in the towns of the Cape and Natal at least until the 1930s. The switch to the industrial production of diamonds and gold with its vastly increased drive for international capital investment, its complex technology and labour process, and its huge demand for a cheap, controlled labour force led to major changes in the form of the state and had ramifications which entered into every aspect of rural society. This went way beyond the earlier impact on South African societies of merchant capital or the existing urban centres,[4] which were themselves drawn into and becoming dependent upon the economic hub first of Kimberley, and then, more importantly, the Witwatersrand.

The essays in this collection, then, represent a preliminary attempt to grapple with some aspects of the African experience of South Africa's industrial revolution. They arise out of the independent researches of a group of scholars, most of whom were able to participate in a small history workshop on this period at the Centre of International and Area Studies, University of London, which was funded by the Ford Foundation between 1976 and 1979. Central to our activities in this period was the work in progress of Charles van Onselen on the social history of Johannesburg between 1886 and 1914, to be published shortly under the title *Studies in the Social and Economic History of the Witwatersrand* (two volumes, London, 1982). Most of the essays were finally brought together at a conference held at Danbury Park, Essex, at the beginning of 1980, also organised by the Centre and funded by the Foundation. We would like to take this opportunity of thanking both the Ford Foundation and the Secretary of the Centre of International and Area Studies, Mr. A. E. Atmore, and his staff for their assistance.

At its inception, there were two spurs to this project, political and intellectual. In retrospect it seems no coincidence that it was conceived in the mid-seventies as African workers and students made their voices heard again after the long silence of the sixties. The 1972–3 strikes which began in Namibia and Natal, at opposite ends of the subcontinent, and spread rapidly through the Republic, together with the revitalisation of the African trade union movement, had a profound effect both politically and intellectually. In South Africa, the latter was evidenced by the establishment of the *South African Labour Bulletin*, the conference held at the University of the Witwatersrand on the history of labour in South Africa in 1976, and the subsequent workshops on the working-class history of the Witwatersrand. The essays on labour history edited by Eddie Webster and the proceedings of the workshops edited by Belinda Bozzoli are, like this volume, the beginnings of a new literature which tries to unravel the historical complexities which have shaped this resurgent working class.[5]

It was the reawakening of the African working class in the early seventies which also in many ways brought to a head the limitations of the existing literature, whether liberal or revisionist. Neither the newer work coming out of the University of the Witwatersrand nor our own book is unique in addressing itself to the history of South Africa's black workers. It was, however, in part our dissatisfaction with the existing literature which led us to launch the workshop. Now is not the time to embark on a lengthy critique of the somewhat slender bibliography. Nevertheless at the risk of unfair caricature we do need to set out some of the ways in which these essays mark a departure from the current orthodoxies.

From what has been said so far, it is clear that our contributers take issue with a dominant liberal view that in South Africa, as Pierre van den Berghe has remarked:

> Social classes in the Marxian sense of relationship to the means of production must exist by definition, as they must in any capitalist country, but they are not meaningful social realities. Clearly pigmentation rather than ownership of land or capital is the most significant criterion of status in South Africa . . .[6]

While we would not wish to deny the significance of racism in South Africa's historical development and its material reality in the lives of all its people, the essays in this collection suggest a rather more complex relationship between class and race than that proposed by van den Berghe, and rather less economistic definitions of class.

Over the past decade and more, the liberal paradigm on South Africa has been challenged on a number of fronts by a growing radical historiography.[7] At the heart of the debate over this period is precisely the relationship between race and class. Essentially the radical literature of the seventies contested the view that racist practices in contemporary South Africa resulted from 'the actions of a state bizarrely following the "logic" of irrational racial prejudice',[8] or the imposition of essentially anachronistic 'feudal rigidities' on an economy moving ineluctably in the opposite direction.[9] Much of the earlier critique was devoted to showing the ways in which racism was built into South Africa's industrial revolution: far from being dysfunctional, it has on occasion been crucial to South Africa's accumulation of capital, making possible the division of the working class and its control, and determining the distribution of surplus.

More recently Rob Davies has argued that

> the racist hierarchical division of labour within the white wage-earning classes came into existence not as some irrational imposition on the bourgeoisie but 1) *because** it accorded with the requirements of capitalist production at the various phases and stages of capitalist production during the period under discussion [1900–1960] and 2) as part of a political 'solution' which served to structure political class relations in the social formation to the advantage of the bourgeoisie under the hegemony of particular fractions at particular conjunctures . . .[10]

The essays in this collection tend on the whole to modify this view also, at least in its mechanically functionalist implications. In particular the essay by Rob

*our emphasis

Turrell as well as those looking at the origins of migrant labour from the rural end are concerned to show the nature of the struggles which produced particular solutions which did not necessarily seem at the time to accord quite so neatly with the needs of capital. And while Turrell shows the instrumental quality of both racist and liberal ideology on the diamond fields, it is clear that neither originated *de novo* in Kimberley.[11]

What it seems important to recognise is that at the same time as 'racism is a social practice with its own changing history and its own symbolic regularities',[12] both capital and the state — and indeed workers — can use this social practice for their own instrumental purposes. Racism was not simply the invention of capitalists to delude white workers, as is sometimes implied in the literature; quite manifestly capitalists were as caught in racist discourse as any worker.[13] It was perhaps for this reason that it was so powerfully available to assist in the securing of very specific material objectives. Clearly the polarities of white equals civilised and black equals barbarous were well established in the European mind before the foundations of Kimberley, and part of a common western culture. Even a cursory reading of the literature of the 1870s reveals the profound impact of Social Darwinism on an already racist imperial and settler discourse, quite regardless of material interest.

Olive Schreiner's description of New Rush (Kimberley), probably written in 1875 or 1876 when she was not yet eighteen, has latched onto all the conventional wisdoms of the time:

> . . . the street was so thronged with the streaming crowd of niggers and diggers returning home from work that they kicked up the red sand into a lurid cloud over their heads — stark naked savages from the interior, with their bent spindle legs and their big-jawed foreheadless monkey-faces, who, though they were getting home to fire and meals, could hardly get out of their habitual crawl — colonial niggers half dressed not half civilized, and with some hundred per cent more evil in their black countenances than in some of their wilder brethren — great muscular fellows, almost taller and stronger than their masters, the white diggers, who formed a thin sprinkling in the crowd, and who, in spite of the thick dust that enveloped them might be distinguished by their more quick and energetic movements.[14]

1875 was of course the year of the Diggers' Revolt which Turrell reminds us was characterised by a virulent racism, which he attributes to the twin threat being experienced by the white diggers, on the one hand of being squeezed out by the cheaper black digger, on the other by the larger claimowners. Yet there is more to it than that. Faced with the crisis of 1875, white diggers could have united across the colour line with black diggers on the basis of a shared opposition to the greater threat of the large claimowners. They did not. Given the instrumentality of certain forms of exclusion from resources, what still needs explaination is why it was almost invariably along the 'faultlines'[15] of race that these divisions and exclusions were made. This is not to advocate a return to the static and idealist interpretations of the past, but to suggest that consciousness does not proceed in an unmediated fashion either from the manipulations of state and capital or from the direct experience of class struggle. As Peter Burke has reminded us, the 'rational' historian has to come to terms with the irrational and emotional in the past: the collective psychology of men and women is as part of their daily reality as their houses and their food and wages.[16] Both magnate and digger shared in this collective psychology and shaped their world in accord with its assumptions about natural aptitude and inferiority, about good and evil. These were not the simple product of calculation based on empirical observation.

Part of the necessary concern with the relationship between class and race in the radical literature of the seventies has led, despite its centrality, to certain silences. We would not wish to distance ourselves from much of this work. Indeed what follows has only been made possible as a result of the break with the liberal paradigm, the resulting emphasis on class analysis, and our enriched understanding of South Africa's capitalist development. Capital did not invent racism, but it has certainly been able to live with it, more or less comfortably. Racism has indeed been built into South Africa's industrial revolution. While not always necessarily functional to economic growth (or 'optimal economic growth' whatever that may mean[17]) there has at least been a certain reciprocity between South Africa's racist practices and its industrialisation. Nevertheless, despite the importance of the recent radical literature in expanding our understanding of twentieth-century South Africa and its political economy, it has been more concerned with the problems of capital accumulation and the state, with so-called 'fractions of capital' and the white workers, than with black class formation and consciousness. The impact of Althusserian structuralism on radical writing in the seventies reinforced this trend: blacks are relegated to being no more than a silent backdrop against which the political drama is enacted, as much 'dominated classes' in these texts as their authors see them in reality.[18]

Curiously, this has its counterpart in the liberal tradition where only too frequently Africans have been reduced into the 'super-exploited' yet passive victims of apartheid or into some kind of statistical migrant, 'men of two worlds', bewildered by the rapidity of urbanisation and social change.[19] Clearly not all works which treat of African initiatives in South Africa share this particular blindspot. Although, for a variety of reasons, South Africa escaped much of the nationalist historiography of the sixties,[20] there are exceptions: most notably, the major study of African nationalist organisations and socialist struggles by Jack and Ray Simons, Peter Walshe's work on the African National Congress, Gail Gerhart on black consciousness and the four-volume collection of documents edited by Gwen Carter, Tom Karis and Sheridan Johns.[21]

Nevertheless, even the most radical of these tend to be a narrative of resistance concerned with political organisations at the purely institutional level. According to Jack and Ray Simons, for example, their purpose 'is to tell a story and at the same time give resisters of today a guide to the background of [past] controversies'.[22] The result is a scholarly and meticulously detailed narrative political history which nevertheless all too rarely moves beyond it to political economy, the relationship between the political and the economic, or, most crucially in our view, the relationship between class formation, political consciousness and culture. In part because – as Brian Willan suggested in 1978 – this body of work fails 'to come to terms with the reality of class differentiation amongst black South Africans and the effects this may have on the development of ideological forms',[23] the counterparts of migrant workers who 'found the workings of a modern economic system far beyond comprehension'[24] are black conservative leaders (of the petty bourgeoisie) who 'never quite understood their society or its power structure'.[25] The essays in this collection confront all these forms of condescension.

Although there has recently been something of a reaction against the overenthusiastic application of Althusser and Poulantzas to South Africa, and there are some attempts to redress the balance and look again at the struggles of black workers in South Africa,[26] a number of problems remain. As Belinda Bozzoli remarked in summing up the proceedings of the first Witwatersrand workshop:

> Time and time again it emerged in discussion that the economic identification of classes is not the *last* word, but merely the first, and that it is the political, social, cultural and ideological character of classes which renders them real and recognisable social categories ... We possess such broad categories as 'white workers', 'black workers' and the black 'petty bourgeoisie' or even the 'old' and the 'new' petty bourgeoisie, and we divide workers into skilled and unskilled, manufacturing and mining, male and female, English and Afrikaans-speaking, but it began to emerge that these are no more than stereotypes whose usefulness in understanding the social ... relationships on the Rand is limited. Our understanding of working-class culture, of petty-bourgeois politics, of social networks, of ideological patterns is crude where it exists at all ...[27]

The essays in this collection try to address at least some of these issues; to show the actual conflicts and struggles out of which classes are born. Contrary to some of the literature which has a ready-made revolutionary working class waiting in the wings for a less timid and moderate leadership, what we see is an immensely complex and often painful making of this working class in all its cultural specificity.

To reject the notion of a ready-made revolutionary working class is not to deny the existence of an African working class, just as to reject the notion of Africans either as passive victims or 'dominated classes' is not to return to an unproblematic African 'initiative'. For all the emphasis in these essays on consciousness and culture, and our quite explicit debt to Edward Thompson, we return with G. A. Cohen to the assertion that 'a person's class is established by nothing but his objective place in the network of ownership relations, however difficult it may be to identify such places neatly'.[28] In the South African case, part of the problem of 'identifying such places neatly' in this period, is that we are dealing with a period of transition and a working class which is not wholly severed from the means of production.[29] African migrants still have access to land, and first-generation proletarians still have a consciousness in part informed by their rural class position.

While shaped by their precolonial social experience, however, the nature of the African working class clearly cannot be understood outside the imperatives of late nineteenth-century imperialism and South Africa's mining economy. It is for this reason that the volume begins with the two long essays on Kimberley and the Witwatersrand by Turrell and Richardson and Van-Helten,[30] both of which place the actual nature of accumulation and the work process at the centre of the stage.

Yet, as both these essays recognise, to establish class position in structural terms *is* only a first step. Consciousness, 'the way in which . . . experiences are handled in cultural terms: embodied in traditions, value systems, ideas and institutional forms',[31] cannot be automatically deduced from an individual's position in 'productive relations', however much the latter conditions the former. In South Africa the sheer speed of the industrial revolution had profound repercussions for the nature of consciousness. Whereas in the metropole in some sense labour and capital grew up side by side, and took each other's measure over time, in Kimberley and the Witwatersrand international capital arrived ready-made, while with the exception of the small skilled workforce imported (also 'ready-made') from overseas, the working class had to be *created* out of the pre-industrial societies of the subcontinent. Africans entered the workforce profoundly shaped by 'the traditions, value systems, ideas and institutional forms' of their own particular pre-capitalist societies. Hence the papers on the mining centres are followed by four essays on the rural hinterland by Shillington, Kimble, Harries and Guy.[32] Incomplete and selective though the picture inevitably is, they collectively make an important contribution to our understanding of the processes of proletarianisation and the origins of the migrant labour system.

The final essays in this volume are an attempt to look at the issues of culture and consciousness in Kimberley and on the Rand. There is no way we can pretend that they give an overall or comprehensive view of either. Nor do we aim to do so. The search for *a* working class culture in South Africa has all the promise and rewards of the search for Prester John. We share with Peter

Worsley the conviction that

> culture is . . . inherently pluralistic and multi-layered. The levels moreover overlap and interpenetrate . . . The very claim that there is a culture common to all is an ideological claim . . . Rather there are many different cultures in a single society [politically defined] and . . . wider cultural attachments that transcend (political) boundaries . . .[33]

While Philip Bonner's paper looks at the highly charged political moment of working-class militancy after the First World War, Willan, Moroney, Couzens, Coplan and Gaitskell[34] begin to unravel the 'practices and institutions' in which town culture was embodied: mothers' unions, literary societies, dance halls and cricket clubs.[35]

Despite the gaps in our jigsaw, it is the essential interrelationships which we wish to emphasise: interrelationships between the political economy, imperial and local, and class formation, between different sections of the working class and different classes, between class, culture and consciousness. There is nothing static or 'given' about these relationships. For ease of explication we have separated out what rightly belongs together and can only be fully understood as a 'total' picture. Historians should be able to write in chords, for our very medium distorts our intentions by its linear imperatives. We can only say one thing at a time, so that our ordering of the essays and in this introduction in part by chronology, in part by theme is necessarily arbitrary and a poor reflection of the rich texture of historical experience.

Our understanding of South Africa's industrial revolution is in its infancy, and it is to this that Turrell's study of Kimberley and Richardson and Van-Helten's essay on the mining industry on the Rand contribute. The task of comprehending this industrial revolution in all its complexity still awaits the kind of devotion economic and social historians have lavished on the earlier experience of north-western Europe and the United States of America. The capitalist development of South Africa was and is in many ways the child of these prior transformations and we have had our analytical armoury reinforced by the insights of those who have studied the European phenomenon. As Stanley Trapido pointed out in a seminal article in 1971,[36] the South African experience has not been unique, although its particularity – the combination of colonial conquest and rapid industrialisation, of imperial capital and a colonial bourgeoisie, of an explosive mixture of race and class stratification, of the long continuation of forms of coerced labour – adds a challenging dimension to the analysis of comparative industrialisation.

By the end of the nineteenth century, the 'peculiarity' of South Africa consisted in the dominance of a highly advanced form of monopoly capital on the gold and diamond fields, with the most sophisticated capital structure and technology,[37] based on a mass of unskilled migrant labour, still dependent on pre-capitalist social formations for its reproduction and controlled by a series of coercive devices such as the compound and pass laws.[38]

The extent of the monopoly's dominance can be appreciated when it is recalled that by 1888 diamond production at Kimberley was effectively controlled by a single company, Rhodes' De Beers Consolidated, which by 1900 was producing 50 per cent of the Cape Colony's exports; on the Witwatersrand, gold production was controlled by a handful of interlocking mining houses which, by the turn of the century, were producing over a quarter of the world's supply of new gold.[39] Of this, one consortium, Wernher-Beit, & Eckstein produced about half. The extent of Wernher-Beit domination can best be gauged from the remarks of the group's historian, A. P. Cartwright:

> the group might well have claimed that it was the fifth province of the Union of South Africa. The combined budget of Wernher, Beit and Company and Eckstein and Company and the Central Mining and Investment Company [all controlled by, or subsidiaries of, Wernher and Beit] was bigger than that of either Natal or the Orange Free State. Its mining organisation on the Rand was the biggest industry in the country, employing more men and certainly producing bigger profits than the amalgamated railways and harbours of the four provinces.[40]

This monopoly sector coexisted with small-scale, undercapitalised and technologically simple forms of agriculture and manufacturing, as the papers by Keegan, Matsetela and Bonner in this collection demonstrate.[41] Thus, even after the mineral discoveries, the vast majority of South Africans remained subsistence farmers, producing small surpluses for the market. Despite the existence of a craft sector in the port towns, connected essentially with the maintenance of shipworks and docks, and minor workshop enterprises in the market towns, concerned with cooperage, blacksmithing, wheelmaking and carpentry, and the innumerable skills that go into the successful prosecution of sheep-farming and sugar production, it would be stretching definitions to suggest that even late nineteenth-century South Africa was in any sense a manufacturing area. It was the mineral discoveries themselves which by the turn of the century had spurred larger-scale industry with the establishment of the largest explosives factory in the world at Modderfontein, for example, and the creation of engineering works on the Rand.[42]

Again, none of this is unique: combined and uneven development is a feature of all capitalist industrialisation. Raphael Samuel has shown that even in England at the height of the industrial revolution the majority of workers were still employed in small workshops in manufacture or in domestic and agricultural labour.[43] Nor should the coexistence of a highly capital-intensive monopoly sector with forms of highly coerced, unfree contract or migrant labour surprise us: as Philip Corrigan has demonstrated, contrary to the orthodox Marxist model, the spread of capitalism in the Third World has probably seen the extension of forms of unfree labour, together with, if not in place of, the progressive 'freeing' of labour in both the senses in which the term is commonly used by Marxists, i.e. labour 'free' from land, and labour 'free' to sell itself (albeit under economic compulsion so to do) on the market.[44]

There was nothing predetermined about the shape of South Africa's industrial revolution, as all these essays make clear.[45] Prior to the mineral discoveries there was little in southern African history which suggested that it would develop in a manner different from areas of white settlement in other parts of Africa. It was not an economy contributing to any large extent to the import needs of the industrial world and conversely was a small market for Britain's manufacturing industry: its exports were mainly wool, some inferior wine and a little sugar, together with a diminishing amount of the product of hunting – ivory and hides – all forced to compete on a cut-throat international market. Its imports were dominated by firearms, agricultural implements and blankets – none of them on a significant scale. Before the 1870s, then, the South African colonies and republics were not regarded by the outside world as very different to other pieces of colonial real-estate. To the British taxpayer they had the additional liability of being costly: the periodic wars on the colonial frontiers as settlers expanded their dominion were a drain on the exchequer not adequately compensated for by its undeveloped economy. Diamonds and, more importantly, gold transformed this situation to the point where, unlike any other African colony, South Africa came to play a major role in the metropolitan and indeed the world economy.[46]

The dependence of South Africa on mineral extraction for its economic growth led to a very different pattern of industrialisation to that of western Europe or the United States of America. In the period covered by this volume, monopoly capital generally had no need for an internal market nor any real interest in the growth of local manufacturing so long as machinery and stores could be obtained more cheaply from abroad.[47] The partial weakening of international capital during two world wars and the Great Depression; the growth of a local bourgeoisie sufficiently powerful to insist on high protective tariffs for national enterprise; the rise in the gold price in the 1930s which enabled the state to cream off enough revenue to foster local agricultural and industrial production – all in the long run enabled South Africa to join the small band of primary producers who in the 1930s were able to expand rapidly into secondary industry. For these countries, as Geoffrey Kay has remarked, 'the depression of the thirties was experienced not as a temporary hiatus but as a sign that a particular phase of productive development was drawing to a close.'[48]

For this volume, too, the thirties constitute the cut-off date. The years following South Africa's departure from the gold standard and the Second

World War saw a new phase of state intervention, economic development, class formation and class consciousness. Nevertheless, it is in the formative years between 1870 and 1930, years dominated by the imperatives of mining capital, that so many of the seeds of what followed were sown.

Kimberley and the Rand are thus the foundations of our story and the essays by Turrell and Van-Helten are central to the entire volume. Yet most starting points, like most cut-off dates, are arbitrary and impose distortions. The mineral discoveries are no exception. They took place in a complex human environment, already affected in a variety of ways by the impact of European capital and colonisation.

There can be no doubt that the mineral discoveries had dramatic and immediate effect. By the end of 1880 there were some 22 000 Africans on the diamond fields, some 9 000 of them permanently resident, beginning to acquire skills and 'to form the nucleus of an African working class'.[49] On the Witwatersrand the creation of a workforce was even more spectacular. By 1899 there were 97 000 black workers and 12 000 white, where a dozen years before there had been a couple of thousand.[50] It is impossible to say how many of the Africans were 'permanently urbanised' or even what exactly this means: the number of women in town is, however, suggestive. African females in Johannesburg rose from just over 1200 in 1896 to 4357 in 1911 to over 12 000 in 1921 and well over 60 000 by 1936.[51] The multiplier effect of the mineral discoveries meant moreover a strident cry for labour from every other sector of the economy: roads and railways had to be built, harbours enlarged, new buildings constructed. The creation of new markets on the mines led to increased agricultural production and therefore, as we shall see, a demand for farm labour; while in the towns, although small-scale at first, manufacturing, initially closely connected to the needs of the mining industry, but soon also food processing, clothing and footwear factories, also required a labour force.

The call for labour at the lowest possible cost and in the greatest possible numbers was ruthless and insatiable. We should not underestimate the violence with which this workforce was created. The wars waged against African communities in the 1870s were, as Duncan Innes has remarked, 'in a critical sense the precondition for the expansion of capitalist relations in South Africa'.[52] As the essays in this volume by Guy, Shillington, Harries and Kimble show, extensive proletarianisation in many cases, though clearly not all, followed directly on conquest.[53] It was only with the enormously important intervention of the state, first in the form of taxation and later in land reservation, together with its increasing ability to intervene in labour markets beyond South Africa's political boundaries, that supplies began to meet demand.[54]

Primitive accumulation in the countryside was paralleled by violence in the towns. In 1886, by which time Company rule had already largely replaced the earlier chaotic conditions on the diamond fields, the veteran Cape politician and later Prime Minister, John X. Merriman, wrote to his wife:

> The misery of this place [Kimberley] grows on one, the appalling crime and the utter hollowness of our civilization which tolerates such things. I verily believe that never was there a labouring population so utterly debased or treated with such complete disregard of their moral and physical welfare. No, not the slaves in the Southern States! . . . I enclose a cutting — two natives were crushed by a large landslip fairly rolling over them — in any other community the suddenness of such a terrible end would have convulsed the community. Here this was absolutely the only notice taken and please note the delicate allusion to the fall not affecting any other company. Next day two more men were killed in an adjoining company — the papers did not even notice the fact.[55]

Few reading Turrell's brief account of mortality rates in the Kimberley compounds or Moroney and Bonner's accounts of Johannesburg slums could imagine that anyone would choose to live and work in such conditions.[56] Compulsion was, for the majority, of the essence, and that compulsion ranged from the insistence of chiefs and homestead heads and the perception of an escape from the constraints of an ascriptive society, to indebtedness to traders and the operations of recruiters and the demands of the state for forced labour and tax.

Nevertheless, the essays in this volume move well beyond any picture of an all-powerful capitalist class using an omnipotent state to mow down all that stood in its path. Whatever the reasons for the new imperialism in the late nineteenth century, the result in the Third World was to create new classes and new class forces. Yet however much the new industrial bourgeoisie may have hoped to shape the colonial world in its own image and in accordance with its needs,[57] its operations were constrained and convoluted by its encounter with pre-existing social formations and their cleavages. The process of proletarianisation was therefore incomplete, often violent, always uneven and idiosyncratic.

In nineteenth-century South Africa, pre-industrial societies, both black and white, could determine, sometimes in significant ways, what was and what was not possible for mine magnates, aspirant capitalist farmers and, later on, manufacturers. They also shaped the form of the South African state which emerged in 1910 out of the welter of African kingdoms, Afrikaner republics and self-governing colonies which had co-existed in uneasy juxtaposition in the 1870s. That this state was an imperial creation there is no doubt: but it could only be fashioned out of local reality. The very failure of Lord Carnarvon's schemes to confederate the South African territories in the 1870s in the absence of sufficiently strong or well-developed class forces working locally to the same end suggests the limitations.[58] And despite the illusions of a Cecil Rhodes or a Lord Milner, even after the devastation of the bitter and costly South African

War, South Africa was not a blank slate for either millionaire or imperial proconsul to write on as he chose.[59] The peculiarities of South Africa's industrial revolution arose out of the conflicts and compromises, the inevitable struggles and alliances between pre-industrial social formations and the new forces of capital. Both were transformed by the experience.

Equally, the very fact that the 'modernisation' of the societies of southern Africa occurred in the wake of and as a result of the massive transformation of north-western Europe and in the context of the new imperialism of the later nineteenth century meant that concerns far more eclectic than those of South Africa alone shaped capital and the strategies it sought to adopt. The accelerated competition for markets and raw materials with the massive industrialisation of Germany, France and the United States, the nature of capital markets in Europe, the possibilities opening up in the Americas, the frequency of booms and slumps over the whole of our period, and a huge battery of additional externally generated factors, acted to spur or constrain investment consolidation, liquidation and diversification in a far from chronologically linear fashion.[60] Turrell, for example, shows the enormous consequences of the slump in the European market for diamonds in the early 1880s for forms of labour discipline employed on the diamond fields, while Richardson and Van-Helten's essay on the Rand illustrates equally the significance for the working class of the position of gold as the international money commodity,[61] and of the nature and timing of international investment flows. In this sense all our actors operated within the boundaries of the possible. Despite the temptation to see millionaire magnates like Rhodes and Beit as superhuman, not merely making their own but also other people's history untrammelled by the constraints suffered by lesser mortals, even their options were limited by the imperatives of the capital markets and the nature of class struggle.

Thus, as Rob Turrell points out, the forms of labour control which emerged on the diamond fields and which spread from there to have a pervasive influence in the rest of South Africa, took time to evolve. By 1900, as the essays by Turrell, Richardson and Van-Helten, and Moroney show, the characteristic nexus of South Africa's labour controls had emerged: the compound system based upon cheap migrant labour, revamped and far more stringent masters and servants laws, pass laws controlling worker mobility, and a colour bar defended by racist discourse. Yet this grew out of a complex set of interactions between the imperatives of profitability, and the actual struggles between white and black diggers, between share-workers and owners, merchant interests, amalgamating companies and black workers. In the early days at Kimberley, the colonial states were weak and fragmented and labour was in short supply: Africans still had access to land and, as Shillington and Kimble show, could fulfil the growing need for cash through petty commodity production. Black workers were thus able to insist on high wages, impose the 'board wage system' on employers and acquire firearms with their cash, despite the opposition of settler states and some capitalist interests to the trade in guns. With a state more receptive to the demands of industrial capital in power after the Diggers' Revolt of 1875, it became possible for larger companies to develop and then to subordinate labour to rigorous industrial discipline for the first time. The development of large-scale systematic mining underground, which doubled the costs of opencast working, made an uninterrupted labour supply and total control over it all the more critical. As Turrell points out, changes in both government and in the labour process transformed the bargaining position of Africans. The construction of the compounds, which was an integral part of the process of underground mining, was the final element in this.

Yet the evolution of the compounded migrant was not something decided upon and simply imposed by the mining industry of its own volition. As we shall see when we turn to the rural end of the story, it was as much a response to the resistance of African social formations to full proletarianisation as any thought-through scheme by mine magnates to cheapen costs. Indeed, both the migrant labour system and the compounds arose out of 'necessity'. Part of the fascination of Turrell's essay is the way in which it traces the many interests involved in the emergence of this particular solution: the white merchants who would have preferred to see the development of Kimberley on the basis of a white proletarian labour force, the white diggers squeezed out by the process of amalgamation, and the new industrialists, who would probably have preferred the solution proposed by T. Collingwood Kitto, a Cornish mining engineer commissioned in 1879 to write a report on the Kimberley mines: 'If natives could be bound to masters for say seven years . . . under strict government supervision, it would be for the infinite benefit of the natives themselves.'[62]

Contrary to most of the previous literature, Turrell stresses the importance of the change in the work process and behind that the widespread crisis of profitability which led to deep-level mining as the major reason for the introduction of the closed compound in Kimberley. He sees the key moment as being between 1880 and 1885 as property on the fields became concentrated and the earlier dominance of merchant capital was replaced by that of industrial capital. The much vaunted need to control Illicit Diamond Buying (IDB) provided the necessary unifying ideology to overcome the protests of merchants and colonial officials, which they couched in terms of 'free trade' and protecting 'native interests'. By 1888, the reality was almost the exact opposite of mid-Victorian capitalist ideology as portrayed by the apologist John Angove in his famous description of the early days on the diamond fields:

> We see here [in Kimberley under De Beers] that just and equal laws are adminstered, and freedom of labour as well as of capital are elements of prosperity in Africa as well as in Europe . . .[63]

Nor could Angove have had in mind the white workers of Kimberley in penning those words. With the formation of companies, independent white diggers or share-workers were transformed into a carefully controlled group of white overseers bought off with higher wages, and collaborating with management 'in disciplining the African labour force'. They were as carefully, if somewhat more congenially, controlled in the white working-class suburb of Kenilworth, effectively isolated from the black working class.[64] Despite some skirmishing between the diggers and capital in the early 1880s when white workers successfully struck work and even on occasion organised black workers in their support in opposition to body searching and wage reductions, the bitterness of the struggle in Kimberley over the drastic reduction of the white working class resulting from amalgamation was muted. The opening up of the gold fields in the later 1880s drew off many of those so displaced; they followed the familiar pattern of the hard-rock miner in moving to the newly opening mining frontier.

The chapter by Richardson and Van-Helten shows how the strategies adopted by both workers and capital were to see their further development, adaptation and development on the Witwatersrand in the following decades. Initially, not only men, but also money flowed from Kimberley to the Rand, although as Richardson and Van-Helten show, with the opening up of the deep-level mines vast amounts of foreign investment soon became necessary if the mines were to be profitably worked. Although both mine magnate and white worker brought their experience of the struggles in Kimberley to bear in the new circumstances of the Rand, the sheer scale of the gold fields, the technological problems involved, the size of the unskilled labour force required and the even greater inadequacy if not unwillingness of the South African Republic's state apparatus to fulfil the needs of mining capital made the Rand 'a wholly new departure', not only 'in the science of recovering gold in South Africa', but also in social, political and economic organisation.[65] The technological demands of an industry based on low-grade deep-level ore and the ceiling on the price of gold had direct repercussions for the labour force, as Richardson and Van-Helten show. If anything the gold-mining industry was operating under even more stringent financial constraints than the diamond fields; and although the position of gold as the international medium of exchange meant that – unlike the situation at Kimberley – there could never be an oversupplied market (an important factor in the centralisation of capital on the fields)[66] cutting costs was of the essence. As de Kiewiet pointed out a long time ago, it is one of the paradoxes of gold-mining in South Africa that an industry 'that was colossally wealthy . . . could be wealthy only on condition that it jealously watched every penny of its expenditure'.[67]

Despite the urgency of cost-cutting, and despite the fact that the wages of the white 11 per cent of the work force amounted to over 28 per cent of all working costs (compared to 25 per cent for black labour),[68] the mine magnates found it difficult to assault the wages of white workers directly in the 1890s. Skilled workers had to be drawn to the Rand from the existing hard-rock mining areas of the world by the lure of high wages. Initially their bargaining power was considerable: many had experience of union organisation, their skills were in short supply, and in the confrontation between mine magnates and the South African Republic both sides looked for allies amongst the skilled workers.[69] Nevertheless, as Richardson and Van-Helten argue:

> The reliance upon relatively scarce and therefore expensive skills of immigrant miners from Europe, North America and Australasia . . . was in direct conflict with the cost-minimising strategies dictated by the imperatives of profitable production. The solution adopted to resolve this contradiction was to develop a production process which satisfactorily exploited the growing reservoirs of cheap unskilled African labour whilst restricting the scope and extent of white employment in a manner consistent with the difficulties of Witwatersrand production.[70]

Thus, although the mine magnates were unable to lower white wages substantially, they were able to control numbers and the allocation of roles in the labour process; according to Richardson and Van-Helten, the industry was able to distribute its skilled and unskilled labour force in this period to reflect its cost constraints. The result was, as F. R. Johnstone and Rob Davies have shown, that white workers occupied a position of 'extreme structural insecurity'.[71] On the one hand, unlike black workers they were fully proletarianised and no longer had access to the land; on the other hand, as African workers began to acquire skills and as the mine magnates began to transform the technology of mining, their position as skilled workers was also undermined. It was in response to this, and to what Johnstone has termed the 'exploitation colour bars'[72] — the migrant labour system, the compounds and pass laws — that white workers established the 'job colour bar', that is the specific measures to reserve certain categories of work and high wages for whites only.

That the measures evolved by way of defence by white workers assumed 'the specific form of racial discrimination'[73] can only be understood in a context wider than simply Kimberley or the Witwatersrand, as we have already suggested. It should not, however, surprise us that by the beginning of this century the white labour movement believed as fervently as any latter-day protagonist of apartheid in an ideology of segregation. To quote the President of the Witwatersrand Trades and Labour Council in 1907:

> If this country is to be a white man's country and a home in a British Colony for white people, then we must take seriously into consideration our attitude to the coloured question. I would strongly advocate a principle whereby certain territories are set apart

for the natives of this country; and with respect to the Indian coolie and the Chinese, I would absolutely exclude them altogether. . . .[74]

If the 'job colour bar' was a response to the 'exploitation colour bars', we should not exaggerate the speed with which mine magnates were able to establish the exploitation colour bar, whether at Kimberley or on the Rand, or to push down African wages. It was crucial that in the 1890s, as so many of the essays in this volume illustrate, social and economic factors in South Africa were insufficient to proletarianise the local populace 'at a pace consistent with the labour demands of mining and other industries'.[75] Despite its attempts to control the recruiting bill, wages and social or reproduction costs of African labour, according to Richardson and Van-Helten the Chamber of Mines' policies in these respects were only fully crystallised on the eve of the First World War. Initially, as Turrell and Kimble show for Kimberley, and Harries suggests for the Rand, migrant labour was regarded as both expensive and inefficient, the outcome of the weakness of colonial authorities, the continued access Africans had to the land, and the cohesion of pre-colonial social formations. Potentially, the mine magnates on the Rand, doubtless drawing on their knowledge of the efficacy of compounds, pass laws and migrancy at Kimberley by the late 1880s, recognised that it was the black wage bill which could most readily be reduced. In practice, through the 1890s competition over labour frustrated the attempts of the leading magnates to force down wages by collective action through the Chamber of Mines and its recruiting organisations, formed explicitly for that purpose.[76] This explains the urgency of the demand from magnates that the state assist them in the creation, coercion and control of the black labour force, demands which always became more strident when the share market was depressed. It was only after the defeat of the South African Republic by Britain that the mining industry found the state more sympathetic to its demands, and more capable of meeting them.

In the early days of the mining industry, capital not only had to come to terms with, and in the end transform, the weak colonial and republican states, and to tread warily in relation to white labour; as the cluster of essays by Kimble, Shillington, Harries and Guy on the rural end of the story show, they also had to come to terms with African social formations and their ruling classes. Thus the migrant labour system, so central to the apartheid state today, was never the conspiratorially planned solution of mining capital to the problem of labour costs suggested by some of the literature.[77] It is clear from the essays by Kimble, Shillington and Harries in this collection, and from Peter Delius's work on the Pedi,[78] that even before the opening up of the diamond fields, Africans were involved both in commodity production and in migrant wage labour. Nevertheless, both these activities were given an immense impetus by the expansion of the commodity and labour markets after 1870. As these papers make clear, however, it is also important to periodise migrant labour and commodity production. A purely descriptive account which sees the continuities in behaviour from the *difaqane** to the present fails to illuminate either the changing social processes involved or their transformed function. These essays demonstrate the immense problems of drawing conclusions from a simple study of behaviour: the motives which drew men onto the labour markets of South Africa in this period before 1900 were closely related to the nature of social relationships in the pre-industrial societies from which they came. Any assumption of motivation according to the norms of *homo economicus* is a manifest over-simplification.[79]

Equally, however, these essays reveal the inadequacy of seeking the origins of migrant labour in the light of the function it and the reserves have come to play in reproducing a cheap labour force in twentieth-century South Africa. Causes are not necessarily found in consequences. Proletarianisation was undoubtedly largely the result of the penetration of capitalist forces of production; that it was 'incomplete' and took the form of labour migrancy was, as these papers suggest, related to the complex struggles between and within ruling classes over the disposal of the labour power of young men. These struggles were extraordinarily diverse, and were shaped by ecology and forms of pre-capitalist production, the configuration of social classes in the rural social formation, the timing of colonial penetration and the nature of the colonial state, and the impact of Christian missionaries. In terms of the historiography, what is significant is the growing picture of structural relations within African societies acting every bit as powerfully on the actions and consciousness of migrants as any 'pull' of market forces, growth of 'new wants', or voluntarist individual choice on the one hand, or the 'determining role of the South African state' on the other.[80]

The essays on the rural hinterland all in some sense relate to the threat early labour migration and commodity production posed to the gerontocratic order in precolonial African societies and the response of chiefs and elders to that threat. Although, with the exception of the Zulu kingdom, all the societies discussed in these pages had some experience of producing for the market and even of labour migration before the mineral discoveries, they were all essentially geared to the production of use and not exchange values. Both production and reproduction centred around the control by chiefs and elders over young men and women through their control of bridewealth (usually cattle) and hence their control over marriage itself.[81] As Patrick Harries points out in the case of the Tsonga, and it is true for all the societies of southern Africa, kinship and kinship ideology was not merely 'superstructure', but actively entered into and structured relations of production.[82] The possibilities of accumulating storeable

---

**difaqane*: the early nineteenth century wars which swept southern Africa in the wake of the rise of the Zulu Kingdom.

wealth which was implicit in any large-scale moves towards producing for external markets, and which were greatly expanded by the mineral discoveries, challenged not merely the rule of chiefs and elders, but also the norms of redistribution and the validity of the rules of kinship. Much of the history of southern Africa in this period, as indeed of Africa as a whole at similar stages of economic development, was characterised by a struggle between the beneficiaries of the *ancien regime* and those who wished, for whatever reason, to escape its constraints. Commodity production for the market carried the individualist implication that single households could accumulate property without reference to the traditional control of wealth exercised by chiefs and headmen, while some of the early labour migration seems to have been part of a general strategy employed by 'cadets' in an attempt to outflank the control of the elders over bridewealth. Nor were the political and social implications of this potential economic independence lost upon the elders: they attempted to control the threat in a variety of ways, with varying degrees of success, as we shall see. That chiefs and elders were trying to retain control over land, cattle, marriage and tribute labour whilst others were trying to establish direct links with colonial markets without chiefly intercession has a double significance when one considers that such internal disruption occurred at the very time that traditional sovereignty was being threatened from without.

The combination of internal and external disruption is very clear, for instance, from Shillington's account of the Southern Tswana. As he shows, even after the annexation of the diamondiferous area of Griqualand West as a British crown colony in 1871, the Tlhaping were able to avoid working on the diamond mines through increased production for the growing urban market. The teeming city had a wide range of needs, and prices were high. Shillington's figures of the prices paid for wood,[83] for example, indicate just how much of a seller's market this new urban agglomeration was. Yet this economic independence was both limited and short-lived. The rapid shift towards surplus production for the market was more than a mere tinkering with economic policy. It greatly increased stratification, undermined an already fragile environment and profoundly disrupted the Tlhaping polity of Jantje Mothibi. That these consequences were not inevitable is well illustrated by Shillington's citation of other Tswana polities, where chiefs were able to retain control over the new economic forces. Nevertheless for Jantje the results were disastrous, partly because of the earlier impact of missionary-inspired individualism, colonial land speculation and the liquor trade. When, in 1878, the chief's son tried to restore chiefly hegemony by rebelling against the colonial order, he met with little popular support. The rebellion simply made matters worse, and Shillington shows how in its aftermath, the colonial administration was able to impose its policies of hut-tax collection and land settlement in reserves. By the

of sharecropping relations in the Orange Free
ere, was the 1913 Natives' Land Act, a piece of
pins South Africa's political economy. Keegan is
ticularities of the Free State and the impact of the
ugh its ramifications were to be as significant for
ndependent African landowners outside of the Free
agriculturalists the act was the final *coup de grâce*,
nquest and confirming expropriation; for others it was
battleground for further struggle between tenants and
wn its conditions. Not only did it definitively limit the
e for African land purchase in the future to the existing
ed landlords to impose stricter terms of tenancy by
s under the Masters and Servants Law and transforming
nto labour tenants.[102]

and Matsetela's accounts it is clear that these changes did
pen overnight. The Pooes, for example, were able to
sturdy independence for a further twenty-five years by
ut of the Orange Free State to the south-western Transvaal.
939 even Naphtali Pooe had been changed from sharecropper
e labourer, albeit a privileged one, while four of his five sons
king in the urban centres.[103]

Act took time to bite should occasion no great surprise. As
ductive relations in the countryside are not simply changed by
fiat.[104] Even after the passage of the Act there were struggling
who saw sharecropping arrangements (now weighted in their
eful transition to more fully capitalised relations of production,
ays of bypassing its provisions. The Act was in any case a
measure which attempted to resolve the contradictory demands of
nine magnate: that it should have fully satisfied neither does not
gnificance in the long run. Passed at a time of political uncertainty,
mpted to be all things to all (white) men: by stabilising the frontiers
rves, the government hoped to satisfy the demands of the mining
or a rural base for cheap migrant labour, the clamour of white workers
gation, and the demands of liberals that African land rights be
ed and protected. Although this frustrated the desire of white farmers
tional land and labour through the expropriation of the reserves, they
o be placated by the increased control they were to have over
opping and non-labour tenants, while the segregatory rhetoric was
also to appeal to the growing number of 'poor whites' being forced off the
by the same processes of capitalisation in this period.[105] For an act that
ed in its preamble to be both temporary and uniform, it was both

1890s, massively impoverished, the Tlhaping were locked into the migrant
labour system, no longer capable even of subsisting on their restricted and
overgrazed reserve lands.[84]

Patrick Harries' description of the Tsonga in southern Mozambique suggests
a more prolonged and ambiguous struggle by chiefs and elders to retain control
over their followers. Tsonga involvement in the labour markets of the Cape and
especially Natal went back to the 1850s and 1860s, long before any direct
colonial administration was established in Mozambique. There the attempts of
chiefs and elders to retain their control over this process took the form of a
manipulation both of bridewealth and of the age of marriage.[85] Despite this,
however, and despite the attempts by chiefs to control recruiting and secure
better conditions for their followers, the Delagoa Bay hinterland lost an
enormous number of its able-bodied, economically active young men to the
mines, farms and plantations of South Africa. According to Harries, by the
1890s about half the able-bodied young men were involved in labour migration,
and of these between 30 and 40 per cent did not return.[86]

There is little doubt that the process was speeded up with the Portuguese
conquests of the mid-1890s. By the turn of the century, the loss of young men
from the agricultural cycle, together with further losses from the spread of
diseases acquired on the mines – TB, miners' phthisis, venereal disease and
consequent infertility – was beginning to have serious repercussions on the
agricultural sufficiency of the area.[87]

In terms of chiefly control, it would seem that of the societies considered in
this volume, in the nineteenth century, and possibly well into the twentieth,
the Sotho ruling lineage was most successful in retaining its position, and
indeed in using the new economic and political order to secure its political
dominance. Thus Judy Kimble sees the great expansion of commodity
production and migrant labour in the period between 1868 and 1880 in
Basutoland as the direct result of Koena determination to secure its continued
power through military organisation.[88] Young men were therefore deliberately
sent to work on the diamond fields to secure firearms: a policy threatened by the
Gun War with the Cape Colony, in 1881, but ultimately vindicated from the
point of view of the Koena rulers in its outcome. When the British were forced
to take over the territory from the Cape Colony which had proved unable to end
the war, the Koena chiefs were able to secure their own continued dominance
over the social formation through their alliance with the colonial authorities. A
not dissimilar pattern was to emerge in the case of Chief Khama of the Ngwato
in Bechuanaland, and the Dhlamini rulers of Swaziland.[89]

Unlike the situation among the Tswana, Sotho and Tsonga, until their
conquest in 1879 and the civil wars of the 1880s, the Zulu participated in
neither the growing commodity nor the labour markets of South Africa. Indeed,

it can be argued that it was their very self-sufficiency which led to their being labelled an 'anachronism' and to their conquest.[90] Yet Jeff Guy shows the complexity of the situation in which there was no simple equation between conquest and total proletarianisation. As he shows, the first concern of the administration was for the wherewithal to pay for its own costs, rather than the labour needs of industrialising South Africa. Hut-tax had to be earned by wage labour outside of Zululand – and secured by tying migrants to continued homestead production. Thus attempts by the colonial state to ensure the continued control of chiefs over *lobola* (bridewealth) and thus marriage and homestead formation, the so-called 'recognition of native law' under the Shepstone system, were not 'just a veneer covering total subordination'. They were based originally 'on a shrewd understanding of the distribution of power in precolonial Nguni societies and the way in which this could be utilised by the colonial state'.[91] The resemblance to the attempts of the Tsonga chiefs to control the return of young men through marriage and bridewealth is thus not coincidental. Yet, as Guy points out, despite certain continuities of form with pre-colonial practices the basic principles of both marriage and homestead formation were dramatically altered 'almost as soon as the colonial state was founded'.[92] With the imposition and successful collection of hut-tax in 1889 – significantly after Dinuzulu, son and successor to the last Zulu king Cetshwao had been exiled – Zululand was fully locked into the colonial economy, and the number of migrants seeking work on the Rand and elsewhere dramatically increased. The contradictions thus set up, Guy argues, cannot be encapsulated within the formula of 'the articulation of modes of production'.[93]

Jeff Guy also reminds us of the disasters of the 1890s which profoundly affected the speed with which Africans were incorporated into the capitalist economy, and the terms on which this occurred.[94] Smallpox, drought, locusts and rinderpest did not in themselves subordinate Africans to capitalist production. Nevertheless in the context of prior colonial conquest and taxation they undoubtedly played a major role in accelerating proletarianisation and undermining many societies which had hitherto been able to stand outside the migrant labour nexus.[95] It is significant that wages on the mines did not reach their 1896 level – the year of rinderpest and of the first deep-level gold mines going into production – until after the Second World War.[96] The consolidation of the settler state after the South African War, the importation of Chinese indentured labour and the formation of the Union of South Africa all greatly strengthened the hold of capital over African societies already weakened by the forces we have been considering. By the beginning of the twentieth century the terms on which Africans entered the labour and commodity markets had inexorably altered, their bargaining position gravely impaired. The Bambatha rebellion of 1906 in which over 3 500 Natal Africans were killed in what in

extraordinarily diverse and complex in its provisions and permanent in its long-term effects.[106] In its immediate application, however, as Keegan and Matsetela demonstrate, it depended very largely on local support and opposition.

If Naphtali Pooe was only finally forced to leave the land completely in 1954 to join his sons in Vanderbijl Park, thousands of others, both black and white had succumbed far sooner. The *bywoners** the Pooes outpaced were only a tiny sample of a far wider group of poor white farmers for whom access to capital was denied and who lacked security. In the ambiguous meeting ground of the slums of Johannesburg they were to rub shoulders with landless black peasants similarly pushed out of the rural areas of South Africa by the capitalisation of agriculture.[107]

To summarise, then, it seems clear that the flow of labour into an insatiable industrial market has to be seen within the context of the changing rural structures of southern Africa as well as within the context of repressive legislation emanating from the industrial centres. Work both within and outside this volume suggests that there was no simple or single route from the pre-industrial systems of farming to proletarianisation. Just as the image of Africans simply as victims of 'ultra-exploitation' needs modification, so too we need to see the rural societies of southen Africa contributing in their own right to the nature of urban change and not merely as part of a periphery soaking up the shockwaves generated in urban epicentres, though undeniably the industrial development of South Africa brought profound structural shifts to their economies. Undoubtedly, some cultivators were forced into wage labour because they were denied access to the means of production by conquest and expropriation,[108] the reservation of land or such measures as the 1913 Land Act. Yet for many, wage labour was only an aspect of a much fuller economic and social existence. In Basutoland before 1900, as in Pondoland until the 1920s,[109] labour migration and increased crop production could go hand in hand. Not the least important aspect of South Africa's industrialisation in this period was the capacity and probably the need for capital to coexist with older forms of production, and this was not merely a strategy for paying lower wages: it was equally a response to African and indeed Afrikaner resistance to proletarianisation. Indeed the increasing recourse to state intervention suggests the resilience.

That there were a variety of routes leading to wage labour and to town had differing implications for consciousness. As Judy Kimble suggests for Basutoland in the 1870s and 80s there were already then three kinds of migrant: adherents of the chieftaincy, whose aspirations were still locked into the pre-industrial moral and political economy; Christians who had accepted the

*White tenant farmers or 'squatters'.

virtues of individual enterprise and private property preached by the missionaries; and a small but increasingly important number of landless peasants.[110] Perceptions of the urban environment were probably at least as coloured by this prior experience as by objective industrial conditions.

It is nevertheless a curiously mechanical, Eurocentric view which would deny these migrants the appellation 'working class' because their consciousness was still partially formed and informed by their very recent experience of contracting rural options, the onslaught on African peasant production and social and political decay in the countryside. As Charles van Onselen showed in a seminal essay on worker consciousness on the Rhodesian gold-mines, their rural roots did not prevent migrants in Central Africa from displaying an acute understanding of the labour market and their position in it.[111] Turrell shows black workers as well as white beginning to organise in Kimberley in the 1880s, while within four years of the opening up of the Witwatersrand, according to Richardson and Van-Helten, the response of Africans to a pay reduction of 14.2 per cent was 'swift and entirely unexpected':

> The mine manager's house at the Anglo-Tharsis mine was blown up by dynamite and the secretary of the Meyer and Charlton mine, F. McMillan, was caught in his burning house on the morning of 24 October 1890 as 'the wage reduction had made the Kaffir take an instant dislike to Mr McMillan who also discharged the duties of paymaster.'[112]

In the following year, a leading magnate, Lionel Phillips, was complaining bitterly that 'of 80 Boys [sic] received yesterday only 18 remain this morning' because their conditions of employment had been misrepresented. Although more workers turned up later in the day, they too 'refused point blank to work for the Company saying they were not "slaves" and refused to be "sold" '.[113] Richardson and Van-Helten record further examples of formal and informal resistance among workers on the mines before the end of the First World War, when Phil Bonner takes up the story among non-mining workers on the Rand.

We are not, of course, in any sense arguing that this was fully-blown class consciousness, or that we are talking of a homogenous working class. Interests, the perceptions of interests, and thus strategies of resistance varied widely both within and outside of the working class, and hence provoked conflict and very different modes of adaptation to, and rejection of, the new colonial order. Moroney shows in these pages, for example, that even among African mineworkers at the turn of the century there were gradations of skill and differing commitments to urban life as well as ethnic distinctions between workers which could be used and manipulated by both the state and the mine magnates.[114] Lack of homogeneity does not, however, deny the existence of a class; even in the 'advanced' capitalist societies of Europe and North America the consciousness of a class 'in itself and for itself' has been the exception rather than the rule – and the rare exception at that.[115] Here too normative values derived from kinship networks, ethnic identification and the pre-industrial moral economy have been part and parcel of working-class cultures.[116] The specificity of the African working class arose from the way in which it emerged from earlier social relationships, and 'made' itself in response to the world of mine magnate, poor Afrikaner, English-speaking worker and capitalist farmer. The sheer speed with which a workforce was hewn out of the non-capitalist, agrarian societies of southern Africa had profound implications, as did the racial categorisation imposed by late nineteenth century colonialism. R. Acutt's observation of a chanting African work-gang encapsulates some of the perception of the resulting experience:

> In this case, they [the Zulu] formed gangs of four, which allowed each man to a corner of the bag. One would act as leader and start as a rhythmical repetition of words chanted over and over again, with the others following . . . They would give one heave and up would go the bag . . . Then they would start off for the stack, chanting Sithi O! Umlungu mubi! Sitho O! Umlungu mubi! (We say: Oh! The white man's bad!)
> Then they would change the rhythm to Isikhalo sempofana (Roughly – The burden of the poor . . .)[117]

For the newly proletarianised Zulu work-gang, though the causal connections may not have been stated, the perception seems clear: the black man is poor, the white man is bad. Racial and class domination were identical. Yet for the 'growing and increasingly coherent class of educated Africans' who were drawn to the burgeoning towns of Kimberley and Johannesburg because of the opportunities they provided 'for employment and for the utilisation of skills associated with the literacy they possessed',[118] neither proposition seemed so clear: there were some rich, or potentially richer, blacks; there were – some – whites who were not 'bad'. As Brian Willan shows in his graphic description of Sol Plaatje's Kimberley in the 1890s, Christianity, colonialism and capitalism had led to the rise of a privileged black elite who had begun to have an identity even before the mineral discoveries. Drawn pre-eminently from the mission stations of the Cape Colony and Natal, they were the living embodiment of the mid-Victorian belief in 'progress' and 'improvement'. 'Progress' and 'improvement' were, like 'Free Trade', code words which evoked an ideological package which included the virtues of free wage labour, secure property rights, linked to a free market in land and individual freehold tenure, equality before the law and some notion of 'no taxation without representation'.[119] This cluster of concepts lay at the base of the Cape liberal tradition, expressed by John Nobel in 1877:

> The aim of the policy of the [Cape] Colonial Government since 1855 has been to establish and maintain peace, to diffuse civilisation and Christianity, and to establish society on the basis of individual property and personal industry.[120]

The essentially optimistic belief of Cape liberalism in the assimilability of Africans as individuals had its roots in the practicalities of Free Trade imperialism: the object of which was, to quote the leading advocate of the abolition of slavery and the fostering of legitimate commerce, to bring forth

> into the markets of the world some scores of millions of customers who may be taught to grow the raw material which we require, and who require the manufactured goods which we produce. [121]

At the Cape the vision always reflected a limited reality. It was never quite so simple to convince Africans living in kinship societies, holding land in a variety of forms of communal tenure, of the moral superiority of individual tenure, nor those settlers who had sources of unfree labour and little cash of the virtues of free wage labour. Nor was the guarantee of equality before the law as colour-blind as it appeared. Nevertheless, liberal bourgeois ideology had had its triumphs at the Cape: the slave trade *was* abolished; Ordinance 50 of 1827 *did* provide a measure of equality before the law and access to the courts for Khoisan, and later African, labour; slaves *were* emancipated in 1834, even if their 'freedom' was far from unambiguous thereafter; attempts were made to establish a settler society in Britain's image, engaged in commercial agriculture and producing raw materials (especially wool) for the British market; a prosperous black peasantry was encouraged to the same end, and was granted a property-based but colour-blind access to the franchise when the Cape was granted self-government in the second half of the century. [122]

Mid-Victorian liberals in Britain and at the Cape had little doubt of the capacity of 'commerce' to transform African societies. The assault of humanitarians on 'savage customs', slavery, polygyny, the conviction that Africans could rapidly and painlessly become sturdy Christian yeomen, arose from what Tony Hopkins has called 'a pervasive vision of a progressive world order'. [123]

Marx was talking about the same thing, though he put it rather differently, when he wrote in the Manifesto:

> The bourgeoisie, by the rapid improvement of all instruments of production, by the immensely facilitated means of communication draws all, even the most barbarian nations, into civilisation. The cheap prices of its commodities are the heavy artillery with which it batters down all Chinese walls . . . It compels all nations on pain of extinction to adopt the bourgeois mode of production; it compels them to introduce what it calls civilisation . . . In one word it creates a world after its own image . . . [124]

The reality was always more complex than this optimistic mid-Victorian passage would allow. It was nonetheless out of this vision that the black Christian elite was born on the mission stations of the eastern Cape and Natal. Clearly, the mission station marked for many a fundamental alteration in style of life, in the aftermath of the *difaqane*. Much of their earliest received experience, as that of their parents (and in the case of Mrs Pooe[125]) testified to the anarchy of that period, to the arbitrary quality of authoritarian chiefly rule, to warfare, hunger. Their enthusiastic acceptance of Christianity and its counterpart, western education, were both deeply felt and highly instrumental: as Bonner remarks of the petty bourgeoisie and aspirant petty bourgeoisie in Johannesburg after the First World War, 'Education and being educated . . . became entrenched as a central value and aspiration in [their] consciousness . . . It was the principal means to breach the citadel of white privilege and the key element in [their] self-identification.'[126] It is fascinating to note from Turrell's piece, for example, that it was a Lovedale graduate and Free Church of Scotland minister, the Rev. Gwayi Tyamzashe, who was the last African to hold a diamond claim in Dutoitspan in 1883.[127] Willan takes up the story with the lamentations over his death in 1896.[128] Crucially, as a minister Tyamzashe was not only literate, but also in receipt of a regular income. Access to mission education provided men like Tyamzashe and Plaatje and their confrères with a set of skills which, for a generation or more, enabled them to escape manual labour.[129] Their escape was to be pre-eminently to the towns where these skills could be best employed, and where they could forge a new and wider identity.

Brian Willan sympathetically traces the educational, friendship and kinship networks, marriage patterns, musical activities, sports clubs, debating societies and churches which 'created a sense of class and community out of the . . . mission-educated Africans who lived on the diamond fields'.[130] He concludes, 'Cosmopolitan Kimberley, the Colony's leading marriage market, contributed more than anywhere else to the process of creating a national African petty bourgeoisie out of a diverse set of regionally and ethnically defined local groupings'[131] – a national petty bourgeoisie who were to figure largely in the creation of African national and nationalist organisations in succeeding decades.

Paradoxically Kimberley, which gave this petty bourgeoisie its greatest opportunity, was also ultimately the harbinger of its destruction. By the time the African petty bourgeoisie was so enthusiastically 'improving' itself, Victorian faith in the prescriptive power of 'civilisation' was waning. As the forces of production expanded and made possible the mid-Victorian vision in a dramatically new way, so imperialists and Cape liberals retreated from the vision.[132] The demands of monopoly capital for vast quantities of unskilled contract labour, the speed with which that labour had to be created and coerced, left little room in the long run for an enfranchised peasantry and black artisan class.[133] In addition, the growing insecurity which underpinned the new imperialist expansion and the parallel changes in ideology increasingly shaped by Social Darwinism, 'Anglo-Saxon race pride' and notions of national efficiency on the one hand, together with the rise of Afrikaner nationalism and the consolidation of settler society on the other rendered them more vulnerable. By

1918, Bonner maintains, the African petty bourgeoisie was 'stunted and repressed'.[134]

Yet to conclude from this that the Kimberley petty bourgeoisie was a doomed and naive group playing at being European while sitting on a time-bomb which would destroy their claim to special consideration and status would be wrong. They never accepted the white man's ways without question even when, as Willan shows, they modelled themselves quite self-consciously on the precepts of the mid-Victorian vision. They used them with a sense of irony and made use of the space this allowed to manoeuvre for status, income and security. They were able to manipulate institutions, concepts of legal equality, and rhetoric to sustain their position long after its material base in the dominance of merchant capital and the prosperity of the black peasantry had passed.[135] We should not underestimate the small victories, even if in the end we judge their faith to have been misplaced. Most notably, their acceptance of British supremacy and imperial ideology and institutions enabled them to appeal for protection against the more immediate violence of settler rapacity by calling on imperial norms. It was of course in large part delusion. But for those who witnessed settler encroachment on African lands,[136] the ferocity with which Afrikaner commandos threatened to end the franchise of black communities in the invaded Cape Colony during the war,[137] or the savagery with which Natal suppressed the Bambatha uprising,[138] the imperial state was the lesser of two evils.

Nor was this the only violence to be escaped by assuming a new identity. By proving their acceptability to whites in terms of education, culture and class, they could hope also to escape the brutalities of the mining compound and underground labour as well as the indignity of the third-class railway department. If, as Bonner says, they were denied the metropolitan petty bourgeoisie's ideology of 'statology, the myth of the ladder and status quo ante-capitalism',[139] they nonetheless drew on an only partially defeated and once hegemonic liberal ideology which still had widespread appeal amongst missionaries, administrators and even some politicians. At least until the Pact government of 1924 they had access to the government and the Native Affairs Department, even if with decreasing hope of making their voices heard.[140] They claimed to speak on behalf of all Africans, and mostly they saw no great contradiction between the needs of the masses and their own self-interest. They struggled for a world of greater equality of opportunity – a world in which they would inevitably and naturally be the black factory-owners, judges, civil servants, professors. For the most part theirs was the path of caution and conciliation.

Yet in moments of great crisis this petty bourgeoisie could be radicalised and adopt a more militant political style, as Philip Bonner shows in his careful delineation and analysis of the upsurge of working-class action in the aftermath of the First World War. The South African economy was perhaps more profoundly affected than we have perhaps fully realised by the First World War.[141] As Bonner shows, it was during the war that manufacturing industry expanded dramatically for the first time, sheltered by the difficulties of wartime communications and the disruption of European production, and fostered by the state and a mining industry anxious to find its necessary stores locally if they could not be obtained abroad; the number of manufacturing establishments on the Rand increased from 862 to 1763, and the number of non-mining workers went up by nearly 50 per cent to over 90 000.[142]

In Johannesburg the petty bourgeoisie and 'aspirant petty bourgeoisie' were a rather wider and less well-defined group than in Plaatje's Kimberley, although undoubtedly there too we were only seeing the more visible, articulate and prestigious segment of the class. At the lower levels, it is rather more difficult to distinguish the store 'boys' and messengers, the mechanics and artisans, the clerks and hospital attendants who carried 'certificates of exemption', 'the badge of the petty bourgeoisie', from the increasing number of urbanised workers in Johannesburg.[143] Wartime inflation had led to a rise in prices and a fall in real income which had acted as the trigger for the most serious outbreak of working-class action to occur in South Africa until the Second World War. Bonner argues that it had also seriously eroded the small wage differential which separated this group from the working class.[144] The racist practices encompassed by the term 'colour bar' seriously obstructed their upward mobility or accumulation of capital, while they shared with other workers the increasingly overcrowded, disease-ridden and squalid housing in the locations, as the rural dispossessed, both black and white, flowed to the city in search of work. The blatant use by the state of the pass laws to put down the sanitary workers' strike in April 1918 was a signal for widespread disaffection for members of the petty bourgeoisie, who came to see 'the law' in a new light: as the Transvaal Native Congress declared in 1919, 'Passes prevent money'.[145]

Drawing on Laclau's analysis of the ideological class struggle, Bonner maintains that the petty bourgeoisie, 'lying between the two dominant relations of production, labour and capital, tended to swing according to the pressures exercised on it by the two contending parties'.[146] In the years after the First World War, he suggests, such was the strength of working-class militancy and action that it posed a severe crisis of identification and commitment for the petty bourgeoisie. For a rare and brief moment, it split, as a number of leading members of the major petty-bourgeois political institution, the Transvaal Native Congress, articulated the demands of workers, were swayed by the radical arguments of African members of the International Socialist League and the International Workers of Africa, and united with them in mass class action.

It was, however, a fragile and short-lived alliance. While the strikes and demonstrations were put down with the full weight of the police and army, a series of measures were adopted by the state and by individual whites to defuse the situation by co-opting the black petty bourgeoisie. And although this reformism made little impact on the broader structures of exploitation, together with rising unemployment and a switch of allegiance by some members of the Congress to action in the rural areas, it did serve to successfully restabilise the situation on the Rand. [147]

It is to the non-coercive elements of this restabilisation that Tim Couzens turns in his essay on 'moralizing leisure time'. Like Willan, he is also concerned with the 'overlapping institutions' in which culture is embodied, and to their active creation. But whereas in the Kimberley of the 1890s the models were classically drawn from Britain, in Johannesburg of the 1920s there is a significant 'transatlantic connection'.

This connection was, of course, not a new one. American missionaries had been active in Natal since the 1830s and had had a profound effect on the formation of Natal's *kholwa* (Christian) community and its ethos, as Deborah Gaitskell also reminds us. [148] Nevertheless, it was on the Rand that the American missionaries came into their own as pioneers of new methods of social control, their expertise drawn from the black American experience and the great northern cities of the United States. Their influence permeated the institutions set up in the wake of the post-war militancy on the Rand, which ranged from movies and football in the mining compounds, to the Gamma Sigma debating clubs and the Bantu Men's Social Centre for the petty bourgeoisie. The American influence entered too through the Phelps-Stokes Commission in 1921, and the support of the Carnegie Corporation for the establishment of a library for blacks and then for the South African Institute of Race Relations — at much the same time as the foundation was also funding a major enquiry into the 'poor white' question in an effort to restabilise another area of potential urban upheaval. In all of this, Couzens is concerned to show the intricate connections between the deliberate attempts to 'moralize leisure time' through the 'channelling of literature and drama' in particular, and the shaping of African artistic sensibility. As he remarks, 'even literary influences do not come floating out of the air'. Nor are they simply a matter of individual choice: we are back again at the question of 'necessity', agency and experience. [149] Couzens deals with this in the context of the apparently chance hearing by Peter Abrahams, the young black writer, of Paul Robeson's recording of 'Old Man River' to which Abrahams 'attributes a large measure of his consciousness'. [150] Unravelling the 'limits and determinants of choice' which are set outside of the dictates of personal biography is thus the main object of the second section of this essay.

At the heart of Couzens's piece is a concept of 'social control'. And both here, and in Deborah Gaitskell's account of women's prayer associations, *manyanos*, which follows it, the concept would seem to have a certain utility despite the debate which its use has aroused.[151] The use of the term does not imply that there was no philanthropic impulse behind the creation of these institutions, though it erodes any unambiguous notion of 'philanthropy'; nor does it mean that attempts at social control were automatically successful. The outcome of conflict, they could in turn become the new arenas for struggle. The existence of institutions of social control does, however, partly explain why the absence of consensus does not necessarily spill over into overt conflict.[152] At the same time, in the South African case we should not forget the role of more explicitly coercive apparatuses of control of which the 'criminalisation' of the black population through the pass laws is perhaps the paramount example.[153]

Increasingly, feminist historians have drawn our attention to the role of the family as an institution of 'social control'. The sensitive essay by Deborah Gaitskell[154] is in part directed to the ways in which adolescent female sexuality is so controlled. The *manyanos* which are her starting point enjoy massive support from Christian women in both town and countryside. Gaitskell argues that these evolved in part to enable women to cope with the new stresses on the family resulting from industrialisation. As yet, we know far too little of what was happening to black women in either town or countryside in the period covered by this volume (or indeed either before or after) and facing, as Jacklyn Cock has reminded us, a triple oppression as women, as blacks, and as workers.[155] Gaitskell's is a pioneering attempt to look at some of the implications for black women of the changed division of labour within the family which came with migrant labour, and the changed ideology of the role of women which came with late Victorian Christianity. As traditional practices of external sexual intercourse were abandoned among Christians and peer-group education through initiation ceremonies was discouraged by missionaries, a much greater burden of responsibility was thrown on mothers to control adolescent female sexuality. At the same time, Christian women in the towns were facing the contradictory demands of a mission ideology which cast them in the role of dutiful housewives, and an economic situation which forced them out of the home if their families were to survive.[156] No longer subject to the control of chiefs and elders over their productive and reproductive capacity,[157] in the towns African women faced the equally constraining demands of 'Gold and God'.[158] The uniformed prayer associations were a creative attempt to meet the challenge.

If Gaitskell's essay takes us to an area of black female initiative, in David Coplan's piece too we look at the emergence of new cultural forms as a result of urbanisation and proletarianisation.[159] His is an ambitious and richly textured attempt to look at the diversity of the African music in South Africa. Starting with the musical innovation already in evidence among the black communities in Kimberley, he traces the varied influences of trade-store instruments, rural culture and Coloured, Afrikaner, British and black American music on African modes of expression. Not the least important aspect of his essay is the clear evidence he offers that African musical innovation in the township depended on the interaction of one African musical mode with another, rather than any simplistic notion of syncretism as a result of the interaction of African 'traditional' forms with European 'culture'. Indeed this very formulation presupposes the existence of a single 'culture', whether black or white, which his and other essays in this collection, we hope, have gone far to demolish. As Coplan illustrates, not only were there the discrete worlds in which musical cultures could develop, as on the mines and mission stations; there was also a constant interaction between mine-compound and urban location (something which Moroney's essay also vividly portrays) between town and countryside, and between the mission and all of these. The result is an immensely fertile range and versatility: from *famo* and *sefela* to *amakwaya* and the music of Scottish regimental bands.[160] Coplan, too, reminds us of the 'multi-layered' nature of popular culture.

Coplan ends, 'what has been important in popular urban culture is that it has not reflected idealised notions of social encapsulation or opposition between "red" and Christian, migrant and town-dweller, proletarian and petty bourgeois, townsman and countryman'.[161] Despite the variety, we are witnessing the creation of a complex urban culture born of shared experience and given a common meaning through shared symbols and practices.[162] It had its roots in a material life which created both divisions and new unities, and gave strategies for surviving and creating a space for living in a new and harsh world, if not, as yet for transforming it.

Notes

1 The phrases from E. Genovese, *Roll, Jordan, Roll* (London, 1975) and E. P. Thompson, *The Making of the English Working Class* (Harmondsworth, 1968) are deliberatively evocative because of the ways in which these powerful and compassionate works have shaped our thinking on South Africa, even where we have parted company from them on specific issues.

2 To cite only the most obvious recent publications: I. L. Walker and E. Weinbren, *2,000 Casualties. A History of Trade Unions and the Labour Movement in the Union of South Africa* (Johannesburg, 1961); E. Katz, *A History of White Workers in the Transvaal and the General Strike of 1913* (Johannesburg, 1976); F. A. Johnstone, *Class, Race and Gold. A study of class relations and racial discrimination* (London, 1976) (which has far more on the state, capital and white workers than on the black working class after its 'super-exploited' position has been established); R. Davies,

Capital, State and White Labour in South Africa, 1900–1960 (Brighton, 1979); and H. Wolpe, 'The "white working class" in South Africa', *Economy and Society*, 4, 2, 1976.

3 For a fascinating discussion of the term 'experience', a key concept in the work of E. P. Thompson, see P. Anderson, *Arguments within English Marxism* (London, 1980), pp. 25–30; we use it here in the 'neutral' sense, 'an occurrence or episode as it is lived by the participants, the subjective texture of objective actions' (Anderson, p. 26).

4 Thus, although in the nineteenth century merchant capital stimulated commodity production and began to undermine pre-capitalist social formations in South Africa (see below, Kimble and Shillington in particular; also S. Marks and A. Atmore, *Economy and Society in Pre-industrial South Africa* [London, 1980]), unlike industrial capital, it did not attempt to transform productive relations or the non-capitalist social structures. It was dependent for its surplus on these exisiting social forms, and so, as Geoffrey Kay points out, 'its revolutionary role has been countered by [a] conservative tendency to protect the status quo' (*Development and Underdevelopment. A Marxist Analysis* [London, 1975], p. 98).

5 E. Webster (ed.), *Essays in Southern African Labour History* (Johannesburg, 1978); B. Bozzoli (ed.), *Labour, Townships and Protest, Studies in the Social History of the Witwatersrand* (Johannesburg, 1979). We are not suggesting the strikes were the only influence. Some of the 'revisionist' literature was already moving in this direction, including van Onselen's previous work on the Rhodesian mineworkers.

6 P. L. van den Berghe, *South Africa: a study in conflict* (California, 1967) p. 267. There has been something of a shift in recent South African and American liberal writings on this issue, whether in response to the events of the 1970s or the radical critique. See, for example, H. Adam and H. Giliomee, *Ethnic Power Mobilized. Can South Africa change?* (New Haven and London, 1979), who find 'the focus on class formation' has 'superior explanatory value' to the emphasis on racism or cultural pluralism, though they allege its proponents have an inadequate 'grasp of the psychological aspects of ethnicity versus class' (pp. 46–50, esp. 46). They do not apply their insights to the black population at all on the grounds that 'cleavages and currents within the ruling ethnic group – rather than the actions of the subordinates – are likely to influence South Africa's future in the short run' (p. ix). Even in the very short run, events have belied their analysis.

7 See, for example, R. Davies, *Capital, State and White Labour in South Africa, 1900–1960*; F. A. Johnstone, *Class, Race and Gold*; M. Legassick, 'Forced Labour, Industrialization and Racial Differentiation' in J. Harris (ed.), *The Political Economy of Africa* (Cambridge, Mass., 1975) and 'South Africa: Capital Accumulation and Violence', *Economy and Society*, III, 3, 1974; S. Marks and A. Atmore (eds), *Economy and Society in Pre-industrial South Africa*; S. Trapido, 'South Africa in a comparative study of industrialization', *Journal of Development Studies*, 7, 3, 1971; H. Wolpe, 'Capitalism and cheap labour power: from segregation to apartheid', *Economy and Society*, I, 4, 1972; and articles in the *Journal of Southern African Studies* and the *Review of African Political Economy* by some of the authors cited above, and B. Bozzoli, D. Innes, D. Kaplan, M. Morris and D. O'Meara.

8 R. Davies, *Capital, State and White Labour*, p. 32.

9 cf. H. J. and R. E. Simons, *Class and Colour in South Africa, 1850–1950* (Harmondsworth, 1969), p. 618: 'South Africa uniquely demonstrates that a dominant racial minority can perpetuate social rigidities and feudalistic traits on an

advanced and expanding industrial base.'

10 R. Davies, *Capital, State and White Labour*, p. 32.

11 R. Turrell, Chapter 1 below, p. 50–2.

12 G. Clarence-Smith, 'Ideology and Racism in South Africa', unpublished paper to the South African social history workshop, London, 1981, p. 3.

13 cf. this passage from Lionel Phillips, Chairman of the Central Mining and Investment Corporation and a leading member of the mining fraternity to his son, F. R. Phillips (2 March 1922):

> . . . the abolition of the Colour Bar [which he considers 'irrational and immoral'] by a stroke of the pen . . . would be an absurdity because, for the proper working of the mining industry a large number of skilled White men of all kinds are essential. . . . Even leaving the human aspect of the matter aside, it would be bad business for any mining company to entrust its winding machines, or the supervision of any work requiring initiative, fortitude and intelligence, to Natives. They would not dream of doing it. But this is not on account of their colour, but of their actual inferiority. You must have learned by this time that Natives are quite intelligent when they have to repeat an operation which they have been thoroughly taught to perform, but they would be most unsatisfactory if they had to meet an emergency in the course of carrying out that operation. . . .

Cited in M. Fraser and A. Jeeves, *All That Glittered. Selected correspondence of Lionel Phillips, 1890–1924* (Cape Town, 1977).

14 O. Schreiner, *Undine* (London, 1929), p. 194.

15 The term is Tom Nairn's in 'The modern Janus' in his *The Break-up of Britain: Crisis and Neo-nationalism* (London, 1977), p. 353: 'as capitalism spread and smashed the ancient social formations surrounding it, there [sic] always tended to fall apart along the faultlines contained inside them . . . these lines of fissure were nearly always ones of nationality (although in certain well-known cases deeply established religious divisions could perform the same function)'. We would argue that racism is analogous.

16 P. Burke, 'Reflections on the Historiographical Revolution in France: the *Annales* School and British Social History', *Review*, I, 3/4, 1978, p. 154.

17 Faced with the evidence of a growth rate second only to that of Japan in the 1960s, when apartheid policies, supposedly inimical to economic growth were being implemented to an unprecedented degree, some commentators argued that had it not been for the irrational intervention of the polity the growth could have been even higher. But this notion of 'optimal growth', of an economy in some way free of political constraints, exists only in the imagination of the wilder exponents of 'free enterprise'.

18 The phrase recurs in R. Davies, *Capital, State and White Labour* and in the work of other South African followers of Poulantzas.

19 See, for example, G. Gerhart, *Black Power in South Africa. The evolution of an ideology* (California, 1978), p. 29, writing of the period before 1948:

> Most rural-born workers, having little or no formal education, found the workings of a modern economic system far beyond comprehension. The fatalism characteristic of the peasant's world view . . . left most with little perspective on their own existence, obliged to take life as it came, without reflection or analysis. How laws were made or who made them, complex issues of political morality such as who should vote and why, the choice between fascism and democracy,

capitalism and socialism, these were questions which the average worker could begin to fathom only after long and patient explanation from someone with a much higher level of political consciousness. . . .

20 S. Marks, 'Towards a People's History? Recent developments in the historiography of South Africa', in R. Samuel (ed.), *People's History and Socialist Theory* (London, 1980).

21 P. Walshe, *The Rise of African Nationalism in South Africa: The African National Congress, 1912–1952* (California, 1971); H. J. and R. E. Simons, *Class and Colour in South Africa*; G. Gerhart, *Black Power*; G. Carter, T. Karis and S. D. Johns (eds), *From Protest to Challenge: A documentary history of African politics in South Africa*, 4 volumes (Stanford, 1972–1977).

22 Simons and Simons, *Class and Colour*, pp. 9–10.

23 B. Willan, 'Sol Plaatje, de Beers, and an old tramshed: class relations and social control in a South African town, 1918–1919', *Journal of Southern African Studies*, 4, 2, 1978, p. 196.

24 See note 19.

25 Simons and Simons, *Class and Colour*, p. 429, cited in Willan, 'Sol Plaatje, de Beers and an old tramshed'; see also Gerhart, *Black Power*, p. 30.

26 For the anti-Poulantzian attack, see, for example, S. Clarke, 'Capital, "fractions" of capital and the state: "neo-Marxist" analyses of the South African state', *Capital and Class*, 1977, and D. Innes and M. Plaut, 'Class struggle and Economic Development in South Africa: the interwar years', Collected Seminar Papers, No. 24, *Societies of Southern Africa in the nineteenth and twentieth centuries*, Vol. 9, 1978; for a reply, D. Kaplan, 'Relations of production, class struggle and the state in South Africa in the inter-war period', *Review of Afrian Political Economy*, 15–16, 1979, pp. 135–145.

   For the new literature on the African working class, see C. van Onselen, 'Randlords and Rotgut, 1886–1903', *History Workshop* (Autumn, 1976) pp. 33–89 and his ' "The Regiment of the Hills": South Africa's lumpenproletarian Army 1890–1920', *Past and Present*, 80, August, 1978, pp. 91–121. These represent two of the essays published in *Studies in the Social and Economic History of the Witwatersrand, Volume I, New Babylon; Volume II, New Nineveh* (London, 1982), completed while he was at the Centre of International and Area Studies, London. Other work in this field stemming from varied vantage points are the recent history of the South African Congress of Trade Unions by K. Luckhardt and B. Wall, *Organize . . . or Starve!* (London, 1981); P. Wickins, *The Industrial and Commercial Workers' Union of Africa* (Cape Town, 1978); D. du Toit, *Capital and Labour in South Africa. Class Struggles in the 1970s* (London and Boston, 1981) which has a fairly long historical introduction. Not yet published is the Ph.D. (Warwick, 1980) by David Hemson on Durban dockworkers, some of which is to be found in his 'Dock workers, labour circulation and class struggles in Durban, 1940–1959', *Journal of Southern African Studies*, 4, 1, 1977, pp. 88–124; and the work in progress of F. du Clerq and D. Innes on South African trade unions, whose main focus is post-Second World War.

27 *Labour, Townships and Protest*, p. 5.

28 G. A. Cohen, *Karl Marx's Theory of History, A Defence* (Princeton, 1978), p. 73. The following pages also have a fine discussion of the problems with E. P. Thompson's rejection of a structural definition of class (pp. 73–7). See also P. Anderson,

Arguments Within English Marxism, pp. 16–43, for a valuable analysis of 'agency', 'human volition' and 'necessity' in class formation.

29 The discussion in Cohen, Karl Marx's *Theory of History* (pp. 70–3), shows South Africa is not alone in this, and his reformulation is helpful:

> It is broadly true that the proletariat was formed when immediate producers were deprived of their means of production. But lack of means of production is not as essential to proletarian status as is traditionally maintained. It is better to say that a proletarian must sell his labour power in order to obtain his means of life. He may own means of production, but he cannot use them to support himself save by contracting with a capitalist (p. 72).

30 Chapters 1 and 2 below.

31 E. P. Thompson, *The Making of the English Working Class*, p. 9.

32 Chapters 3–6 below.

33 P. Worsley, *Marxism and Culture*, Occasional papers No. 4, Sociology Department, Manchester, 1980, pp. 14–15.

34 Chapters 9–12 below.

35 Cf. C. Critcher, who defines culture as 'shared symbols and meanings created and reproduced in shared experiences and interactions and sedimented in practices and institutions', in 'Sociology, cultural studies and the post-war working class' in J. Clarke, C. Critcher and R. Johnson (eds), *Working Class Culture. Studies in History and Theory* (London and Birmingham, 1979), p. 31.

36 Trapido, 'South Africa in a Comparative Study of Industrialization'.

37 R. V. Kubicek, *Economic Imperialism in Theory and Practice: the case of South African Gold Mining finance 1886–1914* (Durham, North Carolina, 1979), especially Chapter 3.

38 F. A. Johnstone, *Class, Race and Gold*, pp. 23–4.

39 The figures are from D. Innes, 'Monopoly Capital and Imperialism in Southern Africa: the role of the Anglo-American Group', Ph.D., Sussex, 1980, p. 103; and Table I, from T. Gregory, *Ernest Oppenheimer and the Economic Development of Southern Africa* (Cape Town, 1962) and Chamber of Mines, *86th Annual Report* (1975) p. 61.

40 A. P. Cartwright, *The Golden Age. The story of the industrialization of South Africa and the part played in it by the Corner House Group of Companies* (Cape Town, 1967), p. 18.

41 Chapters 7, 8 and 10 below.

42 J. J. Van-Helten, 'British and European Economic Investment in the Transvaal with specific reference to the Witwatersrand goldfields and district, 1886–1910', Ph.D., London, 1981, p. 209 (Chapter 6 has a thorough discussion of the explosives industry in this period); for the engineering works, see W. Bleloch, *The New South Africa* (London, 1901) pp. 236–7.

43 R. Samuel, 'The Workshop of the World', *History Workshop*, 3, 1977, esp. pp. 45–54; see also M. Dobb, *Studies in the Development of Capitalism* (London, 1975), p. 258 ff.

44 P. Corrigan, 'Feudal relics or capitalist monuments: notes on the sociology of unfree labour', *Sociology*, 1977.

45 See esp. Turrell, p. 68 below.

46 For the importance of South African gold production in the international economy, see J. J. Van-Helten, 'British and European Economic Investment', Chapter 2; also S. Marks and S. Trapido, 'Lord Milner and the South African state', *History Workshop*, 8, 1979, pp. 56–8.

47 B. Bozzoli, *The Political Nature of a Ruling Class. Capital and Ideology in South Africa, 1890–1933* (London, 1981), esp. pp. 119–120.

48 G. Kay, *Development and Underdevelopment*, p. 126.

49 Turrell, p. 57 below.

50 S. T. van der Horst, *Native Labour in South Africa* (Oxford, 1942), pp. 85, 136; D. Hobart Houghton and J. Dagut, *Source Material on the South African Economy 1860–1970, Vol. I, 1860–1899* (Cape Town, 1972), pp. 310, 317.

51 D. Gaitskell 'Female Mission Initiatives: women in three Witwatersrand churches, 1903–1939', Ph.D., London, 1981, Chapter 3.

52 D. Innes, 'Monopoly capitalism and imperialism', p. 77. See also A. Atmore and S. Marks, 'The imperial factor in South Africa in the nineteenth century: towards a reassessment', *Journal of Imperial and Commonwealth History*, III, 1974, pp. 122–3.

53 Chapters 3–6 below.

54 M. Legassick and F. du Clerq, 'Capitalism and Migrant labour in South Africa', unpublished paper presented to the seminar on Migrant Labour in the British Empire–Commonwealth, Institute of Commonwealth Studies, London, 1978.

55 J. X. Merriman, Kimberley, to A. Merriman, 31 Jan. 1886, in P. Lewsen (ed.), *Selections from the Correspondence of J. X. Merriman 1870–1890* (Cape Town, 1960), pp. 207–8.

56 See pp. 64–5, Chapter 10 *passim*, p. 283; also p. 98 note 84.

57 See the discussion on p. 28 above.

58 The standard works on the confederation policies are C. W. de Kiewiet, *The Imperial Factor in South Africa* (Cambridge, 1937) and C. F. Goodfellow, *Great Britain and South African Confederation* (Cape Town, 1966); for a critique, see Atmore and Marks, 'The imperial factor', and N. A. Etherington, 'Labour supply and the genesis of South African confederation in the 1870s', *Journal of African History*, 20, 2, (1979) pp. 235–53.

59 See Marks and Trapido, 'Lord Milner and the South African state'.

60 R. V. Kubicek, *Economic Imperialism*.

61 See below, Chapter 2.

62 Cited in Turrell, p. 56 below.

63 J. Angove, *In the Early Days: reminiscences of pioneer life on the South African diamond fields* (Kimberley and Johannesburg, 1910). The quotation comes from a chapter entitled 'The diamond fields as a school in which Natives are taught the theory of modern civilization'.

64 Cf. C. Burrows, *A History of South African Medicine before 1900* (Cape Town and Amsterdam, 1958), who talks of

    a rigorously controlled society equipped with a scientifically managed industry, watched by a secret police and dominated by a benevolent autocrat. Kimberley became, for all practical purposes, de Beer's Consolidated Mines Ltd.' (fn. 83, p. 266).

65 Richardson and Van-Helten, p. 78 below.

66 D. Innes, 'Monopoly capitalism and imperialism', pp. 113 ff.

67 C. W. de Kiewiet, *A History of South Africa, Social and Economic* (Oxford, 1941), p. 134.

68 Richardson and Van-Helten, pp. 82 below.

69 Marks and Trapido, 'Lord Milner and the South African state', p. 67.

70 Richardson and Van-Helten, p. 81 below.

71 Johnstone, *Class, Race and Gold*, pp. 57–64; Davies, *Capital, State and White Labour*, pp. 69–70.

72 Johnstone, *Class, Race and Gold*, pp. 26–34.

73 *Ibid.*, p. 65.

74 Cited in M. Mbeki, 'Is there a dialectic between race and class?', *Freedomways*, second quarter, 1981, p. 122.

75 Richardson and Van-Helten, p. 81 below.

76 Johnstone, *Class, Race and Gold*, pp. 29–34. Cf. L. Phillips (Johannesburg) to Messrs Wernher, Beit & Co., 9 Aug. 1890:

> *Chamber of Mines*: With a view to taking united action to reduce Kaffir wages, I am considering ways and means. . . . I think the reduction will be best attained by . . . [getting] all the Companies to send copies of monthly paysheets (Kaffir) to the Chamber. . . . Having once got copies of the paysheets, then by special agreement it can be resolved to reduce the wages a certain percentage. This must not be attempted before October 1st when labour will be coming in plentifully, and at the risk of possibly interrupting the work to some extent I would like to see a reduction of 33 per cent effected at one swoop. . . .

Wages were in fact reduced by the Chamber, though not as drastically as Phillips would have liked. (See M. Fraser and A. Jeeves [eds], *All That Glittered*, pp. 37–8, 41.)

77 See Harries, p. 142 below.

78 P. Delius, 'Migrant Labour and the Pedi, 1840–80', in Marks and Atmore, *Economy and Society in Pre-industrial South Africa*, pp. 293–312.

79 Cf. M. Godelier, *Rationality and Irrationality in Economics* (New York, 1972).

80 Here again our authors are engaged in the issue of 'necessity', 'agency' and 'human volition': see Kimble, pp. 129–30 and Harries, p. 157 below in particular, and note 28 above.

81 Cf. Marks and Atmore, *Economy and Society*, Introduction, pp. 9–13 and the essays therein by Guy, Beinart and Bonner.

82 Harries, p. 145 below.

83 Shillington, p. 106 below.

84 K. Shillington, 'Land loss, labour and dependence: the impact of colonialism on the Southern Tswana', Ph.D., London, 1981.

85 Harris, pp. 151–3, 158 below.

86 Harries, p. 154 below.

87 *Ibid.*, p. 155.

88 Kimble, pp. 132–3 below.

89 Q. N. Parsons, 'Khama III, the Bamangwato and the British with special reference to 1895–1923', Ph.D., Edinburgh, 1973; and M. Fransman, 'The Colonial State and the Land Question in Swaziland, 1903–1907', in Collected Seminar Papers, 24, *The Societies of Southern Africa, Vol. 9*, Institute of Commonwealth Studies, London, 1978.

90 J. J. Guy, *The Destruction of the Zulu Kingdom, 1879–1884* (London, 1979), pp. xxi, xxii, 21.

91 Guy, p. 188 below.

92 *Ibid.*, p. 189.

93 *Ibid.*

94 *Ibid.*, pp. 182 ff.

95 For the impact of rinderpest on southern Africa, see C. van Onselen, 'Reactions to Rinderpest in South Africa, 1896–7', *Journal of African History*, XIII, 3 (1972), pp. 473–88.

96 Harries, p. 159 below: F. Wilson, *Labour in the South African Gold Mines* (Cambridge, 1972), pp. 46, 141.

97 See S. Marks, *Reluctant Rebellion. The 1906–8 disturbances in Natal* (Oxford, 1970), which fails to interpret the material in this light, though it provides the basis for such an interpretation.

98 Below, Chapters 7 and 8.

99 T. Keegan, 'The restructuring of agrarian class relations in a colonial economy: the Orange River Colony, 1902–10', *Journal of Southern African Studies*, V, 2 (1979) pp. 234–54.

100 Turrell, p. 51 below; Keegan, p. 202 below.

101 Keegan, p. 195 below.

102 *Ibid.*, p. 206.

103 Matsetela, p. 229 below.

104 Keegan, p. 207 below.

105 T. Keegan, 'Black peril, lapsed whites and moral panic: A study of ideological crisis in early twentieth century South Africa', unpublished paper, Centre of International and Area Studies, London University, 1979.

106 For an outline of the provisions of the 1913 Natives' Land Act see C. M. Tatz, *Shadow and Substance in South Africa. A study in land and franchise policies affecting Africans, 1910–1960* (Pietermaritzburg, 1962). For the implications, see C. Bundy, *The Rise and Fall of the South African Peasantry* (London, 1979), pp. 213–4, 230–3. For somewhat differing interpretations, see H. Wolpe, 'Capitalism and cheap labour power'; M. Morris, 'The development of capitalism in South African agriculture: class struggle in the countryside', *Economy and Society*, 5, 3 (1976); M. Lacey, *Working for Boroko. The origins of a coercive labour system in South Africa* (Johannesburg, 1981), Chapter 1 and pp. 124–32.

107 Hence the preoccupation of the ruling class with the dangers of racial degeneracy in these years. See Keegan, 'Black peril'; also Davies, *Capital, State and White Labour*, pp. 100 ff.

109 This was clearly the case for example with the Southern Tswana – see K. T. J. Shillington, 'Land loss, labour and dependence'. For the Xhosa in the Ciskei, see, for example, Bundy, *Rise and Fall*, pp. 32, 34–5, 40, 83–6.

109 Cf. W. Beinart, 'Production, labour migrancy and the chieftaincy: aspects of the political economy of Pondoland, c. 1860–1930', Ph.D., London, 1979.

110 Kimble, p. 130 below.

111 C. van Onselen, 'Worker Consciousness in black miners: Southern Rhodesia, 1900–1920', *Journal of African History*, XIV, 2 (1973), pp. 237–56.

112 Richardson and Van-Helten, p. 92 below.

113 Fraser and Jeeves (eds), *All That Glittered*, p. 46.

114 Moroney, p. 267 below.

115 Hence the importance of the structural definition; see especially Anderson, *Arguments within English Marxism*, p. 40, and note 28 above.

116 For a fascinating discussion in relation to the English working class see J. Foster, *Class Struggle and Industrial Revolution. Early industrial capitalism in three English towns* (London, 1974), Chapter 5.

117 W. Saunders (ed.), *R. Acutt. Reminiscences of a Rand Pioneer* (Johannesburg, 1977), pp. 98–9.

118 B. Willan, p. 241 below.

119 Willan, p. 242 below; see also A. G. Hopkins, 'Property rights and empire

building: Britain's annexation of Lagos, 1861', *Journal of Economic History*, XL, 4 (1980), a valuable article which sparked off a myriad of useful comparisons for South Africa.

120 J. Nobel, *The History of South Africa* (London, 1877) pp. 334–5, cited in S. Trapido, ' "The friends of the natives": merchants, peasants and the political and ideological structure of liberalism in the Cape, 1854–1910', in Marks and Atmore, *Economy and Society*, p. 250.

121 CO 2/21 Fowell Buxton to Normanby, 20.4.1839, cited in Hopkins, 'Property rights', p. 796.

122 For the Cape liberal tradition, see S. Trapido, ' "The friends of the natives" ', pp. 247–74; for the ways in which it established its ideological hegemony for blacks, see N. Hogan, 'The posthumous vindication of Zachariah Gqishela: reflections on the politics of dependence at the Cape in the nineteenth century', in Marks and Atmore, *Economy and Society*, pp. 275–92.

124 K. Marx and F. Engels, 'Manifesto of the Communist Party', in *Karl Marx and Frederick Engels. Selected Works in One Volume*, (London, 1968), p. 39.

123 Hopkins, 'Property rights', p. 778.

125 Matsetela, pp. 215, 234 n. 13 below.

126 Bonner, p. 288 below.

127 Turrell, p. 69 n. 6 below.

128 Willan, p. 243 below.

129 *Ibid.*, p. 241.

130 *Ibid.*, p. 244.

131 *Ibid.*, p. 252.

132 This was already evident in the 1870s: see Trapido, ' "Friends of the natives" '; cf. A. Trollope, writing about the fact that black miners from Natal and the Cape were earning at least 10s a week on the diamond fields and would, theoretically, as British subjects be eligible to vote:

> There will be those at home who will say — why should they not vote if they are industrious labourers earning wages at so high a rate? But no white man who has been in South Africa and knows anything of South Africa will say that.

South Africa, Vol. II, p. 350–1 (Cape Town, 1973, reprint of 1873 edition), edited by J. H. Davidson.

133 Trapido, ' "Friends of the natives" ', pp. 255–7; Lacey, *Working for Boroko*, p. 56.

134 Bonner, p. 272, 305 below.

135 The best treatment of this is in B. Willan, 'The role of Solomon T. Plaatje (1876–1932) in South African society', Ph.D. London, 1980.

136 See note 109 above.

137 B. Nasson, ' "These Natives think this war to be their own": reflections on blacks in the Cape Colony in the South African War, 1899–1902', Collected Seminar papers, No. 27, *The Societies of Southern Africa in the nineteenth and twentieth centuries* Vol. 11, (Institute of Commonwealth Studies, London, 1981).

138 Marks, *Reluctant Rebellion*, *passim*, but see, for example, pp. 242–6.

139 Bonner, p. 272 below.

140 Willan, 'The role of Solomon T. Plaatje', Chapters 4 and 9.

141 The subject is under-researched, but see Bozzoli's suggestive remarks, *The Political Nature of a Ruling Class*, pp. 143–6.

142 Bonner, p. 272 below.

143 *Ibid.*, p. 283.
144 *Ibid.*, p. 277.
145 *Ibid.*, p. 279.
146 *Ibid.*, p. 271, 289.
147 *Ibid.*, pp. 303–4.
148 Couzens, p. 314 and Gaitskell, *passim*.
149 Couzens, p. 328 below; see notes 3 and 28 above.
150 Couzens, pp. 328–9 below.
151 For a discussion, see A. P. Donajgrodzki (ed.), *Social Control in Nineteenth Century Britain* (London, 1977), introduction.
152 Donajgrodzki, *Social Control*, p. 15.
153 These are dealt with in detail by Bonner, pp. 281–2 below.
154 Below, Chapter 1.
155 *Maids and Madams, A Study in the Politics of Exploitation* (Johannesburg, 1980), p. 5.
156 Gaitskell, p. 348 below; see also her 'Housewives, maids or mothers: some contradictions of domesticity for Christian women in Johannesburg', paper presented to the Conference on the History of the Family in Africa, School of Oriental and African Studies, London, September, 1981.
157 See below, especially, Guy, pp. 170–2.
158 Gaitskell, p. 338 below.
159 Coplan, Chapter 14 below.
160 Coplan, p. 351 ff below.
161 *Ibid.*, p. 372.
162 See note 25 above.

CHAPTER ONE

Kimberley: labour and compounds, 1871–1888*

Rob Turrell

The mill and the mine were respectively the sources of the growth of industrial wealth in Britain and South Africa. If the 'dark, satanic mill' was the abiding image of new social relationships in Britain, it was the repressive role played by the mine compound that came to symbolise the early development of capitalism in South Africa. But a mill is not a mine; the one processes raw materials, the other produces them, and they differ radically in relation to the organisation and control of labour. The mill organised and coordinated workers under the domination of steam machinery and located the control of workers in the exigencies of the labour market; the potential mine labour force had to be separated from its independent means of production by brute force, as no dull economic compulsion propelled labourers constantly into the pit. Mine employers had to come to terms with migrant African labour, whose rapid turnover and 'shortages' were increasingly to hinder the process of capital accumulation. The compound system, as a particular form of working-class housing, was the institution which simultaneously organised and subordinated the mine labour force to capital. On the one hand, it contributed fundamentally to the organisation of the labour process through the entrenchment of a racial division of labour. On the other hand, it facilitated the exploitation of labour and ensured a constant supply. The extended and often barbaric process of primitive accumulation of capital in Britain gave birth to the mill and its pattern of social relationships as the normal form of a mature capitalism; but in South Africa, conquest and the compound system gave birth through Caesarean section to industrial capitalism.

The prevention of diamond theft and the elimination of the criminal trade known as IDB (Illicit Diamond Buying) have been the most common explanations among historians for the development of closed compounds on the

* I wish to thank Jean Jacques Van-Helten for frequent discussions; for the defence, in my absence, of an earlier version of this paper at the conference on which this book is based; and for incisively cutting this paper to its present length.

Kimberley mines.[1] This view is too simple, extracting one factor from a complex process of capital accumulation. The construction of closed compounds was integrally related to the development of industrial capitalism in the diamond mines. The production of diamonds, a luxury commodity, was crucially dependent on the European market, which throughout the 1870s and 1880s exhibited a long-term decline in rough diamond prices. Expanded production exacerbated this tendency, and it was only through the centralisation of capital and the greater productivity of labour — rather than the elimination of theft — that mineowners could raise the rate of profit. In this process, housing came to be the most important site for the organisation and control of the labour force.

In the early days of diamond digging, Africans lived on their employers' compound, which comprised his tent or frame house, an area for sorting diamond soil and the site of different forms of labourers' housing. The close supervision entailed in this arrangement changed as labourers sought a greater spatial independence from employers in the townships or locations. In the late 1870s, the white bourgeoisie began to build in brick away from the work-place, and the compound took on a new content as an open barracks for African labourers. Closed compounds were introduced only with the development of underground mining in 1885. They can be understood as the end-product of a changing strategy of 'social control', on the lines of van Onselen's *Chibaro*, the pioneering history of the compound as an institution of 'social control'.[2] However, although *Chibaro* is largely concerned with the operation of an established compound system, where the notion of 'social control' illuminates the mechanisms through which labourers were exploited by Rhodesian gold-mining capitalists, the term 'social control' bears a legacy of functionalism, which hinders an analysis of the struggles over the original implementation of the compound system.[3] This essay seeks to set out those struggles within the process of capital accumulation on the diamond fields, a process in which the interests of the mineowners and labourers were never pre-defined.

'The mining and mercantile guerrillas of a new state'[4]

Diamonds were first mined successfully at Kimberley, in the new British colony of Griqualand West, in 1871. The 'dry diggings' which were referred to as Kimberley consisted of four mines: Kimberley (originally known as 'Colesberg Kopje' or 'New Rush'), De Beers, Dutoitspan and Bultfontein. The mines varied in richness and displayed marked differences in the quality of diamonds won from the soil. Kimberley mine, originally containing 470 claims,[*] was the

---

[*] A claim measured 31 × 31 square feet.

richest in terms of the average number of carats found in each load extracted from the pit. De Beers mine, divided into 622 claims, was second to Kimberley in diamond-producing potential. Dutoitspan mine, initially containing 1441 claims, was the largest mine, and, although its diamonds fetched the highest average price per carat, it never matched the productivity of Kimberley. Bultfontein mine, containing 1 067 claims, was known as the 'poor man's kopje', and sections of it earned the name of 'the graveyard'.

These mines were situated on three farms, Kimberley and De Beers on the farm Vooruitzicht, and the two poorer mines on the farms Dorstfontein and Bultfontein. All three farms were bought from their pastoral Afrikaner occupiers by land syndicates soon after diamonds were discovered in their soil. One syndicate, led by John Paterson, Henry Christian and Dunell, Ebden and Company, merchants of Port Elizabeth, purchased Vooruitzicht for £6 000. Another syndicate, dominated by the diamond merchants Maurice Posno and Henry Webb, acquired both Dorstfontein and Bultfontein. By the end of 1875, the Vooruitzicht estate had been bought by the Griqualand West state for £100 000, and the other two farms had been acquired by the London and South African Exploration Company, incorporated in London in 1870 with a capital of £50 000.

Originally, the energy of diggers and labourers was concentrated in Kimberley mine, and the demand for access to diamondiferous ground was so great that the claims were subdivided into quarters and even smaller parcels of ground. In 1872 the mine was split into between 1 600 and 1 800 separate holdings with possibly as many owners.[5] By 1875, although a quarter claim remained the basic unit of production, claims had been concentrated into the hands of 381 owners. All four mines were owned by 757 men and women, of whom 120 were black, mainly Mfengu, Ngqika and Coloureds from the Cape, mining the 'poor man's kopje' of Bultfontein.[6] On the one hand, claims were owned by merchants and others in the Cape, Natal or Europe, whereas on the other hand, some of the 800 tradespeople in Kimberley had invested in the mines. The strong interpenetration of ownership between trade and mining makes it difficult to specify the size of a residential bourgeoisie on the diamond fields. However, at the outside, 1 600 people, in a population of 6 000 whites and 18 000 blacks, either owned claims and/or were their own masters in the town economy of Kimberley.[7]

Africans formed the majority of the wage labour force from the earliest period of mining. At Dutoitspan, family labour was used in the mine throughout the 1870s, but in Kimberley large gangs of labourers were employed to open the pit up. Between 1871 and 1875 about 50 000 'natives from the interior' came to and left Kimberley each year.[8] The majority came from the north-eastern Transvaal and were called 'Mahawas' by the South Sotho and whites in

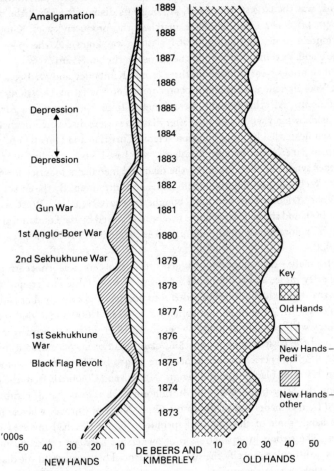

DE BEERS AND KIMBERLEY:
LABOUR CONTRACTS REGISTERED, 1873-1889
Showing Old Hands re-contracted and New Hands with Pedi contracts isolated

Fig. 1.1   Labour contracts registered on the diamond fields, 1873–1889

Notes
Sources: CAD, GLW 55 and 71; *Griqualand West Government Gazette*; G20–81, *BBNA*, pp. 132, 133; G33–82, *BBNA*, pp. 182, 183; G3–83, *BBNA*, pp. 10, 11; CAD, NA, 195, 198, 202.

1. Up to 1875 the Pedi were called Mahawas, the South Sotho term for North Sotho, but in 1876 under the impact of the First Sekhukhune War, the Pedi (Secocoeni Basutos) were registered separately from the Ndzundza Ndebele (Mapoch's Matabella), the

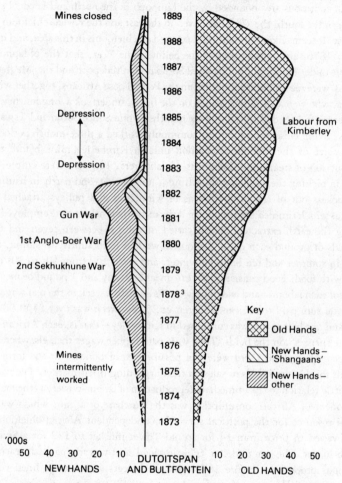

DUTOITSPAN AND BULTFONTEIN:
LABOUR CONTRACTS REGISTERED, 1873-1889
Showing Old Hands re-contracted and New Hands with 'Shangaans' contracts isolated

Fig. 1.1 (continued) **Labour contracts registered on the diamond fields, 1873–1889**

Transvaal Basuto and 'Maghata Basutos'. The term Pedi, as charted here, covers all these chiefdoms.

2. In 1877 17.33% of New Hands were Ndundza Ndebele, that is, composed half of the Pedi.

3. Pedi made up 39.23% of New Hands in 1878 and 18.31% of this were Ndzundza Ndebele.

Kimberley. The Mahawas were mainly composed of 'Secocoeni Basutos', better known as the Pedi, who were supposed, by the Registrar of Natives, to come from an enormous area bounded by the Limpopo in the north and Leydenberg district in the south, the 'Comatie River' in the east and the Kwena chiefdom in the west. It seems likely that the term covered all chiefdoms in this area, and it is only in 1876, after the impact of the Sekhukhune War, that the Ndzundza Ndebele under Mapoch, the Transvaal Sotho under Malepoch and the 'Maghata Basutos' were registered separately from the Pedi. These Africans, together with Tsonga, who were called 'Shangaans' on the fields, undertook a long journey to Kimberley and tended to stay for six months, while South Sotho and Tswana groups, living closer to the mines, commonly worked a three-month period.[9]

The size of the average production unit in Kimberley mine before the introduction of steam machinery was 15 labourers. Ten men were employed partly in picking the earth and shovelling it into buckets and partly in hauling the buckets out of the pit by means of windlasses and pulleys attached to stagings which rimmed the perimeter of the mine. Five others were employed in sorting the earth extracted, which varied in volume between seven and ten cartloads of ground each day.[10] Labourers worked from sunrise to sunset, 14 hours in summer and ten hours in winter, and were paid from 10s to 30s per week with food. Food consisted of *mielie* meal each day and 1 pound of meat a week for each labourer and added between 7s and 10s a week to the real wage.[11] The total sum paid to African labourers at 25s per week was over £500 000 a year, and one half of this was consumed in Kimberley – that is, each African on average spent £5 on the fields. They were paid higher wages than elsewhere in southern Africa, and there were the possibilities of bonuses in the form of rewards for diamond finds or sales on the burgeoning illicit market. The wage bore little relation to the immediate reproduction of labour-power, as the major component of African consumption was the purchase of a gun, which was a crucial resource for the political survival of independent African chiefdoms. Guns varied in price from £4 for an old Tower musket to £12 for a Snider breech-loader. The gun trade, or 'trade in blood' as it was stigmatised, reached enormous proportions before 1875, and the 'streets were almost lined with stands of arms'.[12]

Both Europeans and Africans performed manual labour in the mines. When Africans were in short supply or allegedly unproductive, Europeans were recruited to fill the breach.[13] They earned a higher wage, which was explained by virtue of the greater value of their work; the wages of unskilled European labour on the Cape railways had been accounted for in a similar fashion.[14] A structural explanation of wage differentials in terms of European proletarianisation as opposed to African worker-cultivators with access to rural production has now become the orthodoxy.[15] More descriptively, labour practices and the customary differentials in the port industries of the Cape were reproduced in the mining labour process. European artisans commanded £1 10s to £2 *a day*, whereas 'persons of colour' earned between £2 and £4 *a week* with quarters.[16] Artisanal work was encapsulated within the confines of craft organisation, and the skills of blacksmiths, masons, carpenters and others were jealously guarded. It was only with the development of the engineering trades in conjunction with steam machinery and the emergence of overseers as a substantial stratum of unskilled supervisory workers that the dominance of craft organisation was altered.

Prior to 1875 numbers of Europeans without the capital to invest in a claim worked as share-workers in the mines. Share-working was a system which allowed a merchant or landed gentleman to speculate in claims without bearing the complete cost in terms of capital or time. He arranged with a practical digger, the share-worker, to mine his claim. The share-worker organised and hired a group of labourers to work the ground and in return he received 50 per cent of the diamond proceeds, although the terms of the arrangement and the percentage varied. It was a system which was similar in form to sharecropping in agriculture and had its origins in the tribute system of Cornish mines. When Alfred Aylward, soon to be deeply involved in a rebellion against the Queen, wrote 'the workers on shares are tenants of the claims, and the claimholders' share is rent and nothing else', he was arguing for the maintenance of share-working as a profit-sharing form of sub-contract in the diamond mines.[17] Share-workers, who composed the majority of diggers, were abused by owners, who often sold claims from beneath their feet or took over proved claims on their own account. It was this process that reduced the share-worker from an independent position, with access to a possible fortune, to the occupation of overseer in the ranks of the working class. In this situation European share-workers were caught between the twin threats of cheaper black competition and arbitrary actions by claim-owners.

It was this dual pressure on European share-workers that accounts for the racist discourse of the leaders of the Diggers Protection Association prior to the Black Flag Rebellion of March to June 1875.[18] Share-workers formed the rank and file of the Association, which was led by struggling claim-owners and supported by store-keepers, canteen-keepers and small diamond buyers. In a period of declining fortune, with reefs[19] collapsing and water accumulating in the mines, together with a depressed international market in diamonds, diggers were hard pushed to make ends meet. When the banks refused to finance the diggers, they were driven to borrow money from usurers at rates of interest of over ten per cent per month. At this time the theft of diamonds, largely ascribed to African labourers, assumed great importance in European debate in Kimberley Hall, on Market Square and in the newspapers. The Association embarked on a campaign to deprive all blacks of the legal right to own or work claims on shares. Richard Southey's government in Griqualand West refused to deprive blacks of their legal right to own claims. In the face of this government position the Association announced in a manifesto their intention to protect their 'rights, property and liberty' and assumed the state functions of patrolling the townships to keep Africans 'under proper police surveillance'.[20] The rebellious actions of the Association were a response to the impoverishment of Europeans, but the emphasis on diamond theft and racism concealed more fundamental changes in labour relations.

Labour legislation in Griqualand West was based on the Cape Masters and Servants Law of 1856 and Governor Barkly's Proclamation of August 1872. Under the provisions of Proclamation 14, a servants' registry was established to contract all servants, but in fact this came to apply only to 'natives',[21] who were required to carry a pass at all times. The inability of the state to regulate the supply of labourers and to prevent desertion induced masters to refuse to contract servants. This accounted for the collapse in registration figures for 1875, but it was also true that the numbers of labourers coming to the fields had begun to decline from the beginning of 1874. This was largely the result of the deteriorating condition of the most productive mine. In March 1875 only 181 claims out of 400 in Kimberley mine were workable, while the rest were covered with reef or submerged in water.[22] As a means of overcoming these production problems, some wealthier claim-owners had introduced steam machinery, which exacerbated the differences between consolidating owners and share-workers. With steam-driven hauling and washing machines, 40 or 50 loads of ground could be extracted from the mine, which was now over 160 feet deep in some parts. March 1875 was the nadir of misfortune in Kimberley mine, and, with competent pumping about to conquer the water problem, an expanded labour process and the prospect of renewed production, diggers cried out for labourers.

Africans chose not to work in dangerous claims near the reef or in third-class claims where the finds and conditions were poor. This meant that the 'shortage' of labour was most severe for share-workers, who struggled to make their claims pay. In early 1875, debris washing emerged as a profitable enterprise, and the discarded soil was re-sorted or washed for the first time. Governor Southey estimated that 600 washing machines found diamonds worth £20 000 each week.[23] The growth of debris washing created anger against the diggers over the theft of diamondiferous soil and the avenue it provided for alternative work. 'There are at least 800 savages in the camp,' Alfred Aylward announced at a public meeting, 'registered to other persons of indifferent character and similar colour, apparently for sorting debris.'[24] European debris washing enticed more labourers away from the task of extracting the ground from the pits. The 'shortage' was worsened by the threatening rhetoric of European diggers which not only made Africans wary of travelling to the fields but drove blacks away from the mines in fear of their lives.[25]

At the same time the African labourers on the fields were in a position of strength and imposed the 'board wages' system on their employers. This meant that wages were forced up to 25s per week, and labourers fed themselves at the proliferation of boarding houses, 'Kaffir eating houses' and coffee shops in the main thoroughfares of the townships. The significance of this was twofold: it increased the real wage, and it 'removed them from the immediate control of their masters'.[26] In the early 1870s, contracted Africans (as well as white labourers) lived on diggers' compounds.[27] Shelter was in most cases rudimentary, and bearing in mind the discontinuous nature of mining and the frequency of desertion Africans fended for themselves. They squatted in 'native camps' which sprang up on the outskirts of the towns. The West End was one such area:

> The district lies to the west of the stretched out 'camp' and is bare and flat as the camp itself. It is almost exclusively inhabited by Blacks and Coloureds. The Blacks are mainly Basuto, either subjects of Sekukuni or of other chieftains living beyond the Magaliesberg or they are Moshesh's people. Many of the latter have already worked for years in the Colony or in the Free State; the vast majority however are migrant labourers. The Coloureds are Koranna and Griqua from this area. Zulus, as other Black tribes and Bastards, are scarcely represented.[28]

Other Africans lived independently in the main townships, squatting or renting rooms in Bultfontein, the Malay Camp or Newton. Prior to the rebellion the government insisted that it had no right to dictate where 'natives' should live, but this was to change after the dismissal of Governor Southey in 1875 and the inauguration of a new administration.

The Black Flag Rebellion occurred in a period of transition on the diamond fields. The dominance of merchants with their interests in an expanding commodity market was being challenged by a group of industrialists whose aim was purely the production of diamonds. These industrial capitalists were mainly the great exporting diamond merchants (referred to on the fields as 'shippers') who were increasingly unable to profit from trading in diamonds without investing directly in production. Foreign capital began to pour into the mines after the commercial crisis of July 1876, when diamonds crashed 33 per cent in price. Three years later, the majority of claims in Kimberley mine were in the hands of 12 private companies with a total capital of £2½ million. Diggers in general reaped the enormous return of 30 per cent on their invested capital. The new order that emerged after the rebellion had been more receptive to the requirements of capital accumulation based on industrial production in which share-working was less and less common.[29]

'If natives could be bound to masters for say seven years...'[30]

One of the most important aspects of the systematic development of diamond mining was the attempt to subordinate labourers to rigorous industrial discipline. Major Lanyon set up a Labour Commission in 1876 to investigate how this could be done. The Commission put three basic propositions forward for the 'immediate attention of government'. The first recommended no legislation as to the rate of wages. It was recognised that high wages 'were the surest means of encouraging the introduction of labour'. Secondly, the government was asked to secure the 'safe passage' of migrants to the fields and 'their means of subsistence along the line of route'. This entailed the establishment of government agencies among the labour-supplying chiefdoms and government depots to provide food, shelter and security along the labour routes. The third proposition was the centralisation of the labour supply through the establishment of a labour depot in Kimberley itself. The principal suggestions of the Commission built on practices in force in India, Natal and Mauritius. Its significance lay in the clear conceptualisation of how to solve the 'labour question' through a combination of common sense and coercion.[31]

The central depot in Kimberley was to be the only conduit through which 'native labour' flowed into the mines. It was to be under the control of a Superintendent, whose main task was to contract all 'natives' and to register the labour contracts of all 'servants' in Kimberley. A minimum contract of three months for new migrants – 'mere apprentices learning the use of mining implements' – was to be enforced. The Commission reminded the Administrator, lest he believed otherwise, 'that the compulsion proposed is absolute liberty as compared with the tyrannical rule of their own chiefs'. This caveat applied more particularly to the Superintendent's other functions. He was to adjudicate all cases of conflict between master and servant. The Superintendent was to take over from the Resident Magistrate the task of issuing gun permits to 'natives'. One final function of the Superintendent was to dispose of unemployed 'natives' located in his depot. The Commission reported:

> The compulsory employment of those natives who at the end of 5 days sojourn at a depot, are unable to obtain employment, cannot be considered a hardship, when such Natives are at liberty to contract themselves, and if unable to do so, may very reasonably be looked upon as paupers unable otherwise to obtain their own subsistence. If such men were to be turned out of the depot they would be forced into vagrancy and possible crime.[32]

It is here that the conveyor-belt principle of the depot exposed its true colours as an institution of forced labour. These suggestions were embodied in a Native Labour Ordinance. It was, however, refused ratification by the Colonial Office, which objected to specific laws applying to 'natives' and to the legal blows it struck against the freedom of wage labour. A central depot was established under a previously passed but unpromulgated Ordinance, which made it optional for Africans in search of employment to be located there.[33]

An optional depot did not suit the pressing needs of the diggers, and they turned their attention more decisively to recruitment in three forms: government-sponsored, private or labour touting. Governor Southey had maintained an elaborate system of communication with African chiefs in the interior, through traders, missionaries and agents, but, like Major Lanyon after him, he was loath to give government support to recruitment. For example, Major Lanyon rejected the scheme of João Albasini, 'an old Portuguese slave dealer', and Crowley, a Kimberley merchant, for the recruitment (under government sponsorship) of African labourers from the Zoutpansberg and beyond. Once, however, the Transvaal had been annexed to Britain in 1877, the north-eastern Transvaal and the trans-Limpopo region, unsettled by the 1876 Sekhukhune war, was much more suitable for government recruitment. On the other hand, private recruiters, like the Natalians John Dunn, Arthur Shepstone and Reuben Benningfield, became increasingly important labour suppliers stretching their resources as far north as Inhambane in Moçambique. But many diggers were still forced to rely on labour touting. The labour tout collected bands of Africans *en route* through the Transvaal, at Christiana or Potchefstroom, and promised protection, food and a safe position in Kimberley. When they reached the mines he often sold their capacity to labour on Market Square for £2 a head. Touting played its part in increasing the rate of desertion, and in fact bore a greater resemblance to slavery than ordinary recruitment.[34]

Securing a supply of labour was only half the battle. In an attempt to reduce desertion from one employer to another, the mineowners set about a campaign to tie labourers more effectively to one master for three to six months – the longest period new migrants would remain on the fields before leaving for home. The Labour Commission had attacked the prevalence of the 'board wages' system, and recommended that employers should be forced to house and feed their labourers on their premises. Such an idea, Sydney Shippard, the Attorney-General, had regarded as 'absurd' in 1875, but in August 1879 it was made compulsory.[35] The Labour Commission had labelled 'board wages' a 'fruitful source of temptation to crime', and by 1879 'it had been clearly demonstrated' that the system 'was conducive to the continuance of the Illicit Diamond Trade'.[36] The validity of this argument will be assessed when it re-surfaces with greater coherence and vehemence in the mid-1880s over the introduction of closed compounds. What needs to be emphasised at this point is the genesis of the idea, not in relation to IDB, but in a process of systematic mining development based on steam machinery.

The compound system was conceived to maintain and discipline a migrant labour force. The most explicit statement in this respect came from Thomas Collingwood Kitto, a Mining Inspector, who was commissioned in 1879 to write a report on the Kimberley mines by Sir Charles Warren, the new Administrator and only engineer to hold this post. Kitto wrote:

> The labour question here is, in my opinion, a matter of very great importance, and I think every possible means should be adopted to secure to owners of mines a constant supply. . . . I must say the quality of labour here is the worst I have seen in any part of the world, and I cannot help contrasting it with the black labour of Brazil. I am very certain that one of the Brazilian blacks will do as much work on an average as three Kimberley blacks. The Brazilian blacks are classed from one to four, and are hired out to English companies at per day, the owners receiving for a first class man, one milreis (2s), for a second class man, 1s 8d, for a third, 1s and for a fourth class, about 3d. The companies have to feed them. . . . The blacks are lodged in barracks, which are built in the form of a square, the outer wall being much higher than the inner wall; the roof slopes inside. The entrance to the place is by a large gate, over which at night hangs a powerful lamp which lights up the whole place. Men and women answer to the call of their names while passing out at the gate in the morning and in the evening when entering. They retire to rest early, and an overseer locks up the premises each night and unlocks them in the morning. There is a very good feeling existing between the Brazilian slaves and the owners . . . in another 22 years, or thereabouts, all will be free; by which time, if they continue in their present state of progression, they will be ripe for the occasion.
>
> I believe the natives of South Africa, under European supervision, are capable of being made almost – if not quite – as good as the blacks of Brazil, provided they are dealt with in the same manner.[37]

Kitto was quick to point out that he did not advocate slavery, but the conclusions to be drawn from a comparison with Brazilian slave labour lay precisely in the disadvantages for mining capital of a migrant labour force. He wrote: 'if natives could be bound to masters for say seven years . . . under strict government supervision, it would be for the infinite benefit of the natives themselves'.[38]

The corollary of the attempt to force employers to lodge and feed labourers on their compounds was the elaboration of a policy of 'localisation' of those Africans who were not so accommodated.[39] 'Localisation' substantially meant a policy of residential segregation, which earlier Southey had been disinclined either to legislate for or to pursue. Fears of a black uprising in Kimberley during the 1878 rebellion in the Griqualand West countryside boosted the demands of some white citizens for the 'localisation' of 'natives'. 'Localisation' was seen as a policy of containment, not only against a threatened uprising, but also in response to the mineowners' demands for control of those Africans 'living at large', who were 'lazy', possible deserters from the pits and who lived in 'dirt and plenty without work or visible means of support'.[40] In the following year, Sir Charles Warren emphasised the desirability of locations over and above the revenue possibilities of hut-tax. By the end of the decade there were four laid-out locations on the Vooruitzicht estate and another three on the London Company estate.[41]

At the beginning of 1880 there were 12 000 Africans on the fields, and the Registrar of Natives estimated that 20 000 Africans were required to work the mines properly. By the end of the year, even though there were 22 000 African labourers on the fields, the Registrar wanted another 10 000 to reduce wages to their 'proper level' of 10s per week.[42] African labour was the barometer of diamond wealth:

> Native labour is the life of the Diamond Fields, and just as in proportion as the supply and demand of this commodity varies so in a great measure is the prosperity of the community gauged.[43]

By the turn of the decade 9 000 Africans were estimated as permanently resident on the fields, constituting the nucleus of an African working class which was to have a crucial impact on the pattern of capital accumulation in the 1880s.[44] Cecil John Rhodes, soon to become a public figure and influential representative of mining capital, was pleased to write: 'this is now the richest community in the world for its size and . . . it shows every sign of permanency [and it] would take at our present rate of working 100 years to work out.'[45]

'The native labourer is to us what the Irish labourer is at home – the hewer of wood and drawer of water'[46]

After the slump in diamond prices in mid-1876, mining underwent a process of systematic development. The first industrial cycle of production on the fields (1877–85) began with the extensive acquisition of fixed capital in the form of steam machinery, which stimulated the process of economic recovery. Whereas in 1877 there had been only 16 steam engines in operation on the fields, by 1881 the total number of engines had soared to 306. Productivity grew, not only in terms of output but also in terms of a reduction in mining costs, central to which was an intensification of labour exploitation. But as the expansion of production accelerated, the high rate of profit encouraged the growth of speculation and attracted a large portion of idle capital from the Cape Colony. Beginning in 1880, but largely concentrated in the first half of 1881, 66 joint-stock mining companies were floated on the fields with a total nominal capital of £7 365 390. During the boom, known as the 'share mania', all vestiges of economic rationality were discarded as scrip soared to premiums of between 200 and 400 per cent over their nominal values. This feverish activity of company promotion and speculation successfully concealed the impending over-production of diamonds. Although the boom was punctured by the banks' refusal to extend credit for the purchase of scrip in June 1881, it was not until the collapse of the European diamond market in late 1882 that the impact of the economic depression began to be felt seriously in Kimberley.[47]

The scarcity of African labour was the explanation most favoured by company directors when they reviewed their dismal year's work in 1881. The 'Gun War' in Basutoland over the disarmament of the Basotho people and the Transvaal War of Independence cut off the two major labour reservoirs. It was at this point that merchants and tradespeople in Kimberley argued the case for the employment of a 'superior class of labour' – that is, either unskilled white colonials, or recruited Irish, Italians or Chinese. They weighed the advantages of a white proletarian, as against a black migrant, labour policy.[48] White working-class families settled on the fields would expand the circulation of commodities in Kimberley as long as the value of white labour-power was not depressed below its historically constituted level in the Cape. The higher cost of such labour, compared with cheaper African migrant labour, would be compensated for by its permanence and political security, while wives and daughters would make good domestic servants, unpaid labourers in the home and wage labourers in the town economy. Merchants presented themselves as the guardians of white civilisation and vividly spelled out the social implications of dependence on black labour in terms of black political dominance in the future. For the mineowners, whose interest in the future extended as far as the next dividend date, the cost of white labour at four times the price of black labour tipped the scales against its imagined reliability. By the end of 1881 there was a growing surplus population of white men converging on Kimberley as colonial forces were disbanded and railway works abandoned. However, despite the fact that a number of companies employed white labour throughout the depression period, white labourers were generally employed only when it was impossible to hire Africans.[49]

The employment of whites between 1881 and the depths of the mining depression in 1884 showed a sharp reduction in proportion to the decline in black employment, a reduction most marked in the poorer mines. In 1881 one European (with whom Coloureds were classified) was employed to every five Africans in Kimberley and De Beers, while one European was employed to every six Africans in Dutoitspan and Bultfontein. By 1884 the ratio in the richer mines was one to six while in the poorer mines it had widened to one to nine. Overall, between 1881 and 1884 European employment fell by 61 per cent to 1 210, whereas African employment only fell by 47 per cent to 9 000. Africans made up between 83 and 88 per cent of the mine workforce and were paid 30s per week. Of the small number of European and Coloured workers, 68 per cent were overseers and labourers earning up to £5 per week; 20 per cent were steam engine-drivers earning between £6 and £8 a week; and the remaining 12 per cent were artisans, working as mechanics, smiths, miners and carpenters, commanding up to £8 a week in wages. The employment of artisans and engine-drivers was dependent on the running of steam machinery, which was periodically hindered by reef and water problems in the mines. By contrast, the employment of overseers, a stratum of unskilled supervisory labourers, was more incisively threatened by shortages of African labour. The ratio of overseers and labourers varied between mines according to the size of the diamonds. Consequently, the richer mines employed more overseers than the poorer mines. Nonetheless it was the tighter profit margins in the poorer mines that determined the retrenchment of expensive European workers.[50]

The reduction in European employment involved a change in the racial division of labour. Both European artisans and overseers faced the prospect of displacement through the employment of Africans. Rudolph Heinrichsen, Managing Director of the Victoria Company (De Beers mine), argued at a meeting of mineowners in London:

> For instance while the general run of Kafirs simply work at digging in the mines, others do work above. There are native engine-drivers as well as white engine-drivers, and if the white engine-driver is paid £5 a week the native engine-driver must be paid something more than 15s per week. . . . [He] should be paid 30s per week, but . . . no employer should be allowed to set more than 25% of his native labour at the superior kind of work.[51]

This process of substitution was more common in the poorer mines in this period, and the Machinery Inspector reported that one half of the engine-drivers would not pass muster in England.[52] Symptomatic of both substitution and depression was the collapse of the Savings Bank in Dutoitspan in 1882 and the halving of the depositors in Kimberley.[53] The overseers were in a more vulnerable position. The social and economic gulf between overseer and labourer, whose fortunes were so closely intertwined, was far narrower than the gulf between artisan and labourer, where skill and notions of dignity and respectability fortified the division. The racial and cultural differences between European overseer and African labourer reinforced the pattern of authority in the workplace. Nonetheless it was becoming common for recruited Africans to work under the supervision of their headmen, who were rewarded with a higher wage.[54]

Wage reductions and recruitment were the policies pursued by mining companies during the depression. They combined to agree on a scale of wages to be paid to Africans but signally failed to implement it.[55] This was illustrated through the experience of the largest company in Kimberley mine, the Central Company.[56] The Central arranged to have labour recruited from Inhambane via Natal at a cost of £6 per head in late 1881. Of crucial importance in this scheme was the period of contract, which was one year.[57] However, even recruitment and the length of the contract were not enough to ensure a constant supply and employment of African labourers. Both at the beginning and end of 1882,

William McHardy, the Central manager, increased African earnings, breaking the employer combination to reduce wages. In May 1883, McHardy was forced once again to raise wages to increase the supply of labourers, despite the fact that the mine had substantially stopped production. The mine was crippled through the bankruptcy of the Mining Board, which organised the extraction of reef. The Central, however, continued to wash its accumulated blue ground on the depositing floors. In January 1884 the Central embarked on a policy of employee retrenchment in conjunction with a reduction in wages. Finding it increasingly difficult to raise money to cover working expenses, the Central picked this moment to confront the organisational strength of its workers.[58]

The appearance of explicit class conflict in this period underlined the decline in the standard of living in Kimberley. White mechanics, engine-drivers and overseers had formed the Working Men's Association of Griqualand West in November 1882, initially to oppose wage reductions. But the first test of their strength lay in opposition to the implementation of systematic searching on entry to and exit from the mines. Most mine managers admitted that searching was inadequate and impractical in preventing thefts. However, it did increase the regimentation of the labour force, even though it undermined the relation of domination between overseer and labourer. Initial resistance to the mineowners' attempt to discipline labour came not from the overseers, but from the artisans and engine-drivers. They orchestrated a successful strike in October 1883, when the searching system was applied to the engine-houses and workshops on the edge of the mine and on the depositing floors. This strike was precipitated by the erosion of the dignity of 'respectable' skilled workers. The mineowners capitulated to their demands to be excluded from the regimentation of searching, as they feared a flight of black labour in the event of an extended strike. In early 1884, however, the situation changed. An epidemic of smallpox broke out in Kimberley, and its deadly legacy remained well into 1885. The mineowners used their influence with the local press and medical men to brand the disease non-contagious and not smallpox. They feared that the scare of the 'pokkies' would drive off transport-riders and send the prices of fuel and provisions soaring. They were only partially successful in their designs; but the consequences of this criminal subterfuge, in terms of the loss of life, were astronomical.[59]

It was in the face of this fear of disease and death that the mineowners provoked a clash with their labour force in April 1884, when they reneged on their promise not to strip and search white men. Organised through the agency of the Artisans and Engine-Drivers Protection Association and the Overseers and Miners Association, white workers initiated the disruption of production on the fields. This involved calling out African labourers despite the sectional interests of white men in supervisory and skilled organisations. On 29 April,

250 white men and between 1 000 and 1 500 Africans and Coloureds descended on Kimberley mine in an attempt to stop the engine pumping water from the pit. They were confronted by special constables under the command of mine managers and directors together with a small detachment of police. When the workers attempted to approach the engine-house they were fired on, and six white men died. A controversial inquest exonerated the special constables for their defence of private property. This show of force, the consequent dismissal of white men involved in the strike and the employment of others from the surplus population at reduced wages, demonstrated the resolve of the mineowners to smash worker combinations. But this conflict also raised the spectre of a class alliance between black and white workers, a threat which was not lost on Cecil Rhodes, who raised the issue vociferously in a debate in Parliament on the strike and the 'affray'. Diminished production in Kimberley and a disciplined white labour force prepared the ground for the co-option of white labour and the resolution of the mineowners' most pressing problem: African labourers.[60]

'The folds of the boa-constrictor'[61]

Soon after Griqualand West was annexed to the Cape, the Kimberley representatives in Parliament, Dr Josiah Wright Matthews, Joseph Benjamin Robinson and Cecil John Rhodes, demanded an enquiry into the diamond mining industry.[62] The Parliamentary Enquiry concluded that IDB threatened to jeopardise the entire future of diamond mining, and argued that 'exceptional circumstances' required 'exceptional and stringent legislation for the protection of this industry'.[63] The protective measures demanded were a barrage of labour legislation and enforcement of existing statutes, which promised to tighten employer control over the material and social lives of workers. The canteens, which were the central institutions of African working-class lives, were believed to be the crucibles of the IDB trade. Although a bill was introduced for the total prohibition of liquor to Africans, only the limited object of a prohibition on consumption and sale in the locations and mining areas was achieved. The searching system was recommended and finally promulgated and implemented. The police force was reorganised on the basis of recommendations of B. V. Shaw, a Metropolitan Police Commissioner, who had been invited to review the state of the Griqualand West Constabulary. The expanded police force increased its vigilance in relation to African migrants, and the number of pass arrests and convictions soared throughout the 1880s. But the most important piece of legislation passed was the Diamond Trade Act, an Act which fundamentally undermined the legal rights of British subjects.

This Act abolished the jury system for IDB cases, as the mineowners found the number of convictions too low. A Special Court presided over by a judge was set up to deal solely with these cases. He was empowered to mete out a maximum penalty of 15 years or 5 years and banishment from Griqualand West. Another tenet of British law was discarded: the presumption of innocence until guilt is proved. The Act placed the *onus probandi* of legal possession of a diamond on the suspected party. Furthermore, the officers of the law were given wide powers of search in public and private places. A Detective Department was created exclusively to investigate IDB offences. Although constituted as a state department, it was largely subsidised by mining capitalists, who worked closely with detectives. The use and abuse of detective surveillance for political purposes and labour intimidation excited strong protests from the wider diamond fields community soon after its inception.[64] By placing strict controls on the diamond trade and sanctioning the 'trapping system', by means of which suspects were enticed into criminal activities, the Act created fear and suspicion among Kimberley's 'honest' citizens.

The final salvo in this barrage of legislative activity was the demand for the enforcement of the compulsory feeding and lodging of Africans on their employers' compounds. It was this suggestion that mobilised general merchants and retailers to combine against the designs of mining capitalists. They petitioned Parliament:

> The general spirit and tenor of these rules seem to imply an intention to unduly and unfairly curtail the liberty of the natives engaged in the mines, as well as to foster the establishment of retail shops by Mining Companies, for by entrusting employers with the power to prohibit the natives from leaving their compounds after working hours, it will be in the power of the employers to prevent their servants from going in to the open market to spend their wages, and so indirectly compel them to deal with such shops they might themselves establish in the compounds.[65]

Here the tradespeople of Kimberley presented themselves as the protectors of African liberty in opposition to the mineowners' pursuit of their economic interests through a discourse in which IDB was construed as the greatest threat to the industry, rather than the scarcity and unreliability of African labour. However, it was the political strength of merchants and their rhetoric of 'free trade' which, together with the 'brandy interest' in Parliament, managed to keep compounds off the statute book.

It was clear to dealers in consumer goods, and their suppliers at the coast that compounds were part of a process of reconstruction in the diamond industry after the collapse of the boom. This was strikingly revealed at the time by the attempt of Cecil Rhodes, William Alderson and H. W. Henderson Dunsmure to sell the De Beers mine to Baron Erlanger and Company, bankers of London and Paris, for £3 million. The amalgamation of companies would increase the revenue of the mine from $14\frac{1}{2}$ per cent to $87\frac{1}{2}$ per cent of the proposed capital in two and a half years. Two measures would fundamentally contribute to this fabulous wealth. First, a shaft and tunnel system would increase the output and reduce the labour required. Second, the 1 500 African labourers were to be housed in barracks. What particularly caught the eye of the merchant in the statement respecting this amalgamation was the projected £29 250 per annum profit on African purchases from the 'tommy shops' in the barracks, purchases which totalled one-third of their wages.

More threatening for the future was the effect that amalgamation and compounds would have on the spending power of white employees. Under the existing system in De Beers mine African wages amounted to £121 680 and white wages to £95 000 per annum. With an amalgamated mine African wages would total £90 090 whereas under the impact of redundancies white wages would collapse to £33 100. The 25 per cent saving claimed through the elimination of IDB was not included on the credit side of these calculations. In fact it was easy for the merchant or retailer to conclude that IDB was the Trojan horse which carried the mineowners out of industrial production into the heart of the town economy.[66]

The collection of interests in this commercial opposition to barracks, or closed compounds as they became known, was complex. On the one hand, the interests of landed property were threatened. The expansion of mining operations and the extension of land required for depositing floors had been given preference by the state and the London Company over the established rights of standholders. Financial reconstruction would further jeopardise this investment as it would involve the introduction of foreign capital and the transfer of wealth to Europe in the form of dividends.[67] On the other hand, merchants and retailers benefited from IDB while remaining 'honest' men and women. W. H. Rennie, Inspector of the Standard Bank, reported:

> Illicit diamond buying although being very ruinous to the diamond industry is remarkably profitable to the storekeepers. It is very rife at present and many hundreds of hands are believed to be engaged in it. Men of this nature are simply gamblers, to whom money comes easily and goes easily also. They all of them live in 'good style', at any rate in an 'expensive style' and are all 'good pays'. Herman Willigerod [one of the merchant petitioners] who had a magnificent business here has informed me that few people have any idea of the immense amount of money expended by 'Illicits' upon these Fields, and he attributes his large cash sales of liquor very much to the custom of these illicits to the various canteens and houses throughout the camps, to which he finds the supplies.[68]

Local tradespeople had steered clear of the 'share mania', and this reinforced the separation of their interests from those of the mineowners. They found the custom of black and white workers more profitable than that of shareholders in the mines. They espoused proletarian policies for white workers, spoke of establishing a group of settled Africans in the locations, and began to organise a political challenge to the mineowners' dominance over the Kimberley representatives in Parliament.

Commercial political power lay in the Town Councils of Kimberley and Beaconsfield, but from 1883 a political alliance was struck between tradespeople and mineworkers. Prominent merchants mounted public platforms and supported the strikers; labourers and artisans shunned Good Templary and continued to patronise the premises of hotel and canteen-keepers. Artisans formed Friendly Societies and plumped for commercial candidates; the Licensed Victuallers elected their own candidate, George Garcia Wolf, and supported other commercial representatives. The threat that Rhodes had seen crystallised in the strike of 1884 had its precursor in the formation of an Africander League, which aimed to put a black man in Parliament, and drew support from Coloureds, Africans and white Afrikaners.[69] The De Beers, Kimberley Central and *Compagnie Française* mining companies put up their own candidates and voted large sums of money for campaigns,[70] but it was only at the end of the decade, when De Beers had monopolised diamond production, that the mineowners controlled Parliamentary representation. Even then they went to the trouble of manipulating African and Indian voters off the roll.[71] In 1884, having smashed the white workers' combinations but unable to solicit Parliamentary support for closed compounds, the most powerful companies began to build barracks to isolate Africans from the town. The introduction of the system had fundamental implications for the racial and sexual division of labour in South Africa: it determined the maintenance of an African migrant labour policy and the development of a labour aristocracy of supervisory and skilled white workers.

'Not for the sake of the natives, but for the sake of their own pockets'[72]

The construction of large, central compounds was part of the vertical integration of company management. The Kimberley Central had three open compounds by the early 1880s and, like those of other companies, they were cold and overcrowded. Next to accidents in the mines, exposure and pneumonia were the largest killers on the fields. Corbet, the Central compound manager, provided staggering weekly figures of Africans on the sick list. The number of sick Africans in all compounds in the latter part of 1883 was estimated by Dennis Doyle, the Sanitary Inspector, as 1 in 15, whereas among the night-soil collectors, the unhealthiest employment in Kimberley, it was 1 in 100. Overcrowding was the second remarkable feature of open compounds. Dr Otto visited the North Floor compound of the Central in August 1883 and reported that this was the cause of the extraordinarily high mortality rate. The authorised space per man in a barracks was 600 cubic feet; in compounds the minimum space should not have been less than 330 cubic feet per man, but Doyle found that compounds were generally more congested than this. Mortality, sickness and overcrowding became of grave concern in this period because of the epidemic of smallpox. The large compounds that were closed in 1885 were improvements in terms of space, but the death rate continued to climb after the compound system was introduced. Pneumonia and mine accidents continued to take their toll.[73]

Soon after the strike of 1884, the Kimberley Central Company and the Compagnie Française decided to develop a system of underground mining.[74] In De Beers mine, a rock shaft was commenced on the north side outside the mine at the end of 1884 by the De Beers Mining Company. In the next year it was abandoned in favour of an incline shaft at the West End. The company began hauling blue ground from the shaft in January 1886 but did not abandon open working until the end of the year.[75] An intrinsic part of this move to systematic underground mining was the establishment of closed compounds for a portion of their African labourers. The Compagnie Française began the system in January 1885 with 110 recruited Africans engaged in Natal. The Kimberley Central followed suit in April with 400 Africans, who promptly struck, but once the strike leaders had been dismissed the others began work. This pattern was fairly established when in July 1886 the De Beers Mining Company closed their compound on 1 500 Africans, who immediately struck but failed to hold out long. Prior to this the Company had built a compound for 300 African convicts.[76]

It is in the joint development of both convict and free compounds that the key determinant of a constant supply of labour, rather than the control of IDB, can be seen. De Beers Mining Company first approached the government in connection with the employment of convicts in October 1884. They wanted long-service African convicts who would be contracted for one or two years. These Africans were to be employed on the floors, and once the mine was amalgamated they wanted as many more for work in the mine.[77] The cost of the erection of the convict barracks was £5 200, and in return for this and the expenses of daily maintenance and discipline, the Company was granted a two-year contract, beginning in January 1886, and the free services of the convicts.[78] G. F. Williams, General Manager of De Beers, later explained the advantages of convict labour:

> In the first place we have labour that we can depend on and it is always at hand. The convicts cannot get away like ordinary labourers. We can also prevent theft better than with free boys. If the latter attempt to escape you cannot shoot them, whereas the sworn officials of the Government can shoot a convict if he attempts to escape.[79]

Compounds were, indeed, intended to prevent theft, and they later grew to be structurally identical to convict stations with entrance and exit tunnels to the mine, wire mesh over the barracks and detention cells for workers to flush out stolen diamonds when their contracts expired. But the introduction of the closed compound system and the convict station occurred as the aftermath of a process of centralisation of company production and as a precursor of a fundamental change in mining production. The projected working costs of underground mining were double those of working in the open, and the amount of capital invested in development work and machinery necessitated an uninterrupted supply of labour in crucial departments of mining.

Before the closed compound system could become universal, sections of commercial capital tried to get its operations restricted. The Chamber of Commerce, which represented large general merchants, refused to support the attempt. The expansion of interior trade and particularly the development of the goldfields had opened up new prospects. Besides, they readily perceived that they would receive substantial contracts to supply the compounds and that a captive market had its advantages over a free one. But for the storekeeper and the liquor trade in general, compounds spelled disaster. It was left to the licensed victuallers and their new representative in Parliament, J. J. O'Leary, to propose an anti-truck bill. Its main thrust lay in two points: no wages were to be paid other than in the current coin of the realm, and no goods were to be supplied in the compounds by mining companies. The Parliamentary debate was conducted in a philanthropic discourse in which the compound system was presented as of infinite benefit to Africans themselves. However, one Member of Parliament exposed the venality of both commercial and mining capital when he argued compounds were 'not for the sake of the natives, but for the sake of their own pockets'.[80]

If this bill had been passed it would have meant the end of the closed compound system, and Rhodes did his utmost to effect a compromise.[81] The mineowners made two important concessions. Firstly, they undertook to buy all merchandise required for the compound stores from dealers in Griqualand West. Secondly, they disclaimed any intention of compounding white workers. At stake was the £30 000 per week thrown into circulation as wages. This compromise seemed to save the compound system and give a reprieve to some tradespeople in Kimberley: the legitimate African liquor market was to be locked up and kept dry. The Labourers' Wage Regulation Act was the form in which this compromise became law in August 1887. However, there was no clause in it which forbade the compounding of white workers. After the monopoly of diamond production had been achieved in 1889, white workers were subjected to a 'cantonment' in the model suburb of Kenilworth, and Charles Rudd, a De Beers Director, agreed that the object in amalgamating the mines had been 'to control the white employees'.[82]

It was openly admitted in commissions and private letters that white workers and even managers were as much involved in IDB as black workers.[83] Initially the mineowners had been committed to searching all their workers, but when compounds had been introduced white workers were excluded. At the same time the literature abounded with complaints over the scarcity of African labourers but was silent on the desertion of European employees. The fact that mineowners found it politically impossible to compound white workers was largely the work of commercial capital. But it seems clear that segregated compounds had a divisive effect in a simple and instrumental way – and was seen as divisive by the mineowners.[84] With the power of white workers destroyed in the strikes, their authority in the work place was reinforced by their exclusion from compounding. Overseers, whose employment had been so dependent on the fluctuations in the supply of African labour, found their posts more secure with their freedom intact. Skilled workers, whose attempts at control of entry into their trades had been torpedoed, were co-opted with higher wages and in effect granted a sectional weapon that increased differentials. White workers of different skills became a labour aristocracy that collaborated with management in disciplining the African labour force.

Conclusion

The years between 1880 and 1885 were crucial in the accumulation of capital on the fields. Property ownership in the mines was centralised through the agency of joint-stock companies. The boom on the share market in 1881 was followed by an international depression of critical proportions, and over-capitalised companies battled with severe problems in the labour process. It was this situation which led to the collapse in the average rate of profit, a collapse which was neither created, nor primarily determined, by IDB. Those who make a direct equation between IDB and the introduction of the closed compound system fail to take account of the way in which the issue of IDB entered into the ideological discourse in which industrial legislation was formulated in the Cape Colony. IDB, as a symbol of unity of that discourse, was used not only to secure possession of private property but primarily to enforce and enact legislation involving labour control generally: the Master and Servant Law, Pass Laws, the Liquor Law and an attempt to legislate a closed compound system in 1882.

It was the necessity of underground mining that forced a reconstruction of the labour process, which entailed the development of a closed compound system. The vastly increased amounts of capital required for development work and underground mining dictated the need for a constant supply of labourers. Opposition to closed compounds came from the liquor trade and dealers in 'Kaffir truck'. Supporting the white workers' refusal to be compounded, they reached a compromise with the mineowners. The compound system for African workers alone entrenched an unskilled/supervisory racial division of labour in the mines and a sexual division of labour between African male migrants in wage work and African females in household production.

The institution of migrant labour and compounds was a pattern of labour relations which neither the mineowners nor the workers chose. It was the product of a struggle determined by the changing structure of production in the mines and in the South African countryside. In 1870 numerous independent African policies existed, with chiefly control over the extraction of surplus labour. By the turn of the century, all had finally come under colonial, republican or imperial control, and the process of labour extraction for the mines facilitated. The characteristic institution for African accommodation in towns had become the compound. Its specific features in Kimberley were determined by the nature and size of the commodity produced. The reasons for its introduction are not to be found in the growth of IDB but in the structural conditions of capital accumulation in the mining industry itself.

Notes

Abbreviations

BBNA	*Blue Book on Native Affairs*
BPP	Great Britain, *British Parliamentary Papers* (London)
CAD	Cape Archives Depot
CPP	Cape Colony, *Cape Parliamentary Papers* (Cape Town)
DF	*Diamond Field*
DFA	*Diamond Fields Advertiser*
DI	*Daily Independent*
DN	*Diamond News*
GLW	Griqualand West
GLW I.G & CR	*Griqualand West Investors' Guardian and Commercial Records*
JAH	*Journal of African History*
KCDM	Kimberley Central Company
RHL	Rhodes House Library
SAL	South African Library
SBA	Standard Bank Archive
UCT	University of Cape Town

1 S. T. van der Horst, *Native Labour in South Africa* (Oxford, 1942), pp. 79, 82; G. R. Doxey, *The Industrial Colour Bar in South Africa* (Oxford, 1961), p. 34; J. M. Smalberger, 'I.D.B. and the mining compound system in the 1880s', *South African Journal of Economics*, 42 (4), 1974.

2 C. van Onselen, *Chibaro* (London, 1976).

3 For an analysis of the use of the term, see G. Stedman Jones, 'Class expression versus social control', *History Workshop Journal*, 4, Autumn 1977.

4 *Diamond Field* (DF), 16 Sept. 1874, Letter from Scrutator.

5 T. Reunert, *Diamond Mines of South Africa* (London, 1892), p. 20; A. Moulle, *Géologie générale et mines de diamants de l'Afrique du Sud* (Paris, 1886), p. 103.

6 Cape Archives Depot (CAD), Griqualand West (GLW) 55, *From Inspector of Claims Dutoitspan and Bultfontein*, Wright to J. B. Currey, 1 Oct. 1874; CAD, GH 12/5,

Enclosure in No. 42, Southey to Barkly, 22 April, 1875; *Berliner Missions Berichte*, 1876, p. 112; Methodist Missionary Society, SA XVIII, Bechuanaland File 1872–74, G. Slade to Perks, 26 Sept., 1874; J. W. Matthews, *Incwadi Yami* (London, 1887), p. 209. It is clear that digging options lasted longer on the London Company estate for individual diggers, both black and white. Blacks continued to hold claims throughout the 1870s; most were bought out at the end of the '70s but others took shares in the diamond scrip speculation of 1881. The Rev. Gwayi Tyamzashe was the last African to hold a claim in 1883 in Dutoitspan. Blacks continued to hold claims at the river well into the twentieth century, which was indicative of the greater wealth and competition for claims in Kimberley.

7 CAD, Colonial Office Confidential African Print, No. 96, *Report of Lieutenant-Colonel Crossman, R. E., on the affairs of Griqualand West*, 1 May, 1876, pp. 8, 21. Population figures were all estimates until the first census was taken in June 1877. Governor Southey, who had an interest in enlarging the population of his province, estimated 10 000 whites and 20 000 'native labourers from the interior'. He also mentioned 1 000 'persons of colour', British subjects from the Cape, Natal and Basutoland, who with the families made a total of 3 000 to 4 000 (*BPP*, C.1401, Enclosure in No. 1, Southey to Barkly, 30 June, 1875, pp. 2, 3).

8 *Ibid.*, Southey to Barkly, 30 June, 1875, pp. 2, 3; von Weber, *Vier Jahre in Afrika 1871–1875* (Leipzig, 1878), p. 443; *Crossman Report*, Court of Enquiry, Dutoitspan, evidence of Geo. Manning, p. 34.

9 For chiefly control of migration, see P. Delius, 'Migrant labour and the Pedi, 1840–1880', in S. Marks and A. Atmore (eds), *Economy and Society in Pre-industrial South Africa* (London, 1980); P. Harries, 'Kinship, Cosmology and the Nature of Pre-colonial Labour Migration', Chapter 5 below; R. F. Sieborger, 'The recruitment and organisation of African labour for the diamond mines', unpublished M.A. thesis, Rhodes University (Grahamstown), 1975; for a clear description of the differences between Colonial and interior Africans see O. Schreiner, *Undine* (New York, 1972), p. 281.

10 E. von Weber, *Vier Jahre*, p. 433; P. M. Laurence, 'Diamonds', in C. Cowen (ed.), *The South African Exhibition, Port Elizabeth 1885*, (Cape Town, 1886), pp. 274, 275; *DF*, 13 Jan. 1875, Notes; W. J. Morton, *S.A. Diamond Fields* (1877), p. 21.

11 CAD, GLW 82, *Records* No. 412, Jan., 1876.

12 For wages consumed in Kimberley, *BPP*, C.1401, Enclosure in No. 1, Southey to Barkly, 30 June 1875, pp. 2, 3; von Weber, *Vier Jahre*, p. 433, estimates 20 000 Africans on the fields at any one time and 80 000 working in Kimberley each year. At 10s per week he estimates £450 000 paid in wages each year. Geo. Manning (*Crossman Report*, p. 34) estimates 8 500 Africans on the fields in 1875 paid 25s per week of £60 per annum totalling £510 000; CAD, GLW 80, *Records*, No. 38, Coleman to Chief Clerk, 5 Jan., 1876, estimates 9 000 registered servants in Kimberley, excluding 1 000 domestics, cooks, hotel and restaurant servants at the end of 1875. For the gun trade, CAD, GLW 183, *Semi-official letters*, Southey to Barkly, 2 June, 1874; *Diamond News* (hereafter *DN*) 15 Aug., 1874, Leg. Council debate on Gun tax (15 Aug. 1874), J. B. Currey; *DN*, 27 Feb., 1875, 'Retrospective glances by an occasional visitor'; J. B. Taylor, *An African pioneer looks back* (London, 1939), p. 42; 75 000 guns were sold in Kimberley between 1 April 1873 and 30 June 1874. For total consumption in Kimberley in 1875:

COST PRICE TO IMPORTER AT KIMBERLEY

Ales, wines and spirits	£73,057
Tobacco	£5 497
Arms and ammunition	£47 136
Articles of 'Kafir trade'	£50 670
Building materials	£41 731
Hardware, ploughs, machinery	£22 630
Furniture and household utensils	£16 080
Soft goods, woollens, cottons	£84 240
Edibles of all descriptions	£99 073
	£440 114

Value of Colonial produce imported (brandy, wines, flour, wood, fruit), £100 000 (*Crossman Report*, Enclosure No. 15, pp. 87–9).

13 F. Boyle, *The Savage Life* (London, 1876), pp. 77–9.

14 See A. Purkis, 'The politics, capital and labour of railway building in the Cape Colony 1870–1885', unpublished D.Phil., Oxford, 1978, pp. 341, 352.

15 H. Wolpe, 'Capitalism and cheap labour power: from segregation to apartheid', *Economy and Society*, I, 4 (1972).

16 BPP, C.1401, Enclosure in No. 1 Southey to Barkly, 30 June 1875, p. 3.

17 *DN*, 11 Aug. 1874, Supplement, Letter from Aylward.

18 For a detailed analysis of the Rebellion, see Rob Turrell, 'The 1875 Black Flag Revolt on the Kimberley diamond fields', *Journal of Southern African Studies*, VII, 2 (1981).

19 'Reef' was the term used for the sides of the diamond mines, which were friable and collapsed into the pits on lengthy exposure to the open air.

20 *DF*, 20 March 1875, Manifesto.

21 A 'native' was defined as a member of any tribe whose principal chief lived beyond the borders of Griqualand West (CAD, GLW 80, *Records* No. 38, Lanyon memo, 6 Jan. 1876). 'Natives' who held a cart, claim or debris licence did not have to carry a pass. Africans who carried Cape certificates of citizenship, like 'persons of colour', did not have to carry a pass. In fact 'there is hardly an instance of one of the class of artificers who will submit to have himself registered at an office which is considered to be for Register [sic] of Natives' (CAD, GLW 64, *Letters miscellaneous*, James Hall to J. B. Currey, 29 Sept., 1874).

22 Kimberley Public Library, *Paton papers*, Provincial Engineer's Report, 9 March, 1875, p. 4. The mine was valued at £500 000 and the workable sections at £200 000.

23 BPP, C.1342, *Correspondence relating*, Enclosure 1 in No. 32, Southey to Barkly, 25 Feb. 1975, p. 181. See also Louis Cohen, *Reminiscences of Kimberley* (London, 1911), p. 96; J. B. Currey, 'The diamond fields of Griqualand West and their probable influence on the native races of South Africa', *Journal of the Society of Arts*, XXIV (1876) 337.

24 *DF*, 11 Nov. 1874.

25 CAD, GLW 185, *Semi-official Letters*, Southey to Barkly, 10 April 1875.

26 CAD, GLW 80, *Records*, No. 440, Resolution passed at a meeting of Liquor Licensing Court, 23 Dec. 1875.

27 For a good description, see von Weber, *Vier Jahre*, letter of 1 May 1872.

28 *Berliner Missions Berichte*, Report of Rev. Meyer, April–Nov. 1875, p. 111.

29 Standard Bank Archive (SBA), Inspection Report (Kimberley) 15 March 1879, Report; GM to LO 15 Aug., 1879 (Henry Files). I am extremely grateful to Mr James Henry for having drawn my attention to this superb archive. It also includes typescripts of the extensive material he extracted from the GM/LO correspondence, and I refer to this as the Henry Files. They form the basis of his excellent book, *The First Hundred Years of the Standard Bank* (London, 1963).

30 University of Cape Town (UCT), Smalberger Papers, T. Kitto, *Report on the Diamond Mines of Griqualand West*, 1897 p. 104.

31 *Griqualand West Government Gazette*, 23 May 1876, Report of the Commission upon the Griqualand Labour Question. See also N. Etherington, 'Labour supply and the genesis of South African Confederation in the 1870s', *JAH* (1979), 235–53.

32 *Griqualand West Government Gazette*, 23 May 1876, Report of the Commission upon the Griqualand Labour Question.

33 Ordinance 28 of 1874 had provided for the establishment of depots, where all 'natives' could be located until contracted. This provision had been linked to the compulsory clothing of 'natives', and as the state was unable to bear the expense the Ordinance had become inoperative.

34 CAD, GLW 50, from D. Arnot to J. B. Currey, 29 April 1873; GLW 71, *From Servants Registrar's Office . . .*, Frazer to J. B. Currey, 2 July 1873; GLW 19, *Miscellaneous*, Henry Francis to Southey, 26 March 1874; *DN*, 26 May 1874, Leader; GLW 184, *Semi-official Letters*, Southey to Barkly, 28 Aug.,1874; GLW 82, *Records*, No. 595, Proposal from Albasini and Crowley, 9 Feb. 1876; GLW 93, *Records*, No. 2689, Crowley to Lanyon, 8 Sept. 1876; Natal Archives Depot, T. Shepstone Papers, Vol. 20, Barry to Shepstone, 15 May 1877, 29 May 1877, 19 June 1877; CAD, GLW 17, *Transvaal Despatches*, No. 4, Rose-Innes to Lanyon, 24 Feb. 1880; CAD, CO 3344, No. 129, Coleman to Colonial Secretary (Cape Town), 11 Dec. 1880, Minute of Charles Villiers, 21 Dec., 1880; CAD, GLW 39, 1873 *Mining Commission*, reply of Willis to Q.14; GLW 97, *Records*, No. 3628, Coleman to Colonial Secretary, 14 Dec. 1876; A. Trollope, *South Africa*, II (London, 1878), p. 182; Cohen, *Reminiscences of Kimberley*, p. 292, 'At times when labour was scarce, some speculative spirit would leave the fair town of Kimberley and meet, say, a famished horde of two hundred attenuated wretches on their way to Eldorado or death. He would engage the lot at ten shillings per week, and if when they arrived in Kimberley there was a glut in the labour market, then these poor descendants of Ham were to be seen on the outskirts of Kimberley starving to death.' For the Sekhukhune War, see P. Delius, 'The Pedi polity under Sekwati and Sekhukhune 1828–1880', unpublished Ph.D. thesis, University of London, 1980, chs. 8 and 9. See also R. F. Sieborger, 'Recruitment and organisation', pp. 90–120.

35 CAD, GLW 80 *Records*, No. 440, Shippard, Comment on Resolution passed at Meeting of Licensing Court, Kimberley, 23 Dec. 1875; GLW 133 *Records*, No. 730, Petition against Board Wages; GLW 152, *Records*, No. 625, Government Notice No. 151 of 1879.

36 *Ibid*.

37 University of Cape Town, Smalberger Papers, Kitto, *Report on the Diamond Mines of Griqualand West*, pp. 59, 60.

38 *Ibid.*, p. 104.

39 For a similar process in the countryside see K. Shillington, 'The impact of the diamond discoveries on the hinterland of Kimberley: class formation, colonialism and resistance among the Tlhaping of Griqualand West in the 1870s', Chapter 3 in this volume.

40 CAD, GLW 131 *Records*, No. 301, Webb to Scholtz, 27 Jan. 1879, and Warren's comments thereon.

41 *Berliner Missions Berichte*, 1880, p. 136; GLW 153, *Records*, No. 835, Coleman to Acting Colonial Secretary, 14 April 1880. The three locations on the London estate were in Newton and under the authority of the Kimberley municipality. There were other locations in Dutoitspan. These locations were for 'natives' and were not supposed to include Coloureds or Indians.

42 CAD, GLW 17, *Transvaal Despatches*, Coleman's Minute on the Labour Question, 14 Feb. 1880; CAD, CO 3344, No. 129, Coleman to Colonial Secretary (Cape Town) 11 Dec. 1880.

43 University of Cape Town, Smalberger Papers, *Daily Independent*, 12 Oct. 1880, Leader.

44 Cape Parliamentary Papers (CPP), *Blue Book of Native Affairs*, G8–'83, Appendix, p. 5.

45 South African Library (SAL), Merriman Papers, No. 27, C. J. Rhodes to J. X. Merriman, 16 May 1880.

46 University of Cape Town, Smalberger Papers, *Daily Independent*, 12 Oct. 1880, Leader.

47 *DN*, 8 July 1879, The Bank Statements. £100 000 was the estimated value of machinery purchased between June 1878 and June 1879. *Incwadi Yami* (London, 1887), p. 251, estimated £650 000 as the amount devoted to machinery in the formation of companies; *Mining Journal*, 4 June 1881, letter from R. W. Murray, value of machinery in place of Kimberley estimated at £750 000; *Griqualand West Investors' Guardian and Commercial Record (GLW I.G. and G.R.)*, 21 April, 1881, 'Hints to Investors', states the average cost of hauling and washing the blue ground as: Kimberley, 7s 6d to 15s per load; De Beers, 7s 6d to 10s per load; Dutoitspan, 4s 6d to 7s per load.

KIMBERLEY JOINT-STOCK MINING COMPANIES, 1880–81

Number of Companies		Nominal Capital (£)	Amount yet to be paid up (£)
Kimberley	13	2 733 150	557 000
De Beers	12	1 334 100	137 651
Dutoitspan	19	2 001 140	265 822
Bultfontein	15	276 100	142 950
Jagersfontein*	3	287 400	118 500
Koffyfontein*	4	133 500	34 250
Total	66	6 765 390	1 256 173

* In the Orange Free State.

Source: SBA, GM to LO, 29 April 1881 (Henry Files)

The decline in the price of diamonds was as follows, with the September 1882 selling price representing an immediate 15 per cent collapse on the prior price:

DECLINE IN DIAMOND PRICES, 1882–85

Company	Selling price, Sept. 1882		Selling price, August 1885		Depreciation		%
	s	d	s	d	s	d	
Kimberley	28	2½	14	4½	12	10	46
De Beers	25	10½	15	11	9	11¼	38
Dutoitspan	40	4	23	10¾	16	5¼	41
Bultfontein	31	10½	16	8¾	15	1¼	47
Average	31	2¾	18	0¾	13	2	42

Source: SAL, 'The President and Members of the Board of the French Company', p. 3.

48 For this distinction see C. Perrings, 'The production process, industrial labour strategies and worker responses in the Southern African gold mining industry', *JAH*, XVIII, 1 (1977), 129–35.

49 SBA, GM to LO, 19 Aug. 1881 (Henry Files); Rhodes House Library (RHL), MS. Africa t14, Cecil Rhodes to Charles Rudd, 1 Feb. 1881; SBA, GM to LO, 12 Nov. 1881 (Henry Files); *GLW I.G. & C.R.*, 22 Sept. 1881, p. 5; *Mission Field*, Jan. 1883, No. 55, Letter from 'Layman', 26; *DN*, 24 Dec. 1881, Leader; *GLW I.G. & C.R.*, 24 Nov. 1881, 1 Dec. 1881, 8 Dec. 1881, 29 Dec. 1881, 'The labour question'; *Diamond Fields Advertiser* (*DFA*), 30 July 1880, Leg. Council Debate (27 July 1880) on searching overseers; *DFA*, 23 Dec. 1882, Report of Meeting of Representatives of Diamond Interests held in London (21 Nov. 1882). The Bultfontein Mining Company worked with white labour alone. The Kimberley North Block Company employed white labour and declared a 10 per cent dividend in 1882. The British Company (Kimberley mine) employed white labour owing to a scarcity of African labour. However, most mine owners developed a preference for African labour, and argued as follows:

I have tried white labour. I engaged 50 white men as labourers but it would not answer, they worked one day and got drunk the next. You can always depend on the Kafirs (*CPP*, A9–'82, *Select Committee on IDB*, evidence of S. Marks, Q. 218).

50 *CPP*, G11–'90, *Report of Mining Inspectors*, p. 38; A. Moulle, *Géologie générale et mines de diamants de l'Afrique du Sud* (Paris 1886), p. 116. The occupational breakdown is derived from Moulle, who was the Manager of the *Compagnie*, as the Inspectors' reports are inadequate. Moulle, however, makes a rigid racial division between white artisans and black unskilled labourers, which is incorrect. These figures are only approximate average figures and take little account of seasonality and discontinuities in production.

51 *DFA*, 23 Dec. 1882, Report of London Meeting of Representatives of Diamond Interests (21 Nov. 1882).

52 *CPP*, G34–'83, *Report of the Inspector of Machinery*, p. 50.

53 Cape Blue Book 1881, p. U10; Cape of Good Hope Blue Book, 1882, p. 725. In 1881 the Kimberley Savings Bank had 1 060 depositors, and Dutoitspan 385. In 1882 the Dutoitspan Savings Bank had closed, and there were 570 depositors in Kimberley.

54 *CPP*, A9–'82, *Select Committee on IDB*, evidence of S. Marks, Q.181; evidence of H. J. Feltham, Q.17.

55 CAD, GDM 6/4, *Eagle Diamond Mining Company Letters*, Circular from A. W. Davis, 18 Aug. 1882. 20s per week for general labourers was the figure named. The lowest cost of living for a labourer was estimated at 10s per week, and for an artisan between £2 15s and £3 10s per week in 1884 (G28–'85, *Report of the Inspector of Machinery*, p. 27).

55 The dividends declared by the Central Company were: 1880 – 10%; 1881 – 28% and a bonus of £12 on original shares; 1882 – 26%; 1883 – 5%; 1884 to 1886 – none; 1887 – 34½%; 1888 – 36%.

57 UCT, Smalberger Papers, Kimberley Central Company (KCDM), Directors' Minute Book I, 5 July 1881, f112; 28 Feb. 1882, f236.

58 UCT, Smalberger Papers, KCDM, Directors' Minute Book I, 30 Dec. 1881, f178, 20 Nov. 1882, f346; Directors' Minute Book II, 8 May 1883, f37; 28 Jan. 1884, f255; 29 Feb. 1884, f278; Anglo-American Archive, Gregory Papers, KCDM Directors' Minute Book II, 16 Feb. 1884; 9 April 1884.

59 The official figures are inaccurate, as numbers of death from smallpox were not certified as such. The figures, for what they are worth, are 2 311 cases from October 1883 to January 1885, of which 700 resulted in death (51 European). In 1882 the population of the fields was between 17 000 and 20 000 Europeans and 22 000 Africans, declining to 12 000 in the middle of the year.

60 The searching system, the smallpox epidemic and the strikes are dealt with in greater detail in R. V. Turrell, 'IDB: the ideological discourse of mining capital, 1880–1885', unpublished M.A. thesis, School of Oriental and African Studies, University of London, 1977.

61 SAL, 'Our estate in the Cape Colony and its management' (1886), p. 9.

62 *CPP*, G86–'82, *Diamond Mining Commission*, appointed 7 Sept. 1881, and composed of all the Kimberley representatives and other mining capitalists; G82–'82, Report on IDB appointed by the Diamond Mining Commission, which included a draft bill drawn up by the Board for the Protection of Mining Interests on which the Diamond Trade Act was based; A9–'82, *Select Committee on IDB*, appointed 21 April 1882; members: Cecil Rhodes (Chairman), J. X. Merriman (Commissioner of Crown Lands and Mines), Dr Matthews, Saul Solomon, James Irvine, Anthony Goldschmidt, Jan Hofmeyr, Jonathan Ayliff, Charles Leonard, Joseph Robinson.

62 *CPP*, A9–'82, Report p. iv.

64 For detective surveillance of African combination against searching see UCT, Smalberger Papers, KCDM, Directors' Minute Book I, 28 Feb. 1883, f421; scandals in the Department were to be the subject of Parliamentary enquiry. See G50–'85, *Report by Roper on the Detective Department*, and G3–'88, *Commission on the Diamond Trade Acts*.

65 *CPP*, A100–'82, *Petition of Merchants, Standholders, Storekeepers and others owning real property and engaged in trade in Kimberley*.

66 Anglo-American Archive, Gregory Papers, DMP B–6, 'Statement respecting De Beers Mine', May 1882. The existing and projected variable expenses per annum were:

Existing systems	Expenses (£)	Future systems	Expenses (£)
20 Managers	16 000	2 Managers	1 600
20 Sub-managers	7 000	2 Sub-managers	700
20 Secretaries	8 000	3 Secretaries	1 200
40 Engine-drivers	12 000	12 Engine-drivers	3 600
20 Gangs of 4		10 Gangs of 4	
Africans for fuel	4 680	Africans for fuel	2 340
200 Overseers	52 000	100 Overseers	26 000
2 000 Africans	117 000	1 500 Africans	87 750
500 Horses	39 000	150 Horses	11 700
Total	255 680	Total	34 890

Total saving per annum was to be £206 430: variable (£120 790) and fixed (£85 640).

67 *DI*, 2 Feb. 1883, 'The commercial interests of Kimberley'; SAL, 'Our estate in the Cape Colony and its management' (1886), p. 14.

68 SBA, Inspection Report, Kimberley, 12 Nov. 1881, f495. Herman Willigerod was worth £20 000 and in 1882 turned over between £15 000 and £20 000 each month in liquor sales.

69 *DI*, 13 Dec. 1883, 'Formation of an Africander League'. A form of black consciousness was espoused by Joseph Moss, the High Court Interpreter (who was a Mfengu); DI, 22 Dec. 1883, white Afrikaners, for example George Beet, formed the Griqualand West and South African Political Association, which had no connection with the Afrikaner Bond, and chose its candidates in conjunction with the Africander League.

70 UCT, Smalberger Papers, KCDM, Directors' Minute Book II, 23 April 1883; 19 Nov. 1883; De Beers Mining Company, Director's Minute Book I, 21 Nov. 1883.

71 Rhodes House Library, MS. Africa S228, C2 A, No. 40, Judge Lange to Rhodes, 22 Dec. 1891.

72 Cape *Hansard*, House of Asembly, 1887, speech of de Waal, p. 130.

73 UCT , Smalberger Papers, KCDM, Directors' Minute Book 1, 27 March 1882, f218; 10 Oct. 1883, f138, the lowest figure of 22 sick; 3 Nov. 1882, the highest figure of 105 sick out of 800; Directors' Minutes Book II, 9 Aug. 1883, f126; DI, 10 Nov. 1883, Board of Health; *DFA*, 9 Aug. 1884, Reports of Sanitary Inspectors; Kimberley Public Library, Beaconsfield Municipal Council, *Letters Received*, Vol. 2, No. 404 and Enclosure in 471, Reports of Sanitary Inspector. In 1886 there were 1 384 deaths out of a population of 15 000 in Kimberley alone (DI, 12 Feb. 1887). In 1888 there were 2 131 deaths. Of this increase of 747 deaths, 243 died of pneumonia and 268 of mine accidents, and Africans accounted for $61\frac{1}{2}$% of the increase (G1–'90, *Liquor Laws Commission*, Appendix 1, Letter from Dr A. H. Watkins, p. 1058).

74 SBA, 700: 24, W. Kenrick to Messrs J. & P. Higson, 26 Aug. 1884; 700:006, W. Kenrick to Kimberley Central Mining Company Directors, 6 Oct. 1884; DI, 15 Dec. 1884, KCDM Company Report for half year ended 31 Oct. 1884; *Griqualand West High Court*, Vol. III, pt. IV (Johannesburg, 1973) *Kenrick v. KCDM Company*, 25, 28 Sept. 2, 5, 7, 19 Oct. 1885, pp. 414–28, *DFA*, 3 March 1885. Shafts had been constructed in the blue ground in the mine but were threatened by reef

collapses. Rock shafts outside the mine signified a total commitment to underground mining.

75 T. Reunert, *Diamond Mines of South Africa*, p. 30; DI, 8 May 1886, Yearly Report of De Beers Mining Company.

76 *DFA*, 19 Jan. 1885; *DI*, 28 April 1885; G3–'88, *Commission on Diamond Trade Acts*, evidence of F. R. Thompson, Q 108; N. Rouillard (ed.), *Matabele Thompson: his autobiography and story of Rhodesia* (Johannesburg, 1957), pp. 42, 43.

77 CAD, CO3454, No. 244, Stow telegram to John Graham, 4 Oct. 1884.

78 CAD, CO 3454, No. 244, Wright telegram to Graham, 11 Oct. 1884, CO 3526, No. 166, E. A. Judge to Under Colonial Secretary, 14 April 1886.

79 *CPP*, A7–'91, *Select Committee on Trade and Business in Griqualand West*, Q 4246.

80 Cape *Hansard*, House of Assembly, 1887, p. 130. Speech of De Waal, MLA for Tulbagh and partner in a Cape Town ironmongery firm. Although for the anti-truck bill, he had just earned a handsome commission from D. P. Graaff and Company by securing for them the contract for the supply of the 'tommy shops' on the Kimberley railway extension (SBA, Inspection Report, Cape Town, 14 Sept. 1885, f99).

81 See Lewsen, *Selections from the Correspondence of J. X. Merriman*, I, pp. 213, 214; J. X. Merriman to J. B. Currey, 14 June 1886 and 18 June 1886, for comments on the Parliamentary support of the Bond for the anti-truck bill, which forced a compromise.

82 G3–'88, *Commission on Diamond Trade Acts*, evidence of C. D. Rudd, Q.2046.

83 For example, SBA, Inspection Report (Kimberley), 12 November 1881, f; SAL, Merriman Papers, 1885, G. Smith to J. X. Merriman.

84 See Foster, *Class Struggle and the Industrial Revolution* (London, 1974), pp. 203–50; J. Foster, 'Imperialism and the labour aristocracy' in J. Skelley (ed.), *The General Strike 1926*, (London, 1976).

CHAPTER TWO

Labour in the South African gold mining industry, 1886–1914

Peter Richardson and Jean Jacques Van-Helten

I

When Harrison and Walker lodged discoverers' claims to portions of auriferous ground on the farm of Langlaagte on the Witwatersrand in the South African Republic in 1886, they brought to an end a distinct period in the economic history of southern Africa.[1] Although it was not realised immediately, their discovery effectively marked the end of the era of the gold prospector south of the Limpopo. From the 1850s until the mid-1880s the small-scale digger was the key figure in the winning of the precious metal. As a result of a large number of discoveries in the 1870s and the early 1880s, diggings were scattered across the territory of the more northerly of the two Boer republics from Klein Letaba in the Zoutpansberg district in the north to Klerksdorp in the southern Potchefstroom district. A line of diggings in an east–west direction could also be identified, stretching from De Kaap in the Lydenburg district to Melamanie in the Marico district.[2]

These workings were significant for the small amounts of capital and labour which they employed, and for the particular type of industrial organisation which they required. The largely alluvial nature of early gold production meant that much, if not all, of the diggers' capital was sunk in simple and inexpensive tools, machines and materials, as the following contemporary advice to would-be prospectors reveals:

> Deposits of gravel should be carefully searched, and careful attention paid to the mixture of dirt and gravel on the bed rock, as well as in the fissures of the bedrock. A flat-bottomed pan, provided for panning-out work, will here be found necessary, and the dirt washed and shaken until the lighter particles are separated and lost by the overflow of water, and the heavier metals sink to the bottom. A supply of mercury and cyanide of potassium must be laid in for amalgamating with fine gold.[3]

Such activities could be undertaken easily enough by individual prospectors or small syndicates with a minimum of unskilled assistance. Digging and washing out of gold-bearing gravel were the tasks normally assigned to the small number of Africans employed by the diggers.[4]

Even such individualistic and small-scale production held within it pressures for change. The incessant search for gold led the diggers naturally from the alluvial finds to the mother deposits themselves. Before the discovery of the Witwatersrand, the most important reef finds were made at Barberton in 1885, although other reefs were worked at the Tati and Pilgrim's Rest goldfields.[5] The move from panning to mining, even on such a small scale, heralded important developments. Besides requiring increased capital to cope with the problems of crushing gold-bearing ground, the actual mining required greater resources of unskilled labour for the recovery of the metal than ever before. In 1887 J. W. Matthews reported on a visit to the De Kaap valley that

> The average English labourer will be driven out of the fields by native labour, 1 500 natives being at present employed, and there will be no such thing as a poor man jumping into a fortune except by some extraordinary stroke of luck.[6]

It is indicative of the closing of the mining frontier that Barberton was soon driving out men like Harrison and Walker, and sending them inland in search of additional deposits which could once again be worked by men of small means.

It was Harrison and Walker's ill-fortune that their famous discovery continued and intensified the economic changes that were overtaking gold mining in southern Africa. Within a relatively short time it was recognised that the deposits of the Witwatersrand marked a wholly new departure in the science of recovering gold. In that the Witwatersrand was a larger reef deposit, its exploitation represented a continuation of the developments of the previous thirty years. However, as was recognised by the time of the Anglo-Boer war, the combination of size and regularity ensured not only a revolution in mining enterprise but also in the social and economic organisation of the communities of southern Africa.[7]

II

Between 1886 and 1914, the mines of the Witwatersrand were developed in a virtually unbroken line along the strike of the Reef from Randfontein to Modderfontein, a distance of nearly forty miles. The only breaks of significance in the formation were to be found at Boksburg in the east and Roodepoort in the west.[8] It was soon appreciated that gold-bearing ground was to be found not only in this prolonged outcrop, but at depth, as the southward-dipping reef was increasingly intercepted by vertical shafts in claim areas due south of the strike. Between 1890 and 1895, the proving of the deep-level claim areas opened up whole new areas of mining ground on a scale hitherto unimagined.[9] The sheer magnitude of the new fields to a large extent determined their labour demands. However, as the geological knowledge of the area increased, other features became conspicuous which also influenced the labour requirements of this burgeoning industry.

Despite some very rich ground, particularly to the immediate south, east and west of Johannesburg, Rand ore was on average 4 to 5 dwts (pennyweights) poorer than deposits currently being worked in Australia and Canada.[10] In addition, only one of the gold-bearing reefs or beds identifiable on the fields, the so-called Main Reef series, was consistently payable, and within the Main Reef series itself the basis of payability in each claim area varied quite substantially. Depending upon the prevailing level of aggregate working costs, mines worked richer or poorer reefs within the series, often for considerable periods of time. Generally speaking, in the period before and immediately after the Anglo-Boer war, the level of costs meant that only the richer reefs of the series were worked in any of the Witwatersrand properties. Thereafter, the general decline in working costs enabled mineowners to exploit ores that were closer to the average grade for the whole field.[11]

The pyritic rock in which the deep-level gold was embedded also posed serious technological and economic problems, and directly affected the labour demands of the industry. To extract the gold from this conglomerate of white quartz pebble, cemented together with silica and sand and thickly sprinkled with pyrites, required increasingly sophisticated and expensive plant to ensure maximum percentage of recovery and to offset losses of free-milling gold. Although the industry was successful in overcoming these difficulties in two distinct phases, moving from a single amalgamation system in 1887, through the Plattner cyanide concentration method to the MacArthur–Forrest process by 1893, the costs of these innovations added greatly to the overhead costs of mine investment and greatly increased the pressure for large-scale operations.[12]

The pressures operating on those seeking to accumulate capital on the basis of profitable exploitation of these deposits was further intensified by the economic circumstances in which the industry came into being. Despite the proliferation of diggings in the South African Republic in the 1870s and early 1880s, it still had a largely pastoral economy, lacking any developed infrastructure to supply and support advanced mining technology. With the discoveries of the Witwatersrand, nearly all heavy equipment had to be imported, a fact which made the industry sensitive to changes in the level of world prices.[13] This sensitivity was further increased because under the operation of the gold standard the selling price for gold was in effect fixed, and changes in the value of gold relative to other commodities could not be matched by gold price changes. The purchasing power of the proceeds of gold production therefore rose or fell depending upon the direction of these changes in relative value.[14] This inability to control certain critical elements of the cost structure of the mining industry was made even more significant by the fluctuations in the supply of working capital. The most important periods of speculative inflow before 1914 occurred in 1889–90, 1895–96, 1899, 1902–3, and 1909–10.[15] The intervening periods were often those of fairly acute depression for the industry, which increased the pressures to appropriate capital from internal sources, to control production costs to achieve this, and to maintain the flow of dividends to encourage market confidence.[16] These periods of depression also involved the industry in attempts to seek greater cooperation with the state as pressure on working costs and internal appropriations of capital put additional pressure on the production regime. Thus, in the wake of the collapse of the 1895–96 boom, the industry attempted to reduce African wages, and asked the state to introduce a pass law to control desertion.[17] Similarly, in 1903–4 in the wake of another collapsed stock-market boom the industry sought, this time successfully, state support for control of its Chinese labour force.[18]

III

Variations in the grade of ore mined, technological difficulties of recovery, fluctuating store costs, weak infrastructural development, price control and fluctuating capital supplies all placed a premium upon control of other production costs to ensure profitable working. In the circumstances of the developing deep-level, low-grade industry of the Witwatersrand, this drive to contain costs usually took the form of heavy pressure to contain or reduce those items of working expenditure which were *directly* amenable to management control, the judicious selection of reef workings within the possible permutations presented by the geological configuration of particular claim areas, and continued attempts to lobby the government to secure a favourable fiscal and financial environment.[19] Of these three strategies, the latter two were by their nature restricted in scope. Thus, the options available to mine managements to control the grade of ore mined was subject both to natural constraints and the prohibitive costs of altering mine design once working had already started.[20] Similarly, the amenability of incumbent governments to pressure from the industry was limited by the sources of its political power and its wider function of ensuring the general conditions governing capital accumulation. This was most clearly demonstrated up to 1899 when the Kruger regime, although by no means opposing industrialisation, adopted a strategy which directly raised the cost of mine production.[21] Similar conflicts in interest, although not so prolonged or as serious, can be identified in the Crown Colony period (1900–7), the Responsible Government period (1907–10) and in the early years of the Union.[22]

As a result of the limitations placed on aspects of the mines' cost control strategy, those costs which were directly amenable to management control therefore remained the most effective means of controlling the costs of production and ensuring profitable returns for the investors. As the industry had developed by the time of the Anglo-Boer war, costs actually incurred in the process of production were divided between the purchase of labour-power and the purchase of stores and fuel. In 1898, for example, 58 producing companies spent 53.44 per cent of their total production costs on labour, and the balance on various stores and fuel, the largest single items being explosives (10.95 per cent) and fuel (8.23 per cent).[23] Consequently, commodity price levels and the costs of different types of labour-power were a central concern of the industry's managers. As the industry was not generally able to exercise a controlling influence over commodity prices, 'labour costs thus became the crucial area of cost minimisation'.[24]

For practical purposes the industry's concern with the cost of labour-power centred upon two different issues. The technical difficulties of deep-level mining, the scale of investment that it required, and the absence of an indigenous skilled workforce meant that in the initial stages of capital accumulation the industry was forced to resort to the introduction of skilled immigrant workers to perform certain specific task of production and to oversee the production process in general. However, the reliance upon the relatively scarce and therefore expensive skills of immigrant miners from Europe, North America and Australasia to perform these tasks was in direct conflict with the cost-minimising strategies dictated by the imperatives of profitable production.[25] The solution adopted to resolve this contradiction was to develop a production process which satisfactorily exploited the growing reservoirs of cheap unskilled African labour whilst restricting the scope and extent of white employment in a manner consistent with the difficulties of Witwatersrand production.[26] This reliance upon migrant white and African labour thus gave to the mines a racially defined skill profile which mirrored and extended the differences between the societies from which these labourers were drawn.

In the early years, the social composition of the mine labour force was additionally noteworthy for the reason that Afrikaners, or local-born whites, were by and large not directly involved in the mining industry. During the 1880s some Transvaal Boers had owned claims and possessed diggers' licences, but the nature of the industry precluded Afrikaners, particularly after the reorganisation of 1889.[27] That is not to say that Afrikaners were not employed at all in the mines prior to 1907 when large numbers entered the industry for the first time as scab and then permanent labourers. In 1897, for example, during the height of the recession, Wernher, Beit & Co. noted that H. Eckstein & Co. were having 'good results' from 'the employment of Dutchmen'.[28] Again, in 1902, during the famous experiment with white unskilled labour undertaken by F. H. P. Cresswell at the Village Main Reef Mine, some Afrikaners were also employed.[29] Nevertheless, the extent of Afrikaner proletarianisation, and consequent increase in unskilled labour costs which provision for the reproduction costs would have involved, mitigated against their large-scale employment until technological changes had undermined the value of skilled work sufficiently to permit their employment as overseers, rather than as unskilled labourers.[30]

IV

Despite this racial division of labour, the costs of white labour remained high, amounting to 28.39 per cent of all working costs in 1898, as against 25.05 per cent for African labour costs. In the same year white workers amounted to only 11.05 per cent of the total mine workforce of 92 806.[31] Because of these considerations, the ratio between European and African (and later Chinese) miners, both in terms of numbers and relative costs, became one of the most sensitive indices of the profitability of mining operations on the Rand. As a consequence it became a fixed policy of the Chamber of Mines to claim that expansion depended to a very large extent upon the movement of this ratio in favour of African labour:

> Work among the whites must be confined to skilled departments . . . [whilst] the continuance and expansion of the mines, and prosperity, contentment and existence of the white population depend, in a large measure, on an adequate supplementary supply of cheap labour through the coloured races.[32]

In this situation in which the industry sought to restrict both the numbers, job description and cost of the white workforce, miners of European descent occupied certain distinctive areas of employment on the Rand gold mines. Generally speaking, in the period of the deep-level development and exploitation of the original Witwatersrand between 1893 and 1914, white skilled work was divided into craft work which was done in the mine, but was not necessarily peculiar to mining as an occupation, and work which required certain skills particularly associated with metalliferous mining in hard rock. In the first category were to be found boilermakers, brass finishers and mounders, bricklayers, carpenters, coppersmiths, electricians, ironmoulders, joiners, mechanics, painters, pattern makers, plasterers, plumbers, tinsmiths, turners, wire-splicers and woodworking machinists; in the second category were amalgamators, assayers, banksmen, cyanide shiftsmen, drill-sharpeners, air, steam or electrical drivers, engineers, fitters, gangers, machine rock-drillers, millwrights, onsetters, pipesmen, pumpmen, riggers, samplers, signallers, skipmen, timbermen and time-keepers.[33] The relative importance of these two categories seems to have changed over the period 1893–1914. Thus, while the major deep-levels were being developed and output from the outcrops was predominant, a greater proportion of whites were employed underground than on the surface. The large amount of highly technical and skilled shaft-sinking and development work required to bring the deeps into production required this distribution of skilled labour, and concentrated the majority of white workers into specifically skilled mining jobs. As a larger number of deep levels became working mines after 1895, an increasing proportion of white jobs were on the surface, and probably belonged to the first category. Thus, in 1897, 9 530 whites were employed on the Witwatersrand mines, of whom 7 961 or 83.54 per cent were underground. At that time there were 52 producing mines in operation.[34] By 1907, there were 95 producing mines, with 17 328 whites employed, but only 7 866 or 45.39 per cent were underground miners. Although this proportion fluctuated slightly thereafter, at no time before the First World War did the number of underground whites outnumber those employed on the surface.[35]

The quantity and distribution of unskilled labour reflected similar parameters and constraints to those which affected skilled white labour. Thus, between 1893 and 1914, African unskilled labour became increasingly concentrated underground. In the period up to 1907, as the bulk of the deep levels came into production, the percentage growth of African underground labour was actually slower than that for surface labour, although in absolute terms underground labour always absorbed more than surface work. After 1907, as the remainder of the deep levels came into operation, the percentage increases were reversed and African underground labour increased at twice the rate of surface labour. All of this occurred within the context of a massive extension of the total numbers employed, reflecting the overall growth of the Witwatersrand goldfields as they became the world's pre-eminent gold producer. Thus, although throughout 1890 only 15 000 Africans were employed on the fields, by 31 December 1897 the daily total was 69 127. By 1907 the numbers of Africans at work at a single time had risen to 105 027 despite a serious shortage of labour in the years immediately after the 1899–1902 war. By 1912 this figure had risen again to 189 253, although the number of working mines had fallen from 95 to 59 in five years, reflecting an expansion of the scale of individual units of production following a series of amalgamations between 1908 and 1909.[36]

In a similar manner to white skilled labour, very definite specialisms became associated with African employment during this, the classic period of deep-level, low-grade mining, and put a distinctive stamp upon the production process of the Witwatersrand gold-mining industry. In an important memorandum presented by the Transvaal Chamber of Mines to the Transvaal government in 1906, the situation was summarised as follows:

> The bulk of the work underground, apart from attending to machinery, blasting and other skilled work, consists of (a) drilling; (b) shovelling; (c) tramming; and it is

estimated that about 90 per cent of the whole of the unskilled labour underground is employed on one or other of these occupations. . . . As regards the handling of ore on the surface, where peculiar conditions of working which prevail underground and which to so large an extent prohibit the employment of mechanical devices do not apply, it can be said that in no other mining region has money been spent more lavishly on labour-saving devices than on the Rand. Many new forms of machinery for this purpose have been invented and developed here, and any new methods which have been invented abroad are not long allowed to remain untried on these fields.[37]

The extent to which the mining industry was able to distribute its skilled and unskilled labour forces to reflect so accurately its cost constraints at this time raises important questions. Robert H. Davies has recently suggested that in the first quarter of the twentieth century a twofold change occurred in the relations of production within the gold-mining industry, and that whilst the concentration of powers to 'assign the means of production, resources and profits' took place 'between 1896 and about 1910', the concentration of powers 'related to the direction of internal organisation of actual labour processes' proceeded 'more slowly, [and] was not completed until 1922'.[38] In other words, the centralisation of ownership and control in the form of the group system was established during the early period of the industry's development, but it was not until 1922 and the Rand Revolt that mine management succeeded in breaking down completely the skill division of labour within the industry.

Given the realignment of the group structure which took place after 1913, it is questionable whether the process of concentrating the power to assign the means of production was completed by 1910 as Davies suggests. It is also open to question whether the mines failed to intervene significantly in the organisation of the labour process in the period. According to Davies, the struggle to achieve this control over the labour process took the form of an offensive by capital to bring about a 'greater separation between the tasks of conception, co-ordination and control on the one hand and productive manual labour on the other, in order to restrict white employment to new petty bourgeois mental and supervisory places: principally the latter'.[39] However, as our analysis of the distribution of white and black labour within the prevailing production process on the Rand before 1914 indicates, the experience of white labour was more complicated than this. The concentration of skilled work on the surface suggests that there was more than an attempt to differentiate mental from manual labour underground in this period.[40] Davies' definition appears, in fact, to be drawn from the experience of a part of the working class on the mines. In so doing he does not provide a general analysis of the period or provide a faithful picture of the process of capital accumulation. The problems of accumulation centred upon the combined process of mining and recovery and involved black and white labour across a whole range of occupations. As long as greater returns could be secured by technological innovation above ground and minimal mechanisation below ground, as in the period before 1914, the ability of the mining industry to concentrate skilled men on the surface counterbalanced any threat to accumulation from the resistance of whites to job redefinition underground. Only when economic circumstances changed during the First World War and thereafter, and the need to mechanise below ground became imperative, did underground resistance assume the character of a general threat to accumulation. Before 1914 the power of assignment within the labour process was held by capital, and only thereafter did the struggles between capital and labour assume the character ascribed to them by Davies.[41] The background to this situation must now be examined more closely.

V

The relative balance and aggregate costs of these two types of labour meant that it became a matter of policy to control the real cost of each and to control the ratio of costs between them. Out of these considerations emerged several strategies to meet the differing circumstances of white and African labour.

The success of the industry in restricting the relative size of the white workforce in the face of great pressures to reduce working costs met with fluctuating success before the First World War. Thus, whereas before the Anglo-Boer war the ratio of white or Coloured labour fluctuated around 1:8, between 1901 and 1903 it suffered a sharp decline to 1:4.6.[42] Thereafter the industry succeeded in widening the ratio once more so that by 1912 it stood at 1:7.8, and by 1914 at 1:8.2.[43] As we have seen, this overall ratio was established in the context of significant changes in the distribution of white labour between underground and surface work, with a consequent decline in the relative proportion of underground mining work. In absolute terms the number of white miners actually rose until 1911 and thereafter numbers fell each year until 1914.[44]

The relative, and later absolute, decline in the number of white miners reflected more fundamental changes than those simply associated with a redistribution of skilled work. As Davies has pointed out, the mining industry sought to reduce the skill content, particularly of white underground work. This process was most acutely reflected at the sensitive points of production, and before 1914 was very largely associated with changes relating to the rock-drill. Even before 1900 the actual operation of these machines had passed out of the hands of white operators, who had been reduced to supervising two drills operated by five Africans. The number of drills was increased to three after 1907, and, following the introduction of a new, smaller drill, the number had increased to ten by 1914.[45] By 1913–14, a similar pattern can be observed in other departments and processes, with white engine-drivers and machine operators also becoming supervisors.[46]

The de-skilling of the white work force was only part of the industry's strategy for controlling the total cost of this type of labour. In addition to reducing the actual value of the work involved and reducing the ratio of white to Coloured labour, the industry also sought to protect itself against the possibility of a re-extension of jobs done by whites through the acceptance of the demand by white workers for a legal definition of racially demarcated work. This definition and demand centred upon skilled labour in the first instance, and found its first expression in 1893 when a colour-bar was introduced in respect of blasting. By the time of the Anglo-Boer war the colour-bar also covered the operation of winding and other machinery and jobs performed by banksmen and onsetters.[47] The range of the colour-bar was further extended by the first schedule to the Labour Importation Ordinance of 1904, and consolidated in the Mines and Works Act of 1911.[48] This strategy had a dual function for the industry. Not only did it tend to stabilise the definition of skilled work: by recognising certain realities of economic and political power held by the white working class, it also 'served to maintain and reinforce the prevailing division of labour in the industry, and the prevailing division of the working class generally, the restriction of unskilled work to non-whites and the lack of solidarity between white and non-white workers'.[49]

The obverse of the 'job colour-bar' was to ensure that non-skilled work remained the province of cheap African labour. As Johnstone has observed, few prospects filled the mining companies with greater alarm than that of a widespread extension of white labour into jobs held by African miners and defined as unskilled. Both the immediate impact on costs and profitability and the long-term cost implications of the potential unionisation of large sections of the unskilled work force ensured that from the very beginning the mining industry sought to oppose resolutely any attempt to introduce a general white labour policy.[50] Thus the attempts of Cresswell at the Village Main Reef and on other mines in 1902–3 and in 1907–8 on mines of the J. B. Robinson group to undertake production on the basis of white unskilled labour were denounced as failures.[51] The successful resistance of the mines to this policy was matched by attempts to promote African and Chinese rather than white labourers into the formerly skilled positions of rock-drilling on an increasing scale after 1902.[52] After 1908, it was clear that any full-blooded white labour policy would in effect be in the public sector.[53]

However, the strategies of the industry in relation to white labour did not end there. In the face of a sustained fall in profits after the Anglo-Boer war, the companies sought to effect economies in all areas of working costs. Given the size of white labour costs in this profile, this resulted in a determined effort to reduce white labour costs still further. The industry was greatly helped by the technological developments which enabled African and Chinese unskilled labour to undertake the production tasks associated with machine drilling and which relegated white labour to supervisory positions from an early date. The mine managers were quite explicit about their position, as this statement at the time of the 1907 strike makes clear:

> The main issue of the present strike is Unionism. If the tenor of operations were even it would not be a serious danger, but decreasing yields and other controlling factors make it imperative that costs be reduced with the least possible delay. To do this we must be free to make the most of our labour conditions, and such freedom is manifestly impossible under Unionism.[54]

The attempts to reorganise underground work in the wake of the defeated 1907 strike were particularly successful, for not only were the number of machine drills supervised by white miners increased, but a fundamental change was effected in the economic and social structure of skilled white labour as a result of this victory. As Davies has observed, the number of local-born whites employed by the mines at wages that were significantly lower than foreign-born miners increased by 1 077 between April and June 1907.[55] Thereafter the trend towards the displacement of the high-cost, foreign-born migrant white miners continued unabated. By 1930 only 40 per cent of the workforce was foreign-born, as against 83 per cent in April 1907.[56] Furthermore, not only were the great but declining majority of white workers foreign-born; they were also single men or married men remitting money to their families in their country of origin. In 1897, only 12 per cent of white employees of the Witwatersrand gold mines were registered as married and had their families resident with them in the Transvaal. By 1912, in conjunction with the increasing intake of white miners from the local communities, it had risen to 42 per cent.[57]

The strategies for controlling the labour costs of productive mining operations on the Witwatersrand did not stop short at white labour. The majority of the workforce were racially defined unskilled labourers whose total cost to the industry was only slightly below that of white labour and whose strategic importance in a rapidly changing production process was arguably greater by the end of the first decade of the twentieth century than that of their white counterparts. From the early days, the great problem of unskilled labour on the mines had been how to secure sufficient amounts of labour at a cost compatible with the total expenses admissible under the conditions of Witwatersrand production.[58] There were in essence three aspects to the cost of African labour which the industry sought to control. In the first place there were those costs which were incurred in securing the workforce, specifically through recruiting and government licence fees. Secondly, there were the direct wage costs of African labour. Thirdly, there were its social or reproduction costs. As a result of the conditions in which the industry developed, these three problems often presented themselves as part of a broader development associated with the transformation of the position of African societies in southern Africa generally.

The problem of controlling the costs of recruiting and wages of unskilled labour in a period of rapidly expanding labour demand was one which exercised the leaders of the mining industry from the outset. It was not until the First World War that the Chamber's policies regarding unskilled labour were finalised. The attempts to create an unskilled labour force involved the industry with the state more directly, more closely and for longer than probably any other single problem in this period, although it was not always a wholly cooperative relationship. Thus, between 1890 and 1899, despite persistent requests, the state failed to provide any effective mechanism to meet the demand for a cheap and reliable labour force of Africans because of the impact this would have had upon the agricultural labour market.[59] After the Anglo-Boer war, the state in the Transvaal proved to be much more amenable to the industry's suggestions on setting up a viable and permanent system of unskilled labour employment. Thus, in 1901 and again in 1909, the source of recruits from Portuguese East Africa was more or less guaranteed by the state.[60] At the same time consistent and effective attempts were made to increase the efficiency of unskilled labour after 1903 by controlling the drink traffic and regulating health conditions in the compounds.[61] Furthermore, in a more controversial move, the British administration of the Transvaal agreed to the importation of Chinese labourers to overcome the shortage of African labour which developed after the war of 1899–1902.[62] Although this was discontinued after 1907, the state continued to intervene directly in securing the labour supply through the establishment of the Government Native Labour Bureau in 1907 and through the regulation of recruiting conditions and agreements, a policy which reached a climax in the 1909 Convention and in the passage of the Native Labour Regulation Act of 1911.[63]

Although state–industry collaboration was always a cornerstone of the industry's policy in respect of unskilled labour, it did not of itself provide the means of mobilising labour for the mines. In response to this situation, the industry sought to develop a policy of collaborative monopsony* by which the African labour market could be controlled. In the absence of a complete collapse of traditional African societies, and in the face of varying degrees of state collaboration and inter-group competition, this policy met with varying success. Thus the attempts to control wages through reductions in 1890, 1896, 1897 and 1900 were all failures. Not until the introduction of Chinese labourers

*Monopsony is strictly speaking a situation in which there is only a single buyer in a given market, whose bargaining position is such that the purchaser alone determines the price of sale. In practice, monopsony is often used, as with the case of monopoly, to indicate an advanced state of concentration of purchasing power rather than a complete monopoly.

destroyed the bargaining position of African labourers at a time of severe depression in the southern African regional economy and final military defeat following the collapse of the Bambatha rebellion in Natal, did the mines succeed in controlling the upward movement of wage costs. Thereafter, the control of the mines over the real costs of African wages seems to have been increasingly successful.[64]

The success of the mines in establishing an effective recruiting company was even more belated. The need for such an organisation grew out of the enormously increased demand for labour within the mining industry itself and within southern Africa generally as a result of the economic changes triggered by the development of the Witwatersrand. The need to combine to bypass the speculative labour touts and to control internecine competition for labour were the symptoms within the industry of a phenomenon that was widespread within southern Africa at the time. The first formal attempt at establishing an industry-wide recruiting organisation was made in 1896 with the formation of the Rand Native Labour Association. The failure of the state to administer effectively a pass law and to guarantee contracts of service undermined this attempt.[65] In 1900 a second attempt was made to impose collective discipline upon the companies through the creation of the Witwatersrand Native Labour Association (WNLA). This initiative, although more successful than its predecessor, was only partially so. In 1906, following several months of growing pressure on labour supplies in the light of imminent Chinese repatriation, the agreement broke down, and the J. B. Robinson group seceded from the Association and the monopsony within British South Africa was abolished.[66] Only in Portuguese East Africa was the monopsony retained after 1908, when the rules of the Association were altered.[67]

A more successful attempt was made in the first decade of the twentieth century to set up a disciplined recruiting company with the establishment of the Chamber of Mines Labour Importation Agency in 1904 to oversee the recruiting and importation of Chinese labourers. However, this company was merged with WNLA in 1908, following the decision to repatriate time-expired Chinese labourers.[68] Within a few years of the reorganisation of WNLA, the lifting of the depression and the return to free recruiting were forcing up recruiters' prices and putting renewed pressure on wage rates. Consequently, a further successful attempt was made in 1912 to control recruiting within British South African territories. The establishment of the Native Recruiting Corporation in 1912 was more than a victory for controlled recruiting;[69] it also heralded the introduction of a maximum average wage rate* within the industry which was a

*The maximum average wage was a device instituted to reap the productive benefits of piece-work whilst reducing its cost. Its essence was an average wage ceiling per shift for African miners on piece-work. These rates were set by member companies in the NRC. The agreement was policed by the corporation and enforced through a system of fines

major force for controlling wage costs.[70] However, the Native Recruiting Corporation (NRC) itself experienced difficulties until 1919, when the J. B. Robinson group finally joined it.[71]

Behind these failures to control wage rates or the behaviour of member groups in the face of labour shortages lay an insistent fact about the unskilled labour market which the companies were forced to recognise. The economic and political forces which were operating in southern Africa were insufficient to expand the unskilled workforce at a pace consistent with the labour demands of the mining and other industries. To meet the circumstances of this situation, as Legassick and du Clerq have pointed out, there were two possible alternatives available to the mining industry: either increase the productivity of labour or expand the area from which the workforce was recruited. As the demand of the production process then operating on the Rand mines made the first alternative financially unattractive or indeed impossible, the second was chosen.[72] The most important area in this context was undoubtedly Portuguese East Africa, which between 1904 and 1914 never provided less than 47 per cent of African labour employed in the Transvaal coal- and gold-mining industries.[73] Between 1904 and 1907 the geographical range of this policy was extended even further by recruiting some 63 695 Chinese labourers.[74] The advantages presented by these and other sources of labour were more than those stemming from the addition of considerable numbers of men at wage rates acceptable to the mining industry; for the longer contracts of service which these men worked also significantly slowed the turnover rate of the migrant unskilled workforce.[75]

Even the importation of significant numbers of labourers from areas outside the political boundaries of the British South African territories did not exhaust the need, and therefore the policies, of the mining industry, for unskilled labour. At the time that they actively encouraged the introduction of this so-called foreign labour themselves, they also made use of the growing structural decline of African societies within the High Commission territories by allowing the free engagement of labourers driven out of their traditional societies in this way.[76] The mines also pursued a policy of debt bondage based on a system of advances as a means of drawing out labour.[77] The extent of the decline in areas such as the Transkeian Territories, Natal and Zululand was such that the industry was able to pay wages to single male labourers, as from elsewhere, at rates below the cost of reproduction of this labour-power and still secure a growing army of recruits.[78] Furthermore, in pursuit of this policy the industry supported measures which tended to increase the reliance of African

---

levied on companies which permitted higher than average rates per shift. The advantages of the system were that it permitted a generalised system of productivity-related payments which favoured the marginal mines without wholly destroying the rationale of bonuses for richer companies.

societies upon migrant labour. In this context the industry's support for the 1913 Natives' Land Act was of considerable significance.[79]

VI

These cost-cutting strategies of the mining industry were not met passively by either African or white labour. Before 1914 a whole range of responses to direct and indirect coercion of the labour force can be identified. Nevertheless, the differences in the degree of direct state support for repressive and divisive tactics pursued by the mining industry in relation to the two main sections of its workforce tended to produce appropriately different responses to this situation.

The working and living environment of African labourers tended to be circumscribed in large measure by the directly coercive and ubiquitous compound. This system of housing, which combined cost effectiveness in social provision with widespread means of social control, originated on the Kimberley diamond mines.[80] The extension of the system to the Witwatersrand did not lead to a wholesale adoption of the Kimberley closed compound system on the Rand. Nevertheless, it provided a very effective means of management control over the labour force, and provided the environment within which resistance to work conditions, changes in the methods of production, changes in rates of pay, and general proletarianisation took place at the mines. The increased willingness of the state after 1902 to buttress this system of control through effective Pass Laws and enforcement of the Masters and Servants Law further circumscribed the limits of African resistance.[81]

Conversely, white labourers had a more complex relation to capital by virtue of the economic and political power that they exercised in Transvaal colonial society. Thus, although the state was forced to recognise and guarantee certain economic demands of white workers, and their living conditions were not so directly controlled, coercion still formed the underlying basis of relationships between white labour, capital and the state. Troops were used to control serious outbreaks of conflict between mining capital and labour in 1907, 1913 and 1914,[82] and in terms of the Transvaal Industrial Disputes Prevention Act of 1909, a system of 'compulsory conciliation' was enforced upon the white working class on the mines.[83]

In these circumstances African resistance usually took on a covert although not necessarily disorganised form. Thus, desertion and breach of contract by African miners continued to be a major cause of labour turnover throughout this period, either as a response to wage-rate adjustments or to poor living or working conditions. Between 1902 and 1909, desertions and gaolings for breach of contract accounted for an annual average of 7.2 per cent of total wastage of the unskilled African workforce. With the passing of the Act of Union and the general tightening up of labour legislation there was a significant reduction in the losses incurred by the industry for this reason. By 1912 the annual average loss by desertion was down to 1.83 per cent.[84] Another covert form of resistance to the conditions on the mines came in the form of persistent failure to perform a minimum amount of work. This phenomenon was described as 'loafing' by the mine management. Although by definition this is difficult to measure, there can be no doubt that the mines saw it as a very serious problem. In 1905, for example, they secured an agreement from the Foreign Labour Department which permitted the mine management to deduct pay for failure to complete a 'fair day's work', and at the same time made it legal for days so described to be added to the worker's term of service.[85] Again, in 1909, the companies stipulated that African miners on drill work who failed to drill 30 inches should not be paid and the shift not credited to the contract of service.[86] This 'loafer ticket' system was incorporated in the pay schedule drawn up by the Native Recruiting Corporation in 1912.[87] Other evidence of African resistance to the controls imposed by the mining industry may be found in the progressive growth of urban crime, the emergence of informal housing sectors, prostitution and the drink traffic.

When occasion demanded, African responses could, and did, take the form of open resistance. Thus, in 1890, the Chamber of Mines attempted to introduce a wage reduction of 14.2 per cent in the wake of the stockmarket collapse of that year.[88] The response of African workers was swift and entirely unexpected. The mine manager's house at the Anglo-Tharsis mine was blown up by dynamite, and the secretary of the Meyer and Charlton mine, F. McMillan, was caught in his burning house on the morning of 24 October 1890 as 'the wage reduction had made the Kaffir take an instant dislike to Mr McMillan who also discharged the duties of paymaster'.[89] During the wage reductions of 1896–97, Julius Wernher observed that 'amalgam thefts seem to be carried out on a tremendous scale – no wonder the City [Deep] failed to give satisfaction as gold returns fell off'.[90] In 1902, following the wage reductions which accompanied the formation of WNLA, African miners at the Consolidated Main Reef Mine went on strike in protest against the higher wages being paid to African workers by contractors working outside WNLA agreements.[91] The strike of African workers on the mines in 1913 also revolved around the issue of pay at a time of falling real wages.[92]

Similar patterns of informal and more organised resistance can also be found amongst the white workers on the mines, although the tenor of their actions tended to be influenced also by their industrial experiences in Europe, the United States and Australia. Poor working performances, particularly amongst whites working as unskilled labourers, seem to have been almost as common an experience as 'loafing' amongst African and Chinese labourers. Indeed, a witness before the Transvaal Indigency Commission of 1906 claimed that whites were more likely than Africans to 'work in a slovenly manner or behave uncivilly to employers'.[93] However, more overt confrontations between management and workers tended to be the rule with white workers. As early as 1889 white miners struck for better working conditions at the Salisbury mine,[94] and in 1893 thousands of miners marched through the streets of Johannesburg in opposition to the Illicit Gold Buying bill.[95] In 1902, 1906, 1907 and 1913 miners struck to protect their skilled positions and their rights to organise against the management and have some control over their working conditions.[96] It was in the course of the latter dispute that an even greater threat to the management on the mines became apparent: the possibility that a successful strike by whites would demonstrate to African workers that gains could be made by combination and strike action. Furthermore, there was the added danger that strikes amongst white workers which involved the wide-scale deployment of force could provide the opportunity for a successful African rising against both employers and the state.[97] Thereafter, much of the energy which had been expended on the creation of an unskilled workforce was directed by industry and the state into preventing this, the most dangerous of combinations.

VII

To summarise: the development of the deep-level, low-grade deposits of the Rand represented a revolution in the science and technology of gold-mining which had a decisive impact upon the demand for labour within the industry itself and within southern Africa. Further, in the course of this developing revolution of capitalist industry, labour came to be distributed by the mining industry across a racially defined skill profile which reflected very accurately the cost constraints of this type of mining. In the process of maintaining and refining this sytem in line with technological changes associated with metalliferous mining, the industry was forced to engage in various strategies to control the costs of the different types of labour-power that it utilised. It was in the differing degree of success that it achieved in this field, rather than in that of labour-utilisation as such, that the limits of the mining industry's power within the Transvaal in particular and within southern Africa in general may be found.

Notes

Abbreviations

BRA/HE	Barlow Rand Archives/H. Eckstein & Co.
JAH	*Journal of African History*
JSAS	*Journal of Southern African Studies*

1   W. MacDonald, *The Romance of the Golden Rand: being the Romantic Story of the Life and*

Work of the Pioneers of the Witwatersrand – the World's Greatest Gold Fields (London, 1935), *passim*; J. Gray, *Payable Gold: an Intimate Record of the History of the Discovery of the Payable Witwatersrand Gold Fields and of Johannesburg in 1886 and 1887* (Johannesburg, 1937), pp. 15–90, esp. pp. 79–87.

2   *11th Annual Report of the South African Republic Chamber of Mines for 1899* (Johannesburg, 1899), p. 298.

3   E. Glanville, *The South African Gold Fields* (London, 1888), pp. 112–13, quoted in D. H. Houghton and J. Dagut (eds), *Source Material on the South African Economy, 1860–1970, Vol. 1 1860–1899* (Cape Town, 1972), p. 267.

4   T. Baines, *The Gold Regions of South Eastern Africa* (London, 1877), pp. 75–88.

5   S. T. van der Horst, *Native Labour in South Africa* (London, 1971), p. 125.

6   J. W. Matthews, *Incwadi Yami, or Twenty Years' Personal Experience of South Africa* (London, 1887), p. 486.

7   *13th Annual Report of the Transvaal Chamber of Mines for 1902* (Johannesburg, 1902), Annexure entitled 'A descriptive and Statistical Statement of the Gold Mining Industry of the Witwatersrand', p. 6.

8   Frederick H. Hatch and J. A. Chalmers, *The Gold Mines of the Rand: being a Description of the Mining Industry of the Witwatersrand, South African Republic* (London, 1895), Ch. 2.

9   J. H. Curle, *The Gold Mines of the World* (London, 1899), pp. 73–5; G. A. Denny, *The Deep-Level Mines of the Rand* (London, 1902), *passim*.

10   Transvaal Chamber of Mines, *The Gold of the Rand: a Great National Industry, 1887–1923* (Johannesburg, 1923), pp. 14–15.

11   S. H. Frankel, *Investment and Return to Equity Capital in the South African Gold Mining Industry, 1887–1965: an International Comparison* (Oxford, 1967), p. 28: Table 6.

12   J. Gray and J. A. McLachlan, 'A History of the Introduction of the MacArthur-Forrest Cyanide Process to the Witwatersrand Goldfields', *J. Chemical, Metallurgical and Mining Society of South Africa*, 33 (1933), 375–95.

13   On the generally under-developed nature of the infrastructure of the South African Republic, see S. Marks and S. Trapido, 'Lord Milner and the South African state', *History Workshop Journal*, VIII (Autumn 1979), 74–105; for another interpretation see D. Denoon, 'Capital and capitalists in the Transvaal in the 1890s and 1900s: a non-regressive revision', *Historical Journal*, XXIII, 1 (1980), 111–32; on the scale of imports involved see P. Richardson and J. J. Van-Helten, 'The Gold-mining industry of the Transvaal, 1886–1899', in P. Warwick (ed.), *The South African War: The Anglo-Boer War, 1899–1902* (London, 1980), p. 22.

14   P. Vilar, *A History of Gold and Money, 1450–1920* (London, 1975), pp. 351–2; J. J. Van-Helten, 'British and European Economic Investment in the Transvaal with Specific Reference to the Witwatersrand Gold Fields and District, 1886–1910', Ph.D. thesis, University of London, 1981, Chapter 2.

15   S. H. Frankel, *Capital Investment in Africa, Its Course and Effects* (London, 1938), pp. 92–5; R. V. Kubicek, *Economic Imperialism in Theory and Practice: the Case of South African Gold Mining Finance 1886–1914* (Durham, N.C., 1979), pp. 21–2.

16   Frankel, *Capital Investment in Africa*, p. 95.

17   Van der Horst, *Native Labour*, pp. 130–6.

18   P. Richardson, *Chinese Mine Labour in the Transvaal* (London, 1982), pp. 27–46.

19   C. Perrings, 'The Production Process, Industrial Labour Strategies and Worker Responses in the Southern African Gold Mining Industry', *Journal of African History (JAH)*, XVIII, 1 (1977), 129–35.

20 A. H. Jeeves, 'The Control of Migratory Labour in the South African Gold Mines in the Era of Kruger and Milner', *Journal of Southern African Studies (JSAS)*, III, 1 (Oct. 1975), 3–29.

21 G. Blainey, 'Lost Causes of the Jameson Raid', *Econ. Hist. Rev.*, 2nd ser., XVIII (1965), 350–66.

22 A. A. Mawby, 'Capital, Government and Politics in the Transvaal, 1900–1907: a Revision and a Reversion', *Historical Journal*, XVII, 2 (1974), 387–415.

23 *13th Annual Report of the Transvaal Chamber of Mines for 1902*, Annexure, p. 14.

24 F. A. Johnstone, *Class, Race and Gold: a Study of Class Relations and Racial Discrimination in South Africa* (London, 1976), p. 20.

25 R. H. Davies, *Capital, State and White Labour in South Africa, 1900–1960: an Historical Materialist Analysis of Class Formation and Class Relations* (New Jersey, 1979), p. 52.

26 Johnstone, *Class, Race and Gold*, pp. 24–5.

27 For an early instance of the employment of Afrikaners in the mines, see Barlow Rand Archives (BRA)/H. Eckstein and Co. (HE) 125, J. B. Taylor to Jules Porges, 28 October 1887. We should like to thank Maryna Fraser for her kind permission to use these archives. For the history of early Afrikaner urban employment see C. van Onselen, *Studies in the Social and Economic History of the Witwatersrand*, Volume 2, *New Nineveh*, Chapter 3, 'The Main Reef Road into the Working class: Proletarisation, Unemployment and Class Consciousness among Johannesburg's Afrikaner Poor, 1890–1914', pp. 111–3; E. L. P. Stals, *Afrikaners in die Goudstad, Deel I 1886–1924* (Pretoria, 1979), pp. 19–29.

28 BRA/HE 63, p. 179, Wernher, Beit & Co. to H. Eckstein & Co., 24 September 1897.

29 R. Davies, 'Mining Capital, the State and Unskilled White Workers in South Africa, 1901–13', *JSAS*, III, 1 (Oct. 1976), 63.

30 See below p. 85.

31 *BPP* 1901, LXXXVIII, Cd. 447, *Mines and Quarries General Report and Statistics, Pt. IV, Colonial and Foreign Statistics for 1899*, Table of Persons Employed on all Transvaal Gold Mines at 31 December in each Year.

32 *13th Annual Report of the Transvaal Chamber of Mines for 1902*, Annexure, p. 22.

33 Based on the reserved schedule of jobs in the Transvaal Labour Importation Ordinance, 1904 (No. 17 of 1904) in Transvaal, *A Handbook of Ordinances, Proclamations, Regulations and Instructions Connected with the Importation of Foreign Labour into the Transvaal* (Pretoria, 1906), pp. 5–22; for the difference of opinion as to whether the Ordinance represented the maximum extent of white skilled employment on the mines up to that time see M. Legassick, 'The Mining Economy and the White Working Class', Paper read at the Conference of Southern African Labour History, African Studies Institute, University of the Witwatersrand, 8–10 April 1976; D. Denoon, 'The Transvaal Labour Crisis, 1901–1906', *JAH*, VIII, 3 (1967), 481–94.

34 *BPP* 1899, C.9187, *Mines and Quarries: General Report and Statistics* Pt. IV etc., for 1897, *loc. cit.*

35 *Ibid.*, for 1898–1913 in *BPP* 1899, CVII, C.9527; *BPP* 1901, LXXXVIII, Cd.447; *BPP* 1902, CXVI, Cd. 959; *BPP* 1903, LXXXII, Cd. 1506; *BPP* 1904, CVI, Cd. 2084; *BPP* 1905, XCVIII, Cd. 2600; *BPP* 1906, CXXXIV, Cd. 2911; *BPP* 1907, XCVII, Cd. 3566; *BPP* 1908, CXXXIII, Cd. 4145; *BPP* 1909, CII, Cd. 4739; *BPP* 1910, CIX, Cd. 5284; *BPP* 1911, CI, Cd. 5884; *BPP* 1912–13, CVII, Cd.

6460; *BPP* 1914, XCIX, Cd. 7217; *BPP* 1914–16, LXXX, Cd. 7732.

36 On the amalgamations, see Kubicek, *Economic Imperialism*, pp. 80–1; on labour returns, see *BPP* 1904, XXXIX, Cmd. 1897, Evid. of TCM to the Transvaal Labour Commission, Exhibit I, Native Labour Returns; *24th Annual Report of the Transvaal Chamber of Mines, for 1912*, lxii.

37 *BPP* 1906, LXXX, Cd. 3025, Memorandum on the subject of Labour-Saving Appliances used in the Mines of the Witwatersrand, 2 April 1906, enc. 2 in Selbourne to Elgin, 9 April 1906.

38 Davies, *Capital, State and White Labour*, pp. 46–7, 50.

39 *Ibid.*, p. 67.

40 The concentration of surface workers was not the result of resistance below ground but reflected the degree of technological development on the surface and the consequent need for skilled workers. Nor was the definition of skilled workers merely nominal, reflecting the preservation of defunct categories for judicial purposes. The 1904 Labour Importation Ordinance actually defined a greater number of skilled jobs where the division between mental and manual labour was not far advanced at all (see note 33 above). The only point where de-skilling might be claimed to have reached an advanced stage on the surface before the 1913 strike was where the majority of skilled occupations on the surface were not peculiar to mining as an occupation.

41 The flexibility in the total production process which this argument implies distinguishes this analysis from that put forward by Charles Perrings, 'The Production Process', 131–2. For a further discussion of this point see Richardson, *Chinese Mine Labour in the Transvaal*, pp. 23–4.

42 P. Richardson, 'The Provision of Chinese Indentured Labour for the Transvaal Gold Mines, 1903–8', unpublished Ph.D. thesis, University of London, 1978, p. 368.

43 Davies, *Capital, State and White Labour*, p. 70.

44 *Ibid.*

45 *Ibid.*

46 Johnstone, *Class, Race and Gold*, pp. 142–4.

47 *Ibid.*

48 Van der Horst, *Native Labour*, pp. 172–79.

49 Johnstone, *Class, Race and Gold*, p. 81.

50 Davies, *Capital, State and White Labour*, pp. 59–60.

51 Davies, 'Mining Capital, the State and Unskilled White Workers', 52–6, 63–4.

52 E. Katz, 'White Workers' Grievances and the Industrial Colour Bar, 1902–1913', *South African Journal of Economics*, 42, 2 (1974), 135–8.

53 Davies, 'Mining Capital, the State and Unskilled White Workers', p. 65.

54 BRA/HE 253, f.148, No. 932, Notes on Strike Situation submitted by Mr Hannold at Meeting of Consulting Engineers, 28 May 1907, enc. 2 in Hannold to Phillips, 24 June 1907.

55 Davies, 'Mining Capital, the State and Unskilled White Workers', p. 63.

56 L. G. Irvine, A. Mavrogordato and H. Pirow, 'A Review of the History of Silicosis on the Witwatersrand Goldfields', Paper given to the International Silicosis Conference, Johannesburg, August 1930, p. 194.

57 *Report of the Small Holdings Commission (Transvaal), 1913* (U.G.51–13), p. 12, cited in C. van Onselen, *Studies in the Social and Economic History of the Witwatersrand*, Volume 2, *New Nineveh*, Chapter 1, 'The Witches of Suburbia: domestic service in Johannesburg', p. 9 and note 34.

58 Perrings, 'The Production Process', pp. 131–2.
59 Richardson and Van-Helten, 'The Gold-mining Industry', p. 31.
60 Richardson, 'The Provision of Chinese Indentured Labour', pp. 40–2; Richardson, *Chinese Mine Labour in the Transvaal*, pp. 166–87.
61 C. van Onselen, 'Randlords and Rotgut, 1886–1903', *History Workshop Journal*, II (Autumn 1976), 33–89; Jeeves, 'The Control of migratory labour'.
62 Richardson, *Chinese Mine Labour in the Transvaal*, pp. 27–46.
63 *Ibid.*, pp. 166–87; van der Horst, *Native Labour*, pp. 179–80.
64 Van der Horst, *Native Labour*, p. 206; S. Marks, *Reluctant Rebellion: the 1906–8 Disturbances in Natal* (London, 1970), pp. 338–65.
65 Van der Horst, *Native Labour*, pp. 133–5.
66 Jeeves, 'The Control of Migratory Labour'.
67 Van der Horst, *Native Labour*, p. 192.
68 P. Richardson, 'The Recruiting of Chinese Indentured Labour for the South African Gold Mines, 1903', *JAH*, XVIII, 1 (1977), 85–108.
69 Van der Horst, *Native Labour*, p. 193.
70 Union of South Africa, *Report of the Native Grievances Enquiry, 1913* (U.G. 37–14), paras. 263–9.
71 Van der Horst, *Native Labour*, p. 193.
72 M. Legassick and F. du Clerq, 'Capitalism and Migrant Labour in Southern Africa: the Origins and Nature of the System', Paper presented to the Labour Migration Seminar, Institute of Commonwealth Studies, University of London, 13 June 1977.
73 *15th to 25th Annual Reports of the Transvaal Chamber of Mines*, return of natives in the employ of members.
74 Richardson, 'The Provision of Chinese Indentured Labour', p. 384.
75 Richardson, *Chinese Mine Labour in the Transvaal*, Table A:11.
76 The increase in the number of non-recruited labourers was very striking, particularly after the war of 1899–1902: the number of so-called locals distributed by WNLA between 1902 and 1912 increased from 3 423 in 1902 to 91 590 in 1912 – an increase of 54 per cent of the percentage of labour distributed by the Association – see *Annual Report of the Witwatersrand Native Labour Association for 1912*, return of geographical distribution of natives received by WNLA.
77 The policy of using cattle advances is discussed in W. Beinart, 'Joyini Inkomo: Cattle Advances and the Origins of Migrancy from Pondoland', *JSAS*, V, 2 (April 1979), 199–219.
78 The full extent of the debate about the conditions creating a migrant African workforce on the mines can be traced in the following works: H. Wolpe, 'Capitalism and Cheap Labour in South Africa: from Segregation to Apartheid', *Economy and Society*, I, 4 (Nov. 1972), 425–56; M. Legassick, 'South Africa: Capital Accumulation and Violence', *Economy and Society*, III, 3 (1974), 253–91; M. Legassick, 'Gold, Agriculture and Secondary Industry in South Africa, 1885–1970: from Periphery to Sub-Metropole as a Forced Labour System', in R. Palmer and N. Parsons (eds), *The Roots of Rural Poverty in Central and Southern Africa* (London, 1977), pp. 175–200; Legassick and du Clerq, 'Capitalism and migrant labour'; C. Bundy, *The Rise and Fall of the South African Peasantry* (London, 1979).
79 F. Wilson *et al.* (eds), *Farm Labour in South Africa* (Cape Town, 1977), p. 21.
80 See R. Turrell, 'Kimberley labour and compounds, 1871–1888', Chapter 1 above.
81 For a full discussion of these laws, see S. Moroney, 'Industrial Conflict in a Labour-Repressive Economy: Black Labour on the Transvaal Gold Mines 1901–12',

B.A. Hons. thesis, University of the Witwatersrand, 1976, *passim*.

82 Davies, *Capital, State and White Labour*, p. 83.

83 *Ibid.*, pp. 113–20.

84 *Annual Report of WNLA for 1912*, return of wastage of African workforce, 1902–1912. An indication that desertion was often a perfectly rational response to intolerable working conditions can be gathered from the truly horrific fatality statistics of the Witwatersrand mines: between 1897 and 1910 no less than 5 053 African miners were fatally injured whilst working in the Witwatersrand mines, to say nothing of those who died from diseases contracted at the mines or who were permanently or partially disabled; see *Mines and Quarries, General Report and Statistics for 1897–1910, Pt. IV, Colonial and Foreign Statistics*, return of deaths from accidents on Transvaal gold mines (for full sources see n. 36 above). These figures are an underestimate of the full extent of accidental mortality on the Transvaal miners, as they omit figures for white and Chinese miners. They also omit returns for 1899 and 1900 because of the war. On the admission of the Witwatersrand Native Labour Association, no less than 49 531 African miners died from all causes between 1901 and 1912; see *Annual Report of WNLA for 1912, op. cit.*

85 Richardson, *Chinese Mine Labour in the Transvaal*, pp. 171–2.

86 Johnstone, *Class, Race and Gold*, p. 43.

87 *Ibid.*

88 *2nd Annual Report of the Witwatersrand Chamber of Mines for 1890, passim.*

89 *The Star*, 21 Oct. 1890; *The Star*, 27 Dec. 1890.

90 BRA/HE 167, J. Wernher to G. Rouliot, 29 April 1897.

91 Transvaal Archives Depot, Secretary for Native Affairs Papers, 7/783/02, General Manager, Consolidated Main Reef, to General Manager, WNLA, 2 April 1902.

92 Van der Horst, *Native Labour*, pp. 205–6.

93 *Report of the Transvaal Indigency Commission* (1908), p. 25, para. 48, cited in Johnstone, *Class, Race and Gold* p. 60.

94 BRA/HE 52, p. 367, H. Eckstein to Jules Porges and Co., 13 September 1889.

95 *The Star*, 28 Jan. 1893; H. J. and R. E. Simons, *Class and Colour in South Africa, 1850–1950* (Harmondsworth, 1969), pp. 155–6.

96 On the Village Main strike, see Davies, 'Mining Capital, the State and Unskilled White Workers', p. 53; on the Crown Deep strike see *Transvaal Leader*, 11 Oct. 1906; BRA/HE 218, f.44, No. 39, Memo by Mine Manager, Crown Deep, 26 Oct. 1906; on the 1907 and 1913 strikes see Davies, *Capital, State and White Labour*, pp. 71–2, 81–4, and E. Katz, *A Trade Union Aristocracy: a History of White Workers in the Transvaal and the General Strike of 1913* (Johannesburg, 1976), *passim*.

97 Davies, *Capital, State and White Labour*, pp. 82–4.

CHAPTER THREE

The impact of the diamond discoveries on the Kimberley hinterland

Class formation, colonialism and resistance among the Tlhaping of Griqualand West in the 1870s

Kevin Shillington

It is widely accepted that the year 1870 marked a watershed in South African history. It is to the beginning of the 'mineral revolution' of the 1870s that the origins of South Africa's modern industrialisation can be traced[1] – an industrial revolution which,was to 'set in motion changes which had a profound and qualitative effect over the whole of the Southern African subcontinent'.[2] Some of the clearest manifestations of these changes were the acceleration of two developments within the African societies of the region: peasantisation and migrant wage labour. These two related processes have recently been receiving close attention from historians of central and southern Africa.[3]

These socio-economic structural changes were complex. Their manifestations included the weakening of pre-colonial relations of production[4] and the extension of colonial rule to hitherto independent African kingdoms (and Afrikaner republics) in what was partly an attempt to bring their social and economic relationships into line with the demands of South Africa's industrialisation.[5] They also involved increasing stratification and class formation in rural African society,[6] and the development of a rural proletariat, based in African 'locations' or 'reserves', but dependent for a major part of their livelihood upon wage employment in the urban centres or on privately owned farms.[7]

Ironically, recent historical research has focused upon those African societies which were geographically furthest away from the hub of South Africa's early mineral revolution – from the eastern Transvaal, through southern Mozambique and Natal to the Xhosa chiefdoms of the eastern Cape. The catalogue of names highlights the considerable geographical range of South Africa's early industrial hinterland. Apart from some recent work by Peter Kallaway, however, there has been little attention so far given to the effects of the diamond-mining boom of the 1870s on those African chiefdoms closest to the diamond fields of Kimberley and the lower Vaal.[8]

Although this essay may be seen partially as an attempt to rectify this omission, there are more specific reasons for considering that a study of the Southern Tswana is of special significance to historians of African response to capitalist and colonial penetration in general and to historians of nineteenth-century southern Africa in particular. The region's proximity to the gathering industrial power of Kimberley greatly intensified processes of change. At the same time the peculiar nature of the ecology of the region severely limited the productive options open to the rural population, which further magnified the strains of change within the society.

In addition, the Southern Tswana of Griqualand West, mostly Tlhaping, were the first victims of the extension of colonial rule following the beginning of the mineral revolution. Here in the Griqualand West of the 1870s the British colonial government was confronted with many of the problems which they were to face later in industrialising southern Africa, not least among them being the crucial and related problems of land ownership and administration. The 'solutions' devised in Griqualand West were both shaped by existing colonial practice in the Cape and Natal and helped shape government policy further in the next few decades.

In this study of Griqualand West in the 1870s it is possible to identify two principal sources of strain working on the structure of Tlhaping society, one internally generated and the other externally imposed. Following the pattern of political and economic decentralisation which had been characteristic of the Dikgatlhong polity of Jantjie Mothibi in the 1850s and 1860s,[9] individuals responded to the new market opportunities of the diamond fields with an enthusiasm which led to differentiation within the society through materially-based stratification. The degree of strain generated by this process was partly reflected in the differing reaction of individuals to the colonial encroachment of the 1870s. To these internal strains was added the external imposition of colonial land policy. The combination of the two had provoked a crisis by 1878, the year of 'rebellion' in Griqualand West.

Market response and class formation

Two of the principal economic factors underlying the fragmentation of Jantjie's polity in the 1850s and 1860s had been the large-scale loss of cattle through drought and disease, and a decline in the profitability of the long-distance hunting trade as the 'ivory frontier' retreated northwards towards the Zambezi. Aided by prompting from missionaries of the London Missionary Society (LMS), this state of affairs led to an increasing dependence upon crops for subsistence.[10] The widespread use of guns and the destruction of large game during the 1860s increased both the possibility and the necessity for bringing wider areas under cultivation.[11]

The ecology of the region, however, severely limited the productive capacity

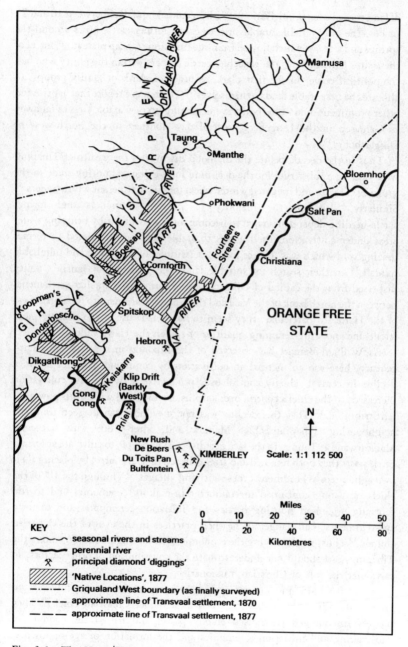

Fig. 3.1 The Harts/Vaal territory and the diamond fields, 1867–1877

of land turned over to cultivation. With an annual rainfall of between 10 and 25 inches, the only reliable arable sites were the former cattle posts around the springs and streams which flowed from the limestone Ghaap plateau. Control of these sites fell largely to the wealthier cattle owners within the polity who had the political power in the first place, as heads of wards or family groups, to allocate the best arable land to themselves.[12] There was a report that Jantjie and other prominent men in his polity were opening up new arable sites as far away as Gamasep in the Langeberg, several days journey to the north-west of Dikgatlhong.[13]

Thus in the decade before the diamond discoveries the wealthier Tlhaping were finding a substitute for the declining long-distance hunting trade in the growing of maize and irrigated winter wheat for sale to itinerant white traders.[14] Similarly, although the majority of poorer commoners and former cattle-herding dependants tried to become more self-reliant by bringing wider areas under cultivation, their access to arable land was restricted to former grazing veld which was subject to the vicissitudes of the sparse and unreliable rainfall.[15] In their search for suitable land, the Tlhaping of Jantjie's polity dispersed from the capital of Dikgatlhong to form many smaller settlements between the north bank of the Vaal and the Ghaap escarpment to the north-west of the Harts. In particular, they seem to have made use of the slightly more fertile and moisture-retaining qualities of soil in the Harts valley.[16]

As William Beinart has observed of the Mpondo in the late nineteenth century, here too an increase in cultivation by commoner families led to a decline in central, chiefly control over productive activities. As cultivation increased, so the chief's control over surplus declined and with it his powers of redistribution.[17] That this decline was not inevitable can be seen from the neighbouring Tlhaping chief Mahura and, after 1869, his successor Mankurwane at Taung. In the face of a dispersal of people to cultivate at former cattle posts they both retained and strengthened central control by placing their own appointees as headmen of these outlying villages.[18] Through the 1870s the chiefs of Taung continued to conduct rain-making ceremonies and to run centrally organised hunting parties and initiation ceremonies and to form age-regiments – all dangerous heathen practices in the eyes of the Christian church.[19] Thus, in identifying the economic basis for fragmentation among the Tlhaping, one should not underestimate the contribution of other factors, in particular the role of Christian missionaries.

Successive LMS missionaries at Dikgatlhong had a strong influence on Jantjie Mothibi, whom they regarded as a model Christian chief.[20] They actively discouraged centralised chiefly power and halted the conduct of rain-making and initiation ceremonies and the formation of age-regiments. They further weakened the chief's redistributive powers by condemning the conduct of cattle raids upon neighbouring polities. In return, the missionaries encouraged the pursuit of individualism through the development of peasantisation, and with the plough and irrigation they demonstrated the technological means for achieving this.

Yet Jantjie's loss of political power in the 1870s cannot be blamed solely on the debilitating effects of Christianity any more than it is to be blamed solely on the economic imperatives of shift in the nature of production. To his north, for example, the Ngwato chief, Khama, managed successfully to use Christianity and the changing nature of production to increase chiefly power.[21] Nor, as this latter comparison might suggest, can Jantjie's loss of political power be blamed on his own personal shortcomings. Any personal determination and leadership ability which Jantjie may have lacked was more than made up for by that of his son, Luka, who was assuming much of the responsibility for the chieftaincy by the 1870s. It may be that Christianity, economic shifts and Jantjie's personal failures combined to weaken the Dikgatlhong chieftaincy in the 1860s. What brought about its collapse in the 1870s, however, was the political and territorial encroachment of colonial officials and settlers combined with the increasing decentralisation prompted by individualist responses to the market opportunities of the diamond fields.

During the period of the early diamond discoveries at the Vaal 'river diggings', 1868–70, individual Tlhaping were extensively engaged in selling diamonds to white traders, prospectors and dealers.[22] Although at least one used the trade to set himself up as a prosperous itinerant trader,[23] most appear to have used the opportunity to reinvest in the rural economy, and cattle, sheep, goats, wagons and horses poured into the region 'at a deuce of a pace'.[24] The impression given by the report of the government land surveyor, John H. Ford, in 1872 is that by the time the British took over Griqualand West at the end of 1871, there were few, if any, completely stockless dependants within Jantjie's polity.[25] From the available evidence it is not possible to estimate the extent to which pre-capitalist relations of production had in fact broken down; a number of villages certainly remained under 'traditional' chiefly authorities. But the dispersal to form many relatively self-sufficient homesteads and small villages in the previous decades and the proximity of the rapidly expanding consumer market of Kimberley offered opportunities to all members of Tlhaping society to achieve greater self-sufficiency. Although Tlhaping diamond prospecting continued on the 'river diggings' after the majority of whites had 'rushed' to the more valuable 'dry diggings' in 1871, direct Tlhaping involvement in the diamond trade declined.[26] As the white prospectors had found, by the end of 1870, most of the readily available surface diamonds had already been picked up and the profitability of the 'river diggings' was limited, while at the new 'dry diggings' township of Kimberley, restrictive legislation discriminated against the casual seller of diamonds, especially if he were black.[27] There were clearly easier ways of producing and accumulating a surplus.

In the absence of detailed evidence of precisely who was doing what in the rural areas of Griqualand West in the 1870s, the strength of the rural economy of the period is perhaps reasonably illustrated by the fact that relatively few Tlhaping men entered wage labour contracts at the Kimberley mines until 1876.[28] An estimate of the total Tlhaping population of Griqualand West north of the Vaal is largely speculative, but it would appear to have been in the region of ten to fifteen thousand.[29] Yet Tlhaping labourers made up at most only a few hundred – some 3 or 4 per cent of the total – of the labour contracts registered at Kimberley in the early 1870s. And it is possible that many of those Tlhaping contracted came from the as yet independent chiefdoms of Taung, Manthe or Phokwani.[30] Migrant labour is of course not necessarily a measure of rural economic decline, and indeed Kimberley labour recruiters complained that the Tlhaping of Griqualand West had no need to engage in wage labour at the mines because they were becoming wealthy through supplying the provisioning market.[31] The government census figures of 1877 would seem to confirm this picture of full productive employment in the rural areas.[32] Magisterial estimates for the rural areas north of the Vaal showed that the numbers of men and women were roughly equal, which suggests that there was no serious labour migrancy from the area. In the urban centre of Kimberley, on the other hand, the more carefully enumerated 'non-European' population was found to be in the ratio of eight men to one woman, reflecting the presence of a large migrant labour force.

No hut-tax was collected in Griqualand West until 1879, and white ownership and settlement of farms did not become effective until about the same time.[33] It was not until after the 'rebellion' of 1878 that any official financial demands in the form of direct tax or rent were made upon the rural African population of Griqualand West by colonists or government. Trade in consumer goods between the rural and urban areas would therefore seem to have been conducted according to socially determined needs, whether in 'luxuries' or 'essentials', rather than in answer to newly imposed financial demands. It cannot be concluded, however, that all of the rural population were trading with the consumer market of the diamond fields, or that all of them were 'becoming wealthy'.[34]

Initially the provisioning trade of the diamond fields was fairly readily accessible to the Tlhaping of the region as it appears to have taken the form of selling off the natural surplus of the rural economy. Those near the river-digging centres sold fresh milk on a regular basis,[35] while those further afield brought in fuel, reeds, mats and long grass for thatching.[36] Even the firewood supplied was in the first instance merely the branches cut from trees.[37]

Soon, however, as the urban population at Kimberley expanded by thousands, the demands for food and fuel increased, and prices soared. Much of the food demand was met by black and white farmers from the Transvaal, Free State and Basutoland,[38] but there is also evidence of a considerable increase in cultivation in the Harts valley. The years 1874–6 appear to have brought sufficient rainfall to secure reasonable sorghum harvests, although in 1872 the government surveyor, John H. Ford, remarked of the Tlhaping in the potentially fertile but arid Harts valley: 'They sow frequently, but rarely reap.'[39] The principal trader of the region, R. Spalding, who set up shop at Spitskop in 1874, claimed that in his first three years of business he sold as many as 600 ploughs to local Tlhaping customers.[40] In July 1876 the post-harvest sorghum supply at Kimberley market was so great that the price dropped to 16–20s per muid, compared to the 'normal' level of 27–36s for the same month in previous years.[41] The period of favourable rainfall, however, was short-lived, and in 1877 and 1878 the grain harvests of the Harts valley were negligible. In the early months of 1878 the supply of sorghum was so scarce as to fetch 50s per muid on the Kimberley market.[42]

The apparent wealth of rural Griqualand West in the 1870s was neither soundly based nor evenly distributed. There were a number of factors which accentuated internal political fragmentation, undermined the basis for a self-reliant rural economy and increased Tlhaping dependence upon the diamond fields. Firstly, much of the apparent 'natural surplus' which was being marketed in the early 1870s was sold off at a rate higher than that of its natural reproduction. Timber for firewood, reeds for thatching and game, especially small antelope, for meat, were all treated as extractive industries, and as such their productive life was severely limited. Springbok carcasses, for instance, which fetched up to 10s each in the early 1870s, had disappeared from the Kimberley market by 1877.[43] By the late 1870s antelope had been all but shot out in the Harts/Vaal region, and so the local population had lost not only a trade item but also an important source of food.[44]

Secondly, with the notable exception of the small irrigable sites, cultivation in the region was not a reliable source of food, and the regular storage of grain was not widespread. Possibly because of a lack of storage facilities, when the rainfall allowed a good harvest, the bulk of the grain was sold off.[45] A tendency to flood the market would seem to be confirmed by the dramatic fall in prices at times of good harvest.

Thirdly, as more of the former pastoral land was brought under the plough, settlement spread out further in search of pasture. It is probable that this in turn led to wider consumption of *veldkos* (wild foodstuffs) as small game declined. There is some evidence that 'migrant' labourers from the diamond fields were beginning to accumulate cattle in the Harts/Vaal region, though it is difficult to tell whether this was widespread enough to have had any serious effect upon available grazing resources.[46]

Finally, the wider access to and use of imported 'luxuries' encouraged a greater dependence upon market relations. Tea and coffee became prominent among articles sold by the new rural white storekeepers who penetrated the Harts/Vaal region in the mid-1870s. Ominous too for the future health of the Tlhaping was the spread of the brandy trade and the rural canteen.[47]

On the whole the wealthier cattle owners were at a distinct advantage as the underlying weakness of the newly stimulated Tlhaping economy revealed itself. Their principal advantage was their ability to buy wagons. A good ox-drawn transport wagon cost in excess of £150, the price of at least twenty cattle, and it required a further twelve to sixteen draught oxen to pull it.[48] Wagon-owners were able to strip the dwindling natural resources of the country far more quickly, besides which their wagons gave them access to the Kimberley market where they received better terms of trade than from the local rural storekeeper. The best opening for the wagon-owners and the one to which they quickly turned most of their attention was the trade in firewood.

In 1873 it was estimated that the average white family on the diamond fields consumed a wagon load of firewood per month.[49] Though this may have been an overestimate, the introduction of steam machinery in 1873 greatly increased the demand for firewood, whatever the domestic consumption.[50] Throughout the 1870s the Kimberley firewood trade was a seller's market. The top price for a fully laden ox-wagon in February 1872 was £2.[51] By the middle of the year it had reached £5 5s, a year later £7 and in 1875 and 1876 it rose to £10 and £11.[52] The Tlhaping wagon-owners were well placed to take full advantage of this booming business. One report in *Diamond News* complained that they were buying cattle with the money and so avoiding wage labour,[53] but there is more significance to it than this. The wagon-owners were enriching themselves at the expense of the less fortunate strata of society in more than one sense. It appears that the wagon-owners were also becoming 'extensive dealers' in brandy. Although this applied particularly to those from Botlasitse's chiefdom of Phokwani, just beyond the border, there is no reason to suppose that those within the Crown Colony were any less involved. They carried loads of reeds and firewood to Kimberley, invested the proceeds in brandy and then traded the brandy at home for sheep, goats and even cattle. The Lieutenant-Governor, Richard Southey, met 'several such wagons' while on a visit to Taung in August 1873.[54]

It is clear that at one end of the spectrum some people were becoming increasingly wealthy. The complexity of a society undergoing such major upheaval, however, defies simple categorisation, and lack of detailed empirical evidence makes the necessary analysis, particularly of what was happening among the poorer people, extremely difficult. There was still wide access to land, but its productivity varied widely and increasing competition for its limited resources, especially game and timber, further reduced its usefulness. In 1877, with very poor harvests throughout the region, the number of Tlhaping seeking labour contracts at Kimberley increased enormously (to over 900 for the eight months recorded), and it is probable that these came as much from within Griqualand West as beyond it.[55] This would appear also to be a time when certain Tlhaping in Griqualand West began to take up residence in the urban centres, particularly in artisanal capacities, such as brickmaking.[56]

In the meantime, although some appeared to be losing ready access to the means of production in the rural areas, a conflict of interests seems to have developed among the wealthier strata of Tlhaping society, especially between the new, 'self-made' men and the 'traditional' chiefly authorities. William Ashton, the LMS missionary responsible for Dikgatlhong, observed in 1876 that although Jantjie and his councillors were worried by the colonial encroachment upon their land and political authority, the bulk of the Tlhaping were little concerned with such matters while they could still make use of Kimberley as a market for grain, firewood and for employment.[57] Not only had the process of social and political fragmentation accelerated as more and more of Jantjie's people sought out 'the fountains in the country beyond the British line' to settle and develop irrigated cultivation,[58] but many of those who remained in Griqualand West were becoming in effect full-time wood-riders.[59]

Only a tiny minority of those Tlhaping who remained in the Barkly district in 1878 displayed any sympathy for their 'traditional' leaders who found themselves at war with the colonists by the middle of that year.[60] Not that they displayed much sympathy *for* the Government, but the wagon-owners took full advantage of the soaring wood prices caused by the war of 1878 which effectively blocked the wagon trade from north of the colony.

In August and September 1878, while the colony's volunteer forces were hunting Tlhaping 'rebels' beyond the border, Ashton, based at Barkly, was issuing between three and twelve wagon passes a day to 'loyalists' within Griqualand West.[61] By pursuing Tlhaping 'rebels' beyond the colonial boundary and disrupting the wagon trade, the colonists of Kimberley were having to pay up to £24 a load for their firewood in the closing months of 1878.[62]

The development of a policy of colonisation

The British government came to Griqualand West with no clearly defined land or 'native' policies. The region had been annexed in an attempt to prevent the Afrikaner republics controlling both the diamond fields and the Cape merchants' trade route to the 'interior'.[63] The purpose of the arbitration held at Bloemhof in 1871 had been to justify British annexation, on the grounds that the whole territory belonged to the Griqua chief Waterboer, who had been prevailed upon to concede his rights to Britain.[64] Tlhaping territorial rights in Griqualand West were therefore overridden, and the Arbitration Commission at Bloemhof refused to hear the case of *Jantjie* versus *Waterboer*.[65]

In order to ensure a smooth takeover of the 'dry diggings', situated on the Griqualand West – Free State border, the Cape Governor, Barkly, guaranteed all land holdings extant on 27 October 1871.[66] The lapse of time, however, since the first discovery of diamonds in 1867 had allowed colonial speculators to build up a mass of rival claims to vast tracts of the most useful land of the territory. When these claims were examined in 1872–3, it was found that much of the land of Griqualand West, which the new government had expected to receive as Crown land, had at least two rival claimants.[67] It was this, rather than extensive 'native' occupancy, which prevented speedy settlement of the question of land ownership in Griqualand West.

Richard Southey, as Colonial Secretary at the Cape until 1872 and Lieutenant-Governor of Griqualand West for 1873–5, retained the sole right to issue land titles in the new Crown Colony and was determined to thwart the grand designs of the two main land-jobbing factions, one of whose leading beneficiaries was his own Surveyor General, F. H. S. Orpen.[68] Hailing from an eastern Cape farming background, Southey hoped to capitalise the farming land, thereby broadening the economic base of the new colony and reducing its dependence upon the fortunes of the nascent mining industry.[69]

By refusing to recognise the more ambitious claims of the speculators, Southey hoped to declare most of Griqualand West 'vacant Crown Land' and thereby auction it off to finance the government of the Crown Colony. He planned to outwit the land jobbers by issuing titles only to those who had taken possession and occupied their claims.[70] As part of this policy Southey was willing to recognise certain Tlhaping land claims, but only as the privately owned property of individuals. Thus he was prepared to recognise Jantjie's private ownership of the 'farm' Dikgatlhong, but he was not prepared to recognise any broader Tlhaping territorial rights of usufruct.[71] To have done so would have been to undermine the legal justification for the very existence of the new Crown Colony which was based upon former Griqua ownership of the whole region.

Despite Southey's claim that he was the protector of 'native interests', he ignored most Tlhaping occupation of Griqualand West in favour of creating a community of colonists based upon 'progressive' white farming.[72] He chose to put aside Ford's revelation of the wide extent of 'native' occupancy of the Harts/Vaal territory in favour of his suggestion that the Vaal river might be 'drawn out' at Fourteen Streams to irrigate the whole region. Sale of land between the rivers was postponed as Southey toyed excitedly with the notion of selling off six times as many productive, irrigated lots of 500 morgen for the same price each as 3 000-morgen ones.[73]

Meanwhile in December 1874 Southey, desperate for government revenue, auctioned off a string of farms to the north-west of the Harts, again overriding known extensive 'native' occupancy.[74] However, Southey's plans fell through. Firstly the irrigation ditch had to be abandoned as too expensive, even with the use of convict labour, and then the government received payment on only eight of the thirty-four farms auctioned in December 1874.[75]

Part of the underlying reason for the failure of white settlement to take effect in 1875 was the colonists' lack of faith in the future of the Griqualand West government. The border dispute with the Free State was still unsettled, and there was mounting opposition to Southey's government within the mining community at Kimberley.[76] Moreover, the purchasers found that those farms with worthwhile water resources were already thickly populated by Africans who seemed prepared to resist encroachment, by force if necessary.[77] And the government had neither the police strength nor the inclination to back up forcible white seizure or even the extraction of rent, should absentee landlordism become the norm. It is significant that half of those farms which reverted to the government through non-payment of quit-rent were reallocated as 'native locations' in 1876–7.[78]

Southey's thwarting of the designs of the speculators and his inability to substitute an alternative land settlement meant that when his successor, Major W. O. Lanyon, took over as Administrator towards the end of 1875, land titles had still not been issued and the policy towards 'native' occupants had still not been decided. The judgment of the subsequent Land Court which sat from November 1875 to March 1876 went against the findings of the Bloemhof arbitration, and recognised that there had indeed been widespread Tlhaping territorial rights north of the Vaal before 1871.[79] So Lanyon, commissioned with preparing the Crown Colony for incorporation into the Cape, proposed the adoption of a system of 'native locations' similar to those in parts of the eastern Cape.[80] The delineation of 'native locations' around the areas of greatest Tlhaping occupancy and the promulgation of hut-tax obligations had the advantage of undermining the unifying strength of the 'traditional' chiefly authorities and drawing the people more fully into the money economy. At the same time it was expected to facilitate peaceful settlement of the remaining areas by colonists who would be able to draw on nearby sources of labour.[81]

Although the 'locations' were promulgated in 1877, collection of hut-tax and the peaceful white occupation of the remaining areas could not become effective, however, until the 'traditional' Tlhaping authorities had been bent to the will of the colonial government. The nature of resistance to this extension of colonial authority was determined by a combination of two things: on the one hand the uncertainties of Southey's government followed by the aggressive assertions of Lanyon's administration; on the other, the increasing divergence of interests within Tlhaping society, as a result of the diamond discoveries. The latter in particular meant that resistance to colonial encroachment in Griqualand West was sporadic and localised.

Resistance to colonialism

Southey's attempts to thwart the schemes of the speculators had led a number of colonists to try to establish occupation of their land claims during 1873–4. Since the irrigable 'farms' around the Ghaap springs of Koopman's, Donderbosch and Boetsap offered the best prospects for permanent white settlement, they first tried to take these over. Thus the Tlhaping who first felt the effects of colonial land encroachment were those with power and influence, the 'traditional' chiefly authorities who had established control over these favourable agricultural sites.[82] On the whole they retained possession, partly because Southey was hesitant to deny the individual claims of Tlhaping farmers and partly because the Barkly magistrate had not the police force to arrest more than the occasional commoner for assault.[83]

On the other hand, Lanyon's administration, which succeeded Southey's in late 1875, committed itself to a firm policy of 'native locations' and a diminution of chiefly power. The conflict which emerged between Tlhaping and colonists in the period 1876–8 reflected the strains on the 'traditional elite' as they opposed or tried to come to terms with the growing challenge to their position of economic strength and political power. Botlasitse, based beyond the border at Phokwani, but with territorial claims as far as Boetsap, frequently tried to reassert his authority in the new colony. He and two of his close relatives, Molema and Mothibi (not to be confused with Jantjie Mothibi), refused to recognise the surveyor's beacons and demanded tribute in cash, brandy or cattle from both white settlers and former members of their own polity who tried to break their ties with Phokwani.[84] Lanyon courted confrontation in deciding that swift military action against 'the native' would solve a lot of problems.[85] However, his punitive expedition against a hastily deserted Phokwani in January 1878 and his confiscation of 445 cattle only increased the incidence of cattle theft in subsequent months.[86]

Meanwhile, in Jantjie's polity the chief's family had similarly been coming into conflict with the colonial authorities. After Luka returned from an unprofitable trading trip to the 'interior' in 1876, he tried to recoup his losses by exacting tribute within Griqualand West. Opposition from the field-cornet, J. G. Donovan, who had claims to farms at Donderbosch and Boetsap, and the threat of police action from Lanyon caused Luka to withdraw temporarily from the colony and to join his father at his up-country village of Manyeding.[87] The following year a warrant was issued for Luka's arrest after he had allegedly assaulted the employee of the field-cornet A. W. Greef, who was trying to establish his claim to Dikgatlhong by occupying Luka's house.[88] Luka once more fled north of the border where he gathered a small band of mounted armed men and prepared to resist the arresting force which he anticipated after Lanyon's expedition against Phokwani in January 1878.[89] It was thus that Luka was prepared for and able to impose a sharp check on J. H. Ford's volunteer column as it hurried to the 'relief' of Kuruman that June.[90] In the meantime a close relative of Luka's, Matsemane, had been arrested for opposing government census officials at his village near Spitzkop.[91] After serving a one-month sentence in February, Matsemane left the colony to join Luka and was among those killed at the battle of Dithakong in July 1878.[92]

During the Griqua rebellion there were in fact only three main acts of violence committed by Tlhaping in the Crown Colony, and an examination of their probable motives reveals that they were far more than mere 'blind acts of protest'.[93] At the end of May a group of about twenty armed men attacked and killed a storekeeper named Burness and his wife and brother near Daniel's Kuil. There was little to loot in the store, but Burness had the previous year been appointed master of the local cattle pound as well as field-cornet responsible for pointing out the surveyor's beacons in the northern border region.[94] Since four of the principal leaders of the attacking group were from just across the border, it seems more than likely that Burness's connection with the land survey was an underlying motive for the attack.[95]

The other two assaults were led by Botlasitse's family in July. The looting of Donovan's store at Boetsap needs little further explanation. He had been in regular conflict with numerous Tlhaping since 1873, and his store was full of brandy.[96] The most brutal assault of all, however, was on Francis Thompson of Cornforth a few days later.[97] His farm had been used as a police post since 1876, which was reason enough, but in January 1878 the police sergeant stationed there had reported that in spite of Botlasitse's indictment against the felling of 'camel thorns' (*Acacia erioloba*) in 1876, Thompson had 'something like a hundred loads on his farm, which to my own knowledge were cut at Poquane [*sic*]'.[98] In the attack on the farm, led by Botlasitse's sons, F. R. (later to be known as 'Matabele') Thompson and his cousin narrowly escaped, but Francis Thompson senior was captured and killed by a ramrod thrust down his throat.[99] Lanyon's volunteer forces pursued the perpetrators of these various assaults beyond the borders of the colony, where they defeated and captured or killed all the leading chiefly authorities of Jantjie's and Botlasitse's polities.[100]

The war of 1878 in Griqualand West seldom receives more than a passing reference in general histories of South Africa,[101] and indeed compared with the scale of conflict elsewhere during the period – in the eastern Cape, Zululand and the eastern Transvaal – this neglect is hardly surprising. Nevertheless, contemporary white commentators sought to interpret the 'rebellion' as part of a widespread anti-white conspiracy, inspired by agitators from the eastern Cape.[102] Inez Sutton, in the most detailed study of the rebellion so far, has pointed out that the contemporary white obsession with conspiracy theory may have been a defence mechanism to absolve themselves of blame for the uprisings.[103] Whatever the causes, the settlement which was imposed revealed a growing awareness of the need for the development of a comprehensive southern African 'native policy' which would reflect the demands of industrialising South Africa.

Conclusion

Significantly, the campaign of 1878 marked the end of 'traditional' chiefly authority in Griqualand West, and the subjection of the African population to the demands of the colonial authorities. After 1878 it was a relatively easy matter to disarm the 'loyal natives' completely and impose a hut-tax.[104] The effective imposition of 'native locations' and hut-tax collection was part of a policy which was in a few decades to become universal throughout South Africa. The adoption and nature of that policy in Griqualand West, however, though apparently borrowed in outline from the eastern Cape and Natal experiences, was the product of conflicting interests between black and black, white and white, and black and white in the Griqualand West of the 1870s.

There has been a tendency among historians of the rebellion to imply that the Tlhaping in general joined with rebellious Griqua against the government because the Tlhaping in general had lost their land and political independence.[105] Yet, as this essay has attempted to show, differentiation within Tlhaping society and the inability of the colonists to effect a speedy land settlement combined to ensure that the majority of Tlhaping did not in fact act against the government in 1878. In 1880 the Crown Colony of Griqualand West was annexed to the Cape, and then the complete dependence of the 'loyalists' upon the diamond fields ensured that they could do little but accept their declining economic role as the diamond industry was restructured during the years that followed.

Notes

Abbreviations

Bloemhof Blue Book   *Evidence taken at Bloemhof before the Commission appointed to investigate the Claims of the South African Republic, Capt. N. Waterboer . . . and certain other Native Chiefs . . . to portions of the Territory on the Vaal River . . .* (see note 16)

BPP	Great Britain, *British Parliamentary Papers* (London)
CAD	Cape Archives Depot
CPP	Cape Colony, *Cape Parliamentary Papers* (Cape Town)
JAH	*Journal of African History*
LMS	*Archives of the London Missionary Society* (School of Oriental and African Studies, University of London), In-Letters, South Africa
OHSA	*The Oxford History of South Africa*
PRO	Public Records Office
TVL	Transvaal Archives Depot
UW	Archives of the University of the Witwatersrand

1 M. Wilson and L. Thompson (eds), *The Oxford History of South Africa (OHSA)*, II (Oxford, 1971), p. 11.

2 M. Legassick, 'Gold, agriculture, and secondary industry in South Africa, 1885–1970: from periphery to sub-metropole as a forced labour system', in R. Palmer and N. Parsons (eds), *The Roots of Rural Poverty in Central and Southern Africa* (London, 1977), p. 175.

3 See the various contributions to Palmer and Parsons, *Roots of Rural Poverty*; C. Bundy, *The Rise and Fall of the South African Peasantry*, (London, 1979); and W. J. Beinart, 'Production, labour migrancy and the chieftaincy: aspects of the political economy of Pondoland, *ca.* 1860–1930', Ph.D. thesis, University of London, 1979. See also H. Slater, 'Land, labour and capitalism in Natal: the Natal Land and Colonisation Company, 1860–1948', *Journal of African History*, XVI, 2 (1975), pp. 257–84; P. Delius, 'The Pedi polity under Sekwati and Sekhukhuni', unpublished Ph.D. thesis, University of London, 1980, and 'Migrant labour and the Pedi, 1840–80', in S. Marks and A. Atmore (eds), *Economy and Society in Pre-industrial South Africa* (London, 1980), pp. 293–312; and J. Kimble, J. Guy and P. Harries in their contributions to this volume.

4 Beinart, 'Production, labour migrancy and the chieftaincy', pp. 74–5.

5 A. Atmore and S. Marks, 'The imperial factor in South Africa in the nineteenth century: towards a reassessment', *Journal of Imperial and Commonwealth History*, III, 1 (Oct. 1974), 122–3; and Legassick in *Roots of Rural Poverty*, pp. 177–8. See also *OHSA*, II, chs. 5 and 6.

6 Bundy, *The Rise and Fall of the South African peasantry, passim.*

7 *Ibid.*

8 P. Kallaway, 'Black responses to an industrialising economy: "labour shortage" and "native policy" in Griqualand West, 1870–1900', unpublished paper to the conference on South African labour history, University of the Witwatersrand, 1976; and 'Tribesman, trader, peasant and proletarian: the process of transition from pre-capitalist "natural economy" to a capitalist mode of production in the hinterland of the Kimberley diamond fields during the nineteenth century', unpublished paper to the African Studies seminar, University of the Witwatersrand, 30 Oct. 1978.

9 These developments, summarised in the following paragraphs, are discussed at greater length in ch. 1 of my Ph.D. thesis: 'Land loss, labour and dependence: the impact of colonialism on the Southern Tswana, *ca.* 1870–1900', University of London, 1981.

10 *Archives of the London Missionary Society* (School of Oriental and African Studies,

University of London), In-Letters, South Africa (*LMS*), 26-1-A; *LMS*, H. Helmore, 'Likatlong Hart River', 1 Jan. 1851; *LMS*, 29-1-A, H. Helmore, Likatlong, 23 Jan. 1854; *LMS*, 30-1-A, W. Ross, Likatlong, 26 Dec. 1856; *LMS*, 30-3-A, W. Ross, Likatlong, 15 April 1857; *LMS*, 32-1-A, W. Ross, Likatlong, 13 Jan. 1860.

11 See W. J. Burchell, *Travels in the Interior of Southern Africa*, I. Schapera (ed.), (London, 1953), II, p. 369, for a remarkably explicit forecast of this eventuality.

12 *Evidence taken before Judge Stockenstrom in the matter of Certain Land Claims* (Cape Town, 1877), pp. 85–6, evidence of Piet Boromelo who, with others, worked Donderbosch and Wolvefontein in the Ghaap escarpment and retained '*une résidence secondaire*' at Dikgatlhong; *LMS*, 35-2-C, W. Ashton, report from Likhatlong, 1868; and J. Mackenzie, *Ten Years North of the Orange River* (Edinburgh, 1871, and 2nd ed., facsimile reproduction, with introduction by C. Northcott, London, 1971), pp. 89–92.

·13 Transvaal Archives Depot (*TVL*), *Helmore Papers*, A 55 1/2, R. Moffat to Helmore, Kuruman, Feb. 1857.

14 *LMS*, 32-1-A, Ashton, Kuruman, 3 Oct. 1860; and A. A. Andersson, *Twenty-five Years in a Waggon* (London, 1887), I, p. 105.

15 *LMS*, 35-2-C, Ashton, report from Likhatlong, 1868.

16 *Evidence taken at Bloemhof before the Commission appointed to investigate the Claims of the South African Republic, Capt. N. Waterboer, Chief of West Griqualand, and certain other Native Chiefs, to portions of the Territory on the Vaal River, now known as the Diamond Fields* (hereafter *Bloemhof Blue Book*) (Cape Town, 1871), evidence of Jantjie Mothibi (p. 100) and John O'Reilly, trader (p. 192), and extract of letter from R. Moffat, to *The Times* (pp. 345–6); *Evidence before Stockenstrom*, pp. 2–7, evidence of various white settlers between Harts and Vaal during 1860s; *Judgement Delivered by Judge Stockenstrom on 16 March 1876* (Grahamstown, 1876), p. 2; and *Cape Archives Depot* (CAD), SGGLW 42, details of Harts/Vaal Survey by J. H. Ford, Sept.–Dec. 1872; and CAD, GLW 49, Preliminary report on Harts/Vaal Survey, J. H. Ford, Government Surveyor, to F. H. S. Orpen, Surveyor General, Grahamstown, 5 July 1873, enclosed in Orpen, 12 July 1873.

17 Beinart, 'Production, labour migrancy and the chieftancy', p. 74; cf. E. Terray, 'Long-distance exchange and the formation of the state', *Economy and Society*, III, 3 (1974).

18 CAD, BBLC 31, claims submitted to the Land Commission at Taung in November 1885, enclosures in Nos. 45 and 59, and Nos. 70, 71, 72, 107, 132, 133; and the proceedings of the Warren/Mackenzie Land Committee held at Taung, Aug. 1885, and published in *British Parliamentary Papers* (*BPP*), XLVIII, 1886, C.4643, *Further Correspondence re. the Affairs of the Transvaal and Adjacent Territories*, evidence of Rev. John Brown (p. 44), Molema, son of Mahura (pp. 45–6), Bogosin, son of Mahura (p. 46), Tokwe, headman (pp. 47–8), and John O'Reilly, trader (pp. 48–9).

19 *LMS*, 39-1-C, Ashton, Barkly, 21 Aug. 1877; and *Daily Independent*, 1 and 13 Sept. 1877.

20 Holloway Helmore (1840–55), William Ross (1855–63), and William Ashton (1864–70). From 1871 Ashton had charge of Dikgatlhong from Kuruman (1871–6) and Barkly West (1876–97). Their correspondence in the *LMS* archives forms a major part of available source material for the pre-colonial period. For mission influence at Dikgatlhong, see also J. Mackenzie, *Ten Years North*, p. 91:

Mackenzie was at Kuruman 1859–60, 1861–2, and from 1876 to 1882.

21 N. Parsons, 'The economic history of Khama's country in Botswana, 1844–1930', in *Roots of Rural Poverty*, pp. 113–43.

22 See ch. 2 of my thesis (see n. 9) for detailed evidence drawn largely from contemporary newspaper reports.

23 E. Holub, *Seven Years in South Africa* (London, 1881), I, pp. 241–2.

24 *Colesberg Advertiser*, 7 Sept. 1869. See also *idem* of 3 and 4 Aug. and 14, 21 and 28 Sept. 1869.

25 CAD, GLW 49, Ford to F. H. S. Orpen, Grahamstown, 5 July 1873, enclosed in Orpen, 12 July 1873.

26 *Diamond News*, 5 Oct. 1873.

27 J. M. Smalberger, 'The role of Kimberley in the formation of the South African pass law system', *International Journal of African Historical Studies*, IX, 3 (1976), 419–34. See also the contribution of R. Turrell to the present volume and his 'The Black Flag Revolt on the Kimberley Diamond Fields', *Journal of Southern African Studies*, VII, 2 (1981).

28 For labour returns see *Diamond News*, 19 Dec. 1872; and CAD, GLW 71, returns of Servants' Registry Office for 1873–4. There do not appear to be any figures for 1875 extant, but for 1876–80 returns were published in the *Griqualand West Government Gazette* (copies held in the Public Records Office [PRO], CO 109/1).

29 These figures are based upon Ford's Harts/Vaal survey report of 5 July 1873 (CAD, GLW 49); Ford's N. W. Harts survey (CAD, GLW 57, report of 9 Dec. 1874); Ford's evidence at RM's Court, Barkly, 18 March 1875, published in *Diamond Field*, 20 March 1875; evidence of English, Bellew and Donovan (purchasers of N.W. farms in Dec. 1874) in *Diamond Field Supplement*, 24 March 1875; letter of Rev. J. Brown, Taung, 26 Jan. 1874, in *Cape Argus*, 24 Feb. 1874; evidence of Ford and Jantjie Mothibi to Land Court of 1875–6 published in *Evidence before Stockenstrom*, pp. 36–7, 133; and *Cape Parliamentary Papers* (*CPP*), A14–'77, *Results of Census in Griqualand West*.

30 *Diamond News*, 19 Dec. 1872; CAD, GLW 71, returns for 1873; and F. Boyle, *To the Cape for Diamonds* (London, 1873), p. 158.

31 Report of Native Dept. for 1876, in *GLW Govt. Gazette,* 20 Oct. 1877.

32 *CPP*, A14–'77 (Cape Town, 30 June 1877).

33 The Administrator, W. O. Lanyon, ordered a hut-tax proclamation to be drafted in June 1876 (CAD, GLW 79, Minute of 1 June 1876). First collections began in the second half of 1879: Return of Revenue GLW, 1870–79, published as CPP, A64–'80, *Despatches from Acting Administrator of Griqualand West forwarding statements relating to finance*.

34 See note 31 above.

35 CAD, *Southey Papers*, A611/43, Campbell to Southey, 16 Jan. 1871; and *LMS*, 37-1-A, Ashton, 26 Nov. 1872.

36 CAD, GLW 49, Ford's report of 5 July 1873.

37 *Ibid.*

38 CAD, A611/44, Campbell, Bloemhof, 15 May 1871; Holub, *Seven Years*, I, pp. 164–6; and Bundy, *The Rise and Fall of the South African Peasantry*, pp. 203–4.

39 See note 36 above.

40 *BPP*, LX, 1877, C.1776, *Further Correspondence respecting the War between the Transvaal Republic and Neighbouring Native Tribes and generally with reference to Native Affairs in South Africa*, p. 28, Lanyon to Barkly, 23 Dec. 1876.

41 For regular market reports, see contemporary newspapers: *Diamond News, Diamond Field, Daily Independent* and *Diamond Fields Advertiser*. A muid is a South African measure of capacity equal to three bushels.

42 *Diamond Fields Advertiser*, 27 March and 20 April 1878.

43 See the Kimberley newspapers for 1877.

44 Holub, *Seven Years*, I, pp. 107, 122, 201–2 for 1873; and C. Warren, *On the Veldt in the Seventies* (London, 1902), p. 115, for his observation that there was 'scarcely any game about' near Fourteen Streams on the Vaal where five years previously there had been 'all kinds of large game'. When there was no game left, observed Warren, 'the Kaffir must either work or starve'. In 1876 labour agent A. C. Bailie saw very few trees in the Harts valley where three years previously Holub had seen plenty (*BPP*, LII, 1878–79, C.2220, *Further Correspondence respecting the Affairs of South Africa*, p. 48, A. C. Bailie to Lanyon, 30 July 1876).

45 See Kimberley newspapers for widely fluctuating market prices.

46 See, e.g., the Mfengu landowner, Piet Manzana, who bought the farm H/V 80 in 1877 in order to accumulate stock for himself and others from Kimberley (CAD, GH 29/4, enclosed in GLW No. 9 of 19 Jan. 1878, affidavit of Manzana, and enclosed in GLW Confidential of 26 Feb. 1878, affidavit of Jappi Ginza (Gaika Xhosa).

47 *LMS*, 36-3-E, Ashton, Likhatlong, 14 Sept. 1871 and 37-1-A, Ashton, Kuruman, 26 Nov. 1872; Holub, *Seven Years*, I, p. 236; and *GLW Govt. Gazette*, 16 March 1878, Attorney General to Lanyon, Kimberley, 11 March 1878. For an example of the scale of the liquor trade in the Kimberley hinterland see *Diamond News*, 25 Feb. 1875: Metrovich, a storekeeper on the Kuruman River, had his supply wagon looted by the Tlharo chief Morwa near Kuruman. The wagon contained 12 *aums* of Cape brandy, 20 cases of French brandy, 3 cases of gin and 2 cases of ale (an *aum* was an old Dutch liquid measure of about 40 gallons).

48 CAD, GLW 184, Southey to Barkly, 24 Oct. 1874.

49 *Diamond News*, 16 Sept. 1873.

50 *Diamond Field*, 9 Jan. 1873.

51 Boyle, *To the Cape*, p. 328.

52 See Kimberley newspapers for market reports.

53 *Diamond News*, 16 Sept. 1873.

54 CAD, GLW 181, Southey to Barkly, 24 Aug. 1873.

55 See note 28 above.

56 CAD, GLW 128, Registrar of Natives, 25 Aug. 1878.

57 *LMS*, 38-3-A, enclosed in Ashton, Kuruman, 23 Feb. 1876: Ashton to Lt-Col. William Crossman, H.M. Special Commissioner, Kuruman, 9 Feb. 1876. See also in *ibid*. Ashton's letter of 13 April 1876; in 40-1-C, Bechuana District Committee to Governor Frere, Kuruman, 25 Jan. 1879; and Mackenzie to Lanyon, Kuruman, 1 Aug. 1878, printed in A. J. Dachs (ed.), *Papers of John Mackenzie* (Johannesburg, 1975), pp. 110–11.

58 *LMS*, 37-3-A, Ashton, Kuruman, 19 Aug. 1874, and 37-3-B, Ashton, 10 Nov. 1874.

59 *LMS*, 39-3-B, Ashton, Barkly, 5 July 1878.

60 *CPP*, G4–'83, *Report of the Commission on Native Laws and Customs*, Vol. II, Appendix E, F. R. Thompson (Inspector of Native Locations), Barkly District, reply to circular of 1881.

61 *LMS*, 39-3-B, Ashton, Barkly, 5 July 1878, and 39-3-C, Ashton, Barkly, 15 Aug.

and 3 Sept. 1878; and Archives of the University of the Witwatersrand (UW), *Mackenzie Papers*, A75/2, Ashton to Mackenzie, 27 July 1878.

62 See market reports in the *Diamond Fields Advertiser*.

63 C. W. de Kiewiet, *British Colonial Policy and the South African Republics, 1848–72* (London, 1929) is still the best published work on the annexation of 1871.

64 See chapter 2 of my Ph.D. thesis where I argue, contrary to J. A. I. Agar-Hamilton (*The Road to the North* [London 1937], p. 88), that the Bloemhof arbitration was far from being impartial. On the contrary, its purpose was to validate British annexation of the diamond fields and curtail the westward expansion of the Transvaal.

65 *Judgement by Stockenstrom*, p. 10.

66 See Barkly's private memo to Southey of 29 Oct. 1872, written on Arnot to Southey, 18 Oct. 1872 in CAD, *Southey Papers*, A611/50.

67 CAD, GLW 180, Southey to Barkly, 28 June 1873, GLW 184, Southey to Arnot, 5 Dec. 1874, and Southey to Barkly, 16 and 20 Jan. 1875; and Boyle, *To the Cape*, pp. 190–98.

68 *Statute Law of Griqualand West*, Barkly, No. 154 (14 March 1872); and CAD, GLW 180, Southey to Barkly, 28 and 29 June 1873, GLW 184, Southey to Barkly, 16 and 20 Jan. 1875; and Boyle, *To the Cape*, pp. 190, 198.

69 See Turrell, 'The Black Flag revolt' and above, for a more detailed view of the opposition fostered by this policy.

70 CAD, GLW 180, Southey to Barkly, 28 June 1873.

71 CAD, GLW 182, Southey to Barkly, 15 Nov. 1873, GLW, 183, Southey to Ashton, 20 Feb. 1874, and GLW 187, Southey to Jantjie Mothibi (draft), 20 April 1874.

72 *Ibid.*, and GLW 182, Southey to Ashton, 12 Dec. 1873, GLW 184, Southey to J. S. Moffat, 29 Aug. 1874, and Southey to Barkly, 9 Jan. 1875.

73 CAD, GLW 180. Southey to Barkly, 29 June 1873.

74 CAD, GLW 57, Records of Surveyor General's Office for 1874, and GLW 184, Southey to Barkly, 20 Dec. 1874 and 9 Jan. 1875.

75 CAD, GLW 184, Southey to Barkly, 21 Jan. 1875; and *Report on the Land Question in Griqualand West by Lt-Col. Warren* (Colonial Office, London, 1880), p. 89.

76 Turrell, 'The Black Flag revolt' and above.

77 *Diamond Field*, 20 March 1875, and *Supplement* 24 March 1875; CAD, GLW 90, No. 2183, Selly Coryndon to Administrator, July 1876.

78 *Report by Warren*, p. 89.

79 *Judgement by Stockenstrom*.

80 PRO, CO 107/2, No. 15277, Lanyon to Barkly, 22 Nov. 1876.

81 PRO, CO 107/4, No. 4452, Lanyon's instructions to Orpen, 15 Feb. 1877.

82 See note 12 above.

83 *Diamond News*, 23 and 30 Oct. 1873, and *Supplement* of 13 Nov. 1873; *Evidence before Stockenstrom*, evidence of P. Boromelo (p. 86) and F. J. van der Venter (p. 94); and CAD, GLW 182, Southey to Barkly, 8 Nov. 1873, GLW 183, Southey to Ashton, 20 Feb. 1874, GLW 65, A. W. Greef to RM, Barkly, 27 May 1874, GLW 19, Jantjie to Southey, 5 June 1874, and GLW 65, Civil Commissioner to Barkly, 13 July 1874.

84 CAD, GLW 79, Report of Orpen, Oct. 1876, GLW 101, No. 633, G. Bradshaw, Constabulary Camp, Cornforth Hill, 27 Feb. 1877; *Diamond News*, 21, 23 and 28 Dec. 1876; *BPP*, C.1776, pp. 26–8, various enclosures for Dec. 1876 in Despatch

No. 21; and Confidential Print 'African 151', Enclosures in Despatch No. 12 for Dec. 1877 and Jan. 1878.

85 TVL, *Lanyon Papers*, 596/13, Lanyon to his father, 8 Jan. 1878.

86 Confidential Print 'African 151', Enclosure in No. 12, Lanyon to Barkly, 31 Jan. 1878; PRO, CO 107/5, various enclosures in No. 32 of 25 June 1878; and *LMS*, 39-3-B, Ashton, 13 June 1878.

87 *LMS*, 38-3-B, Ashton, 13 July 1876; CAD, GLW 91, No. 2236, J. G. Donovan, Klein Boetsap, 21 July 1876; *Diamond News*, 5 Aug. 1876; and *BPP*, LX, 1877, C.1748, *Correspondence respecting the War between the Transvaal Republic and Neighbouring Native Tribes, and generally with reference to Native Affairs in South Africa*, pp. 92–4, enclosures in Despatch No. 66 of 17 Aug. 1876, Barkly to Carnarvon.

88 UW, *Mackenzie Papers*, A75/2 (draft), Mackenzie to Lanyon, 5 Oct. 1877.

89 *Ibid.*, of 1 Feb. 1878.

90 *BPP*, C.2220, pp. 25–6, Ford to Acting Colonial Secretary, 'Mazeppa fontein, near Manyeering', 4 July 1878.

91 CAD, GLW 104, No. 1447, Report of Field-cornet Corus, Spitskop, 15 June 1873, and various minutes thereon, and report of G. Bradshaw (Acting RM), Barkly, 23 Oct. 1877; and CAD, GH 12/9, enclosures in No. 43, Report of C. C. Campbell (RM), Barkly, Jan. 1878.

92 UW, *Mackenzie Papers*, A75/2, Ashton to Mackenzie, 23 Feb. 1878; and *LMS*, 39-3-C, Ashton, 15 Aug. 1878.

93 A. Sillery, *John Mackenzie of Bechuanaland, 1835–1899* (Cape Town, 1971), p. 47.

94 TVL, *Lanyon Papers*, 596/2, J. D. Barry to Lanyon, 12 April 1877; and *CAD*, GLW 109, No. 2397, J. Burness, Daniel's Kuil, 2 Oct. 1877.

95 CAD, GLW 128, Mackenzie to Sam Edwards, 10 June 1878.

96 CAD, GLW 131, inserted after No. 239, correspondence between Donovan, Hunter and Colonial Secretary, Nov.–Dec. 1878.

97 PRO, CO 107/5 enclosures in No. 41 of 7 Aug. 1878.

98 CAD, GLW 114, No. 17, Minute of G. Bradshaw, 17 Jan. 1878. At Kimberley prices, this represented about £2 000 worth of prime firewood stolen from Botlasitse's country.

99 PRO, CO 107/5, enclosures in No. 41, statements by W. Thompson (21 July) and F. R. Thompson (25 July), extract of letter from the Recorder, J. D. Barry to Frere, Kimberley, 23 July, and Dr Murphy to Barry, Spitskop, 22 July 1878.

100 *BPP*, LIII, 1878–79, C.2252, *Further Correspondence respecting the Affairs of South Africa*, pp. 41–2, Warren to Lanyon, Taung, 25 Nov. 1878.

101 Cf. *OHSA*, II, p. 257.

102 Rev. John Mackenzie, 'The disturbances in Bechuanaland', in *Cape Argus*, 15 Aug. 1878. See also *BPP*, LII, 1878–79, C.2222, *Further Correspondence respecting the Affairs of South Africa*, pp. 116–25, enclosures in No. 36, reports by Warren, Lanyon and others, Sept.–Nov. 1878, for the view of the Griqualand West Administration.

103 I. B. Sutton, 'The 1878 rebellion in Griqualand West and Adjacent Territories', unpublished Ph.D. thesis, University of London, 1975, pp. 288–90.

104 *BPP*, XLIX, 1883, C.3635, *Report by Colonel Warren, dated April 3rd 1879*, p. 7.

105 Sutton, 'The 1878 rebellion'; and A. N. White, 'The Stockenstrom Judgement, The Warren Report and the Griqualand West Rebellion, 1876–8', unpublished M.A. thesis, Rhodes University, Grahamstown, 1977.

CHAPTER FOUR

Labour migration in Basutoland c. 1870–1885

Judy Kimble

Introduction

The years 1868–80 saw rapid and traumatic change for Basotho. Between 1868 and 1871, the formal independence of the kingdom was brought to an end; the geographical boundaries of the country were sealed; and the original ruler of the kingdom, Moshoeshoe I, was succeeded by his eldest son. From 1881 to 1884, the country rose in a protracted war against the Cape colonial government, the Gun War, which was followed by a bitter civil war. At the conclusion of this turbulent decade and a half, Basutoland was removed from the political control of the Cape and placed under the direct protection of the British government.

The tremendous increase in the production of agricultural commodities – wheat, sorghum, maize, wool and mohair – during this period confirmed the view of many contemporaries that Basotho were 'the most intelligent and industrious – the most peaceably inclined and tractable – race in South Africa'.[1] During the same period, thousands of adult male Basotho began to move annually onto the colonial labour markets to exchange their labour-power as a commodity. To recognise and explain this movement of labour, it is necessary to examine the structural conditions prevailing in both the settler social formations and the Sotho social formation itself. The uneven and contradictory effects of several decades of penetration of merchant capital into the whole region make it difficult to assess these conditions, but it is important to differentiate between several distinct processes.

This essay seeks to explain this Basotho participation in the labour markets of southern Africa during the years between the diamond and gold discoveries, with particular emphasis on the sale of labour power as a commodity. Basotho experience during the middle and late nineteenth century was not atypical of that of other southern African peoples. The two distinctive features in the economic development of this period – namely, the production and exchange of agricultural commodities and the sale of labour-power – should be seen as two different forms of one fundamental process: the increasing commoditisation of production. In the wider context of colonialism and imperialism, this process represented an important phase in the primitive accumulation of capital and the uneven development of capitalism. For the African populations in the subcontinent, the transition from one form of participation in the commodity markets to another was ultimately made necessary by the changing nature and requirements of gold-mining capital. But the precise manner in which this transition occurred, the form it took and its contradictory results were the product of many complex determining factors, not least of which was the specific character of the pre-colonial social formations involved.[2]

By the time of their original annexation in 1868, Basotho had been renowned for over four decades as good workers on white-owned farms, and in colonial towns and ports. Which settler interests were to continue to exploit this capacity to labour, and in what manner, were two of the issues at stake in the annexation debates of 1868–71.[3] Behind this contemporary perception of Basotho 'labour', however, lay two different types of migration. From the earliest years of Moshoeshoe's reign in Lesotho,[4] general migratory movements of homesteads had taken place. These often originated on a large scale as refugee movements away from the frequent outbreaks of war on the southern highveld; at other times they were produced by local ecological or political crises. Such movements must be treated as part of a wide and fairly amorphous 'ebb and flow' of homesteads, families and sometimes individuals, primarily in search of access to land and some form of political protection.[5] From this perspective, it is possible to compare the position of a male labour tenant, 'bound' to perform a certain amount of labour service to a white landowner, with the position of a male homestead head seeking to settle under Moshoeshoe in the 1840s. The latter would also 'bind' himself as a subject and follower through relations of personal dependence to performance of tribute labour.[6] Such movements of homesteads characterised Basotho history in the early and middle decades of the nineteenth century, and continued in various forms well into the 1880s and 1890s. In the period 1870–85, they were aggravated by the aftermath of the wars of the 1860s by removals from the Orange Free State, and by the Gun and civil wars.

Although such migratory movements served to satisfy a demand for labour among white colonists, it is important to distinguish between these movements and the more regular form of labour migration which is examined in this essay: a movement generally of single adult men, seeking to exchange their labour-power against a wage. Such migration had already begun to emerge prior to annexation in 1868, but it only began to appear on a significant scale during the 1870s. This essay is premised on such a distinction, and seeks to analyse the movements of wage labourers in the period 1870 to around 1885 through an examination of both the character of the demand for labour and the form of migration which it involved.

The central argument is that the structural conditions prevailing in Basutoland in the 1870s ensured that large numbers of adult male Basotho began to sell their labour-power as a commodity regularly – but only in exchange for wages which would ensure them access to certain commodities. As for the demand for labour, it will be shown that the emergence of capitalist conditions of employment on the diamond fields with its corresponding demand for mobile or 'free' labour had dramatic repercussions on a labour market previously dominated by semi-feudal relations of production with its corresponding demand for immobile or 'unfree' labour.[7] In the absence of a dominant mode of production or dominant class, the employers experienced a permanent labour shortage: wages rose steadily and guns were freely supplied to attract workers.

As for supply, it will be shown that, broadly speaking, the primary structural determinant of Basotho labour migration during this decade lay in the role played by the ruling Koena lineage in Basutoland in its attempt to reproduce its position of dominance within the social formation in the new context of formal colonialism. Conditions on the labour markets ensured that one particularly vital product which was needed by the royal lineage was readily available: guns. There were other factors producing a growth in labour migration during these years. On the one hand, as in earlier decades, Christian commodity producers moved into wage employment to obtain goods which would enable them to engage more independently in agricultural export. This was in harmony with their ideology of private property and political distance from the chieftainship. On the other hand, there is evidence of the re-emergence of an old phenomenon with a new significance. Growing social differentiation and the impact of colonial rule began to bear heavily on those homesteads which had been impoverished in the wars of the mid-nineteenth century. Unable to fulfil their various cash requirements through the production of foodstuffs for exchange, such homesteads were increasingly forced to resort to labour migration.

'Labourers, labourers everywhere, and not a man to work'[8]
The fluid nature of the relations of production existing in the areas dominated by white settlers in the nineteenth century makes generalisation precarious. However, overall, before the opening of the diamond mines, relations of production in the subcontinent were predominantly semi-feudal.[9] The years after 1870 marked a new development, since on the colonial public works, in the new employment in the towns, on an increasing number of farms and at the point of production on the diamond mines, relations were now clearly being conducted on a capitalist basis. The difference between these two types of productive relations can be quite difficult to identify, since both appear in various forms. This is particularly so in the case of white farms producing on a

commercial basis, where conditions of payment and service for labour tenancy varied widely from place to place, and often overlapped imperceptibly into seasonal wage-labour. Nevertheless, an essential characteristic of both the dominant forms of semi-feudal relations – 'squatting' and labour tenancy[10] – was that the direct producers remained in effective possession of the means of production, and thus the surplus labour or surplus product extracted remained separate from necessary labour. As was the case within the Sotho social formation, a homestead was not in a position to sell the land it resided on, but within certain limits it was free to work on it with its own tools, and to dispose of the product. In contrast to this, a labourer who entered capitalist wage employment was a 'free' labourer, in the sense that he engaged in the contract as an individual, who neither owned nor possessed the means of production at the point of employment, and hence had no independent or direct accesss to these.[11] The labourer worked completely under the control of the capitalist, to whom his labour belonged and to whom the entire fruits of his labour accrued and who then remunerated him in the form of wages. Paid and unpaid labour were thus inseparably mixed up, and the labourer entirely dependent on the wage for subsistence during the period of employment.

In itself, the establishment of the mining industry in Griqualand West did not signify the dominance or even necessarily the emergence of the capitalist mode of production in the subcontinent. Prior to the investment of substantial quantities of imperial capital and the opening of the gold mines, in the context of different relations of production and rival polities, 'there was no clearly dominant mode and no unequivocally dominant class' in the subcontinent.[12] But once production at the Kimberley blue ground pipes got under way, it had a tremendous impact on the economy of the whole of southern Africa and, above all, on the labour market. The opening of the diamond diggings served not only to aggravate seriously the perennial labour shortage experienced in the colonies and republics before 1870, but also to disrupt the patterns of wages and conditions of employment. It thereby began to threaten the entire labour market.

In the 1870s, conditions of production on the diamond mines were characterised by chaotic competition between small-scale entrepreneurs.[13] When combined with the relative independence of the African workforce, who for the most part still retained access to an independent, viable economic base, this factor guaranteed a constant struggle between the two classes involved on the diggings: the diggers and the labourers. During the 1870s, the black workers generally held a strong bargaining position, and, as a result, wages showed a steady tendency to rise over the decade, while employers were forced to waive colonial restrictions on the sale of arms and ammunition to the African workers. Another consequence of this gradual increase in wages was to divert the already inadequate flow of labour from other, more 'traditional' directions. All other employers in this period – whether 'old' (that is, farmers) or 'new' (for example, the colonial state) – were forced either to raise wages to a competitive level, or to resort to independent, coercive measures in an attempt to divert and secure such labour.

From the beginning, contemporaries observed large numbers of Basotho at the diggings.[14] In the early 1870s, they were said to have predominated, although later the workforce clearly became more diversified. According to one source, Zulu were considered by the Kimberley diggers to be the 'favourite', but Basotho were regarded as the next best because of their reputation for being strong and hardworking, and thus it was often complained that they were 'in short supply'. In the wake of the 1874 war between the Transvaal and Bopedi, another major supplier to Kimberley, diggers were forced to rely more than before on Basotho; and by 1880, one Kimberley newspaper acknowledged that 'We on the Fields depend greatly on Basuto labour for the working of the mines'.[15] The dangers of such dependence became devastatingly clear to the mineowners in that year, when the outbreak of *Ntoa ea Lithunya* (the Gun War) in Basutoland provoked a wholesale 'exodus' of 4 000 Basotho. The mines were brought to a standstill, and the owners were forced to embark on a completely new strategy of recruitment in the north, to lessen their dependence on 'local' labour.[16]

Lack of efficient, diversified recruitment and subsequent labour shortage were not the only problems for the diggers in these years.[17] More important, the very production process and the structure of ownership of claims on the mines prevented any effective combination of employers, who were thus unable to stop the gradual rise in wages. By 1872, the average wage had risen from 10s to 30–40s per month (without rations), and the frequent attempts to reduce these wages failed consistently. The situation came to a head in the depression on the diamond fields of 1874–76, which reduced the number of claimholders in Kimberley by three-quarters. The fall in diamond prices, it was argued by those who remained, made a reduction in wage costs imperative. By the middle of July 1876, diggers had agreed to lower the wages from an average 10–20s per week to 5s. As predicted by pessimistic observers, the move failed, and provoked instead a massive departure of black workers. Within two months, at least 4 000 men left the fields, 1 000 of them from Basutoland. As one newspaper observed with heavy sarcasm, the 'admirable independent strike' produced the desired effect for the workers: by the end of August, wages had been forced back up to their original level. The 'unprecedented scarcity of labour' provoked some of the larger diggers to outbid each other, and others went to Basutoland to recruit directly. Those workers who remained on the fields continued their strike, demanding higher wages and refusing to fulfil their contracts.[18]

It was under these conditions of inter-employer competition and general labour shortage that arms and ammunition were made freely available on the diamond fields.[19] Officials of the imperial government had had a long record of ambivalence towards this trade, but no resolution was reached during this decade. The perennial conflict between the needs of security and the need to encourage commodity production and a regular flow of labour inhibited the Governor of the Cape Colony and his subordinates from restricting the issue of gun permits on the diamond fields.[20] As one writer in a local Free State newspaper commented:

> The mainspring . . . of the prosperity of Griqualand West hinges upon the illicit . . . gun trade. Do away with that and the diamond industry would collapse.[21]

The illegal sale of guns thus continued freely, and it was not until the end of the decade that an abrupt attempt was made by the Cape Colony to reverse the effects of this official laxity, with the implementation of the 'Peace Preservation Act'.[22]

The net effect of high wages and easy access to guns on the diamond fields was to attract labourers – both potential and actual – away from other kinds of employment in the subcontinent. This decade witnessed a comparable growth in the demand for both unskilled and semi-skilled labour in the various towns of the Cape Colony. According to missionaries resident in Basutoland, Basotho were 'very much in demand . . . in various jobs' in these towns, and many thousands made their way there on the basis of 'temporary migrations'.[23] The demand, however, remained unsatisfied: 'Labourers, labourers everywhere, and not a man to work', lamented one Port Elizabeth journalist.[24] Wages were forced upwards, and in turn aggravated the situation in the Cape Colony, where wheat and wool farmers were expanding production for the market. Labour tenancy was still widespread, but in many areas seasonal and temporary wage employment increased. Basotho had long supplied the northern districts of the Eastern Province, and by 1893, according to Griffith, the Governor's Agent in Maseru, these districts drew 'most, if not all of their agricultural and other labour from this territory'.[25]

The Cape colonial government was particularly sensitive to the needs of its white farmers in this decade, and for its own publicly financed programmes of railway construction undertook to send labour recruiting agents to the annexed territories, specifically to 'prevent as much as possible any interference with the ordinary supply of colonial labour'.[26] One such attempt was made in 1873, with the circulation of the Brownlee Document, an initiative designed to encourage mission establishments to send labourers to the railway works in the Eastern Province, and to establish a tradition of regular and stable contracts. In doing so, the Cape government was forced to offer relatively high wages as an attraction.[27]

On receipt of this new scheme for recruitment, Griffith directly broached the matter at the annual government *pitso* (public parliament).[28] Arguing that Basutoland would benefit from the railways, since these would reduce transport costs for exports, open up markets and cheapen the price of imported goods, he advised the Basotho chiefs and their subordinates to send their followers to the works. His exhortations were repeated by several of these authorities. Despite this, the local magistrates noted an initial reluctance amongst Basotho to go, and attributed this, probably correctly, to the difficulty of 'procuring guns' in the Colony as compared to conditions at Kimberley.[29] Indeed, within a short time, even though they continued to refuse to issue gun permits themselves, the colonial public works employers were forced to turn a blind eye to other sources of permits. Once it was discovered by Basotho that these could be acquired by making a detour to other magistracies in the Eastern Province, the numbers at the railway works increased. By 1877, it was estimated that there were 5 000 Basotho selling their labour-power there.[30] In general, however, Griffith became increasingly pessimistic about the possibility of organising recruitment on a systematic basis. As late as 1879, he was arguing that it was simply a question of supply and demand:

> When there is a good demand for labour, and good wages are offered, the supply is generally equal to the occasion, and therefore no number of agents would be able to induce the Basutos to go out to service if their own circumstances did not require them to do so.[31]

Farmers in the Orange Free State were particularly severely affected by the struggles over Basotho labour. The history of Basotho relations with Free State farmers, traders and burghers was immensely complicated between 1830 and 1870 because Orange Free State inhabitants simultaneously sought control over the land, labour and grain of Basotho.[32] Tim Keegan's recent work on the economy of the Orange River Colony in the early years of the twentieth century has convincingly analysed some of the class forces struggling either to break up or to maintain semi-feudal relations of production. He suggests that control of labour supplies was central to this struggle, although the process of 'disintegration/transformation of class relations' was highly uneven and complex.[33] Many of the struggles identified in this later period had their roots in the penetration of merchant capital into the Free State in the mid-nineteenth century, and in the period of increased tension and competition for labour which followed the discovery of diamonds.

Thus, for example, although the Orange Free State government made several attempts during the years 1870–85 to eliminate the practices of 'uncontrolled squatting' and 'uncontracted servants', and to curb the absentee landownership which encouraged these to flourish, they remained widespread. It was widely recognised that 'nothing could excel' the grain-producing potential of the north-eastern districts of the Free State – the 'conquered Territory' previously controlled by Moshoeshoe, seized by Boer commandos in the wars of the 1860s, and handed over to the Free State in the Wodehouse negotiations of 1867–68. Yet the farmers of the Free State not only failed to produce agricultural foodstuffs for the Kimberley markets, but also remained largely dependent on external supplies of grain for domestic consumption. Many Free State farmers apparently found it cheaper and easier to enter the carrying trade than to produce themselves, and in 1873, *The Friend* newspaper lamented:

> As yet most of the grain sold on the Kimberley fields by Free State people is the produce of British Basutoland.[34]

The main problems for those farmers who attempted to expand production on a commodity basis were those of labour shortage and competition from Basotho agricultural producers.[35] In general, those farmers who sought immobile labour, in the form of labour tenants and squatters, were satisfied during this period; those who sought a more mobile, seasonal wage labour force suffered severe shortage. Of course the two demands were often made by the same farmers, and it was the temporary, 'free' labour which proved inaccessible. In most cases, this was particularly so since the farmers offered wages and conditions which were uncompetitive. The continued demand for labour tenants and squatters by a section of Free State farmers during this decade was indeed a vital outlet for thousands of Basotho homesteads. The gradual peeling off of the most fertile parts of the lowlands of Lesotho between 1848 and 1870 began to take its toll on the delicate balance between land for cultivation and land for pastoralism.[36] This imbalance was aggravated by the extensive immigration into Lesotho from the Free State, following the Aliwal Convention of 1868; by the expansion of arable production in the 1870s; by the gradual and constant return of homesteads from the Cape Colony (some of whom had been away for decades); and by the tremendous increase in stock. The pressure on the land was relieved to some extent by the discovery that cereals could be grown in the Maloti mountains, and a 'move to the mountains' began in the late 1870s and early 1880s. But the lowlands were becoming crowded, and in a now familiar pattern of response to the new 'boundary legislation', after the 'clearing' of the Conquered Territory in the wars of the 1860s, many hundreds of Basotho homesteads simply moved back on to land they had previously occupied, and entered into relations with the new owners of the land. In some cases they were actively encouraged to do so by their chiefs; they were certainly welcomed by many farmers. According to one mission report, by the end of the 1870s there were 'thousands' of Basotho scattered 'through the breadth and length' of the Free State, engaged as servants to the farmers.[37]

In contrast, attempts by farmers to secure wage labour on a seasonal basis failed miserably. There was thus an inevitable resort to the violence and obstruction that had characterised Free State dealings with Basotho for decades. This kind of action, not surprisingly, served to lessen the attraction for Basotho of working in such conditions.[38] As soon as the diggings opened in Kimberley, the cry went up in the Free State: 'all our best servants – poor even at the best – are being drawn from us by the superior attraction of the Diamond Fields.'[39] To their chagrin, farmers, builders and transport riders witnessed thousands of Basotho and others passing through their land, 'laughing' at offers of work; even when unable to find work at the diamond mines, Basotho would walk home 'rather than accept the lower wages offered in towns or on farms along the road'.[40] Legislation was introduced by the Free State for the enforcement of contracts and for heavy pass taxation, but the most common response of the farmers to this frustrating state of affairs was the arbitrary arrest of Basotho carrying guns, and the thrashing and flogging of all such travellers.

These attempts by Free State authorities and farmers to attract or coerce Basotho labourers to work in the Republic failed to achieve the desired effect and, instead, tended to reduce the total flow of Basotho workers from Basutoland to all destinations. Naturally this development produced great anxiety on the part of the Cape colonial authorities. In 1874, one local magistrate in the territory reported that the 1s tax imposed for passage through the Free State had caused a drop of 1 000 passes issued annually from his station.[41] Basotho themselves complained bitterly to their new government about the seizure of guns and indiscriminate violence they experienced at the hands of the white farmers – activities which the protection and annexation of 1868 had been expected to bring to an end. As Masopha Moshoeshoe appealed to Griffith in 1875:

> But in the Free State we are not protected, and the Government doesn't stand up for our blood. We are thrashed for nothing – under the Queen's pass, our people have their guns taken from them and are imprisoned and flogged – all under the Queen's pass.[42]

Griffith and the Cape government were well aware, however, that the 'Queen's Government' was unable to take action to ensure that the much-needed labour reached the desired destination, especially since it had itself collaborated with the Free State on the question of arms prohibition in the past.[43] As long as the conditions for the creation of a unified political structure had not emerged, the competition for labour supplies between the republics and the colonies continued unabated.[44]

In the 1870s and early 1880s, then, structural conditions prevailing in the subcontinent created a relatively favourable conjuncture for Basotho engaged on the labour market. In the first place, the very conditions under which the diamond-mining industry emerged made it impossible to structure the labour market effectively in the interests of employers. The actual labour process and the relations of production operating on the mines themselves inhibited the combination of employers for the enforcement of a maximum wage limit. At the same time, the absence of a dominant class with access to political power gave rise to competition between the different branches of production and economic interests, all of which sought to engage labour, whether on the basis of capitalist or non-capitalist relations of production. Out of all these – farmers, government public works' employers, private mining entrepreneurs – the diggers on the mines, with a high turnover of ownership of claims and considerably greater profits at stake, were able to bid the highest price for their labourers, and so to disrupt the entire market, both for mobile and immobile labour.

Secondly, but as importantly, the conditions prevailing within the Sotho social formation were such that there was little internal economic compulsion for Basotho to sell their labour-power at any price and under any conditions. Prices for agricultural produce remained high, and there was no effective competition from white farms. The Sotho nation was still in possession of its means of production and its internal capacity for the production of goods for subsistence and exchange had not been seriously undermined. In these circumstances, Basotho were in a position to accept or reject the wage levels offered on the mines and elsewhere, and thus to perpetuate the conditions of labour shortage. As *The Friend* commented in 1873, the labourer had 'the best of it. He can hold out without employment much better than the masters can without labour'.[45] Yet thousands of Basotho did continue to migrate in search of work during these years. It is to an examination of the internal structural determinants of labour migration that we now turn.

Basotho migrant workers

By the end of the 1870s, according to one report, there were probably some 5 000 adult male Basotho employed on the diamond fields, another 5 000 on the colonial railway works, and perhaps the same number again engaged on farms, in the towns and in miscellaneous employment in the Free State and Cape Colony.[46] The most obvious explanation for the rapid growth of Basotho labour migration in this decade would seem to have been what one district magistrate characterised as the growth of a 'great many artificial wants' on the part of Basotho, as they 'progressed in civilisation':

> Thus it happens that although according to their old native standards they might consider themselves sufficiently rich, yet the constantly recurring pressure of new wants sends them from home and stimulates them to greater exertion.

No better proof of this could be given, he wrote in 1875, than the annual increase in the number of passes issued.[47]

This kind of explanation – perpetuated in various guises in much of the existing literature on labour migration – has been effectively challenged by the work of Arrighi on labour supplies in Rhodesia. Arrighi acknowledges that the pressure of 'new wants' did serve to promote participation in the newly developed commodity markets, but argues that this should be seen in a historical perspective. Under conditions of high prices and a strong demand for agricultural foodstuffs, this participation tends to take the form of production of agricultural commodities for exchange. In itself, 'new wants' cannot explain why labour migration should develop as the form of market participation. His thesis, developed extensively in the context of South Africa by Bundy and others, has provided some important starting points for such an explanation.[48] These writers have insisted that the stimulation of new 'needs' and the imperative to acquire cash to obtain these needs must be seen as a historical product of certain political and ideological conditions. They have also clearly demonstrated that prior to the political manipulation of market structures (both for agricultural produce and labour-power) which ensured that African agriculturalists were no longer able to satisfy these growing cash needs through exchange of their produce (in Arrighi's terms, by raising the effort-price of such participation), African producers were in a position to withhold their labour and frustrate the demand for that labour. By stressing these factors, Arrighi and Bundy have succeeded in bringing the question of the mechanisms of primitive accumulation to the fore.[49]

However, even with these crucial historical arguments, the 'Arrighi thesis'[50] cannot explain why any labour should have been forthcoming before the operation of the relevant political mechanisms, particularly in a period like the one under discussion, when the demand for African food production was high. It may perhaps be argued that this is not a serious criticism: that the favourable conditions in the *labour* market ensured that, in Arrighi's terms, the 'effort-price' of participation in both markets was roughly equal. It could then be suggested that the important factor was the choice of the individual homestead, a choice which might have been influenced by the ready availability of guns, for example, on the labour market. Such an answer may go part of the way towards tackling the problems posed in this essay. But in doing so, it relies on description rather than analysis, and serves to obscure the character of the non-capitalist relations of production in the African social formation, in this case, Basutoland. The response implicitly assumes that the basic unit of production in such societies is the single, structually isolated homestead, which operates on the basis of a particular form of economic calculation and rationality, conceptualised in terms of individual 'choice' and a voluntary 'response' to market pressures. This in turn is based on implicit assumptions about the 'need' for commodities, without taking into account how these were integrated into the circuits of production and reproduction within the total social formation.[51]

With a few exceptions, these are inappropriate assumptions to make in the case of Basutoland in the 1870s, and they make it impossible to interpret either the major wars of resistance fought in the 1880s or the political structures of colonial rule imposed on Moshoeshoe's kingdom. Although the homestead formed an important centre of productive activity in the Sotho social formation, the social organisation of production was dependent on the existence of a chieftainship which was maintained through the surplus labour of the direct producers. The links between a homestead head and his chief were weakened in the case of Basotho resident on mission stations, and temporarily disrupted for those settled on land belonging to the Free State. But amongst Basotho resident in the area demarcated under royal control, these links were still decisive in determining the patterns of production. Thus any discussion of agricultural commodity production and labour migration must take into account the continued existence of the political, ideological and economic levels of the Sotho social formation and, despite large-scale expropriation by the Free State, the maintenance of a firm land base.

To provide an alternative explanation, it is necessary to begin with some understanding of Sotho productive relations. Four decades of penetration by merchant capital had produced certain contradictory effects which played an important part in structuring the development of labour migration in the 1870s, and these enable us to distinguish between different categories of migration taking place. It is possible to identify three such categories: migrants organised by the ruling lineage; Christian migrants; and poor, possibly landless, migrants. This last group was still relatively small during the 1870s, but was a symptom of future developments.

Moshoeshoe's kingdom emerged in the Caledon lowlands in the wake of the *lifaqane** wars, and was characterised from its early days by a social division of labour.[52] The royal lineage which dominated the chieftainship controlled access to land and cattle, and possessed extensive powers of surplus appropriation exercised through the four main branches of production – agriculture, pastoralism, hunting and military organisation. In several respects the powers of this ruling lineage were bounded, but its wealth and dominance increased throughout the early nineteenth century. The emergence of the royal lineage was an important precondition for the extensive development of agricultural commodity production in Lesotho during the years 1830–70. This process in turn served to strengthen and entrench the ruling group, which was thereby able to reproduce its dominance on an expanded scale. The key to the

---

* The *lifaqane*, *difaqane* or *mfecane* were the wars in the wake of the rise of the Zulu kingdom in the first decades of the nineteenth century.

consolidation of Koena power lay in the various modes of appropriation of surplus through which the safety and defence of the kingdom was assured, and every homestead granted access to the essential means of production – cattle and land. Reproduction of its dominant position was achieved by the Koena lineage through realisation of the surplus in the form of both redistribution and, increasingly, exchange. The primary form of redistribution was the loan of cattle and other goods in a relationship of *mafisa*, which carried with it the obligation to perform tribute labour-service in various branches of production.[53]

In quantitative terms, agricultural labour-service (*matsema*) was the most important method of exploiting the surplus labour time of the adult male subjects. With the decline of hunting, cultivation became the most important branch of production, and the scope of its application was extended.[54] However, military organisation remained central to the structure of the production process, particularly since tribute labour was organised through the regiment structures.[55] At the same time, the rapid growth in the armed strength of Basotho during the middle decades of the century had been one of the major preconditions for the retention of a secure land base in the face of constant settler encroachment. According to some contemporary observers, Sotho commanded one of the best armed and mounted forces in the subcontinent: this was in a large part due to their extensive possession of European-manufactured weapons and ammunition.[56] In the years before 1870, the ruling lineage had increasingly begun to realise the surplus it had appropriated through exchange, in the form of guns, which were then redistributed to its subjects on the basis of *mafisa*.

It is thus in the context of the increasing dominance of the Koena lineage, and of the importance of military organisation to the reproduction of this dominance, that any 'desire to get guns' on the part of Sotho labourers should be understood. Beyond this, the character of the colonial threat to Koena power in the 1870s is significant. The various attempts made by the Cape administration to infringe chiefly prerogatives, alongside its overt readiness to work closely with the missionaries, were regarded with great suspicion by Sotho chiefs. The latter were ready to defend their rights of surplus appropriation against the 'Queen's government' – a government, moreover, which by 1875 did not remotely resemble the form of administration envisaged by Moshoeshoe in his requests for British 'protection' a decade earlier.[57]

However, the response of the Koena chiefs to the imposition of colonial power was not unilaterally hostile. As one of the younger sons of Moshoeshoe put it in 1873, there was a general consensus among chiefs and people to 'enter the Queen's government', even if this was 'only . . . with one foot'.[58] For although the colonial administration was clearly determined to reduce the political and economic powers of the chieftainship and to curb what was considered 'excessive' surplus appropriation, in practice the situation demanded that both government officials and chiefs establish a working relationship. In the 'absence of a dependable armed force', the power of the administration was recognised by its own representatives to be more of an 'ideality' than a 'reality', and these were forced to look to the chiefs for execution of the political and economic tasks of the colonial state.[59] Their cooperation was required for the maintenance of 'law and order', for the collection of colonial tax and above all, for the organisation of a regular outflow of agricultural commodities and labour-power.

There are many examples of the contradictory attitude of the colonial administration. On the one hand, for example, we find Griffith and other officials perturbed by what they considered a 'reactionary movement' on the part of the chiefs, who were finding 'their power leaving them'. Some magistrates noted the 'great rush' to the diamond fields in the early 1870s and observed that this movement was almost wholly at 'the instigation of the chiefs'. According to one magistrate:

> The chief Molapo was the first who sent large groups of men to work at the diamond fields, and it was openly said by the natives that he had ordered them not to return without guns and ammunition, which order they scrupulously obeyed.[60]

Others reported these instructions being issued at the annual *letsema* events. On the other hand, we find Griffith himself appealing to the Koena chiefs to organise their men to go to the public railway works. The Koena chiefs translated these requests to their subjects in terms of a demand to attend the 'Queen's *letsema*'. They appealed to the authority of Moshoeshoe, in whose time 'we were simply ordered and went'.[61]

Again, although it was official policy of the colonial administration not to issue passes for employment prior to the payment of colonial taxation (a policy designed to prevent tax evasion), in practice officials would instruct the chiefs to send all those unable to pay 'for passes to enter the Colony for service'. In 1871, one senior councillor from Moshoeshoe's time appealed to Griffith on behalf of those Basotho who were in arrears with their tax that

> . . . although they may not have hut receipts to show, . . . [they] may go at once to the Colony and earn the money . . . and if any are found having such a passport and not using it for the purpose it was given, they may be punished.[62]

The situation was clearly a precarious one for the colonial administration. Not only could the chiefs send their followers to the mines, they could also summon them back at times of crisis in Basutoland, and, furthermore, impose their own system of direct taxation on returning labourers.[63] In 1877, at the time of the Gaika-Gcaleka wars in the eastern Cape and just after the Pedi massacre by the Transvaal mercenaries, it was observed by farmers in the Free

State that Basotho were very uneasy 'about something . . . two petty chiefs have gone down to the Fields to recall all that are working there'.[64] And in 1880, the impending military confrontation with the colonial government over disarmament led the Koena chiefs to issue a general summons to the mines: as we have already seen, more than 4 000 Basotho returned immediately. With this evidence it becomes possible to interpret the massive national resistance to disarmament in 1880–81: not only were Basotho exceedingly bitter at yet another broken promise of the British, but the threat to disarm Basotho struck at the very foundations of royal power, a power which had been considerably strengthened during decades of organising and controlling the movements of labour migration.[65]

The central role played by the Koena lineage in organising and controlling patterns of labour migration during this decade was an expression of its economic and political position within the social formation. This position had been consolidated on the basis of the penetration of merchant capital. Merchant capital, however, did not foster one tendency alone: the effects of penetration were ambivalent and even contradictory. Although it is not legitimate to reduce the nineteenth-century mission theme of 'Christianity, commerce and civilisation' to a reflection of merchant-capital and colonial interests, it is possible to see how the activities of the missionaries, and that of the Paris Evangelical Mission Society (PEMS) in particular during this period, served the interests of merchant capital by providing some of the conditions for the emergence of a group of semi-independent petty commodity producers. Any temporary entry into wage labour by this group was not so likely to be influenced directly by the chiefs as by the missionaries, and tended to have a different significance for the reproductive cycle of the individual household.[66]

The missionaries laid great emphasis on the notion of private property and the right of direct producers to dispose of their own products. They encouraged individual homesteads to abandon their practices of *matsema*, *mafisa*, *mephato* and *bohali*;[67] and they resisted their converts' participation in the various forms of obligatory labour-service. They argued that a man should be free to dispose of his labour-time (and that of his wife and children) as he wished – preferably, in the eyes of the PEMS, either by applying it to the production of agricultural foodstuffs for exchange, or by entering into employment with white colonists and settlers. However, the traditional practices referred to above were not reducible to 'pagan customs', as the most astute missionaries realised. They represented key mechanisms of reproduction within the social formation, both between homesteads, and between commoners and chiefs. Their retention was central to the maintenance of existing relations of production, and their dissolution entailed drastic consequences. The PEMS did not succeed in large-scale, long-term conversion in Lesotho in the mid-nineteenth century.

They were forced to compromise their original aspirations. But the establishment of a growing number of mission stations with virtually autonomous control over the surrounding land areas provided an environment conducive to the two significant processes: an 'atomisation of households' and a weakening of the links between chiefs and their converted followers.[68]

By 1868, the date of British annexation, mission programmes had begun to bear fruit and the colonial administration made clear its intention of working closely with the PEMS. Collaboration between the two forces was evident in all spheres, while the missionaries looked on the Kimberley boom as a godsend for their industrious converts. Indeed, the 'success' of the PEMS in stimulating the emergence of a group of petty commodity producers was to have an influence on the political alliances which developed inside Basutoland during the crisis war years of 1880–81. There is evidence that a large number of Christian converts remained 'loyal' to the colonial administration throughout the war, and that many of these had come to identify their interests in opposition to the national chiefs.[69] Throughout the 1870s missionaries remained in a position to issue official passes to their followers. Although at first they were often quite anxious about the conditions on the mines to which their converts would be exposed – conditions which included the 'vices' of white 'civilisation' – they were happy to respond to the government demand for 'young mission-educated men' at the colonial railway works. One of the more perceptive missionaries in Basutoland at this time, serving also as a colonial offical, realised that in the prevailing conditions there was no need for the demand for labour to disrupt the cherished patterns of agricultural commodity production; indeed, the two could reinforce each other. He urged the purchase of agricultural machines by the colonial administration, which would soon be 'paid for':

> The natives, seeing the advantage of them would then procure them spontaneously, and an amount of manual labour would then be set free for the colonial labour market. Thus the use of plough instead of the kafir pick has enabled the Basutos either to hire ploughmen whilst they went to work, or to proceed to the Free State after a few days' ploughing themselves.[70]

At the other end of the scale, however, it would appear that the 1870s saw the emergence of a new phenomenon: poor and impoverished households forced to migrate in order to fulfil their cash needs, and above all to pay tax. Colonial officials became aware of this development, and in 1875 one magistrate pointed out the need to mobilise this stratum to work:

> I don't mean to say that a person who is rich ought to go out to service, but we all know that everywhere there are poor people who ought to go out as servants and earn their living. There are many in Basutoland who have no stock, and if these people would only work, they would benefit themselves.[71]

It could be argued that from the days of the *lifaqane* wars, Sotho society had embraced such an impoverished stratum of households, which tended to be extremely dependent on the chiefs. The wars of the 1860s had doubtless contributed to the deepening of the division between such households and the majority of Basotho. But it must also be pointed out that all homesteads were subject to an increase in exploitation on several fronts during this decade, a result of the steady growth in the chiefs' power which manifested itself in their growing control over the means of production and intensification of surplus extraction from every homestead, as well as of the imposition of colonial tax. To these pressures should be added those of the subjection of all households to a combination of market and ecological uncertainty. With the decline of other productive activities, there emerged a growing dependence on that branch of . production which was becoming most thoroughly integrated into the commodity circuits — cultivation.

By the early 1870s, there was evidence that some homesteads were unable to pay their taxes. When, in 1879, the colonial administration proposed to double the annual tax rate — a suggestion which was supported by some senior chiefs — the commoners responded with general opposition, and often included the Koena rulers in their public criticism. 'It is true we plough a good deal', argued Smith Posholi, 'but we are impoverished by you chiefs.'[72] One Rakoto, a subject of Masopha, argued his poverty in the following terms:

> . . . the Chief Jonathan said that we are getting rich, he is perhaps rich because he is a chief. I am a heathen, that's my name. I am a very poor man: the blanket I now wear, I have had for three years. My children are naked, and I am too poor to give them clothing. We were first told to pay ten shillings hut tax to the Queen; now we are asked to pay twenty shillings and at the same time to give up our guns. Chiefs, when will you stop killing us?[73]

Basotho military victory in the 1880–81 *Ntoa ea Lithunya* ensured that the tax rate remained at 10s per annum. By the early 1880s, however, as the fixed rate of exchange for agricultural produce set by the colonial administration dropped in line with falling prices, those forced to migrate would have felt the growing burden. As one speaker at a *pitso* complained bitterly:

> We must work for six months for a sheep and now we must sell it for 5s. A beast we work twelve months for and the money will not pay our tax.[74]

The tendency for impoverishment to lead directly to labour migration became more pronounced in the years after the gold discoveries and re-annexation of Basutoland by the British (1884). Land pressure intensified, and some families were unable to obtain access to adequate land.[75] Clearly this was a complex process and raises important questions about the later development of labour migration. When questioned in 1903 as to whether there was any correlation between those 'farmers' who were not 'doing well' and the incidence of labour migration, one missionary, Dyke, replied:

> Not exactly; say a family consists of four sons, one remains at home and [looks] after the farm whilst the other three go abroad: They all belong to the same family and all have the rights to these plots of ground.[76]

To what extent such labour migration was to become more widespread, and perhaps typical of the era of segregation, will have to await later research.[77] However, it is suggested here that the 1870s saw the beginnings of this development, which must be considered as a category of labour migration distinct from the two other categories discussed. In this decade and a half, then, with the exception of the migration characteristic of Christianised petty commodity producers, the primary structural determinant of migration was the concerted action of the Koena royals to direct their subjects to enter the labour markets at the mines and on the colonial railway works. This policy had contradictory causes. It was partly an attempt to strengthen military organisation in response to the threat of colonial rule and to reinforce the position of dominance of royal power, partly a move of collaboration with the same colonial authorities. The net effect, however, was to facilitate the outflow of Basotho labour.

Conclusion

The specific argument of this paper is that any explanation of the development of migrant labour from Basutoland requires a detailed study of the structural conditions prevailing at both the point of supply and that of demand. The years 1870 to around 1880, it has been argued, represented a particular conjuncture when both conditions within and relations between the various white settler and African social formations in the subcontinent were in a critical phase of transition. Decades of penetration by merchant capital into the region had given rise to specific requirements for labour amongst settlers and colonists. The precarious mechanisms of the labour market which had developed by 1870 were put under severe strain with the establishment of the diamond-mining industry. The disadvantageous position of the employers could be reversed only after substantial political, military and economic intervention. At the same time, the penetration of merchant capital had given rise to a process of internal differentiation within the Sotho social formation – a process which continued to develop in a contradictory way under formal colonialism. In this context, it has been possible to separate out three distinct categories of labour migrants at a time when, as a whole, the Sotho social formation still retained a degree of economic integrity.

By way of a more general conclusion, it can be argued that it is necessary to progress beyond the purely descriptive characterisation of migrant labour such as that of Francis Wilson's in *Migrant Labour in South Africa*. According to Wilson, migrant labour is 'the system whereby men oscillate between their home in some rural areas and their place of work'. At this level, it is indeed possible to compare contemporary movements of labour with those of the nineteenth century, and state that 'migrant labour is nothing new in South Africa'.[78] The movement of Basotho out of their country into employment by whites in other parts of South Africa has been in evidence for over a hundred and thirty years, and it might seem legitimate to identify this as a constant feature of interaction between the two which has continued up to the present day. In fact, the economic and political conditions both within the 'rural area' and the 'place of work' have undergone substantial structural change over the decades, and it is possible to identify distinct stages in the development of interaction between the two.[79] Migrant labour needs to be subjected to a rigorous periodisation within the context of capital accumulation in southern Africa.

Notes

Abbreviations

AAVP	Cape Colony, *Annexures and Appendixes to the Votes and Proceedings of the Cape House of Assembly* (Cape Town)
BPP	Great Britain, *British Parliamentary Papers* (London)
CAR	Colonial Annual Report
CPP	Cape Colony, *Cape Parliamentary Papers* (Cape Town)
JME	*Journal des Missions Evangéliques* (Paris), annual journal of the Paris Evangelical Mission Society

1 *Cape Argus*, 14 June 1874. The focus on migrant labour in this paper should not obscure the fact that on a quantitative basis, during the decade of the 1870s, the sale of agricultural produce far outweighed the incidence of migrant labour. According to one assessment given in 1879, the income earned by Basotho as a whole from the former was five times that earned from 'labouring' and transport riding taken together. CAR 1879, quoted in debate on Basotho disarmament, *BPP* C.2755, pp. 295–6.

2 This is the main argument of my unpublished M.A. thesis, from which much of the empirical evidence on which this paper is based has been taken: 'Towards an understanding of the political economy of Lesotho: the origins of commodity production and migrant labour, 1830–*c*.1885', National University of Lesotho, 1978.

3 *Ibid.*, pp. 121–3, 193–5.

4 In this paper, the name 'Lesotho' is used when referring to the kingdom prior to colonial annexation in 1868, and 'Basutoland' for the period under colonial domination.

5 This is not intended to dismiss such a broad movement as insignificant, and is discussed more in my M.A. thesis, *vide supra*.

6 This analogy is limited solely to a comparison of the bonds of personal dependence involved in both cases, and is not intended to suggest that there was no difference between the modes of production in question. For a fuller discussion of the character of Moshoeshoe's kingdom in the 1850s, see Kimble, M.A. thesis (*supra* n. 2), 'Origins of commodity production', ch. 2.

7 The term 'free labour' is used here in the Marxist sense. See also an interesting discussion on the mobility of labour in G. Standing, 'Migration and modes of exploitation: the social origins of immobility and mobility', *Population and Employment Working Paper* 72, International Labour Organisation, June 1979.

8 *The Friend of the Free State and Bloemfontein Gazette* (Bloemfontein), 13 Feb. 1873 (hereafter referred to as *The Friend*).

9 I am basing this general conclusion on evidence in M. Legassick, 'South Africa: capital accumulation and violence', *Economy and society* III, 3 (1974); in T. Keegan, 'The restructuring of agrarian class relations in a colonial economy: the Orange River Colony, 1902–10', *Journal of Southern African studies*, 2, (1979); and in my own M.A. thesis, 'Origins of commodity production'.

10 On the difference between these two forms of feudal relations, see M. Morris, 'The development of capitalism in South African agriculture: class struggle in the countryside', *Economy and Society* V, 3 (1976), 294. For a further discussion, see T. Keegan, 'The sharecropping economy, African class formation and the 1913 Natives' Land Act on the highveld maize belt', Chapter 7 below.

11 The term 'ownership' here refers to the (legal) property relation; the term 'possession' refers to the relationship of the direct producer to the means of reproduction of his own labour-power. In capitalist production relations, both these connections can be characterised by a 'separation', whereas in most non-capitalist modes of production, the direct producer retains possession of the means of production. Here I am using the argument from B. Hindess and P. Q. Hirst, *Pre-capitalist Modes of Production* (London, 1975), pp. 189–90.

12 Legassick, 'Capital accumulation', 259.

13 See R. Turrell, 'Kimberley, Labour and compounds, 1871–1881', Chapter 1 above, for further discussion.

14 Sources for details about the diamond diggings include: R. F. Sieborger, 'The recruitment and organisation of African labour for the Kimberley diamond mines, 1870–1888', unpublished M.A. thesis, Rhodes University, 1975; J. W. Matthews, *Incwadi Yami, or Twenty Years Personal Experience in South Africa* (New York, 1887); S. T. van der Horst, *Native Labour in South Africa*, (London, 1942); R. Turrell, above; and contemporary newspapers: *The Diamond News and Griqualand West Government Gazette*; *The Diamond Fields Advertiser and Commercial Guide*; *The Friend*.

15 *Diamond Fields Advertiser*, 19 July 1880. The 'Gun War' broke out in 1880 as Basotho took to arms to resist the threat of disarmament posed by the application of the Peace Preservation Act to Basutoland. The war with the Cape Colony lasted until 1881, when the latter was shown to be clearly unable to manage the colonial possession given to it by the supreme power, Britain; Basutoland was handed back to the Queen's government henceforth to be ruled from London. For a discussion of the actual status of Basutoland after 1884, see 'Indirect rule and progress towards self-rule and independence: the case of Lesotho', by J. M. Mohapeloa, paper presented at Conference on southern African history, National University of Roma, Lesotho, Roma, 1–7 August 1977.

16 *Diamond Fields Advertiser*, 18 Aug. 1880; Registrar of Natives to Secretary for Native Affairs, 19 Feb. 1881; *AAVP*, G.20–1881, 130.

17 None of the methods attempted in the 1870s, including schemes for labour depots drawn up by the Cape government, succeeded in establishing reliable recruitment. Sieborger, 'African labour', p. 88.

18 *The Friend*, 29 June, 6 July, 13 July, 3 Aug., 31 Aug., 12 Oct., 9 Nov., 14 Dec., 1876; *The Diamond News*, 8 Aug. 1876; *The Daily Independent*, 3 Oct. 1876. Sieborger, 'African labour', p. 159.

19 Workers were not usually paid directly in the form of guns; they exchanged their cash wages for arms on the submission of a permit from their employers. Southey to Barkly, 11 April 1874, *AAVP*, A.68–1881, 6.

20 Matthews, *Incwadi Yami*, p. 278; *The Friend*, 20 Feb. and 27 Feb. 1873.

21 *The Friend*, 1 Jan. 1874.

22 The Peace Preservation Act of 1878 was expressly designed to take away from Africans the guns that they had bought over previous decades. It was held in reserve for two years in the case of Basotho, but the threat was in the air prior to the 1879 rebellion of Morena Moorosi.

23 Editorial, *JME*, 1879, 303.

24 *The Friend*, 13 Feb. 1873.

25 Griffith to Secretary for Native Affairs, 8 Nov. 1879, *CPP*, C.8–1881.

26 *The Friend*, 15 Oct. 1874. Hence the readiness with which the colonial government seized on the opportunity to employ Africans who resisted colonial rule – for example, the subjects of Langalibalele and Moorosi. Brownlee to Resident Magistrate of Lesotho, 9 Jan. 1874, *AAVP*, G.27–1874, 155–6; Ellenberger, undated, *JME*, 1879, 149–50.

27 Circular no. 5 of 1873, *AAVP*, G.27–1874, 152; van der Horst, *Native Labour*, pp. 89–90.

28 After annexation, national *lipitso* continued to be held, but under the auspices of the colonial officials.

29 Rolland, CAR 1874, *AAVP*, G.21–1875, 10.

30 Austen, CAR 1876, *AAVP*, G.12–1877, 4; *Little Light of Basutoland*, 1 Jan. 1877.

31 Griffith to Secretary for Native Affairs, 8 Nov. 1879, *CPP*, C.8–1881.

32 For details of this, see Kimble, 'Origins of commodity production', ch. 3; P. Sanders, *Moshoeshoe: Chief of the Sotho* (London, 1975).

33 Keegan, 'Agrarian class relations', and below, 'The sharecropping economy', Chapter 7.

34 *The Friend*, 9 Oct. 1873.

35 Cf. G. Arrighi, 'Labour supplies in historical perspective; the proletarianisation of the African peasantry in Rhodesia', in G. Arrighi and J. Saul (eds), *Essays in the Political Economy of Africa*, (New York, 1973), p. 288, n. 47.

36 On the importance of maintaining this balance for ecological reasons, see Kimble, 'Origins of commodity production', ch. 1; on the details of land expropriation in the nineteenth century, see Sanders, *Moshoeshoe*.

37 *Little Light*, 3 March 1876.

38 In 1885, there were complaints from Basotho that Free State farmers were in the habit of ill-treating their servants 'when their time had nearly expired', with a view to cause them to desert, 'and so deprive them of the wages which are their due' (Clarke to Brand, 16 Sept. 1885, *BPP*, C.4644, p. 53).

39 *The Friend*, 26 June 1871.

40 *Ibid.*, 17 July, 7 Aug. 1873; 13 Aug. 1876. K. J. de Kok, *Empires of the Veld: being fragments of unwritten history of the two late Boer republics . . .* (Durban, 1904), p. 58.

41 Rolland, CAR 1874, *AAVP*, G.21–1875, 10.

42 Government *pitso*, 4 Nov. 1875, *AAVP*, G.16–1876, 17.

43 Southey to Barkly, 28 Feb. 1873, quoted in Sieborger, 'African labour', p. 54. The Bloemfontein Convention of 1854 between the Orange Free State and the British government prohibited the sale of ammunition to Africans. After this Convention, OFS officials had with impunity harassed Africans carrying guns *en route* through white farming land.

44 'The evident differences between the republics and the colonies presented a good case for Confederation in the 1870s' (Sieborger, 'African labour', p. 57).

45 *The Friend*, 13 June 1873.

46 This estimate was made in 1875, so was probably a serious underestimate for the end of the decade. Rolland, CAR 1875, *AAVP*, G.16–1876, 8. In general, the statistical records of labour migration in this decade are very poor and unreliable.

47 *Ibid.*

48 C. Bundy, *The Rise and Fall of the South African Peasantry* (London, 1979); see also several of the essays in R. Palmer and N. Parsons (eds), *The Roots of Rural Poverty in Central and Southern Africa* (London, 1977).

49 Neither of these two writers actually use the term 'primitive accumulation' (although Arrighi refers to it), but it is quite clear that this concept is appropriate here. See Legassick, 'Capital accumulation'.

50 A phrase coined by Kosmin in his essay in Palmer and Parsons, *Roots of Rural Poverty*.

51 Such assumptions are built into the classic definition of African peasants elaborated by Saul and Woods, and referred to by several contributors in *Roots of Rural Poverty*; J. Saul and R. Woods, 'African peasantries', in T. Shanin (ed.), *Peasants and Peasant Societies* (Harmondsworth, 1971).

52 This summary is a simplified version of chs. 1 and 2 of Kimble, 'Origins of commodity production'. For a detailed political history of Moshoeshoe's kingdom, see Sanders, *Moshoeshoe*.

53 *Mafisa*: the practice of loaning out (primarily) stock, the caretaker being granted certain rights of usufruct, but not of exchange.

54 J. Widdicombe, *Fourteen Years in Basutoland: a sketch of African mission life* (London, 1891), p. 48; P. Hadley (ed.), *Doctor to Basuto, Boer and Briton, 1877–1906: memoirs of Dr Henry Taylor* (Cape Town, 1972), p. 44: J. M. Mohapeloa, *Government by Proxy: ten years of Cape colonial rule, 1871–1881* (Morija, 1971), p. 15; *Leselinyana la Lesotho*, March 1872.

55 Not on a scale comparable with the Zulu social formation, but significant nonetheless. Kimble, 'Origins of commodity production', pp. 38–40.

56 Some contemporary estimates in the nineteenth century: in 1858, Moshoeshoe could muster 10–12 000 mounted warriors with firearms against the Free State; in 1880, Basotho forces consisted of 23 000 well-mounted, armed men; and in 1898, 14 years after re-annexation by the British, out of a population of 220 000, there were 25 000 armed men, of whom 3 000 were mounted and armed with breech-loading rifles. *Ibid.*, p. 36. In 1880, according to the Commandant-General of the Cape forces, many Basotho were armed with 'better weapons' than the Snider rifles and carbines in possession of the Colonial forces, 'whom he thus advised should be given the newest Martini-Henry guns' (Clarke to Sprigg, 22 Oct. 1880, *BPP*, C.2755, 280).

57 For examples of struggle between Koena royals and the Cape administration over the right to hold *matsema*, see Mohapeloa, *Government by Proxy*, p. 15.

58 Tsekelo Moshesh to Griffith, 30 Aug. 1873.

59 Major Bell, quoted in G. Tylden, *The Rise of the Basuto* (Cape Town, 1950), p. 122.

60 CAR 1873, *AAVP*, G.27–1874, 23, 34–6; Griffith to Secretary for Native Affairs, 4 April 1873, Letter Book S91121, Maseru Archives; Austen, CAR 1880, *AAVP*, G.20–1881, 13–14.

61 Government *pitso*, 4 Oct. 1875, *AAVP*, G.16–1876, 11–15.

62 Message from Ratsiu, encl. in Griffith to HC, 18 Aug. 1871, in G. M. Theal, *Basutoland Records*, vol. 6 (unpublished).

63 See, for example, the account in Hadley, *Dr Henry Taylor*, p. 44.

64 *The Friend*, 18 Oct. 1877.

65 For an interpretation of the Gun War, see R. Ajulu, 'The Gun War in Basutoland, 1880–1: some aspects of the destruction of the natural economy and the origins of articulation', unpublished B.A. dissertation, National University of Lesotho, 1979.

66 Kimble, 'Origins of commodity production', ch. 3.

67 *Mephato*: system of age groups, closely associated with *lebollo*, circumcision school; *bohali*: marriage, also refers to cattle transferred between male kin of bride and groom.

68 For an interesting account of aspects of this process among the Mpondo, see W. Beinart, 'Production, labour migration and the chieftaincy, *c.* 1860–1930', Ph.D. thesis, University of London, 1979.

69 Barrett, CAR 1883, *AAVP*, G.3–1884, 96; 'Losses by loyals in the Thaba Bosiu district during the Gun war', *AAVP*, G.47–1882, 115–22; F. W. Chesson, *The Basuto War* (London, 1881), p. 16. This had been hoped for by the administration. CAR 1877, *AAVP* G.17–1878.

70 Rolland, CAR 1875, *AAVP*, G.16–1878, 9.

71 Austen, at government *pitso*, 4 Oct. 1875, *ibid.*, 11.

72 Government *pitso*, 16 and 17 Oct. 1879, *AAVP*, G.13–1880, 46–74; 54. There is a hint in these proceedings that the chiefs used to pay colonial tax for their poorer subjects, but were no longer doing so by the end of the decade.

73 Extracts from minutes of meeting held at Thaba Bosiu by Letsie, 3 July 1880, Maseru Archives.

74 Government *pitso*, 11 March 1886, *BPP*, C.4838, 13–14.

75 Evidence by Lagden, 30 July 1903, Transvaal Labour Commission, p. 134.

76 Evidence by Dyke, 21 July 1903, *ibid.*, pp. 4, 8.

77 There is no simple correlation between landlessness, absence of stock and incidence of labour migration. In conditions where agricultural commodity production depends on acquisition of substantial cash inputs for productive investment, it may well be that labour migration and viable agricultural production are vitally connected. See C. Murray, *Families Divided: the impact of migrant labour in Lesotho* (Cambridge, 1981), for an argument to this effect for Lesotho *c.* 1960–75. However, I would be reluctant to read this analysis back into the 1870s and 1880s when conditions of capitalist penetration were utterly different. Precisely what the relationship between labour migration and agricultural commodity production was in the critical years 1890–1930 forms the subject of my current research.

78 Wilson, *Migrant Labour in South Africa* (Johannesburg, 1972), p. 1.

79 Thus, for instance, Wolpe identifies and explains substantial differences between apartheid and segregation by reference to the changing relations between capitalist and non-capitalist modes of production. H. Wolpe, 'Capitalism and cheap labour-power in South Africa: from segregation to apartheid', *Economy and society* I, 4 (1972), 425–56.

CHAPTER FIVE

Kinship, ideology and the nature of pre-colonial labour migration

Labour migration from the Delagoa Bay hinterland to South Africa, up to 1895

Patrick Harries

I

The function of migrant labour in the development of capitalism in southern Africa has long intrigued researchers. Within the Marxist paradigm, Wolpe and Legassick have examined the low cost of migrant labour, and linked capital's need to exploit this form of labour and thus reduce labour costs, to the transition from the policy of segregation and reserves to that of apartheid and Bantustans.[1] Whereas the analyses of Wolpe and Legassick were restricted to the period following the 1913 Land Act, however, numerous researchers have pushed their analysis back to seek the *origins* of migrant labour in the minimisation of labour costs by mining capitalists.[2] The latter, it is argued, were able to secure a supply of cheap labour through the maintenance of labour reserves where agricultural production acted as a supplement to below-subsistence wages. This supplement ensured the reproduction of the labour force by 'subsidising' low wages and providing for the migrant in old age. The reasons then for both the origin and perpetuation of migrant labour are to be found in capital's need for cheap labour. The state, operating in the interests of capital, enforced and institutionalised a migratory form of labour which ensured the extraction of surplus value from both the migrant worker and his family.

The static nature of this analysis, however, raises a number of problems. In areas free to European control, such as Moçambique before 1895, the colonial state was unable to force workers onto the market. Nor did it wish to institutionalise migrant labour because of its cheapness, for migrant, as opposed to stabilised, labour was not cheap in the nineteenth century. That the importation of labour from economically depressed areas constituted an important mechanism for undercutting local wage levels, and consequently reducing labour costs, is not contested. What is questioned is that the return of such labour to its area of origin after a specified period was a conscious element in the early policy evolved by employers to minimise their labour costs.

During the nineteenth century, the major threat to capitalist control of the wage structure lay in the competition among employers for scarce labour, and attempts to reduce its costs were directed at creating centralised recruiting organisations. These organisations were designed to prevent wage fluctuations through the creation of a regular supply of labour and by ending employer competition for workers, in the areas of both recruitment and employment.[3] These objectives were achieved on the Rand only in the twentieth century with the institution of the maximum average wage system.

Before effective colonial rule throughout the region and the creation of any monopsonistic organisation of recruiting and wage determination, migrant labour proved expensive by European standards. In the nineteenth century, basic African wages on the Rand and at Kimberley compared favourably with the wages paid to agricultural workers in Britain and exceeded those of Irish workers by up to 100 per cent.[4] Informal activities such as brewing, male prostitution and the investment of wages in goods which were sold for a profit as luxuries in the home area further increased the migrants' wages. For Moçambican workers, sterling wages paid in gold were worth up to 30 per cent more in Moçambique when exchanged against the artificially inflated *real*. The super-exploitation of migrant labour was nothing new to nineteenth-century capitalism. The realisation of surplus value through the exploitation of European non-capitalist peripheries was an integral part of nineteenth-century primitive accumulation. In the industrial areas of nineteenth-century Europe, capitalists did not baulk at refusing to pay pensions to workers. Nor did they fail to exploit women and children directly.[5] By international standards, relatively, the wages of nineteenth-century migrant workers employed in the industrial areas of South Africa were not low.

Added to what capitalists considered a high wage, the employment of migrant labour called for recurrent recruiting costs, capitation fees and travel costs, as well as heavy losses through desertion and the theft of gold amalgam and diamonds, whose sale in areas outside British or Transvaal jurisdiction it was impossible to prevent.[6] Generally, short-term migrants did not acquire the skills needed to cut sugar-cane or work underground. Employers were not concerned with restricting periods of service, and where opposition to the permanent settlement of the labour force was expressed, this came from political authorities mindful of the threat posed by a 'foreign', black proletariat.[7] During the nineteenth century much of the labour was supplied by politically independent chiefdoms which, as long as they remained free of colonial controls, could restrict recruiting monopsonies and frustrate attempts to lower wages.

Without effective recruiting organisation and laws controlling the entry and movement of labour on the market, workers could not be compelled to return home. Nor was this a pressing problem: pass laws in Natal and on the Rand aimed at reducing desertion and competition for 'deserters' between employers rather than at curtailing periods of employment.[8] Conditions in the compounds of the Rand and Kimberley presented a real but not overriding reason for a worker to return to his kin, for labour was continually lured onto the non-contracted labour market. To escape the restrictions placed on foreign Africans, bilingual Moçambicans settled under Shangaan chiefs in the Transvaal and Nguni chiefs on the farms and reserves of Natal; in the Cape they joined the ranks of the 'Mosbieker' community. On the farms and plantations, climatic factors, rather than poor working conditions or an employer's wish to exploit cheap 'bachelor' labour, determined the length of the work period.

An alternative approach to the origins of the migratory form of labour may be found in the factors which conditioned the worker's decision to return home after service in South Africa's labour market.

These factors will be examined with reference to labour migration from the Delagoa Bay hinterland of southern Moçambique to South Africa before the destruction of the independent chiefdoms and the final installation of Portuguese colonial rule in 1895–97. During much of this period Portuguese control hardly extended beyond the trading entrepôt of Lourenço Marques, and the colonial state thus had little influence on the pattern of labour migration. Moçambican workers were of particular importance to the South African economy because they were willing to spend longer periods under one employer than other workers. They performed tasks that other workers were able to avoid, such as cutting cane or working underground, and they came on to the market in large numbers. Starting in the 1850s, the movement of labour from southern Moçambique had reached a few thousand every year by the 1860s. By 1879 there were up to 12 000 Moçambicans working in various areas of South Africa; and by 1897, some 60 000 Moçambicans were employed on the Rand alone.[9]

In looking at the origins of the migratory form of labour, it is not the purpose of this essay to examine its material causes. These were probably related to the decline of the local economy caused by the shooting out of game, a restructuring of trade opportunities and the decline of cattle-herding and agriculture in response to capitalist penetration. These problems were exacerbated by the effects of ecological upsets and intermittent warfare which closed, for many, any employment independent of the labour market.[10] The objects of this essay are threefold: firstly, by concentrating on the rural dimension, to offer an alternative to the analysis that gives to the South African state a determining role in the origins of the migratory form of labour; secondly, to show that an understanding of the nature of migrant labour as an institution demands its periodisation, for in its early phases, independent chiefs and elders were able to protect the migrants from the super-exploitation that was to characterise later phases. Concomitantly, the chiefs were able to benefit from migrant labour and, despite its disruptive potential, were thus able to entrench their dominance in the labour supplying rural areas. The third object of this essay is to examine the effect that 'extra-economic' forces had in creating the conditions needed to reproduce a migratory flow. Foremost amongst these was kinship, which was essential to production and crucial in its transformation.

II

In the hinterland of Delagoa Bay in the nineteenth century, kinship structured the social relations of production. Although kinship implied a blood relationship, ties of consanguinity were often fictive in that they did not constitute a biological relationship but rather expressed a social relationship linking members of the same productive unit. Thus real or fictive kinship links generally determined the composition of the productive unit, whether it was the homestead, the lineage, a number of lineages or the clan. Membership of the kinship group determined a man's rights to his means of production and established his position in the redistributive economy. At the political and judicial level, it structured the nature of material and political inheritance and defined the structure of the chiefdom as the political expression of the clan. Kinship defined crime as an offence committed against the kin group; it legitimated the positions of chiefs, sub-chiefs and headmen and, importantly for this essay, allowed them to extract taxes and fines. At the ideological level, kinship determined social avoidances and deference, and defined prospective marriage partners.

Both the politico-judicial and ideological levels influenced kinship at the economic level. Thus inheritance increased a man's access to land, cattle and women, and this gave him the means to attract foreigners as dependants who would be incorporated into the kin group. Similarly, respect for the elders was founded on their control of women and women's productive and reproductive capacities, and of seeds, tools, knowledge and access to land and the ancestors. Respect, as ideology, reinforced the position of the elders in the production process. Thus kinship and kinship ideology played a major role in determining the form of production in the nineteenth-century Delagoa Bay hinterland. As the nature of production changed in response to capitalist penetration and especially migrant labour, so too did the ideological and political factors which structured and conditioned the nature of the production process.

The power base of the chiefs was not confined to the senior lineage and appointed sub-chiefs, but extended to, and depended upon, the support of the *numzane*, or homestead head. These homestead heads were more than merely married men, for they controlled the homestead as a productive unit and often counted married sons and married dependants amongst their homestead's members. Junod referred to them as 'gentlemen' and 'owners of cattle' who ranked 'almost as petty chiefs'. Elsewhere, they were described as 'headmen of the villages, the important men of the country'.[11] *Numzane* came together at national festivals, served in the same age-regiments and on the same councils. A strong relationship existed between the chiefs and the *numzane* as the latter supplied the brideprice for the chief's offical wife. The council of elders, drawn from the *numzane*, confirmed the legality of the chief's position and could overrule and, in extreme cases, even depose the chief.[12] The *numzane* of junior lineages could look to their lineage heads or imposed sub-chiefs to lead them into seceding from the clan if displeased with the rule of the chief. As owners of cattle, it was also relatively easy for the *numzane* to secede with the members of their homesteads and transfer their allegiance to another chief.

The *numzane*'s support for the chiefs was ensured in several ways. The large numbers of wives whom chiefs generally married gave them access to the more powerful *numzane* as affines; concomitantly it was only the wealthy *numzane* who were able to marry a chief's sisters or daughters, due to their high brideprices.[13] Because of their relationship with the chiefs, the *numzane* could benefit from the chiefs' economic control — from the farming out of cattle to the blessing of their first-fruit potions to the redistribution of taxes.[14] But it was the common role of the chiefs and *numzane*, within the production process, that linked them as a group. They organised production through their control of labour, by mediating with other elders over production strategies and distribution, through their decisions about when to plant and harvest and which new areas to cultivate, and through their intercession with the ancestors. It was their common relationship to the means of production, through their control of access to wives, land and tools, however, that determined their dominance.

The quality and amount of land that a young man received was dependent upon the generosity of the *numzane*, as was his access to the iron tools with which to work, and the cattle with which to fertilise, his lands. Yet in a society with a low level of technological development, land and capital goods were generally less important as factors of production than labour. Consequently a man's productive capacity was largely dependent on his ability to attract labour to cultivate his soil and look after his cattle, to increase his military strength and to make him certain payments in labour and in kind. In this way a wealthy man aspired to build a circular homestead consisting of up to thirty huts and more than a hundred dependants.[15] However, the attraction of followers depended on a man's ability to marry. This was because the controls and restrictions of the kinship system precluded the existence of an open wage-labour market. A bride provided a man with children who increased the size of his homestead in terms of access to labour and in terms of rights to cultivable land and pasture. Thus marriage played a central role in the expansion of the homestead where, because of the patrilocality of marriage, the families of male children enlarged and enhanced the father's ability to segment and establish his own settlement. Female children secured the dependence of males on the homestead *numzane*, as it was their brideprice that allowed male dependants to marry. Thus wives were a synonym for wealth, as both the product of their labour and of their fertility gave their husbands access to the means of production.[16]

With the capitalist penetration of the nineteenth century it was the labour of children and dependants, and especially of wives, which determined the reproduction of the social formation. It was their labour that released males from domestic production and allowed them to take part in long-distance trade and hunting. As only males took part in these activities, they monopolised the luxury goods from Lourenço Marques, and women's access to these goods was largely dependent upon their performing services for men. Thus, it was men's ability to exploit female labour that allowed them to realise a profit from hunting and trading. That chiefs and *numzane* could tax trade and distribute the proceeds also proved an important element in their attracting followers.

From the early eighteenth century, cattle as *lobola* (bridewealth) were supplemented, and in hard times even replaced, by other goods such as Venda hoes, bronze and brass neck- and arm-rings, goats and specially imported beads. In the middle of the nineteenth century, cattle were the major medium of *lobola*, and for a marriage to be sanctioned they had to be transferred by the family of the bridegroom to that of the bride. However, because the area was cut off from other sources of cattle by a virulent tsetse belt, access to cattle was restricted; they could be acquired only through inheritance, as *lobola*, by raiding or on loan. Inheritance was adelphic and consequently cattle passed from a father to his younger brothers to his eldest sons. This meant that when men were of marriageable age, they had little chance of inheriting cattle and generally remained dependent on their father or father's brother for bridewealth. The monopoly that these men exercised over cattle bridewealth and the existence of the levirate, by which a man inherited his deceased brothers' widows, enabled a *numzane* to contract several marriages and commensurately increase the productive capacity and size of his following. They were obliged to distribute part of their cattle inheritance only insofar as it consolidated the dependence of younger siblings, sons and male dependents upon them for wives. It was this dependence, and the access to the means of production that it determined, that maintained the cohesion of the homestead, the economic basis of the *numzane*'s political power. The cattle monopoly held by the *numzane* was entrenched by the kinship system which regarded as incest unions between descendants of the same grandparents and favoured marriages contracted between clan members.[17] Thus bridewealth circulated widely amongst the *numzane* and the social unions contracted in this way entrenched the political unity of the clan-chiefdom.

The cadets or *nandja*,[18] because of their restricted access to cattle bridewealth, were dependent on the cattle monopoly of the *numzane* for their brideprices. But marriage did not mean automatic accession to the rank of *numzane*; a bridegroom remained dependent on his creditors until either he inherited a brideprice or a daughter reached marriageable age and her *lobola* could be used to cancel her father's debt. It was the transfer of the *lobola* in its entirety which legalised the man's right to the children of his wife. Thus, father right lay with the *lobola*, and if the wife's kin were to demand the entire brideprice and the husband was unable to pay, they had a legal right to reclaim their daughter and all the children of the marriage.[19] In this way, a man was dependent on his kin not only for the brideprice needed to procure a wife but also for the securing of his rights to his children.

As long as part of a man's brideprice remained outstanding, he was a legal minor, a *de facto* 'cadet', dependent on the goodwill of the *numzane*. This explains the extreme respect for elders and the hierarchical relationship between elder and younger brothers, for *lobola* patrimony passed through the elder brother, upon whom the younger was thus dependent for his *lobola*.[20] The *numzane* were prepared to supply a cadet's *lobola*, as brides increased the power and size of the family and widened social alliances.[21] In turn, the expectation of receiving a brideprice, and the nature of its partial payment, secured the adherence of the cadet to the homestead.

The cadets' dependence upon the chiefs and *numzane* was also structured by the cosmology of a society which engendered the belief that the chiefs and *numzane* had access to the supernatural forces controlling the daily existence and prosperity of the people. As the chiefs and *numzane* were the direct descendants of the most powerful ancestors and could intercede with them, they were thought able to control rainfall, disease and wars.[22]

The real and believed ability of the elders to control daily existence by controlling access to the means of production acted as a mechanism of social control and determined the nature of surplus extraction. Because of the dependence of the cadets upon the chiefs and *numzane*, the latter could extort prestations from the cadets in the form of agricultural produce and joints of game or stock. Hunting taxes, such as certain skins and the grounded tusk of an elephant, were levied, as were fishing, trade and transport taxes. Chiefs used the cadets' labour to till their fields, build and repair their huts and to clean public squares and roads. Cadet labour was also used in porterage and hunting expeditions organised by the chiefs, and in looking after farmed-out cattle and poultry.[23] At least seven words were used by Tsonga speakers to describe the various forms of tax and tribute embodied in these prestations. The accumulated tribute was eventually distributed to followers, and the prestige and power of the chiefs and *numzane* was measured in terms of the generosity of these 'benefices'. Chiefs and *numzane* also acted as magistrates, which allowed them part of any fine. As co-ordinators of most phases of the production process, they gave cadets access to wives, land, sufficient labour, tools, fertiliser and the divine intercession needed to ensure a successful harvest.

The relations between the dominant chiefs and *numzane* and the subordinate cadets were thus a complex interaction of patriarchal and filial bonds and mutual obligations and were very different from the simple wage relationship linking capitalist and worker. It was nonetheless a relationship of exploitation in the technical sense that wives, although they were passed down to the cadets, did not constitute part of the *numzane's* benefices. Until their husbands had fully honoured their brideprice debts, wives remained under the control of the *numzane* and the circulation of their brideprices cemented the social ties linking the *numzane* as a collectivity. The prestations given by the cadets were the product of their labour, whereas the benefices passed down by the *numzane* were the product of their social and political dominance. This dominance was entrenched by the *numzane's* ability to determine the size of the prestations and by the dependence of the cadets, as direct producers, upon the *numzane* not only for access to the means of production but even for the redistribution of the product of their labour. The transfer of prestation and benefices, structured by the kinship system, ensured the reproduction of the relations of dominance and subordination that conditioned the nature of exploitation. The dominance of the chiefs and *numzane* was symbolised in various ways, such as the wearing of headrings and expensive skins, the distribution of the joints of a slaughtered beast and the arrangements of households within the homestead.[24] Junod described a hierarchy in which the chief was

> all powerful . . . an autocrat with power over life and death. In every village the headman possesses similar power over his subjects and the elder brother reigns as a despot over the younger. . . . From the top to the bottom of the social ladder the strong dominate the weak and combine, in a powerful way, to assure the submission of the inferior.[25]

A cadet excluded from his father's patrimony and dissatisfied with his position could always leave the homestead. He would then generally move to his mother's brother (*malume*), as his closest blood relation with property outside of his father's family, or *kondza* to a new chief and, in return for the customary prestations, be assured of the chief's benefices. But a sister's son had no claim on the patrimony of the *malume* and the nature of the *kondza* relationship was determined by the size and importance of the migrant's following; a single cadet would probably be given marginal land and, in terms of inheritance, would be beneath the youngest son of the most junior wife.[26] Thus, in the Delagoa Bay hinterland segmentation was a measure of desperation rather than a mechanism resolving conflict.

This indicates that although kinship laws can be traced to, and were rooted in, the production process, they also structured the reproduction of the relations of exploitation. But underlying the moral inducements to conform that were embodied in kinship ideology lay the threat of force. Nonconformists could be smelt-out for witchcraft or be expelled from the homestead and the kin group. This was a drastic course of action as the *numzane* lost a dependant and the wrongdoer lost his rights to the means of subsistence. In the nineteenth century this often meant that he would be sold into slavery or be forcibly conscripted into the Portuguese army.[27]

Consciousness of exploitation is discernible in folk stories and songs which celebrate the triumph of the young and oppressed over the oppressor.[28] But this consciousness was never transformed into action, for adelphic inheritance ensured that, even though at an advanced age, many cadets became *numzane* while all cadets were separated from women by the sexual division of labour. Even within the homestead, married women were separated from unmarried women, childless women from mothers and junior wives from senior wives; moreover, married women were of diverse origin due to the patrilocality of marriage. Family, lineage and clan ties further prevented the formation of a common class consciousness. Thus in contrast to the elders, the exploited groups had little unity or solidarity.

In the second half of the century, migrant labour markedly changed the level of exploitation in the Delagoa Bay hinterland. It also offered the cadets new strategies for throwing off the dominance of the chiefs and *numzane*.

III

In the early 1860s, a major drought affecting many parts of southern Africa descended on southern Moçambique and was soon followed by a severe lungsickness epidemic. This ecological disaster coincided with the ravages of the Gaza civil war and resulted in a major loss of cattle and a sharp decline in their use as bridewealth south of the Limpopo.[29] Iron hoes imported from Vendaland had been used earlier as a bridewealth supplement and now rapidly replaced cattle.[30] Like cattle, the circulation of these hoes was controlled by the chiefs and *numzane*. Hoes were exchanged for trade goods brought from Delagoa Bay which were, in turn, procured through the exchange of hunting produce such as elephant and hippopotamus ivory, rhinoceros horns and buck-skins. As the chiefs and *numzane* were the only people able to mobilise large hunting-parties, and because they extracted taxes which amounted to more than half the hunted produce, they had a virtual monopoly over marketable products of the hunt. Thus they largely controlled the trade in hoes with Vendaland and consequently monpolised the circulation of bridewealth. These Beja hoes[31] were not used as agricultural implements, as they provided the future brideprice for sons and acted as security for married daughters.[32] As they were largely restricted to the sphere of bridewealth circulation, their socially disruptive potential as capital goods was neutralised.

After the establishment of a French vegetable-oil company at Lourenço Marques in 1869, the importation of industrially-made hoes soared; from 1869 to 1876, almost one million hoes were imported through the trading settlement. This new source of hoes threatened the elders' monopoly of bridewealth, because migrants returning from Natal were able to purchase industrially made hoes around Delagoa Bay at 2s each. With increasing numbers of hoes entering the area, fathers were faced with an effective devaluation of their daughters' worth and a disintegration of the special nature of bridewealth exchange. This was countered by raising brideprices from 10 hoes to more than 100, a move that had the effect of absorbing most imported hoes into the prestige sphere of circulation. Although this allowed the *numzane* to retain their monopoly of bridewealth, in the long term it was an impossible situation as, apart from the difficulties involved in transporting a brideprice weighing several hundred pounds, the ability of young men to purchase hoes rose in proportion to their increasing ability to find wage labour in South Africa.

By the late 1870s, several thousand Moçambicans were employed on the labour markets of South Africa.[33] These men returned to the Delagoa Bay area with large amounts of sterling specie; as early as 1877 the Governor of Lourenço Marques reported that the area was already dependent on money for its imports while the other two major means of acquiring imports, ivory and skins, were in rapid decline.[34] The following year, he estimated that over £33 000 in sterling had circulated and left Lourenço Marques, and traders in the area confirmed the increasing monetisation of the economy.[35] From the mid-1870s, sterling specie rapidly replaced hoes as the medium of bridewealth and the ability of the *numzane* to monopolise bridewealth became increasingly dependent on their control of sterling.[36]

The introduction of a sterling brideprice, which allowed the cadets to circumvent the elders' monopoly of bridewealth, was constantly opposed by the chiefs and *numzane*.[37] They wanted to return to cattle, as cattle produced offspring and were not 'eaten up' in the buying of consumer goods which caused much inter-generational bitterness as it meant the loss of the brideprice normally used to provide the eldest son with a wife. There was, however, little alternative to sterling, as cattle diseases and tsetse continued to plague the area; as late as 1890, the Ronga chiefdoms were reported to be practically without cattle.[38] In order to control the circulation of specie bridewealth, the *numzane* had to control the major part of the 'liquid capital' flowing into the area in the form of migrants' wages. This they were largely able to achieve because of their ability to tax the increasingly monetised economy and because of the nature of bridewealth circulation.

In order to prevent the 'devaluation' of brides and the breakdown of the special-purpose nature of bridewealth exchange, brideprices were continually raised above the level of the returning migrants' wages. Effectively, this meant that the dependence of the cadets on the *numzane* for their brideprices was retained. During the reign of chief Zihlala (1867–83), the Mpfumo brideprice was fixed at £8, but even during his reign this was pushed up to £10 10s by the elders.[39] Chief Maphunga of Nondwane (*ca*. 1860–90) tried to limit to £15 10s the claims of elders to brideprices of £20 and £30. Brideprices continued to rise, and by the 1890s they stood at £15 to £20; and in the Lourenço Marques area, where there was a larger circulation of liquid sterling, they could reach as high as £30.[40]

Another major source of sterling for the *numzane* lay in the direct extortion of a part of the workers' wages on their return from South Africa. These 'labour taxes' were levied by the chiefs and then distributed to the *numzane* or were levied individually by the *numzane*. This form of taxation was recognised in the area as a common practice and generally amounted to £1 to the chief and 2s to the *numzane*.[41] The taxes differed according to the chiefdom and the chief. Thus the Mabudu chief Nozingili demanded an unspecified amount of 'specie', while his wife, the queen regent who succeeded him, levied a tax of £1 on all returning migrants. Her son Ngwanase, who used the labour of his regiments to plant and weed his fields, levied a tax of £5 to £10 on all those males who avoided military service by migrating to South Africa.[42] Added to this source of sterling income, by the late 1880s, the chiefs and *numzane* were able to levy various fines and prestations, previously paid in kind, in sterling specie. They were also able to accumulate sterling by allowing labour recruiters to operate in their areas and by demanding presents and capitation fees for each of their recruited subjects.[43] It was universally recognised that recruiters were unable to operate without the co-operation of the chiefs.[44] A further source of cash income came from the host of taxes levied on Banyan merchants who themselves were drawn by the migrants' sterling wages. With the money thus accumulated, the chiefs and *numzane* perpetuated their control of the bridewealth system and maintained their dominance.

Chiefs and *numzane* were not interested in the accumulation of sterling simply as a source of material wealth but rather as a means of social control. Juniors could be wealthier than elders in material terms, but as long as the elders monopolised access to wives, they were able to dominate and exploit the juniors.[45] This meant that, despite the juniors' participation in migrant labour and thus access to an independent source of bridewealth, they remained dependent on, and open to, continued exploitation by the chiefs and *numzane*.

Instead of leading to the development of the productive forces and bringing about change in the structure of the social formation, migrant labour tended to act as a brake on development, for, while the export of labour depleted the productive forces, migrants' wages were invested in bridewealth and in consumer goods like cloth and liquor. A major part of the migrants' wages was transformed through marriage into sterling which circulated unproductively between the *numzane*. Because of the special-purpose value of sterling as a bridewealth medium, when wages were 'converted' into bridewealth, they took on a social rather than a market value. As bridewealth was kept in trust in order to provide future generations with the means of acquiring wives, it could not be invested or 'eaten' in the expansion of agricultural production. Sterling was thus encapsulated within the system of bridewealth circulation and was seldom exchanged, except in emergency conditions, for common commodities such as food. In some cases, its 'leakage' from one sphere of exchange to another was prohibited, although some leakage was inevitable when sterling bridewealth was exchanged for commodities which were redistributed for primarily social and political purposes. With the constant raising of brideprices and the conversion of most sterling into a social value isolated from market forces, most of the developmental potential embodied in migrants' wages was neutralised within the sphere of circulating specie bridewealth.[46]

Nevertheless, part of the migrants' wages was spent on consumer goods and, increasingly by the end of the century, on food. As people became more reliant on wage-incomes, agricultural production declined drastically, to the extent that by the end of the 1880s Lourenço Marques, which had formerly been an exporter of food, had become an importer of subsistence foods such as maize.[47] Thus migrant labour tended to reproduce and perpetuate itself without meaningfully challenging the existing social relations.

The shift in the bridewealth medium from cattle to hoes and later to sterling, deepened male involvement in the market economy and increased their dependence on external trade and later on migrant labour. This increased the exploitation of cadets in the society as it was the product of their labour power which was exchanged for the hoes and sterling needed to maintain the elders' monopoly of bridewealth. By the late 1880s, migrant workers in Moçambique suffered a double exploitation through the extortion of surplus value by their employers and through the extraction, by the chiefs and *numzane*, of bridewealth and prestations that amounted to the major part of the migrants' repatriated wages.

IV

The social conflict caused by the increased exploitation of the cadets was manifested in several ways. A general decline in cadet respect for their elders was noticed, as was their refusal to perform various 'traditional' labour tasks for the chiefs and *numzane*.[48] By the 1890s there was a definite trend for young men to oppose their elders politically; one contemporary observer stated that during the Luso–Gaza war, the 'uncles' sided with the Portuguese 'in order to get back the power that they had formerly exercised and put aside their nephews'.[49] Other signs of the general social upheavel of the period were the rise in 'witchcraft', spirit possession and alcoholism.[50] For many cadets, their only response to the decline in local economic opportunities and their increased exploitation was to emigrate permanently to the South African labour market.

The permanent emigration of families, which characterised Mabudu migration in the 1850s,[51] was stopped by the 1860s because of official disapproval in Natal, where these people were considered 'drifters' with no 'tribal controls' and by Zulu opposition, as Cetshwayo complained that Mabudu emigration had caused a drop in tribute to Zululand.[52] It also seems likely that the Mabudu elders disapproved of the permanent emigration of their dependants, which the emigration of families encouraged. From the 1860s the movement of labour consisted of single males in their teens and twenties. According to both oral and documentary evidence, many of these men never returned to Moçambique as, after breaking contract to get onto the open labour market, it was easy for the bilingual Mabudu to integrate with the Natal Zulu population and 'disappear'.[53] The same process took place on the Rand, where it was possible to slip onto the non-contracted labour market or settle among the Tsonga-speakers of the north-eastern Transvaal. Several thousand Moçambican workers emigrated permanently to the western Cape, several hundred of whom settled on the Namaqualand copper mines.

Although this emigration of Moçambicans contributed to the growth of South Africa's black proletariat, it depleted the following of the chiefs and elders in Moçambique. In the Mabudu area, permanent emigration to Natal reached such large proportions in the 1880s that the queen regent of Mabudu sent a message to the Natal governor stating that although she was

> very much indebted to the Natal Government for the licence granted to her subjects to enter, pass through or work in Natal without interference or being bound for three years . . . however . . . at the same time she would be very pleased to know that the said government made it compulsory for her subjects to return home after two or three years' service in Natal as many of them forsake their homes, wives and children and never return.[54]

Population and hut-tax returns, as well as travellers' reports, all indicate that at any given time during the late 1880s and 1890s, over half the economically active male population of most areas of the Delagoa Bay hinterland was working in South Africa. Statistics from the Witwatersrand indicate that 30 to 40 per cent of Moçambican migrants settled permanently in South Africa, which meant that there was a permanent emigration of 15 to 20 per cent of the male population with a temporary loss of a further 30 to 35 per cent working as oscillating migrants.[55] The loss of dependants through emigration was worsened by a high mortaility rate of up to 8 per cent in the wage labour areas,[56] apart from those who returned to die from phthisis and infectious tuberculosis. When added to a 2 to 3 per cent loss on the routes leading to and from the labour centres, this meant that in some areas migrant labour resulted in a permanent loss of between 25 and 30 per cent of the male population. The absence of such a large number of males, when combined with the rapid spread of venereal diseases, causing female infertility, resulted in a fall in the overall birthrate.[57] This drop in the population of the area was bitterly decried by the chiefs and *numzane*[58] in much the same way as the 'depopulation' thesis was later described by the Portuguese in their negotiations over labour with the Transvaal and South African governments.[59] The loss of dependants was a serious blow to the chiefs and *numzane* because the cadets, who constituted the vast majority of the migrant labour force, were an important element in the domestic economy. The cadets were not only important in protein-accumulating activities like hunting, fishing and cattle-keeping, but also in various phases of agricultural production.[60] Yet because of the nature of the routes to the plantations of Natal and mines of the highveld, men could not co-ordinate their migratory patterns with the agricultural seasons.[61] This loss of male labour was largely responsible for the decline in agricultural production which, as clearly mentioned, accompanied migrant labour.[62]

A drop in agricultural and other forms of production also entailed a decline in the overall revenue accruing to the chiefs and *numzane*, which adversely affected their ability to centralise goods and attract followers through their redistribution. This in turn diminished the productive potential of the homestead, lowered its defensive and offensive capabilities and threatened the security of the *numzane* in old age. The effect of this loss of male labour on existing social relations should be seen in conjunction with the general loss of revenue caused by shrinking hunting and trading frontiers and by the threat to the *numzane*'s control of access to the means of production that was posed by alternative sources of bridewealth. By securing a part of the migrant's wage on his return home, the chiefs and *numzane* were largely able to maintain both their control of bridewealth circulation and their dominant position in the redistributive economy. In short, the reproduction of the relations of dominance and subordination was dependent on a form of labour movement that ensured the repatriation of the worker and of his wage. But the control by chiefs and *numzane* of the egress and ingress of Delagoa Bay labour was severely restricted by the nature of its movement.

Nineteenth-century 'migrant' labour was far more complex than the push-and-pull migration suggested by some writers for twentieth-century

South Africa. In-migration – movement within the chiefdom and its immediate surroundings – preceded, accompanied and facilitated out-migration, which often took the shape of a stage-by-stage movement onto the labour market. During these various moves it was easy for the worker to loosen his ties with his area of origin. A group of men might move to the railway on the Nkomati where wages were 12s a week, and then move on to Barberton because wages there were 18s a week.[63] It was common for men to use Barberton as a halfway house where money would be earned to complete the journey to the Rand. The same process took place in Natal, where many Moçambicans took advantage of various immigration schemes merely in order to earn enough money to get to the well-paid labour markets of Kimberley and the Cape railways and harbours.[64] Even in the well-paid areas, the men moved from one farm or mine to another so as to benefit from better pay and living conditions, while the next stage was to move on to the non-contracted labour market, which was tantamount to 'disappearing' in the eyes of the plantation or mine owners.

There is evidence to suggest that the chiefs had a good deal of control over Moçambican communities scattered over large parts of South Africa and that they were able to condition, to some extent, the willingness of their dependants to return home. The Moçambicans formed recognised communities in the major labour centres: they were 'amaTongas' in Natal, 'Mosbiekers' in the western Cape and 'Shangaans' on the diamond fields and the Rand. They tended to gather on certain farms or mines, to which they travelled in groups at specific times of the year and along specific routes. A high degree of contact between the various Moçambican communities is evidenced by their reaction to any foreign threat to their home areas. If war threatened a chiefdom, the chief refused to permit the migration of any male followers of military age[65] and recalled his people working in South Africa. Thus with the approach of the Anglo-Zulu war, there was an exodus of Moçambican labour in Natal; in December 1878 alone, 1 300 Moçambicans returned home by sea and more than 5 000 by land. Mabudu fear of Zibhebhu and their support for the Usuthu faction in the Zulu civil war resulted in the mobilisation of the army in 1882 and 1883 to stop Zibhebhu moving north, and this again caused an efflux of Mabudu labour from Natal. The same control was noticeable on the Rand when, because of the outbreak of the Luso–Gaza war of 1894–95, 150 Moçambicans were reported to have left for home each day in order to join the Gaza army.[66]

Just as the nature of the cadets' prestations changed with migrant labour, so too did the nature of the benefices passed down by the chiefs. The latter were able to protect the interests of the migrants in various ways and consequently to encourage them to maintain contact with their home areas. In a society where the term 'recruiter' is synonymous with 'swindler' and 'perjurer',[67] the chiefs and *numzane* played an important role in controlling the operations of recruiters and colonial government agents. The chiefs and elders ensured that recruiters fulfilled the obligations they contracted with the migrants, and they negotiated the terms of new labour-importing schemes.[68] If a young wife did not return to her parents during her husband's emigration, generally because her *lobola* had already been paid, it was the duty of the chiefs and *numzane* to protect her and her children. This function was termed *basopa*, from the Afrikaans *pasop*, and ensured that the cadet's property was protected during his migration and that his family had enough land and labour to provide itself with food; it also prohibited any infidelity on the part of the wife. The benefits of the redistributive economy encouraged workers to return home, as it provided them with the land and labour needed to subsist outside the wage economy. This acted as an insurance in old age and as a weapon with which to combat low wages and poor conditions on the labour market. Thus when the Chamber of Mines tried to reduce African wages in 1890–91, thousands of Moçambicans were able to withdraw their labour by returning home and in this way were able successfully to force a return to the old wage level. To some extent, the chiefs were also able to maintain high wages by using their homesteads as information-gathering centres from where migrants were directed to the best-paid labour centres in South Africa, and by encouraging competition between the freelance and contracted labour recruiters who worked for competing mining houses.[69]

It has frequently been noticed that people become locked into the world economy as former luxury imports become necessities and that this was an important factor in generating migrant labour. It was not merely human nature, however, that encouraged the importation of goods like cloth and liquor; chiefs and *numzane* often conditioned the adoption of these goods by dressing their wives in imported cloth and by using liquor in feasts, festivals and rituals. As the co-ordinators of agricultural production, the chiefs and *numzane* were probably also responsible for the adoption of maize as a staple and for the increase in cassava production at the end of the nineteenth century. Both crops are extremely rich in carbohydrate and consequently provide an immediate source of energy. This, together with the labour-saving techniques used in growing them, allowed a less disruptive transfer of labour from the domestic economy to South Africa.

Several years before the imposition of Portuguese rule, the cosmology of southern Moçambican society had changed sufficiently to accommodate migrant labour as a normal part of attaining adulthood. For many, migrant labour replaced entry into the age-regiments, and labour recruiters in the 1890s were able to refer to migrant labour as 'a form of initiation'.[70] As early as 1891, a missionary wrote of migrant labour as 'a tour of duty' performed at least once if not several times by all young men in southern Moçambique.[71] After a period of service on the mines, young men were treated with new respect as *gayisa*, those who have returned from the mines and are a source of wealth. Red-coats, smoking-jackets, hats and trousers bought on the mines were the symbols of their new status. Men who remained at home and refused to work on the mines were denigrated as *mumparras*, narrow-minded and ignorant provincials.[72]

A migratory form of labour was encouraged in various other ways. As the birthrate fell in the late nineteenth century, the chiefs dropped the marriage age from the mid-twenties to eleven to twelve years old for girls and twelve to thirteen for boys, and there was a withholding of the premarital sexual favours known as *gangisa*.[73] This meant that young men were pushed into marriage before leaving for the mines, and the sexual gratification and security of family life acted as an important attraction for a worker who might be obliged to return home due to accident, disease or an unwillingness to accept a fall in wage-rates. Younger marriages ensured the continued dependence of the cadets on the *numzane* for a brideprice and probably helped offset the falling birthrate. Prohibitions on sexual intercourse during lactation had been a traditional form of birth control that could last up to two years, but with the growth of migrant labour, this period of abstinence was used to encourage men to go to South Africa during their wives' post-natal periods.

A consequence of the reduction in marriage age was that women played a fuller part in homestead production, and became mothers at a much earlier age. Men's dependence on women to supply the subsistence needs of the family increased proportionately with their involvement in migrant labour, and, in this way, much of the exploitation involved in homestead production was passed on to women. By increasing the burden placed on women in the production process, the *numzane* increased the cadets' dependence on women to supplement their wage labour with the agricultural production needed to reproduce the family. This increased exploitation of women was an important reason conditioning the cadet's decision to return home with the brideprice necessary to complete his debt to the elders. For with migrant labour, the establishment and maintenance of the homestead came to rest almost entirely on its female members, and it was the product of their labour and fertility that gave to the cadets the possibility of entry into the dominant *numzane* grouping.

V

The development of reef mining and especially the opening up of the deep-level mines after 1895 called for enormous supplies of cheap labour and a new rate of exploitation. These the Moçambican chiefs and *numzane* were unable to supply because their political position was dependent on the kinship system, with all its rights and obligations, and on the existing relations of production. They were thus constrained to protect the worker's wage and his domestic means of production. Colonialism was fettered by no such encumbrances, and it was only the colonial state, established after the defeat of the Gaza king Gungunyana in 1895, that was progressively able to free labour from its material possessions – and from the rights and obligations embodied in the social relations of the old order. During the pre-colonial period, the chiefs and *numzane*, through what was in effect an alliance with capital, played an important role in directing the movement of labour to and from the markets in South Africa, and in this way maintained their dominant position in the structure of the society. But only the colonial state was able to use organised violence to propel workers onto the market for, unlike the chiefs and *numzane*, its only responsibility towards the workforce was to ensure the conditions of its physical reproduction. The colonial state was able to use the apparatus of government, army, police, prisons and chiefs working as government agents, together with the threat of forced labour and porterage, military conscription, compulsory cultivation, corporal punishment and imprisonment to coerce the workers onto the market, while at the same time restricting Africans to reserves where their access to a means of production outside of wage labour was strictly limited. It was through the partial preservation of the old lineage mode of production in these *regedorias* that the colonial state was able to compel the African homestead to bear much of the cost involved in the reproduction of the labour force.

The qualitative nature of migrant labour from the Delagoa Bay hinterland changed markedly after the defeat of the independent chiefdoms and the installation of colonialism. The colonial period was marked not so much by the increase in numbers of workers forced onto the market, but rather by their increased exploitation. After the Luso–Gaza wars of 1895 and 1897, real wages fell sharply on the Rand, and it was only after World War II that African wages, in cash terms, rose for the first time above the £3 10s wage level of 1896.[74] While short-term wage reductions may be attributed to factors such as rinderpest, the Anglo-Boer war and the introduction of Chinese labour, the long-term debasing of African real wages must be traced to the formation of successful recruiting monopsonies, the prohibition of collective bargaining and the enforcement of cheap migrant labour. This essay suggests that long-term or secular wage reductions resulted, too, from the destruction of independent chiefdoms and the wage protection they ensured. Pressure from the colonial state also increased the number of migrations undertaken by a worker. Pre-colonial labour migration was performed almost exclusively by men in their teens and twenties,[75] but during the colonial period labour migration was commonly undertaken by men who completed up to fifteen contracts and continued migrating in their thirties and forties.[76] During the twentieth century the control of labour on the Rand increased markedly and this restricted 'traditional' wage supplements through theft, trade and informal activities.

Furthermore, Portugal was prepared to accept the low wages paid to its colonial labour in return for rail, labour and fiscal privileges which largely benefited metropolitan coffers.

However, poorly capitalised Portuguese colonialism needed its own source of cheap labour. Thus under colonialism the basic contradiction in the emigration of labour shifted from satisfying the needs of chiefs and *numzane* to satisfying the divergent interests of Portuguese settler and metropolitan fractions of capital. To overcome this contradition, the Portuguese colonial state enforced a migrant form of labour; a policy that was willingly supported by the South African state, whose mining capitalists were anxious for homestead production to subsidise their below-subsistence industrial wages, and whose administration was increasingly able, after the Anglo-Boer war, to enforce short-term labour contracts.

Notes

Abbreviations

AHU	Arquivo Histórico Ultramarino
BMSAS	*Bulletin de la Mission suisse en Afrique du Sud*
BO	*Boletim Official de Moçambique*
CMAR	*Chamber of Mines Annual Reports*
GG	Governor General
GLM	Governor of Lourenço Marques
IAC	Cape Archives, Immigration Agent files
ICE	*Industrial Commission of Enquiry*
II	Natal Archives, Indian Immigration files
JSAS	*Journal of Southern African Studies*
NA	Natal Archives
PI	Protector of Immigrants
SNA	Natal Archives, Secretary for Native Affairs files
TLC	Transvaal Labour Commission
UNISA	University of South Africa

1 H. Wolpe, 'Capitalism and cheap labour power in South Africa: from segregation to apartheid', *Economy and Society* I, 4 (1972); M. Legassick, 'South Africa: capital accumulation and violence', *Economy and Society* III, 3 (1974).

2 e.g. E. Webster, 'Background to the supply and control of labour in the gold mines', in E. Webster (ed.), *Essays in South African Labour History* (Johannesburg, 1978), pp. 9–12; F. Molteno, 'The historical significance of the Bantustan strategy', *Social Dynamics* III, 2 (1977), 16–18; M. Morris, 'The development of capitalism in South Africa', *Journal of Development Studies* XII, (1976), 285, 288–9; N. Nbcasana, 'The politics of migrant labour', *S. A. Labour Bulletin*, I, 8 (1978), 24. In Moçambique, a similar analysis has been used by Marvin Harris, 'Labour emigration among the Mozambican Tonga: cultural and political factors', *Africa* XXIX, 1 (1959), and A. Rita-Ferreira, *O Movimento Migratorio de Travalhadores entre Moçambique e a Africa*

do Sul (Lisbon, 1963), p. 73. Probably the leading exponent of this view is Claude Meillassoux, 'From reproduction to production: a Marxist approach to economic anthropology', *Economy and Society*, I (1972), 103; 'The social organization of the peasantry', in David Seddon, *Relations of Production* (London, 1978), p. 168; and *Femmes, Greniers et Capitaux* (Paris, 1975), pp. 148, 165–6. See also Samir Amin, *Modern Migrations in Western Africa* (Oxford, 1974), p. 110.

3 Natal Archives (NA), Secretary for Native Affairs (SNA) 1/1/79. Lt-Gov. annotating in Goodliffe to SNA, 7 June 1869; *Natal Govt. Gaz.* XXII, No. 1269, 24 Jan. 1871; Keate to Kimberley, 21 Oct. 1870; SNA 1/1/22, Memo by SNA, 5 Nov. 1872; *Chamber of Mines Annual Reports (CMAR)* 1893, p. 43; *CMAR* 1899, p. 57.

4 Pamela Horn, *Labouring Life in the Victorian Countryside* (London, 1976), pp. 30, 119–23, 126; and especially appendix G; L. M. Cullen, *An Economic History of Ireland* (London, 1972), pp. 137, 151–2, 160; John Clapham, *An Economic History of Modern Britain 1887 to 1914* (Cambridge, 1963), pp. 97–9; W. H. B. Court, *British Economic History 1870–1914* (Cambridge, 1965), p. 286; Ronald Blythe, *Akenfield* (London, 1969), pp. 40, 41.

Irish wages were as low as 1s to 1s 6d per day in 1870, and wages of 10s for a working week of over 72 hours were not uncommon in areas like Oxfordshire and Suffolk in the 1890s; *South African Mining Journal*, 28 Jan. 1893; W. Nelson, *Masbro Advertizer*, 19 May 1877, in *Africana Notes and News* XX, 5 (1973). According to K. Hvidt, *Flight to America* (New York, 1975), p. 126, Danish farmhands in 1870 earned wages of approximately £1 per month. Compare this with a basic average wage of £3 10s on the Rand in 1896 and up to £4 at Kimberley in the 1870s.

5 Rosa Luxemburg, *The Accumulation of Capital* (London, 1961); V. I. Lenin, *The Development of Capitalism in Russia*, Collected Works, vol. 3 (London, 1960). On child and female labour, see F. Engels, *The Condition of the Working Class in England* (London, 1926); K. Marx, *Capital* I, pp. 372–80; Horn, *Labouring Life*, pp. 124, 198–218.

6 Labour costs on the Witwatersrand constituted 29.66 per cent of overall costs as against a probable 31.7 per cent in England: *Industrial Commission of Enquiry* (ICE hereafter) (Johannesburg, 1897), evidence of Seymour, p.149; Fitzpatrick, p.47; Hall, p.447. On the costs involved in migrant labour, see *ICE*, Johns, p.256; Transvaal Labour Commission, Johannesburg, 1906, evidence of Breyner, pp. 27–8; Transvaal Archives, SSA 264 R16015 Grant to SS, 19 Dec. 1893; SSA 329 R1959/96 encl. in Ra607, Sec. Robinson Mines to acting SS, 7 Feb. 1897; SSA 330 R5792/79 in Ra607/96 Sec. Assoc. of Mines to State Pres., 14 April 1879; *CMAR* 1894, p. 27. For the 'augmentation' of African wages through theft, see M. Binford, 'Stalemate': a study in cultural dynamics', Ph.D. thesis, Michigan State University, 1971, p. 87; E. P. Mathers, *The Goldfields Revisited* (Durban, 1887), p. 7; A. Schiel, *Drei und Zwanzig Jahre Sturm und Sonnenschein in Süd Afrika* (Leipzig, 1902), p. 282.

7 NA, SNA 1.1.19 No. 122 draft letter SNA to Goodliffe, Oct. 1869; SNA 1.1.22 Memo by SNA on 'Import and control of native labour', 5.11.1872; Transvaal Archives SSA 264, Ra3309/95 encl. R1222/93, SS to ZAR Consul, Moz. 6 Nov., 1890. R16015 Grant to SS 19 Dec. 1893, 'The fixing of service at only six months will very much decrease the value of kaffir labour, because experienced workers are more valuable than raw kaffirs'; *ICE*, p. 183, evidence of Brakham; p. 43, Way;

p. 219, evidence of Jennings; all of whom called for the permanent settlement of labour on the Rand.

8 Transvaal Archives, SS 3294 Ballott to Grant encl. in Ballott to Superintendent of Natives, 2 Nov. 1893; 'I feel persuaded such a pass system will effectually prevent or reduce to a minimum the malpractices of touts, and the wholesale desertion of natives, which so frequently and seriously embarrasses employers at present.' See especially A. Jeeves, 'The control of migratory labour on the South African gold mines in the era of Kruger and Milner', *Journal of Southern African Studies (JSAS)*, II, 1 (1975), 11–12; SS 329, Ra5025/96 in Ra607, Sec. Robinson mines to State Sec., 16 Oct. 1896.

9 Estimates from Natal Archives, Indian Immigration (II) files; R. F. Sieborger, 'The recruitment and organization of African labour for the diamond mines', M.A. thesis, Rhodes University, Grahamstown, 1976; *CMAR*; Cape Archives, Immigration Agent files (IAC) 1 to 12, 21.

10 P. Harries, 'Migrant labour from the Delagoa Bay hinterland to South Africa: 1852–1896', CSP 7; P. Harries, 'Production, trade and labour migration from the Delagoa Bay hinterland in the second half of the nineteenth century', Centre for African Studies, *Africa Seminar, Collected Papers*, I, 1978, University of Cape Town.

11 H. A. Junod, *Life of a South African Tribe*, I, p. 328; II, p. 6.

12 University of South Africa archive, Junod Collection (UNISA/JC), letter to Rossel, 21 Oct. 1896, 'The causes of the rebellion'; Junod, *Life*, I, pp. 408, 423.

13 Mission Romande, *Chez les Noirs* (Neuchatel, 1894), p. 6; JSA, file 74, p. 66. Evidence of Majuba, Junod, *Life*, I, pp. 283, 287.

14 H. A. Junod, *Life*, I, pp. 295–403, 407, 409.

15 H. F. Fynn, 'Delagoa Bay', in G. M. Theal (ed.), *Records of South-East Africa*, II (Cape Town, 1898), p. 480; *Cape Monitor*, 16 July 1853; NA, ZGH, 708, Z 288/87, C. R. Saunders, 'Supplementary Report on the AmaTonga people, 11 November 1887'; M. Morris, 'Tonga settlement patterns', *Anthropology Quarterly*, 45 (1972), 233.

16 Swiss Mission Archives, Lausanne, MS 1760, Grandjean diary, 1889/90 to 1895, p. 272; H. A. Junod, *Life*, I, pp. 210–14, 284, 288, II, p. 7; 'Les Baronga', pp. 40–42; H. P. Junod, *The Wisdom of the Tonga –Shangaan people* (Pretoria, 1936), pp. 121, 137, 145.

17 H. A. Junod, *Life*, I, pp. 118, 254–6, 260, II, p. 182, Junod, 'Les Baronga', 84–6, 257. H. P. Junod, *The Wisdom*, p. 135. On the levirate, see Junod; *Life* I, pp. 202–211, 247, 262, 509. Junod, 'The fate of the widows', *South African Journal of Science*, 1909.

18 The term 'cadet' is used as it implies a member of the family who is junior in status, generally, but not always, the younger brothers. All children of the first house are senior to their siblings by later wives of their father. A *nandja* is a follower, subject or servant. See Junod, *Life*, I, p. 6.

19 MS 1760 Grandjean diary, p. 68; MS 528/A Paul Berthoud to Leresche, 13 Jan. 1893; Junod, *Life* I, pp. 214–16, 241–2, 279, 332, 439.

20 *Ibid.*, p. 229; 'Les Baronga', p. 79.

21 *Ibid.*, pp. 278–9, 332.

22 MS 1760, Grandjean diary, p. 68; Junod, *Life*, I, pp. 395–404.

23 MS 513, Grandjean to Leresche, 15 May 1893; 513/B, Grandjean to Leresche, 5 Sept. 1894; Junod, *Life*, I, pp. 330–2, 404–7, 409, 440; II, pp. 46, 85.

24 Junod, *Life*, I, pp. 329–30.

25 *Ibid.*, II, pp. 224–5.

26 *Ibid.*, I, p. 433, II, pp. 6–8.

27 *Ibid.*, I, pp. 331, 387; II, p. 7; NA, SNA 1/1/27, Du Bois to SNA, 22 March 1876; UNISA/JC, 'The causes of the rebellion', Junod to Rossel, 21 Oct. 1896; PRO. FO 63/1316, Casement to FO, 15 Feb. 1896; SPG, Mission Report, 1892, Bishop Carter, 'A missionary journey into Tongaland', July 1892; Lisbon Archives, AHU; Governor's Correspondence, pasta 32, Governor of Lourenço Marques (GLM) to Governor General (GG), 10 Jan. 1880, in GG to Overseas Ministry, 29 Jan. 1880.

28 Junod, *Life*, II, pp. 213, 221–4.

29 A. Merensky, *Erinnerungen aus dem Missionsleben in Transvaal* (Berlin, 1899), p. 83; NA, SNA/1/96 enclosure in No. 73 'Statement of messenger from Umzila', 16 Aug. 1870; AHU, Governor's Correspondence, pasta 19, GG to Col. Min., 28 June 1862; pasta 21, GLM to GG 8 Feb. 1862 and GLM 'Report for 1864', in *B.O.*, 27 May 1865; St V. Erskine, 'First journey – 1868', p. 40, ms. in Royal Geographical Society.

30 N. J. van Warmelo, *The Copper Miners of Messina*, Department of Native Affairs, Pretoria, 1940, Ethnological Publications, p. 68; A. Grandjean, 'L'invasion des Zoulou dans le sud-est africain', *Bull. Soc. Neuchateloise de Geogr.*, XI (1899); Struthers ms. (private ms.), p. 89.

31 There hoes were called Beja or *landin* by the Portuguese from the Tsonga word for the Venda, 'BeVesha'. The term *landin* was used in southern Moçambique in much the same way as the term 'kaffir' in nineteenth-century South Africa. AHU Moçambique, 2ª Repartição pasta 1. GG, to Col. Min., 28 April 1884, plus enclosures.

32 AHU Moçambique, 2ª Repartição pasta 3, GG to Col. Min., 8 Oct. 1886.

33 R. F. Sieborger, 'The recruitment and organization of African labour', appendices; II; Archives of the Portuguese Consulate, Cape Town.

34 GLM, 'District report for economic year 1876–7', *Boletim Official de Moçambique* (BO), No. 47, 19 Nov. 1877.

35 'District Report 1877–78', *BO.*, No. 4, 21 Jan. 1879; D. Leslie, *Among the Zulu and amaTongas* (Glasgow, 1875), p. 294. A. M. Cardosa, 'Expedição ás Terras do Muzilla em 1882', *Bol. Soc. Geogr. Lisboa*, III, 7 (1887).

36 GLM, *BO*, No. 50, 11 Dec. 1875; Junod, 'Les Baronga', *Bull. Soc. Neuchateloise Geogr.*, 1898, p. 89; Mission Romande, *Chez les Noirs*; MS 513/B, Grandjean to Leresche, 8 March 1894; *JSA*, file 25, p. 235; ZGH, 796, 892/92, Foxon 31 Aug. 1896.

37 Swiss Mission Archives, Lausanne (MS), 502/A, Paul Berthoud to Leresche, 26 Feb. 1889; MS 1760 Granjean, p. 232, MS. 513/B Granjean to Leresche, 8 March 1894.

38 H. A. Junod, 'Les Baronga', *Bull. Soc. Neuchateloise de Geogr.* (1898), 199. F. Cohen, 'Erlautende Bemerkungen zu den Routenkarte einer Reise von Lydenburg nach der Delagoabaai', *Jahres Geogr. Ges. Hamburg*, II, 1874–5, 286; ZGH Z 796, 892/96, Foxon; JSA file 74, p. 9; McKenzie, *The Net*, 1881.

39 UNISA/JC, 'Littérature–coutumes'; 'Les Baronga', 89.

40 MS 528/A. Berthoud to Leresche, 23 Nov. 1893; MS 1642/A Confessions des Négres, 1896; Wits. Univ. Library/A 170 Am. Zulu Mission, Pinkerton diary, July 1880; NA/ZGH 708 Z288/87 Saunders; ZGH 796 892/96 Foxon; *Bulletin de la Mission Suisse en Afrique du Sud*, (BMSAS), No. 116, 1894, 143; No. 122, 1895, 361; A. Castilho, *O Districto de Lourenço Marques no Presente e no Futuro* (Lisbon, 1880), p. 13.

41 PRO, FO 63/1316, Br. Consul, Lourenço Marques to FO, 14 Feb. 1896; UNISA/JC, 'Littérature–coutumes'; ZGH 708 Z 288, Saunders, *CMAR* 1894, p. 34; 'District report for Lourenço Marques, 1876–7', *BO*, No. 45, 5 Nov. 1877; *BPP*, SA corres. 1878–9, C. 2220, No. 66.

42 ZGH 708, Z 288/87, Saunders Report, 17 Nov. 1887; NA/GH 1050 Supreme Court, *Agnew* v. *Van Gruning*, 14 May 1875; FO 63/1316, 'Report for 1876–7', GLM *BO*, 5 May 1877.

43 SNA 1/1/21, Clarence to SNA, 24 April 1871; Leslie to SNA, 28 July 1871; SNA 1/1/25, J. Colenbrander to SNA, 27 March 1880; H. W. D. Longden, *Red Buffalo* (Cape Town, 1950), p. 46.

44 SNA 1/1/24, Dunn to SNA, 21 March 1874; GH 829, Elton to Protector of Immigrants (PI), 25 Oct. 1875; CSO 664, 4069/78 Circular to Magistrates; CSO 677, 2548/78, Bennett to PI, 9 July 1878; CSO 726, 4993/79, Dunn to PI, 1 Nov. 1879; G.H. 1050 Shires to SNA, 7 April 1875; F.O. 63/1449, Crowe to F.O., 15 April 1901. *Transvaal Labour Commission* (1904), p. 47, ev. of F. Perry; MS 542/B Loze-Grandjean, 27 Nov. 1897.

45 MS. 1760 Grandjean Diary, p. 232; Junod, *Les Chants et les Contes Baronga* (Lausanne, 1897), p. 48; *Life*, I, p. 385.

46 Portuguese officials often complained of the withdrawal of sterling from the market through its 'conversion' into bridewealth; Alfredo Andrade, 'As minas de ouro do Transvaal', *Revista de Obras Publicas e Minas*, 1898, p. 330; *Regulamento das Circumscripçoes Civis dos Districtos de Lourenço Marques e Inhambane* (Lourenço Marques, 1908), p. 45; also MS. 513/B.

47 MS. 1256/A Grandjean, 'Report for 1892'; MS. 519/D, Loze to Council, 25 Sept. 1895; AHU, Governor's Corres., pasta 31, GG to Col. Min., 13 Oct. 1877; Report of the Curadoria Geral dos Individuos sujeitos a Tutella Publica, 21 Jan. 1878; GG to GLM, 11 March 1878; Report of the Curadoria in Curator General to Col. Min., 31 Oct. 1880; MS. 517/B Junod to Renevier, 10 Oct. 1895; AHU Moçambique, 2a Rep, pasta 9, GG to Col. Min., 24 Aug. 1890; I. Carmona, 'Replaçoes entre os Portuguese de Moçambique e os Boers', *Moçambique* No. 87, p. 38; A. Castilho, 'Acerca de Lourenço Marques', *BSGL*, IIV, 5 (1895), 14.

48 A. Richardson, *The Crowded Hours – the story of Lionel Cohen* (London, 1952), p. 159; UNISA/JC, 'Les causes'; *Life*, I, p. 157. MS. 1760 Grandjean Diary, 1889.

49 MS 514 Grandjean to Leresche, 5 Jan. 1895. See also Arthur Richter in L. C. von Wissel, 'Reminiscences of trading days in northern Zululand 1895–1919', MS. in Killie Campbell Library, Durban, p. 6.

50 Junod, *Life*, II, pp. 479, 613, 'Les Baronga', pp. 404–7.

51 SNA 1/1/8, Foxon, 6 April 1858; Shire, 10 May 1858; Milner, 11 May 1858; Robinson, 20 May 1858; Foxon, 19 June 1858.

52 SNA 1/1/19, draft SNA to Goodliffe, Oct. 1869; SNA 1/1/22, memo by SNA, 5 Nov. 1872; SNA 1/1/13, Dunn to SNA, 8 July 1863. The last forty families moved from Moçambique to Natal in 1862.

53 NA, Indian Immigration 1/24, 163/85, Andrew to PI, annotated; PI to Col. Sec., 9 Jan. 1885; CSO 682 482/79, PI to Natal govt. railway contractors, Jan. 1879; *JSA*, file 25, p. 260; SNA 1/1/68 936/83, Border Agent, Lower Tugela to Col. Sec., 11 Jan. 1884, annot. encl. in Br. Res. Zululand to SNA, 30 Nov. 1883; H. Junod, *Moeurs et Coutumes des Bantoes* (Paris, 1933), p. 23.

54 ZGH 702 33/87, 'Statement of Grantham and deputation from Zambile', 27 Jan. 1887; see also *JSA*, file 25, p. 260.

55 Population returns for Crown lands are in *BO*, 4, 23 Jan. 1886, for 1884–5; *BO* 4, 22 Jan. 1887 for 1886 returns and *BO* 3, 21 Jan. 1888 for 1887 returns, Hut-tax returns for 1882 are in E. Noronha, *O Districto de Lourenço Marques* (Lisbon, 1895), pp. 54–5; those for 1896 and 1897 are in *Circumscripçoes de Lourenço Marques*, 'Lourenço Marques, 1909', p. 146. See also ZGH 708 Z288/87, Saunders, 'Supplementary report on the character of the AmaTonga people'; ZA 27 'Report of the amaTonga Border Commission', 24 Dec. 1896; Transvaal Archives, SSA 330, 'Aantal Naturellen Vertrokken...', p. 183; *Transvaal Labour Commission*, evidence of Ferraz, p. 246; evidence of Wirth, p. 112.

56 A. Cabral, *Raças, Usos e Costumes dos Indigenas do Districto de Inhambane* (Lourenço Marques, 1910), pp. 86, 102. Moçambicans suffered from mining accidents and diseases more than other workers due to their 'specialisation' as underground labour.

57 MS. 82H Liengme, 'Report for 1892'; MS. 497/B Paul Berthoud, 'State of the coastal areas, 1887'; Junod, *Life*, I, p. 203.

58 MS. 1225, H. Berthoud, 'Expedition to Gungunyana, 1891'; MS. 513/B Grandjean to Leresche, 4 March 1894.

59 E. Noronho, *Lourenço Marques*, pp. 54–5; TA. GOV. 210. Confid. 33/06, Br. Cons. Gen. LM, to Selborne, 27 July; 1906. Cabral, *Raças e Usos*, p. 102.

60 *JSA* file 74, evidence of Mahungane and Nkomuza; file 12, evidence of Ndaba; Junod, *Life*, I, pp. 337–8; II, pp. 12, 14.

61 Malaria and tick-bite fever in the summer months restricted travel to Natal, as did winter weather on the highveld. CSO. 729. 5278/79, S. Smith to Col. Sec., 22 Nov. 1879; *Natal Mercury*, 25 Nov. 1871; *BPP* L11, 1890, Zambile to SNA, 1 March 1889; Berthoud–Junod, *Lettres*, pp. 81, 92, 99.

62 See note 47.

63 MS. 1760, Grandjean diary, 1890; Longden, *Red Buffalo*, p. 46; W. H. C. Walton, *The Story of Lebombo* (London, 1902), p. 31; *ICE*, evid. W. R. Brown, p. 363; Shanks, p. 366.

64 SNA 1/3/26, R233/76, Res. Magistrate, Upper Tugela to SNA, 29 March 1876; SNA 1/1/106, 416/88.

65 II 1/1, Elton to PI, 20 June 1876; G.H. 837, Elton to Lt-Gov., 20 June 1876; *Natal Govt. Gazette*, 24 Jan. 1871; Keate to Kimberley, 21 Oct. 1871.

66 *CMAR*, 1895, p. 42.

67 R. de Sa Nogueira, *O Diccionario Ronga-Portuguêz* (Ba-galantzana).

68 CSO 665, 4069/78: statement of Umango, messenger to Nozingili, 4 June 1875; SNA 1/1/24, Dunn to SNA, 21 March 1874; *Natal Govt. Gazette*, 22 June 1869; CSO 636 154/80, Dunn to Col. Sec., 1 Jan 1880; CSO 677 2882/78, Bennett to PI, 6 Aug. 1878; CSO 665 4069/78, GH 1050, Shires to SNA, 7 April 1875; II 1/1 R53/76 SNA to PI, 24 June 1876; TLC evidence of Perry, p. 47.

69 II 1/1 R496/75, Shires to SNA, 26 Aug. 1875; *CMAR*, 1898, p. 4.

70 Best and Williams in *CMAR*, 1894, p. 34.

71 MS. 1255/B. Henri Berthoud, 'Rapport sur l'expédition'. Berthoud refers to a 'tour de campagneonage'.

72 R. de Sa Nogueira, *O Diccionario*; Junod, *Life* II, p. 601; Gabral, *Raças e Usos*, pp. 99, 182.

73 ZGH. 708. Z288/87, Saunders Report, 17 Nov. 1887; MS. 497/B, Paul Berthoud, 'L'état du Littoral', Sept. 1887; ZGH 796. 892/96 Foxon, 31 Aug. 1896; Junod, *Life*, I, p. 99; *JSA*, file 25, p. 236; MS. 1642/A, 'Premières confessions des Négres'; Robertson, July 1890, in E. and H. Wheeler, *Soldiers of the Cross in Zululand*

(London, 1906), p. 113, *Transvaal Labour Commission*, Evidence of Cohen, p. 163.

74 F. Wilson, *Labour in the South African Gold Mines 1911–1969* (Cambridge, 1972), pp. 45–6, 53, 55, 141. Wilson shows that in 1969, the final year of his survey, African real wages on the Witwatersrand were lower than in 1889. A. Rita-Ferreira, *O Movimento*, pp. 75–79, gives African wage statistics of £2 19s 10d in 1889; an average of £3 10s in 1896; £2 3s 6d in 1897; £1 11s 1d in 1901; £2 2s in 1928; £3 in 1944; and a £3 15s starting wage in 1955.

75 II I/5.81/78. Col. Eng. to PI, 14 Dec. 1878; III6/78 Immigration Agent to PI 18 Sept. 1878; III/20.626/84 De Coster to PI, 8 May 1884; III/55.551/90 Depot Surgeon to PI, 5 July 1890; Cape Archives, IAC 8 to 12, 21.

76 M. Binford, 'Stalemate: a study of cultural dynamics', p. 86; F. Wilson, 'International migration in southern Africa', *International Migration Review*, X, 4 (1976); David Webster, 'Migrant labour, social formations and the proletarianization of the Chopi of southern Mozambique', *African Perspectives*, I (1978), 171; *O Mineiro Moçambicano*, mimeo, Centre of African Studies, Eduardo Mondlane University, Maputo, 1979, 60ff; C. E. Fuller, 'An ethnohistoric study of continuity and change in Gwambe culture', Ph.D. thesis, Northwestern University, 1955, pp. 148–9, 224.

CHAPTER SIX

The destruction and reconstruction of Zulu society

Jeff Guy

In December 1888, ten years after the British invasion of the Zulu kingdom, a Zulu, Msilana, was brought before the Resident Magistrate of the Lower Mfolozi district in the British colony of Zululand. Msilana was the son of an elderly chief, then in hiding, and charged with rebellion against Her Majesty's Government, and he was accused of refusing to assist a party of Zulu who, in the charge of a court policeman, were on their way to work for the Natal Government Railways (NGR). It was alleged that Msilana had abused and threatened the labourers saying that by going to work on the railway they had deserted the cause of the Zulu royal house and allied themselves with the government.[1]

In his anger Msilana had identified a fundamental aspect of the changes which had come to Zululand in the previous decade. The history of Zululand in the 1880s and the 1890s can be seen as the history of the diversion of surplus labour from the service of the Zulu state to the service of developing capitalist production in southern Africa. However, this was not brought about by direct assault – this had failed in 1879 – but by the manipulation of the hitherto existing system, by the adaptation and retention of certain social features, as well as by innovation. Thus Msilana did not rail against the work party itself, but the fact that it was going to labour for the 'government' and was no longer working for the Zulu state.

In the past few years some of the most fruitful analyses of modern southern African history have argued that capitalist production in southern Africa developed in articulation with pre-capitalist modes of production.[2] Recently the idea that pre-capitalist and capitalist modes coexisted has come under criticism.[3] In this paper I examine the impact of capitalism on Zulu society in the late nineteenth century. By comparing the pre-conquest Zulu kingdom with the British colony of Zululand, and by identifying those areas where change took place, and where there was continuity, I hope to give more empirical content to the debate on the specific manner in which capitalism developed in the subcontinent.

The Zulu kingdom in the 1870s[4]

In 1878 the people of Zululand were members of an independent African kingdom. Although the spread of settler colonialism and mercantile capital had affected the kingdom, these phenomena had not caused fundamental changes in its structure. Unlike most African communities in southern Africa at this time the Zulu were still only marginally involved in commodity production; trade had not altered production relations, and their labour was still expended within the kingdom in support of the Zulu state. In spite of some reverses, the Zulu kings, backed by the huge Zulu army, had kept invading forces at bay, and the Zulu retained most of their land together with their political institutions with the Zulu king and his chiefs exercising full political authority.

Production in the Zulu kingdom took place in the homesteads. These formed the productive communities of the kingdom and were made up of the homestead-head, his wives and their children, together with their cattle, and associated arable and grazing lands. These homesteads were divided into houses in the charge of the wives of the homestead, each house forming a unit of production within the homestead with its own land and cattle. The homestead was economically self-sufficient and consumed most of its own produce. There was a rigid sexual division of labour, with the women working in agriculture and performing domestic labour, the men concentrating on animal husbandry, the heavier building tasks and land preparation. The production of handicrafts was also allocated according to sex, but there was no clearly demarcated group of craftsmen or petty-commodity producers. Individuals tended to concentrate on activities for which they had a particular talent, or produced goods made from locally available raw materials. With the possible exception of iron products, and certain wild animal skins, exchange of these goods took place informally, and their production did not affect the existing structure of the homestead. Out of a population of perhaps 250 000 it has been estimated about 90 per cent lived in homesteads such as these – 'commoner's homesteads' consisting of a man, and perhaps two or three wives, and their children.

The homestead was not only the productive but also the reproductive community, and consequently kinship links were not only representations of reproductive, but also of productive relations. Wives, and their houses, were ranked within the homestead. Each homestead had sprung from a house within a previously existing homestead, and was formed when the eldest son of a house broke from the homestead of his father to establish a homestead of his own. This process of 'segmentation' was expressed in terms of the lineage. Aggregations of lineages, all the members of which believed they had descended through the male line from a common founding ancestor, are usually described as clans. These clans were exogamous, and wives had to be introduced to the clan from another one. Nevertheless, it should be remembered that 'lineage' and 'clan' are abstractions which found material expression as the homesteads or productive communities of the kingdom, which came into existence and disappeared with the passing of each generation.

The establishment of a homestead depended on the transfer of cattle: from father to son through inheritance and from the prospective husband to the father of the wife through 'brideprice' or *lobolo*. Homestead formation therefore depended on a vertical link between father and son and a horizontal one between husband and wife's father, and these links were marked by the movement of cattle out of the founding homestead. At the same time, of course, cattle entered the homestead as daughters moved out as prospective wives.

But the Zulu kingdom was not composed of an association of essentially egalitarian homesteads. It was a highly stratified society with great differences in wealth, authority and status, and the homesteads of the kingdom were grouped into large political and administrative units which I shall refer to here as chiefdoms.

Some of these chiefdoms had existed as powerful independent polities before they were incorporated into the kingdom by Shaka; others had reached their positions of dominance during the reigns of the Zulu kings. The chief was responsible for good order within his chiefdom, the allocation of land and the application of the law. He received fees and fines from his courts and a certain amount of tribute both in produce and labour from the members of the homesteads which made up his chiefdom, and delegated authority down to district heads with responsibility resting ultimately on the homestead-head. Nguni societies to the south of the Zulu kingdom were generally organised on a chiefly system of this kind. The Zulu, however, added another level to this system – that of the king who reigned in association with, but over, the chiefs of the kingdom.

The king was supreme ruler in the Zulu state. The basis of his power lay in the Zulu military system by which all males in the kingdom gave service to the king for some twenty years from the time they reached the age of puberty until they were given permission to marry. Apart from providing the force for external warfare, defence and internal coercion, the men of the army herded the royal cattle, and worked in the king's fields where the usual sexual division of labour did not apply. The greater part of the costs of subsistence and reproduction of these state servants was provided by the homesteads in which they were born and grew up. Thus the Zulu state depended ultimately on the massive extraction of surplus labour from the homesteads of the nation.

Furthermore, the fact that males were released from intensive service for the state when they were given permission to marry meant that the king could control the essential processes not only of reproduction, but also of production within the state. For it was only after marriage that men could set up homesteads of their own and thus establish new productive communities. The king also had ultimate control over the allocation of land within the kingdom. Any man who gave allegiance to the Zulu king was entitled to the land necessary for the support of himself and his family. Nominally all the cattle in the land were the king's as descendant of the founder of the kingdom, and anyone who left the kingdom forfeited his cattle. There were, however, clear individual rights to cattle as well – for example, those attached to a particular homestead and those inherited by one house from another.

Order in the kingdom was maintained by a large number of officials. They ranged from the great chiefs of the nation to the lesser chiefs, military commanders, those with special ability in particular fields, the confidential messengers, tribute-collectors and so on. Nevertheless there was no specific official stratum of officials in Zululand; all married men in the kingdom, regardless of rank or status, were homestead-heads and therefore in control of the productive communities of the kingdom.

The homestead of a man of rank was far larger, however, than that of a commoner. There were more cattle and a greater number of houses for his wives and children, and the laws which organised production within the homestead were more complex. The king held vast herds: those attached to his personal homesteads, the herds of his ancestors, those attached to the various royal homesteads or distributed through the kingdom through various forms of clientship. To a lesser degree the same applied to the men of rank within the kingdom, the number of cattle and size of homestead decreasing down the social scale.

The number of cattle to which a man had access was a clear indication of his status and political power. The importance of cattle in Zulu life is well known. Not only were dairy products a dietary staple but also the movement of cattle from one group to another, or their sacrifice to the shades, marked every significant event in an individual's life. Much has been written about the 'cattle complex' of Africa's pastoral peoples, and the tendency has been to see the accumulation of cattle as an end in itself. In pre-conquest Zululand, however, it was the fact that cattle could be transformed into human beings through the *lobolo* system which lay at the root of this accumulation.

In Zulu society there was no large-scale production of any form of permanent, storable wealth; in other words it was not possible for surplus labour to be realised in any permanent, storable form, with the exception of cattle. Moreover cattle could be used to obtain wives, the agricultural producers in the homestead and the reproducers of the homestead whose daughters could in turn be transferred for cattle. In this manner labour was continually being realised in the form of cattle, and cattle in the form of labour. It meant that cattle could be seen as self-reproducing stores of spent labour and of labour power. It is this process which underlies the crucial importance of cattle in the pre-colonial Zulu kingdom, and from which sprung the pride, the prestige and the social strength of the owners of large herds.

The possession of large numbers of cattle testified to the political power of men of rank in the kingdom, and the daughters of men of status commanded more cattle on marriage than those of commoners, a fact which tended towards the perpetuation of social difference and political dominance. For although the most effective way to utilise cattle was through the homestead/lineage system, it must be remembered that lineages were not the political units within the kingdom. Men of rank, therefore, could also utilise their cattle through various forms of clientship, thereby creating political bonds and increasing the number of their dependants and followers.

Thus at the very heart of Zulu society was the drive to accumulate cattle. But it must be stressed that this accumulation was not an end in itself but practised in order to transform these cattle into human beings, thereby increasing the size of the social group and the amount of labour power at the command of an individual. This would seem to be a consequence of production in a society where the level of technical development is low, and there is therefore a significant correlation between social strength and the size of the group.

Meillassoux has argued that in 'agricultural self-sustaining formations' the 'concern for *reproduction* becomes paramount – not only reproduction of subsistence but also reproduction of the productive unit itself', and 'their end is reproduction of life as a precondition to production'.[5] These fundamental characteristics seem to have been shared by the pre-conquest Zulu kingdom, although it also contained a clearly differentiated wealthy ruling group with the king exercising ultimate control over reproduction. In pre-colonial Zululand the producer, once he or she had reached maturity, had access to the means of production. This, together with the undeveloped nature of commodity production, the retention by the productive community of most of its produce and the extraction of surplus labour through the military system all suggest that the kingdom had retained its pre-capitalist character and was indeed a society in which man 'appears . . . as the aim of production' and not production the 'aim of man'.[6]

Pre-conquest Zululand was not, however, sealed from outside forces, and to assert its essentially pre-capitalist nature is not to argue that commodity exchange had not influenced Zulu society. Most Zulu exchanged cattle and hides for blankets, cloth, iron utensils and trinkets, but this trade does not seem to have affected fundamentally the basis of production within the kingdom. A few chiefs were personally involved in trading. The most important of these lived along the coast, and provided the links between the territory to the north-east of Zululand and the commercial houses of Natal. John Dunn, the white trader and hunter who had adopted the life-style of a Zulu chief, and Zibhebhu kaMaphitha, traded and recruited labour in the north-east and supplied the Zulu with guns. Although these men came to play a significant historical role in Zululand, it has to be remembered that before 1879 there were very few Zulu leaders involved in commercial activity of this kind. A decade after the discovery of diamonds in the southern African hinterland the Zulu king could still state that his people had never been to Kimberley to sell their labour.

The destruction of the Zulu kingdom[7]

The very success of the Zulu kingdom in resisting change until the last quarter of the nineteenth century singled it out as the object of an unprecedented demonstration of imperial military might. In the late 1870s the British government attempted to impose 'confederation' on southern Africa's different communities – that is, to bring into being a political union which would, in part, facilitate capitalist production in the subcontinent. The independent Zulu kingdom was seen as a major obstacle to this scheme and as a result was invaded by British and colonial troops in January 1879.

Instead of an easy military victory, however, the British troops suffered severe reverses on the battlefield. The effectiveness of Zulu military resistance played an important part in the British decision to abandon plans for confederation and to adopt a more passive approach. Thus at the end of the war the Zulu were able to retain much of their land, and their formal independence; they did this, though, at the price of the centralised state and its military system, and the rule of the Zulu dynasty was terminated, the king sent into exile and the country divided into thirteen chiefdoms.

The result of this scheme – the notorious British 'settlement' of Zululand – was civil war. Supporters of the old Zulu order came into conflict with the newly appointed chiefs, in particular the trading partners Zibhebhu and John Dunn. These factions were aided and abetted by forces from outside Zululand: from the Transvaal where individuals exchanged fire-power for land, and from Natal where officials saw in control over the Zulu and their resources the answer to many of the problems of African administration which had developed in their colony. The British government, reacting against the aggressive expansionism of the late 1870s, adopted a policy of retrenchment and intervened only when immediate imperial interests appeared to be threatened.

By 1887 both sides in the civil war had fought themselves to a standstill and Britain partitioned the country, giving a district in the north-west to the insurgents from the Transvaal, and assuming sovereignty over the remainder of the country. This latter region became the colony of British Zululand, which remained in existence from 1887 to 1897 when it was incorporated into the colony of Natal. It is British Zululand which forms the focus of attention in the rest of this chapter.[8]

Although formally a British colony, Zululand was from the start dominated by its neighbour Natal. Natal officials had played a leading role in the crushing of the royalists in the civil war, and the administrative system, and the officials who implemented it, were drawn largely from those men who had their initial experience in Natal's Department of the Secretary for Native Affairs. This office in turn still bore the imprint of the man who had been in charge for the first thirty years of its existence, Sir Theophilus Shepstone. Shepstone had retired in 1875 but until his death in 1893 he was consulted by officials on matters dealing with African administration, was the major influence on the development of policy for Zululand, and his friends and relatives filled many of the most important posts.[9]

The Natal officials' attempts to impose their control over the Zulu sprang from the need to bring the country within the colony's economic orbit, to ensure access to the African interior along a route to the east of the Transvaal and, most pressingly, to provide land for Natal's 'superabundant' African population. This latter need was the result of contradictions that had developed in Natal as a result of Shepstone's policy which cannot be dealt with here.

The reconstruction of Zulu society

The 'Shepstone system' was a policy of 'segregation'.[10] It provided a certain continuity with the past by retaining features of the pre-capitalist system, in particular the maintenance of homestead production, by allowing the African population access to land, the application of customary law and the recognition of chiefly authority. In its application to Zululand it was argued that, like Natal forty years before, the situation made it impossible to implement any policy which necessitated too violent a rupture with the past. The recognition of the existing chiefly stratum and the traditional production system would free the people of Zululand from the tyranny of the Zulu dynasty and they would gladly accept the restoration of the 'natural' Nguni system of homestead production under chiefly rule. At the same time, it was said, progress would be ensured by the overall authority of white magistrates and the right of appeal to their courts. The imposition of the hut-tax would substitute the civilising influence of wage labour for the barbaric demands of Zulu military service and would have the added advantage of covering the administrative costs of the colony.

The Shepstone system was devised in a situation in which the African community was strong enough to resist attempts at outright dispossession and the colonial state lacked the facilities and the infrastructure to control large numbers of people who were suddenly proletarianised. It created an administrative system which divided the African community among chiefs, and at the same time incorporated the chiefs by allowing them some authority while diverting a portion of the surplus previously destined for their use to the service of the colonial state.

Thus the laws and regulations for British Zululand left the land in the possession of the Zulu people. The Governor of Natal now assumed the office of the Governor of Zululand as well, and he also became Supreme Chief of the Zulu people with 'the powers and prerogatives hitherto attaching to the position of Supreme Chief over Zululand and its Native population'.[11] In Zululand a Resident Commissioner and Chief Magistrate was placed over six Resident Magistrates who heard the more serious criminal cases and appeals from the chiefs' courts. Officially recognised chiefs had restricted criminal jurisdiction, and applied customary law in civil cases between members of their tribes. The cost of maintaining this administration was met by a 14s hut-tax.

The administrative structure of the colony of Zululand was the result of a conscious attempt to preserve elements of the old order, while at the same time intervening at crucial points to introduce certain 'progressive' factors. However, behind the political and administrative system, and the anthropological justifications and rationalisations with which it was buttressed, lay a triad of social forces around which the reconstructed Zulu society was built. This triad consisted of the hut-tax, wage labour outside Zululand, and the retention of homestead production within the colony.

The similarities between this system and the pre-conquest system in which surplus labour was extracted by the Zulu state from the homestead through the military system are obvious, and the initiators of the new order justified it in terms of reform rather than revolution. In the Zulu kingdom it had been the 'young men' who served most intensively in the royal regiments; in colonial Zululand official reports refer time and again to the 'young men' engaged in wage labour for their homesteads. In both cases this is something of an oversimplification, but nonetheless it does point to the fact that it was the unmarried men in the homesteads who, in both systems, were expected to work outside the homestead for the state, and generally did so.

Thus in 1883 Shepstone wrote of the changes in Zululand since the invasion, and reported that an ex-soldier had told him that since the deposition of the king 'we find that we can go and work and earn money, and buy what we want, and marry and become heads of families while we are yet young', and he told of others who 'had learned that "shillings were better weapons than assegais wherewith to capture property" '.[12] And in 1892 Osborn, Sheptone's intimate friend, and Zululand's Resident Commissioner and Chief Magistrate, Melmoth, defended the new system in these terms:

> The great ambition of all the young Zulu men is to get married and to obtain the necessary cattle to give as lobola or marriage consideration, hence the readiness with which they go to work for wages. The money so earned is, as soon as possible, invested in cattle, and marriages are forthwith contracted. The young man thus becomes a responsible member of the community with a family to care for instead of remaining as

young men had to do under the Zulu Kings' regime, in a state of forced celibacy until over 40 years of age.[13]

Thus from the moment of its inception in Zululand, labour migrancy depended on aspects of both the pre-capitalist and the capitalist systems: wage labour and the payment of hut-tax taking place within the context of homestead production. This in turn required the colonial state to perpetuate the organising principles of the homestead — that is, women as agricultural producers, the transfer of cattle for wives, customary law, the kinship system, the laws of succession and inheritance, organised and controlled by the homestead-heads under the authority of the chiefs.

In this section I want to examine the initial impact of colonial rule and wage labour on selected features of the pre-capitalist system, with the aim of understanding more clearly how the process of 'restructuring', 'conserving' as well as the 'dissolution' of the pre-capitalist mode of production took place in Zululand.

The hut-tax

The collection of hut-tax presupposed the existence of homestead production. And it was not just a 'hut' tax. As Dunn was informed in 1888, not only was a tax imposed on every 'hut' (except cooking huts) but on every wife 'whether she possesses a hut of her own or not'.[14] It was therefore a tax on the potential productive capacity of the homestead, the assumption being that the more wives and the more children within the control of a homestead-head, the greater the wealth of the homestead.

It was the hut-tax which loomed largest in the minds of the officials responsible for the government of Zululand. This is partly explained by the specific history of the relations between the Natal officials and the British Government in the 1880s, when the local officials spent so much energy trying to convince London that there was no need for the cost of the annexation of Zululand to fall on the British taxpayer but that it could be carried by the Zulu themselves. However, when the hut-tax was first imposed officially in the Reserve in 1883 it met with resistance, and although by the time the Reserve became part of British Zululand in 1887 it was covering its costs, the imperial loan made to set up the Reserve was still outstanding. For the Natal officials the successful collection of the hut-tax was a vindication of their policy, and a proof to the economy-minded British government that its reluctance to extend authority over the Zulu had been based on a misconception.

The hut-tax was by far the most important source of revenue, and formed the financial foundation of the colony of Zululand. It contributed over 70 per cent of the total revenue of between £40 000 and £50 000 raised annually.[15] And in the first few years of the colony's existence the officials' predictions of the ability of the Zulu to be 'self-supporting' appeared to have been well founded. By 1889 the Zululand government was able to show a favourable balance after covering the cost of administration (37 per cent of the revenue), the costs of coercion (the Zululand police took about 25 per cent of the revenue),[16] and also repaying the imperial loan and the costs of the special court which had tried the leaders of the 1888 resistance. This favourable situation continued for the next few years, and in 1893 the Crown Agents in London had invested nearly £20 000 for the Zululand government in 'the usual approved securities'.[17]

In June 1888 the first hut-tax in British Zululand fell due, but its collection was disrupted by the Usuthu (that is royalist) resistance of that time – resistance connected with the demands made on the Zulu to ensure the collection of the tax. When the Usuthu disbanded their forces in August 1888, the Resident Commissioner, Osborn, and the Governor began pressing the magistrates to resume hut-tax collection: 'The fact is', Osborn wrote, 'we require all the money we can get to settle up our many liabilities now that the disputes are over.'[18] By September the magistrates were again demanding the hut-tax. Both cash and cattle were hard to come by at this time, especially in the northern districts where the civil war had been most violent, and many Zulu found it difficult to pay. Some sold cattle to raise the cash, some paid in cattle which were valued by the magistrates at 15 per cent below the market price, and others, if it could be shown they had no resources at all, were allowed to defer paying till the next year when they were to be charged double.

Labour migrancy and commodity production

All the evidence suggests that we can date large-scale labour migration from Zululand from this time, the closing months of 1888, immediately after the crushing of the last of the royalists, and in consequence of the demands made for the hut-tax. Magistrates' reports suggest that the number of people going out to work increased steadily during the last months of 1888 and into the opening months of 1889.[19] By the middle of that year there were reports from different parts of Zululand saying that all the potential workers were out, and another that the only men remaining behind were those necessary for the protection and administration of the homesteads.[20]

The economic situation beyond Zululand's borders facilitated the general movement of the Zulu into labour migration in 1888 and 1889. By this time there was an unprecedented demand for labour in the neighbouring territories. The recession of 1886 had been reversed as a result of the discovery of gold in the Transvaal in that year. The comparatively high wages offered on the Rand had attracted thousands of Africans from Natal, driving up wages in that colony and causing a labour crisis, just at the time when Natal was attempting to expand economically in order to take advantage of the opportunities offered by the new developments in the interior. The forced labour system in Natal, which served the Department of Public Works and paid 10s a month, collapsed as Africans fled when requisition orders for labour were served on the chiefs. Natal farmers and labour agents for the NGR urged the authorities to obstruct the movement of labour to the Transvaal where wages were four or five times as high as the 10s to 12s a month paid on Natal farms.[21]

The most urgent programme in Natal at the time was the construction of the colony's railway line towards the Transvaal in order to take advantage of the greatly increased carrying trade to and from the mines. The NGR offered 1s a working day on a six-month contract for African labour, but was unable to meet its requirements, and appealed to the Secretary for Native Affairs (SNA), Henrique Shepstone, for assistance, stating in October that unless labour was found 'work to a great extent will be at a standstill'. Unable to provide labour from Natal, Shepstone turned to the Resident Commissioner in Zululand.[22]

Osborn and his magistrates in Zululand rose to the occasion. In 1888 and 1889 many Zulu had their first taste of wage labour driving the railway through northern Natal towards the Transvaal. They were recruited by the Zululand officials, gathered into labour gangs and marched to the railway works in the charge of a government *induna*, driving the cattle they needed for their subsistence with them. The costs of recruitment were covered by the Natal government.[23]

Some magistrates used force to complete the number of these labour gangs. Knight of the Melmoth district put pressure on the chiefs, saying that he regarded their willingness to co-operate in this as a test of their loyalty to the government.[24] As we have seen, Msilana was brought before the magistrate, and convicted for 'interfering' with just such a labour party.[25]

The widespread movement into migrant labour was sudden, and so was the response of the Zulu to its demands. Although the magistrates assisted in the process initially, by the end of 1889 they were no longer acting formally as recruiters and the chiefs were assuming this role. Dunn, of course, had been recruiting for years, but before the end of 1888 so many other chiefs were participating in the process that Osborn told the SNA that labour agents were giving the chiefs a 'substantial fee . . . [which] makes it rather difficult for us [the officials] to procure men'.[26] By the end of 1889 there were reports in the Natal newspapers of chiefs forcing labour by fining those who did not go out to work and thereby denied the chiefs the capitation fee.[27]

There are also indications that the workers themselves very quickly became wary of taking contracts organised by the officials, and preferred the freedom of negotiating the terms of work independently of them. It was reported in July 1889 that 'for some reason' workers 'preferred to pay a shilling for a pass, and to go on the chance of finding employment, [than] to availing themselves of the more advantageous terms offered in Your Honour's circular'.[28] Moreover, already by this time a knowledge of current wages on the labour market affected recruitment. Thus a magistrate warned a recruiter from Durban that he 'would have to pay current rates at the Point, or your men would become very discontented and probably all desert . . . a great deal would depend upon the rate of wages you offered and whether you are prepared to pay a bonus per head to chiefs as done by other labour agents'.[29]

Thus many of the workers who left Zululand at this time did not go as members of the officially recruited labour detachments.[30] They were either recruited by labour agents, who found increasingly that they had to work through the local chief, or they went out as small, kin-based groups, in the charge of an older 'brother' and sought employment, and returned to the country, together.[31]

We can only speculate on the proportion of the wage brought back to Zululand. Very roughly, a worker could expect about 30s a month in Natal and £4 in the Transvaal, but, of course, the further a man worked from Zululand the greater the costs of transport and subsistence and the more the danger of being robbed. Lagden, after considerable experience in Basutoland with labour recruiters, pointed out the danger of accepting the figure he referred to as the 'pay on paper':

> I found that [the rate of pay] given to me on paper was never verified – deductions were made from the boys' pay. . . . If the boy came to work for six months, he sometimes lost two months' wages by deductions.[32]

The magistrate C. R. Saunders, a generally reliable and intelligent observer, estimated in 1896 that the worker brought back on average about £6 after a contract. There is nothing in the fragmentary evidence we have to suggest that this is an unreliable estimate.[33]

The amount of cash in Zululand increased rapidly with the onset of labour migrancy. After 1889 cattle were no longer tendered for hut-tax, and it was paid completely in cash. Whereas in 1888 some men complained that they could not go out to work as they did not have the shilling needed for the pass,[34] from 1889 magistrates generally reported that large amounts of money were circulating in the country.

It appears as if most of the cash in Zululand had its origin as the wages paid for labour in Natal and the Transvaal. A Zulu peasantry – in the sense of agricultural commodity producers – did not emerge in the 1890s. An initial move in this direction proved to be a disastrous experience. In 1889, under pressure from the authorities to pay the hut-tax which was levied at the end of the harvest, many Zulu sold grain, which fetched about 5s a 200lb muid. A drought early in the next growing season caused severe shortages and storekeepers and traders were able to push the price of mazie up to £3 or £4 a muid.[35] Many Zulu did not even have enough seed for the coming crop.[36] Although there were pockets of people involved in peasant production, these originated from outside Zululand's borders, and lived near Natal or on mission stations. The vast majority of the Zulu quickly learned the dangers of moving too rapidly into commodity production and, while always eager to buy cattle, they sold them only as a last resort, and grain was sold only locally and informally when there were substantial surpluses.

To the end of the 1890s the magistrates wrote of the indifference of Zulu agriculturalists to both the plough and the market. As the Chief Magistrate reported of 1898:

> Natives, as is usual amongst them in this Province,[37] grow only sufficient grain, etc., for their own support. Their methods of cultivation are primitive, small patches of land being broken up by the women with hoes. A few ploughs are in use in some of the districts, though the implement is almost unknown in others. Indications of progress in Agriculture çan hardly be said to appear.[38]

From this it appears that throughout the 1890s the hut-tax was raised for the most part by wage labour outside the country.[39] At the same time, of course, the contribution of homestead production to the whole system was fundamental – it was upon this that the majority of the population depended between contracts – and it was the need to ensure the adequate functioning of homestead production that determined the character of the Zulu administration, its laws and system of control. At a local level this responsibility fell on the chiefs of Zululand.

The chieftainship and the application of customary law
Sir Theophilus Shepstone wrote that

> it may be accepted as an axiom . . . that it is impossible to govern effectively a Zulu population . . . without the aid of their own institutions, at the head of which are their Chiefs or Headmen.[40]

The implication of statements such as this is that the colonial authorities, in the classic pattern of indirect rule, were recognising existing political structures and the office-holders within them. However, the history of the civil war in the 1880s demonstrated what happened when a substantial number of chiefs refused to participate in an attempt to graft their own institutions onto a system of colonial overrule. The civil war can in fact be seen as the consequence of attempts by colonial officials to create a class of compliant chiefs. By 1887 the majority of the chiefs of the old Zulu kingdom were dead, many of them having died violently, and others were in gaol or in exile. The most powerful chiefs in colonial Zululand (in terms of the number of people under them) were foreigners whose appointments had been the reward for faithful service to their colonial masters. The chieftainship was, indeed, a pre-colonial feature; close examination shows, however, that the chiefs, and their duties, had to be altered substantially before they could become a feature of the colonial system.

The chiefs in colonial Zululand had certain important local administrative and judicial functions. These had been granted to them on the insistence of Shepstone when the Laws and Regulations were being drawn up in 1887.[41] They had judicial rights over civil cases between members of their chiefdoms and limited criminal jurisdiction. Other cases and appeals were tried by the magistrates or went before the High Court of Zululand presided over by the Chief Magistrate.

Any analysis of the application of the law in Zululand would lay bare the structure of colonial control. However, there are a number of problems in carrying this out. Although the records of a significant number of cases survive there are only references to the proceedings of the chiefs' courts. A study of the statutes are of limited value: by Proclamation II of 1887 Natal Law was extended to Zululand 'so far as applicable',[42] a clause which obviously gave the magistrates considerable legal leeway, and which makes it difficult to generalise about their application of the law. However, an examination of certain aspects of the operation of the law in Zululand is extremely revealing, particularly in so far as it was applied to preserve the system of homestead production — and at the same time to change it.

Thus the records of cases of 'seduction', 'abduction' and 'adultery' show the severity with which colonial law treated actions which, in effect, disrupted the organisation of the homestead. One example will have to suffice. In 1895 James Stuart found a certain Sembatwa guilty of 'Abduction and Adultery'. Ten years previously a married woman from Natal had left her homestead with Sembatwa and gone to live with him in Zululand. Stuart sentenced Sembatwa to two years' imprisonment with hard labour and fifty lashes in two instalments. The Chief Magistrate, Marshall Clarke, quashed the sentence on the grounds that the original offence was outside Stuart's jurisdiction. The magistrate's defence of the sentence he imposed is interesting. Stuart said that he had tried the case under Section II of the Laws and Regulations of Zululand which made it an offence to bring stolen property into Zululand and 'according to native ideas, women are only regarded as so much property'.[43]

That distortion of traditional law and custom of this kind was widespread is well known, but it must not just be dismissed as a falsification of customary practice. The application of the law in this manner, together with the regulation which made it necessary for a woman to be identified by a man known to the pass officer before she was given a pass to leave Zululand, and the instruction that women's claims for divorce were not to be heard before the courts,[44] worked to keep the women in the homestead — that is, to ensure that they fulfilled their role as agricultural producers and the reproducers of the homestead, either as wives or as daughters. Nevertheless, it was the operation of *lobolo* in colonial Zululand which provides us with perhaps the most significant insights into the changes and the continuities which resulted from the initial impact of wage labour on the Zulu.

In the first section of this chapter I attempted to demonstrate the fundamental role that the transfer of cattle for women played in pre-conquest Zululand. It was through this process that labour was realised and this created more labour, and because women of the politically dominant strata commanded more cattle it was this process which maintained and reproduced existing politically dominant strata. The perpetuation of homestead production in colonial Zululand ensured the continuance of *lobolo*. Its importance is revealed by the fact that the vast majority of civil cases which came before the magistrates were claims for *lobolo*, or claims that had their origin in *lobolo* disputes, either in the form of claims for cattle, or for 'girls'.

Because these *lobolo* cases occupied so much of the magistrates' time, and because of the disparities in the judgments they gave, a number of investigations were held on the subject of *lobolo* in Zululand.[45] From the evidence which emerged during these enquiries, it appears that important features of Zulu custom, usually seen as part of the traditional system, were in fact innovatory: that it was the colonial state which introduced the changes which allowed the *lobolo* transaction to be interpreted as a form of sale; that the colonial state created the 'target' towards which the migrant worker laboured; and that the African 'love of litigation' was a response to pressures which developed within the colonial context.[46]

From the information gathered on the operation of *lobolo* in pre-conquest Zululand it is clear that the transfer of cattle in recognition of marriage took place over an extended period of time, often over generations. After annexation, the tendency developed for the father to demand the payment of a fixed amount, which had to be handed over before the marriage took place.[47] In pre-conquest Zululand the number of cattle to be transferred was not fixed, but depended on a number of factors such as the behaviour of the wife, her fertility, the number and sex of her children (with increases for the number of girls born), the need of the father for cattle and the number of cattle at the disposal of the husband. The husband was referred to as the *isiqodo* – the stump upon which his father-in-law could lean for support.[48] While there was no predetermined, fixed sum, the number of cattle transferred in pre-colonial times ranged from about three to six head. After annexation this number increased to ten – the figure laid down in the Natal Code as the maximum which could be asked in a commoner marriage. Furthermore, in pre-conquest Zululand, claims arising out of *lobolo* transactions were not brought before the courts. They were settled informally by the families concerned. After annexation the Zululand courts spent an increasing amount of time deciding *lobolo* claims. Thus one magistrate could write in 1890:

> The everlasting litigation, at the different Magistracies in Zululand, has only been introduced by our Government since the country became a British possession . . . [He recommended that *lobolo* cases be excluded from the courts] before the love of litigation amongst the Zulus takes deep root, as it has done in Natal.[49]

Other magistrates were aware of these changes. One wrote

> our system has gradually tended to increase the number of *lobola*, demanded with the knowledge that it can ultimately be recovered by law.[50]

And C. R. Saunders believed that

> The system of lobola as at present recognised is just tending to make the people look upon the women as little more than mere chattels for trade & barter, which until the last few years was not the case.[51]

Such shifts seem to be indications of fundamental change; marriage, and the transfer of cattle to mark marriage, were the pivotal transactions in pre-conquest Zululand, and changes like these both reflected and initiated alterations in the whole social structure. Thus the increase in *lobolo* and the intervention of colonial courts made it more difficult for the young unmarried men to obtain the number of cattle they needed to marry and establish independent homesteads. They were changes which worked, in the initial stages of colonial overrule at least, in favour of those with cattle and with daughters, and against the interests of those without. It forced the latter group to work for longer periods as wage-labourers if they were to obtain the necessary cash to buy cattle, or pay the hut-tax on their fathers' houses, in the hope that they would follow the traditional practice and raise the *lobolo* for their sons. Soon instructions were issued which laid down a scale of maximum *lobolo* charges, which enabled chiefs and men of rank to demand higher *lobolo* for their daughters, thus bolstering their dominant positions within Zululand.[52] These alterations in *lobolo* practices signify an increasing concern for individual accumulation and a shift from a practice based on reciprocal obligation to one of direct exchange. Ultimately, they indicate an increasing division between those Zulu with property and those without. Such divisions did exist in pre-conquest Zululand, but they were divisions which were resolved in time – indeed, custom worked towards their resolution; in the colonial system practice and the law worked increasingly against their resolution.

'Natural disasters'
However, before discussing the consequences of such divisions in more detail it is necessary to examine another set of factors which occurred in the 1890s and which had a significant influence on the changes that were taking place. This

was the series of 'natural disasters' which broke out in Zululand between 1894 and 1897 and which seriously affected homestead production.

After the drought of 1889 and the resultant crop failure, the Zululand government had to import seed maize into the country.[53] After this, Zululand experienced three comparatively prosperous years. The 1890–91 harvest was so good that the acreage under cultivation was reduced in the next year, and although local droughts caused a certain amount of scarcity, there was generally a sufficiency of grain in the colony. The 1892–93 harvest gave high yields. Cattle numbers increased steadily through this period. The Zululand treasury showed an increasing surplus, its debts were paid and surplus invested, new magistracies were established in the north-east, and the Resident Commissioner spoke encouragingly of the wealth of the colony and the contentment of its people.

It is true that there were some disturbing aspects. Malarial fever was spreading in the lower districts. *Nagana* (trypansomiasis or sleeping-sickness) was prevalent in regions which in the times of the kings were densely populated, and the Zulu argued that it was the result of the colony's game laws. Lungsickness in cattle was always a problem, and even in years of general prosperity there were always regions affected by local drought and shortages. Smallpox introduced from the mines caused difficulties, because quarantine regulations hindered the free movement of workers, and infected Zulu families had not only to suffer the horror of the disease raging in their isolated homesteads, but were also unable to pay the hut-tax.[54] Nonetheless, the colonial officials felt that such setbacks were more than offset by the healthy balance in the treasury which was based on agricultural production in the homesteads and wage labour beyond Zululand's borders.

Then in 1894 locust swarms arrived from the north, damaging maize in particular, and laying their eggs. These hatched, and the 1894–95 grain crop was virtually wiped out. Magistrates urged all able-bodied men to go out to work and raise the cash they would need to offset these losses in homestead production. The women began to plant root crops. In the 1895–96 season the spring rains were late. The magistrates reported that there was no chance of the wages earned outside the colony covering the shortfalls in homestead production. Even if existing transport facilities could handle the amount of grain needed, it was impossible that sufficient grain could be obtained at the inflated price demanded by traders and storekeepers.[55]

As a result the Zululand government decided to stabilise the grain price by importing maize and selling it at cost, paying local storekeepers and African wagon-drivers to transport it to Zululand. This decision proved an expensive one to implement – especially when rinderpest regulations in neighbouring Natal closed the border to ox-drawn traffic and the grain had to be imported by sea. Revenue decreased as homesteads were made destitute, and in December 1896 the Zululand government could not cover its current expenses and had to ask for a loan on the hut-tax which was to be collected in June.[56]

The one sector of the Zululand economy which had shown a steady improvement since annexation was cattle holdings. In August 1897 rinderpest entered the Nquthu district, spread rapidly through the country, and within a year killed 85 per cent of the cattle in the country.[57] On 29 December 1897 the colony of Zululand, no longer securely based on productive homesteads and dependent on a steady stream of wages entering the country, was incorporated into the debt-ridden colony of Natal.

Drought, epidemic and plague directly undermined homestead production, forcing more and more men out to labour for wages;[58] but it is not valid to interpret them as the major force in the subordination of Zulu society to the demands of capitalist production. As we have seen, the pattern was already being established before 1894. The diseases and droughts which afflicted Zululand after 1894 cannot be categorised as just 'natural disasters': they were natural enough, but the degree to which they were disastrous depended on the social context in which they occurred. After all, Zululand had a serious locust invasion thirty years before; smallpox entered the country in the reign of Mpande; the malaria and *nagana* belts spread and receded with climatic and vegetational changes throughout Zulu history; lungsickness had been present in Zululand since the 1850s and, although less dramatic than rinderpest, it was an endemic, debilitating disease which continually reduced cattle numbers. However, these occurred in a social situation in which more land was available and the local movement of homesteads easier, and custom softened the blows of economic disaster by spreading the impact through the obligations of kinship.

The disasters of the late 1890s took place in a colonial context; in a situation which demanded that every year, regardless of their economic well-being, 14s was collected from every house within every homestead in the country. Earlier in this chapter I described the hut-tax as a tax on the potential productive capacity of the homestead. It was not, as was the labour service demanded in the kingdom, a tax on the homestead's actual productive capacity. In colonial Zululand the failure of the homestead to realise its productive potential was not considered sufficient reason to excuse payment of the hut-tax – indeed, the hut-tax plus a fine in cattle was the penalty for being found guilty of 'evasion of tax'.

The failures in homestead production in the late 1890s and the diversion of wages to cover the subsistence needs of the homestead made it extremely difficult to collect the hut-tax. As a magistrate pointed out:

the absence of cattle creates a difficulty in enforcing payment – there being no property other than food which could be seized for such as might neglect to pay.[59]

The only answer was to make ever-increasing demands on the wage-labourers. Thus in November 1897 the magistrates were ordered to

> Remind all the Chiefs . . . of the necessity for preparing their people to pay the Hut Tax next year by encouraging the young men to go out to work.[60]

And a few months later the chiefs were told

> that any young men who may be loitering at their kraals should be sent out to work with as little delay as possible.[61]

Many went, as a magistrate reported:

> since the loss of their cattle I notice a greater desire on the part of the Natives to proceed to work, in fact kraal heads have informed me that they are now dependent, to a great extent, upon the earnings of young men.[62]

However, the increased exploitation of the younger men of Zululand could not take place without causing tension within the country. We have seen that already earlier in the decade there were indications of an increasing division beteen those with property and those without − between fathers, homestead-heads, men of rank, and those forced to labour for wages. These divisions were made greater in the later 1890s after failures in homestead production made it necessary to impose even more on those earning wages.

Class formation

This added exploitation of the wage-labourers of Zululand manifested itself in a variety of ways. At one level it was revealed in the increasing number of complaints of the lack of respect that younger people were showing for custom and for the older generation, although officials alleged that this was the consequence of their experiences at work. As one magistrate reported:

> They value money only as the means of getting cattle and as the latter are now almost unprocurable the incentive to work is wanting. It is necessary for them to get money, however, and they seek employment in the mines in the Transvaal, where their experiences must tend to demoralise the young men and boys who when they do return to their kraals are found to have lost a good deal of their former respect for elders and kraal influence. The fact that Natives remain away in some instances for lengthened periods likewise tends to lessen kraal restraint and this accounts for women and girls deserting their kraals more than formerly.[63]

In addition, Addison, Magistrate of the Nquthu district, wrote that it was impossible not to

> help noticing the decline of the young generation as compared to their fathers. The honesty, courteous manner, and respect to their elders, which were a characteristic of the Zulu, are gradually disappearing.[64]

Their protest went beyond truculence and bad manners in the homestead.

Some took to stock theft: in Addison's area the convicts 'consist chiefly of young men'.[65] Others disregarded the obligations and laws of homestead formation and marriage. Although in some areas it was reported that the Zulu had reverted to the old system of paying *lobolo* over an extended period of time, the general feeling was that the system was collapsing. 'The losses caused by rinderpest have made it impossible for natives to conform with the customs of *lobolo* hitherto observed. They are anxious for some other system to be proclaimed', wrote one magistrate.[66] Magistrates reported a general increase in 'adultery' and 'desertion' and attempts to avoid *lobolo* commitments. Fathers of girls made the situation worse by forcing their daughters onto those few men who were still in possession of stock.[67] In other cases men simply founded new homesteads regardless of their fathers' wishes and laws of inheritance.

> The heads of houses in kraals will not brook interference from the kraal head, hence break away and build kraals of their own, therefore the supervision and control of families which [was] maintained under the Zulu regime is fast becoming a thing of the past.[68]

However, there was another, more radical way of resisting the increasing demands of the homestead and the colonial state. That was to break away from Zululand altogether, cut links with the homestead and the family and remain at the place of work — which meant, in effect, the Witwatersrand — beyond the reach of the Natal or Zululand magistrates' police. Thus in 1897 the magistrate of Ndwandwe reported that one of the reasons why the people of his district were impoverished was

> the misconduct of the young men who go to Johannesburg to seek work: these have latterly taken to squandering their earnings and staying at the Rand instead of saving and coming home with them for the use of their families.[69]

In 1898 it was reported that

> Husbands are continually deserting their wives by not returning from work.[70]

And

> a great many of the young men are away working, and there are complaints of the reluctance they show to come back again. Many have been absent for years, and it is feared, have permanently deserted their homes.[71]

It must have been difficult to choose between the increasing demands and decreasing rewards of labour migrancy, and the dangers and insecurity of a worker's life on the Witwatersrand. Nevertheless, those who chose the latter course at least avoided handing over a considerable portion of their wages to their families and the colonial state, and as van Onselen's research is showing, the move to the city was not just an 'ineluctable march . . . into the working class'.[72]

The colonial state

However, work taking place on the Witwatersrand denied Natal and Zululand the opportunity of raking off a percentage of the workers' wages. In Natal, all the changes I have described above appear to have occurred earlier and already to have penetrated the social structure more deeply. Thus in 1895 J. S. Marwick was appointed Johannesburg representative of the office of the SNA in Natal. It was his job to ensure that wages were safely remitted to the colony, that men who had failed to pay the tax on their houses in Natal were traced, that Natal debtors who had fled to the mines were brought to book. In some cases workers who had in Marwick's words 'become unmindful of their natural obligations to the community from which they have sprung'[73] and were 'squandering' their earnings, were bundled on the train bound for Natal.

Early in 1896 Marwick was appointed representative of the Zululand government in Johannesburg. He was assisted by Sikonyela, previously *induna* to Mnyamana, chief of the Buthelezi. Sikonyela's rank, however, did not save him from having his three assegais confiscated by the police on his arrival at the station in Johannesburg.[74]

> Will you kindly have Sigonyela asked to hustle the young men a bit about remitting money in view of the near approach of hut tax time?[75]

wrote the Ndwandwe Magistrate, and another official asked Marwick to trace a man's four sons:

> They left their kraal some years ago and have never remitted any money nor have they ever visited home. Their father is much concerned about their conduct and [is] getting old.[76]

Another aspect of this need to ensure that a proportion of the worker's wages reached the colonial treasuries was the attempt to shore up homestead production when it showed signs of failing. We have already seen that in times of shortage colonial funds were used to stabilise maize prices. The placing of limits on *lobolo* reflected the same need. Although *lobolo* doubled or tripled after annexation, and this worked in favour of greater control and increased wage-labour, there was the danger that if the price went too high it would place daughters completely beyond the reach of the earnings of the unmarried men. The absence of limits, it was felt, would result in 'hardship', 'and the privilege would be abused'.[77] Another magistrate felt that lower limits on *lobolo*

> would have the effect of the women being more generally distributed among the men and would increase the necessity of the men to go out and work as I have noticed that in kraals where there are only two or three wives men as a rule go out regularly to work.[78]

Clearly an optimum figure had to be set: one which forced unmarried men out to work without making it impossible for them to achieve the target and thereby undermine homestead reproduction and increase the rate of proletarianisation.

At the end of 1897 Zululand was incorporated into Natal as a province of the colony, and in 1899 the new Natal Pass Regulations applied to Zululand. The major provisions show clearly that the colonial state was attempting to control and confine the African workforce. For example, outward passes were valid for only a year, could be issued only by a magistrate, and the pass-seeker had to be identified by his chief or a representative. Passes had to be refused to anyone already under contract or in service, any male under eighteen years of age, any married woman unless accompanied by her husband, and any unmarried woman unaccompanied by her father or guardian. Applications to leave the colony had to receive the approval of the chief and the magistrate, and procedures were laid down to assist in recording the movements of all pass-bearers. The Tout's Act of 1901 made it illegal to recruit labour to work beyond the colony's borders.

All these interventions sprang from the colonial state's desire to shore up the increasingly unstable foundation of the rural economy; to support homestead production when it showed signs of disintegration, and to re-channel the flow of wages when they spilled over the colony's borders. Whatever form they took later, and whatever specific interests they came to serve, labour migrancy and the ideology of segregation, so far as Zululand was concerned, had their origins in the desire that the colonial state had for a cut of the wages of its first workers.

Conclusion

Early in the 1890s the Resident Commissioner in Zululand described the colonial regime imposed on the country as one which was based on the structure of traditional society, but which introduced certain progressive elements. In particular, it freed the unmarried men of Zululand from the tyranny of the Zulu dynasty, which had drawn on their labour for much of their productive lives, and allowed these young men to labour for wages and establish themselves as free, independent homestead-heads. The colonial system had reconstructed Zulu society, blending the best of the old with the new. It was a system which served progress in southern Africa as well as the well-being of the Zulu people.

By the end of the 1890s all this had been proved hollow; the system was still in existence, but its foundations were already crumbling. Homestead production was failing, wages were not flowing freely back to the colony, and the hut-tax was becoming increasingly difficult to collect. The system survived only through the continual intervention of the colonial state. The Shepstone system which provided the rationale for the particular political and administrative structure imposed on Zululand was not, however, just a veneer which covered total subordination. It was based originally on a shrewd understanding of the distribution of power in pre-colonial Nguni societies and the way in which this could be utilised by the colonial state. That it was not as well suited to the centralised Zulu kingdom as it had been to the Natal chiefdoms of the 1840s was demonstrated with bloody clarity in the Zulu civil war. But it was not totally inapplicable, and it could be argued that Zululand of the early 1890s, with its chiefly rule, African access to land, customary law and favourable balance in the Treasury were indications of the success of the Shepstone system.

Closer examination, however, reveals that this was not so. The imposition of colonial rule in Zululand created within Zulu society fundamental changes and contradictions which could not be resolved within that social context. Similar contradictions had taken a number of decades to emerge in Natal. In Zululand, however, because these developments in Natal tended to spill over their common border, and because of the increased strength of capitalism in the 1890s, these changes and contradictions emerged in a far shorter space of time.

Almost contemporaneously with the imposition of colonial rule, the desire for individual accumulation was causing change and tension in Zululand. This created divisions of a new kind in the country, although they were given social expression as rivalry over access to traditional forms of property. Furthermore, the fixed demands that the colonial state made on the productive communities of the country caused chaos and suffering when natural events undermined productive capacity. As a result, an increasing number of Zulu left the colony permanently, an action which only threatened the stability of the colonial state further.

The effect of the imposition of colonial rule on Zulu society was to create a brittleness in the social structure. Thus we see the emergence of cracks steadily separating the propertied homestead-heads and the younger wage-labourers.[79] There was a loss of flexibility, and the structure now showed a tendency to fragment under the blows of shortage and famine rather than absorb them as it had done in the past.

It seems to me misleading to conceptualise the Zulu social formation in the 1890s as a pre-capitalist mode of production coming into articulation with the capitalist mode. To do this is to confuse form and content. One would have to accept the official rhetoric of the time, for the continuities with the pre-capitalist past were superficial ones. It is true that homesteads still existed and production took place within them, that chiefs were still local administrators who applied the customary law which controlled the polygynous homestead, kinship and the transfer of *lobolo*; but empirical examination indicates that the content of these forms changed rapidly. As each year passed, so more homesteads lost their self-sufficiency as productive units under the supervisory control of the homestead-head. The material basis of the chief's status had begun to change from the moment he was appointed, and he retained his rank only as long as he served the interests of the colonial state. Basic principles of marriage and homestead formation were altered almost as soon as the colonial state was founded. In the 1890s Zulu society had changed fundamentally, from a society in which man was the aim of production to one in which production was the aim of man.

The Zulu kingdom successfully resisted the intrusion of capitalist forces up to 1879. As a result it suffered first invasion and then civil war during which the pre-capitalist system was effectively smashed. Reconstruction followed, but it was the reconstruction of a façade: a façade built from pieces carefully selected from the ruins it was meant to hide. Thus certain pre-capitalist features were retained if they enabled the colonial state to extract a surplus more effectively, and were rejected if they obstructed this. Capitalism dominated Zulu society from 1889, when the first hut-tax was successfully collected. From this time it was made to serve the interest of capitalist accumulation, whether mediated through the colonial state, or, as happened later, mining capital through the South African state.

It is true that the 1890s and beyond was still a stage of transition, but there is nothing in the immediate subsequent developments to suggest that there was a reversal of the trends that I have outlined here. The upheaval of the war at the turn of the century, the depression that followed, the drought of 1903, another devastating cattle disease in the form of East Coast fever, can only have exacerbated these trends. In 1905 over 40 per cent of Zululand was opened to white settlement. In this chapter I have considered only cattle and women as forms of property underlying incipient class divisions; it seems clear that access to land would soon become a crucial factor as well.

In 1905 a poll-tax was imposed on all men not already paying the hut-tax. It was deliberately aimed at those 'Africans who were escaping their tax burden, [and] it was felt that the young, unmarried ones were the worst culprits'.[80] Here, surely, we have a clear indication of the final collapse of the older homestead production system; a recognition that the homestead was no longer able effectively to produce and control surplus labour in the interests of the colonial state. An old man in Zululand caught the essence of the changes which had come to the country when he complained of this poll-tax which meant that

> although a man had a son who by rights ought to work for him, the son was obliged, on account of this tax, to go and work for himself.[81]

Notes

Abbreviations

BPP	*British Parliamentary Papers*
JSAS	*Journal of Southern African Studies*
RM	Natal Archives, Resident Magistrates' record books
SNA	Natal Archives, Secretary for Native Affairs files
ZA	Natal Archives, Zululand Archives
ZGH	Natal Archives, Zululand Government House

1 RM, Lower Mfolozi, 2/7/1, *Supreme Chief* v. *uMsilana*, 22 Dec. 1888.
2 See especially H. Wolpe, 'Capitalism and cheap labour-power in South Africa: from segregation to apartheid', *Economy and Society*, I, 4 (1972).
3 J. Banaji, 'Modes of production in a materialist conception of history', *Capital and Class 3* (autumn 1977); and P. Kallaway, 'Tribesman, trader, peasant and proletarian', *African Perspective*, (1979).
4 I have discussed the nature of the pre-conquest Zulu kingdom a number of times. See 'Production and exchange in the Zulu kingdom', *Mohlomi: Journal of Southern African Studies*, II (1978), and *The Destruction of the Zulu Kingdom* (London, 1979), chs 1 and 2.
5 C. Meillassoux, 'From reproduction to production: a Marxist approach to economic anthropology', *Economy and Society*, I (1972), 100 and 101.
6 E. J. Hobsbawm (ed.), *Karl Marx: pre-capitalist economic formations* (New York, 1965), p. 84.
7 This section is based on Guy, *Destruction of the Zulu Kingdom*.
8 And I deal specifically only with the six magisterial districts which were annexed in 1887, not those annexed later. This affects to a limited degree some of the figures I give later in the chapter. The territories annexed later in the north-east require special treatment as they lay on the periphery of the kingdom, and commerce, trade, and wage labour affected the people living there far earlier than the people of the core of the kingdom.
9 See Guy, 'The destruction of Zulu independence: the part played by the Natal officials', a paper delivered at a conference on the Anglo-Zulu war, a centennial reappraisal, University of Natal, Durban, 7–9 Feb. 1979.
10 See S. Marks, 'Natal, the Zulu royal family and the ideology of segregation', *JSAS* IV, 2 (1978), 174–5.
11 *BPP*: C5331, No. 2, Laws and Regulations for the Government of Zululand, 1.
12 *BPP*: C3616, No. 31, enc., p. 57 and p. 59.
13 ZGH: 741, Z836, Minute, Osborn to Mitchell, 28 April 1892.
14 RM, Eshowe, 5/11/1, Saunders to Dunn, Jan. 1888.
15 These estimates are taken from the Zululand Annual Reports and ZGH, 768, Z201, Statement showing the Revenue and Expenditure 1891–1895.
16 Zululand, Annual Report, 1889.
17 ZGH: 730, Z535, Knutsford to Mitchell, 15 Aug. 1890; Zululand Annual Report, 1893.
18 RM, Nquthu, 5/1/14, Osborn to Tyrell, 29 Aug. 1888 (private).
19 RM, Melmoth, 5/1/3, Knight to Osborn, 27 Oct. 1888. On 24 Dec. Knight

reported, 'There is scarcely a kraal in the District from whence men have not gone.'

20 RM, Melmoth, 5/1/4, Knight to Osborn, 27 March 1889, 6 April 1889, and 1 June 1889, RM, Nongoma, 2/9/5, Gibson to Osborn, 10 Oct. 1889. RM, Lower Mfolozi, 5/1/2, Tye to Osborn, 8 July 1889.

21 SNA: 1/1/106, 335/88 and SNA: 1/1/108, 607/88 and 661/88. Evidence of the problems of forcing labour at this time can be found in SNA: 1/1/110 and 1/1/117.

22 SNA: 1/1/108, 705/88, Minute by District Engineer (Construction), 25 Sept. 1888. SNA to Res. Comm. 2 Oct. 1888 (telegram) and the reply and subsequent correspondence.

23 RM, Eshowe, 5/11/1 correspondence with the RM Ladysmith, Sept. and Oct. 1888.

24 RM, Melmoth, 5/1/4, Knight to Osborn, 7 Oct. 1889.

25 See above, p. 167.

26 SNA: 1/1/134, Osborn to H. Shepstone, 11 Oct. 1888 (private).

27 *Times of Natal*, 23 Oct. 1889.

28 RM, Nongoma, 2/9/5, Gibson to Osborn, 11 July 1889.

29 RM, Melmoth, 5/1/4, Knight to Wilson, 24 Sept. 1889.

30 I have not tried to quantify the figures on labour migration from Zululand in this period. The figures that exist in the records raise many problems, and at this stage of my research any statement on labour migration can only be impressionistic.

31 See the information in ZA69, *Regina* v. *Hlakanyana and Umbumbuluzo*, ZA70, *Regina* v. *Mgitshwa and Mhlutshwa*; ZA78, *Regina* v. *Mtshingeni*. All these cases deal with the theft of workers' wages.

32 Transvaal Labour Commission, evidence of Lagden, p. 136.

33 RM, Eshowe, Saunders to Clarke, 31 Jan. 1896.

34 RM, Melmoth, 5/1/3, Knight to Osborn, 5 Sept. 1888.

35 Zululand Annual Report, 1890 (C.6269).

36 ZGH: 730, Z503, Report, 5 Sept. 1890.

37 On 29 Dec. 1897 Zululand became a province of the colony of Natal.

38 *Natal Blue Book on Native Affairs*, 1898. Chief Magistrate's and Civil Commissioner's report, C14.

39 I am trying to develop a method of assessing the relative importance of the different sectors contributing to the Zulu economy. There are many difficulties arising not only out of the unreliable nature of the available statistics but also because market and non-market sectors are probably not strictly comparable. However, for what they are worth I offer the following estimates based on 1894 statistics and Saunders' estimates for the Eshowe district in 1896. In 1894 the six original magisterial districts paid £35 212 in hut-tax. Workers brought back three times that amount of cash, and the homesteads produced four and a half times that amount of grain at market prices. The cattle holdings were worth twice the annual grain crop. It should be noted, however, that this is based on Saunders' 1896 estimates. Grain actually sold at double the price he estimated. After rinderpest, a magistrate noted that he had underestimated the cattle holdings by half.

40 *BPP*: C5331, No. 2, enc. 3, Memo. by Sir T. Shepstone, 23 April 1887, p. 18.

41 *BPP*: 5331, No. 2 and enc. 3 in No. 2.

42 *BPP*: 5331, No. 2, enc. 1, Proclamation II, 1887.

43 ZA75, *Supreme Chief* v. *Sembatwa*.

44 ZA15, Circular from Resident Commissioner and Chief Magistrate, Feb. 1894.

45 In ZA15.

46 No historical study of *lobolo* can avoid reference to H. J. Simons, *African Women: their*

legal status in South Africa (London, 1968), a book full of insight and significant analysis. I must point out, however, that, in my short treatment of *lobolo* here, I am using evidence which emerged in the 1890s to indicate changes which seem to have been occurring *at that specific period*. Some of these trends appear to have been reversed at a later period, but one should not conclude from this that they necessarily reflect a reversion to an older, more traditional, situation. The greatest challenge to the analyst of change in African societies in this context is to distinguish successfully form from content, apparent correspondence and non-correspondence.

47 ZA15, C. R. Saunders, Memorandum: On the custom of Lobola, 9 Sept. 1896.

48 *Ibid.*, and Addison to Res. Comm., 16 Dec. 1890. See the entry for *umkhwenyana* ('son-in-law') in Doke and Vilakazi, *Zulu–English Dictionary* (Johannesburg, 1972): 'Umkhwenyana yisigodo sokuqhuzula' (A son-in-law is a log for constant chopping).

49 ZA15, Addison to Res. Comm., 16 Dec. 1890. See also Saunders to Ag. Res. Comm., 12 Dec. 1890 (confidential). The adoption by Zulu of practices already in existence in Natal (facilitated by the presence of Natal Africans in the southern districts) is an important factor, and also a frustrating one. It makes it difficult to distinguish developments springing from within the Zulu social formation itself and those which developed by imitation.

50 ZA15, Knight to Ag. Res. Comm., 20 May 1891.

51 ZA15, Saunders to Ag. Res. Comm., 12 Dec. 1890 (confidential).

52 RM, Nongoma, 2/9/6, 29 Dec. 1890: 'the payment of an increased lobola to appointed Chiefs and Headmen is necessary to give them more standing and authority among the people', and ZA15, R280, Lower Mfolozi, statement by Jan: 'I think the daughters of men of rank should be fixed at twenty head, so as to prevent any common man who has ten head of cattle marrying them to which we have a very great objection.'

53 See above.

54 RM, Nongoma, 2/9/7, RM, Ndwande to Res. Comm., 31/10/92. In the same file in his report for the month ending 15 Nov. 1892, he writes: 'I recognize the necessity for taking the greatest precaution against the spreading of so terrible a disease as small pox is, but it seems a pity that such precautions should be carried unnecessarily far when they are of a nature to affect so seriously the industries of neighbouring territories and the welfare of the people of this.'

55 RM, Melmoth, 5/1/6, A. J. Shepstone to Res. Comm., 31 Jan. 1896. RM, Eshowe, 5/11/3, Saunders to Res. Comm., 31 Jan. 1896.

56 ZGH: 773, Z1149/96, Clarke to Hely-Hutchinson, 5 Dec. 1896.

57 For an assessment of the epidemic's effects in southern Africa, see C. van Onselen, 'Reactions to rinderpest in southern Africa, 1896–97', *Journal of African History*, XIII, 3 (1972).

58 See below.

59 RM, Nongoma, 2/9/9, Report for May 1898.

60 Res. Comm., Circular, 19 Nov. 1897.

61 Res. Comm., Circular, 15 Feb. 1898.

62 *Natal Blue Book*, Departmental Reports, Report on the Province of Zululand, 1898, Lower Mfolozi district, BB26.

63 *Natal Blue Book on Native Affairs*, 1898, Eshowe district, C18.

64 *Natal Blue Book on Native Affairs*, 1898, Nquthu district, C28. Addison attributed this to passing of the old Zulu order with its strict military discipline. The irony is that, only a decade previously, Addison himself played a leading role in the pursuit

and defeat of all Zulu who showed the slightest support for this system the disappearance of which Addison now showed such regret.

65 *Ibid.*

66 *Natal Blue Book*, Departmental Reports, Report on the Province of Zululand, 1898, Emtonjaneni district, BB36.

67 *Natal Blue Book*, Departmental Reports, 1900, Nkandla district, B114.

68 *Natal Blue Book on Native Affairs*, 1898. Lower Mfolozi district, C35.

69 RM, Nongoma, 2/9/9, Report of the Res. Mag., 1897.

70 *Natal Blue Book on Native Affairs*, 1898, Nquthu district, C28.

71 *Natal Blue Book on Native Affairs*, 1898, Ndwandwe district, C43.

72 C. van Onselen, *Studies in the Social and Economic History of the Witwatersrand 1886–1914*, Vol. 2, *New Nineveh* (London, 1982), Chapter 2, 'Amawasha: the Zulu washermen's guild of the Witwatersrand, 1890–1914'.

73 *Natal Blue Book on Native Affairs*, 1897. Report of J. S. Marwick, Representative at Johannesburg of the Department of SNA, 28 Feb. 1898, p. 31. It is most unfortunate that most of Marwick's correspondence has not yet been traced. His reports written for the SNA appear intermittently in the SNA files. Those for Zululand were addressed to the office of Res. Comm., and most of the records of this office have yet to be found.

74 SNA: 1/1/125, Marwick, Report for week ending 11 July 1896.

75 RM, Nongoma, Gibson to Windham (private), 22 April 1897.

76 RM, Mahlabathini, Letter book 1898–1900, RM to Marwick, 9 Oct. 1899.

77 ZA15, RM, Melmoth to Res. Comm., 28 Nov. 1893.

78 RM, Nongoma, 2/9/6, Ag. RM to Ag. Res. Comm., 29 Dec. 1890.

79 In her article, 'Natal, the Zulu royal family and the ideology of segregation', JSAS, IV, 2 (1978), p. 190, Shula Marks suggests that within a generation these cracks were now chasms. It seems to me that detailed research would show how the cracks of the 1890s widened as more and more commoner homesteads were impoverished, leaving at the top a smaller number of wealthy chiefs and rich peasant producers, based, I would imagine, on their status within the colonial system and their resultant ability to influence the allocation of land.

80 S. Marks, *Reluctant Rebellion* (Oxford, 1970), p. 141.

81 *Natal Native Affairs Commission*, 1906–7, evidence of Magonondo, p. 750.

CHAPTER SEVEN

The sharecropping economy, African class formation and the 1913 Natives' Land Act in the highveld maize belt

Tim Keegan

The role of African peasants in early capital accumulation in South Africa has only been fully recognised in recent years, due in large part to the pioneering work of Colin Bundy.[1] As yet, however, little detailed empirical research has been undertaken on the nature and significance of the peasant economies in different areas of white settlement in South Africa, and on the precise mechanisms of capitalisation and class formation which have transformed agrarian society and economy in the twentieth century. This is an important task if the dynamics of South African capitalist development are to be fully understood. A range of themes relating to industrialisation, such as the social history of Johannesburg, have begun to receive attention, and work on the transformation of African social formations is increasingly sophisticated and extensive. With some important exceptions, however, the study of agrarian change in white-settled areas has lagged behind. Any attempt to fill this gap must be more concretely empirical than the rather general, theoretical overviews that have dominated discussion in recent years.[2] If the debates on race and class, on segregationist ideology and practice, and on the nature and role of the state are to be rescued from the sterility into which they have drifted, then detailed studies of class relations and their transformation on a local level are required. Hence the focus of this paper is the maize belt of the southern highveld in the early twentieth century.[3]

The mineral discoveries in the South African interior during the late nineteenth century had profound effects on the agrarian formations of the highveld. From its inception with the opening of large urban markets, the South African maize revolution was in considerable measure predicated on black peasant enterprise. In areas of white settlement on the highveld, this enterprise largely took the form of sharecropping – a system in which surplus labour was expended on the tenant's plot, and the surplus extracted by the landlord took the form of a proportion of the crop. This generally amounted to a half, rising in certain cases to two-thirds or even more.[4] This paper examines the sharecropping economy, its significance and characteristics, and its eventual decline and destruction.

Being a highly commercialised relationship, sharecropping generally arose in response to the emergence of the markets at Kimberley and, more importantly, on the Rand. Thus it spread rapidly in the 1890s, particularly in areas with easy access to the markets, such as the northern Orange Free State and southern Transvaal, which were relatively close to Johannesburg and which from 1892 were bisected by the railway. This area, too, was pre-eminently suited for dry-land maize production. In other areas, such as the eastern Free State, the 'Conquered Territory', it was only after the Anglo-Boer war, with the establishment of rail facilities, that maize production and marketing on a large scale became viable for the white landowners. Here, too, with the expansion of maize production, sharecropping was rapidly extended.[5]

The zenith of sharecropping in the highveld maize districts was relatively short-lived, but during the decade following the end of the Anglo-Boer war it seems that sharecropping was the dominant relation of production in most of the arable districts of the white-settled highveld, although quantitive assessments are difficult to make because of the lack of adequate statistics.[6]

Understanding sharecropping demands an enquiry into the peasant–tenant economy and its subsumption within colonial capitalism, along with an analysis of the role of sharecropping in the process of landlord capital accumulation. The rapidity of landlord capitalisation and the related undermining of the commercial peasant tenantry led to a situation by 1913 in which the state was able to intervene (albeit with limited initial success) in the interests of rich white farmers.[7] Capital accumulation in the landlord economy meant that the intensification of exploitation most frequently took the form of expropriation of the sharecropping peasantry rather than increased surplus extraction on the basis of existing landlord–tenant relations.

What made the sharecropping system work despite the implicit conflicts in it[8] was the peasants' own vigorous productive enterprise rather than coercion. Landlords' profits depended upon the capacity of their black tenants to maximise output. Without much supervision beyond that provided by the landlord himself or his agent, and no policing other than the physical presence of the contracting parties at the harvest, the relationship was based on a precarious balance of interests. Despite widespread conflict over the division of the harvest, each party needed the other.

The way in which individual households 'locked into' this commercialised and relatively large-scale cash-crop production requires investigation. Emelia Pooe's testimony, collected by Ted Matsetela of the University of Witwatersrand,[9] provides some illumination. Her family first took to sharecropping in the Heilbron district in the northern Free State in 1897. The rinderpest epizootic and a drought had only recently come to an end. In order to get a ploughing team together, her father had to borrow young bullocks and heifers from their neighbours. What may have led him to commercial sharecropping was the promise of seed and credit from the landlord and the prospect of recovering his stock holdings with the proceeds from his enterprise. As a sharecropper, Mrs Pooe's father had access to more ploughing land; indeed, his acceptability to his landlord depended on his willingness to maximise his crop. Under these circumstances, and given the monetisation of many items of productive and personal consumption, as well as credit relations and tax demands which were already in some degree part and parcel of the peasant economy, economic survival as independent producers for many families meant a decision to throw in their lot with a white landlord who had both land and access to state aid and credit. In this way, many black tenant households came into the capitalist economy as sharecroppers producing surplus crops for the landlords. Economic motivation and market relations should be seen in this material context, for it was these factors which turned black cultivators into commercial sharecroppers, rather than any supposed innate, universal predisposition to respond to market opportunities for their own sake.[10]

Options for Africans were changing in the 1880s and 1890s. They were finding it more and more difficult to exist on the margins of the colonial economy. Those on white-owned farms had to decide whether they were going to become ever more dependent on the alienation of their own labour as labour–tenants or as wage-earners, or to succumb to the colonial economy by transforming and extending their own productive activities. If they chose the latter course – the course of the sharecroppers – they had to do so wholeheartedly, for their security of tenure depended on their capacity to satisfy their landlords' drive for surplus, at a time of increasing commercial opportunity. They had to have the skill and the capacity of commercial farmers, or risk failure. So, despite the structural constraints which pushed households ever deeper into relations of surplus extraction, there was, nevertheless, often an element of choice involved in the way in which individual households responded.[11] Hence observers in the mid-1890s noted that many Africans were moving from other districts into the northern Free State specifically in order to enter sharecropping relationships.[12]

This is not to say that Africans had not produced for the market prior to the mineral discoveries (they had on a considerable scale) or that a rent in the form of a share had never before been extracted from African tenants. But the nature and scale of the landlord–sharecropper relationship were qualitatively different by the 1890s. It was not simply another form of surplus extraction such as Africans living on the white-owned farms had long since grown used to. The sharecroppers were entering a new realm of productive enterprise. The crucial new factor, the growth of a massive home market on the Witwatersrand, stimulated a new cash-crop economy demanding high levels of production. This required a new breed of market-oriented producers, including the black sharecroppers.

The limited evidence suggests that in the early years of the twentieth century some sharecropping families cultivated twenty or thirty morgen. The more prosperous could produce three hundred bags of maize in a growing season, as well as wheat in favourable areas like the eastern Free State, and sorghum, which found a ready market when Africans replaced Chinese workers in the mines after 1906.[13] Although the calculations remain rough and ready, it seems likely that a family unit using its own labour could subsist on a dozen bags of maize a year, and thus some households clearly were producing sizeable surpluses. The mutual profitability of the relationship and the success of the maize export drive after 1907 — which largely depended upon black peasant production irrespective of whether landlord or tenant actually marketed the crop — is evidence that sharecroppers were producing a product fit for international markets.[14]

Such intensive sharecropping seems unlikely without the use of up-to-date ploughs and equipment as well as the intensive mobilisation of family labour.[15] New technology, changes in family labour organisation and new attitudes to productive activity were logically necessary for successful sharecropping.[16]

Another important facet of agrarian formation was stratification amongst the white landlords. Sharecropping took place in the context of an evolving rural capitalism. Incipient class differentiation amongst the tenants coincided with the uneven development of landlord capitalism. Resident sharecropping landlords[17] were usually the poorer and less capitalised white settlers. They were therefore the most vulnerable to expropriation and foreclosure at a time when more and more private capital was seeking profitable investment in land, when mercantile credit was easily obtainable and when the relative self-sufficiency of the settler family was eroding rapidly. The purchase of land for younger sons and the buying-out of co-heirs, common features of Boer property relations and testamentary practice, often involved considerable indebtedness at times of rising land values. On the other hand, some white farmers were able to escape the more debilitating aspects of indebtedness and embarked on a relatively self-sustaining cycle of development of the means and the organisation of production. They were thus able to enter more directly into capitalist relations if the supply of labour permitted. The uneven development of landlord capitalism was therefore intimately related to differentiation amongst black tenants; the large-scale, intensive production of the sharecroppers was indispensable to the poorer white landowners.[18]

The significance of the constraints blocking capitalist agriculture can best be understood by examining the productive processes involved. A one-share plough drawn by oxen can turn no more than about a morgen of ground per day; and by 1894, according to *The Friend*, 90 per cent of the ploughs in the Free State were still one-share ploughs.[19] Climatic conditions on the South African highveld dictate that ploughing be completed in as short a period as possible, since rain comes in sharp, intense thunder-showers and the soil is wet enough for ploughing only for relatively short periods. Before the age of motor traction, farmers who wished to participate in the exchange economy as grain producers were hard pressed to get a competitive acreage under crops.

Thus by the 1890s some white farmers in the Free State used more than twenty ploughs simultaneously.[20] This required the labour of up to sixty males (including young boys as leaders of the oxen), plus 120 or 160 oxen. Not surprisingly, given the labour and capital constraints experienced by white farmers, most were simply incapable of mobilising resources on this scale. Under these circumstances, it was more viable to draw off a surplus from a number of individual peasant households working with their own implements and oxen. Hence the partiality for sharecropping arrangements amongst so many white landlords. G. Tylden, a farmer of Ladybrand district, defended sharecropping relationships in the following terms in 1908:

> Very few of us Boers . . . can afford to keep more than one span of oxen to plough with . . . it means too much capital locked up in animals which do not increase. This means that in our extremely short ploughing seasons we cannot bring a sufficient proportion of our land under cultivation. . . . The farmer therefore gives one or more of these natives, who own perhaps three spans between them, a certain amount of land to plough. The boy finds the labour and often the seed, and gives the owner of the farm half the crop grown.[21]

Thus there was not necessarily a division between sharecropping landlords, on the one hand, and those who directly controlled productive activities on their land, on the other. Both types of relationship generally coexisted on the same farm. There was also a considerable degree of differentiation within the African peasantry. Although many tenants had the wherewithal to succeed as sharecroppers to their own as well as to their landlords' benefit, others were more dependent on the direct alienation of their labour power. Many a white farmer/landlord would use tenant labour to work with his own implements and oxen, while supplementing such production with the surplus production of sharecropping families using their own implements and oxen.

An important factor in the spread of sharecropping arrangements was the proliferation of small farms, particularly after the Anglo-Boer war. Newly established settlers very quickly moved into sharecropping relationships. The larger Boer landowners of an earlier date had managed to maintain themselves on the basis of extensive pastoralism. The smaller landowners (or lessees) who were increasingly becoming a feature of the arable districts had to survive on the basis of grain production, supplemented by dairy farming, or go under. Given high land values and the need to enter debt in order to establish basic improvements on the land, these newer settlers very quickly became dependent on tenant enterprise. Although the Boers had always been dependent to some extent on exchange for commodities and capital, the extent of the dependence of highveld farmers on commodity production was probably far greater by the beginning of the twentieth century than ever before. In the grain districts this increasingly meant intensive cash-crop production, given the declining size of farms. And this in turn meant sharecropping relationships for many, even most. The significance of sharecropping in this context is illustrated by C. Chase, who described himself as a 'young struggling and progressive' farmer in Heilbron. Chase held his farm on lease and hoped to buy it. Yet his limited resources restricted him to the use of one plough and one team of oxen, which, given the soaring price of land, provided insufficient income. He supplemented his own efforts with those of two sharecroppers. With the profits gained from the combined efforts of the three, he hoped to buy his farm and invest in stock and equipment for more intensive exploitation of the land.[22] G. J. van Riet of Thaba Nchu district made the same observation as Chase with regard to the post-war settlers of that district:

> If you look round the country you will see some of our settlers who, were it not for the sowing on shares, could not stand today where they are now. The natives were planting and sowing under their supervision, and where settlers were not in a position to buy cattle those natives helped a lot. It is practised by nearly every farmer in the district and by the new settlers.[23]

Thus the process of capital accumulation in the landlord economy was frequently dependent on sharecropping. The extraction of surplus from the black tenantry was often needed for capitalisation. Indeed, the sharecropping relationship can be seen as a form of primitive accumulation. This is not to say that all landlords were themselves individually capitalising. But their survival in an increasingly capitalist economy was dependent on maintaining a competitive income from their tenants' enterprise. Those white landowners who could not survive the rising tide of finance and mercantile capital in the countryside were bound to lose their land eventually. They could not simply opt out of intensified commodity production. The latter implied either the direct employment of black labour under white organisation and capital or, where capital and labour were the limiting factors, as they generally were, entering sharecropping relationships with the commercially oriented peasant tenantry. Those who failed to survive as landowners were already on the path to proletarian status, and helped swell the ranks of the so-called 'poor whites' during these years.[24]

Further, the subsumption of labour power under white agrarian capital had no advantages in terms of productivity or profitability so long as the agricultural technology available to white landlords was not qualitatively different from that used by black sharecroppers. Thus, for the landowner who was unable or unwilling to capitalise his production, the best course was simply to leave the peasant in command of the means of production and to live off the surplus generated. This was especially so since the sharecropper was likely to devote more care to a crop of which half was to be his own than to a crop which was to be of profit to the white farmer alone. Thus, the 1908 Orange River Colony Natives Administration Commission reported that whites who defended sharecropping asserted that 'some natives are as good or better formers than some white men, and that unless the farmer has a direct interest in the crop, he will not exert his best endeavours towards its successful production'. [25]

Sharecropping thrived because and as long as settler farming was stifled through the lack of capital. In the long run, however, sharecropping was itself to give way to the process of capital formation in the landlord economy. The reluctance or inability of sharecroppers to reinvest in improved technology made them vulnerable to expropriation as land prices rose and the opportunity cost of sharecropping increased for capitalising landlords. Sharecroppers could not increase their output sufficiently to maintain their viability. The limits of production were set by the number of family members available to work and their capacity to intensify their own productivity, and the amount of land they could cultivate. Under these circumstances, sharecroppers were particularly vulnerable to any general flow of capital into the landlord economy. It was this factor, apart from any other, which became more and more important after 1907 when the post-war depression began to break. The intervention of the state in the promotion of settler agriculture was probably a major aspect of the transition to capitalist farming.

State intervention took the form of loans for such purposes as fencing, dam building, stock importation, seed and equipment grants, the extension of the railway network, the building of creameries and experimental farms, and action against animal and crop diseases and pests. Most importantly, after 1907 the South African states set up agricultural loan banks and promoted grain exports by heavily subsidising freight rates. Access to capital and resources on such a scale was a new experience for white farmers, especially as a result of the economic boom which followed unification in 1910, when private finance was made available to maize farmers on an unprecedented scale. [26]

The swing to capital-intensive farming was not yet massive in these years. But good seasons, easy capital and credit, and assured markets all served to create incentives and transform attitudes. Agrarian capital formation was never a simple, evolutionary process. Nevertheless, the half-dozen years after 1907–8 were crucial in the process of capitalisation of settler agriculture and the transformation of productive relations on the farms in the maize belt of the highveld. The vilification of 'kaffir farmers' and landlords who allowed 'squatters' to 'infest' their lands grew more urgent in consequence. Thus, bills were produced before the Transvaal and Orange River Colony legislatures in 1908 designed to prohibit all tenancy by Africans other than labour-tenants. These abortive statutes were forerunners of the anti-'squatting' clauses of the 1913 Natives' Land Act, though it was decided not to implement their provisions in anticipation of the approaching National Convention.

There was not, however, an absolute decline of sharecropping relations. The contrasts between capitalist and peasant farming may have become starker, and the capital base of settler agriculture was probably increasing rapidly, as more rich farmers settled in the maize districts,[29] but there is no evidence that sharecropping was crumbling during these years, although the terms were gradually transformed. Despite the vociferous forces calling for a renewed onslaught on peasant independence, it would be misleading to overestimate their numerical strength. The very shrillness of the anti-'squatting' agitation at the time, both by those seeking a cheaper and more abundant labour supply, and by those for whom black competition was the cause of poor-white degradation, is evidence of the continuing prevalence of sharecropping arrangements. Indeed, it might be that such arrangements reached their widest extent when the post-war drought broke, prices started rising, commerce picked up and export markets opened. Impressionistic evidence suggests that by 1913, sharecropping was still the dominant relationship of production in much of the maize belt. Many landowners at first extended sharecropping arrangements as a cheap and relatively efficient way of exploiting the soil intensively without risking capital investment. Also, for many a landowner during these years, the greater accessibility to capital and credit may have meant greater indebtedness and vulnerability rather than more financial independence. For these reasons, those factors which shored up sharecropping were probably as often strengthened as weakened in the years after 1907–8.[28]

Just as importantly, more and more sharecropping landlords had the will and the wherewithal to subsume their tenants' labour more directly under their own organisation and capital, but were hampered by the alternative access that peasants had to the means of production and their consequent capacity to resist encroachments on their independence. It seems likely that these landlords were particularly strong and vocal supporters of the 'anti-squatting' agitation, especially at a time of increasing opportunities and incentives.[29]

Different attitudes towards sharecropping amongst whites were causally related to the uneven accumulation of agrarian capital. This was at the heart of the conflict between elements of the landlord class in the countryside. On the one hand there were successful, 'progressive' capitalist farmers; on the other there were those who remained structurally dependent on the productive enterprise of the independent tenantry. After 1907 both sought to enlist the support of other interests and, most significantly, the state in the intensified conflict. In essence that conflict concerned the manner in which the state would intervene in the process of African class formation and the precise mechanisms of surplus extraction and exploitation. In short, were the Africans to become proletarians or were they to remain tenant producers?

The basic premise of the anti-'squatter' agitation was that sharecropping and other forms of independent tenancy obstructed and undermined the capitalisation of agriculture as they 'tied up' potential supplies of labour.[30] They provided African households with a degree of independence which obviated the necessity for them to alienate their labour power regularly and intensively. The rapidly growing proportion of land under cultivation and the growing number of capitalist farmers settling in the maize districts intensified the shortage of labour on the farms. The crises over the labour supply – the single most serious obstacle to capitalist farming apart from access to capital itself – fed into and reinforced the contemptuous and derisive attitude towards 'Kaffir farmers' and 'squatter landlords'.

By the time of Union, the absolute shortage of *potential* African farm labour was not a problem in white people's minds; it was rather a problem of realising that potential supply: extracting labour from a black tenant population which did not feel inclined to render it. Thus, in the words of R. N. Rosenzweig, magistrate in Kroonstad, the inadequacy of the labour supply was due 'not so much to the number of natives in the area as to the fact that many of the squatters are rich and unwilling to work except at their own farming operations'.[31] Such independence was also the product of rapid increase in the stock population on the highveld in recent years. African tenants were often very considerable stockowners in the years leading up to 1913. This accumulation of wealth, probably unprecedented since the mineral revolution, may have lessened African dependence on other forms of participation in the colonial economy, notably as labourers.

The five years leading up to 1913 seem to be characterised by the often unsuccessful attempts of white landlords who were capitalising and improving to bring the labour of their tenants more directly under the organisational control of their own capital. Resistance to this attempted coercion led to much displacement of African families, as they sought to maintain their independence as stockowners and commodity producers.[32] It is in this context of struggle and resistance that the most important legislative intervention in the process of agrarian class formation in these years, the Natives' Land Act of 1913, should be understood.

The major provision of the Act in so far as it affected the Free State was that which laid down that the only legal form of rent payment by black tenants to white landlords henceforth was to be labour service. A rent in the form of a share of the crop or in cash was illegal.[33] Those who most welcomed this were the large group of landlords for whom the bargaining power of African tenants and their reluctance to sell their labour were thought to be the major obstacles to productive farming. It would seem to be the labour-starved, 'progressive' farmers who were best served by the Act. The 1913 Land Act was aimed at stifling the independent peasantry, levelling peasant differentiation, and shutting off alternatives such as those offered by sharecropping landlords. J. G. Keyter, Member of Parliament for Ficksburg, a district dominated by 'progressive' farmers, told the Natives' Land Commission that his constituents were:

> glad that the law has been passed because farmers in Heilbron and other districts cannot now entice their natives away to work there on the half share system . . . they would have been forced to adopt the same practice on a larger scale because the others are taking their servants away.[34]

The immediate effect of the Act was a spate of evictions of African tenants from farms, an aspect highlighted in the polemical writing of the time,[35] and stressed by historians.[36] Although it cannot be stated with certainty, it seems logical that those landlords who were in a position to evict African tenants on the grounds that they ran too much livestock or that they refused to become labour-tenants were, in the main, 'progressive' farmers with substantial capital who required statutory backing to enable them to assert their power. The dispersal of sharecroppers or large herd-owners was possible only because of the closing of the arable land frontier and the increasing numbers of Africans on white farms. The rapidly increasing density of black settlement on white-owned farms served to increase the bargaining power of the white landlords in so far as it decreased the tenants' alternative access to good land. But it was the 1913 Land Act which swung the balance in favour of capitalising white farmers. By prohibiting sharecropping tenancy, it severely hampered the independent surplus-producing peasantry on the farms, although it could not immediately destroy it. In so far as the Act declared that the only legal form of rent payment by African tenants in the Free State, although not elsewhere, was labour service, African sharecroppers were stripped of many of their defences.

At the same time, the effectiveness of the Act and its destructive impact should not be overstated. Certainly, given the power of the colonial political economy to shape African class formation, the final victory of capitalist landlords over the sharecropping peasantry was assured, and the conditions of that victory were being laid all the time. In the long run even the most backward of the landlords had to capitalise or lose their land. But by the same token it was impossible for the transformation of productive relations to be engineered artificially by state intervention. As long as some farmers continued to depend upon sharecropping for their survival, their black tenants were assured of survival in one or other attenuated form. The poverty of many white landlords lent to the tenants a degree of immunity from the levelling forces of landlord capitalism for the time being. The state could, however, lay down the conditions and delimit the battleground for the struggle between landlords and tenants. And this is the ultimate significance of the 1913 Land Act. More than anything else, it allowed some landlords increasingly to limit peasant independence and to impose ever stricter labour conditions on tenants. But it was an uneven, gradual and sporadic process.[37] It did not immediately destroy the independence of black tenants any more than it replaced tenancy relations with wage labour. Such an instant transformation was inconceivable whilst the capital base of so much settler agriculture remained meagre. It was this that limited the power of any legislation designed to undermine peasant enterprise and to expand the labour market for richer farmers responding to market opportunities.

Thus, while the capitalising farmers probably used the law for the ultimatums and evictions that were such a feature of the period, it was as much pressure on the land which swung the balance their way as the law itself. To have imposed the same conditions on the poorer or less privileged landowners would have destroyed them, and they continued to be dependent on the surplus produced by their independent black tenants. In fact the Act was not at all rigorously enforced. Prosecutions under the Act seem to have been rare and inconsequential.[38]

Further, there were a variety of ways in which independent African endeavour survived as the basis of productive relationships. For many small farmers of the maize districts, lacking adequate capital or technology, the law meant that the lands ploughed by African tenants were simply divided in two. If the tenant ploughed one field for himself and another for the landowner, he ceased to be a sharecropper in the eyes of the law but became a labour-tenant whose peasant plot was cultivated in lieu of wages. Such legal side-stepping implied no more landowner control over production or the means of production than before.[39] On the other hand, as Cornelius Wessels, Member of the Legislative Assembly, suggested, a farmer could 'sell the produce grown by these coloured persons on the land allotted to them, giving them a portion of the proceeds'.[40] Similarly, a white Thaba Nchu farmer, defending sharecropping in 1912, suggested that the landowner could legally allow the tenants to plough up twenty or thirty acres as usual, take the whole crop himself, and give the tenants a 'bonus' of so many shillings on every bag produced. This, he wrote, would come to the same thing as sharecropping, but would not hurt the susceptibilities of the government or those farmers to whom sharecropping was anathema.[41] Some such arrangement seems to have replaced formal sharecropping on many farms in the aftermath of the 1913 Act. These 'loopholes' were necessary for those who were simply not in a position to transform their farms into capitalist enterprises worked by means of tenant labour. An editorial in the *Farmers' Advocate* in August 1913 understood the limitations of the Act:

> Ostensibly, ploughing on shares, in partnership between white and black in the produce of the land, is forbidden; actually the law leaves a loophole which, to a large extent, enables the old state of things to continue under a different name.[42]

There was, however, another aspect of the 1913 Land Act which was crucial in strengthening the position of the white landlords. The Act laid down that all black tenants and not only contracted wage-earners in the Orange Free State, although not elsewhere, were to be defined as servants under the Masters and Servants Act. This had considerable implications for the legal status of tenants and for the coercive apparatus that the farmer could summon to his aid against recalcitrant or unwilling workers. For J. G. Keyter, Member of the Legislative Assembly for Ficksburg and a major supporter of the 1913 Land Act, it was this consideration which was paramount. In response to comment that the effect of the Act would be to split the lands worked by the tenant into tenant's lands and landlord's lands without any change in the relations of production, Keyter explained the cardinal difference:

> when the boy had his whole piece of ground to sow and be given a half of the crops, he was not a servant but a partner – a master. The moment you draw that line under the new law, that boy becomes your servant at once. . . . As soon as you draw the line on your farm and say 'You can sow this for yourself', he is your servant.[43]

I. J. Meyer, Member of the Legislative Assembly for Harrismith, said, 'The difference . . . is this, that if a Kaffir ploughs for me and ploughs again for himself he looks upon me as his master, whereas if he is working on the halves he looks upon me as his partner or his equal'.[44] The *Farmers' Advocate*, in an editorial in August 1913, concurred. The major difference made by the new law was that the Africans became servants of the landowner, it declared. 'By such means the farmers get a closer grip over the "loose" or unattached natives to whom they may give permission to reside upon their properties'.[45]

African petitions against the Act expressed their deep concern that the term 'farm servant' to describe all Africans resident on white-owned land would render the wives, daughters and minor sons of African tenants 'practically slaves to the owner of the farm'. The head of the family would have 'no right to order his children to attend school, nor may he require his wife to attend to her domestic duties'. As a rule contracts were sufficiently broad to enable landowners to call on the services of women and minors whenever required. The extension of the Masters and Servants Act to all tenants effectively stripped tenant families of their defences against the landowner.[46]

If the 'class struggle' between landlord and tenants revolved essentially around the nature and intensity of extraction of surplus labour by the landlord, then clearly this extension of servile status was a major victory for the entire landowning class. For servile status implied a severe restriction on rights of movement and organisation. The coercive apparatus of the state was now available for the enforcement of the employer's will against the unwilling, tendentious and resistant African, who saw no reason why he or she should sacrifice his or her independence for the enrichment of another.

The editor of the *Farmers' Advocate* wrote that the crucial difference wrought in the Free State countryside by the Act was:

> that the natives declare themselves to be the servants of the farmer and not his tenants, and bring themselves thereby under the provisions of the Masters and Servants Act.... The work that such natives will do will consist as heretofore in ploughing on shares, but they will be nominal servants instead of nominal tenants.[47]

Here again we see the focus on the legal status of the black tenant and the significance that the imposition of statutory servile status had for the balance of class forces in the countryside.

Nevertheless, the independent peasant economy could not and did not disappear, whatever the sanguine rhetoric of the legislators. Traumatic as the evictions were for many, 'sharecropping' in one form or another did not cease altogether. As early as 1908, the Orange River Colony Natives Administration Commission had concluded from its investigations that it was not possible to frame preventive legislation which could not be evaded 'and that to attempt to enforce such legislation would only drive the farmer to resort to subterfuge and evasive expedients'.[48] That expectation was fully borne out after 1913. As the magistrate in Vredefort reported in 1918: 'the great idea of the natives is to plough, sow and reap on their own account. The Natives' Land Act has not materially altered the relationship that previously existed between the European master and the natives . . . in this respect'.[49] As late as the 1930s, sharecropping was quite openly practised on many Free State farms.[50]

A great deal more capital, manpower and expertise than was then available was required if white farmers employing black labour were to make up for peasant–tenant production. Crucial as the 1913 Act was to be in the process of class formation in the years after 1913 it could not totally eradicate the independent tenancy so long as a significant number of landowners remained dependent on their tenants' productive enterprise. If the history of South Africa's countryside demonstrates anything, it is that legislative edict and administrative fiat have little force in shaping the substance and context of class struggle unless the material conditions are also propitious. The struggle was conducted in the countryside, not in parliament. State intervention did, however, alter the power relationships implicit in that struggle. The disadvantages of 'partnership' were removed by the extension of legal servile status to all tenants, while the manifest advantages of peasant surplus production remained in attenuated forms where it was necessary for settler economic survival and capital accumulation.

Notes

Abbreviations

FW	*Farmers' Weekly*
JPS	*Journal of Peasant Studies*
JSAS	*Journal of Southern African Studies*
NLC	*Natives Land Commission*, UG 22/1916

1 C. Bundy, *The Rise and Fall of the South African Peasantry* (London, 1979).
2 The work of S. Trapido, P. Richardson and P. Delius are the exceptions to this general criticism.
3 Analysis of the sharecroppers and the sharecropping landlords apply equally to the regions to the north and south of the Vaal river. However, as we shall see later, the 1913 Natives' Land Act was of far greater importance and effectiveness in the Orange Free State than in the Transvaal, and the transformation of productive relations was more rapid in the former territory than the latter. Therefore the focus of this paper, especially its second half, is on the Free State (the Orange River Colony before 1910).
4 It is probable that the proportion depended primarily on the balance of power in the particular instance, but the landlord would attempt to extract a larger than usual surplus where he had some control over the means of production – for example, if the peasant did not have enough oxen. The landlord's costs might be deducted from the tenant's share – such as the cost of seeds, ploughing shares, maintenance costs, and perhaps also the threshing costs. The landlord also expected labour-service from adolescent members of the tenant family for work such as herding of stock, as well as one or two girls or women for housework. See T. Matsetela, 'The life story of Nkgono Mma-Pooe', Chapter 8 below.
5 See Tim Keegan, 'The restructuring of agrarian class relations in a colonial economy: the Orange River Colony, 1902–1910', *Journal of Southern African Studies (JSAS)*, V, 2 (April 1979), 238–9.
6 But see the evidence before the *Natives' Land Commission (NLC)*, UG 22/1916, e.g. pp. 2, 15, 22, 28, 36, 68.
7 Again, this applied in the Orange Free State to a far greater extent than in the Transvaal.
8 The exact size of the crop which was to be distributed in predetermined proportions was subject to manipulation. The African producer had plenty of opportunity to minimise the actual quantity which the landholder received. Landlords were not unaware that they were being cheated, and often expressed their feelings on the

matter. (See, for example, 'Progress', Kroonstad, to editor, *Farmers' Weekly* (*FW*), 19 July 1911; 'Squatters Unnecessary', *FW*, 6 Sept. 1911). One source of dissension was the African practice of picking ripening cobs and consuming the green maize from about January to the harvest in June or July. (See R. Seggie, 'Squatting and ploughing on shares', *FW*, 8 May 1912, 574.) The landlord insured himself as far as possible against manipulation of another sort by insisting that he have first choice of the reaped and bagged crop. Thus the tenant could not neglect half the fields in the knowledge that that half constituted the landowner's share; nor could he separate off the poor-quality grain after harvest and hand it over to the landlord. (See 'Wepener Congress', *Friend*, 27 Jan. 1909.) On the other hand, the frequency with which white landowners evicted tenant families from the land on flimsy pretexts once they had ploughed and sown and even reaped, was a source of much grievance. (See, e.g., PRO CO 417/394, Basutoland Reports, 1904, 21 Nov. 1904.)

9 See below, Chapter 8.

10 These assumptions have bedevilled much writing on peasantries in southern Africa. For a critique, see T. Ranger, 'Growing from the roots: reflections on peasant research in Central and Southern Africa', *JSAS*, V, 1 (Oct. 1978).

11 This becomes very clear from the testimony of Emelia Pooe (see pp. 218, 230 below).

12 D. J. Jacobs, 'Die Ontwikkeling van Landbou in die Vrystaat, 1890–1910', D. Litt *et* Phil, University of South Africa, 1979, p. 200.

13 R. N. Rosenzweig, magistrate in Kroonstad, wrote in 1913 that the average income of a tenant family would be about a hundred and fifty bags per annum (NLC, evidence, Appendix XI, p. 4). The magistrate in Winburg, R. Harley, gave the example of a landowner who owned 560 morgen and who got a two-third share of the crop. In 1913 he received 400 bags from his three tenants, which fetched £150 (*NLC*, evidence, p. 2).

14 See T. Keegan, 'Seasonality, markets and pricing: the South African maize trade in the early twentieth century', *Collected Seminar Papers on the Societies of Southern Africa*, X, Institute of Commonwealth Studies, London, 1981. The intervention of the state in the provision of quality seed from government experimental farms to white farmers meant that the quality of grain produced on white-owned farms was likely to improve. Many sharecroppers would have had access to such seed on credit from their landlords.

15 Wage labour was exceptional amongst sharecroppers. See Matsetela, Chapter 8 below, p. 227. Nevertheless they were dependent on work parties drawn from neighbouring families and kin at times of peak activity in the annual cycle. But despite the ostensibly reciprocal and cooperative nature of such labour organisation between households, it is not improbable that an embryonic and disguised form of wage labour was emerging. The extent and intensity of commodity production on the part of the sharecroppers would indicate the emergence of a labour-form which was qualitatively different. The differentiation between the sharecropper with twenty morgen and the capacity to cultivate it, and the labour tenant with a couple of morgen and little more than his labour power to alienate suggests that the relations between them were asymmetrical to the point at which they began to seem like class relations.

16 These themes are handled more fully in my University of London doctoral thesis, 'The transformation of agrarian society and economy in industrialising South Africa: the Orange Free State grain belt in the early twentieth century', 1981, ch. 3.

17 Absentee landlords, mining and land companies and land speculators were also an important element, but far less so in the Free State than in the Transvaal or in Natal. It was the considerable political muscle of the absentee landlords which made state intervention in the undermining of the peasant-tenantry so ineffective in the latter provinces. Thus the 1913 Natives' Land Act, as we shall see, was essentially a Free State Act in its anti-'squatting' provisions.

18 See Keegan, 'Transformation of agrarian society and economy', on the operations and spread of finance capital.

19 *Friend*, 18 Dec. 1894.

20 Jacobs, 'Ontwikkeling van Landbou', p. 191.

21 Encl. in CO 224/27, Lord Harris to Secretary of State, 21 Sept. 1908. See also 'Free State farming', *FW*, 27 Dec. 1911.

22 JUS (Department of Justice) 5/262/13, C. C. Chase to Louis Botha, 17 Aug. 1913.

23 *NLC*, p. 15; see also pp. 55, 71 (evidence of J. D. Oberholzer and Francis Carroll respectively).

24 See T. Keegan, ' "Lapsed whites" and moral panic: an aspect of the South African ideological crisis', paper presented to the Social History Workshop, Centre of International and Area Studies, London, Nov. 1978.

25 1908 ORC Natives Administration Commission, Pretoria, 1911, p. 9. Cf. J. K. Rennie, 'White farmers, black tenants and landlord legislation: Southern Rhodesia, 1890–1930', *JSAS*, V, 1 (October 1978).

26 See Keegan, 'South African maize trade'; S. Trapido, 'Landlord and tenant in a colonial economy: the Transvaal 1880–1910', *JSAS*, V, 1 (Oct. 1978); and Trapido, 'Reflections on land, office and wealth in the South African Republic, 1850–1900', in S. Marks and A. Atmore (eds), *Economy and Society in Pre-industrial South Africa* (London, 1980). Both examine the changing nature and role of the state on the highveld, more particularly in relation to agrarian class formation. See also S. Marks and S. Trapido, 'Lord Milner and the South African state', *History Workshop Journal*, IX, 1980, on the significance of the imperial intervention in facilitating the emergence of a capitalist agriculture.

27 Between 1904 and 1911 the number of farms in the Orange Free State increased from about 7 000 to about 11 000.

28 The evidence of C. Chase, p. 200 above, is relevant here.

29 Colonel Byron was referring to these reluctant sharecropping landlords when he told the Legislative Council in August 1908 that he had never come across a farmer who believed in the system of sharecropping. All were ready to point out the disadvantages, he said; but many could not get labour for their farms unless they too did as their neighbours, and took on African tenants on shares. They were compelled therefore to adopt a system which they knew in principle to be wrong, and of which they disapproved, as the alternative to being without labour ('Legislative Council', *Friend*, 25 Aug. 1908). See also A. B. Allison to editor, *FW*, 6 Nov. 1912, p. 697.

30 See, as examples, 'Progress', Kroonstad, to editor, *FW*, 19 July 1911; 'Spes Bona' to editor, *FW*, 30 Aug. 1911; W. Martins to editor, *FW*, 8 May 1912.

31 *NLC*, Appendix XI, p. 4; also Union of South Africa, U.G. 17–1911, *Blue Book on Native Affairs*, 1910, p. 254; NLC, evidence, p. 56. The magistrate in Edenburg understood the paradox: 'Labour no doubt is scarce, but labourers are superabundant if some means could be devised to exact from each able-bodied native his full quantum of work.' (JUS 1/566/11, Annual Report, 1911: Edenburg).

32 See T. Keegan, 'Restructuring of agrarian class relations', pp. 249–50. Many

sharecroppers were at this time buying land in the Transvaal in anticipation of bad times ahead. See Matsetela, Chapter 8 below pp. 232, 236 n. 38.

33 Section 7 (3) of Act 27–1913. In the Transvaal and Natal all existing sharecropping contracts could remain in force and be renewed, again as a result of the powerful influence of the land companies. In the Cape, the provisions were not implemented as a result of constitutional barriers relating to the franchise qualifications. However, in the Cape, the transition to capitalist wine, wheat and wool farming had, by and large, been accomplished by the late nineteenth century, and the efficacy of the Private Locations Ordinances of 1899 and 1909 in controlling squatting meant that the 1913 Act was of no great importance in that province.

34 *NLC*, evidence, p. 34.

35 S. T. Plaatje, *Native Life in South Africa*, London, 1916; R. W. Msimang, *Natives' Land Act, 1913*, c. 1914. See also evidence before the *NLC*, *passim*.

36 See, e.g., F. Wilson, 'Farming, 1870–1966', *Oxford History of South Africa*, II (Oxford, 1971).

37 See M. Morris, 'The development of capitalism in South African agriculture: class struggle in the countryside', *Economy and Society*, V, 3 (1976), for a discussion of the reasons why emergent capitalist relations in agriculture assumed the form of labour tenancy rather than free wage labour. See also Conclusion to Keegan, 'Transformation of African society and economy'.

38 See Plaatje, *Native Life*, pp. 73, 81–90; Matsetela, below, pp. 232–3. See also Edgar J. Webb, Beachfield, Tweespruit, to editor, *Friend*, 22 Oct. 1913; 'Talis Qualis', Lower Vet River, to editor, *Friend*, 29 Oct. 1913, who advised local farmers to ignore the Act and wait for a test case. He thought that under the Act 'no hardship will be experienced, and the result will be the same as before'. In December 1917 the *Farmers' Weekly* reported that 'another' farmer in the Bloemfontein district had been fined £10 for sharecropping. So presumably such cases, though rare, were not unknown. (See *FW*, 12 Dec. 1917, 1503.)

39 See J. N. van Soelen's comments in 'Legislative Assembly', *Friend*, 14 Aug. 1908. Although sharecropping landlords could, and did, get around the 1913 Act by demarcating separate lands for the tenant's sole use, or some such formal device, there were still good reasons why such landlords preferred the established arrangements. If the arable land were split into tenant's plot and landowner's land, the latter would receive scant attention from the tenant, who after all remained the direct producer (see note 8 above).

40 *Ibid.*

41 'No compulsion', Thaba Nchu, to editor, *FW*, 11 Dec. 1912.

42 'The Natives Bill; its probable effects', *Farmers' Advocate*, Aug. 1913, 665–7.

43 *NLC*, evidence, pp. 52–3.

44 *Ibid.*, p. 59.

45 'The Natives Bill: its probable effects', *Farmers' Advocate*, Aug. 1913, 665–7.

46 Bloemfontein Archives, CS 1278/2/08, Colonial Secretary's Office, G 444/1/08, Governor to Secretary of State, 28 Aug. 1908.

47 'The Natives Bill: its probable effects', *Farmers' Advocate*, Aug. 1913, 665–7.

48 ORC *Natives Administration Commission*, p. 9.

49 *Annual Report of the Department of Justice*, 1918, p. 33.

50 *Farm Labour in the Orange Free State*, South African Institute of Race Relations, 1939, pp. 34–5.

CHAPTER EIGHT

The life story of Nkgono Mma-Pooe:

Aspects of sharecropping and proletarianisation in the northern Orange Free State, 1890–1930

Ted Matsetela

Nkgono Mma-Pooe,[1] Emelia Mahlodi Pooe, is a relative of mine. My aunt on my mother's side is married to her eldest son. I first met her in 1957, and each time I visited her at home in Soweto I found it a great pleasure to talk about olden times. Probably because of my own peasant background and my upbringing in the oral tradition her narrations were quite fascinating to me. From the beginning I was puzzled by one thing: as she was so old, surely she had at some time lived in the country? It was about this place, her place of origin, that we talked repeatedly, until she started recounting her rural way of life in the Orange Free State. As a result the Nkgono Mma-Pooe story became the first case-study in the Oral History Project launched at the University of the Witwatersrand in 1979.[2]

The Oral History Project (OHP) was set up to investigate the process of proletarianisation in the South African countryside from the mid-nineteenth century to the mid-twentieth century. It was felt that the existing history of this period, based as it was solely on archival material, did not confront some of the fundamental changes that took place in the agricultural hinterland surrounding major industrial areas, such as the Witwatersrand.

The use of oral evidence in studying the development of capitalism in South African agriculture and the consequent restructuring of the social relations of production both in the countryside and urban centres has hardly been used at all. Given the nature of South African historiography, which has generally largely recorded the history of the ruling classes, the importance of oral history cannot be overstressed. In addition, the neglect of oral history has certainly left analyses of particular historical moments devoid of descriptive and personal material that takes sufficient account of the human dimension.[3]

The story of Nkgono Mma-Pooe was recorded in a series of tape recordings at her home in Soweto between June 1979 and June 1980. I conducted the interviews using an informal, conversational approach which tended to follow her train of thought.[4] All the interviews were preceded by preparation on my part, and on each visit I tried to draw her out on particular issues that she had touched on previously. On one occasion she was interviewed jointly with her second son Abiud and her niece Lulu, who were also well informed about their family's past[5] (see Figure 8.1). Twice she agreed to an audio-visual recording.[6]

In a deliberate departure from much current South African historiography, I have attempted in this essay to leave 'great' names and events to look after themselves and to take the lives of ordinary people as the central theme of discussion. The discussion has therefore taken the form of a retelling of the life history of a single peasant tenant-farmer (hereinafter referred to as a 'sharecropper'[7]) from the northern Orange Free State. She was the direct descendant of the kind of family which emerged from the communities that were settled in the Orange Free State before and at the turn of the nineteenth century. The story consists of ordinary accounts of events as perceived by Nkgono Mma-Pooe, who was born in 1882, and they have been added to by additional oral evidence available from the immediate family (such as accounts of three of her sons and her niece Lulu) or from people who lived in her home districts – namely, Heilbron, Vredefort, Parys, Koppies, Viljoenskroon, Coalbrook, Vereeniging, Potchefstroom and, later Ventersdorp[8]. An attempt has been made to allow her life history to stand on its own, but I have at times included certain historical facts which give this personal story a wider significance. This was not easy to do mainly because of the shortcomings inherent in the nature of oral history – for instance, the incapacity of any given informant to supply 'facts' other than how he or she subjectively experienced or perceived them. Nkgono Mma-Pooe's accounts are, as Paul Thompson says,

> the exact words ... as they were spoken; and added to them are social clues, 'the nuances of uncertainty, humour, pretence as well as the texture of dialect'.[9]

Among the drawbacks were the inconsistencies and gaps evident throughout Nkgono Mma-Pooe's narrations. She is ninety-nine years old, and it has therefore been very difficult to find corroborative witnesses still alive. It is however, encouraging to say that recent historical research in South Africa confirms much of her story as well as suggests that the history of the Pooe family to some extent typifies that of the fast-disappearing African peasantry.[10]

In addition it is significant that Nkgono Mma-Pooe is Sotho-speaking. Her accounts were transcribed from the original tapes and translated into English for a wider audience. A lot of Sotho subtleties and idiomatic feeling has been lost in these processes. Nevertheless, Nkgono Mma-Pooe's story is so vivid and credible that it constitutes an authentic if encapsulated account of peasant life as dealt with by historians such as Bundy, Trapido, Morris, Keegan and Beinart, though naturally not all the details of her life fit in completely with their accounts.[11] This is hardly surprising, because most of the work done on the rural

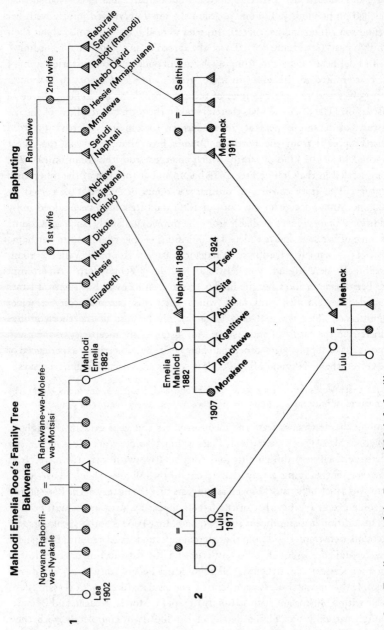

Fig. 8.1   Family tree of the Pooe and Molefe families

economies of the Orange Free State and the Transvaal depend entirely on written records. Nkgono Mma-Pooe's record goes beyond the scope of such written evidence while both corroborating and contradicting it.

After repeated attempts in the interviews I conducted with Nkgono Mma-Pooe I still found it difficult to explain the origin of the Pooe and Molefe clans. What became clear about the two clans was that they had intermarried for a number of generations. Mrs Pooe's marriage (she was born Molefe-wa-Motsisi) was just one of the many marriages that had occurred between Pooe and Molefe clans. The Pooes were of Ngwato-Kwena and the Molefes were of Phuting-Kwena origin, and both became Sotho by adoption. Like all other Kwena groups, they were said to have been settled in the interior of South Africa especially on the Transorangia plateau (the highveld) before the *difaqane* and the coming of Mzilikazi.[12] The Pooes and Molefes fled from what is now the western Transvaal and Orange Free State highveld to cluster around the Lesotho mountains under the protection of Moshoeshoe before or during the devastations of the *difaqane*. Afraid of the anti-foreign sentiment in the emergent South Sotho nation, they relinquished their Ngwato-Kwena origin. The Pooes' grandparents had seen the devastations of the *difaqane*, and in both families there are traces of grandparents commonly referred to as *maja-kgomo-a-basimane-le-a-banana*,[13] 'people who had returned to meat-eating after the starvation of the *difaqane*'.

Nkgono Mma-Pooe's parents were born and grew up during the Sotho–Boer wars, Rankwane in 1853 and her mother in 1862. Her mother was the daughter of Raborifi-wa-Nyakale. According to her story, her grandparents migrated and settled in the Caledon river valley. The communities of which they formed a part reconstructed settled life on the Transorangia plateau in the post-*difaqane* period in 'small scale closely-knit communities based on subsistence agriculture with wealth and prestige concentrated on cattle'.[14] It is also probable that they had moved in or out of Lesotho on a number of occasions depending upon whether there was peace and quiet in the area.

In 1882 when Emelia Mahlodi wa Molefe-wa-Motsisi was born, her parents were staying as labour-tenants on Slangfontein farm,[15] to the south of Heilbron. The Sotho name for the area is Kwakwatsi (Rhenoster river). From Slangfontein the Molefe family moved to Mooikraal (Mmamotlangwe) and thereafter to Rietfontein (Magodiri), which was a farm along the course of Klipriver. In 1897, after the rinderpest, the family moved to Zaaiplaas (Thalle) just to the south-west of Heilbron, which was where her father started sharecropping.[16]

Interviewer: Tell me more about what really happened during that year?
Respondent: I may not remember what else did happen. But I know about the disease. I remember precisely that many cattle died.

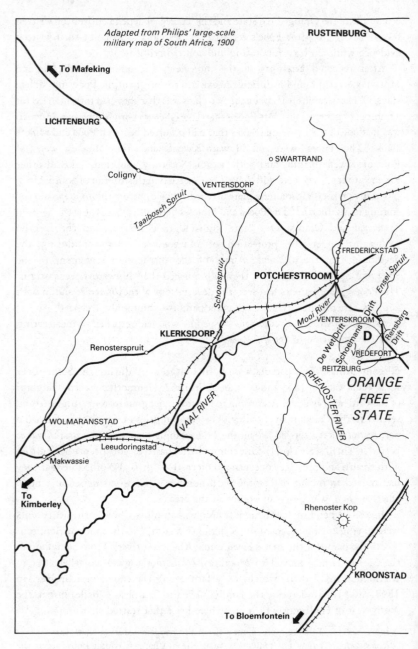

Fig. 8.2 Part of the Transvaal and Orange Free State, c. 1900

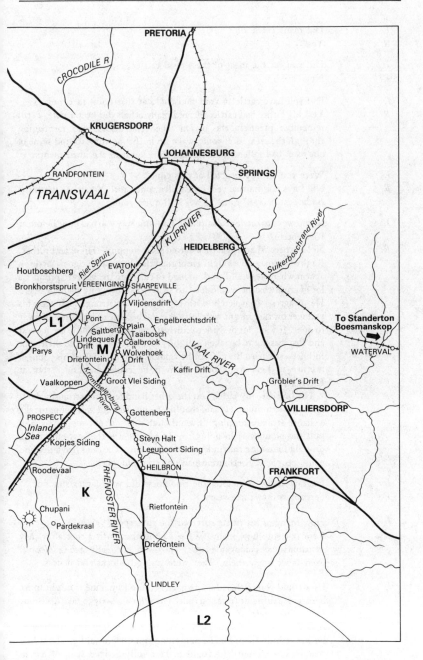

Fig. 8.2 (continued)

I:	Did many cattle die?
R:	Yes.

I:	Did you eat the meat of these dead cattle?
R:	No.

I:	Did you have cattle in your household at that point in time?
R:	Yes! My father had cattle. He and many others did keep cattle. I still remember precisely the period when the disease was rampaging through the area. We would wake up in the morning to find some of our oxen had fallen headlong and stone dead in the kraal manure.

I:	Were you already married at this time?
R:	No! I was not married yet. I was still a young girl. You mean when the rinderpest (*reinpis*) came? I was still quite young.

I:	So you went to settle at Zaaiplaas? The same way you had done before at Rietfontein?
R:	No! It's here where my father started sharecropping. His elder brother, Rankwe, remained though. He argued that he wouldn't go to settle on a farm where he would work so hard to cultivate the lands to produce a lot of crops that he would have to share with the white man, 'a Boer!' He disagreed completely with my father. He strongly felt that his younger brother might have lost his mind because that was not the way to do it. It was a lot of work to cultivate the soil and handle the harvest and that was not to be taken as lightly as his brother did — 'to share your full harvest with a Boer!' That he wouldn't do. He advised his younger brother to look for another farm if he could no longer stay at Rietfontein.
	His brother, my father, on the other hand felt very strongly about leaving Rietfontein. He said that like many others he was going to take a chance at sharecropping. 'Even though there are not enough oxen to pull the plough, I am going to.' In fact, it was the year after a big drought following the rinderpest devastations. The rains had failed and many people at Rietfontein had not even ploughed.

I:	For how many years after the rinderpest did your father stay on?
R:	Perhaps two or three years.

I:	How many of his cattle survived the rinderpest?
R:	I am not sure how many. What I remember is that thereafter they inspanned oxen alongside cows. They were not really strong (*blokosse*) oxen as we knew them. They were young bullocks and heifers.

I:	How could your father then manage because I imagine it might must been a very difficult time and indeed hard for anybody to take decisions such as he took?
R:	In fact, he borrowed some of the cattle from the neighbours. Moreover, he was taming them for the ploughing time. He would go about like that borrowing until he could make a fully-fledged span of ten to twelve. He would then start ploughing the fallow land. I remember

now precisely. We trekked in February and went up to Zaaiplaas to join
my uncle (Raborifi-wa-Nyakale) who was already staying there.

Although my translation cannot capture the subtleties of the Sotho, Mrs
Pooe's description of her early life provides a lively picture of her father taking to
sharecropping. That happened around 1896–97. Before that time she had heard
of sharecropping and they had known people who practised that type of
farming, but her own family had never engaged in it. Clearly her uncle argued
very strongly against his brother's taking to sharecropping, which was an
indication that he was not used to, or in favour of, that way of making a living.
It is also clear, though, that Rankwe was accustomed to giving his labour,
probably in return for residential rights, a piece of land to plough on and another
portion on which to graze his cattle, or perhaps also just farming for the landlord
and receiving in return an allocation in kind from the harvest. There can be no
doubt, however, that these two men were skilled farmers. It would have taken a
lot of courage for an unskilled farmer to take to sharecropping. It seems possible
to deduce from the argument of the two brothers that the one was younger and
more progressive, and the other older and conservative. To prove how skilled
her father was Mrs Pooe recounted vividly what happened upon their arrival at
Zaaiplaas. She said her father ploughed the fallow soil and waited for the early
summer rains. When finally the rains did come, he planted maize and sorghum.
She recalled that after the 'sharecropping ceremony' her father was left with
forty-five bags of maize. No sooner had they settled to sharecropping than a
great drought followed with lots of red locusts (*Monale*) which destroyed
whatever corn was growing. Nkgono Mma-Pooe suggested that in the absence
of any harvest in 1898 at Zaaiplaas she, together with her mother, paid an
extended visit to the youngest sister of her mother who stayed at Boesmanskop
in the Heidelburg district, to assist them in the harvesting and threshing of
corn. They got there by ox-wagon and found that they had had a good harvest.
At the end of the season her aunt gave them ten bags of sorghum.[17]

Nkgono Mma-Pooe's life in 1899 was interrupted by the South African War –
'*die Driejaar Oorlog*', as she calls it. She said they had heard for some time that
there was war coming. Then one evening some black *spijoene* (British soldiers)
arrived[18] in their village at Thalle ahead of the *laager*.[19] They heard some
shooting during the night, and the following day the *laager* appeared.

The *spijoene* drove all their cattle into the *laager*, caught their fowls and the
pigs, and instructed her father to inspan his horsecart so that they could all join
the *laager*. The soldiers then set their huts and corn on fire.[20] The *laager* took
them somewhere near Heilbron and moved to the north-west to a point north
of Koppies and finally stopped at Vredefort.

For the next two-and-a-half years they were interned in the military camp at
Vredefort, where they met people from all over the Orange Free State. Mrs

Pooe's experiences in the camp entailed a struggle for survival on a day-to-day basis, but in very different and difficult circumstances; her life in the camp amounted to a foretaste of urbanisation – 'the location life', as she recounted. She referred to the hardships surrounding the receiving of rations of maize, *mielie* meal, beans, meat; the difficulty in getting the firewood they needed for ordinary household cooking or just open fires for the icy highveld winters; the introduction of coal as fuel; the temporary disappearance of sorghum porridge and certain food items; and the disruptions of ordinary institutions like normal family life and marriage.[21]

Thus she gave an account of the marriage of a certain Basuto *spiejoen* Lekolane with Magdelina Nchabelle in the changed circumstances where it was not possible to pay *lobola* in the usual way. She talked of her father's participation in the war as an *agterryer*[22] for the officers of the mainly youthful British soldiers (*spijoene* or Ma-Johnny)[23] and of the Boer captives herded into railway trucks and taken to Vredefort for internment. Nkgono Mma-Pooe also described the black *spijoene* who, with their knowledge of the terrain, assisted the British in tracking down Boers. She related too what the Boers did to the British and blacks whenever they had an opportunity to retaliate.

She recalled the birth of some Coloured children in the camp and how, just before the end of the war, the internees were forced to work the soil in the vicinity of the camp in order to produce maize which supplemented their rations. She was amazed to see people cultivating vast tracts of land with bare hands and hoes. Although they were accustomed to eating green mielies, they were not allowed to do so in the camp, as it was said that by so doing the projected harvest targets would not be achieved.[24]

After the Anglo-Boer War, Frikkie Els, the owner of the Zaaiplaas farm, came out from Heilbron in search of her father, whom he invited to return to his old home as a sharecropper. Initially her father was reluctant to go back to Zaaiplaas.[25] He argued that it would be difficult for him to do sharecropping without a span of his own. After some discussion in the family and also after Els had promised to supply him with a span of oxen and all the *trekgoed*[26] needed, her father agreed to go. But the terms were different from the pre-war terms. The pre-war sharecropping terms were a 50/50 sharing basis – that is, the harvest was divided into halves after the deduction of costs. The span of oxen was provided by the sharecropper.

For Rankwane the war had brought many changes. Before the war he had a span of his own. He lost all of it in the war. After the war some of the arrangements were such that the owners of the land, who were invariably white, also provided the span of oxen with all its *trekgoed*. The sharing was also on a different basis; the sharecropper who had no span now only received a third or a quarter of the harvest. Mrs Pooe explained how her father found these post-war terms very unsatisfactory. Keegan refers, it is true, to returning sharecroppers, with complete spans, who came from Lesotho after they had taken refuge there during the devastations of the war,[27] but they were the lucky ones.

Referring to their first post-war harvest-sharing ceremony, Mrs Pooe complained: 'We watched tens and tens of bags of maize and grain-sorghum going to the side of the Boer.' Because a considerable number of non-sharecropping tenants on the farms sold their labour to the sharecropper, the distribution of the harvest attracted a great deal of attention from the neighbours.

It amounted to sharing the spoils. Both the sharecroppers and their families who worked daily on their land and neighbours who might have helped in the course of the year in *matsema* (work-parties) watched over this distribution. All took great pride in celebrating their achievement. In later years machines were used to complete the harvesting phases. The very last phase gave the landlord a chance to watch the output, especially to ensure that the *dormasjien* (threshing machine) fee was taken into account as a cost to be subtracted in the same way as were other costs, like seeds, plough-shares and maintenance of the span during the season. It was part of the policing of the process by the landlords. Landlords also made arrangements with sharecroppers on such days for meetings in which new *akkoorde* (contracts) could be entered into for the coming year.[28]

In 1906 Mrs Pooe (then Miss Molefe) married Naphtali Pooe from a farm near Parys called Arkadie (Tlhwaele). After the marriage was solemnized by Rev. Charrelton of the Free Church of Scotland, at Heilbron, the couple moved to Driefontein (Kwenanyane) to stay with one of Naphtali's brothers, David. Driefontein was one of Mmangoloana's farms (Vereeniging Estates Land Company) situated betwen Viljoensdrift and Coalbrook. This was a farm on which sharecropping was being practised. Even before Mrs Pooe arrived at Driefontein there was a field ploughed in her name in the sharecroppers' lot. What she remembered very well about the year 1906 was that the sorghum crop came up very well but was destroyed by *segongoane* (black locusts). She also recounted that it was in that year that she first heard of grain-sorghum fetching a very good price on the local market. She recalled that her own field yielded only three-and-a-half bags of sorghum, and at Viljoensdrift a bag of grain sorghum fetched as much as £1 10s.

In 1907 their marriage was blessed with a baby girl. Her name was Morakane. In that year too, they moved to another farm. This was called Berlin (Tlhankgwe), and was situated south-west of Driefontein on the bank of Kromellemboog river which flows into the Vaal at a point to the north-west of Parys. Here the couple started sharecropping as husband and wife. Their reason for leaving Driefontein was that there was not enough ploughland as it was very crowded. There were many Basotho who had initially come to work on the coal mines in the area but spilled over into the neighbouring farms to engage in sharecropping. In that way the area had become overcrowded, and this made it difficult for any beginner sharecropper to succeed. In fact, Naphtali was invited to Berlin by another of his brothers, Salthiel, to take a teaching post there and to engage in sharecropping at the same time.

At Berlin Naphtali became owner of a full span of oxen, a few horses, a horse-cart, a double-furrow plough (*mmadiketane*) and all its *trekgoed*. In fact Naphtali and his elder brother Salthiel had saved money during the war.[29] Their eldest brother David, who stayed at Driefontein, had some golden sovereigns saved on their behalf in a tin buried at a convenient place in his home. Naphtali and Salthiel used these savings, together with the post-war wages, to purchase spans of oxen, and thus they were able to take part in sharecropping.

Not everybody took part in sharecropping at Berlin. There were a few families, especially those who were long-settled on the farm like the Lebona, Rampa and Ramakhaha families, who were settled just opposite the Pooes to the south of Kromellemboog river, who did sharecropping. The rest provided labour for the landlord in return for portions of land on which they raised their own crops in addition to the allocations from the *baas*, and for grazing rights. These people assisted the sharecroppers since they provided labour, especially during the hoeing, harvesting and threshing seasons. They participated mainly in the work-parties where beer and fresh mutton were served to the workers.

Mrs Pooe recounted that of the non-sharecroppers on the farm, two groups were distinguishable. There were those who owned spans of oxen and those who did not. Those who did could hire out their spans for cash or kind either to the landlord or the sharecroppers. They also provided services such as crop-hauling and general transport services, especially during the peak seasons. Amongst these non-sharecroppers there were also those who kept sheep for wool as well as for meat. In spite of repeated questioning Mrs Pooe could not recall a situation that showed strained relations between the sharecroppers and the labour-tenants. To her they were as much a part of the sharecropping system as the croppers themselves.

Kinship ties were probably important in most of the labour units in sharecropping. The farmers seem to have been aware of these kinship patterns and made use of them when they recruited labour. In the same way as Naphtali had joined his brother Salthiel, Rampa probably invited his next-of-kin, Lebona. Thus patterns of kinship were woven into the new social and productive relations on the farm.

It appears that at this time there was already amongst all the tenant communities in the Orange Free State a distinct group of farmers who had certain skills and capital, such as cattle and all the ploughing equipment. Backed by the tradition of sharecropping in their own families and the little education most of them had acquired, they were in a better position to negotiate for 'reasonable' terms. Not every 'squatter'—peasant could do that. Some of the successful sharecroppers in fact probably had the same class interests as the small white progressive farmers of the time. Even though there may have been a clash of interests between the white progressive farmers and the sharecroppers – the latter did not own the land – it was only at the level of who appropriated how much of the labour power from *akkoord*-workers (tenant-labourers) who practically sold their labour to both.

On being asked whether sharecropping was difficult, Mrs Pooe guardedly replied that it was; one had to plough properly, which was onerous, select good seeds, hoe the field perfectly and have the crop harvested and threshed in time especially when there was need to avert winter rains. Hoeing, harvesting and threshing in particular required strong work-parties, for each of which a sheep would be slaughtered and a number of other food items and beverages served. Only the few people who could, in reality, afford this custom would undertake to go into sharecropping. One also had to be a good farmer. It was not enough to have a span of oxen, a plough and all its *trekgoed*. Skilful farming was an absolute prerequisite.

From the surnames which Mrs Pooe cited, the tenant farmers and sharecroppers in the districts of Heilbron, Koppies, Vredefort, Viljoenskroon, Parys and in the areas bordering Vereeniging, Potchefstroom, Viljoensdrift and Coalbrook, it is clear that they were invariably of Lesotho origin. One of Mrs Pooe's nieces, Lulu, argued that the links were so strong between Lesotho farmers and sharecroppers of the time that this cooperation even went as far as exchanging seeds, strains of cattle and horses, and sheep.[30]

There was, for instance, the case of Lempe's son, Makarapa Elie Marks, who was named after the owner of Mmangolwana's farms (presumably farms owned by Vereeniging Estate Land Company),[31] the name having been given in tribute to their arrival at Mmangolwana's farms when they came from Basutoland. It was clear from the explanation that Nkgono Mma-Pooe gave that the earnings from mines and other areas in the north were used by the Basotho for their transition to sharecropping or tenant farming.

Interviewer:	So at Driefontein you were people who did sharecropping only?
Respondent:	Yes, because these were farms owned by Mmangolwana. A Jew who owned the farms.
I:	When you say Mmangolwana's farms, what do you mean?
R:	I mean that all the farms in that area were under one man, one authority, i.e. this very Jew, Mmangolwana. There were, however, a few other farms in the neighbourhood that belonged to some Boers. If a Boer had a farm, Mmangolwana would buy this farm from him and then put Basotho on this farm so that they could do sharecropping. He

would give this Boer some money so that he could look for a new place where he could stay. This farm that belonged to the Boer would then become his. Usually it would be a farm adjacent to farms that Mmangolwana had bought and put croppers on. As a result the whole countryside was a vast combination of tracts of land that constituted the farms all belonging to Mmangolwana. It is important to note however, that there were other Boers who retained their land and were indeed not prepared to sell (to leave) them to him.

Nkgono Mma-Pooe remarked that maize fetched very low prices on the local market at this time (1909–11). Grain-sorghum could fetch as much as 15s per bag. Their major outlets were Coalbrook and Viljoensdrift, where there were grain merchants. Her husband, Naphtali, remained a maize and grain-sorghum cropper. They kept cattle – but not many; just enough for a good span of fourteen to sixteen *blokosse* (fully-fledged oxen) and a few cows capable of replacing the old oxen and also to provide enough milk for household use and for sale to those who did not have this facility. They had enough milk to produce butter, part of which they sold in the neighbourhood.

According to Mrs Pooe they remained on the Berlin farm until about 1913 or 1914, when they were forced to move because the landlord insisted that Naphtali sell some of his cattle as there were too many. Naphtali refused and instead opted to move to another farm. He soon discovered, however, that it was not as easy as he thought to secure a new place to stay because of the new powers given to landlords under the 1913 Natives' Land Act.

Respondent: In fact, Naphtali and Ramokhaha's eldest son, Mokeri, went places looking for a new place to stay, especially a place where they could do sharecropping once more. Oh! As if Boers had all formed a conspiracy whereby they had vowed never to take any black men on sharecropping terms. In reality Mokeri and my husband did go for many long days in search of a new place where they could do sharecropping. They would use bicycles for travelling on some occasions and horses on others. They would come back to report that one Boer had promised them a farm on which he wanted to settle sharecroppers. They would then go there to see what kind of soil there was and to assess the prospects of settling there. The name of the farm was Ceres. When they arrived there they discovered to their disappointment that it was an area of very poor soil with sour grass cover – a clear indication of poor soil – which would make it very difficult to practise sharecropping profitably.

Ultimately my husband found a place called Oorbietjiesfontein (just opposite Lindequesdrif) on the northern bank of the Vaal river (in the Transvaal). Ramakhaha and the rest of the sharecroppers at Berlin also trekked away. I remember some went to settle near the compounds at Coalbrook, at a place called Saltberry Plain.

Another reason why most landowners could not accept Naphtali and the Ramakhahas on their farms, Mrs Pooe recalled, was that they objected to their having a lot of cattle. The farmers insisted that they should cull their cattle. The Africans refused. Most of the landowners who refused to take them as croppers with their livestock were those settled on good, arable land. Mrs Pooe estimated that they had about twenty-five cattle each. None of them maintained more than one span of fourteen to sixteen oxen. Added to the span were four reserve oxen, four to six bullocks and heifers; she maintained the most reasonable estimate was thirty in total. It should be noted that the Pooes ultimately formed part of the exodus of the evicted of which Plaatje wrote in *Native Life in South Africa*.[32]

The Pooes settled at Oorbietjiesfontein together with their three children. Alice, the eldest, who was born in Driefontein, was eight years old, Ranchawe and Mmatli (Abiud), who were both born in Berlin, were five and three years of age, respectively. Their other children were born in Oorbietjiesfontein (Theuns Lindeque's farm). They were Sita, Khatitswe and Tseko.

The farming started off well except that the price for both maize and grain-sorghum were very low. Nkgono Mma-Pooe recalled that a bag of grain-sorghum fetched as little as 5s per bag in 1915. At Oorbietjiesfontein they settled on a part of an old farm which was an undivided estate. Even sections of it that had been bought still retained the same name. They settled down to sharecropping with people such as Philip Makhene and Willem Seboko as well as some Coloured families. They had their span of oxen which had enough grazing land:

> Oorbietjiesfontein has a section of it which is quite rugged and suitable for pasture. There is also plenty of water because the farm is right on the bank of the Vaal river.

Recounting her experiences about their early years at Oorbietjiesfontein, Nkgono Mma-Pooe explained how far afield they went in search of a good price for their farm produce:

> Yes! I remember very well we would set off to Potchefstroom on an ox-wagon for a two-day journey. Potchefstroom is where for the first time (1916–20) we found grain-sorghum and maize fetching good prices.

There were other sharecroppers at Oorbietjiesfontein, as well as two *bywoners*[33], one of whom had settled there a year before the Pooes arrived. One of the *bywoners* farmed and the other worked for Theuns Lindeque as a foreman over the 'squatter'-tenant workers. The former practised farming almost on the same basis as the Pooes did. Mrs Pooe could not say whether he did sharecropping. What she knew was that in practice they competed, and that the competition was so fierce, and the Pooes were so strong, that the *bywoners* had no choice but to leave the farm in the second year after their arrival.

Interviewer: Did Theuns have *bywoners*?
Respondent: Yes.

I:	How many?
R:	One.

I:	Only one?
R:	Yes, he stayed for one year and left in the second year. We in fact later moved into the house which he had been using.

I:	Where did he go?
R:	I don't know. What I know is that the lands that the *bywoners* were allocated were hired out to another *bywoner*. Theuns actually needed somebody else to replace this *bywoner* who had just left. In fact there was now a lot of ploughland but very few croppers to work on them.

I:	How long did the new *bywoner* stay?
R:	Only for a year. So that all those fields now went back to the control of the owner.

I:	Can you tell me more about the *bywoners*? If there was one such *bywoner* on a farm that was owned by another white man what were their terms?
R:	He ploughs. Almost on the same basis as sharecroppers.

I:	So you competed with him?
R:	Yes. And we beat him by far.

I:	How did you manage that?
R:	With us blacks, I would go out into the fields with my husband and perhaps with my children if they were already old enough. With the Boers as *bywoners* it was different. Normally their wives couldn't go out into the fields to hoe. The husband would have to do the hoeing alone. Or sometimes he would take out money to pay for whomever he could hire. With us we would hoe together with Naphtali or organise a work-party. In fact our competition with the *bywoner* was appreciated by Theuns himself. Theuns would remark that he had at last got the real '*Vrystaatse mense*' – people who are used to work and did do proper farming wherever they came from. He would say that before anyone could wake up Naphtali's span was already in the fields with most part of a day's work behind him.

Around 1920–21 Naphtali clashed with Theuns for some reason that Mrs Pooe cannot exaplain. It had, however, to do with Naphtali's eldest son, Ranchawe, who was about eleven years old. Theuns wanted to beat him because he had failed to perform some chore around the farmstead, and after a heated argument Naphtali decided to leave Oorbietjiesfontein (that is, Theuns Lindeque's section of the farm).

Interviewer:	Why did Naphtali ultimately trek away from Theuns Lindeque's farm?
Respondent:	I forget what it was that they quarrelled about.

I:	What did Naphtali do?
R:	He said give me my 'trek pass'.
	Theuns was unwilling to give it. He argued that it was a mere difference that they had had, and that it had nothing to do with

whether he could stay on at Oorbietjiesfontein or not. Naphtali insisted that he wanted to leave. Theuns reiterated that a difference between him and Naphtali did not spell his expulsion. He further remarked that since he was determined to leave at that time he would allow him to go but this did not mean he could not return in case he could not get well-settled wherever he was going and for that reason wanted to return.

I:	Why did Theuns speak like this?
R:	Naphtali was a hard worker. Indeed, he worked very hard in his fields. He produced a lot from the soil. Hundreds of bags, half of which he gave to Theuns, who in turn would proceed to sell them and get a lot of money from the labour to which he had never contributed anything.

The Pooes left Oorbietjiesfontein around 1922–23 to settle on another section of the same farm, owned by Stoffel van Balle (popularly known as Tol). Tol was a very short-tempered man who did not hesitate to beat anyone, whether black or white. In fact they nicknamed him 'Ra-Sjambok' (somebody who depends on the rhinoceros-hide whip to settle any difference).

At Tol van Balle's farm there were no *bywoners*. However, Tol had an uncle who stayed on the farm under almost the same terms as sharecroppers. He was a relatively poor white who did not even have a span of oxen. Before he could plough the fields that Tol had allocated him he either had to borrow from the Pooes or Tol would lend him his.

Tol had known Naphtali before. He allocated to him very good lands where he resumed sharecropping once more. In the first year of their arrival Naphtali produced a very good harvest from the fields. They used a *dorsmasjien* for the first time at Oorbietjiesfontein. Nkgono Mma-Pooe says it moved from one central place to another, in relation to the various farms it served, and threshed for all, regardless of colour. Around 1922 it cost 9d per bag of maize for threshing. She recalls that even during the period of high labour demand paid labour amongst the blacks was only used in exceptional circumstances – this was if, and only if, one was short of labour – if one had, for example, fewer than four people on one's harvesting and threshing floor. If there were four or more people, there was no need to engage further labour. There was also a practice of a working team from one floor moving to another floor as a friendly gesture to boost morale, which went beyond the rather more regular function of a *letsema*. In this case, however, Naphtali even went as far as hiring labour in the neighbourhood to assist in the harvesting and threshing. Mrs Pooe estimated that the maize crop was about three hundred bags.

People in the neighbourhood of Lindequesdrif, other croppers, tenant-labourers, farm-owners and *bywoners*, black and white alike, talked about Naphtali's harvest. Many whites in fact remarked that Tol should be very pleased that he had engaged a cropper of Naphtali's ability. I remember Piet Smit, a white farmer from another section of Oorbietjiesfontein where Meshack [i.e. Ranchawe's half-brother] stayed, brought his own maize for threshing. His maize stack was far smaller than ours. We beat him by far.

Mrs Pooe has a lot of anecdotes relating to areas of common conflict, racial antipathies and downright oppression between the Boers and the peasant sharecroppers. Most of these relate to the division of labour, for example, as to what the black peasant tenant-farmer or sharecropper should do for the landlord; how many cattle and sheep the tenant might keep and the *akkoord* terms they entered into each year. She also recalled fairly well a court case in which her husband, Naphtali, was charged for failing to keep his lands free of *boetebossie* (burr weed).[34] A policeman for fauna and flora in the district came one afternoon to Naphtali's lands and very aggressively told Naphtali that he was charging him for failing to keep his lands free of *boetebossie*. Naphtali objected that, as a policeman, he was too aggressive in laying the charge. The policeman could not accept this language from a black. He dismounted from his horse and attempted to kick Naphtali:

Moenie vir my boei nie. Ek het niemand dood gemaak.
(Don't handcuff me. I have not killed anyone.)

Short though he was, Naphtali was very strong and a good fighter. He overpowered the officer, threw him to the ground and choked him for a while. The officer left after the skirmish, only to return with two other policemen the following day. This time Naphtali was arrested and taken to Venterskroom. The case was heard at Potchefstroom and he was found not guilty and discharged.[35] The incident provoked great anger and resentment among the local farmers, and the case remained a major topic of discussion and dissatisfaction whenever the farmers who did not like sharecroppers met in the neighbourhood.

By 1930 all Mrs Pooe's children had been born. Morakane (Alice) the eldest and the only daughter had died at nineteen years of age in 1926; Ranchawe was twenty years old, Abiud eighteen, Sita fifteen, Khatitswe twelve, and Tseko eight years old. In other words, around 1930 three of Naphtali's eldest sons were already playing a large part in the labour of the family's sharecropping. Apart from the sons, Naphtali's sister-in-law, Sara, born in 1902, had been staying with them for years. Mrs Pooe confirmed that Ranchawe and Abiud could manage the span of oxen by themselves though they needed assistance during the inspanning in the mornings. The two were also working on the alluvial diamond diggings (*Matikiring*)[36] along the Vaal river, in places like Champagne, and only returned home for ploughing and harvesting seasons. Sita said that they soon discovered that they could work for more money in the towns to the north such as Vereeniging and Johannesburg. While the diggers paid

12s 6d a week at Champagne, the Vereeniging mines paid 18s. In Johannesburg they could work for as much as £1 5s a week. His elder brother Ranchawe went to work at Vereeniging, but they both continued to return home for ploughing and harvesting.

In 1935 Tol sold his farm. After the sale Naphtali too decided to go back to Theuns, who unfortunately died in the same year. Theuns's wife, knowing Naphtali, appointed him as a sharecropper and general overseer of the farm. Naphtali could, however, only maintain this status up to 1939 when white farmers in the neighbourhood objected very strongly to his sharecropping and overseeing at the same time. They demanded that Mrs Lindeque hire a white man in Naphtali's place. Mrs Lindeque gave in to these demands and hired Mr Hamilton Dutton, and Naphtali sharecropped for the last time in 1939. From 1940 onwards he worked on the farm as *voomani* (foreman) and storeman for Mrs Lindeque. He was allocated only three acres of ploughland for his household use. His four eldest sons had long taken up employment as labourers in Johannesburg. Only his youngest son, Tseko, remained with him. Naphtali was now in his sixties. He still kept the span of oxen which was used by Dutton to plough Mrs Lindeque's lands. Tseko managed the span until Dutton bought a tractor. Tseko learned to drive it and to plough practically all the arable land on the farm, but his father now came under pressure to sell all his stock. Naphtali did finally sell all his cattle but continued to work as storeman for Mrs Lindeque until the early 1950s. During 1950–52, construction work started on the Vanderbijl Park iron and steelworks site. Using Dutton's tractor, Tseko hauled sand from the Vaal river as one of the contractors to supply the construction works. He put his name on the waiting list for new residents of Boipatong, the dormitory township for Vanderbijl Park, where he received a house when the township opened. Naphtali left the Lindeque farm to join his son at Boipatong around 1954.[37] Naphtali and Emilia Pooe's sons, Ranchawe, Abiud and Sita, had settled in Soweto (after a spell in the 'squatter' areas around Johannesburg in the 1940s and 50s). The fourth son, Khatitswe, remained at Vereeniging as a prison warder. The Pooes joined their eldest son in the late 1950s in Soweto, where Naphtali died in 1963. He is buried at Swartrand (Ga-Mokgopa) in the Ventersdorp district. It was there that he had jointly bought a farm around 1909–11 with other members of his clan.

Conclusion

The history of Mrs Emilia Pooe's family epitomises the fate of many others in similar communities that were settled in the Orange Free State from the mid-nineteenth century. The Pooes were typical of those black peasant-farmers who had the benefit of agricultural skills passed on from generation to generation. Finally, legislative measures and capitalising forces in South

African agriculture caught up with them and reduced them to proletarians, totally displaced from the land which they had depended on for so long for their livelihood.[38]

The parents of Mrs Pooe were also typical Basotho farmers who by local standards were fairly well educated and skilled in the peasant way of life. Although both the Pooes and Molefes are of (Tswana) Ngwato-Kwena origin, they were settled in Lesotho during the mid-nineteenth century, whence they moved to the Orange Free State as tenant-farmers. They kept cattle and cultivated the soil.

Until 1890 they had lived on various farms in the Orange Free State as 'squatter' peasants paying rent in kind or sometimes in labour. The rapid development of gold mining in the late 1880s ushered in an era in which capital and commerce made their first really significant impact on the class structure of the countryside. Inland markets for agricultural produce were opened as a result of the development of transport. The Molefes and the Pooes responded positively to these developments. Mrs Pooe's father (Rankwane) appears to have been a rational farmer who understood the implications of rising land values in the Orange Free State at that time. His decision to take to sharecropping after the rinderpest, when nobody had any cattle, amounts to an entrepreneur's assessment of a situation that offered great opportunities for the capable. He scouted around for land, an effort which finally took him to the farm Zaaiplaas which had very good soil. Here Rankwane established himself as a succesful sharecropper. In addition, it is possible that he left Rietfontein after the rinderpest partly because of uncertainty over the current anti-'squatting' legislation of 1895 which aimed at limiting the numbers of black families per white-owned farm to five. By moving to Zaaiplaas and taking to sharecropping, Rankwane set the pace for his children, who later became some of the most successful peasant tenant-farmers – sharecroppers – in the northern Orange Free State in the early twentieth century.

According to Colin Bundy, at this time sharecropping meant that

> the white proprietor usually provided the seed and the African peasants farmed the grain, and the returns were shared. The division of the crop varied between the eponymous 'halves' and greater or lesser proportions; particularly in the years before the South African war, sharecropping agreements sometimes overlay or were intertwined with other forms of quasi-feudal relations: thus, the African 'sharer' might also have to render a number of days' labour upon a separate field, set aside as his employer's alone. The relationship was one which afforded the sharecropping peasant a decided advantage in the security of his tenure; inasmuch as his landlord was looking to the same crop for his own share of the returns, he was unlikely suddenly to terminate the squatter-peasant's lease.[39]

Although Bundy seems in general to have captured the spirit of these earlier relationships, it is important to note the various arrangements that obtained at the practical level on most farms and what standard terms most sharecroppers accepted.

At the practical level the relationship depended on the nature of the *akkoord* entered into by the landlord and the tenant-sharecropper. The terms were, by and large, the outcome of the bargaining between the landlord and the prospective tenant-sharecropper. Tenant-sharecroppers who had secured good terms and had an understanding landlord would try to remain with such a landlord for as long as possible, whereas those under harsh terms would not tarry long. Nkgono Mma-Pooe, speaking about the winter season around Heilbron in the 1890s says:

> In fact winter time in the Orange Free State was the time for trekking . . . there was a lot of disagreement between the landlords and the tenant labourers because of the changed *akkoorde*.
>
> After harvesting the landlord would call a meeting and you would hear him say: *'Vandag sal ons weer 'n ander akkoord maak. Ons sal nie weer met daardie akkoord werk nie'* (Today we are going to make another *akkoord*. We are no longer going to work according to the previous aggreement). He would then proceed to explain what they would have to do in the new year. Under such arrangements, no sooner would the year be out than most people showed a lot of dissatisfaction. They would have no choice but to leave.

It is clear from this that the terms of agreements between the landlords and the tenants differed widely from one landlord to another, and when they were changed it was likely that tougher terms were incorporated in the favour of the landlord. Mrs Pooe recalled that as the old sharecroppers trekked from one farm to the next, new ones were engaged under the new terms.

What is striking about the Molefes and later the Pooes was their ability to bargain for satisfactory terms. Almost invariably they achieved satisfactory terms with each of their landlords. Rankwane Molefe managed at Zaaiplaas, and so did Naphtali Pooe at Oorbietjiesfontein.

Interviewer: Wouldn't the white farmers force your father to trek away from the farm or just refuse to engage him as a sharecropper for refusing to deliver your mother's labour?

Respondent: Never ever! Even when he happened to have trekked from somewhere and was looking for a new place to stay on a new farm and perhaps the new [landlord] Boer wants him [my father] to give his wife to wash for the Boer's wife or that I as his daughter to work in the kitchen, my father never accepted such terms in the agreement – terms according to which his wife would have to do washing for the white farmer's wife and the daughter to work in the kitchen. Nor even lend out his son to the Boer to milk the cows or perhaps even look after the Boer's sheep. What did happen we knew was that most Boers wanted to know from any new tenant how many boys he had so that he could determine beforehand whether he had a shepherd for his sheep, the one who would be a *handlanger* on the ploughing span, and finally, a boy who would milk the cows. Only then would he consider entering into an agreement whereby he would be allowed to stay on the farm. We also knew very well that it was like that and no one would ever be allowed to stay unless such terms as already described were met.

I: How could your father manage that?

R: He did! He argued very strongly. He said to the white man: 'I and I only work for you.'

Examining the circumstances under which Mrs Pooe and her husband took to sharecropping one sees that the practice was already entrenched in certain families. As in Naphtali and Emelia Pooe's case, so in the case of Mrs Pooe's father; the Pooes and their cousins, the Rampas, were all veteran sharecroppers who engaged in sharecropping on various farms in the northern Orange Free State. Each time one of them found a landowner prepared to accept him on good terms he would invite his brother or cousin to join him.

The years 1913–20, which coincide with Nkgono Mma-Pooe's middle life, saw considerable numbers of people displaced, especially in the Orange Free State where the provisions of the Natives' Land Act of 1913 were at least initially rigorously enforced. Naphtali Pooe joined in the buying of Swartrand with his next-of-kin, but never went with them to resume peasant farming there. He remained as a sharecropper in the Orange Free State up to 1915, when he moved to the Transvaal to continue there until 1940. His environment was, however, considerably transformed. He had hostile neighbouring farmers and ubiquitous law enforcement agencies who did all they could to force him out of sharecropping. From his wife's accounts, it would seem that Naphtali's skills gave him great staying power as did the extent to which he could mobilise family labour. His sons, although already established migrants, continued to return home for the peak seasons to help their father until around 1940. It is probably significant that only the youngest, who stayed in sharecropping with the father, got married at the 'right' age of around twenty years; the rest did not marry until the early 1950s when they were in their forties. This opens up a number of important questions in relation to the effects of sharecropping and migrant labour on family structure, which remain to be answered.

Finally, it is perhaps important to note that, contrary to much of the historiography, the Natives' Land Act of 1913 did not stamp out sharecropping. It continued to exist in modified forms, with many of its practitioners migrating to the Transvaal where the provisions of the Act were not applicable – at least immediately – though in the long run, these skilful farmers faced ruin here too. Even amongst those who remained in the Orange Free State, the practice in fact continued. In both the Transvaal and Orange Free State research needs to be done to ascertain what forms it took.

Sol Plaatje's accounts, in his *Native Life in South Africa*, which reviewed the immediate effects of the passage of the Land Act showed the hideous and agonising impact following 'the exodus of the evicted' tenants and sharecroppers said to have been 'squatting' illegally on white farms. But Plaatje's account, like that of Bundy, fails to consider the continued existence of African sharecroppers in the Orange Free State long after sharecropping was made illegal in 1913. In addition, Nkgono Mma-Pooe's story brings out very clearly the point that there was a very close relationship between sharecroppers and poor white farmers. The latter's lack of capital and demand for labour meant that they had to rely on wealthier, more skilled peasant sharecroppers who possessed, for example, spans of oxen and modern ploughs, and rent-paying tenant peasants who still occupied the various farms, some of which were owned by absentee landlords.[40] This interdependence also meant that sharecroppers were given a temporary reprieve. Looked at differently, sharecroppers also appear to have been dependent on white farmers because outside the tiny Thaba Nchu and Witzieshoek reserves, Africans were barred by law from purchasing land in the Orange Free State. Further, this symbiotic relationship between the farmer and sharecropper persisted into the mid-century, when competition for labour and the spread of state-backed white capitalist farming finally forced the remaining sharecroppers to move.[41] Most, like the Pooes, escaped to the Transvaal, even though many were forced onto farms far away from the main industrial towns where infrastructural developments were lacking.

Nkgono Mma-Pooe's story therefore serves as an example of a family who, despite the legal onslaughts and blatant discrimination, fought for their way of life until the final blow against sharecroppers and rentier tenants came with the 1959 Du Toit Commission, which warned about '*die beswarting van die platteland*'.[42] This was followed by harsh enforcement of anti-'squatting' measures which resulted in mass relocation of labour-tenants and sharecroppers to the now notorious 'homeland' resettlement camps of the 1960s and 1970s.[43]

Notes

1 *Nkgono* in Sotho means 'grandmother'. Mrs Pooe is commonly referred to as 'Nkgono' as a mark of respect for her advanced age. In this essay I will use 'Nkgono Mma-Pooe' or 'Mrs Pooe' when it is absolutely necessary.

2 See preamble to the written project presented by the Director of the Institute of African Studies at the University of the Witwatersrand in November 1979. I worked for the Institute as a researcher.

3 T. O. Ranger in a review article, *Journal of Southern African Studies* (*JSAS*), V, 2, 1979, 107–33, 'Growing from the roots: reflections on peasant research in central and southern Africa', attributes the thinness of the discussion of both the pre-colonial period and of the period since 1930 as arising partly from the absence of oral

evidence. I firmly endorse this view.

4   In my interviews with Mrs Pooe I repeatedly made use of Paul Thompson's *The Voice of the Past – Oral History* (London, 1978).

5   See the family tree, table adapted from Absolom Vilakazi's *Zulu Transformations: a study of the dynamics of social change* (Pietermaritzburg, 1965), p. 17.

6   Interviews conducted with Mrs Pooe at the University of the Witwatersrand on 29 Aug. 1979 and 29 Oct. 1979. Tapes with African Studies Institute.

7   Sharecroppers in South Africa have been variously known as farmers, half-share farmers, peasants or, pejoratively, as 'Kaffir farmers' or 'squatters'. See Colin Bundy's *The Rise and Fall of the South African Peasantry* (London, 1979), pp. 8, 45 and 52–3; T. Keegan, *The restructuring of agrarian class relations in a colonial economy: the Orange River Colony, 1902–1910'*, *JSAS*, V, 2 (1979), 234–54.

8   See map of the Orange Free State (Fig. 8.2), adapted from *Phillips' Large Scale Military Map of South Africa*, rev. ed., Sheets 1 and 2 (London, 1900).

9   P. Thompson, *The Voice of the Past*, p. 98.

10 The Oral History Project of the Institute of African Studies at the University of the Witwatersrand is accumulating case studies which will not only extend our knowledge in this field but will also allow for comparative accounts of sharecroppers in different districts in South Africa.

11 I have been greatly encouraged by their pioneering work on the peasantry in South Africa.

12 Omer-Cooper in his *The Zulu aftermath* (London, 1966) locates the Kwena groups on the Transorangia plateau (p. 133). This point remains unresolved, as M. Legassick discusses at length in 'The Sotho–Tswana peoples before 1800', in L. Thompson, (ed.), *African Societies of Southern Africa* (London, 1969), pp. 86–125, especially the map on p. 25.

13 Mrs Pooe relates that she has learnt from her own grandparents about the Difaqane and how thereafter people went wild and in fact depended on hunting for their survival. Children who were born when the quiet came and people could once more cultivate the soil were called '*maja-kgomo*', literally meaning 'eating beef'. *Ngwanana* is a girl and *mosimane* a boy in Sotho. See also *abatwa*, referred to in Marks and Atmore (eds), *Economy and Society in Pre-industrial South Africa* (London, 1980), p. 124 in the piece by W. Beinart: 'Production and the material basis of chieftainship: Pondoland c. 1830–80'.

14 S. Marks, 'African and Afrikaner History', *Journal of African History*, XI, 3 (1970), 435–47.

15 The owner of the Slangfontein farm was Piet Cilliers. It appears this farm might have had a name-change.

16 The owner of Mooikraal (Mmamot langwe) was Jan Scholtz; that of Rietfontein (Magodiri), Sher Emmernis; and that of Zaaiplaas (Thalle), Frikkie Els.

17 Their visit to Heidelburg (Boesmanskop) explains much of what happened between the various communities, not only in the Orange Free State but also in the Transvaal. Contact was maintained by extended visits to relatives who stayed too far away. These visits entailed labour export and seed exchanges, and it may have also been a way of disseminating ideas regarding their strategies for circumventing the forces that were closing in on the South African peasantry at the time.

18 *Spijoen*: the Afrikaans word for 'spy' or 'war scout'. Mrs Pooe uses the words *spijoen* and 'soldier' interchangeably. She talks of Basuto *spijoene* when referring to real spies used by British forces to track down Afrikaner commandos. She also speaks of Boer *spijoene*

when referring to their Afrikaner counterparts. Sometimes she refers to ordinary soldiers or Basuto workers, such as *agterryers* in the army, as *spijoene*. See below, note 22.

19 *Laager*: an encampment of wagons lashed together for protection of the people and animals within, and as a barricade from which to fire on attackers; the regular defence of the Voortrekkers and other pioneers (J. Branford, *A Dictionary of South African English* (OUP, Cape Town, 1978), p. 131). Mrs Pooe, in her narrations, seems (incorrectly) to refer to both the military convoy and the encampment as the laager.

20 S. B. Spies, *Methods of Barbarism? Roberts and Kitchener and civilians in the Boer Republics January 1900–1902* (Cape Town, 1977) pp. 228–9.

21 Spies, *Methods of Barbarism?* p. 230. He actually shows at length that the British demand for labour was a major reason for the creation of African concentration camps. They also wanted to prevent any African assistance to Boer guerrilla forces.

22 *Agterryer*: a mounted groom or other attendant. Literal meaning: 'riding behind'; '. . . two Boers on horseback, attended by two Hottentot achter-ryders' (Branford, *Dictionary*, p. 5).

23 When she talks of the British she refers to them as 'Johnnies' or perhaps 'Tommies'. There is a prefix normally added in all Bantu languages designating the plural, hence 'Ma-Johnny'.

24 Spies, *Methods of Barbarism?* pp. 228–9.

25 T. Keegan, *JSAS*, V, 2 (1979), cites a document CS/1019/01 (Governor to District Commissioner of Boshof, 22 April 1901), which explains this reluctance by most blacks to go back to the farms.

26 *Trekgoed*, literal meaning: 'material', goods used for hauling'. Mrs Pooe's usage refers to yokes, oxen, chains and all that went with a plough to make it workable for ploughing or hauling a wagon.

27 T. Keegan, Chapter 7 above.

28 *Akkoord*, literal meaning: 'agreement', 'harmony', e.g., *akkoord gaan met iemand* – 'to enter into an agreement with somebody' ('contract'). To the peasant sharecroppers and Boers in the Orange Free State it meant more than just a paper signifying agreement. It incorporated the sum total of all the terms under which a tenant-labourer or peasant-sharecropper would work, and it was a programme for a year's work. It was entered into in winter, around July (i.e., after harvesting, when the 'real' year for the peasants started). There were various *akkoorde* in the Orange Free State. Basically there were *akkoorde* incorporating terms such as labour-tenancy, labour-rent, cash rent, sharecropping and other semi-feudal arrangements, depending upon the outcome of the negotiations between the tenant and landowner.

29 Bundy, *The Rise and Fall of the South African Peasantry*, p. 208.

30 That numbers of Basotho saw the Orange Free State as a natural area for expansion after the end of the Basuto and Boer wars and, later, after the Anglo-Boer war cannot be doubted. The Molefes and Pooes are reported to have been in the Orange Free State before the mid-nineteenth century. All their neighbours at Slangfontein around 1880 are Basotho (Pooe, Rampa, Ramakhaha, Lebona, Mogatle, Lekima, Ramokonopi). The same surnames are repeated later on the farms owned by the Vereeniging Estate Land Company in the north, with a few additions such as Makhene, Siboko, Ngakane, Thekiso Lekhoathi, Pharumela, Lempe. All these people are said to have had connections with Lesotho.

31 These are presumably Sammy Marks's farms referred to by Stanley Trapido in his 'Landlord and tenant in a colonial economy: the Transvaal 1880–1910' (*JSAS*, V, 2

1979) in which he cites details from a report, Tenants' Census and Report of 1903, which suggests an intense degree of cultivation amongst both its white and black tenants. According to this report, SNA 48/138/04, the VELC owned about fifteen farms in the Transvaal and Orange Free State. The Basuto name for Sammy Marks is Mmangolwane. It is possible Sammy is Ellie's son and Mmangolwane could refer as well to Ellie Marks.

32 S. T. Plaatje, *Native Life in South Africa before and since the European war and the Boer Rebellion* (London, 1916).

33 *Bywoner*: landless white, a sub-farmer, authorised squatter or sharecropper, working part of another man's land, giving either a share in his profits or labour, or both, in exchange (Branford, *Dictionary*, p. 40). Mrs Pooe's understanding of a *bywoner* tallies with the above meaning. Interesting in her narrations is that nowhere does she refer to *bywoners* while they still lived in the Orange Free State, i.e. before 1913. She recalls their first encounter with them in the Transvaal at Oorbietjiesfontein.

34 *Boetebossie*: a plant pest, *xanthium spinosum*, a type of burr weed, the fruits of which do serious damage to fleeces. Its eradication was made compulsory by payment of a fine, by legislation in 1860. *Boetebossie* is so called because a fine is the penalty for failing to keep one's land free from this pest (C. Pettman, Africanderisms [London, 1913]).

35 In another interview with Lulu, Ranchawe and Mrs Pooe, it became clear that the *boetebossie* for which Naphtali was charged had in fact been there before he came to Stoffel van Balle's farm. These were fields that Tol had hired out to a *bywoner*. Naphtali had just settled on that farm and had good cause to argue. On the alternative charges of refusing arrest and attempted assault, Naphtali argued that he had the right to defend himself and that he did not start the fight — it was the policeman who kicked him. Christiaan Smit, Tol's uncle, gave evidence in favour of Naphtali at the hearing.

36 *Matikiring*: place of the diggers. These are presumably the alluvial diamond diggings along the Vaal river.

37 Boipatong is the black township adjacent to Vanderbijl Park which was built in the early 1950s.

38 With the passage of the Natives' Land Act of 1913, or a year or two before its enactment, many sharecroppers left the Orange Free State, having bought properties in the Transvaal. This was possible until 1913 and after it under the moratorium granted to the Transvaal province in respect of the enforcement of the provisions of the Act. The case in point here is that of a Kwena-Phuting group, later to be known as Bakwena ba Ga-Mokgupa, who bought Swartrand farm near Ventersdorp. Naphtali Pooe was a co-buyer there. The Bakwena ba Ga-Mokgupa peasantry is a subject in its own right and deserves a separate study. Peasant production was resumed there after 1913 and has continued up to this day.

39 Bundy, *The Rise and Fall of South African Peasantry*, p. 206.

40 The question of cooperation and the relations between labour-tenants and sharecroppers is not the only one that remains unclear in Nkgono Mma-Pooe's story. For instance, she cannot explain satisfactorily why none of her children went to school while her husband had been to Lovedale, could speak English and Afrikaans fluently and was a teacher on the farm schools.

41 M. Lacey, in *Working for Boroko — the origins of the coercive labour system in South Africa* (Johannesburg, 1981).

42 Union of South Africa, *Report of the Commission of Inquiry into European Occupancy of Rural Areas*, (Du Toit Commission, Pretoria, 1960); see especially the map. This

commission is also cited by M. Wilson, 'The Nguni People', in M. Wilson and L. Thompson (eds), *The Oxford History of South Africa*, Vol. I (London, 1969), p. 105.

43 See the following sources in particular: G. Mare, *African Population Relocation in South Africa* (Johannesburg, 1980); M. Nash, *Black Uprooting from White South Africa* (Johannesburg, *SACC*, 1980); C. Desmond, *The Discarded People* (Harmondsworth, 1971); and A. Baldwin, 'Mass Removals and Separate Development', *JSAS*, I, 2 (1975), 215–27.

CHAPTER NINE

An African in Kimberley: Sol T. Plaatje, 1894–1898

Brian Willan

Sol T. Plaatje (1876–1932) was one of the leading black South African figures of his generation. An immensely talented and versatile man, Plaatje established his reputation as a newspaper editor and journalist, political leader and spokesman, one of the founders of the South African Native National Congress (later to become the African National Congress), author of *Native Life in South Africa* and *Mhudi*, and translator of Shakespeare into his native tongue, Tswana. In many ways, indeed, his career both symbolised and expressed the aspirations and achievements of the generation of mission-educated Africans that he represented. The present essay, however, is concerned with an earlier period in Plaatje's life, before he had become a well-known public figure, when he worked as a messenger, and later as a letter carrier, in the Kimberley Post Office between 1894 and 1898. My objective is not only to throw light upon an unknown if formative period in Plaatje's own life, but also to try to portray through a biographical lens something of the wider social experience of the community of which Plaatje was a part at this time.

For want of a better term I have characterised this community as Kimberley's African petty bourgeoisie. By this I mean to refer to the emergent class of African teachers, interpreters, clerks, ministers of religion, tradesmen and others, who stood between an albeit partially formed proletariat on the one hand, and a propertied bourgeoisie on the other; who shared common experiences, values, and an awareness of an identity of their interests as against those of other socio-economic classes; and who developed most visibly and forthrightly quite characteristic forms of cultural expression which it will be the particular object of this paper to explore.

Kimberley in the 1890s was a supremely British place; indeed daily life in the Diamond City perhaps expressed as clearly as anywhere in the empire the meaning and reality of British imperial hegemony. Well before Plaatje came to live and work there in 1894 De Beers had asserted its supremacy over the town's affairs, and 'the old roughness', as James Bryce put it in the same year 'had been replaced by order and comfort'.[1] Max O'Rell, who had been there a year earlier, was similarly impressed with the fact that Kimberley was no longer 'an adventure camp, but a town inhabited by intelligent people who read and study', pointing particularly to the Public Library ('one of the largest and best stocked that I saw in the Colonies') as evidence of this.[2] The diamond magnates were firmly in control, the white working class had been put in its place with little difficulty, and an atmosphere of bourgeois respectability increasingly prevailed. Kimberley itself was widely regarded as a triumph of English civilisation. To have suggested, for example, that the town's existence revolved around providing profits for magnates like Cecil Rhodes would have been in extremely bad taste; it would also have been a little unwise. Rather, it made possible the furtherance of English civilisation and the imperial mission. Kimberley was, after all, the base of the greatest imperialist of them all, Cecil Rhodes. More than anybody else, he personified and expounded this imperial mission. The supremacy of British culture and institutions was one of those self-evident facts quite inseparable from Kimberley's existence.

Such an outlook on the world would not have been wholly self-evident to Sol Plaatje when he first came to Kimberley. At Pniel, where he went to school, other important influences had contributed towards his world view. One was his deep immersion in Tswana history and tradition through his immediate family and relatives. Another was a commitment to a Protestant Christianity derived from German missionaries; for them, God was presumably not an Englishman. Plaatje was of course not immune to the pervasive influence of British institutions and culture; Pniel was not a totally self-contained community but part of the Cape Colony and subject to its laws and regulations. However, the kind of instruction that the Rev. and Mrs Westphal provided Plaatje with – even when it was in English – can hardly have conveyed to him the subtleties of British culture and the values which an education at the hands of English-speaking missionaries could have done, and indeed did so for his contemporaries elsewhere. Of crucial importance to the process of disseminating and internalising the values of imperial supremacy was a fluent command of the English language, and this Plaatje did not acquire until he went to live and work in Kimberley. The manner in which he achieved this was thus of great significance.

Plaatje's place of employment – the main Post Office in Kimberley – was one of the most important arenas in which this process took place. For the Post Office was, Plaatje recalled many years later, 'his educational institution'.[3] He described also 'the difficulties he experienced with the English language when, as a lad of fifteen, he came from the country to work in the Kimberley Post Office'. Here, he went on, 'an abnormal thirst for knowledge showed him that no one was too humble or too young to teach him something', and 'a keen observation stood him in good stead so that he was soon able to find a footing'.[4] In the Post Office, too, Plaatje learned to attune himself to the values and to the standards of behaviour which were considered to be both acceptable and respectable. As a public servant, an ethos of public service and duty was one important influence which left a deep impression on him. Discipline, too, was of the greatest importance, though having grown up on a German mission station Plaatje was no doubt well used to this. Part of a highly efficient and well-organised Cape Civil Service, the Posts and Telegraphs Department in Kimberley insisted upon an extremely high standard of discipline, work and personal behaviour from its employees. John Henry, the Postmaster, had a reputation for maintaining these standards, and transgressors – black and white – were, when necessary, fined for their misdeeds. 'In my day', Plaatje recalled some fifteen years later, 'when a telegram came to "Robinson, Kimberley", Robinson had to get it or the Postmaster General would know the reason why'.[5]

For Africans other qualities seem to have been considered desirable. These were exemplified in the person of Nelson Lindie, senior messenger in the Kimberley Post Office. As 'sender out' he would in all probability have been Plaatje's immediate superior and as such may well have been an important influence upon him. In 1895 there appeared an article about Lindie in the *Diamond Fields Advertiser* under the title 'A Good Example to his Brothers'. Lindie was, so it said, 'a highly commendable product of native civilisation'. Educated at Lovedale, he had come to Kimberley in about 1880, joined the messenger branch of the Posts and Telegraphs Department, and by 1895 had achieved promotion to the position of 'sender out'. He was, according to the *Diamond Fields Advertiser*, 'a well spoken, well educated native of respectable demeanour', whose 'loyalty to the government was unquestioned', and who was altogether to be commended 'for his extremely creditable record as a private citizen and servant of the government'. Interestingly, he was considered also to represent 'in his own person a satisfactory solution of the native problem', and by his 'general conduct' to provide 'a complete answer to those who are strenuously opposed to native education'.[6]

Such were the qualities regarded as desirable in an African employee of the Post Office. Plaatje undoubtedly responded: according to Dr Molema, he soon became known as 'a clever young man, who is fast, energetic, who had knowledge of his job, and good manners'.[7] But the direct assimilation in this way of the values and standards of behaviour appropriate to the workings of the dominant institutions of the colony was, for Plaatje, only part of a wider process of acculturation and socialisation. He found himself in Kimberley not merely as an individual but as a member of a readily identifiable and quite conscious social class, with whose corporate life he came to be closely associated. This fact not only defined Plaatje's social relations during the time that he lived in

Kimberley, but also gave a quite distinctive flavour and meaning to the process whereby the dominant values of society as a whole were transmitted to him.

Kimberley in the 1890s was the home of some 8–9 000 semi-permanent African residents, employed in a wide range of activities in both 'formal' and 'informal' sectors of the local economy.[8] At one end of the spectrum were the unemployed, the casual labourers, the pimps and the prostitutes – those whom Cecil Rhodes liked to call 'loafers'. But at the other end of this spectrum was what constituted an African petty bourgeoisie: a growing and increasingly coherent class of educated Africans who had been drawn to Kimberley because of the opportunities that it provided for employment and for the utilisation of the skills associated with the literacy they possessed. Kimberley became, in fact, a focal point for the ambitions and aspirations of hundreds of Africans from different parts of the Cape and beyond (especially Basutoland and Bechuanaland) who shared common ideas, values and experiences as a result of education at the hands of Christian missionaries of one denomination or another.

Their presence in Kimberley was noted in the *Report of the Civil Commissioner* for Kimberley in 1892:

> In the townships a considerable number of educated natives are employed. They come principally from Lovedale, and belong as a whole, to the Fingo or AmaXhosa tribes. Three of them are employed as clerks, and several others as messengers, in the Post and Telegraph Department at good salaries. Many others find employment in and about the stores at from £5 to £6 per month.[9]

The most highly sought after and best-paid jobs generally went to those with the best educational qualifications: hence the predominance of Africans from the eastern Cape, the oldest and most successful field of missionary endeavour. Within both the Cape Colony as a whole and Kimberley in particular the Mfengu group especially occupied a role as standard bearers of 'western civilisation'. The earliest arrivals on the diamond fields, they assumed a position of social dominance and leadership amongst the increasingly cosmopolitan African community in Kimberley as a whole. Seeking incorporation into Cape colonial society, they were enthusiastic adherents of its more dominant norms and values. Indeed, they took these rather more seriously than did any other social group, a fact which came to demonstrate quite clearly the ambiguity inherent in such notions as 'Cape liberalism' or the 'imperial mission', and which frequently resulted in considerable embarrassment in ruling circles.

It was largely amongst this eastern Cape group that many of Plaatje's ideas and aspirations took shape. United by a deep commitment to Christian belief and morality, they also shared a firm confidence in the values of British imperial hegemony whose vision animated and permeated Cape society. For most Africans educated in the Cape Colony in the second half of the nineteenth century, the concepts of 'civilisation' and British imperial supremacy were inseparable. There existed a strong belief that the survival of the non-racial Cape franchise, which provided both the hope and means for their incorporation into Cape colonial society by institutionalising 'civilisation' rather than race or colour as the crucial criteria for this, depended upon the maintenance of direct imperial control. Accordingly, expressions of loyalty and attachment to the 'imperial factor' were frequently on their lips, particularly at times when local colonial interests were pressing for more repressive 'native policies'. 'Direct Imperial control', as *Imvo* put it in 1897, 'is the talisman engraved on the heart of every native in the land.'[10] It was a concept that underlay much of the political consciousness of Kimberley's African petty bourgeoisie as well. The law courts were regarded as one of the most important areas for the defence and protection of their civil and political rights, and it was no coincidence that it was to sympathetic liberal lawyers that they 'safely entrusted their interests' (as one member of Kimberley's African petty bourgeoisie later put it).[11]

British imperial hegemony did not simply have meaning for this class as a matter of preference for direct political control from Whitehall; rather, it influenced every aspect of their existence, shaping the moral and intellectual, as well as the political framework within which they lived their lives.[12] One peculiarly important and pervasive symbol of this connection, which gave expression to the values and beliefs that they held, was the figure of Queen Victoria, 'who became depersonalised, as an idea: the idea of the Great White Queen'.[13] One part of this idea was the concept of equality before the law of all subjects of the British empire. For Richard Selope Thema, as for so many of his generation, the association was a very close one. Recalling how it was that he 'learnt to admire British institutions of justice', he wrote in 1925 how he remembered clearly 'the story told me by my father when he returned from Kimberley in 1894, where he had gone to work for guns, that there was a Great White Queen across the seas who made no distinction between white and black in the administration of her laws'.[14]

Queen Victoria's Diamond Jubilee in 1897 both strengthened this association of ideas and provided the opportunity for many of them to be made more explicit. In Kimberley, this task fell to one of the leading figures of its African petty bourgeoisie, the Rev. Jonathan Jabavu, brother of the famous editor of *Imvo*. Addressing his congregation on 20 June 1897, he noted how 'the propagation of the Gospel had put a stop to many evil practices amongst the natives, and tyrannous acts by the heathen chiefs were prevented'; now 'both high and low, if they worked honestly, could attain to the highest positions in the State'; 'by a good system of education . . . the savage had been raised to a better state of life'; and now 'the natives had churches and ministers of their own colour, and were enabled to possess their lands'. For all this, the Rev.

Jabavu concluded, 'might the Lord God bless their gracious Queen and increase her years, and lengthen her days so that she might reign long in the land'.[15]

Many of the elements of the ideological milieu in which Plaatje lived in the 1890s were here: the firm belief in the legitimacy of the imperial order, a Victorian work ethic, a confidence in the possibility, indeed the obligation, of individual advancement through the medium of education, and a sense of optimism about 'progress' and 'improvement' generally. Isaiah Bud-M'belle, the High Court Interpreter, expressed similar sentiments in the opening ceremony for the 'Queen's Jubilee Commemoration Hall' in Kimberley's Malay Camp in November 1897:

> The company then sat down to an excellent spread, at the conclusion of which Bud-M'belle proposed the 'progress of the Natives', and compared their present condition to what prevailed at the time of the accession of the Queen, and pointed out that though then scarcely a native could write his name and there were no Native ministers, now thousands could write, and there were about five hundred Native ministers. There were also flourishing Native educational institutions.[16]

The emphasis upon 'Native ministers' was significant. They not only represented by their example the possibility of advancement for educated Africans in one of the main spheres open to them, but also personified many of the values and qualities which as committed Christians they all held in high regard. Sol Plaatje was quickly aware of the special position and status that they occupied amongst Kimberley's African petty bourgeoisie. It was reflected, for example, in the frequency with which they were called upon to lend dignity and respectability to various clubs and societies. There were three of them: the Revs Gwayi Tyamzashe (Congregational), Jonathan Jabavu (Wesleyan) and Davidson Msikinya (Wesleyan). Of the three, Tyamzashe made perhaps the greatest impact upon Plaatje: some thirty years later he remembered clearly that Tyamzashe was 'the first ordained black minister I ever saw'.[17] Tyamzashe, the senior of the three, had been one of the early arrivals on the diamond fields. Born in 1844, he 'fell into the hands of the missionaries at Dr Love's mission station' (Lovedale). There he and his fellow students 'soon found themselves on the highway to civilisation and education', attended classes which included, amongst their European pupils, two Solomons and a Schreiner, completed his theological training in 1874, and departed immediately for Kimberley.[18] Apart from six years away in the Zoutpansberg in the 1880s he remained there until his death in 1896, the occasion of much sadness not only for his congregation but for the town's African petty bourgeoisie as a whole.[19]

The personal example of individuals like the Rev. Gwayi Tyamzashe was one of the most important means by which Plaatje came to internalise the values and beliefs held by the social group as a whole to which both belonged. But an even more important influence was Isaiah Bud-M'belle himself. It had been altogether appropriate for him to have been called upon to toast 'the progress of the Natives' because he, more than any other African living in Kimberley, personified this progress. Bud-M'belle had been born in 1869, of Mfengu origin, and received his education at Healdtown. Here, as elsewhere, he 'acquitted himself creditably', and taught for several years after his qualification as a teacher.[20] While engaged in teaching he studied privately for the Cape Civil Service examination, and in 1893 became the first African to pass the qualifying examination. After a brief period helping out with interpreting in the Kimberley police station, he accepted an appointment as Interpreter in Native Languages (he spoke a total of six) to the Northern Circuit of the Supreme Court which was based in Kimberley. The salary of £25 a month which this post carried would have made him probably the most highly paid African employee of the government in the Cape Colony: and it was a post, according to *Imvo*, in which there was 'no doubting his usefulness'.[21]

Plaatje's contact with Bud-M'belle was one of the decisive influences in his life. They apparently first met when Plaatje, as a messenger at the Post Office, delivered letters and telegrams to the Supreme Court building where Bud-M'belle worked.[22] They quickly became close friends, and some time later Plaatje went to live in the same house in the Malay Camp. It seems likely that Bud-M'belle played an important role in encouraging Plaatje to become a court interpreter, and may well have provided him with the opportunity to gain some experience in doing this; in due course he was to follow in Bud-M'belle's footsteps.[23]

Individual example and friendship was one way in which Plaatje came to appreciate the values held by Kimberley's African petty bourgeoisie as a whole. Another was through participation in their busy social life. The values and ideas which they held in common – whether these were notions of loyalty to the British empire, or the desirability of 'progress', 'education' or regular church attendance – were shaped, sustained and disseminated not in a fitful, haphazard manner, but through a network of regular activities and involvement in churches, clubs and societies. It was the existence and functioning of these that created a sense of class and community out of the cosmopolitan group of mission-educated Africans who lived on the diamond fields. And it constituted, too, the most important mechanism for the socialisation and incorporation of new members.

For Plaatje, an organisation known as the South Africans Improvement Society was of particular significance, providing him with perhaps his most important ideological, social and literary training ground. The name of the Society itself is significant: 'improvement', like 'progress' was an absolutely key concept in African petty-bourgeois circles. Founded in June 1895, the Society brought together Kimberley's most able and articulate Africans for meetings and discussions at fortnightly intervals. The objects of the Society were as follows:

> firstly, to cultivate the use of the English language, which is foreign to Africans; secondly, to help each other by fair and reasonable criticism in readings, English composition, etc., etc.[24]

The emphasis on the English language is of central importance. The fact that the Society saw it as such reflects the hegemony of English institutions in the Cape Colony generally and the implications of this for anybody who wanted to make his way in this society. *Imvo* made precisely this point in one of its editorials just a few months later:

> The key of knowledge is the English language. Without such a mastery of it as will give the scholar a taste for reading, the great English literature is a sealed book, and he remains one of the uneducated, living in the miserably small world of Boer ideals, or those of the untaught Natives. *But besides, in this country where the English are the rulers, the merchants, and the influential men, he can never obtain a position in life of any importance without a command of English.*[25] (My emphasis)

For Plaatje, learning to cope with English from a humble and subordinate position within an institution (the Post Office) that formed part of the Colony's apparatus of government was one thing. But in the company of his peers, gathered together on an equal basis and for a common purpose in a situation outside the immediate nexus of conventional black/white relations, the circumstances were significantly different. Here the English language was less obviously a vehicle for a ruling ideology, and was more the means of advancement and progress – the means, too, not only of enabling one to do a job properly but also of proving oneself capable of participating in 'civilised' society as a whole. In such a context English was something to be played around with, to be enjoyed and to be developed to the highest possible degree.

Plaatje's participation in the meetings of the South Africans Improvement Society undoubtedly contributed greatly to his acquisition of mastery over the English language. The socially important matter of pronunciation was one of the matters that was attended to. At the Society's meeting on 16 July 1895, Plaatje read a passage from a book which resulted in 'his style of reading and pronunciation' being 'fairly criticized', whilst the 'mistakes corrected did not only benefit the reader, but also the other members'.[26] It was a literary début that perhaps gave little hint of the reader's subsequent achievements in the literary field, or of the fluency he developed as a public speaker. Rather more significant was the book from which Plaatje was reading: Max O'Rell's *John Bull and Co.*, a humorous celebration of the glories of the British empire by an author whose visit to Kimberley (distinguished by three highly popular lectures in May 1893) would have been well remembered by many of those present at the Society's meeting that evening.[27] It was a happier choice of text than the piece which had been recited by the previous speaker, W. B. Kawa. His admittedly able recitation from Milton's *Paradise Lost* was not, according to the unnamed member of the Society who wrote up the meeting, 'highly appreciated by the majority of the members as it was too classical to be comprehended by the average native mind'. Kawa had overstepped, it would seem, the limits of social and literary one-upmanship![28]

Plaatje's contribution to one of the Society's meetings several weeks later seems to have been somewhat better received. Certainly it gave an indication of the direction of his future interests, the essay he read being entitled 'The History of the Bechuanas'. 'Being a Bechuana', it was recorded, with just a hint of condescension, 'he showed great mastery over his subject.'[29]

The Society drew part of its inspiration and its rules and regulations from local white societies. Its members looked particularly to the Kimberley Literary Society and the YMCA Debating Society, reports of whose activities appeared regularly in the columns of the *Diamond Fields Advertiser*. The South Africans Improvement Society, however, combined both functions, and music, in addition, provided a major feature of their activities. Its first meeting was taken up with a paper by Isaiah Bud-M'belle entitled 'My Ideas of a Debating Society', which was found to be 'interesting and instructive', and with the election of office-bearers: the President was the Rev. Jonathan Jabavu; the Chairman, Mr E. Ugesi; Vice-Chairman, Mr W. Cowen; Secretary and Treasurer, Mr S. M. Mokwena (Interpreter to the Beaconsfield Magistrates' Court). The Revs Davidson Msikinya and Gwayi Tyamzashe were elected as honorary members.[30] Meetings of the Society were held thereafter at fortnightly intervals, deferring only to such events as a public lecture by Mr Cronwright-Schreiner on 23 August 1895: as this coincided with a meeting of the Society, and as 'the majority of members intimated to the Secretary their desire of attending' the lecture, the meeting was postponed until the following week.[31] By the end of August the Society claimed more than twenty-five members.

The proceedings of subsequent meetings reflect clearly the concerns and attitudes that characterised this group of people. At the Society's third meeting the debate was: 'Is insurance a proper provision of life?', proposed by Isaiah Bud-M'belle, opposed by Mr Joseph Moss (Interpreter to the Kimberley Magistrates' Court). The Society's own account of the meeting clearly conveys the flavour:

> It was at this meeting that one could notice that there is much native talent in Kimberley, hidden in the ground and unused. Mr Moss led his side in able manner, and tried to prove that insurance is mere speculation, and is therefore a risky investment, whilst the other leader proved that it is a poor man's savings bank and a stimulant and encouragement to industry. After some heated discussion for both sides

by the members, the affirmative side carried the day. In consequence of this debate, many who did not fully understand insurance made proposals to the various companies. Sharp Practice, arranged by Mr Mokwena, concluded another enjoyable night.[32]

The Society played a quite direct function, in other words, in familiarising its members with the customs and requirements of 'civilised' life. This general theme was in fact dealt with at the next meeting, in an essay by Mr W. Cowen entitled 'Civilisation and its advantages to African Races'. On occasion, difficulties could arise when conventions of debating procedure went against personal conviction. At a meeting of the Society early in 1896 the subject debated was: 'Is lobola as practiced at the present time justifiable?', W. B. Kawa for, H. C. Msikinya (school teacher, and son of the Rev. D. Msikinya) against. Not surprisingly, H. C. Msikinya won the debate, but to W. B. Kawa must surely go the credit for maintaining, in the best tradition and in what must have been a very difficult situation for him, a stiff upper lip:

> It is only fair to state that Mr. W. B. Kawa, after having ably led his side, publicly stated that his own personal convictions were entirely against this relic of barbarism.[33]

If the activities and concerns of the South Africans Improvement Society reflected the dominant values of the society to which its members aspired, its meetings were characterised by an exuberance and humour of their own creation. Socialisation and acculturation were not just important sociologically and historically; they were also potentially very funny, and one of the most striking characteristics of this social group to which Plaatje belonged is a fascinating blend of humour and self-confidence, qualities which Plaatje was later to make his own. But they were qualities of a social group as a whole, not just of one individual. The humour arose essentially out of the social situation in which they found themselves. They were frequently willing to make fun not only of the 'ways of European civilisation' but of their own aspirations towards these. It was, after all, potentially a very rich source of humour. Within Kimberley's African petty bourgeoisie, the best-known exponent was Patrick ('Pat') Lenkoane, whose sense of humour made a great impression upon his colleagues, and none more than upon Plaatje himself. For Plaatje, Patrick Lenkoane was the 'humorous black Irishman' whose jokes and humorous stories constituted a special genre called a 'Lenkoaniac', several examples of which, told to Plaatje by a friend who had also known Lenkoane in Kimberley, relieved the boredom of the siege of Mafeking a few years later.[34] Lenkoane's contributions also enlivened the proceedings of the South Africans Improvement Society. On one occasion, in response to Mr W. Cowen's undoubtedly weighty paper, 'Civilisation and its advantages to African Races', Mr Patrick Lenkoane ('the native Artemis Ward') said, 'in his inimitable and humorous manner, "That the natives of this country have caught hold of civilisation by the tail, and not by the head, and it is therefore dangerous to them".'[35]

When Patrick Lenkoane was around, it would appear, the process of acculturation and socialisation was rarely a wholly serious business. That he was found funny by his colleagues is a tribute not only to their willingness to make themselves and their social situation the object of satire and parody, but a reflection at the same time of their underlying optimism and self-confidence: for them, 'progress' and 'improvement' seemed assured, and the future held every promise. They could afford to laugh at themselves now and again.

Other forms of activity on the part of Kimberley's African petty bourgeoisie were perhaps not so deliberately conceived as the South Africans Improvement Society to train its members in their society's norms and values, but were nevertheless equally effective in doing so. Ideology permeated their life and social behaviour. Take the 'social gathering of Africans' which took place on 21 August 1896, to celebrate the impending departure of two of their most distinguished sons for education overseas, an event in which Plaatje played a leading role: for him it was both a means and a measure of the extent of his socialisation into the lifestyle, values and behaviour of this social group. The two young men were H. C. Msikinya and Chalmers Moss (son of Mr 'Interpreter' Moss, as he was known), and both had secured places at Wilberforce University, U.S.A.[36] It was naturally an achievement of which they, their parents and the community as a whole were very proud, for educational achievement was one of the most highly regarded attributes in these circles. And it provided an appropriate opportunity for Kimberley's African petty bourgeoisie to parade itself in all its splendour and self-confidence. Such was the splendour of the occasion, indeed, that Isaiah Bud-M'belle, upon whom devolved the task of writing it up, was lost for the words (probably one of the few occasions in which he found himself in such a situation) to 'convey that anything out of the ordinary run had occurred'. He began, however, by listing H. C. Msikinya's social accomplishments (President of the Come Again Lawn Tennis Club, Secretary to the Eccentrics Cricket Club, member of the Rovers Rugby Football Club, and member of the South Africans Improvement Society), and settled for describing the event that took place as 'really an elegant affair in the fullest sense of the word'.[37]

After dinner – 'a feast fit for the Gods' – Bud-M'belle, 'in obedience to the desire of the committee of arrangements', took the chair as the programme proper began. Letters from the Revs Gwayi Tyamzashe and Jonathan Jabavu were read regretting 'their inability to attend owing to prior engagements', after which Sol Plaatje as secretary of the committee of arrangements, proposed the toast, 'The Queen and the Royal Family', and then a second toast, 'The Acting Administrator'. It was undoubtedly quite a moment for him. There then followed musical contributions from, amongst others, Mrs S. Nkomo (with

'What can the matter be?'), Mr S. M. Crutse (well-known opening batsman for Eccentrics), S. M. Mokwena, and H. C. Msikinya himself (with, appropriately in his case if not that of his colleague, 'We shall meet again'). These were interspersed with further toasts (and replies) to 'Our Guests', 'Africa' and 'Local Black Folk', ending, as was invariably the case on these occasions, with 'God Save the Queen'. Mr Joseph Moss then proposed a vote of thanks to their chair, which was seconded by the Rev. D. Msikinya and 'signified by the ladies and gentlemen with a continued applause'. After a vote of thanks, all present 'were called upon to sing the Kafir hymn entitled "Lizalise idinga lako Tixo", "Fulfill thy promise, O! God!", after which the Benediction was pronounced, and closed a function long to be remembered'.

Sol Plaatje was amongst those to whom special credit was due for making the occasion such a success. Isaiah Bud-M'belle again:

> The entire success of this gathering is due to Messrs Sol. T. Plaatje and E. J. Panyane who got up and prepared everything, to Mr. J. Binase [Captain of Eccentrics, with a reputation also both as a ladies' man and as a musician] who gave the use of his fine organ and accompanied most of the songs, and lastly, but not least, Mr. Patrick Lenkoane, who superintended the waiting during the evening and seemed to be here, there, and everywhere at the same time, arranging the details and looking after the introductions.[38]

The significance attached to musical entertainment is especially interesting and important. Music provided one of the main bonds of interest and association for Kimberley's African petty bourgeoisie. It certainly played an important part in Plaatje's life. It is very clearly reflected, for example, in the diary that he kept during the siege of Mafeking several years later where he refers on several occasions to particular musical events that had taken place in Kimberley whilst he was there, and indulges frequently in the construction of elaborate musical metaphors.[39] Musical instruction was prominent in every mission station's curriculum, and musical societies of various kinds provided one of the most popular forms of activity and entertainment for educated Africans in the Cape generally. In Kimberley this perhaps took place on a more extensive and regular basis than elsewhere. Apart from specially arranged concerts, some form of musical entertainment was usual at any gathering – at cricket or rugby club prize-giving ceremonies, for example, and, of course, the meetings of the South Africans Improvement Society. The form that these concerts took was clearly derived from the Western model, and differed little in this respect from those that catered for white bourgeois society in Kimberley. Both, indeed, shared common venues like the Town Hall. But the mixture of musical influences that is evident in the programmes provides a fascinating example of the way in which a quite characteristic tradition and identity was being forged out of a variety of influences – European, African and American. Music, perhaps more than anything else, demonstrated the intermediate cultural position in which this social group found itself and highlighted the rich possibilities inherent in such a situation.

The American influence was particularly strong in Kimberley as a result of the frequent visits in the 1890s of the well-known and highly popular Coloured American troupe, the Jubilee Singers, and in particular to the fact that one of its leading members, Will P. Thompson, decided to remain in the town. Well known as a 'first-rate pianist', Thompson's 'invaluable services' were constantly in demand, and he was invariably associated with the variety of musical enterprises that catered to the interests of its African society.[40] Sol Plaatje, too, was frequently involved, most notably in the Philharmonic Society, whose début took place – under Will P. Thompson's management – in the Woodley Street Hall on 19 March 1897. Its programme, as the *Diamond Fields Advertiser* put it,

> consists of modern part songs, selected solos, the famous Bushman song, Kaffir ditties, with clicks, the Kaffir Wedding Song, the Matabili War Song, and Ulo Tixo 'Mkulu' (Thou Great God) as sung by the first Christian converts among the AmaXhosa Kaffirs, whose name was Ntsikana Gaba.[41]

There were some familiar names amongst the artistes. The Musical Director was Isaiah Bud-M'belle, who was also a baritone soloist, rendering on this occasion 'Close the Shutters, Willie's Dead', a particular favourite, judging by the frequency with which he sang this at other gatherings.[42] Sol Plaatje (baritone) sang 'Trusting'. Amongst the bassos was the versatile T. J. Binase, and H. R. Ngcayiya, a future head of the Ethiopian Church of South Africa.

Music was also a sufficiently important matter for virtuosity to take precedence over strictly interpreted denominational differences. When the Wesleyan Native Church Choir put on a 'Grand Vocal Concert' in aid of the church at the Kimberley Town Hall, amongst the artistes was Sol Plaatje, a Lutheran. One of the soloists, his rendering on this occasion was 'Chiming Bells'. His presence there was a reflection not only of respect for his musical abilities but a measure also of the extent of his social acceptance amongst the predominantly Mfengu group who belonged to the Wesleyan Church. And the concert as a whole, like most of the others, was a great success: under the able musical direction of Mr H. C. Msikinya (an accomplishment which Isaiah Bud-M'belle had neglected to mention on the occasion of his farewell) the part-songs in particular, it was noted, 'were rendered with precision', whilst 'the pianissimo parts were taken with expression and skill'.[43]

Sport, too, was important in the life of Kimberley's African petty bourgeoisie, providing in addition to exercise and enjoyment a further bond of association and the means of disseminating the hegemonic values of the society in which they lived. Tennis was played at one of three clubs: Blue Flag Tennis

Club, Champion Lawn Tennis Club and Come Again Lawn Tennis Club.[44] The game was played by both men and women amongst members of each club, in club competitions and on occasion against other clubs from the eastern Cape. Altogether more popular, however, were cricket and rugby football, the leading sports in the Cape Colony generally. Native Rovers Rugby Football Club was generally captained by Isaiah Bud-M'belle, and in the 1890s they competed with half-a-dozen predominantly Coloured teams in the Griqualand West Colonial Rugby Football Union, which had begun in 1894 with four teams.[45] Rovers tended to be beaten rather more often than they won. When another team, the Universals, won the competition in 1896, W. Cowen (the Rovers' delegate at the prize-giving ceremony) typically congratulated the victors and assured 'those present that his team, although badly defeated this year, would do its best to come out near the top next season'.[46] Isaiah Bud-M'belle also did much for the advancement of rugby amongst Africans and Coloured people in both Kimberley and beyond. He was for several years the Secretary of the Griqualand West Colonial Rugby Football Union, managed to persuade Cecil Rhodes to present them with a cup to be competed for by clubs from all parts of the colony, and played a leading part in the establishment of the South African Colonial Rugby Football Board.[47]

Cricket, however, was the game that Kimberley's African petty bourgeoisie really made its own. That this should have been the case is perhaps not at all surprising. Cricket, after all, was not just a game. Rather, it was a uniquely British institution that embodied so many of the values and ideals which, individually and collectively, they aspired to. Cricket provided for them an opportunity to assimilate those values and ideals, and to demonstrate that they were capable and worthy of doing so. Cricket was a social training ground: the analogy between cricket and life generally was widely accepted, its value in character development unquestioned. 'Caution, care, patience, and decision', so one writer in the *Diamond Fields Advertiser* claimed in 1893, 'are inculcated by cricket's manly toil.'[48] Cricket both embodied and disseminated the imperial idea: Kipling's assault on the 'flannelled fools at the wicket and muddied oafs at the goal' remained in the future.[49]

The game was widely played by educated Africans throughout the Cape Colony. During the cricket season, every issue of *Imvo* contained columns of cricket results, reports, batting and bowling averages. In Kimberley, the two African clubs (they ran several teams each) were the Duke of Wellington Cricket Club (usually referred to simply as 'Duke'), and Eccentrics Cricket Club: even their names are suggestive, both symbolising qualities upon which the British empire was built. During the 1890s these two clubs competed with eight other (Indian, 'Malay' and Coloured) teams, firstly in the Griqualand West Coloured Cricketers Union (from 1892 to 1895), and thereafter in the Griqualand West

Colonial Union.[50] Fixtures between 'Duke' and Eccentrics came high up on the social calendar of Kimberley's African petty bourgeoisie. It was the major entertainment, for example, of Christmas Day, 1895.[51] However, the participation of the two African clubs in the Union was on occasion a source of tension. When Mr J. S. Moss was elected to the position of Vice-President of the Union in November 1895, three of the Coloured clubs temporarily pulled out, although Moss was, as Isaiah Bud-M'belle, who wrote to the local paper about the whole affair, pointed out, 'a cultured and respectable native gentleman of whom any sensible community can be proud'.[52]

Both Duke of Wellington and Eccentrics Cricket Clubs had long lists of office-bearers. Anybody who was anybody sought to become involved in running the club even if they did not actually play the game. Amongst them was Sol Plaatje. For Sol Plaatje, an upbringing on a German mission station seems to have been too much of a handicap to his ever learning to play cricket well, but in November 1895 he was nevertheless elected to the position of Joint Secretary of Eccentrics Cricket Club.[53] He was in respectable company. The President of the club was Boyce Skota (also an employee of the Post Office and father of T. D. Mweli Skota, who described him in his *African Yearly Register* as 'a very religious and real upright Christian gentleman');[54] the Vice-President was Patrick Lenkoane; team captain was T. J. Binase; the committee included Isaiah Bud-M'belle, James Ngcezula (shoemaker and circuit steward of the Wesleyan Native Church)[55] and S. M. Mokwena; whilst the honorary members included, inevitably perhaps, the Revs Msikinya and Jabavu. It was in the company of such as these that Plaatje came to internalise the qualities and values that cricket embodied. He retained them throughout life. When, in 1930, he chose to dedicate one of his Shakespearean translations to a close friend and colleague of his, Arthur Motlala, his qualities were summed up by Plaatje as follows: 'a loyal friend, a splendid cricketer, and an able Penman'.[56]

Linked by common background, values, organisations and sports clubs, Kimberley's African petty bourgeoisie also intermarried. Cosmopolitan Kimberley, the Colony's leading marriage market, contributed more than anywhere else to the process of creating a national African petty bourgeoisie out of a diverse set of regionally and ethnically defined local groupings. There was no happier example of this (from the point of view of both illustrating and exemplifying this process and of characterising the feeling of the couple involved) than Sol Plaatje's marriage to Elizabeth M'belle in January 1898. This was not, however, how the couple's respective parents saw things. What went in Kimberley was certainly not likely to be considered acceptable at Pniel and Burghersdorp, and both sets of parents and relations evidently disapproved strongly of the match for the same reasons, reacting strongly to the notion of their offspring marrying outside their own ethnic group. Plaatje described the situation in which he found himself:

My people resented the idea of my marrying a girl who spoke a language which, like the Hottentot language, had clicks in it; while her people likewise abominated the idea of giving their daughter in marriage to a fellow who spoke a language so imperfect as to be without any clicks.[57]

Sol Plaatje and Elizabeth M'belle had first met in 1897 when she came to Kimberley to visit her brother, Isaiah.[58] Plaatje then 'became interested in her', according to Dr Molema, and 'there sprang a strong flame of love'.[59] After she returned home to Burghersdorp (where she lived and taught) Plaatje began to write, sending her 'daily epistles' which were, he said, 'rather lengthy, for I usually started with the bare intention of expressing the affections of my heart but generally finished up by completely unburdening my soul'.[60] Not all of his letters got through, however: Elizabeth M'belle's parents expressed their disapproval of the liaison by burning all letters to their daughter which carried a Kimberley postmark.[61] This problem of parental disapproval was no doubt one of the factors that Plaatje had in mind when he recalled, several years later during the siege of Mafeking, 'the long and awful nights in 1897 when my path to this union . . . was so rocky'.[62]

The 'civilised laws of the Cape Colony', however, enabled their marriage to take place, saving them, as Plaatje put it some years later, from 'a double tragedy in a cemetery' after the manner of *Romeo and Juliet* which both were reading at the time.[63] On Thursday 25 January 1898, the couple were married in Kimberley by Special Licence. The marriage ceremony itself was conducted by the Rev. Davidson Msikinya, but nobody, if Dr Molema is to be believed, listened to what he had to say: instead, all eyes were on the happy couple.[64] Reactions from respective parents and relatives, when they were informed of what had taken place, were predictable. In the M'belle household, the question asked was:

What! Is this girl mad that she gives herself away to a coloured boy when there are so many handsome Xhosa boys who loved her? Let them be separated! This is not marriage, it is an attack: the M'belle family has been attacked by robbers and rebels.[65]

At Pniel, where Plaatje's family lived, the reaction was similar:

Can this handsome boy just go and marry a small Nguni girl when there are so many Tswana girls?[66]

Happily, the attitudes of both sets of 'erstwhile objecting relatives' changed, both soon coming around to 'award their benediction to the growth of our Chuana-M'Bo family',[67] a fact which no doubt owed more to the breaking down of prejudice through the sheer fact of human contact than to an objective appreciation of the mechanics of social mobility and class formation. Yet these were of course significant aspects of the whole business. And in a very real sense Plaatje's marriage to Elizabeth M'belle both reflected and summed up much of what was of importance in his four years' experience in Kimberley. It marked, for one thing, the fullest possible incorporation into the Mfengu-dominated petty bourgeoisie with which he had become so closely associated, and whose values he had come to accept. It emphasised the importance also of the hegemonic English language and culture in the lives not only of Kimberley's African petty bourgeoisie as a social group, but as the essential means of communication between Tswana and Mfengu in their courtship. Plaatje put this in the following way:

> I was not then as well acquainted with her language – the Xhosa – as I am now; [he was writing in 1914] and although she had a better grip of mine – the Sechuana – I was doubtful whether I could make her understand my innermost feelings in it, so in coming to an understanding we both used the language of educated people – the language which Shakespeare wrote – which happened to be the only official language of our country at the time.[68]

Finally, the actual marriage ceremony, parental disapproval notwithstanding, was conducted in a style and manner thought appropriate to the social standing of the young couple. It was a suitably formal and ostentatious affair that attracted a great deal of attention. Not all of it was favourable: the following passage appeared in the *Diamond Fields Advertiser* the next day:

> Last evening a couple of 'swagger' looking natives, resplendent in bell toppers, morning coats, white waistcoats, light pants, and patent leathers, with a number of females in holiday attire, were the centre of an admiring group at the Kimberley Railway Station. The rumour had gone forth that they were a couple of Lo Bengula's sons and certain of his wives, and the passengers and platform loungers were deeply interested in watching Master Lo Bengula making preparations for Mrs Loben's comfort for the journey, while when one of the princes of the blood royal deigned to take a long drink of water from an old limejuice bottle brought by one of the porters, excitement 'ran high'. Shortly before the train left, the police sergeant on duty at the station 'spotted' one of the 'princes' as an interpreter at a court down Colony, while his companion was discovered to be a telegraph messenger. It transpired that the former had come up to the Diamond Fields for the purpose of getting married, and that the buxom dusky lady who had been put down as one of the sharers of the late Matabili monarch's joys and sorrows was in reality a daughter of the people and the bride of the 'got up regardless' interpreter.[69]

Notwithstanding the confusion on the part of the *DFA* as to exactly who it was that was getting married, both Plaatje and his friends would no doubt have been much amused by the rumour that he was one of Lobengula's sons. Less pleasing, however, was the tone of the report – a sharp reminder of white resentment at black social aspirations. An altogether happier and more appropriate tribute to the compatibility of the young couple would have been noted towards the end of the year by those accustomed to scanning the personal columns of *Imvo*: in December 1898 these contained the announcement that a son had been born to 'Mr and Mrs Sol. T. Plaatje' at Pniel on 23 November 1898.[70] He was christened St Leger (he became known as 'Sainty'), after the well-known editor of the *Cape Times* whom Plaatje greatly admired.

In October 1899 Plaatje left Kimberley to take up an appointment as interpreter in the Magistrates' Court in Mafeking, and was there when war broke out and the siege began in October 1899. Paradoxically perhaps, the diary that he wrote there stands, more than anything else, as a lasting monument to the historical experience of Kimberley's African petty bourgeoisie, and of their contribution to the making of one of the most distinguished of their number. The personality that comes through so clearly in the diary was, of course, that of an exceptionally gifted individual, but it is at the same time very much a reflection of the collective personality of a wider group of people from whom Plaatje derived so many of the beliefs and values, and so much of the confidence and experience that enabled him to emerge as a national political and literary figure. In particular, the diary itself can be seen, from a literary point of view, as a more or less direct outcome of Plaatje's experiences at the meetings of the South Africans Improvement Sociey in the years before: the line of development between his inauspicious and badly pronounced reading from *John Bull and Co.* at the Society's meeting in July 1895 and the virtuosity, self-confidence and humour evident in the diary is a direct one. In Plaatje, these qualities found perhaps their greatest expression, but they were essentially those of a social group, not of a single individual. The range and mixture of linguistic influences evident in the diary is similarly a reflection of their cosmopolitan lifestyle and social existence, mute testimony to the importance of Kimberley – for its African petty bourgeoisie at least – as a cultural 'melting pot'.[71]

Notes

1 James Bryce, *Impressions of South Africa* (London, 1899), p. 202, quoted by B. Roberts, *Turbulent City* (Cape Town, 1976), p. 295.

2 Max O'Rell (pseud. for M. Blouet), *John Bull and Co.* (London, 1894), pp. 266–9.

3 S. T. Plaatje, 'Light and shade in native questions', *Umteteli wa Bantu*, 11 Oct. 1927.

4 *Diamond Fields Advertiser*, 12 Nov. 1928. Plaatje's statement that he was 'a lad of 15' at this time is rhetorical exaggeration: he was in fact 17.

5 *Tsala ea Becoana*, 16 Dec. 1911.

6 'A Good Example to his Brothers', *Diamond Fields Advertiser* (*DFA*), 4 March 1895.

7 S. M. Molema, MS. Biography of S. T. Plaatje (English translation) (copies in Witwatersrand University and School of Oriental and African Studies Archives).

8 For the source of this and further information, see P. Kallaway, 'Black responses to an industrialising economy: "Labour shortage" and "Native policy" in Griqualand West 1870–1900', paper presented to University of Witwatersrand Labour Conference, 1976.

9 Civil Commissioner's Report for Kimberley, 1892, *Blue Book on Native Affairs*, Cape Government, G7 1892.

10 'Natives and the Jubilee', *Imvo*, 13 May 1897.

11 *Koranta ea Becoana*, 22 Nov. 1902.

12 I am guided here by the definition of hegemony by G. A. Williams, 'Gramsci's concept of egemonia', *Journal of the History of Ideas*, XXI, 4 (1960), 587, quoted by J. Saville, 'The ideology of labourism', in R. Benewick (ed.), *Knowledge and Belief in Politics*,

> . . . an order in which a certain way of life and thought is dominant, in which one concept of reality is diffused throughout society in all its institutional and private manifestations, informing with its spirit and taste, morality, customs, religious and political principlees and all social relations, particularly in their intellectual and moral connotations.

13 A. P. Thornton, *The Imperial Idea and its Enemies* (London, 1966), p. x.

14 R. V. Selope Thema, 'The Bantu and the British throne', *Umteteli*, 23 May 1925.

15 'Native Wesleyan Church', *DFA*, 21 June 1897. 'The service was concluded,' it was also noted, 'by the singing of the National Anthem.'

16 'Jubilee Commemoration Hall', *Imvo*, 18 Nov. 1897.

17 S. T. Plaatje, 'The Joint Council and its constitution', *Umteteli*, 28 Feb. 1925.

18 T. D. Mweli Skota, *African Yearly Register* (Johannesburg, 1930), p. 104–5; see also G. Tyamzashe, 'Life at the diamond fields', *Kaffir Express*, August 1874, reproduced in *Outlook on a Century* (Lovedale, 1973), pp. 19–21.

19 See, for example, 'The Late Rev. G. Tyamzashe', *Imvo*, 5 Nov. 1896.

20 Skota, *African Yearly Register* pp. 104–5.

21 'A Government appointment', *Imvo*, 7 March 1894; 'A scholarly native', *DFA*, 9 Jan. 1893; S. M. Molema, 'Biography' (unpublished), p. 23.

22 Interview with Mrs Martha Bokako (Plaatje's niece), Thaba Nchu, April 1976.

23 Molema, 'Biography', p. 22.

24 'The South Africans Improvement Society', *DFA*, 23 Aug. 1895.

25 *Imvo*, 29 Aug. 1895.

26 *DFA*, 23 Aug. 1895.

27 For Max O'Rell's visit to Kimberley, and his lectures, see *DFA*, 8, 9, 10 and 11 May 1893.

28 *DFA*, 23 Aug. 1895. Milton perhaps represented the point at which many Africans began to question the universality of English culture!

29 *Ibid.*

30 *Ibid.*

31 Separate announcement in *DFA*, 23 Aug. 1895.

32 *DFA*, 23 Aug. 1895; topics of other talks and discussions at meetings of the Society included 'Trade Unions' (talk by Rev. Jonathan Jabavu, see 'Beaconsfield', *Imvo*, 29 Aug. 1895); and – at the beginning of 1896 – 'Youth', 'Kimberley and its young men', and 'The peculiarities of natives under European civilisation' (see *DFA*, 4 Feb. 1896).

33 Letter from 'Biza' (a member of the SA Improvement Society) to *DFA*, 17 Jan. 1896. 'Biza', too, made no secret of his objection to *lobola* 'with its innumerable surroundings'.
    W. B. Kawa was the son of Isaac Tod Kawa, another employee of the Post Office (in Beaconsfield); Skota, *African Yearly Register*, p. 162.

34 *Boer War Diary*, entry for 27 Dec. 1899.

35 *DFA*, 23 Aug. 1895. Born in Basutoland, Lenkoane came to Kimberley (probably in the 1880s) and 'soon became one of the leading citizens among his people'. For further details of his career, see Skota, *African Yearly Register*, p. 163, and *Koranta ea Becoana*, 13 Sept. 1902.

36 Chalmers Moss never returned to Kimberley: after two years at Wilberforce he died.

Rev. Msikinya noted that news of his death would be received with 'great regret and disappointment throughout the Colony, as the family is well known and highly respected'; *DFA*, 18 April 1898.

37 'A little function', *DFA*, 25 Aug. 1896. A similar – but extended – account appeared in *Imvo*, 17 Sept. 1896. Chalmers Moss, much younger than H. C. Msikinya, evidently had far fewer social achievements to his credit: he was, however, 'a promising lad'.

38 *DFA*, 25 Aug. 1896; for Binase's reputation as a ladies' man – also as 'a regular churchgoer', which seems not to have been incompatible – see 'E. Kimberley', *Imvo*, 20 April 1896, a report of an earlier social event where Binase and Plaatje together 'played the piano beautifully for our Kimberley women'.

39 Plaatje himself recalled some years later, at a meeting held in New York under the auspices of Marcus Garvey's UNIA, that he 'met the Jubilee Singers when I was a boy and later when I was a man' (*Negro World*, 12 Feb. 1921). Popular amongst both black and white audiences, the Jubilee Singers were in Kimberley in 1891, 1895, 1896, and again (in effect) in 1897 and 1898 as 'Mr McAdoo's Minstrels', McAdoo being the former leader of the Jubilee Singers before disagreements broke it up; see especially *DFA*, 29 July 1895 for their interesting origin and history.

40 He was involved, for example, in the formation of the Colonial Concert Company (along with another former Jubilee Singer, Miss Mamie Edwards), the Balmoral Minstrels and the Diamond Minstrels, as well as the Philharmonic Society.

41 *DFA*, 17 March 1897; see also *DFA*, 13 March 1897 for the Programme (reproduced as appendix).

42 As he did, for example, at a concert given by the Diamond Minstrels in the Kimberley Town Hall on 11 May 1897; see *DFA*, 11 and 12 May 1897.

45 The four original teams (later joined by Progress) were Rovers, Excelsior, Universals and Violets, the latter two generally being the strongest; see particularly accounts of annual prize-giving ceremonies, occasions of much speech-making, for 1896 and 1897, *DFA*, 1 Oct. 1896 and 10 Sept. 1897.

46 *DFA*, 10 Sept. 1897.

47 *Ibid.* Isaiah Bud-M'belle 'had been a Rover delegate since the infancy of the Union'. Chairman of the SA Colonial Rugby Football Board at the same time that Bud-M'belle was Secretary was Robert Grendon, teacher at the Public School (Matric.) at Beaconsfield, soon to move to John Dube's Ohlange Institute, later to become editor of *Abantu-Batho* and tutor and close associate of the Swazi royal family.

48 'The Value of Cricket', *DFA*, 8 Nov. 1893. Cricket, according to this writer, also instilled discipline. In addition, he advised, 'every good cricketer should have one golden rule: Keep your promise, keep your tongue, and keep your wicket up'.

49 For an elaboration on this theme – particularly the connection between cricket and the idea of the 'gentleman' – see Thornton, *Imperial Idea and its Enemies*, pp. 90–1: cricket was 'a game that only gentlemen could play' and 'only great gentlemen could play really well: one of the few things, indeed, that a gentleman was permitted to do really well'.

50 The clubs were Eccentrics, Duke of Wellington, Good Hope, Oddfellows, Primrose, Red Crescent, Standard and United, making the GWCCU the 'largest coloured cricket union in South Africa'; see especially the account of the prize-giving ceremony for 1897, *DFA*, 19 May 1897.

51 For details of the sides, see *DFA*, 24 Dec. 1895. Matches between 'Duke' and Eccentrics were especially well reported in *Imvo* – for example, that which took place

on 16 Jan. 1897. The result on this occasion was victory for Eccentrics by 138 runs. Isaiah Bud-M'belle made 27 runs, but victory was largely due to a fine tenth wicket stand of 99.

52 Letter from Bud-M'belle to *DFA*, 14 Nov. 1895. Wanderers, Universals and Progress were the three clubs which pulled out, disliking, Bud-M'belle claimed, any official positions in the League being 'held by a native gentleman'. The attitude of Bud-M'belle himself is revealing:

> I could understand if the objection of the three clubs was based on the fact that a barbarous native, a street Malay, nay, even a stupid Cape coloured man had been elected to such a post. As far as ability, education, and all other things – except an almost white(?) colour – are concerned, Mr Moss is far superior to any of the men composing the three clubs.

It is pehaps a measure of the consolidation and growing self-confidence of Kimberley's African petty bourgeoisie by this time, that whereas hitherto, as Bud-M'belle says, 'natives and Malays have always allowed Cape coloured people to fill the official positions' in 'mixed' sports organisations, this was now no longer necessarily the case.

53 'Ibala Labadlali', *Imvo*, 22 Oct. 1896.

54 Skota, *African Yearly Register*, pp. 256–7.

55 *Ibid*., p. 225. Like Tyamzashe, James Ngcezula had also gone to Kimberley 'in the early days'.

56 S. T. Plaatje, *Diposho-posho/Comedy of Errors* (Morija, 1930), dedication at the beginning of the book.

57 S. T. Plaatje, 'A South African's homage', in I. Gollancz (ed.), *A Book of Homage to Shakespeare* (OUP, 1916), pp. 336–9; reproduced in *English in Africa*, III, 2, Sept. 1976, pp. 7–8.

58 Interview with Mrs Martha Bokako, April 1976.

59 Molema, 'Biography', p. 27.

60 Plaatje, 'A South African's homage'.

61 Molema, 'Biography', p. 27.

62 *Boer War Diary*, entry for 25 Dec. 1899.

63 Plaatje, 'A South African's homage'.

64 Molema, 'Biography', p. 27.

65 *Ibid*., p. 28.

66 *Ibid*.

67 Plaatje, 'A South African's homage'.

68 *Ibid*.

69 *DFA*, 26 Jan. 1898.

70 *Imvo*, 12 Dec. 1898.

71 Plaatje used Dutch, Sotho, Tswana, Xhosa and Zulu words and phrases in the *Boer War Diary*; see also J. Comaroff's Introduction for further comments on Plaatje's linguistic usage, in particular the sociological context in which this took place.

CHAPTER TEN

Mine married quarters

The differential stabilisation of the Witwatersrand workforce 1900–1920

Sean Moroney

'The compound is in Langlaagte,' Johannes said softly.
'All the mine boys must live in compounds.'
'And you?' Zuma asked.
'They are not of the city, they come from the farms and some are from the land of the Portuguese and others are from Rhodesia. The white man fetched them. And those that are fetched must live in the compounds. It is the law here. But I came to the city like you and I am the boss boy for a white man so I do not stay in the compounds. They do not take many boys from the city for they do not like them.'

Mine Boy, Peter Abrahams, 1946

Compounds were the predominant form of accommodation and social organisation for African mineworkers on the Witwatersrand. There is no doubt that they played a vital role in controlling workers and in labour extraction. A number of writers have emphasised their coercive function,[1] and have viewed them as 'total institutions' in terms of Goffman's model.[2] It has always been acknowledged, however, that they were not 'closed' compounds in the same way as those of the Kimberley mines. Among the factors which determined that Witwatersrand compounds stayed 'open' was pressure from local mercantile capital. Nevertheless, there is a tendency to view compounds as more or less closed institutions which largely prevent inter-mine organisation and combination amongst workers. Unfortunately, this tends to obscure some of the dynamics of the Witwatersrand's social geography, and fails to take account of the 'freedoms' that workers did possess and of their interaction outside the compound environment, some indication of which Charles van Onselen has provided in his studies of Johannesburg.[3]

Competition for labour was intense after the South African War, despite the attempts of the mining industry to regulate it through monopsonistic recruiting and the maximum average wage agreement. Mine managements devised a number of inducements to attract workers – particularly experienced workers. In terms of the maximum average wage agreement, individual mines were entitled to pay $7\frac{1}{2}$ per cent of their total workforce up to 45s per month and

5 per cent at any rates. This was undoubtedly the most important way in which mines could compete for experienced workers. A 'liberal' compound regime was seen as another important, low-cost way of attracting workers at all levels of experience; and this could be achieved, *inter alia*, by allowing liquor brewing, providing a generous beer issue and improved food rations, and instituting relatively better living conditions. Two of the more important inducements were, first, the discretionary issue of 'special passes' by compound managers to workers, allowing workers to move about the Witwatersrand, particularly on weekends; and, secondly, permitting mine locations or providing married quarters. It is this latter inducement which this essay examines.

After the South African War African workers on the Witwatersrand mines were concentrated in many types of accommodation. Mine compounds dominated: single-sex institutions, controlled with varying degrees of efficiency and mainly occupied by migrant, contract workers. In addition, clusters of shacks and huts on mine property housing the families of mine workers became known as mine locations. These were initially outside managerial organisation and control, but in 1908 were mostly demolished or replaced by recognised married quarters, which were more closely regulated. A variety of labour contractors also had their own locations where they settled their workers with their families. Many other informal or 'irregular' (the term used by officialdom) locations or gatherings of squatters' huts were dotted all over the Witwatersrand, housing mine and other workers as well as members of the lumpenproletariat. After the South African War a variety of empty 'native repatriation' and other military camps were occupied, by workers and others, and added to the number of locations. They were, in addition, sources of illegal liquor and no doubt provided accommodation for some of the Witwatersrand's criminal groups.

Apart from mining compounds and locations, the Johannesburg municipality accommodated its workers in a number of compounds around the city. In 1910 it employed 3 733 workers, mostly housed in compounds. By 1913 about 1 000 sanitary workers were accommodated in the main Johannesburg compounds at the south-west corner of Braamfontein cemetery. A collection of dwellings around Brickfields formed the Brickfields Location, and some Johannesburg employers housed their workers here. Again, these and other slums of shanties in and around Johannesburg were sources of liquor and prostitution as well as providing vibrant venues for town and mine workers, black and white, about which we know so little. Thousands of domestic workers living on their employers' properties also undoubtedly participated in location life.

With the growing number of permanent black workers in Johannesburg and other towns, ideological, economic and political pressures to reduce the disorganised settlement of black workers and their families in the towns led to the development of a variety of 'locations' or black townships. Klipspruit, outside Johannesburg, was started in 1906, Boksburg township in 1909, Germiston township in 1912 and Randfontein township in 1914. As a result of Klipspruit's distance and the lack of public transport to the township, a permit system was introduced in Johannesburg allowing employers to house their black workers (other than domestic servants) within the city. By 1912 approximately 9 000 such permits had been issued.[4]

The social milieu of the Witwatersrand was thus one of great diversity, unlike our usual picture of the controlled monotony of the compound. The Witwatersrand, unlike the isolated mines of Rhodesia, formed a wide network of social and economic relations – unquantifiable, but discernible in their broad impact on industrial relations. J. M. Pritchard, then Chief Inspector of the Native Affairs Department (NAD) and later Director of the Government Native Labour Bureau, complained in December 1902 that 'natives are travelling unhindered from one end of the Witwatersrand to the other due to the lack of proper administration of the existing laws'.[5] The state, in collaboration with management, waged a continuous battle to regulate workers' lives to meet production needs. Workers in turn persisted in asserting their social freedom. It is against this back-drop of diversity and continuing conflict that married quarters on the gold mines should be seen.

As we have seen, a great number of informal mine locations were in existence after the South African War. Mine managements, realising their value as a source of cheap accommodation, sometimes allowed them to develop on their properties. In addition, they established their own locations, loosely administered by their compound managers. Pritchard explained the purpose of such locations as follows to his superiors in 1902:

> The principal reason advanced in favour of mine locations is that certain natives, who have worked for long periods on the mines and whose services are particularly valuable, have become married or 'attached' to women and if they were not permitted to live with these females in some such place as these locations they would leave the mine. Many of such natives, having worked for years on the mines have practically made their homes here and have become skilled labourers.[6]

He went on to argue to the Secretary of Native Affairs that he felt these were sufficient grounds to warrant the establishment of mine locations. A more explicitly managerial perspective on the role of locations was given by J. Wernher of Wernher, Beit & Co., when he wrote to H. J. King in 1906:

> Your principal solution of the native labour difficulty would be the establishment of locations, such locations having been established at the West Rand and Witwatersrand Deep Coys with the result of giving to these mines a constant and rarely-changing supply so far as the number of located natives are concerned.[7]

Thus the value of such locations was appreciated by both mine managements and state administrators. However, in the Milner era, inefficiencies which left loopholes for crime or other economic activities, particularly in the informal sector, and which detracted from the labour force available to mining and its ancillary industries, were deplored by the state. The control of all forms of worker accommodation was deemed necessary, and the state began a campaign to eliminate the informal or 'irregular' locations which were seen as havens for criminals and deserting workers. Pritchard outlined this strategy as follows:

> In my opinion, the whole question of the control of the Witwatersrand native population revolves on the question of residence. The policy, I consider, should be to enforce the residence of all native employees either in the property of their employers or in a licensed location. All unemployed natives found living elsewhere than in a licensed location should be arrested and punished under the vagrancy law.[8]

The police, in particular, waging their fight against illegal liquor,[9] lobbied for the elimination of uncontrolled locations and submitted numerous memoranda to that effect.

The police and the NAD soon encountered the opposition of location inhabitants, who tended to re-erect their shanties elsewhere soon after a 'raid'. In addition, they faced the opposition of landowners or leaseholders who often earned high rentals from otherwise unproductive land. Nor was mining capital itself united in its approach to such informal settlements on mining property. They provided a cheap form of readily available accommodation for permanent workers, and to replace them with the regulated married quarters the state was advocating entailed additional costs. Broad differences of approach emerged between deep-level mine managements, which were prepared to undertake such capital investment in worker accommodation in view of the long-term returns, and those of non-profitable or outcrop mines with short lifespans which were not prepared to incur any additional expenses, however minimal. The state, represented by the NAD, was prepared to adopt a flexible approach. Outcrop mines which were close to being worked out were allowed to keep their unregulated locations, and legislation to enforce standardised married quarters was delayed.

In 1907 the Department assessed the Witwatersrand's informal location population as follows:

TABLE 1 WITWATERSRAND LOCATIONS, 1907: POPULATION

A. Situated on mine property

		Approximate total population
Johannesburg	11 Mines	1 690
Germiston	3 Mines	700
Natalspruit	Diggings	150
Krugersdorp	1 Mine	120
Randfontein	2 Mines	100
		2 760

B. Locations not controlled by mining companies

	Approximate total population
Alberton Wash (south of Cleveland)	400
Cashulies (Klipriviersburg)	80
Coal Siding (Germiston)	50
Durandti (near Natalspruit)	50
Georgetown (Germiston Location)	2 574
Human's farm	40
Munroe's (near Natalspruit)	40
Newclare Wash (N.W. of Langlaagte)	50
	3 284
Grand total	6 044

Source: Government Native Labour Bureau Archives (GNLB), Vol. 1, File 2245

Although the Milner administration was prepared to adopt a piecemeal approach, eliminating particularly troublesome locations but leaving the rest alone, a more hard-line, comprehensive location policy can be discerned with the granting of self-government to the Transvaal in 1908. The anti-location lobby was given useful ammunition in 1907 when a storekeeper was murdered, allegedly by location inhabitants. A meeting was held in March 1908 between a Chamber of Mines committee, Captain Mavrogordato of the Transvaal Police, Dr Porter, Johannesburg Medical Officer of Health, and representatives of the Government Native Labour Bureau (GNLB). Proposals were accepted to abolish all informal locations on mine property and to establish regulated married quarters.[10] Regulations were drafted and, in conjunction with the Department of Mines, were framed in July 1906 in terms of the Gold Law. The Chamber cooperated by encouraging mine managements to implement them.

Captain Mavrogordato wrote to the Director of Native Labour on 27 July 1908:

> I think pressure should now be brought to bear on the Chamber of Mines in order that the proposed compounds [married quarters] should be provided without delay, so as to enable us to do away with irregular locations along the Reef as soon as possible.[11]

The Chamber circulated mine secretaries accordingly in September 1908, and increased pressure was applied to mine managements to eliminate 'troublesome' locations.

The demolition of the Stanhope/Simmer and Jack location of sixty huts in January 1908 provides a typical example of state action and was described as follows by the Germiston NAD inspector:

> On Sunday 19th the usual large number of natives assembled to drink, etc. and they disturbed people passing on the Reef Road. The manager of the Witwatersrand compound warned inhabitants that the location would be demolished by 26 January. Yesterday I called together all I could and told them it would be demolished the next

morning. I arranged to have a couple of mounted Transvaal policemen on the spot. This morning I witnessed the pulling down of the whole location with the exception of one tin hut in which a woman was giving birth to a child. The women belonging to the natives working on the Witwatersrand Gold Mine Co., will be moved into a walled-off part of Contractor Mostert's compound. The other women must go elsewhere.[12]

This particular demolition took place with the assistance of the mine management after two nearby mines had complained that there was an increasing rate of absenteeism as a result of liquor consumption at the location. As another example of this series of demolitions, the George Goch mine location, particularly notorious as a source of crime and liquor, was demolished in 1909, and mineworkers and their families moved into a new married quarters. By March 1911 the police were able to report that most 'irregular' locations had been eliminated, replaced usually by regulated married quarters.[13]

Basic provisions contained in the regulations for married quarters required that a high fence or wall be erected around the quarters with only one entrance; supervision was to be by a white superintendent responsible to management; a register of all residents was to be kept, and only *bona fide* mineworkers and their families (children under 14) were to be allowed residence. From the police point of view, these restrictive measures were intended to prevent illicit liquor brewing and sale and other forms of crime. In April 1909, after all, the assistant compound manager of the Village Deep mine was killed in the mine's married quarters.[14]

Some mines provided married accommodation free of charge to selected workers. Most required a payment ranging from 5s to 10s a month per family, usually deducted from pay. Some mines even gave free accommodation and rations to all those in the quarters. Quarters varied in size from populations of fifteen on the Robinson Deep to 1 207 on the East Rand Proprietary Mines. Families were usually accommodated in single or double rooms 10 feet by 10 feet, built in rows, side on. In 1908 the Wolhuter Mine built married quarters for black workers consisting of 150 houses on stands 25 by 30 feet. Occupants were allowed to build their own houses according to certain minimum standards. Many quarters, however, were in poor sanitary condition, without washing facilities. As in the case of compounds, the GNLB negotiated with the various managements over long periods to reduce some of the more obvious health dangers and improve control over workers' movements.

Although management tended to exclude non-mineworkers after 1908, others – for example, women posing as wives and making a living out of liquor brewing and prostitution, craftsmen and evangelists – were tolerated. In 1908 an inspector reported that an African evangelist named Simon actually managed the Langlaagte United married quarters and reported 'anything suspicious' to the management. Compound police were also accommodated in the married quarters in many cases. NAD population estimates for 1913 and 1918 are reproduced in Tables 2 and 3.

TABLE 2 MARRIED QUARTERS ON MINES, 1913–14

Location	No. of mines	Men	Women	Children	Total
Johannesburg					
Central	4	84	78	79	241
East	3	131	95	66	292
West	3	224	236	190	650
Jhb total	10	439	409	335	1 183
Germiston	7	204	244	190	638
Benoni	8	292	225	232	749
Roodepoort	6	584	568	407	1 559
Krugersdorp	4	508	352	326	1 186
Randfontein	4	707	244	270	1 221
Klerksdorp	4	481*	481*	288*	1 250
Boks'burg	4 (9 quarters)	1 207	987	1 112	3 306†
Springs	6 (9 quarters)	318	274	164*	756
Total	53	4 740	3 784	3 324	11 848

* Figures imputed from the recorded total.
† There were 3 married quarters on the Witwatersrand Deep. Figures were recorded for both 1913 and 1914 and indicate a fluctuation in women and children which is not explained in the correspondence. Figures for 1913 are used in the table.

Year	Men	Women	Children	Total
1913	510	451	603	1 564
1914	527	332	227	1 086*

* An imputed figure.

Source: GNLB 78/2843/12/D94 Replies to Director's Circular 2 of 1913

TABLE 3 MARRIED QUARTERS ON MINES, 1918

Location	No. of mines	Total population
Johannesburg	9	1 162
Boksburg	5	3 264
Springs	6 (8 quarters)	712*
Benoni	7 (8 quarters)	749
Germiston	6 (7 quarters)	738
Roodeport	6	1 559
Krugersdorp	4	1 182
Randfontein	4	1 221
	Total	10 587

* Figures imputed from following data: 44 single men and 274 families
Source: GNLB vol. 78/2843/12/D94, Schedule of Native Married Quarters within Labour Districts

TABLE 4 RANDOM SELECTION OF MINES IN 1918, INCLUDING THOSE WITH
HIGHEST OR LOWEST PERCENTAGE OF WORKERS IN MARRIED QUARTERS

	Total workforce	Location population	Imputed no. of family heads	Percentage of work-force
Benoni: ERPM	10 213	1 207	500	5.0
Johannesburg: Nourse Mines	4 079	140	60	1.5
Springs: Springs Mines	3 662	106 families	106	3.0
Roodeport: Aurora West	1 248	446	175	14.0

Source: GNLB 294/238/18/D54, Schedule of Native Married Quarters within Labour Districts

Comparing the 1913 and 1918 figures, it appears that by 1914–18 an optimum number of mineworkers had been shifted from the informal locations and, together with others, installed in married quarters. I have as yet been unable to clarify if and how these figures were determined by management. It seems likely that they were based on the requirements of the production process and the degree to which white workers would tolerate blacks moving into skilled and semi-skilled positions. Unfortunately, I have been unable to obtain post-1918 figures. It may have been that with increasing capital intensity, especially after the Low-Grade Mines Commission, there was a tendency to stabilise more of the black workforce by means of married quarters and other measures. On the other hand, management, like the state, was very conscious of the hazards involved in permanently settling a large proportion of the workforce on the Rand.

As an example of the make-up of married quarters, 276 of the 331 male inhabitants in the three Randfontein mine locations in May 1918 were mineworkers from the Robinson group mines. Of the other 55, 15 were daily labourers, 4 were shoemakers, 1 a cab-driver, 6 were evangelists, 16 worked for the Railways, Native Affairs Department or municipalities, 9 were in other private employ and 5 were listed as having no occupation. In addition, there were 7 unattached washerwomen. The level of diversity was typical of many married quarters which, in addition, served as meeting places for numerous compound-dwellers and town-workers. Nevertheless, tensions developed between compound and married quarters, symptomatic of the clear differentiation, both residential and economic, among their respective inhabitants. There was sporadic conflict between such groups, as the following example makes clear.

On Sunday, 27 September 1914, a riot broke out at the Witwatersrand Deep compound and married quarters. The married quarters had a total population of 1 564 at that time. It was close to the main compound building, and the correspondence indicates that there had been free access by compound inhabitants to the quarters. One of the groups in the quarters was a gang of contractor's workers, identified by management as Xhosa. According to the official account, the fight broke out when some of the eastern Cape (Xhosa) workers attacked a Moçambican (Shangaan) worker whom they accused of giving information about the whereabouts of some *khali* (illicit liquor) in one of the rooms of the quarters, thereby causing a search by the compound police. The Zulu sided with the Moçambican worker, and the fighting spread to the central compound. The police were called, and when they arrived the compound police (identified as being Zulu) and the manager alleged that Basotho compound dwellers were responsible. Basotho workers were attacked in their rooms (while they were sleeping, they subsequently claimed). One was shot dead by the police and two were *sjamboked* to death, probably by compound police.[15]

The conflagration was one of many intra-worker disputes that occurred on the Witwatersrand mines and which became termed 'faction fights'. However, it is particularly interesting because it sheds light on the tensions which built up between compound and married quarters. Differential access to liquor and female company seem the most obvious cause for discontent. The evidence is scanty, but it seems likely that some of the tension arose out of differentiation in the workforce. The eastern Cape workers were under a labour contractor, engaged in different work and possibly on a higher pay scale than the Moçambican workers, who would have been recruited by the Witwatersrand Native Labour Association. As a result of the fight, high fences were constructed to separate the compound and married quarters more effectively.

Although the group of workers accommodated in married quarters formed a small percentage of the total workforce (see Table 4) and showed no increase over the period up to 1918, its significance is that it comprised permanent, fully proletarianised, skilled and semi-skilled workers whom management could not easily replace. Yet their differential accommodation and status in relation to the total workforce may well have reduced their potential as a vanguard of worker resistance.

The co-optive function of mine married quarters was described by an inspector of the NAD as follows in 1912:

> It appears to have been the custom to permit unmarried natives working under some of the smaller mining contractors to live in the locations. These boys appreciate the comparative freedom of this manner of life, and knowing that they are there on sufferance give little or no trouble.[16]

In 1914 Pritchard argued at a meeting with Police and Mine Department officials for the complete abolition of mine locations and the more extensive introduction of married quarters of 'villages', as he called them. The minutes record that his department was anxious to uplift the natives who were coming [to the Witwatersrand] voluntarily in large numbers. He thought the contract system would break down and he wished to provide for the future. With the establishment of these villages you would have a larger permanent force, and a more contented force. If you give the native better living conditions he would be more contented . . . van der Merwe, the Johannesburg Mining Commissioner, thought that the establishment of properly controlled married native quarters would tend to secure a permanent supply of labour, would encourage family life among the natives, would render native risings difficult and would diminish the 'black peril' danger. It would also be helpful to the domestic service question.[17]

As in so many other areas of labour control, the state here seemed to show more foresight and breadth of vision than management, particularly individual local mine managements. Sections of management were relatively slow to realise the benefits of more sophisticated social engineering. Particularly under the Milner administration, the needs of capital were often anticipated by administrators. In the end, despite some conflict, they were sufficiently harmonised, and 'enlightened' administrators would usually have their way. Administrators, like the Chamber of Mines, without the limitations imposed by short-term individual profit-seeking, could perceive the requirements of the industry as a whole and not be diverted by sectional interests. Pritchard, for example, following in the tracks of the Milner administration, imposed improved standards of health, accommodation, recruitment and general worker treatment in all mines in order to improve the labour position of the industry overall.

Evidence of this foresight can be seen from a memorandum in 1917 submitted by the NAD inspector for Johannesburg Central. He adjured the mines to acknowledge the fact that all workers in the married quarters were 'a certain class of native' who had assumed responsible positions, and had themselves and their families to support. He pointed out that 'a state of discontent' was developing 'amongst a certain class of the more enlightened married labourers' because they were not receiving free accommodation and rations for their families and had to pay for accommodation in the married quarters. 'As the mining industry cannot do without this peculiar class of labour, may I suggest,' he wrote to his superior, 'that representations be made to the heads of the industry for the granting of free quarters, rations and medical attendance.'[18]

The mine stores boycott which followed shortly after the 1918 strikes and stoppages, and the widespread 1920 strike suggest that management gave little attention to these warnings about the economic grievances of the growing proletariat. The pressure of wartime demands and inflation and a certain tunnel vision meant that, as Phil Bonner has shown, in the immediate post-war years management allowed this group to develop into a core of resistance rather than the co-opted elite it was intended to be.

Notes

1 E.g., S. Moroney, 'The compound as a mechanism of worker control 1900–1912', *South African Labour Bulletin*, IV, 3 (May 1978).

2 P. Pearson, 'Authority and control in a South African goldmining compound', University of the Witwatersrand African Studies Seminar, 1976.

3 C. van Onselen, *Studies in the Social and Economic History of the Witwatersrand*, Vol. 2, *New Nineveh*, (London, 1982), Chapter 1, 'Witches of suburbia: domestic servants in Johannesburg; Volume I, *New Babylon*, Chapter 4, 'Johannesburg's Jehus, 1890–1914',.

4 Municipality of Johannesburg, *Report of the Medical Officer of Health on the Public Health and Sanitary Circumstances of Johannesburg, 1 July 1909–30 June 1911*, 16 May 1912.

5 Government Native Labour Bureau Archives, Pretoria (GNLB) 1/614/07.

6 *Ibid.*

7 J. Wernher to H. J. King, 14 July 1906, Eckstein Archives 134:820. Local management adopted this view. In 1923 the Manager of the West Rand Consolidated Mines wrote to the Sub-native Commissioner, Krugersdorp: 'With regard to native married quarters I have instructed the compound manager that houses becoming vacant should not be re-let. At the same time, there is a large number of natives extremely anxious to obtain these quarters, and I think in many cases it would be policy on our part to meet their wishes and allow them to occupy these houses as many of these boys are valuable to the company.' Letter dated 9 Aug. 1923, GNLB 204/1644/14/97 (12).

8 GNLB 1/614/07.

9 C. van Onselen, *Studies in the Social and Economic History of the Witwatersrand*, Volume 1, *New Babylon*, Chapter 2, 'Randlords and rotgut', pp. 44–103.

10 Report of the sub-committee of the Chamber of Mines appointed to confer with Captain Mavrogordato and Dr Porter on the question of irregular locations on mines, 10 March 1908, HE 149:973.

11 GNLB 20/2192/11.

12 GNLB 1/614/07.

13 Assistant Commissioner, Transvaal Police to Secretary of Native Affairs, 17 March 1911, GNLB 20/1091/1.

14 Protector, Western District to Director GNLB, November 1909, GNLB 4/1736/09.

15 GNLB 197/1440/14/D48.

16 GNLB 78/2843/12/D94.

17 Notes of a meeting held in New Law Courts, 30 July 1914, GNLB 78/2843/12/D94.

18 Memorandum, Oct. 1917, GNLB 78/2843/12/D94.

CHAPTER ELEVEN

The Transvaal Native Congress 1917–1920:

The radicalisation of the black petty bourgeoisie on the Rand

Philip Bonner

Introduction

The radicalisation of black politics on the Rand during and immediately after the First World War has often been noted by writers on South Africa.[1] Accounts of the origins of the movement share a number of points in common: the growing impoverishment of the reserves (whether it be explained in terms of structural underdevelopment or merely contingent effects of droughts); the growth of a concentrated black urban proletariat as a result of the secondary industrialisation promoted by the war; the concomitant shortage of housing and the emergence of teeming urban slums; the steeply rising cost of living during the war and the stimultaneous pegging of black wages at pre-First World War levels; various direct and indirect taxations on African earnings; the example of white worker action, and the continued inflexibility of the job colour bar. Although there is great unevenness of treatment in these accounts, the interpretations provided are not mutually contradictory, and it is possible to stitch together a composite account.

The same cannot be said of the shape and dynamics of the movements which were spawned by these pressures, and more particularly of the role and class basis of the Transvaal Native Congress (TNC). Here, two broad and mutually contradictory positions emerge. The first, articulated most explicitly by Walshe, is that the TNC and the South African Native National Congress (SANNC, later African National Congress – ANC) more generally, retained their conservative petty-bourgeois orientation and never effectively transcended their class origins or adequately mobilised the political constituency that the times had placed in their grasp. 'While unrest was widespread, if sporadic in expression,' Walshe argues, 'agitation was difficult to maintain and Congress soon lost the initiative against the authorities.... A determination systematically to build up mass membership and branch organisations so as to assert the power of the African majority against European domination had not matured amongst a leadership inclined to moral assertion and concerned with equality of opportunity for progressive individuals. The tactics of extra-constitutional opposition were not easily learnt by those who still retained a vision of peaceful, perhaps spasmodic, but inevitable political evolution.'[2]

Simons and, less explicitly, Benson take a diametrically opposite line. Criticising 'the binary model of standard Marxist theory' espoused by the International Socialist League (ISL) at the time, which denounced the ANC as 'Labour Fakirs of black South Africa, black bell-wethers for the capitalist class', Simons suggests (somewhat obliquely) that African nationalism was the authentic vehicle of black proletarian aspirations, by virtue of its effective mobilisation of agitation, and its identification with British imperial capital against its more immediate white working class and farming oppressors.[3] Taking an almost totally different route Johnstone arrives in the same camp. Concentrating on the functionality of the exploitation colour bars to imperial capital, and the reactions of black workers to a steadily deteriorating position, he equates Congress campaigns with working-class resistance, and treats African politics in this period as a largely homogeneous movement.[4]

The purpose of this piece is to explore more sensitively, and in more detail, the class dynamics of the black population on the Rand between 1917 and 1922. Its main focus is the role and activities of the black petty bourgeoisie, and to this extent it takes off from Brian Willan's fascinating account of the black petty bourgeoisie in Kimberley. As Willan argues there, 'Little scholarly analysis has been devoted to the historical evolution of class difference amongst Africans in twentieth-century South Africa or to the ideological forms that accompanied this', and he goes on to explore the significance of liberal ideology to the black petty bourgeoisie in Kimberley, and how De Beers deliberately fostered an alliance with this group to forestall its radicalisation and identification with an increasingly militant black working class.[5] Willan's analysis raises questions which will be taken up in this piece; it also neglects important issues which have to be considered if we are to have a satisfactory profile of the black petty bourgeoisie. Why, for example, was it so susceptible to liberal ideology and co-option from above? Of whom precisely did it consist? And to what extent was it a homogeneous group? This study hopes to take up these points in more detail, and does so by working from three central premises. The first is that the petty bourgeoisie as a class stands between the dominant relations of production of capitalism – that is to say, the capital/labour relation – and as such is pulled two ways. The second is that

> the more separated is a social sector from the dominant relations of production, and the more diffuse are its 'objective interests' and consequently, less developed its 'class instinct' – the more the evolution and the resolution of the crisis will tend to take place on the ideological level.[6]

And the third is that the black petty bourgeoisie in a colonial racist society was a fundamentally different creature from that found in the developed capitalist world. As Godley noted in his 1921 report on passes, 'a large majority of [the] . . . members [of the SANNC] is comprised of natives who have acquired a certain amount ¬f education only to find the professional, clerical and skilled avenues of employment closed to them'.[7] The colonised black petty bourgeoisie was therefore both stunted and repressed, and unable to articulate with conviction its characteristic metropolitan values of statology, the myth of the ladder and *status quo* ante-capitalism.[8] Finally, for every one of those admitted to its ranks, there was always a correspondingly great substratum among the upper levels of the working class – generally described at the time as the 'educated' or 'civilised' – who aspired to their position and struggled to get in. Indeed it was the mobility between these categories and their imperceptible blending into one another which makes them such a difficult object of analysis. A downward identification towards this group, at least by a section of stunted petty bourgeoisie, was therefore always on the cards. How far it would proceed, and the extent to which this class which was united only by ideology and its intermediary position would cohere on this issue, or split, would be determined by economic, political and especially ideological class struggle. It is therefore to the class struggle on the Rand and its co-ordinates in this period that we must look for an answer to the questions we have posed.

Work, wages and class

In June 1917 the leadership of the ANC shifted decisively to the Rand. Pixley Seme and John Dube were ousted, and S. M. Maghatho and S. Msane were elected respectively President and Secretary-General. Walshe explains the realignment in terms of different tactics in response to the policy of segregation, personality conflicts between Dube and Seme, and the remoteness of Dube in Natal. Almost certainly the reasons went deeper than that, as Walshe himself recognises when he indicates that much of the impetus for the purge came from the Transvaalers and those involved with the Johannesburg newspaper *Abantu-Batho*.[9] The Rand was now overwhelmingly the largest centre of black urban population in South Africa, both of workers and the incipient black petty bourgeoisie.

During the war industrial development had taken off, sucking in huge numbers of those displaced from the land. Between 1915–16 and 1921–22 the number of industrial establishments on the Rand increased from 862 to 1 763, while the black working class engaged in non-mining activities (including 'works') swelled from 67 111 in 1918 to 92 597 in May 1920.[10] Such an environment provided the natural locus of political organisation, more especially as nearby Pretoria was the seat of political power,[11] and it was to here that the centre of gravity of black political organisation naturally moved.

Equally important in forcing the pace of this change was the growth of the black petty bourgeoisie. As industry and the black working class expanded, so opportunities for the black petty bourgeoisie opened up. Teachers, and others with basic educational qualifications, flocked to try their luck in the economic heartland of the Rand.[12] The size which this community had reached by the end of the war is difficult to judge. However, a rough and ready indication may be provided by the number of registration certificates (primarily granted to the self-employed) and letters of exemption (accorded to those with over Standard 3 educational qualifications) issued on the Rand. At the end of May 1920, these, together with under-age certificates stood at 2 497.[13] How they broke down among the three categories is difficult to judge, since only consolidated figures are furnished in the 1920 statement. A more detailed analysis for 1923 may, however, provide some clues. According to this, those in possession of juvenile certificates on the Rand amounted to 257 (191 domestic servants, 66 golf caddies). Daily labourers – a substantial number of whom must have possessed registration certificates – totalled 1 001.[14] This general profile is confirmed by Cooke who, in evidence to the Moffat Commission, spoke of 1 078 Africans holding registration certificates in the proclaimed labour district in 1917.[15] A rough computation would therefore suggest that the salaried or professional section of the black petty bourgeoisie on the Rand numbered almost a thousand; and the self-employed small businessmen or craftsmen slightly over that figure. It was these men who formed the organisational core of the TNC and it was on them that the mantle of leadership now increasingly fell.

The year 1917 was also important on the Rand for an additional reason. In the middle of 1917 inflation began to bite (see Table 1[16]).

TABLE 1 RETAIL PRICE INDEX ON THE WITWATERSRAND (1938 = 100)

Year	Food	All items
1913	97·7	84·5
1914	94·3	82·4
1915	99·2	85·2
1916	104·3	90·7
1917	113·3	98·2
1918	115·7	105·6
1919	124·9	116·5
1920	163·9	144·0
1921	133·9	130·8
1922	109·9	109·6
1923	105·8	105·5
1924	108·3	107·2
1925	108·3	106·4
1926	107·1	104·9

Prices of certain commodities had been rising since the beginning of the war, but for a range of basic African consumer goods, mine stores at least had expended old stocks at old prices which ran out only in the middle of 1917. It seems likely, given the dominance of mine and concession stores in this sector of the market economy, that other traders followed suit. The dammed-up effects of inflation were therefore unleashed only late in 1917.[17] Prices spiralled, and black wages, unlike those of whites who received war bonuses and cost-of-living allowances, remained relatively unchanged. The political atmosphere on the Rand — and, indeed, in most other urban areas in South Africa — became correspondingly charged. In 1918 a boycott of mine stores was organised by Shangan miners on the East Rand, and in June 1918 Johannesburg's sanitary workers struck in support of higher pay — an event which, together with the harsh sentences handed down by Magistrate McFie, galvanised migrant workers, industrial workers, urban lumpenproletarians and the petty bourgeoisie into two years of militant agitation beginning with the so-called 'shilling strike' of 1 July 1918.

The rise in prices and falling real incomes which followed the war led to the most radical black agitation to be seen in South Africa prior to the Second World War, which in turn provoked a systematic rethinking of 'native policy' in the Union, and more particularly in the urban areas of the Rand. Yet it would be a serious mistake to exaggerate the importance of this factor at the expense of the wider range of repressive, discriminatory mechanisms which bore on virtually the whole of South Africa's black population at this time. The grievances of mineworkers, which eventually erupted in the 1920 black mineworkers strike, have been explored in some detail by Johnstone and also in my own article on the subject. What still requires investigation is the structurally ultra-subordinate position (to use Johnstone's expression) of more permanently urbanised workers and the black petty bourgeoisie.

Without wishing to do violence to the essential integrity of the labour repressive system which governed the daily lives of virtually all Africans on the Rand, five main areas of control can be discerned — wages, passes, housing, constraints on upward mobility and capital accumulation, and education. All are interrelated; each fell differentially on different sections of the African population. Yet although their differential incidence provided scope for future reformist initiatives, aimed at driving wedges between black people, their effects were sufficiently pervasive during and immediately after the war to provide the basis for a broad populist movement of agitation. It is to these that we shall now turn.

The most burning grievance of the day for all classes in society was that of wages. For the permanently proletarianised it was just not possible to make ends meet at the prevailing rates of pay. In 1921 the Johannesburg Joint Council of

Europeans and Natives calculated the essential expenses of a family of four living at Klipspruit at £5 3s 11d a four-week month, excluding 'luxuries' such as clothing, furniture and entertainment.[18] Adjusted for town dwellers, average expenditures would have been even higher, the increase in rent exceeding the saving in travelling by from 5s to 10s, and the same is probably true of areas of freehold tenure like Sophiatown, Martindale and Newlands.[19] If we extrapolate back to 1917 on the basis of the retail price index, this figure could be depressed by perhaps 25 per cent (prices of food having risen by roughly 18 per cent and those of all goods by about 33 per cent), leaving us with a minimum living wage of 84s 6d, calculated on the basis of a $4^1/_3$-week month. Very few African workers on the Rand earned this sum of money. A survey of wages paid by private employers in July 1914, for example, shows the following distribution:[20]

TABLE 2 DISTRIBUTION OF WAGES PAID BY PRIVATE EMPLOYERS TO AFRICAN RAND WORKERS, JULY 1914

Wages per month	Conditions	No. of employees	No. of employers
Under 60s	Mostly with food	2 559	40
60–70s	70% without food & quarters	2 859	55
70–80s	No food & quarters	1 280	33
80–90s	No food & quarters	691	13
90–100s	No food & quarters	180	4

Note: The figures furnished are averages for industrial establishments and so do not take account of income distribution *within* each industrial concern: weekly figures calculated on a $4^1/_3$-week month.

Little had changed by July 1918. Figures presented by Cooke, Acting Director of Native Labour, show the distribution of wages outside the mining sector as follows:[21]

TABLE 3 DISTRIBUTION OF WAGES OUTSIDE THE MINING SECTOR, JULY 1918

Category	Non-mining working population (%)	Average wages
House boys	50	40–60s
Store boys	23	70–80s without quarters
Stable boys	3	60–70s
Municipal and allied workers	9	50s with food & quarters
Industrial workers	—	15–22s 6d a week*

*: Calculated on $4^1/_3$-week month = 65–97s 6d: on a 4-week month = 60–90s.

African testimony to the 1918 Moffat Commission confirms this picture of working-class penury, and draws attention to the omissions and understatements of the Joint Council budget calculations.[22] Perhaps the most common complaint expressed by African miners and migrant labourers to the Moffat Commission was the rise in the cost of jackets and shoes and other items of clothing.[23] If these had entered into the realm of necessary as opposed to discretionary expenditure for this section of the working population, how much more essential must they have been to the educated and 'civilised' of the African petty and aspirant petty bourgeoisie?

To exclude such items from the budgets of permanently urbanised African families thus seems unreasonable and arbitrary, as do many of the other estimates of expenditure contained in the Joint Council's budgetary forecasts. Elias Chake, for example, estimated his outlay as: coal, paraffin and wood at 10s, 10s and 5s per month respectively, church fee/school fees £10 and £8 a year, passes £3 5s 0d annually and rent £2 10s 0d a month, each of which were appreciably higher than the Joint Council's 1921 assessment; and the drift of evidence of other witnesses to Moffat lends substance to his claims. Of course, Chake, as an interpreter in the Magistrate's Court in Pretoria, was quite clearly located among the African petty bourgeoisie, yet like many others of the African working class, he was living in a shack in a yard, and his life style and daily needs cannot have differed very much from at least those of the aspirant African petty bourgeoisie.[24]

The generalised poverty of the African working class is readily apparent, but it is more difficult to plot the income and economic fortunes of the African petty bourgeoisie. The most common wage for mine clerks, if one accepts the testimony of R. W. Msimang, who seems to have held a special brief for this group on the Moffat Commission, was between £3 and £5, with food and quarters added.[25] Benjamin Phooko, who was one of two mine clerks to appear before the Moffat Commission, was earning £3 15s 0d a month, again with food and quarters added.[26] More typical, however, were slightly higher rates of pay. According to William Taberer, the Director of the Native Recruiting Corporation, the average payment to clerks in twelve mines chosen randomly across all the mining areas of the Rand was £4 7s 6d a month, once more with food and quarters included, and this we may perhaps take as a more representative rate of pay.[27] What other sections of the petty bourgeoisie were earning is, at the present stage of my investigations, a matter of speculation. Jeremiah Dunjwa, head teacher at the independent school in Klipspruit, which seems to have attracted the children of the more affluent sections of that community, earned £5 a month, which perhaps indicates the salaries commanded by his peers.[28]

If this is so, then one thing emerges starkly from these figures, and that is the small differential between the wages of the black petty bourgeoisie and the rest of the black working class. As we have seen, wages in the non-mining sectors ranged from 65s to 97s 6d, while even underground work in the mines commanded an average of £3 5s 2d per 30-day shift.[29] The objective conditions for an alliance of convenience centred on the demand of 1s a day therefore clearly existed, and render intelligible the universal support accorded to this demand in 1918 and 1919.

At the same time the lines of potential cleavage within this alliance should not be ignored. Most obvious perhaps were those which existed between teachers or others who held good educational qualifications, who 'come to the Rand thinking they would get better work' and found that as mine clerks they were 'only getting the same as received by a blanket man underground', from whom they strove to set themselves apart.[30] Less striking, but nonetheless important, was a more blurred line of demarcation between those who thought of themselves as educated and civilised and those they deemed were not. As Msimang put it:

> Many Europeans do not understand these people. They do not understand that he lives at a fairly high standard of living. These people need – in fact they require – all the things practically required by the European. Take the food bill. Most Europeans seem to think these people are content with porridge, but you will find they have quite a representative table. Meat, tea and so on.[31]

Elias Chake, court interpreter, testified in similar terms. It was not true, he insisted, that blacks had few requirements. No consideration was paid to the educated who had different tastes and different needs. It was time for some differentiation of treatment, he seemed to be saying, between those who were educated and civilised and those who had yet to reach that stage.[32] I. Bud-M'belle, ex-interpreter from the High Court in Kimberley, echoed Chake's views, while the Reverend Ncayiya went as far as to offer some practical suggestions, intimating that the salaries of 'civilised natives' should be considered separately from those of others by boards of arbitration comprised of representatives of both sides.[33]

The message that is conveyed in these representations is one of a perceived community of interest between the black petty and aspirant petty bourgeoisie. In part this was the product of what Laclau would call their 'interpellation' as 'educated' or 'civilised' – that is to say, their mode of self-identification on an ideological plane.[34] The possibilities that this presented for straight ideological co-option have already been mentioned, but there was more to their community of interest than mere ideological forms. Many, though by no means all of this 'community', were permanent urban dwellers who were struggling against the odds to raise their families in town. This meant that their total costs of reproduction had to be covered by incomes generated in the cities, which in the case of urban workers simply did not stretch that far. Powerful pressures therefore existed for their wives to go out to work, which seems to have been as true of all but the most affluent sections of the petty bourgeoisie as it was of those who aspired to join their ranks.

All this both served to unite the petty and aspirant petty bourgeoisie, and paradoxically to drive them closer together with the rank and file of the working class. As Deborah Gaitskell has shown, two broad categories of women came to be settled in the towns: firstly, those coming unattached or fleeing from their homes, who became domestic servants, washerwomen or prostitutes, or took up illicit liquor selling to earn an income; secondly, the wives and daughters of families of those who came to settle permanently in town. Perhaps the most striking characteristic of this group was their relatively high literacy levels; 4·71 per cent of rural Transvaal women were literate as opposed to 31 per cent of their urban kin.[35] The majority of the latter probably provided spouses for the urban petty and aspirant petty bourgeoisie, thereby serving to unite it even further around the values of education and civilisation. Yet their openings for employment were almost as limited as those of the urban unattached. Opportunites for domestic service were limited, besides separating them from their families and homes, and wages had in any case been depressed between 5s and 10s at the beginning of the war.[36] Washing was back-breaking and low-paid,[37] and, for the women of Klipspruit location, it involved travelling costs which virtually cancelled out any profits to be made. As Charlotte Maxexe and Rev. Ncayiya complained to the Moffat Commission, echoing the plea of 122 Klipspruit women uttered eight years before, 'much of the work formerly done by women is now taken over by men'.[38]

The only alternative in these circumstances was the illicit brewing of liquor, which automatically thrust them back into the arms of their lumpen and proletarian brethren in the locations and in the towns. William Letlalo, for example, recalls how his wife was forced into illicitly brewing liquor to provide funds to send his children to school. Letlalo was at that time a Transvaal Native Congress member and a storeman, and the number of complaints to official bodies and government commissions from members of the petty bourgeoisie about police raids for liquor seem to indicate this was an important occupation of this class.[39] Once again, in the particular conditions of the wartime economy two contradictory trends emerged. On the one hand, the cohering of the urban petty and aspirant petty bourgeoisie: on the other, the possibilities of mobilising a broad class alliance comprising the proletariat, lumpenproletariat and petty bourgeoisie. Only the day-to-day flux of the class struggle, and the respective pressures and inducements offered by the main protagonists in the conflict – capital and labour – would determine the eventual position of the petty bourgeoisie.

If the black petty bourgeoisie and working class were thrust together on the issues of wages and cost of living, they found themselves equally close in relation to housing and passes. Both issues occupied a central place in their representations to official commissions and government bodies, and in their campaigns of 1918–20. Passes were perhaps the most bitter source of grievance, and by their multi-functional nature afflicted and hence united all sections of the black urban population. For the labourer in wage employ they represented the means whereby his contract of employment was attested and could be enforced, and his opportunity to seek new employment or improved conditions effectively curtailed. A sense of this repressive function of the pass law was probably present in the minds of black workers from the earliest days of the system, but it only emerged fully blown in the consciousness of the black petty bourgeoisie with the sanitary workers' strike on the Rand in April 1918. Sentenced to three months' hard labour on the jobs they had previously performed, for presuming to strike for higher wages, the helplessness of the 'bucket boys' before the interlocking mechanisms of Pass Laws and Masters and Servants legislation clearly revealed the repressive functions of the law. As Benjamin Phooko, a clerk representing 5 000 City Deep labourers protested:

> Allowing prices to rise alarms us because we have entered into contracts that cannot be broken, so as to demand a higher price for our labour. We therefore record our sympathy with the Municipal workers who were forced to break their contracts.[40]

Nine months later the same point was driven home in a pamphlet issued by the TNC. 'At our meeting at Vrededorp on 30.3.19,' it bluntly proclaimed, 'we came to the conclusion that passes prevented money.'[41]

Passes did indeed prevent money, and in a variety of more subtle and disguised ways. On the monthly pass, renewed each month by the employer, workers' wages were recorded, and this served to peg them indefinitely at low levels, since new employers could always see what wages had been paid before. Any upward drift that might have been effected by withholding of labour and holding out for higher pay was further inhibited by the 6-day pass which obliged the worker to find new employment within six days; the travelling pass which required the payment of a shilling before the worker was allowed to seek employment outside of the district of his registration; and the 'special', which, strictly interpreted, needed to be carried by the worker when he left his employer's premises.[42]

Government spokesmen stoutly defended these measures. The justification furnished by Herbert Cooke, Acting DNC, in an open letter to 'the natives of the Witwatersrand' at the height of the anti-pass law agitation, is typical:

> In Johannesburg and other reef towns unless the native's name and place of residence is written on his pass he is lost to his people. Messages cannot be sent to him. If he dies

no-one knows where his money is to be sent. If he does not get money written in his pass he can complain to the pass officer.[43]

Cooke's argument was reproduced in several official submissions to the Inter-Departmental Pass Laws Committee in 1920, but the essential hypocrisy of at least the last part of his argument was exposed by the Inspector (Central) NAD, Johannesburg. 'The existing regulations regarding the non-payment of wages,' he said,

do not sufficiently protect the natives. Under the Pass Regulations the intent to defraud has to be proved which in most cases is impossible. The Masters and Servants Act only protects servants to a slight degree, the penalty provided being insufficient to deter employers from defrauding their natives.[44]

The real thrust of the Pass Laws was to enforce contracts, prevent desertion and deliver a submissive low-paid workforce to the tender mercies of employers. As A. C. Lawrence, Acting Chief Pass Officer on the Rand, argued when defending Night Passes for women:

There is the Masters and Servants Act, but it is very difficult indeed to trace women. They simply disappear in the night... under the Night Pass Ordinace she is frightened to go out without her pass and you [presumably the employer and the authorities] are not so liable to lose her.[45]

R. M. Tladi's passionate denunciation of the system to the Superintendent of Native Affairs at Benoni underlines the point:

(1) A Passport is supposed to be a protection to natives and regarded as an agreement made at the Pass Office between the employer and the employee.
Question:
    (1) (a) If so why should I be compelled to carry this agreement or document with me?
    (2) (b) Why should the Police run after me day and night asking me to produce this document and cause me to be absolutely restless?
    (3) (c) Why can't I place it in my box for safety?
    (4) (d) Why if I happen to have this in my house the Police must arrest me, and that I have to suffer the penalty before any dispute arises between myself and my employer?[46]

Both Tladi and Letanka also drew attention to the wage-depressing functions of the laws.

When a Native, after being forced to come out of his kraal, got to the Mines or the towns, the Pass Law forced him to get work as soon as possible. That is when the 6-day pass was instituted. When it expires the Native is afraid he may be arrested. He has not sufficient time to find more remunerative employment, and is perhaps forced to accept £1 or 30/- a month. The first white man who hires him gives him as little wages as possible because the unfortunate Native is forced by the Pass Law to take anything that is offered to him. His Pass is marked £1 or 30/- and thus his first employer is his valuator. He cannot get more.[47]

Letanka was implicitly excluding the possibility of worker pressure on employers driving wages up, but here two final aspects of passes came into play: the character column on passes and the endorsement of the stamp *FIRD* for anyone convicted of a criminal offence. The way in which the character column on passes served to suppress employee unrest or resistance has been mentioned by van Onselen, and is graphically illustrated by H. S. Mgqamo's speech to the Superintendent, Native Affairs, Benoni:

> A native works under a white man for 5 years or more. He by mere misfortune breaks a glass or any article in the house. His master gets annoyed and forgets this man worked for such a long time under him. He discharges him and on his character he writes 'bad boy'. This character disables the man to obtain work anywhere and in some cases even if engaged by another white man, when registering him at the Pass Office seeing his character on the Pass the Pass Officer turns to the employer and states 'I advise you not to take this boy', then the man is stranded.

Mgqamo then went on to trace this hypothetical individual's descent into depravity – he meets a 'white hooligan' who gets him a forged pass in turn for selling liquor: he is arrested and convicted, and on discharge has the hated words 'FIRD' imprinted in his passport. He is now of necessity condemned to a life of permanent criminality from which he will never escape.[48]

The connection between criminality and the Pass Laws was indeed intimate, and is worthy of special consideration. An enduring concern of the urban authorities was the canker of criminality in the black community on the Rand, and the threat that this volatile constituency could constitute (particularly if allied to poor white lumpen slum dwellers) in times of hardship and political instability.[49] The Pass Laws were the principal means of policing and if possible of rooting out this 'evil', since by definition the unemployed could not possess a pass stamped with the appropriate contract of employment, unless, of course, this was obtained by extra-legal means. This in practice was what often happened, and so the Pass Laws were faulty in respect of this particularly crucial function. Nevertheless, to the extent that they obliged recourse to such expedients, with the various costs which they entailed, they were as unpopular with the lumpenproletariat as they were with the African working class. It was for this reason that they came to constitute a key component of the anti-pass agitation and infused the movement with much of the volatility and violence that it came to possess.[50]

This criminal function of the Pass Laws was not limited to policing the lumpenproletariat, but also spilled over and infected their application to the black populace as a whole. 'The Pass Laws as applied in the Labour districts,' commented the Native Affairs Inspector for Krugersdorp,

> appear to be based on the assumption that every native is a criminal from whom the rest of the community has to be protected, hence the introduction of the Finger Impression system.

Furthermore, it was

> the continual harassment by police and others, often in an officious manner demanding the production of passes at all times and places,

which he felt was probably at the root against the grievances of the Pass Law system as a whole.[51]

Other evidence confirms at least the earlier part of his assessment,

> The pass [T. M. Tladi protested] persecutes and disappoints [you]. . . . In the first place when you meet a Policeman you'll have to take off your hat and then produce your pass otherwise you will be knocked about and after all you will be arrested and charged for resisting or failing to satisfy the Police and you will be convicted accordingly.[52]

Others endorsed Tladi's views: Mvabasa spoke of 'deficient policemen who do not know the nature of the charges',[53] while 'Comrade Sebeho' at a meeting of the Industrial Workers of Africa (IWA), during the 1s-a-day agitation, gave some clue as to why those adopting 'civilised' manners might be more open to harassment and victimisation. 'The whites are wise,' Sebeho pointed out, 'they do not appoint natives born in town to the police, only those from the kraals.' This is evidence of van Onselen's suspicion of the divisive objects of this pattern of recruitment.[54]

To sum up, passes clearly 'prevented money', whether of a legal or extra-legal variety; they also delivered a submissive, vulnerable workforce, which would not lightly run the risk of crossing the wishes of their masters. It is hardly surprising that they became the focus of militant agitation on the Rand in March and April 1919. Yet while oppressing all sections of the African community and providing a focus of cross-class opposition, they did not oppress all black urban dwellers in the same way, and thus simultaneously furnished a means of fragmenting and defusing the agitation to which they had given birth. The irreducible core of the Pass Laws was designed to maintain a politically stable low-wage economy by enforcing contracts and inhibiting mobility, and by policing and rooting out the criminal lumpenproletarian mob. This was a point on which virtually all submissions by officials to the Interdepartmental Pass Laws Committee agreed.[55]

Equally striking, however, was one other area of unanimity, and this was in respect of relaxing the regulations governing the granting of exemptions and certificates of registration. The recommendations put forward here are particularly interesting since they may help us to define a little more closely the amorphous group described until now as the aspirant petty bourgeoisie. The potential beneficiaries of this largesse, where specified, were store boys, bank messengers of long service, 'the respectable educated and partly educated', the skilled artisans, mechanics, tradesmen, clerks and skilled hospital attendants –

which is perhaps as close as we will get to delineating this rather intangible group.[56]

To mollify these groups fully, reforms in the policing of passes and the abolition of the £1 fee for registration (both of which were recommended in the evidence) were also necessary, yet even without them such a policy carried the germ of success. Registration and exemption certificates freed their holders from the normal operation of the Pass Laws, from the night curfew and from 'native' taxation – all of which were major grievances of the urban populace at the time. They also virtually automatically entitled the possessor to higher rates of remuneration, since the pass could not now fulfill its customary wage-pegging function, and since exemption was taken as an index of potential for a higher calibre of work.[57] Like the agitation on wages, therefore, the agitation on passes was a double-edged weapon since its central target could, as it were, be dismantled and used to disorganise the alliance it had occasioned.

'The Pass Law is . . . slavery.'[58] Housing ran close second for the prize of the most hated single institution governing black urban life on the Rand. Conditions were truly appalling. Existing accommodation fell into five distinct categories: in townships like Klipspruit which served Johannesburg, or others like the Blue Sky location which were dormitories for other towns along the Rand; in areas of freehold occupation like Sophiatown, Martindale, Newclare or Alexandra; in the urban slums of Vrededorp and the Malay location, Fordsburg, Doornfontein, Ferreirastown, Jeppestown, Marshalltown and Prospect Township, where rooms in yards could be hired; on the premises of employers or in compounds they built to house their employees; and in barrack-like compound accommodation such as that at Jubilee and Salisbury which the municipal councils built to accommodate their own and other private businesses' employees.[59]

Material conditions were uniformly squalid and depressed. Klipspruit, Sophiatown, Martindale, Newclare and Germiston and a number of other East Rand locations were built immediately adjacent to municipal sewage depositing sites, which was the principal reason for their becoming available for African occupation. Klipspruit was the worst. By 1917 it was virtually surrounded by the sewage farm, with many huts being within 300 yards of its perimeter.[60] Most families lived in the municipality-built V-shaped huts, which were 'no more than an iron roof placed over the floor';[61] virtually no facilities were provided;[62] the mortality rate was staggering (20:100 adults in 1914/15 and 380:1 000 infantile mortality);[63] and the transport cost of the ten-mile journey to Johannesburg bit deeply into the earnings of those who had to work in town (sixpence daily return, 2s 6d weekly and 8s 6d monthly).[64] In addition, residents were subjected to a highly autocratic location administration. One of the principal inducements held out for moving to Klipspruit in 1906 was the availability of mealie plots and grazing for those who hired stands, but by 1910 most grazing had been fenced off, the owners of strayed cattle being fined at a rate of 5s or 10s a head, and the area available for cultivation having been drastically reduced.[65] Arbitrary actions of all kinds were a regular feature of location life. Among them there were raids to counteract the brewing of illegal liquor; auctions were held, the proceeds going to the municipality, of owner-built accommodation when the owner had fallen behind in stand-rent of property valued at anything up to £100, for ludicrous sums such as 7s 6d or £1 10s – the accommodation was re-let at rentals from between £1 and £2 a month; a charge of 2s 6d was made to ride a bicycle – and so on.[66] Other locations along the Rand endured equally austere and insensitive regimes. Rents were often higher, even less municipal housing was provided, facilities were miniscule and the same continual harassment took place.[67] Small wonder that 'the better class of educated and skilled native dislike[d] the name "location" [and] compared them with compounds'.[68] The functions and objectives were in essence the same. Conditions were little better in the freehold areas of Sophiatown, Martindale, Newclare and so on. Prices of property were two to five times higher than those in neighbouring white suburbs; facilities were non-existent; overcrowding was rife and diseases endemic. Moreover, while they were located considerably nearer town, no municipal transport was provided.[69]

Yet there were long waiting lists for accommodation in each of these locations.[70] A brief review of the housing ecology of the Rand helps suggest some of the reasons. The massive increase in the Witwatersrand black urban population, as a result of the war, had created a tremendous demand for African accommodation, which the building industry had conspicuously failed to meet. Costs of building materials, which had soared during the war, provide part of the reason, but much more crucial was the inability or unwillingness of the municipal authorities charged with the responsibility for black housing to undertake the necessary programme of relief.[71] White rate-payer opposition, commercial and speculative interests who profited from the high rentals yielded by the slums or looked for windfall gains on sale of land to the municipality, mining company reluctance to part with the surface rights to their land, and the overlapping jurisdictions of municipal, provincial and central authorities, all served to paralyse any action in this field.[72] There were, as a result, at least 10 000 blacks in Johannesburg alone without authorised accommodation in municipal compounds, locations or black freehold areas.[73] Their needs were met, though hardly satisfactorily, by a municipal permit system which allowed employers to house employees on their premises, in small, employer-constructed compounds, or in rooms hired in adjacent multiracial slums.[74] Each

– and certainly the last – was less satisfactory than accommodation provided in locations and hence helps explain further why such urban dwellers were so anxious to move out. On the premises of employers heavy rentals were often charged, leading to overcrowding;[75] In compounds, there was no provision for families to stay, and the slums were characterised by the most degrading conditions to be found anywhere on the Rand. Tenants were housed in insanitary yards, divided up into numerous tiny rooms; they lived cheek by jowl with criminals, prostitutes and other members of the lumpenproletariat; rents were extortionate, usually averaging 25s to 30s per month for a room; disease was rife (these areas usually being the source of epidemics that periodically ravaged the Rand); and infant mortality rates were higher than anywhere else (355:1 000 in 1919–20).[76]

The grievance over housing was thus one which could mobilise virtually all sections of the African community. At the same time it should also be recognised that it was felt most keenly by the same 'educated' and 'civilised' Africans who were struggling to construct a tolerable family life in the towns. Jammed together in disease-ridden hovels with the poorest strata of black society, they were the most anxious to escape to the dubious advantages of the location. To the extent that the authorities could provide housing for this sector and introduce a few elementary reforms in the running of the locations, these people were open to being detached from the radical populist alliance that emerged in 1918–19. The authorities themselves were not slow to take the point. Disease and the influenza epidemic were jeopardising the reproduction of the more permanently urbanised population on the Rand.[77] Shortage of housing was breeding intense disaffection both in the locations and the volatile urban slums. As Major Cooke observed in discussions with the Parks and Estates Committee:

> The Committee is perfectly aware the period has been marked by a considerable amount of industrial unrest, and that no longer did the native take up that docile attitude which he had done in the past. This is a result of education which has been instilled in him . . . with the result that we must look for more increased difficulties and we must be more careful than in the past . . . the time was by no means inopportune for reviewing the procedure regarding native administration [and in particular] housing.[78]

H. S. Bell, Native Sub-Commissioner, embroidered on the theme. After commenting on the unsympathetic treatment meted out to 'the better class of educated and skilled', he went on to say:

> There are the educated and skilled native labourers, many of whom are of decent class and desire to live decently, and many young men and women growing up of the same class, who have nowhere to go for any sort of recreation after their daily labours, nowhere where they can go in the evenings . . . it is surely the duty of the Public to

assist them to become respectable, and try and alienate them from the illicit liquor evils and other evils to which so many are driven. . . . As far as I know there is absolutely nothing being done to meet the requirements of this class, who claim to be the leaders of the natives and some grow into bitter agitators.[79]

The government was not slow in grasping the nettle (although it should be noted that its grip quickly slackened when the urban agitation died down after 1921). In September 1918, Louis Botha urged the Administrator of the Transvaal to take up the housing question urgently with the local authorities. 'The present state of affairs,' he emphasised, was 'not only a grave menace to public health, but in addition the social and moral evils accruing from the indiscriminate herding together of Europeans and natives in slum quarters in Johannesburg are incalculable.'[80] Shortly afterwards, the Public Health Act was passed, empowering local authorities to prevent or remedy unhealthy housing conditions, and this was followed in 1920 by the Housing Act, which authorised the central government to assist local authorities in preparing housing schemes and which allowed them to raise loans either privately or from government sources.[81] Clearly the needs of 'the better class of educated and skilled' were finally receiving some attention, which may provide one part of the explanation as to why the urban militancy on the Rand flickered out in 1921.

Thus far in this Chapter the black petty bourgeoisie has been treated as a relatively homogenous group. This it clearly was not. In common with the same class in other parts of the capitalist world the group can be divided roughly between the small business owners/petty commodity producers, and professionals and the salariat, although there were those who straddled the divide. One thing that united both strata of this class, however, was the tight limit placed on their capacity for capital accumulation. To both, this was what was signified by the ubiquitous 'colour bar'. Most areas of government service were closed to blacks; private enterprise enforced its own 'customary colour bar'; blacks were not allowed to own businesses or black eating-houses in white areas, and the pressures of white labour and segregationist ideology had forced many of the marginal but fairly successful purveyors of services out into the economic wilderness of the townships, or back into the ranks of the working class.[82] Even in black residential areas a number of other constraints were felt. In Klipspruit, where the purchase of land was prohibited, no one could lease more than one stand or one mealie plot, and licences for trading and petty vending were both discriminatory and prohibitive.[83] In 1910 business stands cost 36s a month, as opposed to 7s 6d in Vrededorp (by the end of the war they had risen to 38s); and trolleys for hawkers were licensed at £3 each[84] (this of course was in addition to the 2s payment for a monthly pass).[85] Even then black businessmen did not necessarily enjoy a monopoly of the trade. Some locations, according to Bell, the Native Sub-Commissioner of the Witwatersrand, were monopolised by

European traders, and Kagan gives examples of such intrusions into Alexandra and Klipspruit.[86] In the freehold areas the situation was in many respects worse. Properties in Sophiatown cost two to five times the going price in neighbouring white areas, and were beyond the reach of most of the African petty bourgeoisie, while trading was dominated by 'coolies and foreigners'.[87] Perhaps the clearest evidence of the slender resources of the African petty bourgeoisie, however, is the small number that could afford to build their own houses even under leasehold arrangements in places like Klipspruit, and the frequency with which those that were built were auctioned to cover arrears of stand-rent.[88]

The African traditional petty bourgeoisie (small-scale businessmen and petty vendors) were clearly a highly marginalised group. Some indication of this is given by a return of daily labourers for Johannesburg in 1923 (see Table 4).

TABLE 4 DAILY LABOURERS, JOHANNESBURG, 1923[89]

Nature of employment	Number
Shoemakers and cobblers	198
Tailors and clothes-menders	83
Clothes cleaners	15
Pedlars and hawkers	387
Carpenters	21
Tinkers and plumbers	36
Trolley drivers and dray carters	34
General dealers	57
Wash boys	29
Brickmakers and builders	25
Paperhangers and painters	19
Ornament makers	14
Butchers	10
Miscellaneous Bootblacks, musicians, quarrymen, coal heavers, hedge trimmers, hairdressers, bakers, bicycle mechanics, well sinkers, insurance canvassers, wagon makers, thatchers, jobbing gardeners, evangelists, purse makers, grass mowers, eating-house keepers, bangle makers, mattress makers, blacksmiths, harness stitchers, sock and cap knitters, laundrymen	73
Total	1 001

Possibilities for capital accumulation were clearly small, at least in the lower and middle ranges of the spectrum, and it was for this reason that many chose to enter the salariat, and use this as a springboard into more substantial entrepreneurial ventures. S. M. Maghatho and C. S. Mabaso of the TNC apparently chose this route, as did Josiah Sibiya, Klipspruit's most successful business 'tycoon'.[90]

It is hardly surprising in these circumstances that the professionals and the salariat came to be viewed as the most prestigious section of the petty bourgeoisie, and the principal reference group for those aspiring to its ranks. Education and being educated became entrenched as a central value and aspiration in the consciousness of the black petty and aspirant petty bourgeoisie. 'During the past half dozen years,' wrote M. C. Brice, the Honorary Secretary of Native Girls Industrial School Committee,

> The kaffir has been educating himself in his little tin shack in our back yards to a degree that might astonish the average Johannesburger to think about.[91]

Education thus became the principal means to breach the citadel of white privilege, the key element in the self-identification of the petty and aspirant petty bourgeoisie and a major demand in the agitations which arose in the years 1918–20.

The black petty bourgeoisie and the TNC

It is striking that prior to the sanitary workers' demand for higher pay in June 1918 there is scarcely a hint of the impending radicalisation of the black petty bourgeoisie. The most militant posture struck was a threat of a strike in response to the Native Administration Bill of 1917 uttered at an ANC meeting at Phokeng, and this seems to have been little more than a rhetorical flourish which came to nothing in the end.[92] Even the East Rand boycott of mine stores in February 1919, which was recognised retrospectively by the leaders of Congress as the beginning of the agitation, elicited scarcely an expression of concern, and certainly no involvement, from the leaders of the petty bourgeoisie.[93] As I. Bud-M'belle said in answer to a question about the stores boycott addressed to him by the Moffat Commission, 'We [the TNC] did not know [what led to it] . . . we were waiting for people to come and explain to us. No people did.'[94] As late as March and May 1918 no single reference was made to the need for higher wages at the SANNC and TNC Congress meetings held at Bethlehem and Pietersburg on 29 March and 24 May respectively.[95] The Congress leaders can hardly have been accused of having their finger on the pulse of the working class. Only with the bucket boys' strike, which provided the first visible expression of a broader ground swell of opposition among the industrial working class, and whose suppression challenged one of the key petty bourgeois values of the time – the impartiality of the law – was the Congress leadership finally stung into action.[96]

At the outset of this Chapter I argued that the petty bourgeoisie, lying between the two dominant relations of production, tended to swing according to the pressures exercised on it by the two contending classes. Laclau develops this point specifically with regard to ideological class struggle:

> In periods of stability, when the social formation tends to reproduce its relations following traditional channels and succeeds in neutralising its contradictions by *displacements*, this is when the dominant bloc in the formation is able to absolve most of the contradictions and its ideological discourse tends to rest more on purely implicit mechanisms of its unity. This is when, generally, the correlation between the logical consistency of the elements of the discourse and its ideological unity reaches its lowest point (religious interpellations of an ascetic type can, for example, co-exist with an increased enjoyment of wordly goods without the social agents 'living' them as incompatible).
>
> In a period of generalised ideological crisis . . . the opposite tends to occur. The crisis of confidence in the 'natural' or 'automatic' reproduction of the system is translated into an exacerbation of all the ideological contradictions and into a dissolution of the unity of the dominant ideological discourse. As the function of all ideology is to constitute individuals as subjects, this ideological crisis is necessarily translated into an 'identity crisis' of social agents. Each one of the sectors in struggle will try and reconstitute a new ideological unit using a 'system of narration' as a vehicle which disarticulates the ideological discourses of the opposing forces.[97]

The events of 1918–20, I would tentatively suggest, bear out these propositions. The ideology of one wing of the petty bourgeoisie was clearly disarticulated and re-articulated to that of the working class. A middle section vacillated continually and experienced an identity crisis in response to the contradictory pulls of capital, state and the black working class, and the more established affluent and reactionary section sustained, with occasional deviations, an ideology articulated with that of the ruling class.

The speed with which substantial sectors of the petty bourgeoisie swung in mid-1918 is clear evidence of the precarious ideological hegemony exercised by the ruling classes over a racially repressed petty bourgeoisie in a colonial situation. It is also testimony to the depth of working-class resentment that had built up in the course of the war. According to Fenias Plaatjes of Randfontein Block, this was a complaint that went back to 1917 (namely, when inflation began to bite).[98] Benjamin Phooko of City Deep put the issue in a little more perspective. Workers had wanted an increase even before the war, but now the demand had intensified. Individual workers had been asking for an increase for some time. It was in fact an everyday occurrence.[99] What prompted the move to collective action is a more complex question. A major precipitating factor, however, was the municipal engineers' strike of 11–14 May 1918, which put out the town's lights for five nights. The speed with which the municipality caved in and awarded a 23 per cent increase to *all* white municipal workers as a result of their action was an object lesson to black workers on the Rand.[100] Indeed, all the major strike movements on the Rand in this period coincided with actual or impending white worker action. In 1913, it was the white mine workers' strike;[101] in 1918 the engineers' strike; in April 1919 (the time of the anti-pass agitation) a building strike together with a ballot for a general strike;[102] and in February 1920 a ballot for another white mineworkers' strike. In part the synchrony may have arisen from the 'demonstration' effects which have been noted by other commentators,[103] but equally important, probably, was a sense of weakening in the power bloc, which black workers felt they would be able to exploit. Certainly the repressive capacities of the state were stretched to their limit at these times.[104]

Whatever the precise interplay of such factors, the black workers employed on the mechanical section of the South African Railways soon got the message. On 13 May – in the middle of the engineers' strike – they also demanded and secured an increase of 3d a day.[105] The success of the railways workers' action rippled through the Rand. 'This constitutional [method],' reported the Town Inspector of the Native Affairs Department, 'has evidently been copied by the Municipal natives.' On 20 May one hundred workers at the Destructor Compound, Newtown, followed suit, and a few days later similar requests were made in nearly all the other municipal compounds. In the latter case there seemed, in the view of the same official, to have been 'more concerted action,' which 'would appear to indicate that correspondence and organisation is being evolved among the natives employed in large concerns.'[106]

On 1 June the Council's answer was delivered to the workers at Vrededorp. No increase would be granted; contracts would have to be worked out, and workers would then be free to leave or disengage. Those re-engaging would then be considered for a small increment.[107] The workers expressed disappointment but appeared to accede, and the Town Inspector departed completely oblivious of the trouble that was about to erupt. As workers reflected on the decision their anger evidently deepened. They were among the worst-paid workers on the Rand, earning £2 10s a month for a seven-day week; they were contracted for 180 days (the sanitary section at least); their work was 'degrading'; and their wage packets were being progressively eaten away by the continuous inflation. As many testified to the Moffat Commission: prices were up; taxes and school fees consumed most of their income; and they could neither clothe themselves and their families, nor afford to feed their children.[108] The Natalspruit compound was first to react, and it was only after fifty arrests had been made that the trouble was put down. Fifty arrests, however, meant fifty vacancies, and when Bezuidenhout Valley Compound refused to do their Natalspruit colleagues' work, thirteen more ended up behind bars. The climax of the episode was, however, yet to come. Those in the Vrededorp Compound allocated to the vacant jobs were extremely reluctant to comply. First they demanded – and were promised – double pay, and then on the 9 and 10 June they too decided that black-legging was not for them, and refused to do the job. Wolhuter Compound adopted a similar attitude, and Springfield was described as 'wavering and unwilling'.[109] The upshot was 152 arrests and the callous sentence handed down by Magistrate McFie (see above). The fat was truly in the fire. Congress and the African public generally were outraged and the 1s-a-day campaign was about to commence.

The first TNC meeting on the matter was held on the evening of the 10 June, although its executive, through the offices of D. S. Letanka, had taken up the case of the strikers when the first arrests were made.[110] Its proceedings soon revealed many of the cleavages, as well as the preoccupations, that were to characterise Congress over the next two years. S. M. Maghato, President of SANNC, opened the proceedings by observing that the municipal workers had struck because they were united and had been arrested because of the Pass Laws. If the blacks just folded up their arms and stopped work, they would surely hurt the white man.. H. L. Bud-M'belle, by contrast, proposed that they should petition the Governor-General for a relaxation of the penalty, to which Mtota (probably a member of the IWA) retorted they should forget the Governor-General and if no satisfaction was given they should strike. I. Bud-M'belle then intervened and made a plea for moderation, which he thoughtfully made available to the Moffat Commission. 'In coming here tonight,' he announced,

> we have not come to pray, we are here on a very important matter. In rising I wish to express my concurrence with the proposal of M'belle Junior, opposing altogether Mtota's proposal. My countrymen, do not forget we are in a critical time. Do not forget that we have not a single greyheaded man among us, therefore when the fat is in the fire we must remove it ourselves. We must extinguish the fire when we see it burning outside . . . the Congress at Bloemfontein decided that its sentiment was against any form of strike. We have therefore also to be careful about what we do and must avoid putting our people into trouble. . . . If we do not stop the strike the whole of Johannesburg will be in flames. . . . I therefore entreat you to stop the strike. I entreat you to help those people financially, protect them and help them in the appeal required against the Magistrate's judgement. At the same time, let us make it quite clear that we are opposed to strikes.

Bud-M'belle however was quite out of his depth. 'Let it burn' (whether it was the fat or Johannesburg we are never informed) was the audience's reply, and M'belle retired in disarray.[111] The working class was already beginning to exercise its sway.

At this stage the proceedings of the meeting become shrouded in mystery. The Moffat Commissioners obviously had secret police reports of the meeting which I have not been able to trace, when they interrogated those prominent in the agitation, and from their cross-questioning it appears that preparations were now undertaken, at the direction of Mvabasa, to organise a strike. One man,

Mhlonga, was apparently detailed to canvass the idea in Springs, another was to work between Cleveland and Block B, and a third was given responsibility for Randfontein and Roodepoort.[112] Still others were charged with visiting white employers and households to propagate the idea among their employees, the name of a newspaper vendor called Shabalala being mentioned in this context.[113] On 11 June, if Moffat's evidence is to be believed, a report-back took place, and on the thirteenth or fifteenth at a meeting at the African Club the Springs and Benoni delegates detailed their progress.[114] Witnesses naturally denied these allegations when confronted with them by the Moffat Commission, but there was one piece of evidence to suggest that something of this kind was undertaken. On 26 June a worker reported that about two weeks before a man had come to his place of employment and invited them to a meeting (presumably that of the nineteenth).[115]

For Isaiah Bud-M'belle and the older, more established and more affluent section of Congress things were now getting out of hand. On 13 June he telegrammed the Minister of Justice the following appeal:

> Honourable Sir. . . . Your attention may already have been drawn to the severe criticisms of Mr McFie's remarks that appeared in the daily Press of Johannesburg and other centres, characterising the sentence on strikers as unduly severe. In addition I have the honour to inform your honour that this has created an unfortunate situation for the leaders of our Congress, as it has had a painful effect upon the native labourers of the Rand. During the past three days matters grew so serious that two days ago I telegraphed for the senior officers of our congress to help calm the natives. Mr Mgato, our President, Mr Saul [sic] Plaatje, Mr Saul M'aana [sic] and the senior Vice President, Mr D. S. Letanka have had various consultations with the native sections on the Rand, which culminated in a largely attended public meeting at the Pilkington Hall last night, of which this application is the result. I think we have most of their machinations under control, but as I understand that some counter meetings are to take place under socialist auspices next Sunday and Wednesday, the Government would strengthen our hands considerably by extending its clemency to the prisoners, and by altering Mr McFie's decision before the week-end.[116]

The next public meeting on the strike took place on the nineteenth. Until this point *no single formal demand had been made for an increase in wages*, although it is safe to assume that complaints had been registered from the floor at Congress meetings. That, and the whole direction of the TNC over the next two years, was about to be changed. The meeting was a set-piece occasion. A thousand Africans attended (and twelve whites), who had travelled in from all parts of the Rand; the hall was overflowing; and all the TNC dignitaries were there – Maghato, Mabaso, Msane, Letanka, Msimang, M'belle, Maxexe and others. The Rev. Lebalo opened with a prayer, but from that moment a different spirit gripped the assembled throng. Mabaso started with what was to become a familiar diatribe against the location system:

He pointed out Klipspruit and Germiston location as the place of the natives where all the dirt from the towns is deposited or thrown. This aims at making natives bring forth unhealthy children, who would soon die away.

Mvabasa and Selope Thema then launched into an attack on Christian missionaries and Christian teaching:

> The white people teach you about heaven and tell you that after death you will go to a beautiful land in heaven. They don't teach you about this earth on which we live . . . if we cannot get land on this earth neither shall we get it in heaven. . . . The God of our Chiefs, Chaka, Moshoeshoe, Rile, Sandile, Sobuza, Lentsoe, etc. gave us this part of the world we possess.

These were Mvabasa's sentiments, which Thema closely echoed.

What is interesting about these (and other) speeches, aside from the evident passion, is the transformation of consciousness which they seem to entail. The logical inconsistency of elements in their previous ideological discourse had been exposed; Christian values like submissiveness and expecting one's due reward in heaven had been found wanting and discredited. In their place we see in process the construction of a new ideological unity with popular appeals to the land of our chiefs and the God who brought us our customs being re-integrated into a new populist discourse. Politically and ideologically the tide was on the turn.

As significant were the continued cleavages within Congress that emerged at this meeting. All were infected by the atmosphere of the gathering, but there was a limit beyond which some of the leadership would not go. S. M. Maghato, for example, swam with the tide in his rhetorical passages and used the appropriate biblical imagery of the Children of Israel in the Land of the Pharaohs, but mainly in the hope of diverting the agitation into safer, less violent channels. 'The International Socialists . . . and the Labour Parties,' he argued,

> are all white people. I understand they want the natives to strike. If you listen to them and go out on strike they will be the very persons who will be around with rifles to shoot you in the street. I am absolutely opposed to the idea of a strike. I maintain that we shall get our grievances rectified if we only ask through the proper channels. . . . I tell you we are not afraid of white people. We can destroy Johannesburg in a day; we can stop the mines in an hour. But we respect the Union Jack and are loyal to the British Government.

This last was of course a characteristic element of the earlier ideological discourse.

C. S. Mabaso, always to the left of Maghato, adopted a more qualified position:

> There is a section of white people called the International Socialist League. These men appear to sympathise with black people. . . . I cannot tell whether these men are honest or not . . . [but] in my opinion they are friends of the black people.

But it was left to Mvabasa to articulate the militant class position in its most unadulterated form. To the horror of his more moderate colleagues on the platform he moved a resolution, seconded by Thema, that Congress request the authorities and employers to increase wages of black workers by 1s a day as of 1 July 1918. In introducing his motion his remarks clearly betray the influence of the ISL, whose meetings Mvabasa had attended since late the previous year. 'The capitalists and workers,' he said,

> are at war everywhere in every country. . . . The white workers do not write to the Governor-General when they want more pay. They strike and get what they should.

Despite interventions by the Rev. Lebalo and Caluza, which were respectively ignored or shouted down, the die was now cast. It only remained for Herbert Msane of the ISL to propose a secret committee of five from the ISL and TNC (to avoid detectives) to work on a strategy and for a collection to be made before the main business of the meeting was over.[117]

From the report of Native Detective Moorosi (there were several others which confirm the general content of the speeches), it would appear that no decision was actually taken on the question of a strike, although this was clearly the sanction that was in the back of peoples' minds if the 1s request was turned down. Another informer, however, came away with a different view. According to him, Mvabasa had proposed that another meeting be called before the 1 July, and if the employers did not accede a strike would take place on the second.[118] This was certainly the impression gained by the meeting at large. While Mvabasa and Herbert Msane denied at an IWA meeting of 27 June that any such decision had been taken, most of the others who were present (Sebeho, Ntholi, Tinker and Ngoji) insisted that it had.[119] 'All the natives on the Rand knew it,' asserted Comrade Ntholi, and he is supported by a report from the employees of Felber and Jucken whose recollection of the meeting was 'more pay, the abolition of passes and stop work on 1st July'.[120] Even for the more radical wing of Congress the situation was acquiring an alarming momentum of its own.

If the Congress leaders were becoming uneasy, the government was also clearly getting cold feet. To begin with, they had taken up an extremely hard and uncompromising line. When it had seemed that the municipality might be caving in to the muncipal strikers' demands, the Magistrate, Johannesburg, the Deputy Commissioner of Police and the Acting Assistant Director of Native Labour, had written to the council in the following peremptory terms:

> We desire to state . . . that for the Council at the present time to consider even, much more to concede, any claim of bodies of native servants of the Municipality for an increase of wages is a course which would, in our judgement, be fraught with the most serious danger, not only to industry but also to public safety on the Witwatersrand.
>
> We desire also to state formally for the information of the Council that the Government is prepared to deal sternly and immediately with any criminal disorder by

the Natives or by Europeans should any disorder follow from a refusal of the Council to consider the question. We wish to repeat that for the Council even to consider such claims, is in our opinion fraught with the most serious danger to the public welfare.[121]

The prospect of a general strike of black workers quickly concentrated their minds. On the fourteenth, the Minister of Justice replied to M'belle's telegram, saying he would place it before his colleagues at the earliest opportunity; and opportunely, from the point of view of the timing of the strike, the Director of Prisons was able to inform M'belle on 26 June that the Governor-General had agreed to the release of the municipal workers on probation.[122]

The Congress and IWA leaders were getting more than a little jittery themselves. On 13 June, 118 workers at Premier Milling had struck for higher pay, to be followed by nearly 500 workers from eight other firms (not all had struck, but many gave a month's notice when pay increases were refused).[123] Nor was trouble confined to industrial plants. From 20 or 21 June Taberer reported that it became apparent 'that there was an uneasy feeling among the natives on some of the mines', while shortly afterwards workers from Crown Deep went to Western Section to propagate the strike.[124]

The committee of five responded with an attitude of masterly inactivity. H. L. Bud-M'belle issued a circular to all employers on the Witwatersrand on 20 June, drawing attention to the increase in prices and to the fact that 'the native workers of the Rand are a valuable and perhaps indispensable class of the community', and requesting an increase of 1s a day, but beyond that little was done.[125] Part of the reason was that no one was clear whether a strike call had been made on the nineteenth. In any case, as Mvabasa pointed out, it was foolish to strike on the first day of the demand.[126] Equally important, however, in the eyes of Tinker, Ntholi and other members of the ISL/IWA was the belief that the black working class was not yet well organised enough to strike.[127]

It came as some relief, therefore, when the bucket boys were released and other overtures were forthcoming from the authorities. Taberer met Letanka, Msimang and M'belle to warn them that black workers would be shot if they struck and that the mines would close down, while General Botha received a delegation to hear grievances, and promised that an enquiry would be made.[128] A range of co-optive strategies was being quickly brought to bear.

Nevertheless, the terms upon which different parties to the movement capitulated varied according to their ideological and political creed. Mvabasa, at a meeting on 28 June, attended by some 1 000 Africans, was at pains to denounce rumours of a 1 July strike and to explain why there should be delay:

> I see that some of you think that we are too slow with the thing, but it is not so, we are first trying to make you understand and put you on the right way because we don't want any of you to be hurt or get into trouble.

He went on to explain what the right way would be:

our strike won't be like the white man's strike. You could see the white men when they pick stones and break the stores, etc., stop all the trams and railways . . . we won't do [that] . . . but will be in our blankets naked . . . and we shall then see if any Government servant will then come and shoot you while lying in your bed fighting nobody. . . . You must leave your sticks behind in case you strike. . . . The white men will say you were assaulting them with sticks . . . the Sanitary boys were arrested while having sticks with them . . . we natives of Johannesburg are to show the other natives of South Africa. If we do a thing every native in South Africa will do it; as you have seen in the papers that Natal is shaking, asking for more money, and it will be the same in the Cape and the Free State . . . the whole of South Africa will one day go on strike.[129]

Comrade Ntholi begged to differ on Mvabasa's rather naïve approach. On the mines, he accurately predicted,

the white people will place a few armed Policemen or soldiers at the gates [and] . . . the poor natives will be starved into submission in less than two days.

As for kitchen and shop boys:

the boss will only kick him and he will go out to work. He himself [would not] sleep on a strike day. He [would] fight any man that came his way.[130]

Yet for all these differences of emphasis it is clear the strike idea was still alive and well in the minds of some of the Congress leadership.

Those who had always been opposed to the movement were no more convinced. Saul Msane, an old Congress leader, circulated a pamphlet denouncing strike action, which was subsequently reproduced in the white Sunday press, and which was to earn him widespread opprobrium and the title *Isita sa Bantu* (Enemy of the People).[131] Maghato, at a further meeting of 29 July attended by 900 blacks and three whites, struck a more ambiguous note. Once again his speech was laced with militant rhetoric:

The God of the white people was Gold, their heaven was money. . . . We are told by the missionaries that there is a place called Hell, he cannot pray because the devil won't have that nonsense in his place. We black people in this land are in hell already, the owner of the hell, which is the white man, will not allow the blacks to pray . . . the blacks are tormented in this land and the white man does what he likes.

At the same time it was riddled with contradictions.

McFie has opened our eyes and made us see what we had never seen before. The natives had been made to realise their power and its utility. . . . They know by organising they can make their voices heard. The white people have got maxim guns ready to shoot unarmed natives . . . the white people are afraid to talk with us because they know well they would be defeated. I am loyal to the King. I am not afraid of General Botha as I am keeping within the law.

Clearly if anyone was grappling with an identity crisis it was Maghato, as he continually vacillated between the two sides. I. Bud-M'belle was clearer: he supported the 1s demand (he hardly dared not), but he was absolutely 'against any idea of strike'. Mvabasa was clearer still. If people were opposed to the strike they should hold their own meetings. 'If the 1s increase is not given we shall certainly strike.'[132]

Nevertheless, it appeared that for the time being at least the strike had been postponed. On the following day (Sunday), partly at the instance of E. Dower, the Secretary for Native Affairs, a mass meeting was held at New Market, Newtown, attended by 'thousands of natives' which Maghato addressed, telling them there was no strike, and that they would be told what to do the following Sunday. Dower also spoke, eliciting a noisy response, above which nothing could be heard. When Dower departed, Ntholi, who had draped the Union Jack around his body, publicly tore it to shreds. The report concludes, 'the natives were very angry and making rows, some white men hitting them, etc.'[133]

The leadership might have compromised, but as the foregoing report suggests the workers were in no mood to be fobbed off. On 1 July 'Practically all the natives employed by the various firms . . . put forward an application for an increase of wages at a rate of 1s a day', and were waiting for a reply; 'all disclaim[ed] any intention of striking, but I [E. Berg, Town Inspector] very much doubt whether they will continue that attitude were they to meet a general refusal'.[134] Others were not so long-suffering. Several industrial concerns struck, while at Ferreirasdorp, Robinson Deep and Crown Mines, 4 000, several hundred (?) and 2 000 mineworkers respectively refused to go down the shafts, only complying once they had been charged by bayonet- and rifle-wielding police.[135]

Opposition had been temporarily stifled by a mixture of force, disagreement and confusion in the ranks of the Congress leadership, and the conciliatory noises being made by the authorities. At the meeting at Newtown Market, a message had been delivered by Dower from the Prime Minister (which nobody had heard above the din) announcing the appointment of the Moffat Commission. A few days later, on 9 July, Botha agreed to entertain a deputation of the black community to listen to their grievances. The list they presented was a judicious mixture of working-class and petty-bourgeois concerns, providing plenty of scope for cosmetic concessions. It is worth reproducing in full.

TABLE 5   LIST OF GRIEVANCES[136]

(a)   The economic position of the natives on the Rand having regard to:–

    (1)   increased cost of living due to the war;

    (2)   the consequent desire for increased wages;

    (3)   housing accommodation in the case of those not directly employed on the mines and the incidental disadvantages of the existing systems;

    (4)   inability under existing conditions to give proper support to wife and family, more

particularly in the case of those resident in labour areas;
(5)   disabilities and disadvantages imposed by 'the colour bar' in law and the consequent artificial interference with progress;
(6)   payment of compensation in respect of miners' phthisis, death or incapacitation from accident;

(b)   enforcement of the Night Passes Ordinance in respect of women;
(c)   non-availability of letters of exemption in the different provinces owing to the operation of the different pre-Union laws;
(d)   restriction on employment of natives as interpreters in Courts of Law;
(e)   non-employment of natives in post offices and unsuitability of post office accommodation for natives;
(f)   multiplicity of passes in labour districts;
(g)   residential passes and disadvantages owing to the distance of the native locations from the towns, together with a request for suitable housing provisions;
(h)   lack of facilities for education.

On 24 July a further delegation was admitted, representing black residents in the Pretoria district. The process of token conciliation was clearly in full swing.[137]

The latter part of 1918 marks a lull in African opposition, and this is perhaps the appropriate point to draw some general conclusions about the agitation that emerged. One thing that is absolutely clear is that for the Congress leadership at least, and probably also for the mass of the African working population, these events provided the first full realisation of the strength of the organised working class. As Saul Msane said in evidence to the Moffat Commission,

> The masses in the native population are beginning to realise that they are an indispensable factor in the natural and social fabric of South Africa. They are beginning to see that the whole industrial system in this land is based and must be based on their willing co-operation.[138]

Numerous speeches at meetings in this period corroborate this impression. Also apparent is the polarisation among the leadership of the TNC. The older, better established section who were also frequently residentially divided from the working class (for example, Msane lived in Bree Street),[139] proved extremely reluctant to throw their lot in with the working people, having more to lose in terms of their standing with the authorities, and the favours which this might ultimately provide. On the other side, there were those whose outlook was profoundly transformed by this period of working-class mobilisation – people like Mabaso, H. L. Bud-M'belle, Selope Thema, Mvabasa and, to a certain extent, Letanka too. Nor should the influence of the ISL and IWA be underestimated here – as it often is – since it was their members (Ntholi, Kraai, Cetiwe, Sebeho and others) who often held the line when it came to more militant action. Finally, there were those – most classically Maghato – who were caught between and remorselessly pulled two ways, men who were nevertheless important in Congress because they could speak to both factions, and who eventually helped it back on a constitutionalist path.

The Moffat Commission's recommendations, which were published in September, were received differently by different sections of the black population. Another meeting was called by the Prime Minister to acquaint Congress with the substance of its findings, though in the event Botha was indisposed. The Secretary for Native Affairs, Malan, stepped into the breach and announced concessions on the following issues:

(1) Recommend increases in wages for those permanently resident in towns not enjoying the benefit of employer-provided accommodation and rations.

(2) Wage increases for black soldiers and policemen in the SAMR (South African Mounted Rifles) and SAP (South African Police) (5s a month for a single man; up to 12s 6d a month for a married man, plus a war bonus for those married and earning over 3s 6d a day), and special allowances not exceeding 25s a month for those employed in the higher ranks of interpreters.'

(3) Conciliation boards (under very restricted circumstances).

(4) Removal of the 1s a day fee for a travelling pass.

(5) Removal of night passes for women.

(6) Improved Post Office accommodation for blacks with the possibility of the employment of black clerks being considered.

(7) Court interpreters to be chosen exclusively on the basis of merit.

(8) Attempts in progress to improve black education.

(9) Pending the passage of the Native Affairs Administration Bill, *ad hoc* conferences to be convened between the Minister of Native Affairs and black representatives.[140]

Although some were mollified by these concessions (and the Johannesburg Chamber of Commerce agreed to a 25 per cent increase over pre-war rates of pay in the categories Moffat specified),[141] the vast majority were not. Moffat had barely touched on the broader structures of exploitation and oppression, and as inflation bit deeper, a further explosion was on the cards. As early as late August or the beginning of September, at a meeting in Johannesburg, 'one firebrand . . . wanted those present to urge the natives along the reef to come out on strike', until 'Wiser and saner counsels prevailed and it was decided to wait until the Moffat Report was published'.[142] And at a meeting of the executive committee of the SANNC at Bloemfontein at about the same time, Sol Plaatje was horrified at the attitude of the Transvaal delegates:

[They] came to the Congress with a concord and determination that was perfectly astounding to our customary native demeanour at conferences. They spoke almost in unison, in short sentences nearly all of which began and ended with the word 'strike'. . . . It was only late in the second day that we succeeded in satisfying the delegates to report, on getting to their homes, that the Socialist method of putting black against white will land our people in serious disaster.[143]

The influenza epidemic of September/October 1918 temporarily took the steam out of further agitation, but by December of that year Congress was once again meeting with F. S. Malan, the Secretary for Native Affairs, and parading a familiar list of complaints.[144] They received short shrift from the Secretary, although he couched his responses in the most courteous terms. The colour bar could not be removed due to pressure of public opinion, and the use of force would only have the effect of alienating whites; the cost of living would go down now that the war was over; the concession stores were not exploiting their custom; passes did not exist for slavery but for mutual protection and would gradually disappear as blacks moved up the scale of civilisation; housing was high on the Government's agenda; and if the complaints about post offices remained he would bring it to the attention of the Minister.[145]

Nevertheless, inflation kept on rising; no new housing was forthcoming; and passes continued to be viewed as the principal means of obstructing higher pay. Early in 1919, therefore, African leaders began to advance a new tactic in the campaign for extra wages – passive resistance against passes.[146] The anti-pass campaign precipitated one of the more dramatic expressions of African cross-class unity to be seen in this period – not surprisingly, since the incidence of the Pass Laws across the African population served as a focus of grievance for virtually all classes. On 3 April the newspaper *Abantu-Batho* reported that the previous Sunday (30 March), the delegation which interviewed the NAD, the Chamber of Mines, the Native Recruiting Corporation and the Municipal Council on the question of the 1s a day had held a mass meeting to communicate the substance of the discussion. 'The report,' according to *Abantu-Batho*, 'didn't please the meeting as this question was an old one. It was therefore agreed that passes be thrown away as passes are the foundation on which the refusal of the Europeans is based.'[147]

Why, however, did the focus shift so suddenly from wages to passes when no serious demand for their outright abolition had been voiced until this stage?[148] Obviously, the connection between passes and wages had been made as early as June 1918, but, as the *Rand Daily Mail* commented, in successive meetings with the authorities in October and December 1918, and again on 21 March of that year, the question had simply not been raised in that form.[149]

Part of the answer emerges from the meeting between the TNC and various employer bodies that preceded the 30 March meeting. Cooke had been asked there to appeal to the employers in getting higher wages, but had replied he had no power to interfere.[150] If employers would not respond to the Commission's recommendations and government urgings, and if Pass Laws prevented the successful prosecution of strikes, then the obvious target was the Pass Laws themselves. It was here it seems that the link was finally made.

The movement got into full stride the following day. Lawrence, Acting Chief Pass Officer, arrived at his office at 8.30 the next morning to find a large gathering being addressed by M'belle and Mabaso. After brief discussion he agreed to receive a delegation consisting of Mabaso, M'belle, E. Dunjwa, Cetiwe, Nshoko, G. Mapikela, Kraai, J. Khatlane and two others. The message they delivered was that after repeated representations they had received no increase in wages and they had therefore decided to refuse to carry passes.[151] Lawrence made the unremarkable observation that they would be breaking the law, after which they proceeded to hold a mass meeting at Von Brandis Square, and hundreds present began to hand in their passes. In the afternoon, pickets in the suburbs demanded passes from employees in white businesses, and collected probably 2 000 or more.[152] The following day even more militant agitation threatened. The Director of Native Labour cabled the Native Affairs Department in Pretoria that the movement was still growing and that a meeting of 3 000 blacks had been in progress for the previous four hours. A cordon of friendly pickets surrounded the meeting which would only allow entry if passes were surrendered. At this stage inadequate police forces were available, and he urged the despatch of the SAMR. Such action, he added, would not complicate the European strike, members of which fully appreciated the native unrest.[153] Much the same pattern of events was expected for the 2nd April, it having been decided on the previous day that a new mass meeting should be held; that all blacks working in town were to be pulled out by pickets – special attention being given to the municipal compounds; that mine clerks were to cooperate in getting the mine labourers to come out; and that delegates from Pretoria, Potchefstroom, Boksburg and Benoni were to secure the surrender of passes and the cessation of work in those areas.[154] Police reinforcements being by now available, the strike leaders were arrested, and a large crowd followed the arrest to the charge office. Here, further demonstrations took place and new arrests were made.[155] Finally, on the 3rd, mounted police charged a large crowd demonstrating at the Court, many being injured and many arrests being made.

Sporadic incidents occurred for the rest of the month. Violent clashes took place between black and white civilians in Vrededorp on the 3rd and 4th, resulting in 108 arrests; on the 9th, when a meeting was urged to release the prisoners from gaol; on the 14th, when those arrested on the 4th handed in their gaol tickets and with other passless Africans were arrested once more; and on the 25th, when an unsuccessful rescue attempt was made on a police escort taking prisoners from the court house to gaol, a total of 306 being detained on these occasions.[156] Meanwhile similar outbursts were taking place all over the Rand. Benoni was perhaps most seriously affected. At a meeting on 2 April, fifteen arrests were made, after which large crowds gathered at the charge-office behaving, in the language of the police report, in a disorderly fashion. Sixty-nine women and 49 men were thereupon arrested, to which the crowd responded by stoning the police. On the third, 100 Africans appeared carrying a sack containing their passes and 67 arrests were made, and on the 4th all available European constables were summoned to round up 20 male Africans who were travelling the district 'spreading disaffection among the mine natives'. In total, 231 arrests had been made.[157] Similar episodes were reported from Maraisburg and Springs, in which latter instance 50 ringleaders were incarcerated in gaol.[158] Only Boksburg for a time seemed relatively immune, owing largely to the 'moderation' of its branch chairman, Wessells Morake. As early as February 1919 there had been agitation against passes, but this had been successfully stifled by Morake's insistence that they keep within the law. An East Rand Proprietary Mines' clerk, J. G. Matshiqi, soon put an end to that. With the support of the radical Johannesburg branch, and physical reinforcements from Johannesburg, Germiston and Benoni, he arranged counter-meetings, against the express ruling of the Location Superintendent, to advocate the destruction of passes. Morake, 'a moderate man' in the old SANNC mould, naturally informed the Superintendent, with the result that a fracas broke out when the police and the Superintendent arrived, and 60 arrests were made.[159]

What conclusions can we draw from this new phase of political radicalisation? Firstly, although it cannot be traced so readily through the reports of meetings, the process of polarisation was still going on. At the very beginning of the disturbances Maghato hurried off to the Native Sub-Commissioner, Pretoria, to say that the situation was getting out of control.[160] On the other hand it was the familiar figures of Mabaso, H. L. Bud-M'belle, E. Dunjwa, Cetiwe and Kraai who led the march to the Pass Office which started the affair. At the same time we see a new element entering the agitation, no doubt because it was passes that were under attack – the lumpenproletariat of Vrededorp and other urban slums. Of the 316 arrested on 4 April in the Vrededorp disturbances, 45 had previous convictions for serious crimes, 15 for desertion, and 10 for minor offences (for example, pass laws, drunkenness, habitual loafing). One enterprising individual had 26 previous convictions; another had 22, and 15 Pass Law offences; and another two had convictions for issuing false passes. A similar pattern emerged from the arrests of the 14th.[161] Clearly a new and dangerous element was entering the movement, with the arrival of the urban mob, which was to prompt serious reflection as to what course of action to pursue with the radicalised petty bourgeoisie.

A section of the TNC leadership now seems to have drawn back from the brink. The violence unleashed by the anti-pass disturbances, from workers and the lumpenproletariat, as well as from the police, seems to have given rise to serious misgivings. Official soft-soaping once more served to reinforce this feeling. On 1 July 1919 the Director of Native Labour, Pritchard, summoned a TNC delegation to announce the appointment of the Low Grades Mines Commission, and suggested that Congress itself might wish to give evidence. But if they did, he counselled, they 'should go with a clean slate. A great blunder had been made by them in starting the "Throw away passes" agitation', and he advised them to consider what their attitude would be. He was prepared to grant all blacks who had thrown away their passes one week's grace to go to the various pass offices and get duplicate passes.

The deputation then retired and on returning thanked Colonel Pritchard for his offer. They admitted they had made a great blunder, and gratefully accepted his offer. Overjoyed, Pritchard went on to consolidate his gains. The FIRD and the character column on passes, he said, had already been abolished, and his objective was to get the government to agree to a far more liberal granting of exemptions from passes, such exemptions being given free. He felt that 'a great majority of natives would still require a lot of control, but the exempted ones would gradually make a buffer population and readily increase'. Clearly the spectre of a militant petty bourgeoisie once again unleashing the passions of the urban mob and working class was one that he was anxious to exorcise straight away. Concluding, he went on further to sugar the pill by reporting that an inter-departmental Pass Laws Committee was about to be set up, and that he was having discussions with the municipality to expedite the provision of housing and to see what could be done about prosecutions in Klipspruit for illicit brewing of liquor.[162]

Reporting to a TNC meeting in Vrededorp on 6 July, Mabaso got a hotter reception than he can possibly have expected. Thibedi cross-questioned him about his position, eliciting the accusation that 'he was only a youngster and would get us into trouble', and another unnamed member of the audience bluntly accused Mabaso of being bribed. At this Mabaso promptly closed the meeting, and was only with difficulty saved from public assault. The meeting was rescued only when M'belle pointed out that Mabaso was merely reporting back and if they were not in agreement another interview should be arranged.[163]

At meetings on the 8 and 10 July similar criticisms were voiced, it being argued that Pritchard would inform the Commission of Enquiry that blacks had no grievances against passes now they had agreed to take them back. On the 8th Mabaso tried to defend his position by saying, 'We have broken the law: Congress has no money to assist workers. It behoves us to be penitent and to honour the Director who will intercede for us.' However, like Maghato before him he was clearly being pulled two ways, and at the meeting of the 10th he finally caved in. 'Those who want to follow the Director's advice,' he argued, 'can. For those who don't I inform you of a General Strike in the Transvaal on

October 1st.' Already three 'natives' were organising for a strike in Potchefstroom, Middelburg and Rustenburg.[164]

The militant constituency of Congress seemed to be maintaining its grip, but another movement was stirring which would ultimately create a new set of rifts. Both Maghato and Ramailane (another important Congress leader) were becoming increasingly preoccupied with rural problems, and in the process striking a closer alliance with chiefs.[165] What this heralded, in part, was the growth of a rural populist movement, which would reach fruition after the decline of urban agitation in late 1920.[166] From the point of view of the urban agitation, however, the *rapprochement* was to exercise an increasingly conservative drag. Even Mabaso became infected with the conservative spirit that this bred. On 8 February 1920, just before the black mineworkers' strike, he spoke out strongly against Africans causing any trouble over the £2 Poll Tax of the Transvaal. The Native Congress and the chiefs, he added, were not in favour of strikes, but wanted to submit to the laws of the country, trusting that in the end the government would redress their grievances. The *mabalans* (clerks) at Crown Mines, he went on, should use all their influence in preventing trouble taking place, adding that the Transvaal chiefs were going to Basutoland to hear Chief Griffiths' report.[167] Mabaso returned to the same theme on 20 and 22 February. Congress did not want to go against the government. It was trusted by the chiefs, who regarded it as an intermediary between the authorities and 'the natives'.[168]

Chiefly influence and conservatism was clearly pulling a section of the Congress leadership one way, and Ramailane was at pains to emphasise that Congress had no part in the 1920 black mineworkers' strike.[169] Yet it was still not possible to ignore more radical kinds of pressures being exercised on the other wing of Congress or the political polarisation within its ranks, that would persist until as late as 1921. At the 'native strike' meeting, for example, on 20 February, 'a Zulu' announced that he wanted to speak about the strike. 'They must do what they were told,' he said, 'because the strike was organised and directed by educated people.' The strike was to take place on Monday morning, and the strike headquarters was at 21 Delvers Street. Its telephone number was 5791 to which all news should be sent.[170] Similarly, in response to Mabaso's plea for moderation on 22 February, the crowd replied that Congress had failed to accomplish anything, and their faith in it had vanished. The only thing for them to do was to go out on strike.[171]

Other evidence of the continued radicalisation of Congress, in at least its middle ranks, is supplied by a report of a Congress meeting at Boksburg on 8 February 1920. At this, Mgoja got up and gave a speech in a more familiar vein.

> The black race must know that white people are thieves and devils. . . . God did not want cowards. They must look to the gaols as their homes. The mine natives must

know they are producers of wealth and must get better pay. . . . There must be unity among blacks. The town lights can be put out. . . . America said they would free all natives and they will help. . . . America had a black fleet and it is coming.[172]

A millenarian and apocalyptic vision was also beginning to intrude. The Congress wing that would win this battle would be the product of changing rhythms in the economic life of the country and their effects on class struggles.

Conclusion

The period 1918–20 represents the most intense radicalisation of black political leadership in South Africa prior to the Second World War. This piece has attempted a fuller examination of this much-neglected area of black working-class and nationalist mobilisation. In particular it has sought to dissect the movement that arose and to understand the class alliance that was struck. In this latter respect it must be regarded as a preliminary account. The delineation of an indigenous petty bourgeoisie in a colonial situation is an exceptionally difficult task. Not only is the class stunted and repressed, but a fair degree of mobility exists between it and the higher-paid working class. It thus becomes highly problematic to draw a sharp boundary between either wing of the petty bourgeoisie and the working class or to fix its composition at any particular point in time.

Given these analytical and allied empirical problems the most effective approach to the question is an examination of the political leadership of the major political organisation of the time – the Transvaal Native Congress – who fall most clearly into the ranks of the petty bourgeoisie. Here in a period of intense agitation and working-class mobilisation one sees the instability of the group, and the extent to which its ideology was articulated with and moulded by pressures and inducements from capital and labour. This is not to suggest that petty bourgeois political leaders were mere cyphers or vessels of external pressures. Clearly they perceived their own sectional interests and placed their own stamp on events. Equally clearly, however, the political leaders were not mere manipulators – as they are so often depicted in the literature – shaping political movements to suit their own particular needs. As the events of 1918–20 show, the petty-bourgeois political leadership was swept away by an immensely powerful upsurge of working-class agitation, being radicalised and fragmented at the same time.

Nevertheless those lines of internal cleavage were not stable or well defined, and varied according to the extent of working-class pressure, the inducements offered by other protagonists in the struggle and the changing incidence of shared oppression with the working class. Each of these factors appears to have played a part in neutralising the movement and deradicalising the Congress leadership as the 1920s wore on. Working-class agitation diminished from

1921 as deflation and unemployment set in. The main flash-points of tension now shifted from the town to the country, where Congress leaders found themselves in the ambiguous embrace of the chiefs. The inducements offered by this group further stifled the militant spirit that was spawned in the towns. Finally, although arguably least importantly, the petty bourgeoisie's experience of shared oppression with the working class also underwent change. As has been argued, important aspects of shared oppression were experienced differentially by the petty bourgeoisie, providing scope for reformist initiatives to detach them from a broader cross-class alliance. Each of these questions requires further examination in the context of the early 1920s, and is the area which in my future research I hope to explore.

Notes

1 H. J. and R. E. Simons, *Class and Colour in South Africa 1850–1950* (Harmondsworth, 1969); M. Benson, *The Struggle for a Birthright* (Harmondsworth, 1966); P. Walshe, *The rise of African Nationalism in South Africa* (London, 1970); P. L. Wickens, *The Industrial and Commerical Workers' Union of Africa* (Cape Town, 1978); T. Karis and G. Carter (eds), *From Protest to Challenge. A documentary history of African politics in South Africa 1882–1964* (Vol. I, Stanford, 1972); E. Roux, *Time Longer Than Rope* (Madison, Wisconsin, 1964); M. Legassick, 'The rise of modern South African liberalism: its assumptions and its social base', unpublished paper, University of London, 1972; F. A. Johnstone, *Class, Race and gold* (London, 1976).

2 Walshe, *African Nationalism*, pp. 73, 83.

3 Simons, *Class and Colour*, pp. 210–14.

4 Johnstone, *Class*, pp. 174–80.

5 B. Willan, 'Sol. Plaatje, De Beers and an old tram shed: class relations and social control in a South African town, 1918–1919', *Journal of Southern African Studies (JSAS)*, 4, 2 (Oct. 1977), 195, 196–215.

6 E. Laclau, *Politics and Ideology in Marxist Theory* (London, 1977), p. 104.

7 *Report of the Interdepartmental Committee on the Native Pass Laws*, UG 41, 22, 5.

8 N. Poulantzas, *Classes in Contemporary Capitalism* (London, 1975), pp. 290–97.

9 Walshe, *African Nationalism*, pp. 50–60.

10 Transvaal Archives Depot (TAD), Municipal Co. Archives, Box 823, 18/37. Minutes of Evidence to Moffat Commission – Evidence of H. S. Cooke, Acting DNL, 423–4. DNL, Box 323, File 84/20, 243, Local Government Commission, Statement of numbers of natives employed in proclaimed labour districts of Transvaal on 31 May 1920.

11 Interview with William Sebina Letlalo, Soweto, 10 Dec. 1979.

12 Cf. for example TAD, Municipal Co. Archives, Box 823, 18/37, Minutes of Evidence to Moffat Commission, Taberer 481.

13 DNL Box 323, File 84/243, Local Government Commission, Statement of numbers of natives . . . (the figures for the Rand have been extracted from the wider submissions made from the Transvaal).

14 DNL Box 2, 323, File 84/20/243, Replies to circular B.4/23 Chief Pass Officer to DNL, 29 Jan. 1923.

15 TAD, Municipal Co. Archives, Box 823 18/37 Minutes of Evidence to Moffat Commission. Evidence of H. S. Cooke, Acting DNL, 442.

16 Bureau of Census and Statistics, *Union Statistics for Fifty Years, Jubilee Issue 1910–1960*, H.24.

17 TAD, Municipal Co. Archives, Box 823 18/37 Minutes of Evidence to Moffat Commission. Evidence of P. W. McKie, representing Transvaal Mines' Traders Association, 576.

18 The Johannesburg Joint Council of Europeans and Natives, *The Native in Industry*, p. 2, and Report of the Wages Committee, 19 Aug. 1921, cited in N. Kagan, 'African settlements in the Johannesburg area 1903–23', M.A. thesis, University of the Witwatersrand, January 1978, p. 99.

19 For example, Mun. Co. Arch. 823 18/37 Mins. of Evid. to Moffat Commission, 230, Msimang, 151–2 Maxexe, 131, Ncayiya, 565, Chake.

20 DNL 310 File 125/19/48 Native Wages.

21 Evidence to Moffat Commission, Cooke, 442–3.

22 See Note 29.

23 P. L. Bonner, 'The 1920 mineworkers' strike: a preliminary account', in B. Bozzoli, *Labour, Townships and Protest* (Johannesburg, 1979), p. 279.

24 Evidence to Moffat Commission, Chake, 565–6.

25 *Ibid.*, Msimahg, 229.

26 *Ibid.*, Phooko, 317; see also Filiso, 94.

27 *Ibid.*, Taberer, 481.

28 *Ibid.*, Dunjwa, 218.

29 *Ibid.*, Cooke, 459; see also above p. 275.

30 *Ibid.*, Msimang, 229–30.

31 *Ibid.*, 2.

32 *Ibid.*, Chake, 565.

33 *Ibid.*, Ncayiya, 135–6.

34 Laclau, *Politics*, pp. 100–11.

35 D. Gaitskell, 'Laundry, liquor and "playing ladish": African women in Johannesburg 1903–39', unpublished paper, 22 June 1978.

36 TAD, Municipal Co. Archives, Box 823, 18/37, Minutes of Evidence to Moffat Commission.

37 *Ibid.*, evidence of Msimang.

38 *Ibid.*, 338/10/F164 Klipspruit Disturbances 1919, Petition by Ellen Leeuw and 122 native women to the Mayor of Johannesburg, 23 March 1910, 'It is well known that our husbands are getting very low wages and cannot afford to discharge their liabilities unless they get our assistances'. 'All classes of work formerly performed [by women] are now in the hands of men – e.g. kitchen or general servants work, washing and ironing, eating houses for natives, nursing in native hospitals.'

39 Interview with William Sebina Letlalo, Soweto, 10 Dec. 1979; TAD, Municipal Co. Archives, Box 823, 18/37, Minutes of Evidence to Moffat Commission, Charlotte Maxexe, who links the temptation to brew illicit liquor to the reduction of jobs available to women; DNL Box 313 File Part 125/19/48. Industrial unrest 1919 Benoni, H. J. Mgqamo to Inspector NAD Benoni, 30 May 1919, Encl. R. M. Tladi's speech, 2 May 1919; DNL 323 File 84/20/243, Local Government Commission, Evidence H. S. Bell; DNL 281 446/17/D48, Native unrest, Native Detective Sergeant Moorosi to Det. H/Const. Hoffman, 21 June 1918 – speech by Charlotte Maxexe.

40 TAD, Municipal Co. Archives 823 18/37, Minutes of Evidence to Moffat Commission, Benjamin Phooko, 318.

41 DNL enc. pamphlet signed H. L. Bud-M'belle and C. Mabaso, April 1919.

42 C. van Onselen, *Chibaro* (London, 1976), pp. 231–2; TAD, Municipal Co. Archives, 823, 18/37, Minutes of Evidence to Moffat Commission, H. S. Cooke.

43 DNL 309 125/19/48 Anti-Pass Agitation, Cooke to Natives of the Witwatersrand. For other examples, the Pass Officer, Boksburg (19 Dec. 1919) argued, 'As many natives are ignorant and uncivilised this is necessary as an identification and check against crime, and a protection against Europeans'; Protector of Natives (11 Dec. 1919), 'The pass system protects them against unscrupulous employers and when a dispute over length and conditions of service arise. Also in event of accident or demise it makes it possible to inform relatives and remit money.'

44 DNL 320 301/19/17, Evidence to Inter-Departmental Pass Laws Committee, Inspector (Central) NAD Johannesburg to DNC, 19 Dec. 1919.

45 TAD, Municipal Co. Archives, 823 18/37, Minutes of Evidence to Moffat Commission, W. C. Lawrence, Acting Chief Pass Officer, 342.

46 DNL Box 313 File Part 125/19/48, Industrial Unrest 1919 Benoni, H. S. Mgqamo to Inspector NAD Benoni, 30 May 1919, encl. R. M. Tladi's speech, 2 May 1919, Benoni.

47 DNL 313 File Part 125/19/48, Industrial Unrest 1919 Benoni, H. S. Mgqamo to Inspector NAD Benoni, 30 May 1919, encl. R. M. Tladi's speech, 2 May 1919. SN Box 85 527/17/F164(1) Transvaal Native Unrest (1) Stubbs Commission, Letanka's statement.

48 DNL 313 File Part 125/19/48, Industrial unrest in Benoni, Mgqamo.

49 See, for example, DNL 309 Part File 125/19/48 Vrededorp Riot.

50 See below, p. 302.

51 Inspector NAD Krugersdorp to DNL, 17 Dec. 1919.

52 DNL 313 File Part 125/19/48, Industrial Unrest in Benoni, Mgqamo to Inspector NAD Benoni, 30 May 1919, encl. Tladi's speech 2 May 1919; for other evidence to the same effect, see Mgqamo to Inspector NAD Benoni, 30 March 1919.

53 338/19 F164 Klipspruit Disturbances 1919 encl. L. T. Mvabasa to DNL, 1 Aug. 1910.

54 DNL 281 446/1710D48, Police report on IWA meeting, 27 June 1918; 'A native Police who could neither read or write happened to meet one Alfred Barnabas, a clerk at Kleinfontein G. M. Co. Ltd., an exempted man. The Police asked him for his special. He told him that he carried an exemption which he produced to him. The Police insisted on him producing a special "not this", then took him to the Benoni Charge Office . . . [and claimed] he had refused to produce [the exemption]. He was charged and convicted accordingly.' Mgqamo also gave details of two similar cases. DNL, Box 313 File Part 125/19048, Industrial Unrest in Benoni. For the divisive effects of this pattern of recruiting, C. van Onselen, 'The role of collaborators in the Rhodesian mining industry 1900–1935', *African Affairs*, 72, 289 (October 1973).

55 DNL 320 301/19/72, Evidence to Inter-Departmental Pass Laws Committee, *passim*.

56 *Ibid.*, Inspector Central NAD Johannesburg to DNL, 19 Dec. 1919; Pass Officer Roodepoort to DNL, 18 Dec. 1919; W. Walker, Inspector NAD Johannesburg to DNL, 6 Jan. 1920.

57 Interview Letlalo, 10 Dec. 1979.

58 S.N. Box 85, 527/17/F164(1) Stubbs Commission, Transvaal Native Unrest, Letanka.

59 N. Kagan, 'Settlements', pp. 35–66, 111–2, 115; A. Proctor, 'Class struggle, segregation and the city: a history of Sophiatown 1905–1940', in B. Bozzoli (ed.), *Labour, Townships and Protest* (Johannesburg, 1979), p. 53.

60 *Ibid.*, Kagan, 'Settlements', pp. 35–6, 93; DNL 281 446/17/48, Report on SANNC meeting, 19 June 1918.

61 Kagan, 'Settlements', p. 101.

62 338/19 F164 Klipspruit Disturbances 1919, encl. Supplementary Report of the Parks and Estates Committee on the Klipspruit Disturbances, Minutes of 383rd meeting, 27 Jan. 1920.

63 Kagan, 'Settlements', p. 101.

64 *Ibid.*, 92.

65 *Ibid.*, 64, 95; 338/19 F164 Klipspruit Disturbances encl. Evidence of H. S. Cooke, Assistant DNL; *ibid.*, encl. L. T. Mvabasa to DNL, 1 Aug. 1910.

66 *Ibid.*; *ibid.* encl. evidence of H. S. Cooke; Kagan, 'Settlements', pp. 156–7, 93.

67 DNL 323 File 84/20/243 Local Government Commission, Evidence of H. S. Bell, Native Sub-Commissioner Witwatersrand, n.d.; DNL . . . Report by Detective Brandon, 30 April 1919; DNL Box 313 File Part 125/19/48, Industrial Unrest Benoni, H. S. Mgqamo to Inspector NAD Benoni, 30 May 1919, and encl. R. M. Tladi's speech, 2 May 1919.

68 DNL 323 File 84/20/243 Local Government Commission, Evidence of H. S. Bell.

69 Kagan, 'Settlements', pp. 35–7, 87–9.

70 DNL 323 File 84/20/243 Local Government Commission, Evidence of H. S. Bell.

71 *Ibid.*; Kagan, 'Settlements', p. 45.

72 Kagan, 'Settlements', pp. 67–74, 135–6; Proctor, 'Class struggle', p. 53.

73 Kagan, 'Settlements', pp. 41, 52, 115; Proctor, 'Class Struggle', p. 53.

74 Kagan, 'Settlements', pp. 42, 65.

75 *Ibid.*, p. 42, who cites £3–£4 a month; TAD, Municipal Co. Archives, Evidence to Moffat Commission, 296, Jackson Koza who cites 15s a month.

76 Kagan, 'Settlements', pp. 46–50; TAD, Municipal Co. Archives, Evidence to Moffat Commission, R. W. Msimang, E. Chake, C. Maxexe, H. Ncayiya.

77 *Ibid.*, 142, 152–3; my thanks to Doug Hindson for drawing my attention to this point.

78 DNL Box 323 File 84/20/243, Local Government Commission, Parks and Estates Committee, Minutes, 21 July 1919.

79 *Ibid.*, H. Bell, Native Sub-Commissioner, Witwatersrand, to DNL, 26 June 1920.

80 *Ibid.*, L. Botha to Administrator, Transvaal, 11 Sept. 1918.

81 Kagan, 'Settlements', pp. 80–81.

82 S.N. 85 527/17/F164(1) interview between F. S. Malan, Acting Minister Native Affairs and delegation of natives on Reef, 12 Dec. 1918; TAD, Municipal Co. Archives, Mins of Evidence to Moffat Commission, Msimang 230, C. Maxexe 153, I. Bud-M'belle 275, Rev. H. R. Ncayiya, 132, Msane, 401, J. W. O'Hara, 371; C. van Onselen, *Studies in the Social and Economic History of the Witwatersrand*, Vol. 1 (London, 1982), Chap. 4, 'Johannesburg's Jehus, 1890–1914'; Vol. 2, Chap. 2, 'AmaWasha: the Zulu washermen's guild of the Witwatersrand'.

83 Kagan, 'Settlements', p. 60.

84 338/19/F164 Klipspruit Disturbances 1919, enc. L. T. Mvabasa to DNL, 1 Aug.
    1910; TAD, Municipal Co. Archives, Evidence to Moffat Commission, Rev.
    H. R. Ncayiya, 129. According to Kagan ('Settlements', p. 63), in 1906 16
    applications for trading stands had been granted, 11 for African eating-houses and 6
    for church stands.
85 For example, TAD, Municipal Co. Archives, Evidence to Moffat, Ncayiya, 132,
    Cook, 447.
86 DNL 323 File 84/20/243 Evidence of S. Bell; Kagan, 'Settlements', pp. 89, 95;
    see also 338/19/F164 Klipspruit Disturbances, encl. L. T. Mvabasa to DNL, 1
    Aug. 1910.
87 Kagan, 'Settlements', p. 35; TAD, Municipal Co. Archives, Evidence to Moffat
    Commission, Benjamin S. Dlepu.
88 Kagan, 'Settlements', pp. 155–8.
89 T. D. Mweli Skota, *The African Yearly Register* (Johannesburg, 1932), pp. 174,
    254; TAD, Municipal Co. Archives, Evidence to Moffat Commission, evidence
    Moffat, 539.
90 DNL Box 323, File 84/20/243, Chief Pass Officer, Johannesburg to DNL
    Johannesburg, 29 Jan. 1923.
91 Quoted in C. van Onselen, *Studies in the Social and Economic History of the
    Witwatersrand*, Volume 2, *New Nineveh*, Chapter 1, 'The witches of surburbia', p.
    33.
92 Evidence to Moffat Commission, S. M. Maghato, 540.
93 For example, *ibid.*, R. W. Msimang, 228–9.
94 *Ibid.*, I. Bud-M'belle, 279.
95 *Ibid.*, I. Bud-M'belle, 262; S. M. Maghato, 542.
96 B. Willan, Chapter 9 above, pp. 242–3.
97 Laclau, *Politics*, p. 103.
98 Evidence to Moffat Commission, 324, Plaatjes.
99 *Ibid.*, 320–1, Phooko.
100 *Ibid.*, J. W. O'Hara, Johannesburg City Council, 360–1.
101 Johnstone, *Class*, pp. 168–70.
102 DNL 309 125/19/48, newspaper cutting.
103 Simons, *Class and Colour*, p. 230; see also DNL 206 1697/17/17, Report of TNC
    meeting, 13 Feb. 1920.
104 R. H. Davies, *Capital, State and White Labour in South Africa 1900–1960* (New
    Jersey, 1979), pp. 83–4 – see especially Smuts's statement to Parliament in 1922,
    'The fear that obsessed me above all things [during the course of the armed struggle
    of March 1922] was that owing to the wanton provocation of the revolutionaries,
    there might be a wild, *uncontrollable* outbreak among the natives' (emphasis added).
105 DNL, Brown manilla file, Native unrest reports from Town Inspectors and others,
    E. Berg to DNL, 28 May 1918.
106 DNL, Brown manilla file, Native unrest reports from Town Inspectors and others,
    E. Berg to DNL, 28 May 1928; see also Evidence to Moffat Commission, Alfred
    Poolson, Manager, Vrededorp Sanitary Compound, 160–4; *ibid.*, E. C. Berg,
    Acting Town Inspector Native Affairs.
107 *Ibid.*, Berg to DNL, 1 June 1918.
108 *Ibid.*, Number of natives in the employ of the Johannesburg Municipality; evidence
    to Moffat 13–41, Nonjane, 'Willie', 'Tony', 'Frank'.
109 TAD, Municipal Co. Archives, Evidence to Moffat Commission, E. C. Berg;

A. Poolson (the sequence of events given by Berg and Poolson do not tally – where there are disagreements I have followed Berg).

110 DNL, 281 446/17/D48 Native unrest; Native Detective Moorosi to Det. H. Const. Hoffman, 21 June 1918 – speech by Letanka.

111 *Ibid.*, Report on meeting of TNC, 10 June 1918, Ebenezer Hall; Evidence to Moffat Commission, 267–8, I. Bud-M'belle.

112 *Ibid.*, 261, A. Mzimba.

113 *Ibid.*, 221–3, H. Dunjwa.

114 *Ibid.*, 241–2, R. W. Msimang.

115 See notes 125, 126, 127; DNL 281/446/171D48, Deputy Commissioner of Police Johannesburg to DNL, 26 June 1918.

116 TAD, Municipal Co. Archives, Evidence to Moffat Commission, 269–271, I. Bud-M'belle.

117 *Ibid.*, Deputy Commissioner CID Transvaal Division to DNL, 21 June 1918; reports by Native Detective Sergeant Moorosi, 21 June 1918; G. S. Broodryk, 21 June 1918; Sergeant Mbusani, 21 June 1918; Constable J. J. Jordaan, n.d.; Sergeant J. Bland and two others headed, 'Details of Mass Meeting of the Johannesburg Natives 19.6.18', and 'Transvaal National Native Congress and Industrial Workers of Africa'; for Mvabasa and the IWA, see F. A. Johnstone, 'The IWA on the Rand: socialist organising among black workers on the Rand, 1917–1918', in Bozzoli, *Labour*, p. 260.

118 DNL 281 446/17/D48. Report on 'Transvaal National Native Congress and Industrial Workers of Africa'.

119 *Ibid.*, Native Detective Sergeant R. Moorosi to Hoffman, 28 June 1918.

120 *Ibid.*, Deputy Commissioner of Police Johannesburg District to DNL, 26 June 1918, encl. statement Major Bell, Basuto Boss Boy, n.d.

121 TAD, Municipal Co. Archives, Evidence to Moffat Commission, 381–2, Samuel Hanrock.

122 *Ibid.*, 271–2, I. Bud-M'belle.

123 DNL, Brown manilla folder, E. Berg, Town Inspector to DNL, 13 June 1918; *ibid.*, 27 June 1918.

124 TAD, Municipal Co. Archives, Evidence to Moffat Commission, Taberer, 477, Filiso, 90.

125 *Ibid.*, Dunjwa, 223–5; DNL 281/17/D48, Native Detective Sergeant Moorosi to Det. Head Constable Hoffman, 28 June 1918.

126 *Ibid.*

127 *Ibid*; Report of ISL meeting, 25 June 1918, under heading International Socialist League, n.d.

128 DNL 281 446/17/D48 Native unrest, N.D. Sergeant Moorosi to Det. Head Const. Hoffman, 30 June 1918.

129 *Ibid.*, report on meeting, 28 June 1918, headed 'The Transvaal National Native Congress meeting connected with other societies'.

130 *Ibid*; N. Det. Sergeant Moorosi to Hoffman, 29 June 1918.

131 Cited in Willan, 'Class relations', 207.

132 DNL 281 446/17/D48 Native Unrest, Moorosi to Hoffman, 30 June 1918.

133 *Ibid.*, Report on meeting, 30 June 1918, headed 'Transvaal Native Congress and Industrial Workers of Africa', n.d.

134 DNL, brown manilla folder, E. Berg to DNL, 2 July 1918.

135 *Ibid.*, Berg to DNL, 3 July 1918; Evidence to Moffat Commission, Cooke, 431;

G. St Leger Devenish, 173–5; Weaver, 180–2; S. K. Mackenzie, 186–8, 'John', 60–1; 'Richard', 72–6.

136 *Ibid.*, 4–6.

137 DNL 294 243/18/48, Deputation of representative natives to General Botha encl. Report of preliminary meeting, 24 July 1918.

138 Evidence to Moffat Commission, S. Msane, 405.

139 *Ibid.*, 412; see also Kagan, 'Settlements', 98.

140 DNL 243/8/48 (8) Deputation of representative natives to Gen. Botha, 9 July 1918, encl. Notes for Minister's interview with native delegates.

141 DNL 310, 125/19/48, Johannesburg Chamber of Commerce, Report of Executive Committee, 24 Jan. 1920.

142 DNL 243/8/48 (8) Deputation of Representative Natives to Gen. Botha, encl. DNA to DNL, 4 Sept. 1918.

143 Cited by Willan, 'Class relations', p. 206.

144 P. L. Bonner, 'The 1920 black mineworkers' strike: a preliminary account', in Bozzoli, *Labour*, p. 277.

145 S.N. 85 527/17/F164 (1). Transvaal native unrest (Stubbs Commission), Interview Malan and others with TNC delegation, 12 Dec. 1918.

146 This period has as yet not been adequately covered in my researches. I rely on Johnstone: *Class, Race and Gold*, pp. 176–7.

147 DNL 125/19048 Anti-Pass Agitation April 1919 encl. *Abantu-Batho*, 3 April 1919; see also SN 85 527/17/F164 (1), Transvaal Native Unrest, Stubbs (1); *ibid.*, M. Natlab to Natives Cape Town, 31 March 1919.

148 Johnstone, *Class*, 177, fails adequately to answer this.

149 DNL 309 125/19/48 encl. *Rand Daily Mail* (early April 1919).

150 SN 85 527/17/164 (1), Transvaal Native unrest (1). Stubbs Commission, Minutes of meeting between TNC delegation and government officials headed by N. J. de Wet, Minister of Justice.

151 *Ibid.*, Affidavit W. C. Lawrence, Acting Chief Pass Officer, 1 April 1919.

152 *Star*, 31 March 1919, quoted by Roux, *Time Longer Than Rope*, p. 117; DNL 309 125/19/48, statement showing class of natives concerned in recent 'no pass agitation'; *ibid.* Telegram DNL to NAD Pretoria, 1 April 1919.

153 S.N. 216 389/19/F473, Teleg. Natlab to Natives, Pretoria, 1 April 1919.

154 DNL Telegram DNL to Dept. Native Affairs, Cape Town, 2 April 1919, 11.20 p.m.

155 Johnstone, *Class*, p. 177.

156 *Star*, 4 April 1919, quoted by Roux, *Time Longer Than Rope*, pp. 119–20; DNL 309 125/19/48 Anti-Pass Agitation, April 1919; Sergeant F. Gallop to Officer L/C SAP Western area, 9 April 1919; *ibid.*, statement showing class of natives concerned in recent no pass agitation; SN 216 389/19/F473, Statement M. Sibisi, 14 April 1919; DNL Tel. Natlab to Natives Cape Town, 10 April 1919.

157 SN 216 389/19/F473, C. Loftus (inspector, SAP, Benoni) to District Commissioner, Boksburg, 4 April 1919.

158 *Ibid.*, Wilfred Jali, C.I.D. Maraisburgh to Mr King, April 1919; *Cape Times*, 7 April 1919.

159 DNL Inspector Rawlinson NAD Boksburg to DNL, 28 April 1919; *ibid.*, Location Superintendent Boksburg Location to Inspector NAD Boskburg, 29 April 1919; *ibid.*, Det. Head Constable H. St O. O. Brandon to District Commissioner SAP, Boksburg, 30 April 1919.

160 SN 85 527/17/F164 (1), Transvaal unrest, Stubbs Commission, teleg. Natives Pretoria to Natives Cape Town, 1 April 1919.
161 DNL 309 125/19/48, Statement showing the class of natives concerned in the recent 'no pass agitation'.
162 DNL 206 697/14/76, Interview Pritchard with TNC delegates, 1 July 1919.
163 *Ibid.*, Report of TNC meeting, 6 July 1919.
164 *Ibid.*, Report of TNC meetings, 8 July and 10 July 1919.
165 *Ibid.*, Report of meeting, 22 July 1919.
166 SN 85 527/17/F164 (1) Transvaal Unrest, Stubbs Commission, Statement by Detective Kleinbooi, CID Johannesburg, 21 May 1919.
167 DNL 206 1697/17/76 Report of meeting of 8 Feb. 1920.
168 *Ibid.*, Report of meeting, 20 Feb. 1920; *ibid.*, 22 Feb. 1920.
169 *Ibid.*, 20 Feb. 1920.
170 *Ibid.*, Report of Native Strike meeting, 20 Feb. 1920.
171 *Ibid.*, report of meeting, 22 Feb. 1920.
172 Justice Department, Det. Constable Brandon to District Commissioner SAP, 9 Feb. 1920.

CHAPTER TWELVE

'Moralizing leisure time':

The transatlantic connection and black Johannesburg 1918–1936

Tim Couzens

> He scans the world with calm and fearless eyes,
> Conscious within of powers long since forgot;
> At every step, new man-made barriers rise
> To bar his progress – but he heeds them not.
> He stands erect, though tempests round him crash,
> Though thunder bursts and billows surge and roll;
> He laughs and forges on, while lightnings flash
> Along the rocky pathway to his goal.
> Impassive as a Sphinx, he stares ahead –
> Foresees new empires rise and old ones fall;
> While caste-mad nations lust for blood to shed,
> He sees God's finger writing on the wall.
> With soul awakened, wise and strong he stands,
> Holding his destiny within his hands.
>
> James Edward McCall, 'The New Negro'[1]

Contact between black South Africans and America has a long history: American Board missionaries came to Natal in 1835; a number of black Americans visited South Africa in the nineteenth century and several South African blacks, including John Dube and J. Msikinya,[2] went to be educated in the United States; and the foundation of the African Methodist Episcopal Church in South Africa in the 1890s established a direct link with the mother church in the U.S.A. It is, however, with the period after the First World War that this paper is concerned. Martin Legassick has demonstrated this to be a period in which 'the consolidation of a new liberalism was needed' urgently in place of the previous 'rather disparate and empiricist thinking on native policy by individual liberals'.[3] Liberalism, he suggests, was 'a force trying on the one hand to minimise or disguise the conflictual and coercive aspects of the social structure, and on the other to convince selected Africans that the grievances they felt could be ameliorated through reforms which liberals could promulgate'. He suggests that 'The rise of modern South African liberalism as a specific social doctrine . . . stems on the one hand from an attempt by liberals to demonstrate that the specific forms of oppression in the country could be eliminated by the creation of a society based on the principles of political and economic liberalism, and on the other hand from the development of social forces (secondary industry of a particular kind) which appeared to create the basis for such a change'. The years 1917 to 1920 constituted a period of considerable militancy amongst black workers and, to some extent, the urban black petty bourgeoisie, which culminated in the African mineworkers' strike of 1920. The period immediately following was one in which the petty bourgeoisie were, in Philip Bonner's words, 'completely bought off',[4] while rising real wages in the towns and growing unemployment in the reserves led to 'the displacement of agitation to the farms and to the black rural areas which paved the way for the I.C.U. in its more populist, rural based millenarian form'.[5] Legassick and Baruch Hirson have both pointed in different ways to the institutions and groups which were created in response to this militancy. Key amongst these institutions were the Joint Councils for Bantu and Europeans founded in 1921 as a direct result of American intervention.[6]

In her will in 1909 an American, Miss Caroline Phelps-Stokes, left almost £1 million 'for education of Negroes, both in Africa and the United States, North American Indians and the needy and deserving white students'.[7] A survey of black education in the United States was conducted in 1913 and 1914 by Dr Jesse Jones, who had served for eight years at Hampton Institute, one of the major colleges devoted to black education in the United States since the latter part of the nineteenth century. It was decided that a similar survey should be undertaken in Africa and Jones headed this, most of the funding being supplied by the Phelps-Stokes Trustees. After travelling through Africa, two members of the Commission arrived in South Africa early in 1921. They were Dr Hollenbeck, a white, and James E. Kwegyir Aggrey, born in the Gold Coast, who had spent more than twenty years in America, first as a student, then as a teacher.

Aggrey's tour of South Africa caused a sensation. Everywhere he went he was received enthusiastically by initially sceptical whites and blacks alike. His message was primarily one of racial peace, of mutual cooperation between white and black. D. D. T. Jabavu, lecturer at the South African Native College, Fort Hare, was among the most impressed, writing of his 'captivating personality and his versatility as a public speaker'.[8] Jabavu wrote that Aggrey had, without doubt, 'done more than any other visitor I know of, in the brief space of time, to persuade people in our circumstances of the necessities of racial cooperation between white and black'.[9] Aggrey was to be offered the Professorship of Sociology and Education at Fort Hare, a post he eventually reluctantly declined.

Aggrey's stance was not unlike that of Booker T. Washington, the famous founder of Tuskegee, the agricultural-industrial college for blacks founded in Alabama in 1875. The main thrust of Washington's doctrine was the belief that what black people in the South of the United States needed was practical education, 'a foundation in education, industry and property', and for this 'they could better afford to struggle than for political preferment'.[10] In his famous address at the Atlanta Exposition he propounded one of his most famous metaphors. 'In all things that are purely social,' he told his audience of black and white, 'we can be as separate as the fingers, yet one as the hands in all things essential to mutual progress . . . . Nearly sixteen million of hands [i.e. the hands of the black American population] will aid you in pulling the load upward, or they will pull against you the load downward.'[11] His autobiography *Up From Slavery* was one of the most popular books read by South African blacks, and an edition was even published within South Africa by a South African publishing firm.

Washington was strongly opposed by some of his fellow Americans. Most prominent of these was W. E. B. Du Bois, whose name became known after his book *The Souls of the Black Folk* was published in 1903. In 1905 Du Bois helped inaugurate a meeting at Buffalo, New York, in the first stage of what became known as the Niagara Movement. He preached racial equality and political involvement in order to achieve it. 'We will not be satisfied,' he said in his 1905 address, 'to take one jot or tittle less than our full manhood rights. We claim for ourselves every single right that belongs to a free-born American, political, civil and social; and until we get these rights we will never cease to protest and assail the ears of America. The battle we wage is not for ourselves alone, but for all true Americans.'[12] In 1910 Du Bois founded *The Crisis*, as the monthly organ of the National Association for the Advancement of Colored People (NAACP). Less intellectual, more populist than Du Bois, but equally implacably anti-Washington was Marcus Garvey, a Jamaican who came to the United States in 1916. In the early twenties Garvey led a 'Back to Africa' movement which counted millions of supporters and which swept up the black population of America in a fever of expectancy.[13]

Aggrey's style, however, resembled Washington's in both doctrine and metaphor. Thus he calmed South African whites and gave hope to 'progressive' blacks. He encouraged whites and blacks to cooperate in terms echoing the Atlanta Exposition address of his mentor – though his terms were slightly more demanding. 'We [the natives] did not know we had any rights in South Africa. Now we know it and we want them. This newly awakened passion is a Niagara Falls and will engulf you, or it may be a dynamo to drive the wheels of a new civilization.'[14] His best-known parable in South Africa was that of the 'piano keys': 'You can play a tune of sorts on the white keys, and you can play a tune of sorts on the black keys, but for harmony you must use both the black and white.'[15] This, for instance, inspired another version, called 'A Game of Chess', in the pages of *Ilanga lase Natal* in 1924 by a local poet who went under the pseudonym of 'P.Q.R'.[16]

'Neither will win,' the watchers say
  Now that the contest starts,
'For Black men move without their heads,
  And White without their hearts.'

'And if one shall advance,' they said,
  'So much as one short pace,
His fellow-men will shun him then
  A traitor to the race.'

'You wooden men give up the game
  For what are all these squares
But black and white and black again,
  The pattern of your cares?'

The Chessmen quiver into life,
  For love has conquered pride,
Those that were angry face to face
  Are quiet side by side.

Partly as a result of the visit of Aggrey and Jones and influenced by the ideas of the Inter-Racial Committees of the American South, in 1921 a group of whites and blacks set up the Joint Councils, inter-racial discussion societies dedicated to fostering greater understanding between racial groups. One of the main participants in the Joint Councils explained their function:

> The relations between the Europeans and the Natives are today more strained than they have been for more than a generation, and unless the temper of both races is altered, we are heading for disaster. The greatest need is for an increase in the number of Europeans and Natives who have confidence in each other, and who can cooperate to avoid conflict.
>
> The best means of securing this is to be found in the Joint Councils of Europeans and Natives in which Europeans and Natives work together to remove causes of irritation, and to improve racial relations.[17]

Aggrey's own effect on the black elite had been startling and was clearly perceptible to the whites in his audiences. His biographer gives us a picture of Aggrey in action:

> In the evening of April 19th a great meeting was held in the Cinema Hall at Marabastad, the Native section of the city, under the auspices of the Pretoria Native Welfare Society. More than a thousand persons crowded the hall, the heat was intense, the atmosphere suffocating. Mr Magatho, a Wesleyan local preacher and President of the Native Congress, occupied the chair and spoke with a good deal of heat against the Whites in general and the Government in particular. . . . The audience became

excited, there was loud applause, and sometimes the clamour caused a shiver to pass through the twenty or so white people who were present. . . . Then Aggrey arose, and in a few minutes held them in the hollow of his hand as he talked about his own life and the loyalty and patience of the Blacks. He uttered no condemnation of the Whites and pleaded that the Blacks should make themselves indispensable. 'Many imagine that all Whites are bad,' he said, 'that you have not a single friend among them; but I have found that you have more friends than you think.' He besought Blacks and Whites to have patience – it would work miracles. 'We Africans must, like infants, learn to stand before we can walk, and to walk before we can run.' He insisted that Whites and Blacks have need of each other.[18]

As Legassick points out, the same group of people who formed the Joint Councils sponsored other 'liberal' institutions specifically designed to cater for, and encourage, the 'moderate' blacks. Hence the Bantu Men's Social Centre (BMSC) (1924)[19] and the South African Institute of Race Relations (1929) and a number of other social-welfare institutions such as the Helping Hand Club for Native Girls and the Bridgman Memorial Hospital (a maternity hospital for black women). In the universities, departments of Bantu Studies were formed. In 1918 the University of Cape Town appointed a Professor of Bantu Philology and in 1921 A. Radcliffe-Brown became Professor of Social Anthropology; in 1921 Rev. A. T. Bryant was appointed Research Fellow and Lecturer in Zulu History at the University of the Witwatersrand, and in 1923 C. M. Doke was made Senior Lecturer in Bantu Philology and Phonetics and Mrs A. W. Hoernlé, Research Fellow and Lecturer in Social Anthropology. In Pretoria, at the Transvaal University College, Dr Edgar Brookes taught similar courses. The University of the Witwatersrand started publishing its magazine *Bantu Studies* in 1921 with Rheinallt Jones as editor.[20] The Chamber of Mines began its newspaper *Umteteli wa Bantu* in 1920 to counter the ANC newspaper *Abantu-Batho*. The original function of *Umteteli wa Bantu* was clearly stated in an editorial in 1924:

Rather more than four years ago *Umteteli* first appeared to educate white and black and to point out their respective and their common duties. At that time much of the Native press was bitterly anti-white in policy . . . the need for a mediator was felt by a number of far-seeing natives, men prominent among their people and gravely concerned for their people's welfare, and it was due to their representations that this paper was launched.[21]

Nor were the formal 'liberal' institutions documented by Legassick, Hirson and Bonner the only response to militancy. This paper hopes to show how culture and entertainment were also used as auxiliary forces in this context of 'defusing Native passions': conversely, a proper understanding of the literature, the drama, the music, the arts and other related cultural forms of this time needs to take this process into account.

Once again an American connection reveals itself, for the American Board missionaries were by this time active in Johannesburg in many fields. Aside from Bridgman, who had a large hand in setting up the Bantu Men's Social Centre (BMSC), the most prominent was Rev. Ray Phillips who was also very active in that organisation. Phillips's book *The Bantu Are Coming*, published in 1930,[22] a classic of its kind, is infinitely revealing. It opens with an attack on heathenism and witchcraft, in the words of General Smuts, which Phillips quotes, the 'one perpetual nightmare on the African continent'.[23] He then goes on to describe the challenge and wonderful opportunity for a Christian missionary in Johannesburg. Painting a colourful picture of the typical mine compound on a Sunday where '4 000 men are dressing, washing, putting on their best attire for the day' and where he and Bridgman conduct services, he contemplates God's wisdom in attracting so many to one place.

> As we sit facing these scores of young men, two or three random thoughts pass through our minds. First of all, how many clergymen in white churches would be quite willing to have their churches packed, as this one is packed, with virile young men! How strategic is Johannesburg for reaching, and for good, the young men of the whole African sub-continent! These young men will return home at the end of their year of work at the mines. Many will go back to heathen villages in far corners of the land where, perhaps, a white man's face has never been seen. There the seed here sown will bear fruit – a little bush school started, a sod and grass church erected, and, behold, a Christian village! Again, the thought comes pressing in – how fortunate we are to be on the inside of this thing, to be allowed to lend a hand at transforming a people, to be one of the channels through which the Almighty works to bring His will to pass in this great continent! There's nothing else like it for satisfaction.[24]

God, then, works in mysterious ways. Johannesburg has been created to draw men closer to God! There were problems, however: the 1913 Land Act, the World War, the recession and depression between 1920 and 1922 had all combined to cause a large influx of population into the cities, vast social problems and, in the words of a visitor at the time, slums which were 'absolutely the worst in the world'.[25] Phillips saw his role as missionary and social worker as twofold. Firstly to awaken whites to these problems: according to C. T. Loram in the Foreword, Phillips believed 'that the white people of South Africa . . . are fundamentally fairminded and willing to be just to the natives' but 'are ignorant or unmindful of the depths of native feeling' and so he sought 'to rouse them to a sense of the really dangerous position of the present racial situation in South Africa'.[26] Secondly, to counteract the work of agitators (communists, 'Moscow emissaries' and others whom he frequently excoriates through the book) by ameliorating the conditions which breed such 'discontent' and 'agitation'. He saw the great task of the missionary as being 'to devise a "Social Gospel" ' solving 'the whole great problem of *moralizing the leisure time* of natives in City and country alike'.[27] To counteract the city slums, the reformatories full of children and the lack of schools (only 25 per cent of black children of school-going age were at school in 1929), institutions like the Boy Scouts (the Pathfinders) and Girl Guides (the Wayfarers) and Sunday schools and choirs were begun. By 1920 Athletics Leagues had been set up and the head teacher of one night school's 'method of overcoming the hostility that existed between his school and various neighbouring ones has been to buy a football and to organise regular matches in which all participate'.[28] Two kinds of adults had to be catered for: the blacks who lived and worked in the city and the mine labourers in the compounds. Each presented a different and difficult problem.

In the designing of entertainment, the 'moralizing of leisure time', for the city blacks we find the beginnings of the channelling of literature and drama of this period. The passage must be quoted at length because it specifically links the creation of an important institution in the history of black literature, drama and art with the unrest of 1917–20. Phillips wrote:

> It was in 1918 that we found the keen-witted native leaders at their wits' end in Johannesburg, ready to try anything. Repeated representations had been made to the Government on the land question, the Pass Laws, Housing, etc. Deputations had even been sent to England to voice the feelings of the oppressed peoples to the King himself. But the petitioners had failed in every quarter.
>
> A strike was organised at the Village Main Reef Mine. Five thousand native workers refused to work on a certain morning. A lightning strike! It was only on the third day that they were forced back to their work at the point of the bayonet. The strike failed of its purpose – but it was a glorious success in the minds of the leaders. Why? Why, because it demonstrated that *they could do it*! The white man had said the natives couldn't organize effectively. They couldn't keep their mouths shut long enough to stage a strike. The secret would leak out because the natives were such chatterers. But now they had shown that they could, and they were anxious to try this weapon again.
>
> A new strike was being talked about, but on a larger scale. We tried to gain the confidence of these embittered native leaders. They said to us, 'You are not wanted here. You had better go back home. There's not a white man in South Africa who cares the snap of his fingers for the black man. Peaceful measures have failed. We are being forced to try violence!'
>
> We persisted in cultivating their acquaintance, and were finally rewarded to the extent of being able to start a small debating and literary society.[29]

This was the Gamma Sigma Club, and that such an institution had the desired effect Phillips went on to testify:

> These meetings were a good thing for the native men. They began to see that things were not as simple as they looked, nor remedies so easily found. They discovered that the white man had many aspects of these questions to consider. And, most important, they learned that they had friends, many of them, among the white people. . . .
>
> As the result of the Gamma Sigma Club meetings, sentiment among the native leaders changed. One of the most bitter had been Mr M——. Well educated, he had been to England and seen the respectful treatment which men of his colour receive there. On his return to South Africa he saw again the colour line drawn hard and fast. When he spoke at some of the earlier meetings there was a hard bitterness about his

fiery speeches that made the cold shivers run up and down our backs. With a logic that no one could challenge, he painted the conditions of the black man with a brush dipped in gall. He could see no way out except through revolution. Mr M—— became much interested in these club meetings. He was usually present and took an increasingly prominent part in the discussions. As time went on a gradual change took place in his attitude.[30]

The Gamma Sigma Club continued to meet until the mid-thirties, becoming an integral part of the BMSC when it was built in 1924, though the Joint Councils did usurp some of the Club's functions and overshadowed it. Parallel to this Club, the BMSC organised free weekly cinemas and concerts, wherein boys and girls acquitted themselves 'with credit in music and dramatics'.[31]

The compounds, with up to 4 000 males in each – in all, 200 000 – provided a somewhat different problem. Church on Sunday was of course the prime way to occupy the compound dwellers, but 'We must capture the physical and mental life of these young men during six days of the week besides preaching the Gospel to them on the seventh', wrote Phillips.[32] At all times 'with the backing of the mine authorities',[33] the missionaries began their 'experiments'. Volley ball and football partly caught on, as it did for the town workers, but afternoon athletics were a failure because the large meal consumed at four-thirty by the miners after coming off shift militated against strenuous exercise following immediately after. Phillips and friends then turned to evening games such as 'Hunt the thimble' and 'Who's got the ring?' Finally, they hit on the solution of movies.

> The result was immediate and gratifying. The thousands gathered around the screen and showed their appreciation by filling the compounds so full of joyful sound that outsiders often decided that a riot was occurring. With amazed delight the happy crowds went off on trips on the modern magic carpet to other lands; saw the surf riders of Honolulu, and explorers in the Arctic, the reindeer of Lapland and the potter's wheel in India. They followed with quaking breath the adventures of some of the early pioneers among the Indians in Western America; saw King George go to open Parliament in his curious equipage. But they shook their heads at pictures of mining in England and America, showing white men at work with pick and shovel and drill: 'Ai kona! No, that is not right! Mfundisi is fooling us here! No white man works like that. Only black men!'[34]

Indeed, so gratifying were the results that the Chamber of Mines agreed to finance an overall scheme run by Phillips's mission to the tune of £1 500 for equipment and an annual expenditure of £5 000. Inside a year, 'clean, wholesome pictures were being shown regularly in each of the great compounds' – a mixture of 'topicals, interest and dramatic films, enlivened by comedies and acrobatic reels'. At least one 'native sketch', entitled 'A Zulu's Devotion', was shown, indicating the existence of films specially made for a local black market.[35] Elsewhere Phillips noted that 'every foot of film' was 'carefully censored'.[36] Phillips's greatest boast was his use of his movies as peacemaker during the Great Strike of 1922. According to his account, 200 000 black miners were cooped up all day, 'their animal energies accumulating day by day and with no outlet'. Frustrated by the failure of the blacks to rise (according to Phillips), the white strikers attacked the compound at the New Primrose Mine. The compound became a powder-keg awaiting the tiniest flash. Phillips rushed out to the mine and showed Charlie Chaplin movies. 'There was,' he proudly claimed, 'no murder that night at the New Primrose'.[37] Phillips was a city missionary, however. The rural areas did not come within his ambit, and rural blacks hardly seem to have come in for any 'moralized leisure time'.

Just as the BMSC and the Institute of Race Relations sprang from the Joint Councils and the American Board missionaries and other liberals, so a second generation of institutions and clubs derived from the BMSC and its sisters.

On 3 June 1934, 'Great National Thanksgiving Celebrations' were held with performances by a choir of 65 voices, speeches by Dr A. B. Xuma, R. V. Selope Thema and Mrs F. Bridgman, and a 'Great Dramatic Display'. The happening went under the title of the *Emancipation Centenary Celebration*, and revolved around a play, written 'at short notice' by R. R. R. Dhlomo, and the entire proceedings, including the play, were produced by his brother, Herbert Dhlomo.[38] This performance clearly grew out of the formation in June 1932 of the Bantu Dramatic Society, very much a child of the BMSC where all its performances were first held. In April 1933, its first production, *She Stoops to Conquer*, was heralded with a photograph of the cast headed by the caption, 'The Bantu are coming'.[39] The 1934 Emancipation play by Rolfes Dhlomo was 'performed by native children and adults, who made the past live by their realistic performance of the suffering of the American negroes on the slave market, in the cotton fields, and at home, until the joyful news of liberation'. All the music dealt with 'aspects of the struggle for freedom', and in his speech Dr Xuma said that 'it was a striking fact that the first slaves had been introduced into the United States in the same year that the Pilgrim Fathers arrived seeking religious freedom'. Both speakers paid tribute to the work of Wilberforce, Lincoln and others who had 'worked for the interest of humanity' but added that 'the negroes themselves had taken an active part in making the emancipation possible'. In the 'cooperation between black and white' Dr Xuma saw 'the origin of the present European–Native Joint Councils'. Mrs Bridgman established her legitimacy in her speech by saying that 'My father fought in the Civil War and my State was the first to admit Negroes to its university. I am proud of both these facts.'[40]

What is significant, however, about the description of the above activities and an examination of the programme is that, although the whole evening was designed to celebrate the centenary of 1834 (when Britain abolished slavery), *almost the entire proceedings concentrated on American slavery*! Clearly, identification was with the freeing of American slaves in 1863, not with the freeing of South African slaves in 1834. This seems to be a remarkable bias in consciousness.[41] One has to wait for Peter Abrahams' novel *Wild Conquest* (1951) – which may not be a great novel but seems to be truly innovative in the field of literature – for a book that deals, at the beginning, with the 1834 abolition of slavery in South Africa. There is a further American influence – the veneration of Abraham Lincoln. Oddly, his influence seems to have been mediated through an Englishman, the playwright John Drinkwater. Drinkwater wrote his play *Abraham Lincoln* in 1918. His immediate purpose in the play seems to have been to justify a nation's (specifically England's) participation in a just war and to press the theme of the necessity for national unity (Abraham Lincoln being a figure who managed to encompass both: preserve the Union and abolish slavery). But the play, in its more generalised themes, had obvious attractions for whites and blacks in the South Africa of the late twenties. Such statements as the following by one of Lincoln's friends, a character in the play, were not inimical to pacifying interests:

> Abraham's all for the constitution. He wants the constitution to be an honest master. There's nothing he wants like that, and he'll stand for that firm as a Sampson of the spirit, if he goes to Washington. He'ld give his life to persuade the state against slaving, but until it is persuaded and makes its laws against it, he'll have nothing to do with violence in the name of the laws that aren't made. That's why old John's raiding affair struck in his gullet [i.e. John Brown's abortive attempt to overthrow slavery].[42]

Drinkwater implicitly propagates the Great Man theory of history – only Lincoln was capable of directing history so successfully. At the same time he spells out the desirable or inevitable characteristics of the 'genius' – humility, capability of making a lonely decision, the common touch, compassion, firmness. It was this 'intriguing English play' that the Bantu Dramatic Society decided to put on as its second production. It was scheduled to be performed in December 1933, and was being rehearsed late October. Although I can find no record of its actual performance it no doubt inspired the Emancipation play of R. R. R. Dhlomo a few months later (Herbert Dhlomo had certainly read the play by 1938.)[43] Although black South African newspapers often referred to black American writers and politicians, there was another source through which local blacks were introduced to them.

In the late twenties the Carnegie Corporation of New York became interested in South Africa and appointed a Commission to examine the 'Poor White problem'. In 1930, the Carnegie Corporation offered the sum of £1 000 for the establishment of 'a Non-European Library' in the Transvaal. The Carnegie Non-European Library, Transvaal, came into operation in 1931 with its headquarters in Germiston.[44] Initially, it provided books for recreational reading which were distributed among some eighty centres in townships, schools, missions, compounds and hospitals. Blacks were excluded from public libraries at the time (the restriction was lifted in Johannesburg only comparatively recently), so the library undoubtedly served an important function. Yet it is clear that white liberals saw reading, and, more particularly, correct reading as being socially and politically desirable. In his second book, *The Bantu in the City*, Ray Phillips was explicit about the desirable function of libraries and reading rooms. 'It should be borne in mind by White South Africans,' he wrote, 'that Bantu who can read are able – if they have the money – to purchase books and magazines of all sorts in the local news stands. The opposition which has been voiced in the press against the unrestricted importation of undesirable literature has had in mind young European readers. It has equal application to African readers.'[45] Quoting newspapers that Johannesburg was 'being flooded with evil literature', he went on to state that this 'reading material is going to be read by Africans, which seems to point to the need for placing good literature before location dwellers and an attempt, at least, being made to inculcate standards of judgement as to what is wholesome and what is less worthy'. White university students had helped increase interest in the BMSC library and 'reading circles' in locations, 'for the purpose of having books read aloud and discussed might result, as it had in the rural areas of the American South, in stimulating the reading of good literature'. Phillips concluded that 'A practically virgin field here needs exploring'.[46]

The same theme was taken up in another book published in the same year, 1936. R. H. W. Shepherd's *Literature for the South African Bantu: a comparative study of Negro achievement*[47] came about as a result of a visit to the U.S.A. by the author the previous year under the auspices of the Visitors' Grants Committee of the Carnegie Corporation.[48] Shepherd (editor of *South African Outlook* from 1932, principal of Lovedale from 1942 and hence extremely influential) noted the consolidation of efforts to co-ordinate black social activities. 'Recent years,' he wrote, 'have been marked by a new or increasing interest in some quarters concerning the provision of literature for the South African Bantu. The more scientific study of African life, customs and language which has been a feature of the modern age; the danger lest the missionary agencies, having taught vast numbers to read, should leave to non-Christian and even anti-religious elements to supply the reading matter . . . have presented a challenge to different groups to make their contribution towards more effective and co-ordinated production and distribution of literature suited to the Bantu.'[49]

Shepherd (and, presumably, others) regarded a study of black Americans as being particularly suitable for South Africans. Following a racial stereotype, Shepherd regarded black Americans as 'essentially African people, with the spiritual, mental and physical characteristics of Africans' but, 'in every aspect of literary movement – intellectual, industrial, and commercial' he regarded them as 'further along the road than the Bantu, and yet not so far in advance as to render valueless the lessons they can teach to their African kinsmen'.[50] Shepherd fondly quoted James Weldon Johnson, one of the best-known of black American writers, in a saying which must certainly have influenced Herbert Dhlomo's theories of art: 'A people may become great through many means, but there is only one measure by which its greatness is recognised and acknowledged. The final measure of the greatness of all peoples is the amount and standard of the literature and art they have produced. The world does not know that a people is great until that people produces great literature and art. No people that has produced great literature and art has ever been looked upon by the world as distinctly inferior.'[51] Shepherd studied the library system, literacy and education, literary and history magazines, sociological studies and publishing houses of the black Americans. Of great interest to him was 'race relations literature', and his conclusions concerning America were strikingly similar to those Loram, Rheinallt Jones, Henderson and others had come to, under the influence of Aggrey, regarding South Africa.

> Thanks largely to the leadership of Dr Thomas Jesse Jones and others, recent years have witnessed throughout the United States a growing interest in different quarters in the subject of race relations, particularly as they affect White and Black. Race riots during the war and post-war years helped to accelerate the movement. Numbers of the best men and women of both sides felt that the position was becoming intolerable and that the races must get together with a view to mutual understanding, sympathy and service. From organisations so formed considerable quantities of literature have come.[52]

While he noted the popularity of the magazine *The Crisis*, which W. E. B. Du Bois had started in 1910, Shepherd was particularly impressed with *Opportunity*, organ of the National Urban League, whose editor, Elmer A. Carter, stated that the magazine sometimes had difficulty in obtaining suitable material because its 'viewpoint and standard eliminate many, because they want to slap-bang, agitate and protest'.[53] This clearly attracted Shepherd's prejudices as to 'literature in its truest sense'.[54] For Shepherd 'the development of literature as pure art is greatly needed amongst the Negro group'.[55] With apparently altruistic intent, Shepherd advocated even for the black Americans a form of co-ordination of research and writing.

> It has seemed to the writer that one of the pressing needs of to-day is for the setting-up of some form of organisation – call it a Bureau of Negro Literature or by any other name – which would bring co-ordination and correlation into the effort of to-day and which would evolve a more masterly and more united plan for research into Negro life, would give a helping hand to authors, particularly in the early stages of their career, and would tackle problems of the production and distribution of literature suited to the needs of the Negro people.[56]

Turning to South Africa, Shepherd made various recommendations. To further his aims for the spread of 'good literature' he hoped a magazine like *Opportunity* could be founded,[57] and he strongly advocated the extension as far as possible of libraries and reading-rooms, hinting that black librarians should be trained since, as the nineteenth-century clergymen had found in regard to Tiyo Soga and others, people 'of their own race' would 'know best the background and conditions' of the people.[58] He believed too that the time had come for 'a great forward movement in the production and distribution of Christian literature of the best type'. What was wanted, he wrote, was 'a united plan for co-operative effort'.[59] He pushed for the idea of a Bureau:

> In all their work on behalf of vernacular literature there should be the closest co-operation between the University Departments of Bantu Studies and the missionary forces. Their respective efforts, particularly if more closely welded together, would ensure that all the functions of a Bureau of Literature for the Bantu, similar to that advocated for the Negro people, were being performed.[60]

There is no evidence to suggest that Shepherd's ideas for a Bureau and central publishing house[61] ever got off the ground. But an idea closely related to these did have tangible results. Seeing the task of the European in regard to literature was 'to organise and promote its production and distribution', as well as to 'emphasize the value of the use of literature', Shepherd suggested that it 'might be helpful were there called together in the near future a conference of Bantu authors'.[62] On 15 October 1936, Shepherd convened in Florida, Transvaal, 'a unique gathering'.[63] This was a conference of African authors, 'the first of its kind'. Present were D. D. T. Jabavu, R. T. Caluza, B. W. Vilakazi, Mangoaela, R. V. Selope Thema, D. M. Ramoshoane, Mafoyane, and H. I. E. Dhlomo 'as an African who has used English as a medium of his literary efforts'. Apologies were received from J. J. R. Jolobe, H. M. Ndawo, S. E. K. Mqhayi, T. Mofolo, H. Maimane and R. R. R. Dhlomo. Shepherd was in the chair. Miss Margaret Wrong, Secretary of the International Committee on Christian Literature of the International Missionary Council, London, was also present, as were Professor C. M. Doke and J. D. Rheinallt Jones, the editors of *Bantu Studies*. The conference specifically followed a conference of missionary and other bodies held in Bloemfontein in June the same year to discuss with Miss Wrong the 'literature needs of the African people'. The conference discussed many issues. It was particularly concerned about the lack of publication outlets. A cited example of the difficulty of getting a manuscript published 'was that of the late Sol T. Plaatje whose *Mhudi* was rejected by many publishers'. Other examples were given of manuscripts being lost because of lack of opportunity for publication — a brief insight into the grave loss sustained by early South African literature. The kind of material for publication, the need for training in literary criticism, competitions, standardisation of orthography, the use of newspapers and magazines, the distribution and the desirable media for literature were all discussed. The idea of 'a Bureau' surfaced in modified form – two years before Professor Doke had submitted a scheme for 'an academy of Bantu languages and literature' to the Inter-University Committee for African Studies – and Vilakazi and Selope Thema were appointed by the 1936 Authors Conference to serve on a Joint Council to be formed by the Conference, the Inter-University Committee and the Christian Council to discuss the issue.

Although there is no evidence for insincerity or hypocrisy on Shepherd's part, there is, running through his actions and writings, a distinct drift in his underlying assumptions. Clearly the activity of reading and the institution of libraries was one of the important ways in which blacks could be acculturated into the 'new civilisation' whose value was scarcely doubted. The values of 'good literature' would thus be inculcated, and the calm, dispassionate, sedentary nature of the activity would no doubt be salutary. Certainly the combination of the transatlantic example, the reading habit, and the creation of the Carnegie Library had an effect on contemporary writers.

In December 1936, the following poem was published in *Bantu World*:

> He stood alone
> A Negro youth.
> What of his future?
> His cap was worn,
> This Negro youth.
> Why was he born?
>
> Born to lead an empty useless life,
> Born to mar the record of his race,
> Or born to lead his race?
> Locked are the doors,
> Locked – the doors of his future.
> His burden to bear,
> To suffer the pain of life's cruel ways,
> That is why he was born.[64]

The poem was written by a sixteen-year-old, classified as a 'Coloured', Peter Abrahams, living in Pietersburg. What is it that makes a young, Coloured South African identify with a black American poet[65] and write his poem about a lonely and thwarted potential leader using the American expression 'negro'? What is it that makes T. D. Mweli Skota affix to his seminal book *The African Yearly Register* the grandoise subtitle, 'Being an illustrated national biographical dictionary (Who's Who) of black folks in Africa'? Clearly there is a strong measure of identification, but of what kind? It is not really enough to point to the influence of black Americans on black South Africans and say that there is a measure of identification simply because of the colour of the skin. Even literary influences do not come floating in the air. A schoolboy in Pietersburg in 1936 does not totally by accident happen to pick up a poem by a black American and start imitating. There are choices made and choices discarded, and the writer may not always be aware of the limits and determinants of his choice. It is now commonplace to discuss the American influences on black South African writers of the fifties (the influence of Damon Runyon on Casey Motsisi, for instance) or of the seventies (Black Power and Black Consciousness), but the problem with dealing with such ideas as though they are disembodied entities is that their perpetrators are then open to the accusation of arbitrarily adopting 'foreign ideas' and 'foreign ideologies', and 'a handful of agitators' become blamed for all protest.

We can, in fact, be very precise about Peter Abrahams's experience. Almost certainly in that very year, 1936, the young Abrahams nervously walked into the BMSC and, while he waited for the secretary, he heard, in the next room, a deep voice, 'touched with the velvet quality of organ notes',[66] singing (on a gramophone record) the song 'Ol' Man River'. Abrahams's biography, *Tell Freedom*, describes his subsequent reactions.

> That was a black man, one of us! I knew it. I needed no proof. The men about me, their faces, their bearing, carried all the proof. That was a black man! The voice of a black man!
>
> The glorious voice stopped. The men went back to what they were doing. The moment that had given us a common identity was over. Robeson the man had called him. A name to remember, that. I would find out about that man.
>
> 'Some voice, heh, son,' a man said to me.
>
> 'Yessir!'
>
> 'He's an American Negro,' the man said and moved away.
>
> I followed him through the door where the greatest number went. It was a long room, spacious, and with big windows that let in light. At one end was a billiard table. Two men, in shirt-sleeves, played. At the other end were shelves filled with books. Comfortable settees were ranged about the room. Men sat reading or talking. Others watched the game. They all spoke English here.
>
> I moved over to the bookshelves. I wanted to touch the books but held back. Perhaps it was not permitted. Typed slips showed what each shelf held; novels, history, sociology, travel, Africana, political science, American Negro literature. . . . I stopped there. American Negro literature. The man had said Robeson was an American Negro. . . .
>
> A man got up and came over. He ran his finger along the American Negro literature shelf and took out a book.
>
> 'Excuse me. . . . Can I look at these?'
>
> 'Of course,' he smiled.
>
> I reached up and took out a fat black book. *The Souls of Black Folk* by W. E. B. Du Bois. I turned the pages. It spoke about a people in a valley. And they were black, and dispossessed, and denied. I skimmed through the pages, anxious to take it all in. I read:
>
> 'For this much all men know: despite compromise, war, struggle, the Negro is not free'[67]

Peter Abrahams thus attributes a large measure of his consciousness, perhaps even the beginning of the inspiration for writing, to his reading of black American writers.[68] But the circumstances, the history of his coming to read those authors, are not to be found simply in his own biography. He himself, at the time, could not have been aware of the conjuncture of events that brought about his revelation: the troubles of 1917–20, the visit of Aggrey, the establishment of the Joint Councils, the ideology of the American Board missionaries and their liberal allies, the founding of the BMSC, the spread of the British and American film and gramophone industries, the Carnegie Commission and the establishment of the Carnegie Non-European Library.

> In the months that followed, I spent nearly all my spare time in the library of the Bantu Men's Social Centre. I read every one of the books on the shelf marked: American Negro literature. I became a nationalist, a colour nationalist, through the writings of men and women who lived a world away from me. To them I owe a great debt for crystallizing my vague yearnings to write and for showing me the long dream was attainable.[69]

Abrahams went to Grace Dieu School, near Pietersburg, in the northern Transvaal. From there he sent a few of his poems to *The Bantu World*, which published them. 'The Zulu poet, Dhlomo, wrote me a letter of encouragement. Some months later, I sent another batch. A new editor had taken Dhlomo's place.'[70] The reason for this replacement of Dhlomo was that, perhaps in fulfilment of Shepherd's recommendation as a result of his trip to the United States at Carnegie's expense, Herbert Dhlomo had been appointed Librarian–Organiser under the Transvaal Committee of the Carnegie Library Service for Non-Europeans. It was 'the first appointment of its kind in South Africa', and it was 'made possible by special grants from the Carnegie Corporation of New York and from the Witwatersrand Council of Education'. Dhlomo and his appointment were hailed as 'welcome signs of the cultural advancement of Non-European peoples of the Union'.[71]

The BMSC seems to have started its own library soon after its own initiation. Certainly, by 1929 it was functioning, as a contemporary report indicated:

> There is a small library stocked with valuable books, and here a man who wishes to drink deep and still deeper in the fountain of knowledge can spend his leisure hours among great thinkers of the past and the present. It is hoped very soon the library will be well supplied with books, as the Bantu Men's Social Centre will probably be one of the distributing centres for the Carnegie Circulating Library, which is being established for non-Europeans under the auspices of the Carnegie Corporation of New York.[72]

However, by August 1931, Dhlomo himself complained that the BMSC no longer had a library. This was revealed in an interesting article entitled 'Bantu and Leisure' which must have pleased Phillips.[73]

'The Bantu,' Dhlomo began, 'have now reached the stage where the question of leisure enters into their life.' Such aspects of leisure as holidaying, motoring and hunting were 'out of question at this stage of their development'. 'If the work of the blacks,' he wrote, 'is unsuitable, and recreational facilities lacking, the surplus energy they possess finds expression, more often than not, in mischievous and even dangerous habits and actions.' He examined sports, where he found that 'only a small minority indulge in this form of leisure . . . the chosen few monopolise' while huge crowds must remain content with the position of onlookers. He looked at ballroom dancing, which involves 'active participation', and at the cinema, which is 'limited to mental exercise only'. He also warned, though that, 'leisure intoxication is often as harmful as liquor intoxication' – in other words, when recreation was 'made to act as liquor to drown our fears, troubles and problems', then, he suggested, 'we are deteriorating'. These forms of leisure fulfilment are insufficient, according to Dhlomo, however, and it is clear that he sees art, music, literature and reading as developing individualism with a hint of class differentiation. (Certainly, much of his subsequent poetry deals with the desire for individual seclusion, loneliness and the need to be alone.)

> Leisure is no doubt essential. But there are times when surging, frolicking crowds, and bright, thrilling games of captivating spectacles leave one cold and unresponsive. The mind and the spirit should have leisure to refresh themselves by literature, music, art or seclusion. . . . Sports grounds, dance halls and athletic societies are springing up like mushrooms all over the country. This is excellent. However, there is a danger of developing a one-sided complexion in our youth. Not a few leaders of Bantu thought rightly feel that mental recreation must be provided for if we would avoid shallowness, frivolity and deterioration. We have no public libraries, and we cannot afford building good private ones. Even useful institutions such as the Bantu Men's Social Centre have no library. One need hardly mention the glory and wealth of thought and experience, knowledge and real joy our people miss by lack of such provision.

Leisure time must therefore not only be organised and controlled, it must also be *moralized* in a correct way.[74]

On 14 June 1932, however, the BMSC opened its library as a receiving depot of the Carnegie Non-European Library, a fact reported by Dhlomo himself.[75] We therefore know that he was closely associated with the BMSC library as early as 1932 (if not even in 1929). With his job as Librarian–Organiser he would have been in charge of this library by 1937 – this library to which Peter Abrahams had come the year before.[76]

It was Herbert Dhlomo who was to articulate most specifically the concept of 'The New African' – the detribalised, 'progressive', adapted adaptor of the modern South Africa – in his two articles in *The Democrat* at the end of 1945.[77] However, he almost certainly adapted the phrase (and perhaps fitted some of the ideas to his own concept) from a black American, Alain Locke. Locke published, in 1925, his book, *The New Negro*.[78] In the opening paragraph of his introduction to this selection of the 'Renaissance' writers of black America (including Jean Toomer, Countee Cullen, Claude McKay, James Weldon Johnson, Langston Hughes, Arna Bontempt and R. R. Moton), Locke announced the new day, the future which Abrahams's poem awaited.

> In the last decade something beyond the watch and guard of statistics has happened in the life of the American Negro and the three norns who have traditionally presided over the Negro problem have a changeling in their laps. The Sociologist, the Philanthropist, the Race-Leader are not unaware of the New Negro, but they are at a loss to account for him. He simply cannot be swathed in their formulae. For the younger generation is vibrant with a new psychology; the new spirit is awake in the masses and under the very eyes of the professional observers is transforming what has been a perennial problem into the progressive phases of contemporary Negro life.[79]

For page after page the style and thought of Locke (in its exhortatory tone of hope) is so much the style and thought of Dhlomo.

> The Negro today is inevitably moving forward under the control of his own objectives. . . . Up to the present one may adequately describe the Negro's 'inner objectives' as an attempt to repair a damaged group psychology and reshape a warped social perspective. Their realisation has required a new mentality for the American Negro. And as it matures we begin to see its effects; at first, negative, iconoclastic, and then positive and constructive. In this new group psychology we note the lapse of sentimental appeal, then the development of a more positive self-respect and self-reliance; the repudiation of social dependence, and then the gradual recovery from hyper-sensitiveness and 'touchy' nerves, the repudiation of the double standard of judgement with its special philanthropic allowances and then the sturdier desire for objective and scientific appraisal; and finally the rise from social disillusionment to race pride.[80]

The whole trend was summed up in the poetry of Langston Hughes.[81]

> Because my mouth
> Is wide with laughter
> And my throat
> Is deep with song,
> You do not think
> I suffer after
> I have held my pain
> So long.
>
> Because my mouth
> Is wide with laughter,
> You do not hear
> My inner cry,
> Because my feet
> Are gay with dancing,
> You do not know
> I die.

For Dhlomo replied with his own 'Because I'm Black'.[82]

> Because I'm black
> You think I lack
> The talents, feelings and ambitions
> That others have;
> You do not think I crave positions
> That others crave.
>
> Psychology
> And Zoology
> Have proved that Race and blood
> Are a fiction. . . .
> All men are Man;
> Diversity means not disunion –
> It is God's plan;
> White blood and black in test transfusions
> Answer the same.
> They harbour childish vain delusions
> Who better claim.
>
> Because the people eat and sing
> And mate,
> You do not see their suffering.
> You rate them fools
> And tools
> Of those with power and boastful show;
> Not Fate, but chance, has made things so.
> Beware! these people, struggling, hold
> The winning card;
> And when they strike, they will be bold –
> And will strike hard!

When Peter Abrahams had perused some of Du Bois' *Souls of Black Folk* in the library of the BMSC, he 'replaced the book and reached for others'.

> There was *Up From Slavery*; *Along This Way* by Weldon Johnson; a slim volume called *The Black Christ*; a fat volume called *The New Negro*. I turned the pages of *The New Negro*. These poems and stories were written by Negroes! Something burst deep inside me. The world could never again belong to white people only! Never again!
> I took *The New Negro* to a chair. I turned the pages.[83]

Perhaps as Peter Abrahams sat in his chair reading, Eslanda Robeson, wife of Paul Robeson, the very singer who had helped get Abrahams into that very chair, was in Johannesburg, for she visited it between 3 July and 7 July 1936, staying with Dr Xuma in Sophiatown (Robeson himself never came to South Africa; his wife, an anthropologist, was on her way to Uganda, and managed to get into South Africa despite some problems). On the night of Sunday, 4 July, she walked into the BMSC for an evening of entertainment. She noticed that the

'Africans making up the membership of this club' were 'quite European' and the two items on the programme which interested her most were 'a recitation of an alliterative story made up almost entirely of clicks – very humorous and fascinating – and a song about the Johannesburg mountains, a real African ballad which was beautiful in itself and beautifully sung' and which she thought would be 'fine' for her husband to sing. She was presented with a collection of African records which could not have been 'more welcome or of more practical value'. Her perceptive diary[84] is one of the small gems of South African literature. It was probably about this time too that a young musician was completing his course at Tuskegee. In 1952 Ralph Ellison published *Invisible Man*, which is the most devastating attack in literature upon Booker Washington, R. R. Moton, Tuskegee, white liberals and hence, indirectly, on all their intellectual offspring.

Notes

1 Published in Alain Locke, *The New Negro* (New York, 1925).
2 See S. Marks, 'The ambiguities of dependence: John L. Dube of Natal', *Journal of Southern African Studies*, I, 2 (April 1975), 162–80. See also R. Hunt Davies, 'John L. Dube: a South African exponent of Booker T. Washington', *Journal of African Studies*, II, 4 (Winter 1975–76), 497–528. For Msikinya's poem, 'Africa's Tears', in which he asks America to return Africa's children who have been sent there to study so that they can bring light to the 'Dark Continent', see *Koranta ea Becoana*, 7 Sept. 1904.
3 M. Legassick, 'The rise of modern South African liberalism: its assumptions and its social base', University of Sussex African Studies Graduate Seminar paper (mimeo).
4 'The 1920 black mine workers' strike: a preliminary account', in *Labour, Townships and Protest*, edited by B. Bozzoli (Johannesburg, 1979), pp. 273–97.
5 *Ibid.* p. 289.
6 B. Hirson, 'Tuskegee, the Joint Councils, and the All Africa Convention', *The Societies in Southern Africa in 19th and 20th Centuries*, Vol. 11, *CSP*, Institute of Commonwealth Studies, London, 1981.
7 Edwin W. Smith, *Aggrey of Africa: a study in black and white* (London, 1929), p. 143.
8 *Ibid.*, p. 165.
9 *Ibid.*, p. 166.
10 *Up From Slavery* (Cape Town, 1958), p. 52.
11 *Ibid.*, p. 97.
12 *The Souls of the Black Folk*, introduced by C. L. R. James (London), p. x.
13 See, for instance, E. David Cronon, *Black Moses: the story of Marcus Garvey and the Universal Negro Improvement Association* (Wisconsin, 1955).
14 See, for instance, *Aggrey of Africa*, p. 118.
15 *Ibid.*, p. 123.
16 *Ilanga lase Natal*, 15 Feb. 1924. This was, in fact, almost certainly William Plomer.
17 J. D. Rheinallt Jones, 'The Joint Council Movement', in *Christianity and the Natives of South Africa*, Rev. J. Dexter Taylor (ed.) (Lovedale, n.d. [1928?]), pp. 152–3.
18 *Aggrey of Africa*, pp. 174–5.

19 For a fuller account of this institution, see T. Couzens, 'The social ethos of black writing in South Africa 1920–1950', in *Aspects of South African Literature*, C. Heywood (ed.) (London, 1976), pp. 66–81.

20 J. D. Rheinallt Jones, 'Native studies in our universities', in *Christianity and the Natives of South Africa*, pp. 155–8.

21 *Umteteli wa Bantu*, 30 Aug. 1924.

22 Student Christian Movement Press, London. See also Ray Phillips's *The Bantu in the City* (Lovedale, 1936).

23 *The Bantu are Coming* (London, 1930), p. 22.

24 *Ibid.*, p. 31.

25 *Ibid.*, p. 52.

26 *Ibid.*, pp. 8–9.

27 *Ibid.*, p. 58.

28 *Ibid.*, p. 105. See also R. Phillips, 'Social work in South Africa', in *Christianity and the Natives of South Africa*, pp. 145–51.

29 *The Bantu are Coming*, pp. 116–19.

30 *Ibid.*, pp. 120–2.

31 *Ibid.*, p. 104.

32 *Ibid.*, p. 139.

33 *Ibid.*, p. 30.

34 *Ibid.*, pp. 141–2.

35 *Ibid.*, pp. 144, 145, 150.

36 *Christianity and the Natives of South Africa*, p. 148.

37 *The Bantu are Coming*, pp. 147–50.

38 *Umteteli wa Bantu*, 19 May 1934; *Bantu World*, 2 June 1934; *Bantu World*, 9 June 1934; handbill advertisement, Rheinallt Jones papers, University of the Witwatersrand archives.

39 'Bantu dramatic society stages its first show: the Africans invade the stage: dramatic events of history', *Bantu World*, 15 April 1933 (the writer was H. I. E. Dhlomo).

40 'Unique function at B.M.S.C.', *Bantu World*, 1934.

41 This tendency in the work of R. R. R. Dhlomo is already discernible in a poem 'My Country', which he published in *Ilange lase Natal*, 12 Feb. 1926, the sixth stanza of which went as follows:

> Here and there poor whites claim you,
> My country – leaving Natives helpless;
> Here and there cotton planters claim you,
> My Country – leaving Natives hopeless
>   All appear to love you.

42 J. Drinkwater, *Abraham Lincoln* (London, 1918), p. 8.

43 'Reef Gossip', *Ilanga lase Natal*, 28 Oct. 1933. H. I. E. Dhlomo recommended it for reading after he became Librarian–Organiser of the Carnegie Non-European Library (*Reader's Companion* No. 3, Sept. 1938, p. 5). It is almost certain that he read it at the time of the proposed production in 1933 (very possibly he would have been *in* the production) if not before.

44 *Brief History of the Non-European Library Service, Transvaal, 1931–1939* (Pretoria, 1969).

45 *The Bantu in the City*, p. 313.

46 *Ibid.*, p. 314.

47 The Carnegie Corporation Visitors' Grants Committee, Pretoria, 1936.

48 When he returned from the United States trip Shepherd said in an interview 'I was astonished at the quality and quantity of the literature being produced by Negro authors and the publishing houses. Some Negro poets are taking their place in the front rank of American literary men' (*Bantu World*, 20 July 1935). See also the article 'Negro libraries in America', *Bantu World*, 19 Dec. 1936, probably by Shepherd, although possibly by Rheinallt Jones (who was in the United States in October 1934). Phillips had been in America for eighteen months, returning in September 1927, 'full of praise for the famous Professor Carver' and having visited Tuskegee and the colleges where he 'saw the excellent effect these were having on the character of the race' (*Umteteli wa Bantu*, 8 Oct. 1927).

49 *Literature for the South African Bantu* (Pretoria, 1936), p. 10.

50 *Ibid.*, pp. 14–15.

51 *Ibid.*, p. 20. Herbert Dhlomo certainly knew Johnson's work. He quoted Johnson in an obituary on the late John Dube (*Ilanga Lase Natal*, 19 Aug. 1944), and he undoubtedly knew Shepherd's book.

52 *Ibid.*, pp. 37–8.

53 *Ibid.*, p. 25.

54 *Ibid.*, p. 42.

55 *Ibid.*, p. 46.

56 *Ibid.*, pp. 44–5.

57 An anonymous writer (possibly Herbert Dhlomo) was already very aware of both *The Crisis* and *Opportunity* several years before Shepherd's recommendation. See 'African Vernacular Literature', *Umteteli wa Bantu*, 2 May 1931.

58 *Literature for the South African Bantu*, p. 58.

59 *Ibid.*, p. 72.

60 *Ibid.*, p. 73.

61 He himself was advocating 'an All-African publishing house' many years later. See 'Wanted African Authors', *Ilanga lase Natal*, 1 Dec. 1951.

62 *Literature for the South African Bantu*, p. 66.

63 J. D. Rheinallt Jones, 'African authors' conference: a unique gathering', *Bantu World*, 14 Nov. 1936, and 21 Nov. 1936.

64 *Bantu World*, 5 Dec. 1936.

65 In his review, *Bantu World*, 26 April 1941, Walter Nhlapo is aware of the influence when he said that when Abrahams expressed himself it was 'in poetry of unmeasured cadence, metre and rhyme, following in the wake of American negro poets'.

66 *Tell Freedom* (London, 1954), p. 191.

67 *Ibid.*, p. 192.

68 Many black Americans became hero figures: 'What are we doing,' wrote Walter Nhlapo in compiling his pantheon in *Bantu World*, 22 June 1935, 'to find counterparts of such famous Negro Men as Booker T. Washington, Robert Moton, educationalists; Dr Ernest Everritt, scientist; Jack Johnson, Larry Gains, boxers; J. C. Johnson, 'Fats' Waller, dance number composers; Mabel Brooks, artist; Layton and Johnstone, Mills Brothers, jazz singers; Duke Ellington, Lucky 'Blue' Milinder, band conductors; Marcus Garvey, orator; Paul Robeson, John Ross, actors; and Aubrey Pankey, a singer?' Joe Louis, the boxer, became the heroic predecessor of Muhammed Ali. Ernest Gaines in *The Autobiography of Miss Jane Pittman* has his aged heroine say: 'It was way back there in the thirties. Joe had just tanned S'mellin'. We all knowed Joe was from Alabama, and we said if Alabama could give One that good,

Samson, Luzana could do the same.' Paul Robeson was perhaps the greatest hero of all, especially with his message 'I am Coloured and Proud of It.' (See *Cape Standard*, 31 Jan. 1939). The whole position of black Americans as example and inspiration is perhaps best summed up by Simon Lekhela (now in exile in England) in his poem 'A Bantu Lament', published in *Umteteli wa Bantu*, 10 June 1933.

> Black folk, kindred of Africa,
> 'Mongst folk who live in light we dwell:
> Behind we are in deeds – But ah!
> Do we endeavour to do well?
>
> Their intellect we've got to seek:
> Of enterprise we need not speak,
> For lackadaisical we are.
>
> But to endeavours let us turn
> Which give our race what it most needs,
> And by them we will surely earn
> A history of worldly deeds.
>
> For inspiration we may reach.
> Beyond the seas to Negro soil.
> In schools our children, let us teach
> Of Carver, Garvey and Du Bois.
>
> And aye in reverence we pause,
> When Aggrey's deeds our minds imprint.
> Their hero-worship then must cause
> Them to be proud of their dark tint.
>
> We little know what life can hold,
> In vain we strive accomplishment,
> For riches, fame and power loaned
> To them who seek advancement.
>
> Oh Spirit! Thou knowest all,
> Do wake us children from our doze.
> That we may noble deeds recall,
> And in them find a safe repose.
>
> Hasten Black folk, time now arrives,
> Let unity our ideal be.
> Union our destiny decides,
> Endeavour for it each colleague.
> By fate or chance depressed we are
> Oh Spirit Great! we trust in Thee.

A number of institutions were begun or suggested in imitation of black American counterparts – e.g. J. G. Coka's International Negro Youth Movement, possibly a Garveyist movement ('Reef Gossip', *Umteteli wa Bantu*, 28 Oct. 1933) and A. S. Vil-Nkomo's proposed parallel to the National Negro Health Movement (*Bantu World*, 25 Feb. 1939). There was even, in the Johannesburg Bantu Football Association, a team called the 'Negroes' (*Umteteli wa Bantu*, 30 April 1932)! For the most sustained newspaper coverage of black American achievement, see ten articles entitled 'Brief survey of Negro's part in American history', published between 11 March and 20 May 1939, in *Bantu World*.

69 *Tell Freedom*, p. 197.

70 *Ibid.*, p. 227.

71 *Bantu World*, 20 Feb. 1937.

72 *Ilanga lase Natal*, 11 Oct. 1929.

73 *Umteteli wa Bantu*, 15 Aug. 1931.

74 Compare this with D. D. T. Javavu's *The Black Problem* (Lovedale, 1920), p. 77, where he gives advice to teachers: 'You need a room that you can regard as private to yourself for meditation and reading. . . . Move heaven and earth to get this.'

75 'The Bantu Library', *Umteteli wa Bantu*, 25 June 1932 (written by H. I. E. Dhlomo).

76 Dhlomo organised two lectures on the subject of America in the BMSC in 1938: the first, by Dr A. W. White, 'himself a Negro', was 'a learned discourse on Negro literature, tracing the beginnings and the development of Negro literature back from the days of slavery up to the present time' (*Bantu World*, 6 Aug. 1928); the second, by Mr Borland, Secretary of the Carnegie Non-European Library, was on 'Negro libraries in the United States' (*Bantu World*, 27 Aug. 1938). See also James Korombi's letter in appreciation of White's talk (*Bantu World*, 20 Aug. 1938).

77 17 Nov. 1945, pp. 19, 24; and 1 Dec. 1945, pp. 21, 24.

78 A. Locke, *The New Negro* (New York, 1925).

79 *Ibid.*, p. 3.

80 *Ibid.*, pp. 10–11.

81 *Ibid.*, p. 144.

82 *Ilanga lase Natal*, 22 Jan. 1949.

83 *Tell Freedom*, p. 194. I first came across substantive evidence that Herbert Dhlomo might have read *The New Negro* when I found a copy in the library of Professor Hoernlé which is still preserved as a special collection in the Wartenweiler Library, University of the Witwatersrand. Dhlomo knew Hoernlé well and, since Hoernlé's copy was inscribed 'To Professor and Mrs. Hoernlé, in appreciation and remembrance, Alain Locke, Aug. 30, 1928', it seemed not unreasonable to assume that Hoernlé might have talked about it extensively after 1928 when he was probably in America. The nearest I could get to evidence that Dhlomo knew directly of Locke's idea of 'the new Negro' was that he owned and had carefully annotated a copy of E. R. Embree, *Brown America: the study of a new race* (New York, 1932), which was clearly influenced by Locke (as even its title suggests). It was only afterwards that I came across the even more direct evidence in *Tell Freedom*. Five pages of manuscript notes were paper-clipped into Hoernlé's *The New Negro*, indicating that Hoernlé had read it quite carefully. 'We cannot escape external influences,' he wrote.

Dhlomo himself actually used the phrase 'the new Negro' in his weekly 'Busy-Bee' column in *Ilanga lase Natal*, 30 Sept. 1944. Dhlomo was generally well-informed on American writing – for instance, he quoted Pearl Buck that it 'was for the Negro to create his own original drama' (*Ilanga lase Natal*, 28 Jan. 1950) – read Moby Dick (*Ilanga lase Natal*, 15 Aug. 1953) and knew biographies on Washington, Robeson and Carver (*Ilanga Lase Natal*, 18 June 1949). The last-mentioned was no doubt Rackham Holt's *George Washington Carver: an American biography* (New York, 1944).

84 *African Journey* (New York, 1945). For the above quotations, see p. 76. Dhlomo at least read reviews of this book (*Ilanga lase Natal*, 26 Oct. 1946).

CHAPTER THIRTEEN

'Wailing for purity': prayer unions, African mothers and adolescent daughters 1912–1940

Deborah Gaitskell

The uniformed prayer associations or *manyanos*[1], so well-attended every Thursday afternoon by African married women in South African churches today, derive much of their relevance from the family role and responsibilities of the African mother. Only an investigation of the historical origins and early development of thse unions, however, can uncover the precise nature of the strains within the family which it was hoped maternal solidarity in prayer would help to ease. In the course of such an investigation of three denominational prayer unions with Witwatersrand branches, it became clear that the views of mission Christianity on courtship, marriage and the role of the mother within the family ran counter to the assumptions of African, particularly Nguni, society. Consequently, the evidence suggests, the *manyano* and its American Board equivalent, the *isililo*, should be seen in part as the attempt by African women converts to internalise new domestic norms or perhaps lament the difficulty of doing so under the destructive influence of South Africa's industrial revolution. The demands of both God and gold removed key supports from the married woman, while pressing her to accept new responsibilities. Thus, as new economic and social forces increasingly conflicted with new religious prescriptions, certain features of the Christian culture which female Africans were being urged to adopt, struggled to take root in urban working-class society.

The Christian gospel can never be transmitted absolutely 'pure', however desirable such an untrammelled transmission may be; the Christianity exported at any particular juncture of missionary endeavour is itself a historical product. As Adrian Hastings notes, it was only well after the Reformation that 'absolute monogamy, absolute indissolubility, and the celebration of marriage by Christians in a form recognised by the Church' became virtually inflexible requirements among western Christians themselves.[2] Yet it was these norms which clashed with polygynous African marriage. But polygyny is not only 'above all a problem relating to conversion';[3] it is also obviously a male rather than a female 'temptation'. For African Christian mothers, isolated in a smaller monogamous household, and then deprived of relatives as neighbours in town, it was the obligation to guard their daughters' virginity that proved particularly difficult to fulfil.

The home was the centre of Southern Bantu religion, with the father as 'priest' interceding with the ancestors.[4] Mission Christianity, though using extra-domestic buildings for public worship, similarly nurtured family religion, but gave to the mother a spiritual role equal with if not greater than the father's. This reflected social and economic developments in the metropolitan countries which were sending missionaries. From the beginning of the nineteenth century in industrialising Britain and the United States, 'motherhood stood out as a discrete task' for women who were increasingly segregated at home with their children, with their domestic manufacturing diminishing, and their husbands and older children drawn into non-agricultural jobs away from the household. Religious and educational ideology confirmed the importance of women's domestic influence in the spheres of family spirituality and child nurture. Although British working-class families depended on an economic contribution from women and children as well as men, by the end of that century prevailing middle-class domestic ideology was producing even among them something closer to its ideal through measures like factory reform and compulsory elementary education.[5] The persistence of this ideology into the twentieth century can be illustrated in a Methodist missionary's rhetoric:

> Do we ever try to imagine what our England would be without its home life, that most treasured of our nation's possessions? The home where the mother is enthroned as queen, where peace and concord dwells, and where love, emanating from the hearts of Godly parents, holds impartial sway!

Johannesburg women missionaries would not have quarrelled with the sexual division of labour endorsed by one of their number, Mrs Clara Bridgman, who described approvingly those thoughtful young African couples in the 1920s 'founding comfortable and happy homes where the man earns the money and his wife keeps the home and really tries to bring up the children'. Thus, clearly a crucial presumption of the Christian emphasis on the mother's primary domestic role was that wives were able, because of their husbands' financial support through a 'family' wage, to devote themselves full-time to caring for their children and home.

As if to confirm its ideological exportation, there survives a suitable exposition of this doctrine of maternal responsibility by a second-generation black South African Christian woman educated in the United States:

> The woman, the wife, is the keystone of the household: she holds a position of supreme importance, for is she not directly and intimately concerned with the nurturing and

upbringing of the *children* of the family, the future generation? She is their first counsellor, and teacher; on her rests the responsibility of implanting in the flexible minds of her young, the right principles and teachings of modern civilisation. Indeed, on her rests the failure or success of her children when they go out into life. It is therefore essential that the home atmosphere be right, that the mother be the real 'queen' of the home, the inspiration of her family.[6]

Missionaries of this era further assumed that it was the mother's duty to tell her daughter 'the facts of life' and appropriately mould her attitudes towards sex. As one wrote:

Even in the earliest days of a girl's life the mother should find a way so to inculcate those attitudes of self-respect and regard for womanly purity, of reserve and modesty, of dignity, of appreciation of the position of wife and mother, that these things will consciously or unconsciously influence every later act.[7]

Although in African society training children was primarily the parents' duty and in early childhood more directly the mother's, other relatives shared these responsibilities more than was usual in nineteenth-century English or American nuclear families. Furthermore, the peer group in whose company a child learned and performed its economic tasks had a key role in its sexual instruction, as did the community at large in initiation. An adolescent girl refrained, on grounds of respect, from speaking about sex in the presence of her mother, feeling less restraint with her grandmother.[8] In this important aspect of socialisation, then, mothers were not customarily expected to be the sole or even primary teacher. Though African society did not share middle-class Victorian reticence about sex – there was a matter-of-fact acceptance of marriage as 'an essential step for every normal person to take' and a familiarity with the nature of sexual intercourse from an early age – the most explicit sex education did not come from a girl's mother. Female initiation schools among the Lobedu, Venda, Pedi, Southern Sotho and Tswana gave instruction on women's rights and duties, and etiquette in marriage, while a sexual frankness, which would have been considered obscene out of context, characterised Zulu girls' coming-of-age songs. This adolescent group instruction, given under 'unusual and dramatic circumstances', was meant to uphold traditional marriage ideals, not promote sexual licence; initiates had to be virgins.[9]

Like the Victorians, African traditionalists condemned premarital pregnancy; they fined the lover and subjected the girl to public disgrace. Aspects of her dress marked her out, and her peer group mocked her at night in obscene songs.[10] However, although such pregnancy was deprecated, the Nguni, unlike the Sotho-Tswana peoples, practised an approved form of premarital sexual intimacy, intracrural intercourse, which conflicted sharply with the Christian ideal of premarital chastity. These contrasting attitudes to the value of virginity at marriage Goody links fairly convincingly with opposing inheritance patterns: in Eurasian society, where women can inherit family property, female premarital sex is more controlled than in African society. The Nguni form of courtship was more than tolerated — it was deemed socially desirable. Traditionalist Nguni still take the view that 'It is bad to break the rules [i.e. by making a girl pregnant] but it is also bad not to play at all', for the inference then is that the non-participant is being caressed by witch-familiars. Among the Zulu, a group of older girls would control the younger girls, granting permission first to talk to sweethearts, then for external intercourse between the betrothed. Among the Southern Nguni, adolescent night-time song and dance gatherings would end in couples pairing off to sleep together in this way. A daughter might be given a special hut a little apart from the others in which to meet her lover, who paid a 'fine', perhaps a beast, to become 'accredited'. More gifts might be demanded from him subsequently, for 'men regard their daughters as banks', as Bhaca informants told Hammond-Tooke in the 1950s.[11]

It was these two issues arising out of Nguni courtship practices — lovers' gifts and parentally-condoned private lovemaking — which sparked off the spiritual upsurge among Natal American Board Mission women that resulted in the formation of the *isililo* prayer union at the Native Annual Meeting of the Church at Groutville in mid-1912:

> As a result of very powerful sermons preached here, many people were moved to tears over the matter of low morals among the youth during those days. Young girls were getting pregnant before marriage whilst living at their parents' homes.
>
> The male members complained that it was the women who were giving the youth opportunities for immoral behaviour, accepting gladly and without reproach, gifts from their boys' and girls' lovers and also helping to entertain their daughters' lovers in their homes and giving them opportunities for privacy. Then there followed a great spiritual uproar, as at Pentecost, where women who were present confessed their own sins and failure in this matter.

When the movement spread to other Natal ABM stations through a series of revival meetings led by itinerant bands of female preachers, it was on the new Christian basis that mothers were responsible for their children's immorality: one meeting took the text, 'You shall perish with your children.'[12] So the *isililo* is to be interpreted in part as an attempt by African Christian women to take responsibility as seniors for Christian girls, and establish effective communal Christian sanctions against premarital pregnancy at a time when adequate supervision of relationships and punishment of unchastity by the age-set or older girls, persisted only among pagans.

Concern over premarital pregnancy among Christian girls also surfaced vociferously in other churches at the beginning of the second decade of the twentieth century. There was a whole range of circumstances conspiring to produce this phenomenon at this particular time. Because puberty rituals were outlawed by horrified missionaries, the explicit advice given to initiates on how to avoid conception through sex-play became increasingly less accessible to girls from Christian homes precisely at a time when other influences combined to make premarital sexual experience easier to acquire. From the late nineteenth century onwards, missionaries, especially in Natal, encouraged female self-assertion against parental authority by sheltering runaway brides, and obtained legislative backing for the right of women over eighteen to choose their own marriage partner. Rev. Tsewu of Johannesburg, lamenting how out-of-hand girls had become, protested to the South African Native Affairs Commission at the way the state sanctioned daughterly disobedience to paternal wishes. Mission education further eroded parental domination – children who knew more than their parents became defiant, and parents tended to abdicate their religious responsibilities to the school. It also gave adolescents the chance to meet away from home supervision in a coeducational environment. Less peer group pressure was exerted in schools. Western Christian individualism weakened group solidarity, while missionary scrutiny and western norms of romantic love gave school affairs a privacy which, because of its contrast with 'the publicity and control in the Red youth groups', was even more likely in Mayer's view to lead to pregnancy than was ignorance of 'safe' external intercourse.[13]

Economic changes in the wider society – industrialisation, rural impoverishment, African urbanisation – played a crucial part in altering sexual behaviour and customs. Enforced labour migrancy by young men delayed marriage for rural girls, who found themselves competing in a marriage market glutted by a surplus of marriageable girls. The old ways of compensating for premarital pregnancy were also becoming less effective: holding young men responsible for their illegitimate children proved much more difficult in town as well as in rural areas from which men had a chance to escape to town.[14] The absence of fathers left discipline to mothers, who were customarily expected to be more indulgent. It is striking that, the same year as the *isililo* was founded, one of the key ABM stations reported what a 'very serious question' efficient mission administration presented because of the 'new feature in all our churches – the very few men who are at home'.[15] The greater sense of freedom and autonomy which education and wider marriage choice had given to young African females was reinforced materially by their increasing urbanisation in the years between the South African War and the First World War. Poverty and ecological crises forced women and girls to town; we should not minimise their continued financial hardships once there, but some were also attracted to opportunities for economic self-support and independence.

In accounting for the lapses of which the men accused the women at the 1912 ABM Conference, a possible line of argument seems to be that Christian mothers, standing in for paternal authority, feared that harshness would drive their unmarried daughters away to town, where it was becoming obvious that they could earn their own living. More information about the nature and extent of *lobola* payments among ABM members at this time would be illuminating. Perhaps, like Bhaca fathers of the 1950s, women regarded their daughters 'as banks' and welcomed lovers' gifts at a time of financial stringency; if the Mission forbade *lobola*, gifts may have provided an acceptable substitute. The fact that the men berated the women is noteworthy. Fathers may have been worried at the 'spoiling' of daughters under lax maternal control during their absence at labour centres, and the consequent loss of the *lobola* which a virgin could bring. The African account gives no hint of these sorts of factors, but it seems unlikely that the response engendered owed its power entirely to notions of premarital chastity and maternal responsibility propagated by the missionaries. The 'sins' to which the women confessed clearly came out of traditional norms.

The name chosen for the American Board prayer union, *isililo*, is very significant. It means 'wailing' or 'lamentation', and is the term used for the protracted ritual keening of Zulu women after the burial of the deceased. This wailing reflected the helplessness and submission of women at such a time of sorrow, whereas men traditionally ended mourning with an aggressive act of ritual hunting, a sign of their dominance.[16] Now, the *isililo* movement spread through revivalist preaching seeking to produce a kind of mourning in its female hearers; they were to bewail and confess their sins as irresponsible mothers of adolescent daughters, then commit themselves to a new start spiritually. Although the evidence suggests that the style of these gatherings drew on experiences of fervent revivalism dating back at least to the late 1890s,[17] the resemblance between the emotional response elicited by revivalism and routinised female Nguni funeral behaviour was obviously not lost on the black women who chose the name. They held on to the name tenaciously, too. When the white American women missionaries urged them, characteristically enough, to change it to 'Women's Welfare Group of the American Board', the 'old women firmly opposed' any such step, saying, 'We love our name'.[18] The emotional scenes of the first recruitments to the *isililo* denoted mourning and repentance for maternal shortcomings. The persistence of wailing, weeping, sighing, cathartic extempore prayer and sharing of personal troubles in the *isililo* and other *manyanos*,[19] however, seems to reflect in part the increasing helplessness and powerlessness many African women felt in the face of daughterly waywardness and the social and economic forces which exacerbated their problems as mothers.

The *isililo* considered that 'White weddings took place frequently' as a result of their work. The organisation gave presents which were displayed on a table in the church on the wedding day by way of tribute to couples who had succeeded in staying pure. Young women were also enrolled by the *isililo*, initially wearing white ribbons for purity; from the 1940s, they wore pink collars instead.[20] The mothers' uniform consisted of black skirts, white blouses and pink ribbons. But despite the clear centrality of the issue of their daughters' sexual behaviour to the formation of the *isililo*, the organisation, once established, developed an interest in revivalistic religious gatherings for their own sake, rather than to reform attitudes to premarital chastity.[21]

Although 'purity', or premarital chastity, was a perennial concern among ABM women in Johannesburg, the Church's other main centre of operation, the question did not arise organically out of the anxieties of an elite rural Christian community, as in Natal, nor did it provide the stimulus for prayer union formation. In the 1920s at any rate, it was apparently left to missionaries or the wives of church officials to handle. At the annual meeting of the *isililo* in Johannesburg, 'talks on the training of the children, young people in the home and definite Purity talks' were given by the women missionaries. These must have stressed the role of the mother. Mrs Bridgman also periodically gave 'purity talks' to the older boys and girls of the Mission's Johannesburg day schools, 'taking them separately'. Some of the black pastors' wives had 'private talks with girls in the Enquirer's classes', but the fact that one deacon's wife was singled out approvingly in a report for 'fearless talk recently to her class of young women on relations with men', suggests that the task was not generally taken on very enthusiastically or frequently. In fact, probably the most systematic purveyor of 'social hygiene' propaganda within the American Board in Johannesburg was the missionary Ray Phillips, who wrote a book on the topic. Particularly alarmed at the breakdown of taboos on premarital sex and illegitimacy towards the end of the 1930s, he and his wife lectured quite extensively to various African groups – wives, young people, priests – on sex.[22]

Even this brief look at adolescent sexual socialisation in Johannesburg has demonstrated the missionary propensity to rely on 'talks'. However, the verbal reticence and fondness for euphemism about life's central physical experiences which early missionaries displayed, had had the effect of reinforcing in female converts their customary reluctance to speak to their daughters about sex. As the twentieth century advanced, the style and approach of some missionaries changed. The youthful, scientifically trained American Phillips, while reminding readers of his sex-education manual that, in approaching the subject of human reproduction, the proper mood was 'that of awe and humility', urged the need for frankness as well as reverence: 'Veiled allusions only pique the curiosity and excite unwholesome imagination.'[23] However, for many of the older generation of African women, who had seen initiation songs and teaching condemned as obscene, it was too late to remove the tinge of obscenity from this new candour. As late as the 1950s, when Mia Brandel-Syrier spoke to a *manyano* about the problems of mothers in giving their daughters sex-education, several members went to sleep as 'their form of protest, for it is unbefitting for a mother to discuss the Facts of Life with her daughters, and it is even more unbefitting to speak about such "heathenish" matters in church'. Several women explained to her, 'A girl never went to her mother. She could not be so free with her mother.'[24] The fondness for talks had a further dimension. The effectiveness, such as it is, of Red youth group socialisation comes from peer-group pressure in a positive kind of 'on-site' education. By contrast, the mothers' idea of 'educating' adolescent daughters was ' "to preach at them" and "to tell them the rules" '. The pride and privilege of old age were 'hammered into the poor daughters on all occasions'; 'maternal admonishments and commands' were the staple of contact between mothers and daughters.[25] In this the women followed both models evolved in the lecturing of English working-class girls by middle- and upper-class 'purity' advocates, and African ideals of the deference and obedience parents should exact from their children.[26]

While African mothers opted for corporate maternal supervision and admonition, at least two other approaches to the Christian socialisation of adolescents tried in the decade after the First World War merit a mention: the all-African peer group with members of both sexes, and adult-led single-sex youth movements. The objects of *isililo* concern, the young people of the American Board Mission, themselves founded an organisation 'laying emphasis on conduct during courtship, betrothal and marriage and standing firm against all-night wedding feasts'. When the Purity League was set up at Inanda in July 1919 after a weekend convention organised by Charles Dube and Robert Ngcobo, over a hundred young men and women signed the purity pledge. This movement should probably be seen not merely as an attempt to entrench new Christian moral attitudes and standards, but also as one of those expressions of African initiative in religion like temperance movements, from which they no doubt adopted the idea of the pledge. Further, its members were trying to consolidate the new, better-educated, young Christian elite, and enlisted puritanism to assist in forging the respectable, progressive, westernised identity to which they aspired. Sibusisiwe Violet Makanya, the Purity League's Secretary in the 1920s, told the Natal Missionary Conference that in the League's meetings, talks were given not only on bodily purity and abstinence from alcohol and tobacco, but also on anything else that elevated the conduct of youth and made them (in the word she chose) 'respectable'.

The League had a Junior and a Senior division, for twelve- to sixteen-year-olds, and those seventeen and over respectively. Its use of games and music at meetings brings out its similarities to white-initiated African youth organisations of the 1920s. It was the progressivist strain in the Purity League which endured, rather than its stress on a sexual purity deeper than that honoured by 'the mere getting married in the church and the wearing of veils'. In the 1930s, the movement became known as the Bantu Youth League. Under the direction of Miss Makanya, it tried to interest young people in Natal in programmes to uplift the community, while nurturing good citizenship, encouraging pride in African customs and fostering inter-racial co-operation.[27]

White church leaders made a concurrent attempt to establish uniformed youth organisations. Although in the nineteenth century they had found both African dancing and traditional initiation obscene in their sexual explicitness, by the 1920s some missionaries recognised that Christianity had failed to provide meaningful replacements in these spheres of recreation and sex education. The missions consequently promoted African adaptations of Scouts and Guides, called Pathfinders and Wayfarers, to provide adult-supervised Christian socialisation in these respects. As regards recreation, the Girl Wayfarers' Association, set up in October 1925, aimed to supply

> 'the fun of the Fair' to our Christian girls whom we have cut off from all the fun and excitement of heathen life. We don't want them to dance and yell and sing as the heathen girls do, and if we put nothing in the place of that, we have the danger of the empty house into which the seven devils enter.[28]

The lives of adolescent girls were to be enriched, and simultaneously guarded from sexual temptation, by weekly meetings for games, singing, drill, country dancing, and the learning of practical skills rewarded by proficiency badges. On the point of sex education, it was particularly the hope of Mrs Edith Rheinallt Jones, Superintendent of the Transvaal Wayfarers until her death in 1944, that the movement's health and social teaching would, for Christian girls, replace the initiation schools.[29] The claim was made from time to time in the inter-war period that Pathfinders and Wayfarers filled the gap in discipline and training left by the abandonment of tribal circumcision and initiation schools, or that the Christian movements could be shaped 'into something closely akin to age-sets but without some of the heathen presuppositions of the system'.[30] There is little evidence, however, that this was more than wishful thinking or that the substitution was much more than vague and indirect. In any event, Wayfaring was not immune to the problem of 'fallen' girls, even though it hoped to teach purity and self-control – 'A Wayfarer is clean in thought, word and deed' was added to the Law at the start of the 1930s. Mrs Jones thought dismissal necessary if a Wayfarer became pregnant before marriage, but she would always consider applications for readmission on their merits where the girls were received back into the church, claiming that some of her finest workers were 'girls who have gone through this and have suffered and are determined to protect their girls from the like'.[31]

There is no indication that concern about Christian premarital pregnancy played any part in the founding of the Methodist Manyano in the Transvaal, although the women's group gathered by a Potchefstroom minister's wife in 1907 as its nucleus did pray 'for their families and for the common unity and for their sins'.[32] Discussion about children at the 1912 Manyano Convention, however, focussed 'especially on the care of girls, who so often fall into evil ways'. The year 1912, it should be remembered, was that in which the *isililo* was founded in Natal. It is very striking how church synods and committees, the General Missionary Conference and African church members were all showing a heightened interest in the topic of black female adolescent sexual behaviour in the period 1911–12, which is when the 'black peril' scare was also at its peak and missionary advocacy of urban hostels for African girls was building up support. This was clearly a crucial time as regards the urbanisation of young African women and their increasing assertion of independence in the rural areas as well.[33]

Like the American Board, the Methodists set up a junior section of the prayer union for these unmarried girls and young women; the Young Women's Manyano was started at some stage in the second decade of this century by Mrs Elizabeth Kumalo, Manyano Vice-President, with the help of Mrs Burnet, the white District Chairman's wife, who stressed the importance of mothers training 'their children for the Lord'. They drew up some simple rules which were, explained Mrs Burnet's successor, mostly directed towards the moral life of members and intended to strengthen them along the path of 'their greatest danger', which was of course seen in terms of threats to their virginity. The 'unwonted freedom' of coming to town to work, Mrs Allcock went on in the vein of white hostel supporters, was 'fraught with much peril to the native girl' who had 'learnt no control of herself'. She admitted that the Young Women's rules were so binding and restrictive that at first not many girls were found who would conscientiously try to keep them. The movement was able to capitalise, though, on that new, earnest self-confidence general among young educated mission Africans after the First World War. In 1920, a year after the Purity League was founded, there was a special young women's session at the Manyano Convention, since some thirty young educated women, day-school teachers or fresh from the teacher-training course at Kilnerton, wished to speak. The young women continued to contribute at conventions, though generational norms were satisfied by their being given their own session. Their powerful testimonies were especially noted in 1934, for instance. Mrs Allcock promoted the Young Women's Manyano vigorously – seventeen new branches were started in 1924 alone – but recorded 'the hard struggle the young women have to keep true to the rules'. Membership nevertheless increased, 'despite many lapses'.[34]

In the case of the Methodists particularly, wailing and lamentation were not the only reaction of the mothers to their daughters' situation. Both the

Transvaal Methodist Manyano and the Natal Isililo showed great zeal in raising large sums of money for meaningful projects which advanced their children's financial security. The Methodist women funded a Domestic Science Training School, opened at Kilnerton in 1929, to offer their daughters a fuller life. As Mrs Kumalo was the driving force behind both this scheme and the Young Women's Prayer Union, it is quite possible that she envisaged better educational opportunities and consequent well-paid employment as the way forward for young Christian girls, offering something positive in addition to the negative protective sanctions of Manyano rules. The American Board women bought a farm in 1928 'as a memorial of the work of Isililo . . . and if their children became destitute, they could live there'. These projects, with their realistic awareness of life's financial struggles, perhaps indicate a contrast with the missionary approach of guarding female chastity by means of protective supervision through the hostel. In the early 1920s, when the Transvaal Methodist women were set on establishing the school, they could not be brought to see a Johannesburg Methodist hostel as an urgent priority, as the leading missionaries did.[35] African Christian women were well aware of the need to enhance their daughters' ability to earn wages or otherwise support themselves. Indeed they had seen the poverty of their families in town make a mockery of the middle-class missionary hypothesis of the exclusively domestic responsibilities of mothers. Prayer-union members, no less than other women, had to work to supplement male earnings, and even when this was done at home to make some simultaneous child-care possible, beer-brewing and laundry-work made time-consuming demands on the 'queen of the home'.[36]

Already in the Transkei by the turn of the century, Christian Methodist young people, 'giving increased trouble by the vice and follies they run after with greediness', had evolved a substitute for the courting parties denied them, namely 'night Tea-parties under the pretence of helping Church Funds'.[37] The explicit connection of the Transvaal Methodist Young Women's Manyano with resistance to such traditional initiation and courtship practices was underlined in the Union's aims as originally set out:

> To abstain from all youthful lusts, remembering that the body is the temple of the Holy Spirit. To take no part in unbecoming songs, nor spend the night at wedding feasts unless prayer be conducted there by the Association. To avoid the company of the wicked and all unprofitable social gatherings. To resist sin under all circumstances and not to be unequally yoked with an unbeliever or one of questionable character. To avoid superstitious and idolatrous practices and belief.

However, the draft constitution reported to Synod in 1940 was more restrained:

> 1. To encourage members to read the Scriptures every day and to keep their bodies and habits pure as Temples of the Holy Spirit.
> 2. To honour parents as becomes a Christian.

3. To keep the home clean and tidy.
4. To visit the sick, pray for and speak the word to those who are not Christians.
5. To promote the Missionary spirit and help in Church efforts.

That mothers were supposed to help daughters to shun the customary lovemaking was emphasised in the constitution adopted for the Manyano throughout South Africa in 1933, when the Transvaal joined with the movement in the rest of the country. One provision stressed that ' "Night-singing" (Imbolora) and dancing by young people are forbidden'.[38]

The Young Women's Prayer Union remained a relatively small movement (it had 1 655 Transvaal members in 1940 to the adult women's 9 421), and is sparsely documented. For rural members in Swaziland, we know that a number were the daughters of heathen parents and faced opposition to their Christian stand, frequently having to resist arranged marriages with heathen husbands. Of the urban members on the Reef even less is recorded, but membership figures tell their own tale. Whereas adult female membership on the Witwatersrand remained a constant 27 per cent of total Transvaal Methodist Manyano membership between 1933 and 1940, the Young Women's percentage plummeted from nearly 27 per cent to just under 17 in the same period.[39]

The movement was geared to help rural girls resist traditional premarital party-going; in town, the opportunities and distractions took a different form, in the face of which the Young Women's Manyano proved even more ineffectual and unable to attract members. Boksburg in 1940 had only two, for instance. In the 1930s, commercially-run dances, African shebeens and the independence of employment combined to offer young unmarried black women enjoyment and freedom. There was little in town which could by way of counter-incentive make it seem worthwhile or sensible to large numbers of Christian girls to guard their virginity interminably.

Hellmann's survey of almost 350 Johannesburg African families at the close of the 1930s found that one-third of the girls over sixteen had or had had illegitimate babies. Africans thought, wrote Hellmann, that marabi dances were largely responsible for this extensive illegitimacy.[40] In Dikobe's novel, The Marabi Dance, set in Johannesburg in 1938, the story turns on precisely such an event. Martha meets George through marabi parties and bears his child out of wedlock, although the happy ending has the couple marrying eventually seven years later. At several points the book illustrates vividly the argument of this paper, particularly regarding maternal sex-educational reticence and the female self-assertion and male non-accountability of the urban adolescent.

Martha is withdrawn from school by her parents after physical examination by her 'grandmother', albeit at her mother's request, verifies that she has had intercourse several times. Her mother then dresses Martha 'like a woman' so that she can attract a wealthy suitor, but instructs her only in a woman's household work. Her father rebukes his wife for not telling Martha 'women's things', saying, 'you are a mother, and a mother is the one to give law to her child if she is a girl'. When he warns Martha not to be a sexually unresponsive wife – 'A woman who refuses her man the blankets loses him to other women' – his wife hides her face in shame thinking, 'These are man's things which should not be told to children'. Her mother accurately sums up the likely effect of the town's attractions on Martha: 'Soshal Senta and baiskopo will give you a baby and no father.' George, who already has 'girls all over Johannesburg and in the kitchens', persuades Martha to sleep with him on the grounds that he needs proof, via children, that she is a woman. But Martha does not curse her 'sin' when she becomes pregnant, determining 'This child is going to work for me.' Afraid that the girl he has spoiled will get him into trouble, George secures a job transfer to Durban. Martha refuses an arranged marriage with a rustic relative, saying defiantly, 'I don't care if I get a child without a father. It is my child. God has willed that I should get it.' Her parents accept the situation philosophically, and the hardship that Martha suffers comes not from society's disapproval or her peer group's ridicule of her premarital pregnancy, as would have happened in a rural past, but rather from her long abandonment by George. She copes virtually alone with the child's birth, finding work and moving house, a vivid literary representation of what was forced on many young urban African women of that era.[41]

In the case of the Reef Anglicans, the initial impetus to tackle the problem of the premarital pregnancy of African Christian girls derived from the familiarity of the women missionaries with the extensive, somewhat punitive religious and charitable work among unmarried mothers in England. With time, instead of instructing only the girls involved, the missionaries stressed the mothers' responsibilities. Members of the Anglican prayer union, the Women's Help Society (WHS), like other black Christian women, lamented their powerlessness and lack of influence with their daughters and asked for assistance in fulfilling this onerous new duty.

At first, then, in line with the double standard so long entrenched in western Europe,[42] the main approach to female sexual purity was negative and retributive. Penitents' classes for girls under Christian discipline for premarital pregnancy were started in Johannesburg in 1911 – again a significant date – to test 'whether they really understand what they have done', and effect a year's disciplinary probation until the priest throught they were fit to be restored and their babies baptised. Of forty voluntary members in 1912, only two 'fell back into sin' soon after joining, so classes perhaps served for some as a preventive sanction in the absence of traditional penalties. The church also evolved visible punishments, again falling on the female offender, but not dissimilar in kind to those current in traditional morality. In a number of Anglican mission districts in South Africa by 1913, African Christian girls who had had an illegitimate child were not allowed to wear a white dress, veil or wreath on marriage, and the ceremony had to be performed outside the church door or in the church porch.[43]

More positive efforts were made later in the second decade. Amy Kent started branches of the WHS for young girls all over the Reef in 1917, to counteract what she saw as growing immorality and the feeble Christian preparation provided by black male catechists; thus the adolescents were linked for the first time with the mothers' organisation. All but one of these branches collapsed within two years, however, for lack of missionary visits. Perhaps these staffing difficulties reinforced the missionary desire to devolve more responsibility on black mothers. Already in 1911 one missionary had voiced the encouraging opinion that the moral standards of Reef African Christian women were rising,

> that a moral downfall is no longer looked upon as an almost inevitable incident, that there is a growing responsibility of the elder women for the younger and a desire of the mothers to see their daughters, not only better educated and more 'advanced' in the matter of hats and boots (that much desired mark of civilisation) but purer and more womanly than themselves.

The special subject at the WHS conference in 1919, attended by fifty Anglican Church women, was 'Our girls, how to train and teach them when young'. Though women from the country congregations on Reef farms particularly faced the problem of daughters running away from home to town and were 'earnestly desiring help', it was still, a woman missionary reported, 'quite a new idea to some of our more ignorant women' that they could by home teaching and influence help their girls later to be strong in facing temptation. (The unspoken assumption always was that the predominant temptation was sexual.) They had just learnt Christian ways themselves, they said; how could they teach others?[44] Probably their instinctive reticence at taking on the unaccustomed role of sex educators fed into this reaction too.

In 1929 at an Anglican women's conference in Sophiatown, the topic surfaced again. 'One and all who got up to talk about prayer, spoke about girls.' As a result, on the prompting of the mothers, Dorothy Maud, a Sophiatown missionary, started a guild for the girls. They were uniformed like their mothers, but in white veils with their white tops and black skirts, and they met on Friday afternoons. Maud reported the women 'in despair' about their daughters, 'saying that they pay not the slightest attention to them: simply going their own way, and getting into trouble right and left'. By 1940, this guild for confirmed girls in the years between leaving school and qualifying for membership of the adult union had been established further afield, for example in Orlando. Its inability to guarantee premarital chastity amid Reef social conditions is confirmed by the discussion at the Mothers' Union conference in

1946 of the eligibility of girls who had 'fallen by the way to become or remain members of St Mary's Guild'. Most African mothers favoured a lenient approach to the question.[45] The original disciplinary emphasis was retained, though, along with these girls' guilds. Miss Happer at Buxton Street confessed in 1927 that she found her penitents 'a great problem and a great mystery' and could only appeal to the girls to be good mothers 'for the sake of these sweet scraps of humanity'. In Sophiatown and Orlando, penitents' classes formed part of the routine church work, but they were taken, as ever, by the spinster women who were strangers to child-bearing and had presumably resisted premarital sexual temptation. The celibacy of these female missionaries not only accounts for their bafflement, as with Miss Happer, but was a positive disadvantage in their attempts to inculcate maternal responsibility for adolescent girls. Dorothy Maud, for instance, had to get Mrs Bridgman (a Congregationalist, not an Anglican), to talk to the mothers of Wayfarers, admitting wryly, 'The trouble is they don't like mere spinsters talking to them, so we think we shall probably have to rush into matrimony in order to be listened to!'[46]

By the 1930s it was becoming clear in urban churches at any rate that religious sanctions were insufficient to control a social phenomen like premarital pregnancy. Location churches did not generally differentiate, as many rural mission stations did, between the bridal attire and marriage ceremonies of virgins and mothers of illegitimate children. The forceful public disgrace meted out in traditional society had no effective Christian urban equivalent. Eileen Krige commented after investigations in Pretoria:

> A church member who has had an illegitimate child hardly connects the penalty of attending a purification class for six months with moral obliquity, and such purification has almost become a functional constituent of, or a necessary prerequisite to, baptism of the child.[47]

In essence, then, while the resolve to prevent their daughters' premarital pregnancy only sparked off the establishment of the rural Natal ABM Isililo, other women's prayer unions, such as the Anglican and the Methodist, shared the desire to assume responsibility as Christian mothers for the sexual purity of unmarried girls. In all three missions, this impulse led to the creation of a special association for such girls under the protective aegis of the older women's organisation, with which the link appears to have been closest in the Methodist case. However, within a short time a note of persistent lament crept into these efforts at socialisation. Urban, no less than rural, women found themselves compelled to channel their major energies into economic survival. The absence of a family wage from their husbands meant that, even where willing, they were not generally able to devote their days to the pious nurture and sexual guidance of their infant and adolescent children as the Church envisaged. African Christian mothers confessed themselves unable to counteract with religious exhortation and maternal admonition the far-reaching changes set in motion – initially in the countryside but soon prominently in town – by western education, industrialisation and urbanisation.

Notes

I gratefully acknowledge the financial assistance of the International Federation of University Women and the Central Research Fund of London University towards the research from which this paper is drawn.

Abbreviations

ABC   Papers of the American Board of Commissioners for Foreign Missions, Houghton Library, Harvard University

CPSA   Archives of the Church of the Province of South Africa, Witwatersrand University Library

MMS   Methodist Missionary Society Archives, School of Oriental and African Studies Library, University of London

USPG   Archives of the United Society for the Propagation of the Gospel, London

1 *Manyano* (union) comes from the Xhosa *ukumanyana* (to join), and is the most widely-known term for these organisations. The only book-length treatment of them is M. Brandel-Syrier, *Black Woman in Search of God*, (London, 1962), a vivid description of Reef *manyanos* in the 1950s. B. Pauw, *Christianity and Xhosa tradition* (Cape Town, 1975), 93–6, discusses the phenomenon in the eastern Cape in the 1960s.

2 A. Hastings, *Christian Marriage in Africa* (London, 1973), 5–6 and *passim* for examples of how these 'absolutes' were for centuries not rigidly applied.

3 *Ibid.*, p. 18.

4 See D. W. T. Shropshire, *The Church and Primitive Peoples* (London, 1938), pp. 355–7. Perhaps this is an over-simplification; the lineage was the cult group and the genealogically senior male, priest.

5 N. F. Cott, *The Bonds of Womanhood: 'woman's sphere' in New England, 1780–1835* (New Haven, 1977), p. 84; also pp. 46–7, 62–70. See Anna Davin, 'The working-class family: co-operating to survive in early industrialisation', unpublished paper presented to the African History Seminar, Institute of Commonwealth Studies, London, 1980.

6 *Advance* (April 1916), 56; ABC: 15.4.v.39, no. 131, 'The place of women in the Church on the mission field'; C. Maxeke, 'Social conditions among Bantu women and girls', in Students Christian Association of Southern Africa, *Christian Students and Modern South Africa* (Alice, 1930), p. 311.

7 R. E. Phillips, *African Youth and Sexual hygiene* (Durban, 1935), p. 43.

8 I. Schapera, *Married Life in an African Tribe* (London, 1940), pp. 244–7; A. R. Radcliffe-Brown and D. Forde (eds), *African Systems of Kinship and Marriage* (London, 1950), p. 28.

9 Schapera, *Married Life*, p. 38; A. van der Vliet, 'Growing up in traditional society',

in W. D. Hammond-Tooke (ed.), *The Bantu-speaking Peoples of Southern Africa* (London, 1974), pp. 227–37.

10 I. Schapera, 'Premarital pregnancy and native opinion: a note on social change', *Africa*, VI (1933), 65–6.

11 J. Goody, *Production and Reproduction: a comparative study of the domestic domain* (Cambridge, 1976), p. 14; P. and I. Mayer, 'Socialization by peers: the youth organization of the red Xhosa', in P. Mayer (ed.), *Socialization: the approach from social anthropology* (London, 1970), p. 175; E. J. Krige, *The Social System of the Zulus* (Pietermaritzburg, 1936), pp. 104–6, and 'Girls' puberty songs and their relation to fertility, health, morality and religion among the Zulu', *Africa*, XXXVIII, 2 (1968); W. D. Hammond-Tooke, *Bhaca Society* (Cape Town, 1962), p. 95, also pp. 92–6.

12 *Umlandu Wesililo Samabandla 1912–1962* (A history of the *isililo* of the churches), p. 2. This fiftieth-anniversary booklet was compiled by the daughter of one of the founders. I am very grateful to Mrs I. Mkwayi for the loan of this pamphlet and to Mr M. B. Yengwa for translating it. See also ABC: 15.4.v.29, Annual Report American Zulu Mission, 30 June 1913, p. 37, and Walter Foss newsletter, 20 June 1913. These accounts are by comparison unilluminatingly brief and give a consultative role to Mrs Foss which *Umlandu* omits.

13 *South African Native Affairs Commission, Minutes of Evidence*, IV (Cape Town, 1904), p. 794. For a Zululand missionary's condemnation of co-education, see A. W. Lee, *Once Dark Country* (London, 1949), pp. 87–8. He comments further (pp. 109–10), 'The girls, over-sexed, impetuous, and romantically-inclined, fell in and out of love with an enthusiasm credible only if actually seen.' Mayer, 'Socialization', p. 178. A. Vilakazi, *Zulu Transformations* (Pietermaritzburg, 1962), pp. 47, 57–8, also blames Christian secrecy for premarital preganancies. For the earlier emphasis on puberty rituals, see M. Gluckman, 'Kinship and marriage amongst the Lozi of Northern Rhodesia and the Zulu of Natal', in Radcliffe-Brown and Forde, *Kinship*, p. 203; he suggests research showed that all Southern Bantu women initiated into age regiments had frequent illegitimate births after the destructive impact of westernisation.

14 See, for example, *1930–32, Native Economic Commission*, SOAS M4581, pp. 990–1, for Rev. J. C. E. Penzhorn's evidence on how parents in the Rustenburg district 'het gehandsop' in trying to trace those who had caused their daughters' premarital pregnancies in Pretoria and Johannesburg. Men from Pietersburg, Mafeking or Swaziland were too elusive, unlike locals.

15 ABC: 15.4.v.29, Annual Report 1912 Adams and Imfume Stations, 2.

16 H. Ngubane, *Body and Mind in Zulu Medicine* (London, 1977), pp. 84, 93–4.

17 *Annual Report of the American Board . . . 1897*, 30; 'The Volunteers', *Missionary Herald* (Dec. 1905), 638–41, and 'Zulu Women's Weekly Prayer Meeting', *Life and Light for Women* (March 1904), 109.

18 *Umlandu*, 4–5.

19 See Brandel-Syrier, *Black Woman*, pp. 34–40.

20 *Umlandu*, 10. Ribbons were a favoured device in ABM work. See Mrs Cowles's letter, *Missionary Herald* (April 1926), 152, describing how those who took a definite stand for purity, renounced beer and gave up tobacco wore respectively white, blue and red ribbons to proclaim the fact.

21 See the somewhat despairing comments in ABC: 15.4.v.28, Amy Cowles to Miss Lamson, 22 April 1926.

22 ABC: 15.4.v.39, no. 131, 'The place of women', 3; ABC: 15.4.v.44, 'Report – Johannesburg Social Work – 1937–1938' (filed under 1939). The increase in illegitimacy attracted anthropological comment in the 1930s. Schapera, 'Premarital pregnancy', records how widespread the phenomena was among the Kgatla by the end of the 1920s, while E. J. Krige, 'Changing conditions in marital relations and parental duties among urbanized natives', *Africa*, IX, 1 (1936), notes its prevalence in Pretoria locations in the early 1930s. Her figure, that 60 per cent of brides in the Skoolplaas Lutheran Church marriage register 1931–34, were known to have children, can perhaps be related to the economic depression of those years. Cf. D. Levine, *Family Formation in an Age of Nascent Capitalism* (New York, 1977), ch. 9, 'Illegitimacy: marriage frustrated, not promiscuity rampant', which links the peak years of English illegitimacy samples to years of bad harvest or fluctuation in industrial prosperity. Fascinating though this approach is, however, even were such figures available for South Africa, the intention of this paper is rather to focus on the mothers' response than the statistical details of illegitimacy.

23 Phillips, *Hygiene*, pp. 17, 5.

24 Brandel-Syrier, *Black Woman*, p. 95.

25 *Ibid.*, pp. 29, 86.

26 E. Hellmann, *Problems of Urban Bantu Youth* (Johannesburg, 1940), pp. 4–8, stresses particularly the parental strictness which in town was usually not tempered by indulgence and familiarity from maternal relatives.

27 'The place of women', 3; *Missionary Herald* (Jan. 1920), 35–6; *Natal Missionary Conference 1922; Fifth National European-Bantu Conference ... 1933 Report* (Johannesburg), 62–3.

28 L. M. Forrest, 'Evangelism and the Bantu girl', in *Report of Proceedings of Eighth General Missionary Conference of South Africa* (Lovedale, 1932), p. 140. For the importance of clean, wholesome recreation in countering impure thoughts, see the chapter 'Winning through' in Phillips, *Hygiene*.

29 See SOAS, International Missionary Council Archives, Box 1229, 'Girl Wayfarers Association. Sixteen Years of Wayfaring' (Nov. 1941); and Witwatersrand University Library, South African Institute of Race Relations Papers, Note by Mrs Rheinallt Jones to the Adviser, 11 June 1942, for plans for a course on such replacement training in 1942 in Vendaland, an area famed for its female initiation ceremonies.

30 See H. P. Junod, 'Anthropology and mission education', *International Review of Missions*, XXIV, 94 (April 1935), 221; *Umteteli wa Bantu*, 9 June 1928; *1930–32 Native Economic Commission*, SOAS M4581, Evidence of J. D. R. Jones, p. 9032; Mrs. Jones in *Report of the National European–Bantu Conference 1929* (Lovedale), p. 207; R. E. Phillips, *The Bantu Are Coming* (London, 1930), p. 106; 'Do native customs prepare for Pathfinding?', *South African Outlook* (Jan. 1935), 19–20. That a substitute for initiation instruction was desired is indicated by the plea of educated Johannesburg Africans to a leading British moral welfare worker touring South Africa in 1932, for definite teaching to replace the old tribal sanctions. CPSA fAB 329, Report of Miss Higson's Tour, 6.

31 South African Institute of Race Relations Papers, Mrs Jones to Mrs H. Gibson, 10 Dec. 1934.

32 See 'The Story of the Manyano' by Mrs A. E. N. Bolani and Mrs J. Duiker in 'The Methodist Church of South Africa: Transvaal and Swaziland District', African Women's Prayer and Service Union; Manyano-Kopano Jubilee Celebrations, 1959.

33 *Foreign Field* (April 1913), 253. For further discussion of the General Missionary Conference's interest in 'Native girls in town' and of the rationale behind hostels, see D. Gaitskell, ' "Christian compounds for girls": church hostels for African women in Johannesburg 1907–1970', *Journal of Southern African Studies*, VI, 1 (Oct. 1979), 44–51.

34 *Foreign Field* (Feb. 1916), 133; Allcock Papers (in possession of Miss Ruth Allcock), Ts. 'Girls of South Africa'; *Foreign Field* (Sept. 1921), 233; *Transvaal Methodist* (Dec. 1934), 7; *Wesleyan Methodist Transvaal Directory*, 1925–6, 43; 1928–9, 30.

35 *Umlandu*, 5–8; SOAS MMS Box 1052, Mabel Allcock to Miss Bradford, 4 Sept. 1922.

36 On the remunerative occupations of Witwatersrand African women, see E. Hellmann, *Rooiyard: a sociological survey of an urban native slum yard* (Cape Town, 1948); and D. Gaitskell, 'Laundry, liquor and "playing ladish": African women in Johannesburg 1903–1939', unpublished paper presented to the workshop on South African social history, Centre of International and Area Studies, London, 1978.

37 Rev. Hargreaves's Diary, 17 Jan. 1900, quoted in W. G. Mills, 'The role of African clergy in the reorientation of Xhosa society to the plural society in the Cape Colony, 1850–1915', Ph.D. thesis, UCLA, 1975, p. 75. See M. Wilson, S. Kaplan, T. Maki and E. M. Walton, *Social Structure, Keiskammahoek Rural Survey*, III (Pietermaritzburg, 1952), 158–63, for later manifestations of 'school' partyings. See also the essay by David Coplan in this volume.

38 Central Methodist Church, Johannesburg, Transvaal Methodist Synod Minutes 1940, Report of the Women's Manyano; *Minutes of the Annual Conference of the Methodist Church of South Africa . . . 1933*, p. 259.

39 Figures calculated from Cory Library, Grahamstown, MS15 855 . . . *Membership Returns 1933* and Transvaal Methodist Synod Minutes 1940, Manyano Financial Statement and Membership Returns.

40 Hellmann, *Problems*, pp. 16, 51.

41 M. Dikobe, *The Marabi Dance* (London, 1973), pp. 10–11, 64, 66, 78–9, 83–4, 90–1.

42 K. Thomas, 'The double standard', *Journal of the History of Ideas*, XX, 2 (1959), 195–213, attempts to account historically for the centuries-old persistence in western Europe of this assumption that, while unchastity in men is mild and pardonable, for a woman it is 'a matter of the utmost gravity'. But he concludes by wondering whether it simply follows in practice from the fact that female premarital or extramarital sex is more detectable since women can conceive and men cannot.

43 USPG Women's Work Letters Africa, Miss Williams to Miss Trollope, 10 April 1911; Committee of Women's Work, Miss Williams to Miss Saunders, 15 Dec. 1912; CPSA fAB 226, Short Report of the First Conference of Women Missionaries of the Church of the Province of South Africa. See Brandel-Syrier, *Black Woman*, p. 52, for an account of how this sort of rule was observed one Sunday at the established Roman Catholic centre, Mariannhill, in Natal in the 1950s: nine out of ten weddings performed had the bride wearing pink. Women of other South African churches besides the three of this study took on this supervisory role over girls' sexuality. M. Hunter, *Reaction to Conquest* (London, 1936), p. 184, noted that two representatives of the Women's Association of the Bantu Presbyterian Church had to certify, after a physical examination, that a girl was a virgin before she could be married in church with a veil. Contrary to the then accepted view, Hunter claimed, incidentally, that Christian premarital pregnancy was not more frequent than that

among pagans in the same district. Mayer's research from the 1950s distinguishes between the two groups on grounds of age: Christian unmarried mothers are teenagers, while their Red counterparts are in their mid to late twenties. P. Mayer, *Townsmen or Tribesmen*, 2nd ed. (Oxford, 1971), pp. 38–9.

44 USPG E, A. M. Kent, 1917–19; *Mission Field* (Nov. 1911), 349; USPG E, 'Work amongst the native women in Johannesburg and the Reef', 1920; *The Kingdom* (March 1920).

45 CPSA *Litaba tsa Kereke* (Sept. 1929), 3; USPG Ekutuleni Papers, Maud newsletter, 17 Sept. 1929; *The Watchman* (Feb. 1946), 6. But this very fact – that they wanted to let unmarried mothers belong to the girls' guild – underlines Mayer's perceptive observation that the Church prefers unmarried mothers to 'act as if they were still girls' rather than 'as if they were already wives'. Mayer, *Townsmen or Tribesmen*, p. 236. Marriage, not children, transformed a Christian 'girl' into a 'mother'.

46 USPG E, C. Happer, 14 Dec. 1927; CPSA AB 396, Maud newsletter, 3 July 1934.

47 Krige, 'Changing conditions', 6.

CHAPTER FOURTEEN

The emergence of an African working-class culture

David Coplan

If we are to understand the cultural components of African class formation, historical and social anthropological research methods need to be integrated. Together the two approaches help identify both external pressures on colonised societies and their reactions to colonisation, including processes of adaptation and resistance, and attempts to create alternatives to social and cultural patterns that colonialism has disrupted or destroyed.[1] Changes in African culture did not result mechanically from 'contact' with Europeans. New forms arose from processes within the total field of relations of power and production within the South African social formation. Patterns of differentiation and the emergence of new classes within African society reveal how urban and rural areas were linked within the structure of colonial economic and political relations. The purpose of this essay is to review some of what is known about African cultural expression in the period of South Africa's rapid industrialisation, with the focus upon African proletarian culture.

To some extent, the social differentiation implied in such terms of the period as *amaqaba* ('red' pagan), *amakholwa* ('believer'; mission-school African), *amakumsha* (deceiver; freely, lumpenproletarian),[2] 'blanket kaffir', 'civilised native' and 'town boy' was more apparent than real. These categories were only instruments in the complex relationship between the perception of social alignments and divisions, and actual patterns of behaviour.[3] The dichotomy between migrant and urban-dweller, and the social isolation of rural-oriented *amakhaya* ('homeboys') in the city and of westernised *amakholwa* on rural mission stations have been emphasised in much anthropological and historical literature.[4] Despite their empirical validity, these concepts have diverted attention from the equally real, though less visible, continuities of communication and experience among sectors of African society and between town and countryside. To establish the nature and significance of these continuities is as important if we are to understand the strategic responses of Africans to the trauma of proletarianisation.

Excluded both from traditional kraal and white-dominated mission station, African workers had to devise their own flexible patterns of meaning, value and organisation. Their cultural and social forms developed from the manipulation of available resources in adapting to conditions of mine, factory, town location, squatter camp, farm-labour quarters, back-country *shebeen* and, not least of all, the open road. The reciprocal influences of urban and rural communities on the emergence of these forms occurred, moreover, within the encompassing structure of colonial capitalist expansion.

Cities of the New Rush

From at least the mid-nineteenth century, Africans worked in Cape Town and Durban and in the smaller towns of the eastern Cape and Natal, although as yet we know relatively little about class formation and incipient working-class culture in these largely non-industrial urban settings.[5] It was the mineral revolution beginning in Kimberley in the 1870s, however, that stimulated the development of patterns of large-scale African urbanisation which exert their influence even today. Early Kimberley had the reputation of being rougher, more boisterous and more crime-ridden than the worst of the 'roaring camps' of the California gold-rush.[6] Physical conditions were appalling, but perhaps more significant for the process of class formation was the unprecedented mixing of ethnic and racial groups in all spheres of activity.

Ironically, the African workers in Kimberley often had more contact with whites and more experience of the reality of capitalism than did their mission-educated brethren. As W. E. B. Du Bois noted of turn-of-the-century America, 'In the higher walks of life . . . the colour-line comes to separate natural friends and co-workers; while at the bottom of the social group, in the saloon, the gambling hell, and the brothel, that same line wavers and disappears.'[7] Certainly the high rate of desertion (66 per cent) among newly arrived workers[8] and the involvement of up to half of Kimberley's population in the illicit diamond traffic[9] indicate that Africans had ample opportunities to engage in independent entrepreneurial activity. An independent black community arose in the Malay Camp, where new patterns of socialisation and cultural innovation developed that had great influence on the evolution of working-class institutions in both urban and rural areas.

Among the agents of urban social and cultural transmission were the so-called Coloureds, who brought two-hundred-year-old traditions of professional musicianship and the institution of the illegal, private drinking house, or *shebeen*, with them from the Cape.[10] Through Coloured influence and the experience of labour and transport-riding for Afrikaner farmers, western 'trade-store' instruments, including the guitar, concertina, violin, auto-harp and mouth-organ, became popular among migrant and farm labourers as well as among urban workers. These instruments and many urban stylistic influences were incorporated into traditional music and dance culture. Similarly, the *shebeen*, which began to replace the traditional communal beer-drink in town, was taken by migrants into remote corners of rural southern Africa.

In Johannesburg, comparable processes of class formation and cultural transformation affected 'this welter of the tribes', as Maurice Evans put it.[11] The contributions of those who already had experience of work or urban residence in Cape Town, Queenstown, Durban, Kimberley, Port Elizabeth or Rustenburg was crucial to the establishment of socially viable communities in Johannesburg's black squatter camps and slumyards. Although Johannesburg lacked diamonds, the illicit liquor trade created an African home industry which became central to African working-class social and cultural as well as economic reorganisation.

The model of western civilisation presented by the heterogeneous urban whites of Kimberley and Johannesburg was hardly exemplary, and provided a stark contrast to the teachings of missionaries. Although John X. Merriman may have exaggerated in calling Johannesburg, in 1909, the African 'university of crime',[12] the Rev. F. W. Bridgman put it in more neutral a fashion when he observed in 1920 that:

> For weal and woe Johannesburg has become unwittingly the greatest educational agency among the Native people . . . introducing tens of thousands to the White man and his civilization. . . . There are today very few, if any, 'raw' Natives in the sense which the term signified thirty years ago.[13]

The lessons in survival taught in the cities became the basis for an indigenous proletarian culture which made its way into every region of South Africa.

Mine and migrant culture

From the beginning, large-scale mining created a discrete social world among African miners with its own ethos, forms of cultural expression and patterns of affiliation and opposition. It was essentially a male industrial subculture, in which as early as the 1870s group dancing became a major form of recreation and a means of expressing ethnic–regional identification and rivalry. Interested in ways to keep order and healthily occupy the leisure time of their workforce, mine management in Johannesburg sanctioned Sunday displays and competitions between dance teams from the 1890s. Although the original dances were drawn from rural traditions, the urban compound environment stimulated the creation of new patterns directly relevant to life of the mines.

Clegg's research[14] identifies processes of diversification in Zulu dance forms which have been in operation among migrants for at least seventy years.[15] The competitive element so prominent in male dancing in rural society[16] assumed an intra-ethnic, regional–kinship focus on the mines, where the now-close contact of groups from formerly separate Zulu chiefdoms and clans produced rivalries among 'homeboy' dance teams. This concern for local group identity and prestige, arising in part out of their daily work experience, led to the development of more rigorous aesthetic criteria and structure. A new individualism encouraged stylistic innovation as the status of workers rose or fell on the basis of their achievements in the dance arena. In Durban, hostel-dwellers developed new dances in the traditional idiom, such as *ingoma*, and performed rural dances such as *ndhlamu* as members of employer-sponsored teams boasting distinctive colours, banners and uniforms.[17]

The development of such teams in the cities is of particular interest, since though dance and poetic song provided the organisational focus, they took on additional functions as voluntary associations. Homeboy dance clubs in Johannesburg served as vehicles for the expression of identity, solidarity and leadership ability, and as the basis for social networks and both urban and rural faction fighting. The intensified competitive ethos influenced the development of Transvaal Sotho *amalaita* teams, who regularly battled and performed the *mokhorotlo* military dance in the location streets during the early twentieth century. Dance structure itself became an index of adaptation and changing world view, evident also in the fierce contests between male dancers supporting the bride or groom at non-Christian weddings in the rural areas.

As the vocabulary of movement became more spectacular and assertive, means were found to achieve some 'psychic distance' from the intense, winner-take-all atmosphere of the dance arena by performing *ukukomika* ('comic'), steps infused with humour and parody and derived from the emerging culture of the nearby urban locations.[18] The Moçambican tradition of court jesters or *marombes*[19] also appeared on the mines, where Bachopi comedians in European formal wear performed acrobatic and mimetic turns, comic praises, satires of European mine personnel, and even parodies of the ordinarily serious practice of trance-divination.[20] Such attempts at psychocultural adaptation were necessary in an environment where, as at one Crown Mines programme, the internal seriousness of group dance competition was combined with the externally imposed humiliation of ricksha races.[21]

Equally important were individualised modes of performance which were related to the special character of the social experience of migrants. Among the Basotho, for example, social identity was traditionally articulated and reinforced through forms of poetic–musical recitative composition. On the long journeys by foot, and later by train, to Kimberley or Johannesburg, or during leisure hours on the mines, Sotho men adapted elements of these forms into a new vehicle for the expression of their experience and its personal significance. Drawing on forms of *lithoko* (praise poems) and *mangae* songs associated with initiation into 'regimental' age sets, they developed *sefela* (pl., *lifela*), a distinctive genre of self-praise, social commentary and personal address. Prizes are still given in *sefela* competitions on the mines, more than a century after their first appearance. Expressions of pride or challenge form the core of *sefela*, but the more admired composers weave in subtle commentary on religion, history, work, geography and social behaviour.

Lifela are important in the release of the psychological stress which results from arduous, nerve-racking and dangerous work underground. The sense of elated pride in their ability to do 'men's work' persists strongly in the miner's outlook when above ground, and is evident in the wry self-praise of *lifela*. Many of these melodic poems also express the insecurity and emotional suffering of men who toil in the face of death for a pittance, far from home and family and always subordinate to the harsh authority of a white supervisor.

With the institutionalisation of migrant mine labour as the principal means by which young men earned the money for *bohali* (bride wealth), tax and other necessities, a period of service away at the mines largely came to replace traditional initiation into adulthood for the Basotho. Young men travelled to the mines to gain a more worldly, urban experience and to earn the respect of potential wives through their bravery, as well as to demonstrate economic and social independence.[22] Reflecting the increased individualism and competitiveness of the urban-industrial environment, *sefela* became a way of gaining personal recognition, in which the performer could boast about himself and derogate others. Evident also in many *lifela* is the transformation of the miner's self-image from rural-pastoralist to modern industrial man capable of full participation in the urban environment. Rycroft[23] and Schapera[24] have noted similar developments in the praise-poetic traditions of Zulu and Tswana migrants. Sung by migrants in rural as well as urban areas, many examples of these forms have become part of the permanent corpus of African vernacular art. In view of the close association of verbal expression and social process in traditional life, it is regrettable that these sources of information about migrants' historical experience have barely been explored.[25]

An examination of some of the processes involved in other changes in performance culture reveals much about the dynamics of adaptation among African workers. The tradition of performing indigenous music upon western instruments or homemade facsimiles, for example, began with the Khoisan people of the Cape Colony in the eighteenth century.[26] Among Africans, Mayr[27] noted the rapid spread of trade-store instruments among the Zulu in 1908, but both he and von Hornbostel[28] were wrong in assuming that this meant that indigenous music would be discarded along with traditional instruments. Kirby observed in 1934[29] that rural Africans never seemed to play European music upon western instruments, and Rycroft has recently discovered how indigenous musical principles 'in some cases can be more effectively realised through these new media than could be done on the traditional instruments they have replaced'.[30] In the cities, the use of western instruments has facilitated the incorporation of diverse cultural influences into indigenous musical structures. New instruments and stylistic materials enjoyed a high status among migrants and urban workers, who considered them indispensable to the display of modernity and sophistication, reflecting expanded cultural horizons and social interests.

By the turn of the century, syncretic blends of Coloured–Afrikaans, British, black American and African music were emerging as part of urban African cultural patterns. Migrants were among the first instrumentalists to perform in the city streets and *shebeens*, contributing to the development of distinctively urban African performance styles. Just as important, however, was their introduction of urban influences into rural musical and dance forms. It is thus difficult to discern whether *ukuxhentso*, *isiphethukane*,[31] or *mbayizela*,[32] all concertina dances popular with rural Xhosa by 1930, were among the *sources* or the *results* of the development of urban syncretic styles. So common did trade-store instruments become among migrants and rural people that Christian Africans identified them as pagan, 'traditional' instruments and abandoned their use in favour of choral, keyboard and brass music.

Visitors to the countryside can easily see that migrants do not return home untransformed by urban experience. Among the Basotho, for example, returning miners are still known categorically as *sekoata* (pl., *likoata*), from the English, 'squatter', referring to migrants who took up residence in the unauthorised shanty-towns of Newclare and other areas of the Witwatersrand at the turn of the century. In Lesotho, the term refers to the rude, aggressive, ruffianly behaviour of compound-hardened mine veterans home on leave.[33] Returning migrants often find they have little in common with the families they have worked so hard to support,[34] and take refuge in the group support and *ésprit de corps* of men like themselves. Their pockets bulging with holiday or severance wages, they gather as outsiders in *baras* (bars) in their home villages to drink, dance and entertain women with neo-traditional *focho* ('disorder') music played on the concertina and drum. Thus styles and patterns derived originally from traditional models in places like Newclare find their way back to rural areas with young miners who, belonging neither to town nor country, are truly at home only among themselves.[35]

The female counterparts of the *likoata*, the abandoned women, prostitutes and 'shebeen queens' (bar owners) developed parallel forms of expression focused in what has been known among Sotho workes for at least sixty years as the *famo* dance. As a dance, the term *famo* refers to a rather wild type of choreographic striptease performed to attract the attentions of male spectators.[36] Quite distinct from the dance, *famo* involves the performance of lengthy recitative songs paralleling in form and purpose the men's *safela* compositions. *Famo* songs are often addressed to men and other women, and consist of extemporised verses in which the singer laments her abandonment, loss of family ties and home, and the general hardness of her lot, while criticising the bad character or anti-social behaviour of others and praising her own personal qualities and attractions.

The hardships of social disaffiliation were often even greater for women than for men. Most women who left home did so facing grave personal crisis, and returned only if they had established themselves as persons of independent means in liquor or other trades. *Famo* may appear as the emotional response of demoralised workers to a predatory social environment, yet there is evidence in the songs of an underlying sense of community and a system of values retained from rural society. Amidst extremely harsh circumstances, *famo* provided a cathartic medium for moral comment and the expression of common problems. *Famo* occasions helped to establish social networks which brought female-dominated, urban, working-class social institutions such as the *shebeen* and the *stokfel* and *mohodisana* (rotating credit and entertainment clubs) back to the country, where they were further modified to meet the needs of a changing rural society.[37] In both urban and rural areas, emerging patterns of social and economic relations among Africans have depended as much upon the innovative roles of women as upon the activities of men.

Dressed people and urban proletarians

In rural areas, the social and economic disruption of African life produced another category of persons whose activity and influence are worthy of greater attention. These were the *amakumsha* (Sotho–Tswana: *makgomocha*), *abaphakathi* ('people in-between'), or 'dressed people', terms invented by Africans to describe those who were neither pagan nor Christian – those disengaged from traditional communities, yet not incorporated into mission-school culture and its normative social system. Most had acquired sufficient knowledge of western culture through work and travel to enable them to manipulate it for their own benefit. Thus they were considered merely 'dressed people' displaying a veneer of westernisation symbolised by a suit of clothes. They were despised by traditional Africans as exploiters and deceivers, and by the African petty bourgeoisie, who regarded them as immoral, anti-social purveyors of the worst African and European social traits, undermining the claims of Christian Africans to 'civilised' status. Characteristically itinerant, the dressed people were notorious during the latter part of the nineteenth century, and were blamed for the prevalence of drunkenness and crime among Africans in villages and towns.[38]

Though viewed almost unanimously as the human detritus of informal culture contact and modernisation by black and white writers alike,[39] the dressed people were in many ways leaders in the formulation of individualised economic, social and cultural strategies of adaptation, and even resistance to the colonial system. Involved from the beginning in informal and illegal economic enterprises, the dressed people devised ways to manipulate the contradictions of the system while retaining a certain freedom of action. Among their innovations, partly aided by Coloured predecessors, was professional African dance musicianship. Mobile African musicians functioned as cultural brokers, reinterpreting and transmitting new cultural influences as they entertained members of different social groups and geographical communities.

In the cities, categories such as dressed people lost their significance amid the large-scale processes of social marginalisation and proletarianisation affecting Africans. Professional musicians found their services in great demand in urban areas, and provided cultural entertainment for *shebeens*, *famo* dances, and *stokfel* parties, as well as for the concerts, tea-meetings and soirées of petty-bourgeois voluntary associations. In so doing these versatile performers blended musical materials from every available tradition into a syncretic style that became a pervasive aspect of working-class culture in towns throughout South Africa. This culture, called *marabi*,[40] influenced migrant musicians and dancers, who brought it back to the rural areas. In Lesotho, for example, a genre of *marabi* wedding songs known as *wa sala wena* ('we are leaving the bride behind') developed and, according to Guma[41] totally replaced traditional wedding songs among peasant Basotho.[42]

By the end of the First World War, popular culture in Johannesburg was centred in the slumyards of Doornfontein and Prospect Township,[43] where people ranging from petty-bourgeois professionals to domestic servants and industrial migrants gathered for social recreation. As F. W. Bridgman pointed out, 'these slum districts constitute the rendezvous for all classes of Natives. . . . In fact the yards have perforce become the Native pleasure resort during holiday and leisure hours'.[44] It was there, and in the *shebeens* of the city's Western Areas, that one could find the most urbanised of the Sotho *likoata*, the *sebhunu morao* ('buttocks to the back'), migrant contract workers who had left their homes permanently and thus 'showed only their ass to Lesotho'.[45] Similarly, the slumyards attracted many Zulu workers who had severed their ties with the country, and who were considered *udliwe i'intaba*, 'eaten by the hills' (mine dumps) of Johannesburg.

Many other slumyard residents belonged to the fully urbanised and partly westernised African working class, yet retained strong links with rural kin. These links provided a psychosocial defence against an environment of racial hostility, legal restriction and residential and economic insecurity. Such ties were strengthened by the common practice of sending urban children to stay with relatives in the country during periods of family difficulty.[46] For many of these people, Christianity also had an important place within the framework of adaptation.

Part of the attraction of Christianity for Africans derived from the collective power of its white adherents. Africans probably responded to mission teaching according to their perception of its value for material improvement, social advancement and cultural reintegration within the structure of colonial relations. Although Christianity has been an ideological component of colonial domination, Africans have also continually used it in attempts to increase their autonomy in all spheres of activity. In various forms, then, Christianity has influenced the form and direction of change and the flow of cultural communication between African social classes and urban and rural communities.

Christianity and African culture

Much of what has been written about Christian missionary efforts among black South Africans in the nineteenth and twentieth centuries[47] has emphasised the social and cultural discontinuities between mission station and pagan African community life. These discontinuities have been shown to be among the sources of the categorical opposition of 'red' and 'school' Xhosa, for example,[48] and of early class formation among Cape Africans.[49] The mission centres may have had little effect on purely traditional communities, but it is clear that migratory labour and proletarianisation prepared the ground for significant missionary influence on large sectors of the non-mission black population. The mission stations themselves tended to attract refugees, former servants, itinerant marginals and 'characters of the worst description'[50] as well as whole groups, such as the Mfengu, in search of new opportunities under white protection. Missionaries often demanded the complete abandonment of traditional culture, and strove with the help of local magistrates to suppress African social customs and institutions. A number of converts suffered suspension from the stations for beer-drinking with animist kinsmen or attending non-Christian dances.[51] Mission Africans therefore developed alternative institutions strategically combining pagan and Christian traditions in providing a basis for community life.

At least as early as 1866,[52] the English church 'tea-meeting' had been adopted by Cape Nguni converts as an evening entertainment. As in traditional society, music was a central feature of social recreation, and in Kingwilliamstown, at the turn of the century, Scully noted that Christian Saturday evening tea-meetings lasted all night and took 'the place of the European ball with the Natives'.[53] Another important activity was the status competition involved in fund-raising, and in 1897, missionary C. J. Wychk described how money was raised by competitive bidding or 'auctions' for the performance of songs at such occasions.[54] Variants of the tea-meeting soon became popular among African proletarians and magistrates became preoccupied with 'brandy parties' and 'immoral night meetings' held in conjunction with African marriages, or secret occasions called *umngqoungqa* where 'women danced half-naked before men'.[55] In 1900, Rev. Hargreaves reported that even among church members, young converts were causing trouble by 'introducing night tea-parties under the pretence of helping church funds'.[56]

New skills and newly inculcated needs and aspirations made the move to the urban areas more attractive to rural Christians than to non-Christians.[57] Mission education united an emerging petty bourgeoisie organised around the flow of individuals and communication between rural centres such as Lovedale and Adams College and urban schools such as Lyndhurst Road in Kimberley and St Peter's and St Cyprian's in Johannesburg.[58] Mission institutions in both urban and rural areas also contributed much to the formation of working-class patterns of social organisation and cultural expression. At the same time that the *itimiti* (tea-meeting) was becoming generally popular in the eastern Cape, tea-meetings in Johannesburg were providing a model for neighbourhood concerts. These activities brought together mission-school and proletarian participants, and new cultural patterns and social institutions were developed within the framework of communal recreation.

In Johannesburg, the tea-meeting and church *manyano* women's groups helped give rise to primary urban working-class associations, the *stokfel* and *mohodisana* rotating credit and entertainment clubs.[59] In the countryside, the tea-meeting and its bidding custom helped similarly to integrate traditional reciprocity and beer-drinking with the money economy among working-class people, who adopted not only the *stokfel* but also created occasions such as the Xhosa *bungela*, where people bid for beer.[60] Weddings had become a major focus of rural social interaction among all categories of Africans by the early twentieth century. By 1930, working-class Xhosa had adopted the Christian *amabaso* custom where neighbours reciprocally contribute money and gifts at each other's weddings, along with *isipho* (gift) savings associations used to assist in marriage expenses,[61] and *nkazati* clubs in which families unite to buy refreshments for any large communal celebration.[62]

Migrant workers had their most direct contact with mission-school African institutions on the mine compounds. Xhosa *omabalani* (mine clerks) and mission-educated employees from Rhodesia and Nyasaland brought the tea-meeting to Johannesburg, where non-Christian miners transformed it into *amatimitin*: occasions for music, individualised dancing and beer-drinking. Among Basotho, these developed into *famo*, accompanied at first by a concertina and, by the 1920s, a pedal organ. In some cases, this migrant-proletarian form of tea-meeting was returned to school Africans in the rural areas. Graduates of Lovedale and other institutions who went into teaching often found the profession underpaid, unpleasant and lonely, especially in the more remote places.[63] Returning migrants and local proletarian musicians were frequently requested by the teachers in country districts to entertain at weekend *amatimitin* such as the Pedi *sitebi*, where people were entertained by town dance music played on trade-store instruments.

On the mines, workers were also subjected to direct forms of Christian influence through the efforts of a number of mission churches directly encouraged by management. Forced to compete with Sunday traditional dancing, some missions made good use of music in evangelisation. The Methodists had a band of African preachers who 'made their entrance singing, shouting, and moving to the rhythm of their song, and went round the compound inviting men to their service'.[64] Perhaps the most culturally influential mission was the Salvation Army, which used brass bands, tambourines and singing brigades in both the mine compounds and city streets.

Missions established brass bands and choirs in every region of the country during the late nineteenth century, profoundly influencing the development of both working-class and mission-school African performance culture. Evidence from living informants and some documentary evidence[65] suggests that music was possibly as important as education or economics in drawing Africans into the evangelical movement. European military bands, particularly evident during the South African War, also provided a model for the collective cultural representation of working-class solidarity. In Johannesburg, for example, young Northern Sotho *amalaita* gangs formed marching pennywhistle and drum bands in Scottish dress, in imitation of the Scottish regimental bands seen parading in city parks.

As the urban locations developed in the years prior to the First World War, versatile independent bands arose, performing an assortment of church hymns, European marches, popular syncretic dance tunes, and traditional African melodies for every type of community social event.[66] These bands were a major source of public entertainment in the locations, and played a key role in the development of *marabi* and other forms of proletarian culture and social organisation. Bands organised on a 'homeboy' basis often returned to their places of origin on important occasions or holidays, brining the cultural vitality of the urban locations to the African countryside.[67] As early as the 1880s, traditional Tswana chiefs in the Transvaal sponsored their own uniformed brass bands, or remodelled traditional reed-pipe ensembles (*Lethlaka*) along European military lines as a means of symbolically displaying their authority and cultural aspirations within the colonial context.[68]

Music and dance were also central to the development of independent or separatist church movements in both urban and rural areas. In late nineteenth-century Natal, racial discrimination in mission churches coupled with the desire for land led African converts to unite to buy property and set up independent Christian peasant communities of their own.[69] African church hymns were used for worship, but for purposes of work and recreation, these *amakholwa* combined traditional and proletarian-migrant styles of music and communal dancing into new forms such as *umkhukhumbela*, which again spread into the wider environment.[70]

In the early twentieth century, as the economic and legal position of Africans within colonial society deteriorated, independent churches proliferated as Africans tried to regain some control over the process of cultural change.[71] Among the largest and still most influential of these has been Zulu prophet Isaiah Shembe's Church of the Nazarites.[72] In the nineteenth century the Zulu, along with the Pedi, who have given rise to the equally large Zion Christian Church movement of E. Lekganyane,[73] were among the most resistant of South African peoples to mission Christianity. Shembe's 'Zionist' movement began in part as a response by non-mission Africans to the destruction of independent Zulu political power and social structure in the late nineteenth century, and may have represented 'a struggle by traditional society against colonialism, carried on with new weapons'.[74] Proudly acknowledging his lack of western education, Shembe styled himself a deliverer of his people, but set about revitalising Zulu cultural identity and creating the broad structure of a national religious community rather than engaging in overt political organisation.

Borrowing from the 'ecstatic' religious performances of the American Pentecostalists and Baptists, Shembe united traditional aspects of possession, ritual and ancestor cults with Christianity. Ignored or despised by most mission Africans, he attracted thousands to his movement by the use of traditional dances and music in worship, and by his message of cultural and spiritual autonomy. In his collection of hymns, *Izihlabelelo zaNazarethe*, he demonstrated his ability to translate western hymnody into the idiom of traditional African performance practices, and these are considered to be among the first imaginative compositions produced in Zulu under western influence.[75]

In addition to distinctive music and dancing, the Nazarite church provided new modes of communal integration for Africans. Active in both rural and urban areas, the church created intimate support groups with important mutual aid and welfare as well as moral and spiritual functions within the wider fellowship of a national ethnic religious community. Yet because its solidarity has been rooted in shared cultural and political traditions of regional Zulu origin, Shembe's following has not attained the significance of a broadly-based South Africa-wide movement.

By the late nineteenth century, bitterness over white control over the economy and settler refusal to extend social acceptance or political rights even to the educated petty bourgeoisie led to movements in pursuit of religious independence and cultural nationalism among mission-school Africans as well. These movements contained revivalist tendencies as mission Africans began to re-examine the value of traditional culture for self-expression and identity.[76] Amid the generally sombre Victorian sobriety of mission life, religious and secular music-making was a major focus of communal recreation and celebration. Although the psychosocial sacrifices exacted from Christian Africans had made any return to 'heathen' performance culture difficult, some nineteenth-century composers, in particular Lovedale's John Knox Bokwe, tried to repair some of the damage done to the Xhosa language in mission hymnody, and inserted indigenous melodic and structural features into their songs.[77] The attempts of Bokwe to arrange traditional songs in western four-part harmony proved popular with African choirs during the 1890s. Also performed were the hymns of the early nineteenth-century Xhosa prophet Ntsikana Gaba, standard English and African hymns, hymnodic songs of political protest, English secular part songs and American Negro spirituals.[78]

During the first half of the twentieth century, well-known composers such as Benjamin Tyamzashe, R. T. Caluza, and J. P. Mohapeloa succeeded in achieving stylistic continuity in African choral music. It is significant that most such composers come from a rural Christian rather than an urban background. Exploiting the sketchiness and simplicity of the tonic-solfa notation system used to teach music in mission schools, they created room for innovation and flexibility in choral performance and developed an Afro-western style called *makwaya* (choir).

In South Africa as elsewhere in the colonial world, 'traditional' culture is not unified but consists of the traditions of several peoples. One of the dilemmas of cultural nationalism, therefore, has been how to mobilise the symbols of tradition without retreating into the divisiveness of ethnic–regional parochialism. Mission-educated performers and composers played a crucial role in resolving this problem by capturing for black South African Christian nationalism the primary loyalties, images and rhetoric of Xhosa, Zulu and Sotho ethnicity.[79] *Makwaya* remains among the richest and most vital modern musical traditions south of the Sahara, and many compositions have passed into the corpus of urban African popular song. Throughout the twentieth century, *makwaya* has served as an important vehicle of protest, emotional commitment and racial identification in African labour and political agitation.

Black America has been one of the most important external influences on the performance culture of black South Africans. The real influence of black American stage performers on South African black culture began with the visit of McAdoo's American Jubilee Singers to Cape Town in 1887,[80] followed by a series of tours to other towns, including Kimberley and Johannesburg, in the 1890s. From these performances, the minstrel parade clubs of working-class

Coloured men developed, in the famous New Year's 'coon carnival'. The term 'coon' became synonymous with black American popular performance styles among Africans after the turn of the century. By 1912, almost every town had its youthful bands of Coloured and African coon street musicians, and every mission school its student coon groups performing early ragtime.[81] Urban *Shebeen* musicians used the minstrel bones (Zulu: *amatambo*; Tswana: *marapo*) for rhythm, and migrants introduced this instrument into rural culture as well.[82]

Other sources of black American influence were tonic-solfa song albums and recordings which made early ragtime coon songs available in trade stores as early as 1904.[83] Fortunately perhaps, few black South Africans could understand the crude sexual or racist lyrics which American record companies obliged performers to put on these early discs. The appeal, it seemed, 'was not in what they said, but in the rhythm and swing in which they said it'.[84]

In the religious sphere, black American spirituals were popularised by mission churches, in particular the African Methodist Episcopal Church. Other independent churches were also influenced: Enoch Mgijima's millenarian Israelite movement, famous as the victims of the Bulhoek massacre of 1921, used a hymn book blending Xhosa words and melody with spirituals taught them by black American Baptist missionaries of the Church of God and Saints of Christ.[85]

Mission-school people were among the primary transmitters of black American cultural influence to the wider African population. This process is exemplified in the career of one of South Africa's greatest musical innovators, Reuben T. Caluza. A product of the Edendale-Pietermaritzburg community, Caluza's background reflected rural independent Christian culture and bitterness over the suppression of successful African peasant farming.[86] As a teacher at Ohlange Institute, Caluza's musical talents soon proved of economic as well as cultural value to the school. Not content with winning provincial concert competitions with groups of coons and choristers, Caluza set about using his student ensembles to help keep Ohlange financially afloat.

From 1911 he organised pennywhistle and brass bands, full choirs and double quartets to tour first Natal and then the entire Union.[87] A series of Christmas tours to Johannesburg, beginning in 1917,[88] helped make the Caluza choir famous among Africans, who acclaimed the conductor an apostle of African national culture.[89] As a composer and performer, Caluza was strongly influenced by black American music, especially ragtime, during a period when black American culture was coming to be regarded by school and urban Africans as a solution to yet another dilemma: how to create a new identity at once modern and 'civilised', yet authentically African.

Not fully literate even in tonic-solfa before his musical training in America in the 1930s, Caluza was sufficiently nationalist in outlook and close enough to his indigenous heritage to blend Zulu music with western choral and American ragtime idioms. Caluza's Double Quartet recorded more than 120 of his compositions in 1930, which were classified by Africans into three categories: *eMusic* (western choral music in Zulu), *eRagtime* (ragtime piano and vocal songs in Zulu), and *eSizulu* (traditional songs arranged for choir).[90] A complete professional, Caluza performed for any audience or occasion that could make him a profit, helping to make choral music popular and ragtime somewhat respectable. His groups used elaborate stage choreography derived from both traditional and western sources to accompany Zulu ragtime, leading to the introduction of a new verb into the Zulu language, *ukureka* (Eng:rag) 'to play ragtime music; engage in movement during music of African songs'.[91] Caluza's songs were also highly regarded for the topical content of their lyrics, which commented upon social personalities and issues of the day.

Caluza's style had important effects upon African proletarian performance, including the development of *marabi* piano music. In the country as well as the city, his influence helped bring into being migrant and working-class forms of choral music such as *ingoma ebusuku* (night music) that became an important focus of group cultural expression and status competition among industrial and domestic workers. Like Shembe in the field of religious music, Caluza and followers such as William Mseleku revolutionised modern Zulu composition among all categories of performers.

Cultural communication has clearly not reflected idealised notions of social encapsulation, or opposition between 'red' and Christian, migrant and town-dweller, proletarian and bourgeois, or townsman and countryman. On the contrary, communication between members of different social groups in urban and rural environments, and between people in both, has resulted in the emergence of class-based cultures and social institutions keyed to specific adaptive needs and spanning town and countryside. The dynamic of such communication has been the struggle of a dominated people to retain and even regain cultural autonomy through the manipulation of colonial relations and the creation of unifying identities, perceptions, values and patterns of action. The process of syncretisation reveals not only incipient racial and class consciousness but also the continuing value and power of indigenous world views among colonised people. The analysis of African working-class culture should be broadened to include the totality of urban–rural relations, shaped by national and world economic and political forces and historical processes.

Notes

1 Georges Balandier, *The Sociology of Black Africa* (London, 1970), p. 24.

2 S. M. Molema, *The Bantu Past and Present* (London, 1920), p. 319.

3 J. Clyde Mitchell, 'Perceptions of ethnicity and ethnic behavior', in *Urban ethnicity*, A. Cohen (ed.), (London, 1974), p. 14.

4 Philip Mayer, *Townsmen or tribesmen* (London, 1961); B. B. Keller, 'The origins of modernism and conservatism among Cape Nguni', Ph.D. thesis, University of California, Berkeley, 1970; N. A. Etherington, 'The rise of the Kolwa in southeast Africa: African Christian communities in Natal, Pondoland and Zululand, 1835–1880', Ph.D. thesis, Yale 1971 – since published as *Preachers, Peasants and Politics in Southeast Africa, 1835–80: African Christian communities in Natal, Pondoland and Zululand* (London, 1978).

5 S. Judges and C. Saunders, 'The beginnings of an African community in Cape Town', *South African Outlook* (August 1976).

6 Gardner F. Williams, *The Diamond Mines of South Africa* (New York, 1902), p. 189; J. T. McNish, *The Glittering Road* (Cape Town, 1970) p. 57.

7 W. E. B. Du Bois, *The Souls of Black Folk* (New York, 1903), p. 138.

8 R. Turrell, 'The development of diamond mining, 1871–1889', paper presented to African History Seminar, Institute for Commonwealth Studies, London, 17 May 1978.

9 W. T. E., *IDB, or the adventures of Solomon Davis* (London, 1887), p. 217.

10 P. W. Laidler, *A Tavern of the Oceans* (Cape Town, n.d.), p. 40.

11 Maurice Evans, *Black and White in Southeast Africa* (London, 1911), p. 170.

12 Allister MacMillan, *The Golden City, Johannesburg* (London, 1935), p. 149.

13 *Star* (Johannesburg), 2 June 1920.

14 Jonathan Clegg, 'Dance and society in Africa south of the Sahara', B.A. Hons. thesis, University of the Witwatersrand, 1977.

15 Ethel Getliffe, Interview, April 1977.

16 E. Krige, *The Social System of the Zulus* (London, 1936), p. 110.

17 Clegg, 'Dance and society', p. 39.

18 *Ibid*.

19 G. M. Theal (ed.), *Records of Southeastern Africa* (Cape Town, 1901), pp. vii, 202.

20 Alice Balfour, *Twelve Hundred Miles in a Waggon* (London, 1895), p. 63.

21 *Ilanga lase Natal* (Durban), 24 March 1916.

22 P. Sebilo, 'What do the miners say?' B.A. thesis, University of Lesotho, 1976, p. 17.

23 D. Rycroft, quoted in R. Finnegan, *Oral Literature in Africa* (London, 1970), p. 144.

24 I. Schapera, *The Praise Poems of Tswana Chiefs* (London, 1965), p. 4.

25 C. Adams, 'Ethnography of Basotho evaluative behavior in the cognitive domain Lipapadi (Games)', Ph.D. thesis, Indiana University, 1974, p. 128.

26 P. R. Kirby, *The Musical Instruments of the Native Races of South Africa*, 3rd ed. (Johannesburg, 1965), p. 246.

27 F. Mayr, 'A short study of Zulu music', *Annals of the Natal Government Museum*, I, 2 (1908).

28 E. von Hornbostel, 'African Negro music', *Africa* (1928), 42.

29 Kirby, *The Musical Instruments*, p. 257.

30 D. Rycroft, 'Evidence of stylistic continuity in Zulu "Town" music', in K. P. Wachsmann Festschrift Comm. (eds), *Essays for a Humanist* (New York, 1977), pp. 219, 221.

31 M. Hunter, *Reaction to Conquest* (London, 1936), pp. 325, 357.

32 D. Coplan, 'Marabi culture: continuity and transformation in black South African urban music', paper presented to the Society for Ethnomusicology, Annual Meeting, Montreal (October 1979), p. 6.

33 Sebilo, 'What do the miners say?' p. 38.

34 A. Vilakazi, *Zulu Transformations* (Pietermaritzburg, 1965), p. 146.

35 Sebilo, 'What do the miners say?', p. 44, notes that miners with but a few years' schooling suffer the greatest psychological stress; unlike the better educated, they have no chance to move on to better employment, and unlike non-class-conscious traditional men, no attitude of fatalistic resignation to their lot.

36 E. Mpahlele, *The Wanderers* (New York, 1971), p. 45.

37 C. Adams, 'Ethnography of Basotho', p. 150.

38 Etherington, 'The rise of the Kolwa', pp. 233–4.

39 Vilakazi, *Zulu Transformations*; Molema, *The Bantu Past and Present*; Mayer, *Townsmen or Tribesmen*.

40 Coplan, 'Marabi culture'.

41 S. M. Guma, *The Form, Content and Technique of Traditional Literature in Southern Sotho* (Pretoria, 1967), p. 107.

42 John Thamanga, 'Ausi Selena', TREK-GRC DC. 315 SABC Transcription Service Series LT11.

43 E. Hellmann, *Rooiyard* (Manchester, 1948).

44 *Star* (Johannesburg), 21 June 1920.

45 Joachim Ntebele, Interview, June 1978.

46 Hellmann, *Rooiyard*, p. 67.

47 Etherington, 'The rise of the Kolwa'.

48 Keller, 'The origins of modernism'; Mayer, *Townsmen or Tribesmen*.

49 Colin Bundy, 'African peasants and economic change in South Africa, 1870–1913', Ph.D. thesis, Oxford, 1976, p. 137 – since published as *The Rise and Fall of the South African Peasantry* (London, 1979).

50 Etherington, 'The rise of the Kolwa', p. 201.

51 M. Hunter, 'The Bantu on European farms', in I. Schapera (ed.), *The Bantu-speaking Tribes of South Africa* (London, 1937), p. 402.

52 *Cape Standard* (Cape Town), 11 Jan. 1866.

53 W. C. Scully, *Daniel Venanda* (Cape Town, 1923), p. 62.

54 C. J. Wychk, U.S.P.G. EMSS Keiskammahoek, II, 31 Dec. 1897.

55 Scully, *Daniel Venanda*, pp. 79–81.

56 G. W. Mills, 'The role of the clergy in the reorientation of Xhosa society to the plural society in the Cape Colony, 1850–1915', Ph.D. thesis, University of California, Los Angeles, 1975, p. 75.

57 Vilakazi, *Zulu Transformations*, p. 122.

58 Kelwyn Sole, 'Class continuity and change in black South African literature, 1948–60', African History Workshop, University of the Witwatersrand, 2–5 Feb. 1978, pp. 8–9 – since published in B. Bozzoli (ed.), *Labour, Townships and Protest: studies in the social history of the Witwatersrand* (Johannesburg, 1979).

59 Brain Du Toit, 'Cooperative institutions and culture change in South Africa', *Journal of Asian and African Studies*, IV (1969), 282.

60 *Ibid.*

61 M. Hunter Wilson, *et al.*, *Social Structure* (Pietermaritzburg, 1952), pp. 165–6.

62 Du Toit, 'Cooperative institutions', pp. 282.

63 Keller, 'The origins of modernism', pp. 234–5.
64 Donald Vysie, *The Wesleyan Methodist Church in the Transvaal 1823–1902* (Grahamstown, 1969), pp. 132.
65 S. Ramhlala, Interview, May 1977; *Cape Standard*, 11 Jan. 1866; MacMillan, *The Golden City*, p. 61.
66 S. Ramhlala, Interview, May 1977.
67 Walter Pitso, Interview, May 1978.
68 *Standard and Diggers News* (Johannesburg), 4 June 1891; D. M. Wilson, *Behind the Scenes in the Transvaal* (London, 1901), pp. 91–2.
69 Vilakazi, *Zulu Transformations*, pp. 120; B. Hutchinson, 'Some social consequences of 19th century missionary activity among the South African Bantu', *Africa*, XXVII, 2 (1957), 162–3.
70 Dan Twala, Interview, March 1977.
71 Bundy, 'African peasants'.
72 B. Sundkler, *Bantu Prophets of Southern Africa*, 2nd ed. (London, 1961).
73 *Ibid*.
74 Etherington, 'The rise of the Kolwa', p. 322.
75 Albert Gérard, *Four African Literatures* (Berkeley, 1971), p. 193.
76 *Ibid*.
77 A. M. Jones, *African Hymnody in Christian Worship* (Gwelo, 1976), pp. 17–19.
78 *Diamond Fields Advertiser* (Kimberley), 13 March 1897.
79 Anya P. Royce, *Ethnic Identity: strategies of diversity* (forthcoming, 1981), 143.
80 John Lovell, *Black Song: the forge and the flame* (New York, 1972), p. 415; *Diamond Fields Advertiser*, 29 July 1895.
81 *Ilanga lase Natal*, 5 July 1912.
82 Kirby, *The Musical Instruments*, pp. 10–11.
83 *Ilanga lase Natal*, 3 June 1904; 24 Jan. 1908.
84 Alain Locke, *The Negro and his Music* (New York 1936), p. 59.
85 Rev. Alan Lea, *The Native Separatist Church Movement in South Africa* (1925), pp. 15–16; R. Edgar, 'Enoch Mgijima and the Bulhock massacre', unpub. Ph.D. thesis, UCLA, 1977.
86 Gérard, *Four African Literatures*, p. 201.
87 *Ilanga lase Natal*, 23 June 1911.
88 *Ibid*., 4 Jan. and 8 Feb. 1918.
89 *Ibid*., 15 Feb. 1924.
90 *Ibid*., 27 April 1923.
91 C. M. Doke and B. W. Vilakazi, *Zulu-English Dictionary* (Johannesburg 1953), p. 719.

Index